CW00515216

ZAGATSURVEY®

2004

NEW YORK CITY SHOPPING

Editors: Catherine Bigwood, Randi Gollin and Troy Segal

Published and distributed by
ZAGAT SURVEY, LLC
4 Columbus Circle
New York, New York 10019
Tel: 212 977 6000
E-mail: nycshopping@zagat.com
Web site: www.zagat.com

Acknowledgments

We thank Joyce Bautista, Donna Bulseco, Amy Chozick, Erica Curtis, Jacques Dehornois, Ilyssa Diamond, Laurie Dwek, Ed Dwyer, Kimberly Forrest, David Goldman, Dana Gordon, Sohrab Habibion, Ki Hackney, Amanda Hallowell, Nancy Hawley, Evie Joselow, Martin Kaufmann, Althea Keough, Ann Lewinson, Diane Maglio, Elise Maiberger, Nikki Moustaki, Frank Oteri, Dori Perrucci, Steven Shukow, Melissa Sones, William Stout, Matt Sullivan, Edina Sultanik and Carole Therie.

This guide would not have been possible without the hard work of our staff, especially Betsy Andrews, Reni Chin, Liz Daleske, Griff Foxley, Schuyler Frazier, Jeff Freier, Katherine Harris, Natalie Lebert, Mike Liao, Dave Makulec, Lorraine Mead, Laura Mitchell, Jennifer Napuli, Rob Poole, Robert Seixas, Kelly Sinanis and Sharon Yates.

Contents

Home/Garden

Lifestyle

Special Features

About This Survey

Over the past 25 years, Zagat Survey has reported on the shared experiences of people like you. This *2004 New York City Shopping* guide is an update reflecting significant developments as reported by our editors since our last *Survey* was published. For example, we have added over 250 important new places, as well as indicated new addresses, phone numbers and other major changes. All told, this guide now covers 2,021 establishments, ranging from fashion to furniture.

What started in 1979 in New York as a hobby involving 200 friends rating local restaurants has come a long way: Today we have roughly 250,000 surveyors with hundreds of thousands more registered to vote. And over the years we have branched out to publish books on entertaining, golf, hotels, movies, music, nightlife, resorts, shopping, spas and theater. Our restaurant *surveys* are also available by subscription at **zagat.com,** where you can vote and shop as well.

By regularly surveying large numbers of avid customers, we hope to have achieved uniquely current and reliable guides. A quarter-century of experience has verified this. In producing this guide, nearly 7,200 New York City shoppers participated. We sincerely thank each of these people; this book is really "theirs."

We are especially grateful to our key local editors: Joyce Bautista, senior editor for *Real Simple* magazine, Donna Bulseco, a fashion editor who has worked at *WWD* and *W*, and Althea Keough, style editor for *BabyTalk* magazine.

To help guide our readers to New York's best places, we have prepared a number of lists. See Most Popular (page 8), Top Ratings (pages 9–19) and Good Values (page 20). In addition, we have provided handy indexes and have tried to be concise. Finally, it should be noted that our editors have synopsized our surveyors' opinions, with their comments shown in quotation marks.

To join any of our upcoming *Surveys*, just register at zagat.com. Each participant will receive a free copy of the resulting guide when it is published. Your comments and even criticisms of this guide are also solicited. There is always room for improvement with your help. You can contact us at nycshopping@zagat.com. We look forward to hearing from you.

New York, NY
March 23, 2004

Nina and Tim Zagat

What's New

New York's economy may have suffered from the recent recession and the aftermath of the vicious 9/11 attack, but that's barely put a damper on the vibrant retail scene. Quite simply New Yorkers like to shop and they proved it in the last few years. Now with recovery underway, the biggest complaints at most stores are crowding and getting a salesperson's attention. While we can't help in that regard, there's something for every budget and taste in this guide, which covers over 2,000 stores.

Upscale Arrivals: With the economy's rebound, there has been an influx of luxury purveyors along Fifth and Madison Avenues including Swiss sophisticate Akris, furrier Dennis Basso, Dior Homme, bridal designer Reem Acra, haute English import Asprey, now in a new space near Trump Tower, and the Louis Vuitton flagship. Downtown, there's Balenciaga in Chelsea, Carlos Miele in the Meatpacking District and Santa Maria Novella, NoLita's latest status scent store.

Fab Finds: While chic-seekers have a penchant for bold-faced names, many also take a shine to emerging talent. Showcasing fashion's new guard, bazaarlike incubators such as SoHo's 30 Vandam are fueling the fires of discovery – and so is a different type of hipster, style-supermarket, The Lounge.

Home Sweet Home: Two top home-furnishings catalogues came to life – West Elm, Williams-Sonoma's sibling, sprang up in Dumbo, while Design Within Reach debuted in both Brooklyn and Manhattan. Prestigious Parisian furniture designer Catherine Memmi premiered in SoHo, as did Italian imports Natuzzi and tile-titan Bisazza.

Tip-Top Time Warner Center: Revered labels Kangol, The North Face and Theory lured loyalists to the Upper West Side. And as we went to press, the Time Warner Center unveiled The Shops at Columbus Circle, a glorious, must-visit four-story shopping/dining/entertainment destination featuring over 40 big-name merchants and restaurants. Judging by the crowds and lines, New Yorkers have already bought into the new TW shopping experience.

New York, NY
March 23, 2004

Catherine Bigwood
Randi Gollin
Troy Segal

Ratings & Symbols

Name, Address, Subway Stop, Phone Numbers & Web Site

Hours, Credit Cards, Return Policy

Zagat Ratings

	M	P	S	C
Tim & Nina's ◐Ⓢ≠ⓒ	▽ 23	9	13	I

*Time Warner Center, 10 Columbus Circle (8th Ave.),
A/B/C/D/1/9 to Columbus Circle, 212-977-6000;
www.zagat.com*

◪ Packed with "enough merchandise to fill a walk-in closet",
this "world-class canine clothing boutique" on the 157th
floor of the new Time Warner shopping mall at 10 Columbus
Circle attracts an international mix of "stylish spaniels" and
"bargain hounds"; P.S. "delish doggie biscuits" are doled out
if you roll over and bark at Tim's command.

Review, with surveyors' comments in quotes

Stores with the highest overall ratings and greatest
popularity and importance are printed in CAPITAL LETTERS.

Before reviews a symbol indicates whether responses
were uniform ■ or mixed ◪.

Hours: ◐ usually open after 7 PM
Ⓢ open on Sunday

Credit Cards: ≠ no credit cards accepted

Return Policy: ⓒ store credit only

Locations: For chains with more than 10 locations in NYC,
the flagship address is listed with their reviews.

Maps: Maps show locations for stores with the highest
overall ratings and greatest popularity and importance.

Ratings: Merchandise, Presentation and Service are rated
on a scale of **0** to **30,** except for newcomers or write-ins,
which are listed without ratings. The Cost (C) column
reflects our surveyors' estimate of the store's price range.

M Merchandise	**P** Presentation	**S** Service	**C** Cost
23	9	13	I

0–9 poor to fair	**20–25** very good to excellent
10–15 fair to good	**26–30** extraordinary to perfection
16–19 good to very good	▽ low response/less reliable

The price range is indicated by the following symbols:

I	Inexpensive	**E**	Expensive
M	Moderate	**VE**	Very Expensive

Most Popular

1. Bloomingdale's	26. Daffy's
2. Century 21	27. Sephora
3. Saks Fifth Avenue	28. MoMA Design Store
4. Bed Bath & Beyond	29. Scoop NYC
5. Barneys	30. J.Crew
6. Macy's	31. Zabar's
7. Banana Republic	32. Filene's Basement
8. Bergdorf Goodman	33. Kate Spade
9. Anthropologie	34. Takashimaya
10. Costco Wholesale	35. Kiehl's
11. Met. Museum of Art	36. Pearl Paint
12. ABC Carpet & Home	37. FAO Schwarz
13. H&M	38. Old Navy
14. Henri Bendel	39. Brooks Brothers
15. Kate's Paperie	40. Gracious Home
16. Loehmann's	41. Virgin Megastore*
17. Ann Taylor	42. Paragon
18. Ann Taylor Loft	43. Intermix
19. Tiffany & Co.	44. Syms
20. Gap	45. Kmart
21. T.J. Maxx	46. Express
22. B&H Photo-Video	47. Nine West
23. Crate & Barrel	48. Tower Records
24. Lord & Taylor	49. Club Monaco
25. J&R Music/Computer	50. Prada

While the above list contains many obvious big names, it's interesting that a number of the stores, such as ABC Carpet & Home, B&H Photo-Video, Bergdorf Goodman, Gracious Home, Kiehl's and Kate's Paperie, are of the "born in NY" variety, proof that New Yorkers love – and support – individuality in their shopping choices. What's more, if you turn to page 20 you'll see that shopping here can also be a world-class bargain.

---

* Indicates a tie with store above

subscribe to zagat.com

Top Ratings

Department stores are separately rated for their various categories. Top lists exclude places with low voting, except where noted.

Top Fashion/Beauty

29 Harry Winston
Graff
Van Cleef & Arpels
Creed & Bond No. 9
Cartier
Turnbull & Asser
28 Elizabeth Locke
Breguet
Loro Piana
Piaget
Reinstein/Ross*
Mikimoto
Stuart Moore
Manolo Blahnik
Hermès
Bulgari
A La Vieille Russie
Buccellati
Reem Acra
Asprey
Cellini
Eugenia Kim
Brioni
Morgenthal Frederics
Eres

Chopard
Christian Louboutin
Bottega Veneta
Selima Optique
Catimini
Little Eric*
27 La Perla
Ascot Chang
Diane von Furstenberg*
Robert Talbott*
Sergio Rossi*
Chanel
Alain Mikli
Ermenegildo Zegna*
Santa Maria Novella
Yohji Yamamoto
Allen Edmonds
Bergdorf Goodman
Jimmy Choo
Giuseppe Zanotti
John Lobb*
Sigerson Morrison
Carolina Herrera
Tiffany & Co.
Kiehl's

By Category

Accessories
28 Eugenia Kim
27 Bergdorf Goodman
Bergdorf Men's
26 Dunhill
25 Barneys

Activewear
26 Patagonia
25 North Face
Super Runners Shop
24 Puma
22 Adidas Originals

Bridal
28 Reem Acra
27 Selia Yang
26 Vera Wang
Bridal Atelier
Bergdorf Goodman

Clothing: Children's
28 Catimini
27 Bonpoint
Au Chat Botte
Spring Flowers
26 Ralph Lauren Baby

Clothing: Designer (Men's)
27 Ermenegildo Zegna
Giorgio Armani
Paul Smith
26 Hugo Boss
24 John Varvatos

Clothing: Designer (Men's/Women's)
28 Hermès
27 Yohji Yamamoto
Etro
Issey Miyake
Gucci

Top Merchandise

Clothing: Designer (Women's)
27 Diane von Furstenberg
   Chanel
   Carolina Herrera
26 Dior New York
   Chloé

Clothing: Discount
23 Giselle
22 Century 21
   Find Outlet
21 Aaron's
   S&W

Clothing: Men's (Classic)
28 Brioni
27 Oxxford Clothes
   Bergdorf Men's
26 Paul Stuart
   Saks Fifth Ave.

Clothing: Men's (Contemporary)
26 Barneys
24 Ted Baker
23 Scoop Men's
   99X
   Jeffrey

Clothing: Women's (Boutiques)
26 Language
   IF
25 Ibiza
   Kirna Zabête
   Foley & Corinna

Consignment/Vintage
25 What Comes/Goes Around
   Fisch for the Hip
24 Amarcord Vintage
   Resurrection
23 Ina

Cosmetics/Toiletries (Dept. Stores)
28 Bergdorf Goodman
27 Barneys
   Bergdorf Men's
   Henri Bendel
26 Saks Fifth Avenue

Cosmetics/Toiletries (Specialists)
29 Creed & Bond No. 9
27 Santa Maria Novella
   Kiehl's
   Fresh
   Floris of London

**Department/
Large Specialty Stores**
28 Asprey
27 Bergdorf Goodman
   Bergdorf Men's
26 Barneys
   Saks Fifth Avenue

Eyewear
28 Morgenthal Frederics
   Selima Optique
27 Alain Mikli
   Robert Marc
   H.L. Purdy

Fashion Chain: Men's
25 Rochester Big & Tall
22 Brooks Brothers
20 Banana Republic Men's
   Club Monaco
19 J.Crew

Fashion Chain: Women's
23 Eileen Fisher
21 Anthropologie
20 Banana Republic
   Ann Taylor
   Club Monaco

Handbags (Specialists)
28 Bottega Veneta
27 Lana Marks
26 Marc Jacobs Accessories
25 Sigerson Morrison Bags
   Prada

Hosiery/Lingerie
28 Eres
27 La Perla
   Joovay
   La Petite Coquette
26 Wolford

Jeans
27 Barneys
25 Diesel Denim Gallery
   Henri Bendel
24 Earl Jean
23 Scoop NYC

Jewelry: Classic
29 Harry Winston
   Graff
   Van Cleef & Arpels
   Cartier
28 Elizabeth Locke

Top Merchandise

Jewelry: Contemporary
28 Reinstein/Ross
27 Bergdorf Goodman
    Fragments
    Aaron Faber
25 Barneys

Maternity
26 Liz Lange
24 Mommy Chic
22 A Pea in the Pod
21 Mimi Maternity
20 Bloomingdale's

Newcomers/Rated
28 Reem Acra
27 Santa Maria Novella
26 Ralph Lauren Baby
    Akris
25 Theory

Newcomers/Unrated
    Carlos Miele
    Custo Barcelona
    Dennis Basso
    Dior Homme
    Pharma

Shirts/Ties
29 Turnbull & Asser
27 Ascot Chang
    Robert Talbott*
25 Thomas Pink
22 Charles Tyrwhitt

Shoes: Children's
28 Little Eric
26 Shoofly
23 Harry's Shoes
    Great Feet
22 Tip Top Shoes

Shoes: Men's
27 Allen Edmonds
    John Lobb
24 Church Shoes
23 Bergdorf Men's
22 Johnston & Murphy

Shoes: Men's & Women's
27 Jeffrey
    Sergio Rossi
    J.M. Weston
26 Barneys
    Otto Tootsi Plohound

Shoes: Women's
28 Manolo Blahnik
    Christian Louboutin
27 Jimmy Choo
    Giuseppe Zanotti
    Sigerson Morrison

Sneakers
25 Paragon
    Super Runners Shop
24 Puma
23 Niketown
    New Balance

Watches
29 Cartier
28 Breguet
    Piaget
    Cellini
    Chopard

Top Merchandise

Top Home/Garden

29	Steuben	Simon Pearce
	Pratesi	Poggenpohl
28	Thos. Moser	Moss
	Bernardaud	B&B Italia
	Christofle	Simon's Hardware
	Ann Sacks	Hastings Tile
	Artistic Tile	Maurice Villency*
	Baccarat	Zabar's
	Sherle Wagner	Bergdorf Goodman
	James Robinson	Barneys
	Troy	Kraft
	Buccellati	Broadway Panhandler
	Waterworks	Dean & Deluca
	Avventura	Aero
	Lalique*	Stickley
27	Country Floors	Gallery Orrefors
	Frette	Totem Design
	Léron	25 Just Bulbs
	Urban Archaeology	ABC Carpet & Home
	Knoll	ABC Carpet (Carpets/Rugs)
	Tiffany & Co.	Baker Tribeca
	Cassina USA	Scott Jordan
	Bridge Kitchenware	E. Braun & Co.*
	Ceramica	Artemide
	Scully & Scully	ddc domus design*
26	Schweitzer Linen	Jonathan Adler

By Category

Accessories
- 26 Moss
- 25 Jonathan Adler
- 24 Terence Conran
  - Mxyplyzyk
  - Pierre Deux

Bathroom Fixtures
- 28 Sherle Wagner
  - Waterworks
- 27 Urban Archaeology
- 26 Hastings Tile
  - Kraft

Cookware
- 27 Bridge Kitchenware
- 26 Zabar's
  - Broadway Panhandler
  - Dean & Deluca
- 25 Williams-Sonoma

Department/ Large Specialty Stores
- 26 Bergdorf Goodman
  - Barneys
- 25 ABC Carpet & Home
  - Gracious Home
  - Takashimaya

Fine China/Crystal
- 29 Steuben
- 28 Bernardaud
  - Baccarat
  - Avventura
  - Lalique*

Furniture
- 27 Cassina USA
- 26 B&B Italia
  - Maurice Villency
  - Aero
- 25 Scott Jordan

Top Merchandise

Garden
26 Lexington Gardens▽
25 Treillage▽
Chelsea Garden
24 Smith & Hawken
22 Mecox Gardens

Hardware Stores
26 Simon's Hardware
25 Gracious Home
23 Vercesi Hardware
Pintchik
22 Home Depot

Linens
29 Pratesi
28 Porthault▽
27 Frette
Léron
26 Schweitzer Linen

Lighting
25 Just Bulbs
Artemide
24 Lighting by Gregory
23 Lee's Studio
21 Bowery Lighting

Major Appliances
26 Poggenpohl
Drimmers
24 Krups Kitchen & Bath
Gringer & Sons
23 Expo Design

Newcomers/Rated
25 Archipelago
Design Within Reach
24 Butter and Eggs
21 Natuzzi

Newcomers/Unrated
Arredo
Bisazza
Catherine Memmi
Style by Annick de Lorme
Sublime American

Silver
29 Cartier
28 Christofle
Buccellati
27 Tiffany & Co.
25 Georg Jensen

Tiles
28 Ann Sacks
Artistic Tile
27 Country Floors
Urban Archaeology
26 Hastings Tile

▽ Indicates low votes

Top Merchandise

Top Lifestyle

29	Dempsey & Carroll	Joon
	B&H Photo-Video	Dinosaur Hill
28	Tender Buttons	Toys in Babeland
	Sound by Singer	MoMA Design
	Leather Man	Knitting Hands
	Footlight Records	Crouch & Fitzgerald
	Mood Fabrics	New York Golf Center
27	Smythson of Bond St.	Flight 001
	Kate's Paperie	25 Generation Records
	B&J Fabrics	Montblanc*
	Crane & Co., Paper	Other Music
	Fountain Pen Hospital	Colony Music
	Apple Store SoHo	Il Papiro
	Pearl Paint	Hyman Hendler
	FAO Schwarz	New York Central Art
	Tumi	Geppetto's Toy Box
	TLA Video	Annie & Co.
	City Quilter	World of Golf
	M&J Trimming	Paragon
	Tent and Trails	Paper Presentation
	Louis Vuitton	Yarn Co.
26	T. Anthony	J&R Music/Computer
	Soccer Sport	Purl
	Lyric Hi-Fi	Manhattan Doll House*
	Fetch	Vespa*
	Saks Fifth Ave.*	String*
	Harvey Electronics	Lincoln Stationers

By Category

Art Supplies
27 Pearl Paint
25 New York Central Art
24 Art Store
   A.I. Friedman
23 Sam Flax

Audio/Electronics
28 Sound by Singer
26 Bang & Olufsen
   Lyric Hi-Fi
   Harvey Electronics
25 J&R Music/Computer

Baby Gear
25 Albee Baby Carriage
24 Kid's Supply Co.▽
23 buybuy Baby
   Just for Tykes
22 Schneider's▽

Cameras/Video
29 B&H Photo-Video
25 Adorama Camera
21 Olden Camera
20 Alkit Pro Camera
19 Willoughby's

CDs/Vinyl
28 Footlight Records
25 Generation Records
   Other Music
   Colony Music
   Virgin Megastore

Computers
27 Apple Store SoHo
25 J&R Music/Computer
   Tekserve
22 Best Buy
20 CompUSA

▽ Indicates low votes

Top Merchandise

Fabrics/Notions
28 Tender Buttons
Mood Fabrics
27 B&J Fabrics
City Quilter
M&J Trimming

Gifts/Novelties
24 Dylan's Candy Bar
23 Alphabets
Papyrus
Carnegie Cards/Gifts
21 E.A.T Gifts

Knitting/Needlepoint
26 Knitting Hands
25 Annie & Co.
Yarn Co.
Purl
String*

Luggage/Leather Goods
27 Tumi
Louis Vuitton
26 T. Anthony
Saks Fifth Avenue
Crouch & Fitzgerald

Museum Stores
26 MoMA Design
25 Met. Museum of Art
24 AsiaStore/Asia Society
23 Neue Galerie
22 Jewish Museum

Newcomers/Unrated
American Girl Place
Museum of Arts & Design
Nalunyc

Pet Supplies
26 Fetch
24 Beasty Feast
23 Doggystyle
Doggie-Do/Pussycats
22 Furry Paws

Sex Shops
28 Leather Man
26 Toys in Babeland
23 Noose, The
DeMask
Purple Passion/DV8

Sporting Goods
27 Tent and Trails
26 Soccer Sport Supply
New York Golf Center
25 World of Golf
Paragon

Stationery
29 Dempsey & Carroll
27 Smythson of Bond St.
Kate's Paperie
Crane & Co., Paper
25 Il Papiro

Toys
27 FAO Schwarz
26 Dinosaur Hill
25 Geppetto's Toy Box
Manhattan Doll House
24 Enchanted Forest

Videos/DVDs
27 TLA Video
25 Virgin Megastore
Kim's Mediapolis
24 J&R Music/Computer
Tower Records

By Location

Chelsea
27 City Quilter
26 New York Golf
25 Myoptics
AFNY
Williams-Sonoma

Chinatown
27 Pearl Paint
24 Kam Man
19 Pearl River Mart
Canal Hi-Fi
16 Loftworks

East Village
28 Eugenia Kim
Footlight Records
Selima Optique
27 Kiehl's
Selia Yang

East 40s
28 Cellini
27 Allen Edmonds
Robert Marc
Tumi
26 Paul Stuart

Top Merchandise

East 50s
29 Harry Winston
 Van Cleef & Arpels
 Cartier
 Turnbull & Asser
28 Bernardaud

East 60s
29 Graff
 Steuben
 Creed & Bond No. 9
 Pratesi
28 Breguet

East 70s
29 Creed & Bond No. 9
28 Elizabeth Locke
 Reinstein/Ross
 Morgenthal Frederics
 Christian Louboutin

East 80s
29 Dempsey & Carroll
28 Little Eric
27 Au Chat Botte
 H.L. Purdy
26 Schweitzer Linen

East 90s & Up
28 Catimini
27 Robert Marc
 Bonpoint
26 Soccer Sport
25 Annie & Co.

Financial District
27 Fountain Pen Hospital
 Tent and Trails
26 Joon
25 World of Golf
 J&R Music/Computer

Flatiron District
28 Ann Sacks
 Artistic Tile
27 Paul Smith
26 Bang & Olufsen
 Jo Malone

Garment District
29 B&H Photo-Video
28 Mood Fabrics
27 B&J Fabrics
 M&J Trimming
26 Tourneau

Gramercy Park
27 Pearl Paint
26 Simon's Hardware
25 Manhattan Doll House
24 Park Ave. Audio
23 Vercesi Hardware

Greenwich Village
27 Kate's Paperie
 La Petite Coquette
 TLA Video
 C.O. Bigelow
26 Fetch

Lower East Side
26 Toys in Babeland
25 Foley & Corinna
24 Seven New York
 Lighting by Gregory
 Harry Zarin

Meatpacking District
27 Diane von Furstenberg
26 Alexander McQueen
25 Bodum
 Stella McCartney
24 Yigal Azrouel

Murray Hill
25 Shiseido
 ddc domus Design
 Roche Bobois
23 Doggie-Do/Pussycats
22 Ethan Allen

NoHo
29 Creed & Bond No. 9
25 Other Music
24 Tower Records
 Art Store
23 Bond 07 by Selima

NoLita
27 Santa Maria Novella
 Sigerson Morrison
 Hollywould
 Fresh
26 Language

SoHo
28 Reinstein/Ross
 Stuart Moore
 Morgenthal Frederics
 Eres
 Troy

South Street Seaport
25 Met. Museum of Art
24 Coach
21 Sharper Image
 Brookstone
19 Guess?

TriBeCa
27 Urban Archaeology
 Issey Miyake
26 Shoofly
 Totem Design
25 Baker Tribeca

Top Merchandise

Union Square
28 Ann Sacks
Sound by Singer
27 Country Floors
26 Poggenpohl
25 Paragon

West Village
28 Leather Man
27 Fresh
26 Marc by Marc Jacobs
Marc Jacobs Accessories
Betwixt

West 40s
27 Crane & Co., Paper
Tumi
26 Harvey Electronics
25 Sephora
Colony Music

West 50s
28 Manolo Blahnik
27 Ascot Chang
Smythson of Bond St.
Kate's Paperie
Aaron Faber

West 60s
27 Robert Marc
25 Gracious Home
Lincoln Stationers
Bonne Nuit
L'Occitane

West 70s
26 Bang & Olufsen
Sephora
25 Theory
North Face
Super Runners Shop

West 80s
28 Avventura
26 Schweitzer Linen
Patagonia
Zabar's
25 Laina Jane

West 90s
25 Albee Baby Carriage
24 Mommy Chic
21 Metro Bicycles
Petco
19 La Brea

Outer Boroughs

Brooklyn
26 Carol's Daughter
Knitting Hands
Green Onion*
25 ABC Carpet & Home
Jacadi
Clay Pot
Boss, The
Design Within Reach
24 M.A.C. Cosmetics
Amarcord Vintage

Queens
26 London Jewelers
Sephora
23 Expo Design
Thomasville
Nemo Tile
22 Ethan Allen
Home Depot
Bed Bath & Beyond
Best Buy
Smiley's

Staten Island
26 Sephora
22 Ethan Allen
Best Buy
Costco
21 Petco
Crabtree & Evelyn
Mimi Maternity
20 Circuit City
Gymboree
19 Guess?

Top Presentation

29 Graff
Harry Winston
28 Steuben
Creed & Bond No. 9
Cartier
Waterworks
Turnbull & Asser
Takashimaya
Apple Store SoHo
Bernardaud
Breguet
Van Cleef & Arpels
Elizabeth Locke
Baccarat
27 Chopard
Hermès
Bulgari
Carolina Herrera
Moss
Smythson of Bond St.
James Robinson
Fresh
Buccellati
Michael Dawkins
Ralph Lauren Baby

Hastings Tile
Hervé Leger
Santa Maria Novella
Dylan's Candy Bar
Enchanted Forest
Frette
Piaget*
Reinstein/Ross*
FAO Schwarz
Ann Sacks
Tiffany & Co.
Lalique
26 Stuart Moore
Reem Acra
Issey Miyake
Dior New York
Lana Marks
Kentshire Galleries
Bonpoint
Bang & Olufsen
Morgenthal Frederics
Giuseppe Zanotti
Penhaligon's
Troy
Comme des Garçons

Architectural Interest

Adidas Originals
Alexander McQueen
Apple Store SoHo
Asprey
Baker Tribeca
Balenciaga
Calvin Klein
Carlos Miele
Cartier
Comme des Garçons
ddc domus collection
Donna Karan
Fred Leighton
Henri Bendel
Helmut Lang
Hugo Boss

Issey Miyake
Jean Paul Gaultier
Jil Sander
Louis Vuitton
Maurice Villency
Neue Galerie
Nicole Farhi
Niketown
Prada
Ralph Lauren
Rubin Chapelle
Stella McCartney
Terence Conran
Versace
Vitra
Yves Saint Laurent Rive Gauche

Holiday Decoration

ABC Carpet & Home
Barneys
Bergdorf Goodman
Bloomingdale's
Cartier
Catimini
Disney
Dylan's Candy Bar
FAO Schwarz

Henri Bendel
Kate's Paperie
Lord & Taylor
Macy's
Ralph Lauren
Saks Fifth Avenue
Sony Style
Takashimaya
Tiffany & Co.

Top Service

28 Turnbull & Asser
Toys In Babeland
Breguet
27 Elizabeth Locke
Bridal Atelier
City Quilter
Graff*
Piaget
Van Cleef & Arpels
26 Harry Winston
John Lobb
Carolina Herrera
Reem Acra*
Scott Jordan
Ascot Chang
Tekserve
Dempsey & Carroll
Verdura
25 Santa Maria Novella
T. Anthony
Buccellati
E. Braun
Fountain Pen Hospital*
Leonard Opticians
Robert Talbott*
Hooti Couture

Penhaligon's
Jo Malone
Super Runners Shop
Thos. Moser
Valentino
Lana Marks
Dunhill
Annie & Co.
James Robinson
Crouch & Fitzgerald
Beasty Feast
Vercesi Hardware*
Malia Mills
Oxxford Clothes
Robert Marc
24 Fetch
Geppetto's Toy Box
St. John
Hickey Freeman
Kiehl's
Michael Kors*
Cartier
Joon
Asprey
Bulgari*
Mary Arnold

Free Delivery in NYC

Apple Store SoHo
Chanel Fine Jewelry
C.O. Bigelow
Disney
Eric

Gracious Home
Pet Stop
S. Feldman Housewares
Spoiled Brats
Stickley, Audi & Co.

In-Store Dining

ABC Carpet & Home
American Girl Place
Barneys
Bed Bath & Beyond
Bergdorf Goodman
Bloomingdale's
Bodum
Compact-Impact by TKNY
DDC Lab
Dean & Deluca
DKNY

Kiehl's
Lord & Taylor
Lounge, The
Macy's
Neue Galerie
Nicole Farhi
Pearl River Mart
Saks Fifth Avenue
Takashimaya
Target
Virgin Megastore

Good Values

Agatha Paris
Aldo
Alexia Crawford
Altman Luggage
Ann Taylor Loft
American Eagle Outfitters
April Cornell
Babies "R" Us
B&H Photo-Video
Best Buy
Bis Designer Resale
Bodum
Body Shop
Broadway Panhandler
Burlington Coat Factory
Carol's Daughter
Casual Male Big & Tall
Century 21
Container Store
Costco
Crate & Barrel
Daffy's
Dave's Army Navy
David's Bridal
Dö Kham
Dr. Jay's
Filene's Basement
Find Outlet
Fishs Eddy
For Eyes
Fossil
Gerry's Menswear
Giselle
H&M
Home Depot
Housing Works Thrift Shop

Jam Paper & Envelope
J&R Music/Computer
Kam Man
Kartell
Kiehl's
Kmart
LeSportsac
Liliblue
Loehmann's
Loftworks
M.A.C. Cosmetics
M&J Trimming
Marshalls
Maternity Works
Mavi Jean
Mexx
Old Navy
Orchard Corset
Pearl River Mart
Petco
Pookie & Sebastian
Purdy Girl
Ray Beauty Supply
Skechers
Smiley's
Sol Moscot
Super Runners Shop
Swatch
Syms
Target
T.J. Maxx
Watch World
West Elm
West Side Kids
William-Wayne
Zara

Store Directory

A. ◐[S][C] ▽ 23 | 21 | 19 | E

(fka A. Atelier)

125 Crosby St. (bet. Houston & Prince Sts.), R/W to Prince St., 212-941-8435

■ At first, this SoHo boutique, now renamed and solely devoted to menswear, seems somber, with masonite floors, black leather couches and white marble tables, but the decor provides a dramatic backdrop for presenting the "wonderful handpicked selection" of cutting-edge clothing from highly coveted lines like Carpe Diem and Rick Owens; killer shoes and boots complete the handsome picture.

Aaron Basha [C] 23 | 21 | 20 | VE

680 Madison Ave. (bet. 61st & 62nd Sts.), 4/5/6/F/N/R/W to 59th St./Lexington Ave., 212-935-1960; www.aaronbasha.com

■ Many a "most-prized piece of jewelry" comes from this East Side retailer, whose whimsical designs – flowers, "multicolored" bugs and of course the famed, "absolutely adorable baby shoe" charms – often become "status items"; "celebrity moms" are often spotted here picking up a "customized" gift for a "new grandmother" or themselves; naturally, popularity comes at a price.

Aaron Faber Gallery [S][C] 27 | 25 | 21 | VE

666 Fifth Ave. (53rd St.), E/V to 5th Ave./53rd St., 212-586-8411; www.aaronfaber.com

■ So what if MoMA's moved temporarily – entering this chicly minimalist space on West 53rd Street "is like going into a craft museum"; some know this "true gallery" (they hold exhibitions as well as sell stuff) as a "standby for vintage watches" that has the "best service department around"; to others, the draw is the one-of-a-kind, "eclectic, handcrafted jewelry" from studio artists like Tod Pardon and Marco Borghesi that complements the "wonderful estate pieces"; "from antique to ultramodern", it's "the best wearable art in town."

Aaron's 21 | 15 | 18 | E

627 Fifth Ave. (bet. 17th & 18th Sts.), Brooklyn, M/R to Prospect Ave., 718-768-5400; 888-768-5400; www.aarons.com

◪ "Very expensive clothing is now only expensive" at this family-owned "old-timer" "off the beaten path" in south Park Slope where "eager-to-help" salespeople "call you when what you like comes in"; a "comfy" waiting area for "hubby to sit" sipping free coffee and "great purses", accessories, jewelry and womenswear divided into "displays of name designers" like MaxMara and Elie Tahari make this "a shopper's dream" despite the communal dressing room and prices that are "not that cheap."

ABC CARPET & HOME ◐[S] 25 | 24 | 17 | VE

888 Broadway (19th St.), 4/5/6/L/N/Q/R/W to 14th St./Union Sq., 212-473-3000

20 Jay St. (Plymouth St.), Brooklyn, F to York St., 718-643-7400 [C]

www.abchome.com

■ Each "nook and cranny" of this "dazzling", "dizzying" Flatiron District "decorating wonderland" is crammed with everything from "the most luxurious table and bed linens", "beautiful pillows", "über-chic sofas" and chandeliers to French, Italian, Asian and American "antique-y looking things" and "unique" ephemera from "unknown and well-known designers"; if the eight floors of "ever-changing", "quirky" displays of "pseudo-bohemian elegance" don't make you light-headed, the prices "poking holes in the ozone layer" may; N.B. the Brooklyn Dumbo branch opened last year.

ABC Carpet & Home (Carpets/Rugs) ⊘❺☐
| 25 | 22 | 17 | E |

881 Broadway (bet. 18th & 19th Sts.), 4/5/6/L/N/Q/R/W to 14th St./ Union Sq., 212-473-3000; www.abccarpet.com

■ Don't go to this "expansive carpeting mecca" in the Flatiron District "looking for presentation" (like you would at its stylish big sister across the street), but do make a pilgrimage for "piles and piles" of "excellent" "upscale" rugs "from around the world"; some say the staff is "willing to bargain", but for a sure thing wallet-watchers head for the basement and check out the clearance items and remnants "for great buys."

ABC Carpet & Home Warehouse Outlet ⊘❺
| 21 | 13 | 15 | E |

1055 Bronx River Ave. (Bruckner Expwy.), Bronx, 6 to Whitlock Ave., 718-842-8772; www.abchome.com

◪ Supporters say "the occasional find makes the trek" to this Bronx warehouse outlet of the famed Flatiron District duo "worth it" for "seek and ye shall find" "good deals" on furniture, bed and table linens, textiles and rugs, though they warn "you have to remember how high-end they were to begin with"; still, cynics cite the "hit-or-miss" selection of "random pieces" and caution prices "still ain't cheap."

Abercrombie & Fitch ⊘❺☐
| 16 | 18 | 13 | M |

South Street Seaport, 199 Water St. (Fulton St.), 2/3/4/5/A/C/J/M/Z to Fulton St./B'way/Nassau, 212-809-9000
Staten Island Mall, 2655 Richmond Ave., Staten Island, 718-698-9480
888-856-4480; www.abercrombie.com

◪ "Get your libido going" at these national chain "playgrounds" for the "pouty young"; the South Street Seaport and Staten Island "hangouts" are "constantly crowded" with college students and teens pawing the "sexy", "preppy" wear, even though detractors dis "blaring music" and "eye-candy salespeople" lacking "any ability to fold shirts or keep the store orderly"; bring a "fat allowance from mom and dad", as the "hipness quotient" costs aplenty.

ABH Design ☐
| – | – | – | E |

401 E. 76th St. (bet. 1st & York Aves.), 6 to 77th St., 212-249-2276
Costume designer Aude Bronson-Howard's appealing Upper East Side yearling features mostly her own stylish takes on fashion and home accessories, although there are some unusual imports as well; *pour la maison,* there are striped silk napkins, lacy-edged Italian plates, fanciful French candlesticks and terry towels trimmed with pom-poms, and *pour madame,* faux mink slippers, sporty down stoles and cashmere, cotton and cut-velvet robes.

Abracadabra
| 21 | 17 | 17 | M |

19 W. 21st St. (bet. 5th & 6th Aves.), R/W to 23rd St., 212-627-5194; www.abracadabrasuperstore.com

■ "You're sure to learn a good trick or two" at this Flatiron hocus-pocus shop that's "full of curiosities" – and "far more than a toy store"; "you'll find a myriad of costumes" and "simply incredible masks" for you and the kids to buy or rent (it's "the place to be for Halloween" or even an "offbeat date") plus "sections dedicated to wigs, swords and fake jewelry."

Academy Records & CDs ⏺🅂🅲 | 23 | 12 | 15 | I |
77 E. 10th St. (bet. 3rd & 4th Aves.), 6 to Astor Pl.; R/W to 8th St., 212-780-9166
12 W. 18th St. (bet. 5th & 6th Aves.), 4/5/6/L/N/Q/R/W to 14th St./ Union Sq., 212-242-3000
www.academy-records.com
■ You'll have to "go elbow-to-elbow with fellow browsers" to "unearth" "musical treasures" at this "ultimate source for used classical" LPs in the Flatiron District; the "tightly packed" selection also turns up jazz, rock and show-tune CD "rarities and staples", VHS tapes and DVDs at "rock-bottom prices"; P.S. the East Village outlet sells mostly jazz, blues, Latin and reggae music.

a.cheng ⏺🅂🅲 | ▽ 20 | 19 | 23 | M |
443 E. Ninth St. (bet. Ave. A & 1st Ave.), 6 to Astor Pl.; L to 1st Ave., 212-979-7324; www.achengshop.com
■ "Very cute", "girlie creations" rule at this "tiny East Village store", the brainchild of owner and shopkeeper Alice Cheng; her signature corduroy shirtdresses, available in new colors each season, plus vintage "kimono-fabric" touches on tailored jeans, denim jackets and Mandarin-collared dresses ensure "everyone's compliments" when worn.

Active Wearhouse ⏺🅂 | 20 | 14 | 13 | M |
514 Broadway (bet. Broome & Spring Sts.), 6 to Spring St.; R/W to Prince St., 212-965-2284
■ This hopping, "so urban" SoHo shop for men and women features a fly selection of "all the activewear and streetwear you need", from jerseys, team caps and ENYC sweatshirts" to Sean Jean jackets, North Face parkas and Baby Phat hoodies and sweatpants; denim is also in the house, while "the newest funky kicks on market" take center stage to the rear, with a wraparound wall devoted to major playas like Puma, Timberland and Adidas.

Add ⏺🅂 | 22 | 22 | 20 | M |
461 W. Broadway (bet. Houston & Prince Sts.), F/S/V to B'way/ Lafayette; R/W to Prince St., 212-539-1439
■ "Spiffy Manhattanites" fall for the "great shawls", "kitschy handbags", "eclectic costume jewelry" and "unique hats" from a host of fresh, new designers at this SoHo accessories "gem"; the "friendly staff" is "happy to let you open the cases to try things on" and will even "offer great gift ideas – even if that gift is for yourself."

Addison on Madison 🅲 | 19 | – | 21 | E |
29 W. 57th St., 9th fl. (bet. 5th & 6th Aves.), N/R/W to 5th Ave./59th St., 212-308-2660
■ For "shirts you don't see anywhere else" – including some with "unusual ¼-inch collar sizes" – gents look to this specialty store and showroom whose styles favor the "comfortable, baggy American look"; shoppers savor the "accommodating" services: "sleeves are shortened to fit" and "care is taken to get you a tie that works with the shirt"; N.B. it moved to these Midtown digs post-*Survey*.

Adidas Originals 🅂 | 22 | 21 | 17 | M |
136 Wooster St. (bet. Houston & Prince Sts.), R/W to Prince St., 212-777-2001; 800-289-2724; www.adidas.com
■ "You're bound to run into a movie star", or at the very least, fashionistas and club kids, at this garagelike "trendy" SoHo

"pillar of downtown footwear" and "hip athletic wear for both non-athletes" and jocks where the goods are displayed on "cool" low white tables and ultra-futuristic ice-blue boxes and the music's always pumping; "if you want the Originals Collection" – "updated" "retro" "classics from your youth" – plus limited-edition items "that can't be found at Foot Locker", make tracks.

Adorama Camera S | 25 | 12 | 15 | M |
42 W. 18th St. (bet. 5th & 6th Aves.), 4/5/6/L/N/Q/R/W to 14th St./ Union Sq., 212-741-0052; 800-223-2500; www.adorama.com
■ Shutterbugs hoping "to avoid long lines" find that this Flatiron photo palace is "the best one-stop shopping for all your camera needs and wants"; you can expect "great prices" on a "very large stock" of new and used equipment for "professional and beginner" shoots and darkroom work, but "don't expect coddling" since the staff "can't be bothered with stupid questions from amateurs."

Adrien Linford S C | 25 | 25 | 18 | E |
1339 Madison Ave. (bet. 93rd & 94th Sts.), 6 to 96th St., 212-426-1500
927 Madison Ave. (74th St.), 6 to 77th St., 212-628-4500
■ Upper East Side duo devoted to Asian-oriented items – from home accessories like pottery, furniture made of abaca (banana fiber) and golden Buddhas to "upscale geegaws" like "handmade jewelry"; since "they have something for everyone", it's a "great place to get a gift."

Aedes De Venustas ◖ S C   ▽ | 29 | 27 | 24 | E |
9 Christopher St. (bet. 6th Ave. & 7th Ave. S.), 1/9 to Christopher St./ Sheridan Sq., 212-206-8674; 888-233 3715; www.aedes.com
■ "The products, packaging and salespeople are all beautiful" at this tiny, gilded-brick-and-burgundy Greenwich Village home and body fragrance boutique with "gorgeous and unusual" scents, along with candles and bath and beauty products from the likes of Diptyque, Creed and Christian Tortu; "service is superb" (they'll let you "take home samples to try before you buy"), and gift-wrapping ($4.50–$7.50) is as chic as the shop's fabulous floral arrangements.

Aero C | 26 | 21 | 19 | VE |
132 Spring St. (bet. Greene & Wooster Sts.), R/W to Prince St., 212-966-1500; www.aerostudios.com
■ Inspired by the élan of '40s and mid-century furnishings, "bright, young" interior designer and owner Thomas O'Brien fills his two-story SoHo shop with a "brilliant selection" of his own designs along with "well-chosen" vintage items from around the world; aesthetes assert that "he could be this generation's Jean-Michel Frank", but even if he's not, the pieces are "clean, fresh and so very New York."

Aerosoles ◖ S | 18 | 16 | 16 | I |
36 W. 34th St. (bet. 5th & 6th Aves.), B/D/F/N/Q/R/V/W to 34th St./ Herald Sq., 212-563-0610; 800-798-9478; www.aerosoles.com
Additional locations throughout the NY area
☑ "A whole lotta comfort", "a twinge of style" "and a teeny tiny price" prompt boosters to bellow "bravo", this chain is "finally" "making great strides"; scores of surveyors insist these shoes feel "like you're walking on a cloud", plus they're so "fetching" ("not as unhip as they used to be") it "almost makes you forget your mother would like them"; "how boring" yawn the "blasé", who also find service "so-so" and the decor downright "antiseptic."

AFNY C
25 | 16 | 14 | E

22 W. 21st St., 15th fl. (bet. 5th & 6th Aves.), F/N/R/V to 23rd St., 212-243-5400; 800-366-2284; www.afnewyork.com

☑ Loyalists of this converted loft space in Chelsea head here "for ideas" and a "fabulous selection" of plumbing and bath fixtures (from basins to bathtubs and bidets) "in all styles"; while surveyors are split on service ("informed" vs. imperfect), they agree "prices are high."

Agatha Paris ⦿ S C
19 | 18 | 15 | M

159-A Columbus Ave. (67th St.), 1/9 to 66th St./Lincoln Ctr., 212-362-0959
611 Madison Ave. (58th St.), N/R/W to 5th Ave./59th St., 212-758-4301
www.agatha.fr

☑ East Side or West Side, browsing for "cheap and chic", "colorful costume jewelry" is a cinch at these "fashionable" French chain links, which "neatly lay out the wares in glass cases and on the walls"; the "fun-faux", "throwaway" pieces, including the signature Scottish Terrier line, won't "break the bank" – but you also "get what you paid for" say those who quibble over the "quality."

Agent Provocateur S C
26 | 26 | 21 | VE

133 Mercer St. (bet. Prince & Spring Sts.), R/W to Prince St., 212-965-0229; www.agentprovocateur.com

■ "Heidi Fleiss, hold onto your brassiere" – this pink-and-black SoHo "paradise" for "deliciously sexy, tawdry lingerie from the UK" proves "there's no substitute for kink with style", "delivering lacy nothings and marabou-trimmed satin ensembles" for those "bawdy nights" "with a wink and a smile"; "just tittering around" this "world of pure glamour and fantasy" "makes you feel like Marilyn Monroe", plus "even men", mesmerized by the "plentiful" staff clad in "revealing", "retro" "beauty school drop-out uniforms" "love to shop here."

Agnès B. S C
21 | 20 | 15 | E

13 E. 16th St. (bet. 5th Ave. & Union Sq. W.), 4/5/6/L/N/Q/R/W to 14th St./Union Sq., 212-741-2585; 888-246-3722
103 Greene St. (bet. Prince & Spring Sts.), R/W to Prince St., 212-925-4649
1063 Madison Ave. (bet. 80th & 81st Sts.), 6 to 77th St., 212-570-9333
www.agnesb.com

■ "For days when you feel like being French", these "appealing" boutiques beckon with "classic T-shirts", "adorable" separates and "career clothing with a twist", most of it cut "for the thin crowd"; each can be "a fun place to shop", but bring along *beaucoup* bucks, as the merchandise is often "*très cher*"; N.B. the SoHo branch also sells maternity and children's fashions.

Agnès B. Homme S C
20 | 20 | 18 | E

79 Greene St. (bet. Broome & Spring Sts.), R/W to Prince St., 212-431-4339; www.agnesb.com

■ Conveniently close to the chain's female flagship in SoHo, this masculine counterpart is "a must-stop for your man", thanks to the "great selection of shirts, pants and accessories" arrayed in a clean, spare space; the "terrific, sleek designs" of its "offbeat" classics appeal to the "Francophile in all of us."

A.I. Friedman [S]
24 | 22 | 19 | M

44 W.18th St. (bet. 5th & 6th Aves.), 1/9 to 18th St., 212-243-9000;
www.aifriedman.com

◪ In a "chic, airy" Flatiron space, this "quality" art "warehouse" stocks "for the weekend dabbler"; there's only a "small selection of premium supplies" for "real" painters and sculptors, but it's "great for elegant frames, fancy Italian office furniture, inventive journals" and "interesting knickknacks", plus "they don't treat you like a moron if you don't know exactly what you're looking for."

Airline Stationery
22 | 12 | 18 | M

155 E. 44th St. (bet. Lexington & 3rd Aves.), 4/5/6/7/S to 42nd St./
Grand Central, 212-532-9410
284 Madison Ave. (bet. 40th & 41st Sts.), 4/5/6/7/S to 42nd St./
Grand Central, 212-532-6525
www.airlinestationery.com

◪ This affordable, "old-time" family-run stationer and office supplier on Madison Ave. with an East 40s outpost has a similar "feel to a hardware store" – "utilitarian" and "cluttered" with a staff that ably "helps the pickiest of customers" – but it "sure beats the national chains" with its "complete selection" of "business necessities for today's world."

Air Market [S][C]
21 | 17 | 12 | M

97 Third Ave. (bet. 12th & 13th Sts.), 4/5/6/L/N/Q/R/W to 14th St./
Union Sq., 212-995-5888

◪ Fashionistas swayed by "cool", "kitschy", "cartoony Asian tchotchkes" say "Hello Kitty" to the selection of Sanrio's "cutesy Japanese" gift items that fill this East Village "hideaway" that's also stocked with super-hip threads for men and women; while the "funky Japanese accessories" and reworked vintage tees provide "a lot of fun", a few vent that some items are "wildly overpriced."

Akris [C]
26 | 23 | 20 | VE

835 Madison Ave. (bet. 69th & 70th Sts.), 6 to 68th St., 212-717-1170

■ "Just go in and touch" the "sumptuous" women's clothing from this "luxurious" Swiss designer collection, now available at its new tri-level East 60s "shopping haven"; the minimalist interior spares no expense with its floating staircase and horsehair walls, which show off several collections, in a range of price points, of "well-styled merchandise" with "plenty of attitude", including "beautifully tailored suits" and "exquisite" knitwear.

Alain Mikli [S][C]
27 | 25 | 20 | VE

880 Madison Ave. (bet. 71st & 72nd Sts.), 6 to 68th St., 212-472-6085;
www.mikli.com

■ "If you want to be noticed", this East 70s mecca features "fashion-forward" frames that ensure you "won't see yourself coming and going"; the pale-wood setting is "equally beautiful", the "service is impeccable", and even if "people with heart conditions should beware of the sticker shock" that accompanies such "high-end" wares, it's well "worth it" for the "coolest specs in town."

A la Maison [S][C]
22 | 24 | 19 | E

1078 Madison Ave. (81st St.), 6 to 77th St., 212-396-1020;
www.alamaison1.com

■ Like a "French version of Ralph" is what surveyors say about this two-story Upper East Side home-furnishings emporium featuring

European imports like settees, commodes, china, crystal and candlestick lamps; it's "great for picking up gifts for the hard-to-buy-for person" or for pretty, pricey "pieces to perk up your own place."

Alan Moss ⊅ C
▽ 29 | 26 | 19 | VE

436 Lafayette St. (Astor Pl.), B/D/F/S/V to B'way/Lafayette St., 212-473-1310

■ East Village stalwart showcasing "museum-quality" 20th-century furniture, art, glass and lighting; loyalists "love" the owner's "great eye" for "fabulous things" but caution that the cost of benefiting from some of the "best taste" in NY can often be "out-of-bounds."

A LA VIEILLE RUSSIE
28 | 26 | 24 | VE

781 Fifth Ave. (bet. 59th & 60th Sts.), N/R/W to 5th Ave./59th St., 212-752-1727; www.alvr.com

☑ It's "like shopping in Old St. Petersburg" at this "purveyor of high-end Russian artifacts" where the famed Fabergé eggs, "often-rare" European jewelry and "antique place settings" coexist in a "luxurious", "museumlike" setting "across from the Plaza"; the staff is "pleasant and professional" (as long as you "dress like the czar"), and if the prices seem as "royal" as the pedigrees – well, "just [gazing at] the windows is a turn-on."

Albee Baby Carriage Co.
25 | 8 | 19 | M

715 Amsterdam Ave. (95th St.), 1/2/3/9 to 96th St., 212-662-5740; www.albeebaby.com

■ Family-owned since 1933, this "old faithful" on the Upper West Side "carries everything you could possibly need for your babe", from furniture, layettes, cribs and strollers to toys, all "packed into a very tight space"; sure, it can be "chaotic to navigate", but the "helpful staff" "really knows its stuff"; P.S. "free delivery is a dream", plus "they repair Maclaren strollers for a reasonable cost."

Albertine S C
▽ 21 | 22 | 23 | E

13 Christopher St. (bet. Greenwich Ave. & Waverly Pl.), 1/9 to Christopher St./Sheridan Sq., 212-924-8515

☑ Charming windows lure style-mavens into this parlor-level walk-up, a "gem" on the edge of the West Village that prides itself on handmade, one-of-a-kind garb, including items fashioned from vintage fabrics and screen-printed tees; owner Kyung Lee has an eye for young, original design talent, featuring edgy lines like Cinderloop, Kathy Kemp and Christopher Dean; still, a handful huff the reworked clothing resembles "shreds of fabric."

Alcone
25 | 15 | 22 | M

235 W. 19th St. (bet. 7th & 8th Aves.), 1/9 to 23rd St., 212-633-0551; 800-466-7446; www.alconeco.com

■ Tiny, family-owned Chelsea storefront that's packed with professional and theatrical cosmetics "makeup artists can't live without" like such hard-to-find faves as Visiora Foundation, "the best sponges" and beauty editor's picks like Face-To-Face SuperMatte Antishine; manned by an "expert staff" this "user-friendly" shop should also appeal to the "average consumer."

Aldo S C
16 | 17 | 15 | M

15 W. 34th St. (bet. 5th & 6th Aves.), B/D/F/N/Q/R/V/W to 34th St./Herald Sq., 212-594-6255; www.aldoshoes.com

☑ "Your feet can look good without costing an arm and a leg" applauds the "hip crowd" that falls for this "trendy" Canadian chain's "chunky, funky and borderline cheesy" his-and-her shoes; but bashers give it the boot, blasting they "look better than they actually feel" – "boy, do my little piggies hurt" – and find the "psuedo-helpful" staff has all the "personality of a cardboard box."

Alexander McQueen S | 26 | 26 | 19 | VE |
417 W. 14th St. (bet. 9th & 10th Aves.), A/C/E/L to 14th St./8th Ave., 212-645-1797; www.alexandermcqueen.com
■ "The British bad boy makes good in the Meatpacking District", showcasing his "witty, historically flavored, totally hip and absolutely fantastic" designs, from "sexy, edgy frocks" to "fabulous" jewelry, eyewear and shoes in this "funky", futuristic flagship; don't be "intimidated" – the "staff is helpful" and "it's great to just browse" in the "mind-blowing" "museum", with its curved walls and ceilings and mirrored cylindrical dressing rooms that evoke a *Close Encounters of the Third Kind* feel – and it's "even more fun if you can afford to buy here."

Alexia Crawford ●SC | 24 | 21 | 22 | M |
199 Prince St. (bet. MacDougal & Sullivan Sts.), C/E to Spring St., 212-473-9703; www.shopalexiacrawford.com
■ "Tucked away on the outskirts of SoHo", this "cute" accessories shop owned by Aussie Alexia offers "great, offbeat" "treasures" "that won't break the bank"; the "trendy but wearable jewelry", made mostly from sterling silver, freshwater pearls and semi-precious stones, and the "unique" colorful handbags "look modern and stylish" – no wonder "young, cost-efficient shoppers" keep coming back for more.

Alice Underground ●S | 18 | 15 | 12 | M |
481 Broadway (bet. Broome & Grand Sts.), 6/J/M/N/Q/R/W/Z to Canal St., 212-431-9067
☑ For an experience akin to "raiding your eccentric aunt's closet", "go ask Alice", whose creaky-floored, "spacious store" in SoHo carries an array of men's and women's vintage threads, toys and home furnishings; prices are "not the cheapest" (though the "old linens are still a bargain") and sophisticates sniff the "leather jackets, formalwear and funky stuff" are "not top-of-the-line – but it's worth checking out" for the occasional "incredible find."

Alife Rivington Club SC | ∇ 24 | 27 | 18 | E |
178 Orchard St. (bet. Houston & Stanton Sts.), F/V to Lower East Side/ 2nd Ave., 646-654-0628
158 Rivington St. (bet. Clinton & Suffolk Sts.), F/J/M/Z to Delancey/ Essex Sts., 212-375-8128
■ "Push a buzzer to get into" Alife Rivington's "fantastic" Lower East Side "underground" "country club for sneakers" where you'll "catch glimpses of people you'd know if you were cooler"; "if you're an old-school aficionado", the "limited-edition, imported" and vintage "kicks", displayed in cubbyholes, "will bring back tons of memories"; older sibling Alife nearby on Orchard Street feels like an "exhibit space", with artwork in the windows offset by "hip footwear" and an "enticing" mix of apparel and accessories.

Alkit Pro Camera | 20 | 18 | 19 | E |
222 Park Ave. S. (18th St.), 4/5/6/L/N/Q/R/W to 14th St./Union Sq., 212-674-1515 S
830 Seventh Ave. (bet. 53rd & 54th Sts.), 1/9 to 50th St., 212-262-2424
(continued)

(continued)
Alkit Pro Camera
820 Third Ave. (50th St.), 6/E/V to 51st St./Lexington Ave., 212-832-2101
www.alkit.com
◪ There's a lot of contrast to the picture of this camera shop/lab chain: photo buffs impressed with the "professional-quality developing" and "helpful, knowledgeable" service, including free tutorials with digital purchases, say it's "good all-around"; while their Advantage Club offers discounts, others sniff it's "not the best place to buy", given the "expensive but mediocre processing" – perhaps it's all that "arrogance bubbling over" into the chemicals?

Allan & Suzi [S] 21 | 16 | 17 | E
416 Amsterdam Ave. (80th St.), 1/9 to 79th St., 212-724-7445; www.allanandsuzi.net
◪ "If your style is flamboyant", you'll enjoy exploring this long, narrow Upper West Side consignment/vintage clothing store, "crammed to the gills" with "fashions that range from funky to haute couture", from 1950s prom dresses to last season's Roberto Cavalli to new pieces from the likes of Gucci and Prada; regulars warn "beware the costs" and, occasionally, the owners (who "can be moody", though knowledgeable); still, be it a feather boa or a pair of Jimmy Choos, "everyone needs something from here in his or her closet."

Allen Edmonds [S] 27 | 22 | 23 | VE
24 E. 44th St. (bet. 5th & Madison Aves.), 4/5/6/7/S to 42nd St./ Grand Central, 212-682-3144
551 Madison Ave. (55th St.), E/V to 5th Ave./53rd St., 212-308-8305
877-817-7615; www.allenedmonds.com
■ "Without question, some of the most comfortable" men's "shoes on the planet" are walking out of these veteran Midtowners, best known for their handcrafted "quality, conservative" business footwear (though they actually offer a "wide range of styles", from dress to casual), meticulously fitted by "excellent" staffers; yes, the goods are geared to "rich feet", but "for hard-to-find sizes, they're worth the bucks."

Alpana Bawa [S][C] – | – | – | E
70 E. First St. (bet. 1st & 2nd Aves.), F/V to Lower East Side/2nd Ave., 212-254-1249
41 Grand St. (bet. Thompson St. & W. B'way), A/C/E to Canal St., 212-431-6367
www.alpanabawa.com
The stripped-down interiors of this East Village shop and its SoHo offshoot serve as a blank canvas for the "vibrant" wake-up-call colors of this radiant, directional his-and-her collection of "comfortable" Indian shirts, dresses and separates; splendid fabrics, artfully placed embroidery, whimsical appliqués and fanciful stripes and dots make these "ethnic-inspired", "very original" collectibles stand out from the pack – what a "fun" "deviation from classic black!"

Alphabets ◐ [S] 23 | 20 | 15 | M
115 Ave. A (bet. 7th St. & St. Marks Pl.), 6 to Astor Pl., 212-475-7250
2284 Broadway (bet. 82nd & 83rd Sts.), 1/9 to 79th St., 212-579-5702

(continued)
Alphabets
47 Greenwich Ave. (bet. Charles & Perry Sts.), 1/2/3/9 to 14th St.;
1/9 to Christopher St., 212-229-2966
www.alphabetsnyc.com
■ You'll encounter "kitsch galore" at this "eclectic", "quirky" mini-chain that caters to "the child within" with loads of "campy" housewares and novelties like Rosie the Riveter action figures exhibiting a "wink-and-nudge irony" that's catnip to "baby boomers"; those who know their ABCs also revel in the merch "of the decidedly adult variety" that, along with "the best cards", "makes gift-giving so easy"; P.S. the East Village shop also stocks upscale candles, frames and bath products.

Altman Luggage ⑤   23 | 11 | 19 | I
135 Orchard St. (bet. Delancey & Rivington Sts.), F/J/M/Z to Delancey/
Essex Sts., 212-254-7275; www.altmanluggage.com
■ Expect "Lower East Side prices and atmosphere" at this Orchard Street luggage "institution" "jammed" with "every type of bag for every type of traveler", from Andiamo to Kipling to Timberland and more; while "all the major brands are always discounted" "below department-store prices", "don't be afraid to ask for a better deal" – insiders insist "there's room for bargaining."

Amarcord Vintage Fashion ◑⑤   24 | 21 | 23 | M
84 E. Seventh St. (bet. 1st & 2nd Aves.), 6 to Astor Pl., 212-614-7133
223 Bedford Ave. (bet. N. 4th & 5th Sts.), Brooklyn, L to Bedford Ave.,
718-963-4001
www.amarcordvintagefashion.com
■ "Sophisticated vintage shoppers" visit this East Villager for its "wonderful selection" of "witty clothes" and "unusual bags", "mostly by Italian designers" from the 1960s–80s and its newer Williamsburg sibling for men's and women's finds, plus Army/Navy wares from abroad; everything's "reasonably priced and in mint condition", but "luck's in the cards if the owners are around", as they'll "tell you exactly which part of Europe each item came from."

American Eagle Outfitters ◑⑤   15 | 15 | 15 | M
575 Broadway (bet. Houston & Prince Sts.), R/W to Prince St.,
212-941-9785
South Street Seaport, 89 South St. (Fulton St.), 2/3/4/5/A/C/J/M/Z to
Fulton St./B'way/Nassau, 212-571-5354
Staten Island Mall, 2655 Richmond Ave., Staten Island, 718-494-2885
www.ae.com
◪ If their producers ever cut them off, the "young, cute cast of *Dawson's Creek*" just might shop for "weekend duds" at this "Abercrombie-esque" chain for teens of both sexes "with a smaller budget" and "less attitude"; cop that "rumpled, wrinkled" "classic look" "for frat boys and the girls who love them" at South Street Seaport, on Staten Island and, now, in SoHo.

American Folk Art Museum ⑤Ⓒ   19 | 19 | 17 | M
2 Lincoln Sq., Columbus Ave. (bet. 65th & 66th Sts.), 1/9 to 66th St./
Lincoln Ctr., 212-595-9533 ◑
45 W. 53rd St. (bet. 5th & 6th Aves.), E/V to 5th Ave./53rd St., 212-265-1040
www.folkartmuseum.org
◪ "Descend through the new jewel box of a building" designed by Tod Williams Billie Tsien & Associates in Midtown "to the store

tucked into a ground-floor corner and shop for bottle-cap bowls", "pine cone, corncob and starfish Santas" and other "fun stuff" "from the heartland"; "they know their merchandise and give you history" as well as an artist's bio with your purchase, but the "uneven" collection has antagonists arguing "you'll do better at a craft fair"; there's another branch in the museum's Upper West Side gallery.

American Girl Place 🆂🅲 — | — | — | E
609 Fifth Ave. (49th St.), B/D/F/V to 47-50th Sts./Rockefeller Ctr., 212-371-2220; 800-845-0005; www.americangirl.com
Gotham's latest toy extravaganza, a sprawling Fifth Avenue showcase modeled after the Chicago original, goes way beyond the expected, captivating girls with a dazzling array of dolls, many inspired by historical events and available with companion books that relay fictional roles in, say, World War II or the Great Depression, plus matching outfits for owners; dollies can change their 'dos in the '50s-style hair salon, visit the hospital, accompany kids and moms in the cafe, overseen by chef Michael Lomonaco, and even catch live performances in the 130-seat theater.

American Houseware and Hardware 🆂 20 | 13 | 17 | M
95 Court St. (bet. Schermerhorn & Livingston Sts.), Brooklyn, 2/3/4/5/M/R to Court St./Borough Hall, 718-858-5250
85-91 Court St. (bet. Schermerhorn & Livingston Sts.), Brooklyn, 2/3/4/5/M/R to Court St./Borough Hall, 718-243-0844
◪ Brooklyn Heights duo divided into two storefronts: 81-91 Court Street is a general housewares store offering air conditioners, potting soil, paint, grills and cookware; 95 Court Street, a few doors down, is an old-fashioned "real hardware shop" "crammed" with an "in-depth selection" of drills, plumbing, wiring and lumber; in short, it seems "they have a lot of everything – except salespeople."

American Kennels ◑🆂 18 | 14 | 15 | E
798 Lexington Ave. (bet. 61st & 62nd Sts.), 4/5/6/F/N/R/W to 59th St./Lexington Ave., 212-838-8460
◪ At this East 60s pet shop, you'll find almost "anything you need" for the "pampered" pooch and kitty, including "fashionable dog collars", cat accessories and "cute clothes", plus the "helpful staff" can guide you; however, wallet-watchers warn it's strictly for those with "endless budgets."

American Museum of Natural History 🆂 21 | 20 | 16 | M
79th St. & Central Park West, B/C to 81st St., 212-769-5100; www.amnh.org
◼ With a main store and "many theme boutiques" throughout the museum, treasure hunters "don't have to dig too hard" for riches here; the "extensive selection" of "innovative toys" makes it "one of the best places to shop for kids' gifts" – though there's "stuff that's equally fascinating for parents", such as "archaeological models", "nifty" "nature books, videos", "unique jewelry" and cultural crafts from all over the world; best of all, the purchases "won't break the bank", "especially with a member's discount."

Amsale 24 | 23 | 20 | VE
625 Madison Ave. (bet. 58th & 59th Sts.), N/R/W to 5th Ave./59th St., 212-583-1700; www.amsale.com
◼ Amsale Aberra "fulfills every woman's Grace Kelly–inspired wedding dream" at her "airy", by-appointment-only "Madison

Avenue bridal boutique" with "classic", "elegant gowns" that are "feminine without being frothy" and finished with "unique details"; while a bevy of betrothed applauds the "phenomenal service provided by patient, no attitude saleswomen", a few find the staff a "bit haughty"; N.B. as a bonus, the designer also creates eveningwear and bridesmaid's dresses.

Amy Chan 🆂🅲   20 | 21 | 21 | E
247 Mulberry St. (bet. Prince & Spring Sts.), 6 to Spring St., 212-966-3417

☑ Established at the forefront of the NoLita boom, this "very cool" shop boasts old-world tiled floors and fresco-ish walls, a "hip" backdrop for the "hippie rock star merchandise", including "interesting", one-of-a-kind clothing from emerging designers, Chan's signature "cute" clutches and "stylish" handbags sporting mosaic details, plus "chic" purses from other lines; the "friendly staff" is so welcoming, "you don't even mind that everyone in there" seems to be a "size 0."

An American Craftsman ◐🆂🅲   22 | 21 | 18 | E
Rockefeller Ctr., 60 W. 50th St. (bet. Rockefeller Plaza & 6th Ave.), B/D/F/V to 47-50th Sts./Rockefeller Ctr., 212-307-7161
790 Seventh Ave. (52nd St.), 1/9 to 50th St., 212-399-2555
www.anamericancraftsman.com

☑ Fans of these gallery-style stores in the West 50s say their "handmade" home furnishings – many of them crafted of "wood, ceramic" or metal and ranging from trickling fountains and wind chimes to "decorative boxes", bowls, chopping blocks and "beautiful art glass" – make for "unique gifts", but some critics call them "knickknacks" that are "kitschy" and "common."

Andy's Chee-Pees ◐🆂   15 | 9 | 10 | M
691 Broadway (bet. 3rd & 4th Sts.), 6 to Bleecker St.; B/D/F/S/V to B'way/Lafayette St., 212-420-5980

☑ "An enormous selection of old Levi's, corduroys, [rock] T-shirts and other typical thrift-store fare" – plus "Cinderella-style prom dresses from the 1950s" and '60s, and even 21st-century merch – fills this NoHo retailer, itself a veteran of the vintage scene; however, many reviewers rant it's "not so chee-pee", given the "quality of the merchandise" and its "cramped" presentation.

Angela's Vintage Boutique ◐🆂   21 | 15 | 17 | M
330 E. 11th St. (bet. 1st & 2nd Aves.), L to 1st Ave.; 6 to Astor Pl., 212-475-1571

■ Though barely bigger than a shoebox, this East Village vintage clothier boasts a 20th-century-spanning array of "top-notch" merchandise for madame; "what a steal!" – the "excellent choices" range from fun (1950s ballerina bags) to buttoned-up post-Victorian (circa 1900s), with an emphasis on party-perfect 1920s flapper dresses; shoppers also snag "solid designer pieces" from status-y names like Dior and Geoffrey Beene from more modern times, up to the 1980s.

Angel Street Thrift Shop 🆂   16 | 15 | 16 | I
118 W. 17th St. (bet. 6th & 7th Aves.), 1/9 to 18th St., 212-229-0546; www.angelthriftshop.org

☑ "You have to dig and go often", but this Chelsea thrift shop yields "great finds", particularly "excellent furniture", "gently worn designer" threads and "fun records", with proceeds benefiting the Lower East Side Service Center; the "setup" in a 19th-century industrial building and "low prices" are heavenly, but the service veers from "friendly" to "unhelpful."

Anik 🅂 | 22 | 19 | 16 | E |

1122 Madison Ave. (bet. 83rd & 84th Sts.), 4/5/6 to 86th St., 212-249-2417
1355 Third Ave. (bet. 77th & 78th Sts.), 6 to 77th St., 212-861-9840
☑ "A bit of everything for fashionably wise" and "svelte", "trendy women" can be found at these "Upper East Side destinations", from "career classics with flare" to "sexy evening clothes" to "everyday staples, including Juicy Couture sweats", and "decent deals" in the "sale room"; but customers are split when it comes to service with supporters praising the "courteous" staff and snipers sniffing "if they were nicer maybe I'd go more often"; N.B. they now sell children's cashmere sweaters too.

Anna 🅂🅲 | – | – | – | E |

150 E. Third St. (bet. Aves. A & B), F/V to Lower East Side/2nd Ave., 212-358-0195
"Friendly" designer-owner Kathy Kemp is a "doll" and she knows what makes urban women tick, selling her eponymous line of "adorable", pared-down, body-hugging and coyishly sexy tops, dresses and pants from this pert East Village boutique that has less of a vintage focus than at its outset in 1997; among the hotter items in the "intriguing mix" is the 'seven-way silk shirt', complete with instructions on how to maximize its effect.

Anna Sui 🅂🅲 | 22 | 22 | 18 | E |

113 Greene St. (bet. Prince & Spring Sts.), R/W to Prince St., 212-941-8406; www.annasui.com
■ "Adventurous" SoHo shoppers dig the "fanciful bohemian chic" (think purple walls and red floors) in this "funky little boutique" that takes you "back in time", "blasting '60s music" as a backdrop for the eponymous designer's "girlie, sexy", "hippyish clothing"; prices are "a little high", but the "attentive" service isn't overbearing, so feel free to "sit, shop, browse" or "check out the really fun cosmetics."

Ann Crabtree 🅲 | 20 | 20 | 21 | E |

1260 Madison Ave. (90th St.), 4/5/6 to 86th St.; 6 to 96th St., 212-996-6499
☑ A must-stop for young Carnegie Hill moms who rely on the racks of "wearable as well as elegant" women's separates from a variety of European labels for their fashionably understated wardrobes; "pleasant sales help", "beautiful smelling soaps and bath things", plus "lovely" accessories enhance the appeal, but a few crab that the selection can be "limited."

Anne Fontaine 🅂 | 27 | 25 | 24 | E |

610 Fifth Ave. (bet. 49th & 50th Sts.), B/D/F/V to 47-50th Sts./Rockefeller Ctr., 212-489-1554
93 Greene St. (bet. Prince & Spring Sts.), C/E to Spring St., 212-343-3154
687 Madison Ave. (bet. 61st & 62nd Sts.), 4/5/6/F/N/R/W to 59th St./Lexington Ave., 212-688-4362
www.annefontaine.com
■ Lovers of this Parisienne trio, furnished with European antiques and fabrics, call it the "ultimate store for the classic white blouse" with "a zillion styles" (in black too!), each "so well made it's worth every penny"; ooh-la-las also go to the "big-sizes range for us not-so-skinny people" and "nicest-ever" sales associates who

"give honest opinions about the fit"; so, no wonder "you can't resist purchasing three or four at one go."

Anne Klein ●S
| 22 | 21 | 20 | E |

417 W. Broadway (bet. Prince & Spring Sts.), C/E to Spring St.; R/W to Prince St., 212-965-9499; www.anneklein.com

■ "The name says it all" concur kindred Klein-philes who feel this "sleek, airy, split-level SoHo" designer store with soaring ceilings and an "elegant" central staircase offers the "perfect combo of quality and service"; the "always classic, yet imaginative" "New Yorker's staples", now created by Christian Frances Roth, come in several "sophisticated" style ranges, with the sportier "latest fashions for casual Fridays" and secondary AK line housed upstairs and the "higher caliber" "classics" housed below.

Annelore SC
| – | – | – | VE |

636 Hudson St. (Horatio St.), A/C/E/L to 14th St./8th Ave., 212-255-5574

You might miss this tiny, quaint West Village shop if you blink, but stay alert and you'll be rewarded by the "impeccable tailoring on the chic" yet non-fussy creations within its spare confines; designer-owner Juliana Cho, a Catherine Malandrino alum, "wants you to look pretty" in her "beautiful", ultra-femme pieces, many fashioned from menswear fabrics or printed silks with handmade buttons – and if celeb customers like Julianne Moore and Stella Tenant are any indication, she certainly succeeds.

Annie & Company Needlepoint C
| 25 | 23 | 25 | E |

1325 Madison Ave. (bet. 93rd & 94th Sts.), 6 to 96th St., 212-360-7266; www.annieandco.com

■ "Sit and stitch" in one of the "comfy areas" at this large, "bright, cheerful" Upper East Side "needlepoint nirvana" with a "great" French country feeling and "top-notch service"; enthusiasts enjoy the "camaraderie among the clientele" ("there are always helping hands") and give the "wide variety" of "starter projects for the beginner", custom accessories, "intricate painted canvases" and "unbelievable choice of fibers" two needles up.

ANN SACKS
| 28 | 27 | 16 | VE |

204 E. 58th St. (bet. 2nd & 3rd Aves.), 4/5/6/F/N/R/W to 59th St./Lexington Ave., 212-588-1920
37 E. 18th St. (bet. B'way & Park Ave. S.), 4/5/6/L/N/Q/R/W to 14th St./Union Sq., 212-463-8400
800-278-8453; www.annsacks.com

◪ "You can do some serious damage to your bank account" at these "pricey", "stylish" stores near Union Square and in the East 50s showcasing "absolutely amazing tile", including versions in copper or mosaic glass, and "cool", "up-to-the-moment" fixtures like faucets and sinks; still, a few naysayers throw cold water on things by commenting that the wares are "stunning but so is the attitude."

ANN TAYLOR ●S
| 20 | 20 | 18 | M |

645 Madison Ave. (60th St.), 4/5/6/F/N/R/W to 59th St./Lexington Ave., 212-832-9114; 800-342-5266; www.anntaylor.com
Additional locations throughout the NY area

■ "The mother ship" for NYC's crew of "businesswomen" carries a cargo of "day-to-night frocks" with "a look that's sharp but not edgy"; "conservative", "classic", "clean" and "friendly", the city's innumerable outlets offer "cuts to fit a real woman's body", whether she's petite or size 16, and though the goods might be too "bland" for "hanging out on an East Village stoop", if you're in the job market, the clearance rack "doesn't disappoint" for a "great bargain" on the "perfect corporate interview suit."

ANN TAYLOR LOFT ⏻S   18 | 19 | 17 | M

150 E. 42nd St. (Lexington Ave.), 4/5/6/7/S to 42nd St./Grand Central, 212-883-8766; 800-342-5266; www.anntaylor.com
Additional locations throughout the NY area

■ Go "on the fly", "check out the sales" at this "no-frills" but "appealing" Ann Taylor alternative "catering to the 30s crowd"; you'll "walk out with money in your pocket" and a bagful of "really cute", "good-quality, basic things that will not go out of style"; it's "more trendy, more casual and a better value" than its namesake, so there are "massive lines at lunch hour."

ANTHROPOLOGIE   21 | 24 | 16 | E

375 W. Broadway (bet. Broome & Spring Sts.), C/E to Spring St., 212-343-7070
85 Fifth Ave. (16th St.), 4/5/6/L/N/Q/R/W to 14th St./Union Sq., 212-627-5885 ⏻S
www.anthropologie.com

◪ "Bohemians at heart" hanker after the "fantasy-driven designs" at these Flatiron and SoHo national chain links with their "shabby chic", "flea-market feel"; the "fab merch for a fab crowd" features "street-meets-runway fashions", "whimsical" jewelry and "home furnishings with European flair and funk" – all of it carrying irritatingly "eye-popping price tags"; still, "from the delicate lingerie to the wrought-iron table lamps", the scene "makes you feel like a fairy princess", so it's impossible to "walk out empty-handed."

Antiquarium Ancient Art Gallery   ∇ 26 | 23 | 23 | E

948 Madison Ave. (bet. 74th & 75th Sts.), 6 to 77th St., 212-734-9776

◪ Specializing in original Greco-Roman, Egyptian and Near Eastern art and antiquities, this Upper East Side boutique seems "a gallery more than a store"; each piece is delivered with a certificate of authenticity and origin, and while the number of zeroes in an item's price roughly equals the number of zeroes in its date, "where else can you find a 5th-century BC ring?"

Anya Hindmarch ⏻C   25 | 21 | 18 | E

29 E. 60th St. (bet. Madison & Park Aves.), N/R/W to 5th Ave./59th St., 212-750-3974
115 Greene St. (bet. Prince & Spring Sts.), R/W to Prince St., 212-343-8147 S
www.anyahindmarch.com

■ You can always spot this British designer's "adorable" purses – just "look for the telltale little bow", her dime-size logo; the "sweet shops" in SoHo and on the Upper East Side also stock luggage and small leather goods that are "gorgeous in a sleek, cool sort of way", a newly introduced line of "whimsical shoes", plus "clever accessories", all at "heart-stopping prices"; fans with a healthy sense of self also "love the 'be-a-bag' service" that puts "your picture on" your tote or evening clutch.

Apartment 48 ⏻SC   ∇ 26 | 28 | 24 | M

48 W. 17th St. (bet. 5th & 6th Aves.), 1/2/3/9/F/L/V to 14th St./6th Ave., 212-807-1391

■ "Warm and inviting" Flatiron home-furnishings "gem" where "items are displayed" as if they're in an actual apartment (albeit the seven-room one "you wish you had"); "every piece of furniture is for sale", along with vases, glassware and a "great assortment" of both contemporary and classic accessories for every space in the house, including must-haves for that mudroom in the country.

A.P.C. ●ⓈⒸ 　　　　20 | 19 | 15 | E

131 Mercer St. (bet. Prince & Spring Sts.), R/W to Prince St., 212-966-9685; www.apc.fr

☑ "Definitely a stop" worth making, this airy SoHo loft with rough-hewn wood-plank floorboards and "surprisingly friendly" service houses the "minimalist" French line of men's and women's "just yummy" crisp shirts, tees, low-rise jeans, suits and sweaters, providing "staples for any New Yorker"; while these "great basics look simple", they're "cut to perfection" and "very well made"; those less spellbound find the "fit limited" and the staff "snippy."

A Pea in the Pod ⓈⒸ 　　　22 | 21 | 20 | E

860 Madison Ave. (70th St.), 6 to 68th St., 212-988-8039; 877-273-2763; www.apeainthepod.com

☑ "You can still feel cool while pregnant" at this Madison Avenue flagship of the national chain, a "fantastic one-stop shopping source for work-to-play wardrobes" where "it's all about maternity Seven jeans", "very current styles" from such designers as Anna Sui, and Diane von Furstenberg for label-conscious moms-to-be and "fun, fashionable" store-brand threads; while there's "not a grosgrain bow to be seen", wallet-watchers whine that it's "a little pricey for about four months of wear."

APPLE STORE SOHO ●Ⓢ 　　27 | 28 | 22 | E

103 Prince St. (Greene St.), R/W to Prince St.; C/E to Spring St., 212-226-3126; 800-692-7753; www.apple.com

■ "Mac geeks" and "newbies alike" agree it's "all about the Apple fetish" at this two-floor "electric playground", a "masterpiece of minimalist design" in a former SoHo post office offering such a "glimpse of the future" you almost wonder "am I on the set of a sci-fi movie?"; "state-of-the-art-merchandising" and "knowledgeable" tech support "make you want to touch" all the software and hardware and there's even a theater at the top of the "excellent glass staircase" where acolytes "attend fantastic seminars."

April Cornell ●Ⓢ 　　　　21 | 22 | 20 | M

487 Columbus Ave. (bet. 83rd & 84th Sts.), B/C to 81st St., 212-799-4342; www.aprilcornell.com

☑ "Take a step back to the Victorian era" at this Upper Westsider abloom with "sweet and romantic" attire, "darling baby clothes", "gorgeous linens" and gifts galore; while devotees delight in the "floral dresses" and "matching mother-daughter" outfits, urbanites call the "country charm" "a little corny" – but even they confirm the "high quality" of the goods.

Arche ⓈⒸ 　　　　　　21 | 19 | 19 | E

10 Astor Pl. (bet. B'way & Lafayette St.), 6 to Astor Pl.; R/W to 8th St., 212-529-4808
995 Madison Ave. (77th St.), 6 to 77th St., 212-439-0700
1045 Third Ave. (bet. 61st & 62nd Sts.), F to Lexington Ave./63rd St.; 4/5/6/F/N/R/W to 59th St./Lexington Ave., 212-838-1933
128 W. 57th St. (bet. 6th & 7th Aves.), N/R/Q/W to 57th St., 212-262-5488

(continued)

(continued)

Arche

123 Wooster St. (Prince St.), R/W to Prince St., 646-613-8700
www.arche-shoes.com

◪ "Arty, hippie", "all-purpose" shoes with "primarily nubuck uppers" in "wild colors for all seasons" and "ultra-comfy", "squishy soles" are "served up with French attitude" and a "Cartier price tag" at this Manhattan outfit; admirers declare they're a "delight to walk in" and especially "great for new moms and baby boomers looking for something different", but detractors denounce the "slightly bizarre" designs, concluding "I'd rather go barefoot."

Archipelago 25 | 25 | 17 | E

38 Walker St. (bet. B'way & Church St.), A/C/E to Canal St., 212-334-9460; www.archipelagoinc.com

■ "Oh-so-TriBeCa" linens newcomer where seven "fashionable" beds dressed to the nines in "appealing" contemporary coverlets, sheets and pillows dominate the sprawling space; there are 170 fabrics to choose from – suede, satin and sharkskin among them – for custom-made goods; on a smaller scale, embroidered hemstitch napkins and placemats add impact to any table.

Arden B. [S] 18 | 18 | 15 | M

104 Fifth Ave. (bet. 15th & 16th Sts.), 4/5/6/L/N/Q/R/W to 14th St./ Union Sq., 646-638-0361
1130 Third Ave. (66th St.), 6 to 68th St., 212-628-2003
532 Broadway (bet. Prince & Spring Sts.), 6 to Spring St.; R/W to Prince St., 212-941-5697
877-274-6722; www.ardenb.com

◪ "Teenyboppers, "the Britney generation" and the "young at heart" flock to this "cheap and chic" chain for "hip", "hot" clothes that can even "turn the girl next door into a gorgeous" gamine; Arden acolytes adore the mix of "super trendy" "club-going" attire and "romantic date looks" that are "always on top of fashion"; still, a few are B-wildered by the "hype" finding it "pricier than you would expect" for "knockoffs" and "very hoochie" mama for adolescents.

Armani Casa ◐[S] 22 | 26 | 20 | VE

97 Greene St. (bet. Prince & Spring Sts.), R/W to Prince St., 212-334-1271; www.armanicasa.com

■ This "architecturally cool" and "calming" "minimalist slice of heaven" in SoHo showcases "beautiful", "highbrow home fashions" drawn from "the master's aesthetic" and "translated into wood, ceramic and glass"; fashionistas feel you "can't go wrong" with the signature subdued colors and "clean" lines, evidenced in shagreen side tables and pillows made of luscious leathers; of course, these "creature comforts" come at couturelike prices.

Arredo – | – | – | VE

23/25 Greene St. (bet. Canal & Grand Sts.), A/C/E to Canal St.; 1/9 to Canal St., 212-334-2363; 866-427-7336; www.arredousa.com

New SoHo showroom showcasing two floors of "excellent" high-end kitchen (including an all-aluminum version), bath and home-office systems from seven stylish Italian manufacturers, including furniture from Lema, seating from Matteograssi, fixtures from Rifra and lighting from Album; in all, there are more than 10,000 products.

Art and Tapisserie [S] — | — | — | E

1242 Madison Ave. (bet. 89th & 90th Sts.), 4/5/6 to 86th St., 212-722-3222

It may be "small", but this Madison Avenue infants' and children's wonderland staffed with "lovely clerks" crams in "unique gifts and toys", from whimsical costumes to nursery items and even offers temptations for grown-ups; your child's name can live on in infamy as jewelry and rocking chairs can be personalized, plus they carry chess sets – in case you're raising the next Bobby Fisher.

Artbag [C] 22 | 18 | 20 | E

1130 Madison Ave. (84th St.), 4/5/6 to 86th St., 212-744-2720; www.artbag.com

■ Nestled in an East 80s brownstone, this family-run shop features a "contemporary" collection of "beautifully made", quilted, woven and one-of-a-kind bags and belts in an array of leathers and exotic skins so "original" "you won't see yourself coming and going"; service also takes center stage: the "excellent" European-trained craftsmen can copy a favorite piece or custom-design a couture number, plus they do a "marvelous job of repairs" ("it'll cost you but they can fix anything" – "worth it for a treasure").

Artemide [C] 25 | 23 | 14 | VE

46 Greene St. (bet. Broome & Grand Sts.), A/C/E to Canal St., 212-925-1588; www.artemide.us

◩ "If you delight in contemporary lighting", this SoHo showroom of the Italian-based company will "inspire" you with its "gorgeous", "high-tech" offerings, including iconic "modern classics" such as Richard Sapper's Tizio desk lamp; opponents call it "overpriced" and a bit "snooty", but "if you're concerned about quality" and "great design", "this store will satisfy your cravings."

Arthur Brown & Brothers 22 | 15 | 18 | M

2 W. 46th St. (bet. 5th & 6th Aves.), 7 to 5th Ave.; B/D/F/V to 42nd St., 212-575-5555; 800-772-7367; www.artbrown.com

■ "Just walking in makes me feel creative" profess pals of this pen shop in Midtown that's a "reliable" "resource for all things" related to writing instruments (both new and antique); the staff is "helpful", as befits an 80-year-old establishment, and it's "very good for picture framing", stationery and art supplies as well.

ARTISTIC TILE 28 | 25 | 20 | VE

150 E. 58th St. (bet. Lexington & 3rd Aves.), 4/5/6/F/N/R/W to 59th St./Lexington Ave., 212-838-3222

79 Fifth Ave. (bet. 15th & 16th Sts.), 4/5/6/L/N/Q/R/W to 14th St./Union Sq., 212-727-9331

800-260-8646; www.artistictile.com

■ An "incredible selection" of "truly artistic tiles" in a variety of "quality" materials, from metal and marble to glass, pebbles and even leather, along with bathroom fixtures like faucets and sinks, are showcased at these East 50s and Flatiron stores; while surveyors are split over service ("very informed" vs. "spotty"), they agree that prices are "high."

Artsee [S] [C] 22 | 24 | 19 | VE

863 Washington St. (bet. 13th & 14th Sts.), A/C/E/L to 14th St./8th Ave., 212-414-0900

◩ Vintage Hollywood specs along with "Elton John looks", custom buffalo-horn frames, international designer versions that represent the "best of the best" and various accessories are available in the Technicolors of your dreams at this Meatpacking District newcomer; service ranges from "great" to "snooty" and the "prices are sky-high", but aesthetes "love the gallery atmosphere" that's appropriate for such "must-see glasses."

Art Store, The [S] 24 | 22 | 19 | M

1-5 Bond St. (bet. B'way & Lafayette St.), B/D/F/S/V to B'way/ Lafayette St., 212-533-2444; www.artstore.com

■ "Experienced" painters, "students and high-class crafters" give "two thumbs up" to this "well-stocked" NoHo supply shop offering an "inspiring" "selection of quality materials" that are "easy to find" in a trim, "uncluttered" space ("no overstuffed warehouse feeling here!"); the staff is "knowledgeable" and "courteous", and if prices sometimes seem "better suited for trust-fund artists", be sure to visit "during the crazy sales" when "bargains" abound.

ASCOT CHANG 27 | 25 | 26 | VE

7 W. 57th St. (bet. 5th & 6th Aves.), F to 57th St.; N/R/W to 59th St./ 5th Ave., 212-759-3333; 800-486-9966; www.ascotchang.com

■ "If you find a man who wears Ascot Chang, marry him" – after you buy a custom shirt for yourself – advise the enamored of this beige-walled, wood-paneled shirtmaker on 57th Street; you'll be "pampered like a prince" as, from "thousands of fabric choices", you "pick the pattern, collar and cuff and let them craft" "the best [garment] you will find in the world" (there are "equally fantastic off-the-rack" models too); of course, "with exclusivity comes a hefty" tab, but "when you can't get to Hong Kong", this is "the cat's meow in bespoke."

A Second Chance Designer Resale 17 | 12 | 15 | M

1109 Lexington Ave., 2nd fl. (bet. 77th & 78th Sts.), 6 to 77th St., 212-744-6041

◪ When "you hit it right, you can score still-respectable designer or designer-ish clothes, shoes, bags" and jewelry say supporters of this East 70s crammed-to-the-gills consignment store; but second-story surroundings that are "kind of scruffy" and prices that are "kind of expensive" (for "ordinary" pieces) stop skeptics from coming back for seconds.

AsiaStore in the Asia Society and Museum [S] 24 | 21 | 19 | E

725 Park Ave. (70th St.), 6 to 68th St., 212-288-6400; www.asiasociety.org

◪ "The best place to find unique things" from all over Asia is this Park Avenue shop boasting a "lovely presentation" of clothing, jewelry, teapots, vases and one-of-a-kind merchandise that is "custom-made or usually found only in the East", plus "books that no one else has", many of which are set on "the best half-price table in the business"; but a few intrepid shoppers would rather "fly to Thailand and buy it themselves for the cost of some items."

ASPREY 28 | – | 24 | VE

723 Fifth Ave. (bet. 56th & 57th Sts.), E/V to 5th Ave./53rd St., 212-688-1811; www.asprey.com

■ "A taste of upper-class England can be had strolling" through this recently expanded and totally refurbished three-floor "elegant, precious" off-white, black and bronze Midtowner in Trump Tower; browsing among the "exquisite" jewels, watches and the "finest silver and leather goods", plus men's and women's clothing now designed by Hussein Chalayan, is made easy by the "beautiful" displays as well as by the "proper British service" dispensing the "royal treatment" ("if they don't carry it, they'll custom-order it"); "hefty prices" prevail, but it's rather nice "not having to cross the pond to pick up a bauble or two."

Assets London ●⚫🅲 | 23 | 21 | 19 | E |
464 Columbus Ave. (bet. 82nd & 83rd Sts.), B/C to 81st St., 212-874-8253 🆂
152 Franklin St. (bet. Hudson & Varick Sts.), 1/9 to Franklin St., 212-219-8777
☑ "Fun and funky" pair that's "a must" for women desiring a wide selection of "stylish"-to-"trendy" clothing and accessories; though some feel the Zen-ish "TriBeCa branch has more interesting stock", the pink-and-lilac "Upper West Side shop has better sales"; they're worth waiting for, lest the "exorbitant prices" lead you to liquidate your own assets.

A. Testoni ●🆂 | 25 | 22 | 22 | VE |
665 Fifth Ave. (bet. 52nd & 53rd Sts.), E/V to 5th Ave./53rd St., 212-223-0909; www.testoniusa.com
☑ A Fifth Avenue leather goods shop that fits in "alongside its posh neighbors", this swanky stalwart, run by a 79-year-old Bologna-based, family-owned company, primarily caters to meticulous gents (i.e. Mikhail Gorbachev and Jean-Paul Belmondo) seeking handmade luxury, soft "like buttah" shoes in "classic" "Euro styles" and "super quality" luggage, with a smaller collection of "great designs" for women; still, the "heart-stopping price tags" make you walk, not run, except at sale time.

Athlete's Foot 🆂 | 17 | 14 | 13 | M |
1460 Broadway (bet. 41st & 42nd Sts.), 1/2/3/7/9/N/Q/R/S/W to 42nd St./ Times Sq., 212-391-9382; 888-801-9157; www.theathletesfoot.com
Additional locations throughout the NY area
☑ Mega-chain that's "a treasure trove of inexpensive sneakers, but only if you are lucky in timing your visit" – if so, you'll find "a decent selection" of "all the major sports brands" alongside "your basic activewear" and you'll be "in and out in no time"; flip a coin and it's a "very disorganized" "disaster" of "middle-of-the-road" merchandise with "no personality" and a "staff that works at the speed of molasses."

Atrium 🆂🅲 | 21 | 18 | 15 | E |
644 Broadway (Bleecker St.), 6 to Bleecker St., 212-473-9200
☑ Offering "downtown fabulous at a price", this "one-stop shopping" spot set on a NoHo corner carries a "mishmash of designer duds" for "stylish twentysomethings" and "urban metrosexuals"; with men's apparel near the entrance and women's to the rear, there's "more variety than a 7-11", including "an awesome selection of the 'it' jeans of the moment"; still, a handful aren't high on the vibe, deeming it a "hipster-wannabe" hang.

Au Chat Botte 🅲 | 27 | 25 | 19 | VE |
1192 Madison Ave. (bet. 87th & 88th Sts.), 4/5/6 to 86th St., 212-722-6474
■ "Ooh-la-la" fawn fans of this Upper East Side infants' shop where "you pay for the fabulous" "French fashions for babies", "precious" outfits that mirror the latest in mom-size Parisian styles;

the "great selection" of "beautiful classics includes European shoes" for wee ones, accessories, bedding and nursery furniture; but a few faultfinders feel that it's only worth a visit "if you can get past the attitude wafting from the salespeople."

A-Uno – | – | – | E

198 Spring St. (bet. Sullivan & Thompson Sts.), C/E to Spring St., 212-343-2040

123 W. Broadway (Duane St.), 1/2/3/9 to Chambers St., 212-227-6233

Advocates attest this women's boutique is A-one indeed, given its smartly edited selection of "interesting clothing for grown-ups" from such labels as Marithé + François Girbaud, Elm Design Team and the intriguing Pier Antonio Gaspari, whose sweaters look chic either right-side-up or upside-down; the decor at both its TriBeCa and SoHo locations may seem stark, but the "unparalleled service" warms things up.

auto [S] [C] – | – | – | E

805 Washington St. (bet. Gansevoort & Horatio Sts.), A/C/E/L to 14th St./8th Ave., 212-229-2292; www.thisisauto.com

This tiny, "minimalist" space in the Meatpacking District displays a decidedly eclectic assortment of gifts like sweater-clad rocks, porcelain pigs, retro trays and Christian Tortu candles, along with colorful bed linens; devotees defend the seemingly "random" selection as being "paired down to what you now find you cannot live without" after shopping here.

Aveda Environmental Lifestyle Store [S] 24 | 22 | 21 | E

140 Fifth Ave. (19th St.), 4/5/6/L/N/Q/R/W to 14th St./Union Sq., 212-645-4797

509 Madison Ave. (bet. 52nd & 53rd Sts.), E/V to 5th Ave./53rd St., 212-832-2416

1122 Third Ave. (bet. 65th & 66th Sts.), 6 to 68th St., 212-744-3113

866-283-3224; www.aveda.com

■ You "come away feeling refreshed from shopping" at this "environmentally conscious" beauty pioneer offering a vast array of "wonderful-smelling natural products" that include "can't-live-without-them" cosmetics, aromatherapy oils, hair and skincare lines; "just walking in here takes the stress meter down, although paying for items takes it back up a bit"; N.B. a new branch has opened at The Shops at Columbus Circle at Time Warner Center.

Avirex [S] [C] ▽ 25 | 22 | 18 | M

652 Broadway (bet. Bleecker & Bond Sts.), 6 to Bleecker St., 212-254-3030; www.avirex.com

◪ "Wow! It's worth going just to see the store" exclaim aviation aficionados of this fly NoHo haven known for its reproduction WWII leather bomber jackets, pilots' scarves and collectibles; it's also a source for "quality" men's and women's sportswear, including jeans, T-shirts and dancewear, all at "great prices."

AVVENTURA ◐ [S] [C] 28 | 23 | 21 | VE

463 Amsterdam Ave. (bet. 82nd & 83rd Sts.), B/C to 81st St.; 1/9 to 79th St., 212-769-2510; 888-640-9177; www.forthatspecialgift.com

■ The "best place to shop for art glass and ceramics" assert aesthetes about this "must-see" Upper Westsider with "stunning windows" and three large museumlike rooms filled with "one-of-a-kind", "beautiful handmade items" like Venini vases, Venetian chandeliers and Deruta pottery that make for "memorable gifts";

while it can be "annoying that it's not open on Saturdays", the fact that they "gift-wrap and ship anywhere" in the U.S. helps offset the inconvenience.

A.W. Kaufman

| 22 | 7 | 18 | M |

73 Orchard St. (bet. Broome & Grand Sts.), F/J/M/Z to Delancey/Essex Sts., 212-226-1629

■ "Worth the pilgrimage" and the "Lower East Side atmosphere" laud lingerie lovers who uncover "great prices on expensive" bras and panties from the "finest-quality brands" like Chantelle, La Perla, Hanro and Joelle at this "jam-packed" 80-year-old, family-run standby; the "sales staff must know every piece they carry", since there's "no hands-on" browsing allowed and no "trying on" either – unless you consider the storage area a dressing room.

A/X Armani Exchange ●⊠

| 18 | 19 | 16 | E |

568 Broadway (Prince St.), R/W to Prince St., 212-431-6000
645 Fifth Ave. (51st St.), E/V to 5th Ave./53rd St., 212-980-3037
129 Fifth Ave. (bet. 19th & 20th Sts.), 1/9 to 18th St., 212-254-7230
www.armaniexchange.com

☑ "Sleek basics" and "fashionable jeans" satisfy the "slim, trendy" "club kids" who "pack" these "hip" SoHo, Midtown and Flatiron stores, finding logo-laden "clothes with attitude" at "more reasonable prices" than the designer's Emporio and Collezioni lines (even so, sticker-shocked savants say "wait for the sales"); but while devotees deem it perfect for "Armani wanna-bes", others axe it as a "glorified Gap"; N.B. a new branch has opened in The Shops at Columbus Circle at Time Warner Center.

Azaleas ⊠⊠

| ▽ 24 | 23 | 19 | M |

223 E. 10th St. (bet. 1st & 2nd Aves.), 6 to Astor Pl., 212-253-5484; www.azaleasnyc.com

■ It's hard to resist picking up a few sweet nothings at this East Village sugarplum specializing in lingerie (On Gossamer, Woo) "just sexy enough to make your mouth water", plus some "unique" camis and clothing items that can be worn beyond the boudoir; the "always-on-hand" owners are two witty chums, whose snapshots of scantily clad loyalists take the place of mannequins while those of male customers sauce up the changing rooms.

Babies "R" Us ⊠

| 20 | 16 | 12 | M |

395 Gateway Dr. (Erskine St.), Brooklyn, A/C to Euclid Ave., 718-277-3400
139-19 20th Ave. (Whitestone Expwy.), Queens, 718-321-8166 ⊠
www.babiesrus.com

☑ "Find anything you need" and "goodies" "you never knew you needed" "for that new baby in your life" at this "one-stop" "mom-to-be-heaven" that "brings suburban convenience to urban life"; parents applaud the "reasonably priced" "basics and supplies", from "formula and car seats" to "cute clothing", while grandmas and shower attendees embrace the "can't-be-beat registry"; but "bring your mom for advice" or "do your homework" first because service is nearly "nonexistent", plus "checkout may require another nine months."

Baby Bird ⊠⊠

| ▽ 23 | 23 | 21 | E |

428 Seventh Ave. (bet. 14th & 15th Sts.), Brooklyn, F to 7th Ave., 718-788-4506

■ Nestled next to Bird, a fave of stylin' Park Slopers, this hip little "companion" boutique offers "unique" infants' and tots' togs that are just as snazzy as mom's; staples like Petit Bateau T-shirts layer wonderfully well with Levi's, and for future artists and rock stars, there are limelight-worthy onesies in colorful prints and whimsical bibs, plus novelty knockouts from pet lines like Electric Polka Dot and Lucky Wang; N.B. there are purchasable toys to entertain little ones while mother shops.

BabyGap ●S `22` `19` `15` `M`
60 W. 34th St. (B'way), B/D/F/N/Q/R/V/W to 34th St./Herald Sq., 212-760-1268; www.gap.com
Additional locations throughout the NY area

■ "A godsend for all those baby showers" (and it's "easy to exchange") and "cute, practical" infants clothes, this ubiquitous chain is such a "perennial favorite" fans can't imagine "where we would be today without it"; this is "clothing that can last and be handed down", so "stock up on the basics" and "check back often" – "things go on sale frequently"; but a jaded few jab "if you want your child to literally wear what every other New York City child is wearing, shop here."

BACCARAT C `28` `28` `24` `VE`
625 Madison Ave. (59th St.), N/R/W to 5th Ave./59th St., 212-826-4100; www.baccarat.fr

■ This "classic", 240-year-old French manufacturer of "gorgeous" fine crystal "has branched out into colors and diversified their merchandise", so their "superb" stemware, decanters, rings and other "lovely things" continue to "wow" the crowds; it's also clear that the "beautiful" Upper East Side venue with a second-floor showroom is "as good as the one in Paris – without the jet lag."

Bag House, The S C `22` `17` `17` `M`
797 Broadway (bet. 10th & 11th Sts.), R/W to 8th St.; 6 to Astor Pl., 212-260-0940

■ A "cornucopia of possibilities" awaits at this Village "one-stop shop" specializing in luggage, sports duffels and leather goods; customers get carried away over the "extensive" "selection of school bags, travel bags and just everyday bags", including "backpacks galore", at "prices that seem competitive"; but it's not an open-and-shut case for all – a handful feel they "can be beat with a little legwork."

Bagutta Life S C `▽ 24` `–` `23` `VE`
76 Greene St. (bet. Broome & Spring Sts.), C/E to Spring St., 212-925-5216

☑ Downtown divas and dudes find happiness at this luxurious, "chic" two-floor SoHo boutique recently relocated to Greene Street, that's "perfect if you have lots of money" to spend; label-conscious customers thumb through the well-edited, "super" collection, snapping up European designer wear from bold-faced names like Alexander McQueen, Dior and Zac Posen, all housed on the main floor; you can now also shop for furniture and housewares downstairs.

Baker Tribeca S `25` `24` `21` `VE`
129-133 Hudson St. (Beach St.), 1/9 to Franklin St., 212-343-2956; www.bakerfurniture.com

■ This over-100-year-old "tried-and-true" manufacturer from the Midwest recently opened an "impressive" 12,000-sq.-ft., two-story store in TriBeCa designed by Bill Sofield; his "elegant", "expensive" furniture collection along with award-winning California designer Barbara Barry's "gorgeous" line is on the first floor, while more traditional designs dominate the lower level.

Balenciaga 🚇🅲   25 | 23 | 19 | VE

542 W. 22nd St. (bet. 10th & 11th Aves.), C/E to 23rd St., 212-206-0872; www.balenciaga.com

◪ Wander into this "highly conceptual", Zen-like designer den in Chelsea resembling the "art galleries that surround it", and experience the "edgy, yet elegant" aesthetic of house creator Nicolas Ghesquierre; the "lovely" luxe pieces, perfect for "the next time you're invited to the Oscars", are assembled in modular "mouthwatering displays" highlighted by fake boulders and fluorescent tube 'clouds'; still, mystified browsers decree the "military bondage look" "bizarre", and "not compatible" with the "old-guard luxury" brand.

Ballantyne Cashmere 🅲   24 | 23 | 21 | E

965 Madison Ave. (bet. 75th & 76th Sts.), 6 to 77th St., 212-988-5252

■ It's all cashmere all the time at this East 70s boutique, which for years has been offering men and women the plush, two-ply "top-notch stuff", not just in the usual sweater suspects, but in pants, hats and gloves; it now exclusively carries the venerable Scottish label, and once you finger the merchandise, it might be hard to escape without "treating yourself" to a twinset or two in "classic" intarsia, stripes or "wonderful colors."

Bally 🅂   25 | 23 | 20 | E

628 Madison Ave. (59th St.), N/R/W to 5th Ave./59th St., 212-751-9082; www.bally.com

◪ "Gotta love the Swiss" for the "buttery-soft leather" in the "fine handbags, belts and shoes" at this streamlined East 50s boutique; "excellent quality", "comfort and luxury" combined is the "novel concept" ballyhooed by "serious shoppers", but despite efforts to "update the image", hipper heels huff that the merchandise is "still too conservative."

Bambini 🚇🅲   25 | 22 | 18 | VE

1088 Madison Ave. (82nd St.), 4/5/6 to 86th St., 212-717-6742

◪ The "adorable items" at this Madison Avenue mecca "remind me of the things my mum used to dress me in" sigh the smitten who like to outfit their "little ones like little princes and princesses"; it's stocked with "everything you need", from "beautiful layettes" to "gifts for baby showers" to children's togs from a "lot of European designers"; still, a few fret it's "too hoity-toity" and a "bit pricey."

BANANA REPUBLIC ◖🅂   20 | 20 | 16 | M

626 Fifth Ave. (bet. 50th & 51st Sts.), E/V to 5th Ave./53rd St., 212-974-2350; 888-277-8953; www.bananarepublic.com
Additional locations throughout the NY area

◪ Service "can barely keep up" with the "yuppie" "hordes" going bananas over "Garanimals" for grown-ups at the "ubiquitous" "Starbucks of retail"; the "reliable classics" can be a bit costly, but "keen-eyed bargain hunters" stalk the "awesome" sale racks "in the back" of the "well laid-out" stores; fashionistas who find the "four-color repertoire" "not as ripe" as it once was warn "standing next to someone on the train who's wearing your exact same outfit" might make you wanna peel off the "cookie-cutter" clothes.

Banana Republic Men's ◐Ⓢ
| 20 | 20 | 16 | M |

528 Broadway (Spring St.), R/W to Prince St., 212-334-3034
114 Fifth Ave. (17th St.), 4/5/6/L/N/Q/R/W to 14th St./Union Sq.,
212-366-4691
888-277-8953; www.bananarepublic.com

◩ If he's a "professional on a budget", these chain "staples" in the Flatiron and SoHo might be your "husband's favorite stores"; the "helpful, friendly" clerks guide him through the "ever-changing selection of casual shirts, pants, shorts", "stylish shoes" and accessories, and if he "waits for sales, it's almost like getting free clothes"; though they publicly call the threads "bland", even iconoclasts whisper "I wish the Banana Republic clone look would go out of fashion so I could wear it again."

B&B Italia
| 26 | 25 | 18 | VE |

150 E. 58th St. (bet. Lexington & 3rd Aves.), 4/5/6/F/N/R/W to 59th St./
Lexington Ave., 212-758-4046; 800-872-1697; www.bebitalia.it

■ For "modern furniture" fanatics, this gleaming, white two-story space by Antonio Citterio in the East 50s is the apotheosis of "cool", "clean" Italian design; contemporary seating by Jeffrey Bernett, pieces from Gaetano Pesce and the "elegant" accessories and linens upstairs are "drool"-worthy, but far from "minimal" prices leave some frugal fans out in the cold.

B&H PHOTO-VIDEO PRO AUDIO Ⓢ
| 29 | 20 | 19 | M |

420 Ninth Ave. (bet. 33rd & 34th Sts.), A/C/E to 34th St./Penn Station,
212-444-6600; 800-947-9950; www.bhphotovideo.com

■ This shutterbug's "Wonkaland", with purchases in "little baskets whizzing on overhead tracks", spans a Garment District block; "New York's photographic supermarket" "runs like a well-oiled machine" in which the "vast selection" of film and new and used equipment may be "overwhelming", but the "surly yet efficient staff" "can help anyone from a newbie homeboy to a grizzled war photographer find what they need at a reasonable price"; just "don't go Friday night or Saturday", when it's closed for Shabbat.

B&J Fabrics
| 27 | – | 20 | E |

525 Seventh Ave., 2nd fl. (38th St.), 1/2/3/7/9/N/Q/R/S/W to 42nd St./
Times Sq., 212-354-8150

■ "Anything your heart desires is here" at this textile "lover's dream" which recently relocated, after 50 years, to this larger, one-floor store in the Garment Center; over the years, customers like the cast of *Hairspray* and *Kiss Me, Kate* have come to realize "it's well worth" a stop just to "poke around" one of the "best selections of fine European fabrics", including "current fashions" from "designer" collections, "at reasonable prices", plus the "very knowledgeable staff" is on hand to help.

BANG & OLUFSEN Ⓢ
| 26 | 26 | 22 | VE |

927 Broadway (bet. 21st & 22nd Sts.), R/W to 23rd St., 212-388-9792
330 Columbus Ave. (bet. 75th & 76th Sts.), 1/9 to 79th St.,
212-501-0926
952 Madison Ave. (75th St.), 6 to 77th St., 212-879-6161
www.bang-olufsen.com

■ "Is it art, or is it a stereo?" – the "friendly" staff at this "museum of audio" might say it's both; the "avant-garde" Danish company has been creating "sleek and functional" home entertainment products for "design-minded" "well-to-do's" for over 70 years, and if the "gorgeous" "gadgets" exceed your budget, there's always the "cool, cool" pleasure of "walking in just to dream."

Barami Studio ◐🅂 | 16 | 16 | 15 | M |

136 E. 57th St. (Lexington Ave.), 4/5/6/F/N/R/W to 59th St./Lexington Ave., 212-980-9333
535 Fifth Ave. (bet. 44th & 45th Sts.), 4/5/6/7/S to 42nd St./Grand Central, 212-949-1000
375 Lexington Ave. (41st St.), 4/5/6/7/S to 42nd St./Grand Central, 212-682-2550
485 Seventh Ave. (36th St.), 1/2/3/9 to 34th St./Penn Station, 212-967-2990
www.barami.com

☑ "Upcoming professionals" purchase career clothes at these all-around-town women's apparel shops; but while advocates applaud their "feminine and refined", "perfect-fit suits" as "worth it for the money", cons complain the goods "used to be nicer"; service, too, can range from "attentive" to "practically on top of you."

Barbara Bui ◐🅂🅲 | 26 | 24 | 20 | VE |

115-117 Wooster St. (bet. Prince & Spring Sts.), R/W to Prince St., 212-625-1938; www.barbarabui.fr

■ "Unusual" window displays "entice" you into the "hushed galleries" of this SoHo shop, where contemporary, striking "Zen-like designs" appeal to women who want "wearable" yet "sophisticated, cutting-edge" clothing, especially in pants ("the best"); just expect to pay dearly for the "details and quality" when the "helpful salespeople" ring up the bill.

Barbara Feinman Millinery ◐🅂🅲   ▽ | 23 | 20 | 22 | M |

66 E. Seventh St. (bet. 1st & 2nd Aves.), F/V to Lower East Side/2nd Ave., 212-358-7092; www.feinmanhats.com

■ Fans flip their lids for "toppers in all shapes and sizes" with glamorous names like Bogie, Bacall and Ingrid at this "frilly" and feminine, modern yet retro East Village atelier; "wonderful" Barbara "remembers her customers" and "knows her hats", in fact, she'll "pick out the most unlikely thing and it will look good on you", plus "most can be customized"; P.S. it's also "good for costume jewelry."

Barbara Shaum | – | – | – | VE |

60 E. Fourth St. (bet. Bowery & 2nd Ave.), 6 to Astor Pl., 212-254-4250
Have your gladiator footwear custom-made by this "cool" East Village eponymous cobbler who has been crafting sandals, earthy shoes, belts and "real old-fashioned pocketbooks" since the '50s but still retains her "downtown hip" cred; you may have to "take a second mortgage on your house" to afford these leather goods, but they'll "last forever", so join the peace train of cultists who "can't get enough of them."

Barbour by Peter Elliot | – | – | – | E |

1047 Madison Ave. (80th St.), 6 to 77th St., 212-570-2600; www.barbour.com
Whether for pheasant-chasing on the moors or ranging the East Side in your Rover, this very British line of insouciantly elegant, sporting apparel for men and women cuts a dashing figure and is now sold out of preppy clothier Peter Elliot's Upper Madison adjunct devoted exclusively to it; in addition to having timeless style, these togs, especially the waxed cotton jackets, are dutifully durable and can be passed, like peerage, onto future generations.

Bardith 🚫 – | – | – | VE
901 Madison Ave. (bet. 72nd & 73rd Sts.), 6 to 68th St., 212-737-3775
Since 1965, this Madison Avenue purveyor of posh 18th- and 19th-century English porcelain and pottery has offered complete sets of formal china service by all the legendary companies, as well as Dutch delft and papier-mâché trays and glassware.

Bark ◐ [S] [C] – | – | – | E
369 Atlantic Ave. (bet. Bond & Hoyt Sts.), Brooklyn, A/C/G to Hoyt/ Schermerhorn Sts., 718-625-8997
Sharing the same space and address as the hip Boerum Hill store Breukelen is this home-furnishings shop selling handblown crystal from Mexico and Scandinavia, along with sumptuous Italian sheets and silk comforters.

Barking Zoo ◐ [S] ▽ 24 | 22 | 25 | M
172 Ninth Ave. (bet. 20th & 21st Sts.), C/E to 23rd St., 212-255-0658
■ "Stylish" canines crave the "cute accessories" (yes, even Aquascutum) on offer at this Chelsea pet boutique where a "great variety of toys" and other "nice merchandise" also get tails wagging; humans "love" the "extremely helpful staff" and the fact that "they deliver" to the neighborhood; it also offers zoo-tably fashionable hard-to-find premium cat and dog foods.

Barneys Co-op [S] 22 | 19 | 15 | E
236 W. 18th St. (bet. 7th & 8th Aves.), 1/9 to 18th St., 212-716-8816
116 Wooster St. (bet. Prince & Spring Sts.), C/E to Spring St.; R/W to Prince St., 212-965-9964
◩ "Wild and unpredictable", this "decadent emporium of fun" for "trendier-than-thou shoppers" in SoHo and Chelsea is familiar to fans of its floors in parent Barneys; its airy, "well laid-out" interior is a clean backdrop for "a hodgepodge of retro-futuristic designs" from the likes of Tree, Theory, Mayle and Marc by Marc Jacobs, arrayed alongside a "scoopful of small international labels", shoes and the "best cosmetics" and jeans; "Downtown doesn't mean downscale, so don't expect a bargain" – or co-operation from salespeople who seem "more interested in themselves" than you.

BARNEYS NEW YORK ◐ [S] 26 | 25 | 19 | VE
660 Madison Ave. (61st St.), N/R/W to 5th Ave./59th St., 212-826-8900; 888-822-7639; www.barneys.com
◩ A "fantasyland for the well-heeled", this East 60s department store "exerts a gravitational pull" on "chic urbanites" with its "premier men's shop" ("grab that wild Commes Des Garçons shirt while heading for an Armani suit"), "ultrahip-to-traditional" designer duds for dames, "the best jeans in NYC", "unique [Goyard] handbags", "great jewelry", "fabulous footwear" ("from Blahnik to their own brand") and a beauty floor; from the restaurant to Simon Doonan's "genius" window displays, "taste, luxury and humor" abound – even the "outrageous prices are good for a laugh" – except perhaps with the infamously "self-important" salespeople (though they are trying harder "to be civil").

Barton-Sharpe Ltd. – | – | – | VE
200 Lexington Ave., Ste. 914 (bet. 32nd & 33rd St.), 6 to 33rd St., 646-935-1500; www.bartonsharpe.com
Murray Hill furniture maker employing traditional cabinetmaking techniques such as tenon and mortise joints, which turn up in

"well-made" reproductions of 18th-century American furniture; in addition, French-Canadian–style pieces and English Georgian and Regency replicas are available.

Bath & Body Works ●⑤ | 18 | 20 | 18 | I |

141 Fifth Ave. (bet. 20th & 21st Sts.), R/W to 23rd St., 212-387-9123; 800-395-1001; www.bathandbodyworks.com
Additional locations throughout the NY area

☑ For a "flowery, fruity" "pick-me-up present", teens and "tweens" hit this "sweet-smelling" toiletries chainlet for "all kinds" of soap, bath gels, lotions, candles and perfumes at "inexpensive prices"; but sophisticates simply sniff at the "cutesy" "limited merchandise" and "overwhelming mixture of scents."

Bath Island ●⑤⓪ | 21 | 21 | 21 | M |

469 Amsterdam Ave. (bet 82nd & 83rd Sts.), 1/9 to 79th St., 212-787-9415; www.bathisland.com

■ This "oasis on the Upper West Side" has "no fancy bottles, just simple, great products", like "unique bath items", candles, custom-blended skincare lines and scented lotions, making it "the perfect place to buy a gift for someone who has very specific tastes."

BCBG Max Azria ⑤⓪ | 23 | 20 | 17 | E |

770 Madison Ave. (66th St.), 6 to 68th St., 212-717-4225
120 Wooster St. (bet. Prince & Spring Sts.), R/W to Prince St., 212-625-2723
www.bcbg.com

☑ "Phenomenally fitting", "flashy", "feminine and sexy" clothing – "what the young, single manhunter wears to stalk her prey" – takes center stage at this Upper East Side and SoHo duo that offers everything from "bathing suits and business suits" to formal gowns (the scene is "prom dress central come June"); "service varies" ("nice if they think you'll shell out money, rude if not"), and definitely love it before you buy it, warn those who decry the "no-refund policy" (store credit/exchange for 10 days only).

BDDW ● | – | – | – | VE |

5 Crosby St. (bet. Grand & Howard Sts.), 6/J/M/N/Q/R/W/Z to Canal St., 212-625-1230; www.bddw.com

Soaring SoHo space that's a "cathedral" for handcrafted wood furniture like stunning dining tables, platform beds and cool, wood-encased speakers; whether purchasing a piece off the showroom floor or custom-ordering one, the converted pay a pretty penny for such purchases.

Beacon's Closet ●⑤ | 21 | 15 | 16 | I |

220 Fifth Ave. (bet. President & Union Sts.), Brooklyn, M/R to Union St., 718-230-1630
88 N. 11th St. (bet. Berry St. & Wythe Ave.), Brooklyn, L to Bedford Ave., 718-486-0816
www.beaconscloset.com

■ "Go Beacon!" cheer Closet cohorts crazy for the "kooky", "super-cheap secondhand and vintage threads" culled from the "1950s to yesterday" at this recently relocated warehouse setting in Williamsburg, and its "smaller Park Slope" sibling; you may have to "fight off the hipsters with trucker hats" while "thrifting it up" but fans feel "it's worth it", especially for wardrobe "overhaulers" who adore trading or selling "stuff" for store credit or "cash-on-the-spot."

Beads of Paradise ◐ [S] [C] — 23 | 20 | 18 | M

16 E. 17th St. (bet. B'way & 5th Ave.), 4/5/6/L/N/Q/R/W to 14th St./ Union Sq., 212-620-0642

◪ "Transporting little store" in the Flatiron District that's "a bead wonderland where wanna-be children" are busy "stringing trinkets" in the back, while others peruse the "one-of-a-kind" African artifacts up front; experienced jewelry makers say "there are less expensive suppliers", but neophytes can benefit from the "make-your-own" workshops or simply buy one of the finished pieces made by the "soft-spoken staff."

Bear's Place, A [S] [C] — ▽ 24 | 19 | 20 | E

789 Lexington Ave. (bet. 61st & 62nd Sts.), 4/5/6/F/N/R/W to 59th St./ Lexington Ave., 212-826-6465

◪ There's barely a bear to be had, still, there's a "varied selection" of "unique", "good-quality toys" and educational playthings, especially for "younger children", at this Upper East Side plush-animal-and-puppet pad, as well as hand-painted kids' tables and chairs; let the "knowledgeable" staff guide you – "the store's layout can be cramped."

Beasty Feast ◐ [S] [C] — 24 | 17 | 25 | M

237 Bleecker St. (bet. Carmine & Leroy Sts.), 1/9 to Christopher St./ Sheridan Sq., 212-243-3261

630 Hudson St. (bet. Horatio & Jane Sts.), A/C/E/L to 14th St./8th Ave., 212-620-7099

680 Washington St. (Charles St.), A/B/C/D/E/F/S/V to W. 4th St., 212-620-4055

www.beastyfeast.com

■ If you "prefer to give your business to the little guys", this longtime trio of Downtown pet shops will reward you with "great personalized service" from "friendly" owners and staff ("if they don't have it, they'll order it"), "healthier food than you'd find in the superstores" and a "very homey feel"; there's also a "good selection" of accessories, plus "all sales are inspected by house cats" at the Bleecker and Hudson Street locations.

Beau Brummel ◐ [S] [C] — 23 | – | 20 | E

347 W. Broadway (bet. Broome & Grand Sts.), R/W to Prince St.; C/E to Spring St., 212-219-2666; www.beaubrummel.com

◪ When you want to "dress like Regis", head to this recently relocated "classy store" in SoHo for "superb" dress and casual clothing with "lots of funk and color" (their own label as well as others of the Cerruti/Gianfranco Ferre/Zegna ilk); while there are "attentive" – some say "aggressive" – people "to help you shop", opponents opine the offerings "often seem overpriced", which is why the savvy wait to "hit the sales."

Bebe ◐ [S] — 16 | 17 | 14 | M

100 Fifth Ave. (15th St.), 4/5/6/L/N/Q/R/W to 14th St./Union Sq., 212-675-2323

1127 Third Ave. (66th St.), 6 to 68th St., 212-935-2444

805 Third Ave. (50th St.), E/V to 5th Ave./53th St., 212-588-9060

Staten Island Mall, 2655 Richmond Ave., Staten Island, 718-697-0070

www.bebe.com

◪ "Perfect body required" (read: "size 0") at this women's fashion chain, where "gear for girls' night out" "with a wild streak" appeals to "trashy high school" and "twentysomething" "babes" who plunk down dough for "sexy" eveningwear, sparkly jewelry, "slutty" shoes and active apparel "too cute for the gym"; frank-talking foes dub it "harlotwear", but who's to say that's not a compliment?

Bebe Thompson C

22 | 18 | 20 | E

1216 Lexington Ave. (bet. 82nd & 83rd Sts.), 4/5/6 to 86th St., 212-249-4740

☑ "Wonderful choices" of "so expensive but so beautiful" infants and children's clothing from such high-end lines as Lili Gaufrette, Malina and Petit Bateau, all "selected with a critical eye", keep customers coming back to this East 80s boutique; still, a handful smart at the "high prices" quipping, sure, "your child will look extremely elegant, but will there be any money left for dinner?"

Beckenstein Fabrics & Interiors S

21 | 16 | 14 | M

4 W. 20th St. (bet. 5th & 6th Aves.), F/V to 23rd St., 212-366-5142; 800-348-1327

☑ Interior decorators and do-it-yourselfers rely on this Flatiron fabric destination for its "great selection" of "interesting", "good-quality" home-furnishings textiles at "reasonable" prices; "they do wonderful work with upholstery" and custom draperies, but pressed patrons take heed: "special orders can take a long time."

Beckenstein Men's Fabrics

22 | 11 | 14 | M

257 W. 39th St. (bet. 7th & 8th Aves.), A/C/E to 42nd St./Port Authority, 212-475-6666; 800-221-2727

☑ "If you're looking to match a designer fabric", this Garment District shop "is the place" fawn fans who bolt over for the "great selection" of "fine-quality" cloth at "good prices."

BED BATH & BEYOND ◑S

22 | 18 | 15 | M

410 E. 61st St. (1st Ave.), 4/5/6/F/N/R/W to 59th St./Lexington Ave., 646-215-4702

620 Sixth Ave. (bet. 18th & 19th Sts.), 1/9 to 18th St., 212-255-3550

459 Gateway Dr. (Fountain Ave.), Brooklyn, L to Canarsie/ Rockaway Pkwy., 718-235-2049

96-05 Queens Blvd. (63rd Dr.), Queens, G/R/V to 63rd Dr./Queens Blvd., 718-459-0868

800-462-3966; www.bedbathandbeyond.com

☑ "The one-stop shopping spot for furnishing a dorm room or first apartment" ("or whenever the urge to redo gets overwhelming"), this "football-field-size" chainlet is a "household treasure chest"; "whether for bathroom, bedroom, kitchen or garden", fans find it "truly goes beyond", with "interesting new" appliances ("even the gadgets you see on TV"), "fresh and fun" toiletries and "all manner of seasonal, holiday-specific items"; however, its "vastness" "can be a mixed blessing – there's no such thing as a quick trip" through the "meandering displays", and while "every single salesperson says hello to you", "they need more help."

Belgian Shoes

24 | 16 | 20 | E

110 E. 55th St. (bet. Lexington & Park Aves.), 6/E/V to 51st St./ Lexington Ave., 212-755-7372; www.belgianshoes.com

☑ "It's worth it indeed" to "wait up to a year" for "handmade", "built-to-last" shoes from this Midtown "home of the pink-and-green loafer" (founded by Henri Bendel in 1956) laud loyalists who flip for the "most comfortable flats in the world" that "feel every inch like slippers"; you'll find a "limited selection" in stock – "only a couple of styles with dozens of color combinations" – and "tassels, tassels everywhere", but cutting-edge critics sniff it's "not for fashionistas."

Bellini 🅂🅲 | 25 | 25 | 21 | VE |

1305 Second Ave. (bet. 68th & 69th St.), 6 to 68th St., 212-517-9233; www.bellini.com

■ "Great Italian imports made to last and grow with your child" abound at this Upper East Side branch of a furniture chain offering "very high-quality", "solidly made timeless designs" "at a price"; choose from a "wide selection" of "cream-of-the-crop" cribs, chairs, bedding and nursery accessories "to decorate the little one's room", plus "beautiful" stuff for kids and teens; N.B. custom-made goods are also available.

BERGDORF GOODMAN 🅂 | 27 | 26 | 22 | VE |

754 Fifth Ave. (bet. 57th & 58th St.), N/R/W to 5th Ave./59th St., 212-753-7300; 800-558-1855

■ "Posh and classy", this "grande dame" near the Plaza Hotel retains its "charming old-school vibe", but has a "new edge and flair" with "every designer label your heart desires" and a "subterranean dream" of a cosmetics department (whose "madcap beauty" events are "like disco night with your girlfriends"); "you could spend all day staring" at the "great assortment of dainty-to-chunky" modern jewelry and the recently expanded "stellar shoe selection", while brides can seek out "sleek or fairy-tale dresses"; the "courteous", "professional" salespeople "actually follow up", and while the price tags are (of course) "outlandish", end-of-the-season "serious markdowns make it affordable."

Bergdorf Goodman Men's 🅂 | 27 | 26 | 24 | VE |

745 Fifth Ave. (58th St.), N/R/W to 5th Ave./59th St., 212-753-7300; 800-558-1855

☑ "An essay in understated elegance", this "dignified" (some say "stuffy") "island of calm in Midtown" is "as complete a men's store as exists anywhere in the world", offering "superior" suits and "high-end" sportswear ("the prominent designers are all on board"), "English shirts", "custom-made Italian shoes", seemingly "500 kinds of cufflinks" and a "massive tie selection"; of course, you'll "pay top dollar" for "upscaling the man in your life", and while the atmosphere "borders on the elitist" – you may "spot a star from Broadway or Hollywood" among the displays – "dress well and you'll be treated right."

Berkley Girl 🅂 | ▽ 21 | 23 | 19 | E |

410 Columbus Ave. (bet. 79th & 80th Sts.), B/C to 81st St., 212-877-4770; www.berkleygirl.com

■ Tween-friendly to the max, this "so-cool-to-shop" Upper West Side yearling (named after the owner's golden retriever) outfits trendy girls from top to bottom; kicky T-shirts are stacked on a table flanked by racks of bright, funky togs from labels like Lucky Brand, Riley and Tessuto, while whimsical handbags, barrettes and accessories fill the shelves above; as daughter browses, mom can kick back on the way-cool comfy chair and ottoman in the corner.

BERNARDAUD 🅲 | 28 | 28 | 22 | VE |

499 Park Ave. (59th St.), 4/5/6/F/N/R/W to 59th St./Lexington Ave., 212-371-4300; 800-884-7775; www.bernardaud.fr

■ "If you entertain elegantly", this Eastsider is "a wonderful source" for this "fabulous" French manufacturer's Limoges porcelain patterns like Ithaque and Fusion White, which are accented with gold and platinum; the "beautiful shop" also offers crystal and silver flatware, along with furniture; just be prepared to pay an "arm and a leg for the privilege of shopping here."

Best Buy ●S
22 | 19 | 16 | M

1280 Lexington Ave. (86th St.), 4/5/6 to 86th St., 917-492-8870
60 W. 23rd St. (6th Ave.), F/N/R/V to 23rd St., 212-366-1373
Caesar's Bay, 8923 Bay Pkwy. (Shore Pkwy.), Brooklyn, M/W to Bay Pkwy., 718-265-6950
50-01 Northern Blvd. (bet. 50th St. & Newtown Rd.), Queens, G/R/V to 46th St., 718-626-7585
88-01 Queens Blvd. (55th Rd.), Queens, G/R/V to Grand Ave./Newtown, 718-393-2690
2795 Richmond Ave. (Platinum Ave.), Staten Island, 718-698-7546
888-237-8289; www.bestbuy.com

☑ "All the toys are out", and "there's nothing better than being able to test" LCD monitors, notebook computers, TVs and other stuff before you buy at these "huge stores" glutted with "competitively priced" electronics; "though it's merely a chain, they've managed to make the experience almost pleasant" – just "don't expect the royal treatment" from the staff.

Betsey Bunky Nini C
▽ 23 | 21 | 22 | E

980 Lexington Ave. (bet. 71st & 72nd Sts.), 6 to 68th St., 212-744-6716

■ Open since 1969, this relaxed, elegant and comfortable Upper East Side boutique was founded by designer Betsey Johnson and two friends (who all cashed out awhile back); loyalists say it's "still great after all these years" for its "interesting clothes" – the Piazza Sempione line is a big seller – that, while "pricey, are usually worth it for something different."

Betsey Johnson S C
21 | 21 | 20 | E

248 Columbus Ave. (bet. 71st & 72nd Sts.), 1/2/3/9/B/C to 72nd St., 212-362-3364
251 E. 60th St. (bet. 2nd & 3rd Aves.), 4/5/6/F/N/R/W to 59th St./Lexington Ave., 212-319-7699
1060 Madison Ave. (bet. 80th & 81st Sts.), 6 to 77th St., 212-734-1257
138 Wooster St. (bet. Houston & Prince Sts.), R/W to Prince St., 212-995-5048
www.betseyjohnson.com

■ "Mainstream funky" sums up the "ever-eclectic stylings of Ms. Johnson" that are popular with (and seem primarily sized for) "well-heeled teenagers" who "dare to stand out" in her "frivolous", "flirty" party clothes; "it's a blast" to browse these "upbeat", pink-walled shops, especially as the "sweet staffers" will "run over in a second" to "help you get over any inhibitions."

Betwixt S C
26 | 22 | 21 | E

245 W. 10th St. (bet. Bleecker & Hudson Sts.), 1/9 to Christopher St./Sheridan Sq., 212-243-8590; www.betwixt.com

■ "Stock up on" "trendy togs" "for stylish kids" from brands like Miss Sixty and Roxy at this West Village teen and "tween heaven" staffed with "helpful" salespeople; "whether you need an outfit for school, the prom" or "those important" betwixt and between "bar and bat mitzvah years", "you can't choose wrong" at this "good find"; green-with-envy moms can't help but wonder "where were cool stores like this when I was growing up?"

Beyul S | – | – | – | VE |

353 W. 12th St. (bet. Greenwich & Washington Sts.), A/C/E/L to 14th St./8th Ave., 212-989-2533
Way west on a quiet block in the Village, an old warehouse space has been transformed into a Far East temple – a traditional moongate guards the front of the store, and in the rear a Tibetan shrine watches over its wares, which consist of 18th-, 19th- and 20th-century Asian antiques; standouts include a collection of Chinese ancestral portraits, nearly life-size scroll paintings integral to honoring the spirits of long-gone family members.

Bicycle Habitat S | 24 | 16 | 22 | M |

244 Lafayette St. (bet. Prince & Spring Sts.), R/W to Prince St.; 6 to Spring St., 212-431-3315; www.bicyclehabitat.com
■ "Fair dealing, excellent mechanics" and a "good selection" of bicycles and "accessories, especially for the urban" cyclist, make this SoHo "standout" a "pedal-pusher's delight"; "it's a great place to shop" for everything from Trek to BMX models, plus they're "really helpful in repairs and ordering parts for special models – service the way we all want it."

Bicycle Renaissance S | 24 | 15 | 18 | E |

430 Columbus Ave. (bet. 80th & 81st Sts.), 1/9 to 79th St.; B/C to 81st St., 212-724-2350
◪ "A busy bike store" in a "convenient Upper West Side location" within pedaling proximity to Central Park, this "comfortable" 30-year-old stalwart is where "cyclists in-the-know" turn for a "good selection" of bicycles (including wheels for kids), apparel and accessories; while some surveyors salute the service, others opine "make sure you've got one of the top guns working with you."

Big Drop ●S C | 23 | 18 | 14 | E |

174 Spring St. (bet. Thompson St. & W. B'way), C/E to Spring St., 212-966-4299
1321 Third Ave. (bet. 75th & 76th Sts.), 6 to 77th St., 212-988-3344
425 W. Broadway (bet. Prince & Spring Sts.), C/E to Spring St., 212-226-9292
www.bigdropnyc.com
◪ "Always on target with trends", this sleek trio of women's boutiques (the lollipop-bright West Broadway locale's the latest) showcases "unusual selections from up-and-coming" designers (plus "favorites" like Ella Moss and Seven) whose wares often have a handcrafted appeal; however, a Big Drop between the Merchandise and Service scores suggests the staff needs to mend its alternately "pushy" and "too-cool-to-help" ways.

Billy Martin's Western Wear S C | ▽ 23 | 21 | 18 | E |

220 E. 60th St. (bet. 2nd & 3rd Aves.), 4/5/6/F/N/R/W to 59th St./Lexington Ave., 212-861-3100; www.billymartin.com
■ "Yee-haw", the vintage bar and Coca-Cola machine aren't the only reasons why everyone from celebs like Billy Bob Thornton to Jewel to good ol' Western-wear aficionados find this East 60s retailer "a fun place to shop"; patrons pony up big bucks for some of the "best" colorful, novelty alligator "boots in town", "great" silver and turquoise jewelry, belts, buckles and rodeo-ready rhinestone cowboy shirts.

Bird ●⬤🅢🅒   23 | 25 | 21 | E

430 Seventh Ave. (bet. 14th & 15th Sts.), Brooklyn, F to 7th Ave.,
718-768-4940; www.shopbird.com

■ "Style-starved Slopers" pigeonhole this Brooklyn boutique as "providing SoHo fashion without the attitude"; the "color-coded" stock is "an addiction" for "boho girls with a French flair" who want "intelligent", "whimsical" yet "utilitarian clothing and accessories" (exclusive labels "complement the store's own design"); however, even high-fliers warn prices aren't "cheap-cheap"; N.B. there's now a new comfy shoe and lingerie annex to the rear.

Birnbaum & Bullock   ▽ 22 | 15 | 23 | E

151 W. 25th St., Ste. 2A (bet. 6th & 7th Aves.), R/W to 23rd St.,
212-242-2914; www.birnbaumandbullock.com

■ "If the bride wants something special", this by-appointment-only showroom, now in Chelsea, is "the place to go"; these "two very talented designers" create clean-lined "gorgeous gowns", plus components comprised of interchangeable bodices, including corset and tank styles, and skirts that run the gamut from full silhouettes to satin A-lines; the icing on the cake: "wonderful and caring service"; N.B. a post-*Survey* move may outdate the above Presentation score.

Bisazza   – | – | – | VE

43 Greene St. (bet. Broome & Grand Sts.), R/W to Prince St.,
212-463-0624; www.bisazzausa.com

Shoppers are limited only by their imaginations at this new SoHo shop swimming in a sea of stylish mosaic tiles in glass, gold and enamel; the Italian-based company has been creating fantastic custom designs for bathrooms, kitchens and pools for nearly half a century.

Biscuits & Baths Doggy Village 🅒   18 | 18 | 20 | E

701 Second Ave. (bet. 37th & 38th Sts.), 4/5/6/7/S to 42nd St./
Grand Central, 212-692-2323 ●🅢
1535 First Ave. (bet. 80th & 81st Sts.), 6 to 77th St., 212-794-3600
www.biscuitsandbath.com

■ An "adorable day camp for dogs", this pet spa, now in the East 30s, and its Upper East Side satellite ensure its clients "live better than most New Yorkers", offering a "nice array" of "luxury items" and "great toys" for sale, as well as grooming services; it's the "ultimate in pampering" for pups and kitties too, but a few wonder if four-legged friends "really need a birthday party?"

Bis Designer Resale ●🅢   22 | 21 | 21 | M

1134 Madison Ave. (bet. 84th & 85th Sts.), 4/5/6 to 86th St.,
212-396-2760; www.bisbiz.com

■ This "tiny treasure" is a "temple of temptation" to consignment shopaholics for its often-"brilliant designer finds" – "everything from Ralph Lauren loafers to Hermès pullovers" – plus a "nicely edited collection of bric-a-brac"; a "refined" setting makes this ladies' place "the next best thing to shopping retail on Madison Avenue – at about a quarter of the price."

Blacker & Kooby 🅢🅒   22 | 14 | 16 | E

1204 Madison Ave. (88th St.), 4/5/6 to 86th St., 212-369-8308

■ On the Upper East Side, this "convenient" family-owned shop has been "meeting the needs of the neighborhood" for nearly 40 years with a "good selection of stationery, pens and novelty items" and "great office supplies and prepacked invitations"; "locals" love it for "pickups in a pinch", "competitive" prices and an "always helpful" staff.

Blades Board and Skate S
22 | 16 | 21 | M

659 Broadway (bet. Bleecker & 3rd Sts.), 6 to Bleecker St., 212-477-7350 ◐
Manhattan Mall, 901 Sixth Ave. (bet. 32nd & 33rd Sts.), B/D/F/N/Q/R/V/W to 34th St./Herald Sq., 212-563-2448
Pier 61 (23rd St. & West Side Hwy.), C/E to 23rd St., 212-336-6199
Pier 62 (23rd St.), C/E to 23rd St., 212-336-6299
120 W. 72nd St. (bet. B'way & Columbus Ave.), 1/2/3/9 to 72nd St., 212-787-3911
888-552-5233; www.blades.com

■ "If you are into extreme skating and surfing" or "just looking for" "cool stuff" like in-line blades, snowboards and accessories, gyrate over to this Northeast chain; the "genuinely interested", "knowledgeable" staff may "look like the kids you avoided in high school" (i.e. "tattooed, pierced skate rats"), but "who better to buy from than those who live" the rad life?

Bleecker Bob's
Golden Oldies Record Shop ◐ S
22 | 10 | 14 | M

118 W. Third St. (bet. MacDougal St. & 6th Ave.), A/B/C/D/E/F/S/V to W. 4th St., 212-475-9677; www.bleeckerbobs.com

◪ "Browse" through the "dust-filled bins" at this Greenwich Village "institution" "for all those records you thought were lost forever", from "hard-to-find rock" "imports" and "out-of-print" "goodies" to "old vinyl", especially "super-rare punk LPs" (and CDs); while the staff can be difficult, they "know everything they have and where it is."

Bleecker Street Records ◐ S
22 | 15 | 16 | M

239 Bleecker St. (bet. Carmine & Leroy Sts.), A/B/C/D/E/F/S/V to W. 4th St., 212-255-7899

■ "No-frills" late-night Village CD and LP haunt that's "perfect for hunting down" "something you're not likely to hear on the radio", as well as "good bargains, especially in jazz and blues"; the staff is "beyond informed" – they really "know the obscure and offbeat artists" – so chances are you'll "never leave empty-handed."

Bloch S C
– | – | – | M

304 Columbus Ave. (bet. 74th & 75th Sts.), B/C to 72nd St., 212-579-1960; www.blochworld.com

A dance presence for over 70 years, this Australian company makes its U.S. debut with this West 70s flagship, just leaps away from Lincoln Center; high ceilings, stark white counters and a dramatic velvet curtain form the backdrop for cool, comfy leotards, bra tops, hoodies, tights and leggings in high-tech fabrics; the back room is devoted to jazz and pointe shoes, and even flexible trainers, with a barre, huge mirror and TV camera to audition purchases.

Blockbuster Video ◐ S
18 | 15 | 10 | M

849 Eighth Ave. (51st St.), C/E to 50th St., 212-765-2021; www.blockbuster.com
Additional locations throughout the NY area

◪ "You have the best chance of getting a newly released movie" at "the McDonald's of video stores", "a family values–oriented", "convenient" chain where you "can't beat the selection" of "the latest blockbusters"; but critics bash a "staff that knows nothing about film and couldn't care less" and the "mainstream" monolith's "very Hollywood" "pop fluff" titles ("don't go here for any obscure cinema" – it's "not for the arthouse set.")

Bloom C | 20 | 22 | 18 | M |
361 Madison Ave. (bet. 45th & 46th Sts.), 4/5/6/7/S to 42nd St./Grand Central, 212-370-0068
■ Asian flair and pristine lines prevail in this "well laid-out" "Midtown find", a New York City branch of a Japanese jeweler, where those in-the-know buy a "wide variety" of "sleek" silver, titanium and white-gold creations at "all price ranges"; the staff "really knows the pieces", but make sure to inquire about the stringent return policies.

BLOOMINGDALE'S ● S | 23 | 18 | 14 | E |
1000 Third Ave. (bet. 59th & 60th Sts.), 4/5/6/F/N/R/W to 59th St./Lexington Ave., 212-705-2000; www.bloomingdales.com
☑ "From cheap to couture", nearly "everything the discerning shopper needs" lies within this most "upscale" of the "all-around department stores"; there's "almost too much choice" among the "wide variety of clothing", "fashionable necessities", "high-end" cookware, "well-presented" furniture and "wowza array of cosmetics" that's worth running the "perfume-spritzing gauntlet" for; critics cry over a "no-show sales force" that's "rarer than rain in the Mojave", but for better or worse, "nothing in NY comes close" to this "landmark", and maybe that's why it's ranked this *Survey*'s Most Popular store; N.B. at press time, a scaled down SoHo branch was slated to open in 2004.

Blue ● S | ▽ 21 | 13 | 18 | E |
137 Ave. A (bet. 9th St. & St. Marks Pl.), 6 to Astor Pl., 212-228-7744
■ Owner-designer Christina Kara is a "godsend" to fans who make tracks to her East Village boutique for retro-cool "custom-made" cocktail dresses, suits and formalwear "in every imaginable pattern"; the "funky" threads put oh-so-groovy bridesmaids and those seeking stand-out-in-a-crowd party garb in the pink at prices that won't bring on the blues; N.B. a post-*Survey* move may outdate the above Presentation score.

Blue Bag | 24 | 24 | 22 | E |
266 Elizabeth St. (Houston St.), 6 to Spring St., 212-966-8566
■ "Why bother flying to France" when you can breeze over to this NoLita boutique for "totally charming" European accessories, including "fabulous bags" from an array of independent designers that "span all styles" and "dictate trends before they happen on the street", all displayed on easy-access wood shelves; staffed with "extremely nice salespeople", it's "a wonderful place for special gifts" that can "create covetousness."

blush S | 22 | 23 | 20 | E |
333 Bleecker St. (Christopher St.), 1/9 to Christopher St./Sheridan Sq., 212-352-0111
■ "The clothes are so pretty it makes me blush" sigh "anti-Scoop girls" who skip over to this "gorgeous" West Village boutique for their "I don't want to look like every other fashionista-wannabe fix"; the "funky merchandise", arranged in light-colored wood racks and shelves, "has its own New York City flair" and so does the

"accommodating to a Juicy T" staff who coo "lots of 'sweethearts' and 'dears'", making for a "fun shopping experience."

BoConcept **S**   20 | 24 | 19 | **M**
105 Madison Ave. (30th St.), 6 to 33rd St., 212-686-8188;
www.boconcept.com
■ Ample, new "easy-to-navigate" Murray Hill store that's an offshoot of a Danish contemporary furniture chain; "moderately priced", "functional but not too funky" flexible modular sofas, chairs, coffee tables and cabinets along with accessories like plates and pillows make it a "welcome addition to NYC."

Bodum **S** **C**   25 | 24 | 20 | **M**
413-415 W. 14th St. (bet. 9th & 10th Aves.), A/C/E/L to 14th St./8th Ave.,
212-367-9125; 800-232-6386; www.bodum.com
■ "Chic design ideas combined with practicality and modest pricing" make this "hidden gem" in the Meatpacking District "a hit" "for the home"; it's a "supermarket" for the European company's "cool", "sleek" stuff like glass teapots, steel fondue sets and "French-press coffeemakers galore", plus there's a "nice" little in-store cafe too.

Bodyhints **O** **S** **C**   25 | 22 | 24 | **E**
462 W. Broadway (bet. Houston & Prince Sts.), C/E to Spring St.,
212-777-8677; 866-334-3433; www.bodyhints.com
■ Take a hint and give in to this "wonderful", "spacious" SoHo "superstore's" "great assortment" of "moderate to expensive" "skimpy treats", ranging from "unusual undergarments" to "irresistible lingerie" to "great swimwear", all "peddled by a helpful, unintrusive staff"; no matter your heart's desire – satin chemises from Mary Green or "everyday" lounge pants by James Perse – it's all here for the lusting; P.S. "check out the velvet dressing rooms" "so plush you wish you could rent" one.

Body Shop, The **O** **S**   20 | 19 | 18 | **M**
747 Broadway (bet. 8th St. & Waverly Pl.), 6 to Astor Pl.; R/W to 8th St.,
212-979-2944; 800-263-9746; www.thebodyshop.com
Additional locations throughout the NY area
■ Devotees declare that this U.K.-based chain is "the one that started it all" in 1976 in terms of "non-animal-tested toiletries" and "environmentally conscious" products that "don't look as if they belong on a rural commune"; "yummy-smelling", natural-ingredient bath-and-body items, massage creams and cosmetics are "well priced" and displayed in "cheerful", "well-organized" shops.

Boffi SoHo **O** **C**   ▽ 29 | 28 | 22 | **VE**
31½ Greene St. (Grand St.), 6 to Spring St., 212-431-8282;
www.boffisoho.com
■ This Milan-based international bath-and-kitchen chain's sprawling SoHo showroom is a mecca for loft-dwellers who covet the "cool" custom-made cabinets, appliances, sinks and lighting; the minimalist, "high-end", high-tech style incorporates concrete, steel, glass and wood, and several designs have been shown at the Louvre and MoMA.

Bolton's **O** **S**   11 | 9 | 9 | **I**
27 W. 57th St. (bet. 5th & 6th Aves.), F to 57th St., 212-935-4431
◪ "Moderately fashionable", "matronly clothing" makes this "zero-atmosphere" discount chainster a "good low-end place"

for "older types" to solve "pantyhose crises" and other "workwear" dilemmas, since "there are so many" "small, easily negotiated" branches "that if you cannot find your size, you can walk around the corner to the next one and they'll have it" – if you're in the average range, that is, as "they stopped carrying plus sizes", and "the smalls aren't so small."

Bombalulus ●⑤ⓒ　　24 | 18 | 22 | M

Grand Central, Vanderbilt Hall (42nd St. & Park Ave.), 4/5/6/7/S to 42nd St./Grand Central, 212-661-7505
101 W. 10th St. (bet. Greenwich & 6th Aves.), 1/2/3/9/F/L/V to 14th St./ 6th Ave., 212-463-0897
www.bombalulus.com
■ "Absolutely adorable and just a little offbeat", this colorful Greenwich Village children's boutique and its new Grand Central sibling are crammed with "cute, bright" clothing and "different baby gifts" "for the chic city kid"; most of the merchandise is made in-house, "so you won't find it in many other stores", plus there are toys on-site to busy little ones while you browse; N.B. the Midtown shop opened post-*Survey.*

Bombay Company, The ⑤　　17 | 18 | 15 | M

900 Broadway (20th St.), R/W to 23rd St., 212-420-1315 ◐
441 Columbus Ave. (81st St.), 1/9 to 79th St., 212-721-1417
1542 Third Ave. (87th St.), 4/5/6 to 86th St., 212-987-3990
Bay Terrace, 23-88 Bell Blvd. (24th Ave), Queens, 7 to Main St., 718-224-2998
Staten Island Mall, 2655 Richmond Ave., Staten Island, 718-494-0426
800-829-7789; www.bombaycompany.com
◪ "If you're looking for things for the home that aren't expensive", this chain is "the place for you" praise penny-pinchers in pursuit of "reproduction" "traditional-style" "dark wood" furniture and "interesting accent pieces" like prints, mirrors, frames and lamps; but snobs simply sniff at the "same old, same old" "faux upscale" furnishings and "kitschy bric-a-brac."

Bond 07 by Selima ⑤ⓒ　　23 | 26 | 18 | VE

7 Bond St. (bet. B'way & Lafayette St.), 6 to Bleecker St., 212-677-8487; www.selimaoptique.com
■ Owned by the lady behind Selima Optique, this "eye-catching" NoHo boutique sells the designer's "ultrachic" frames, plus a jolly "jambalaya" of "kooky", "cutting-edge" "bohemian dresses", "beautiful handbags" and "even some vintage" eyewear and jewelry; "original is the operative word here", but "beware – you might have to sell your goldfinger to afford" the "sumptuous array."

Bonne Nuit ●⑤ⓒ　　25 | 21 | 19 | E

30 Lincoln Plaza (bet. 62nd & 63rd Sts.), 1/9 to 66th St./Lincoln Ctr., 212-489-9730
■ Tucked away in a "hidden location" in Lincoln Plaza, this "unique" lingerie-and-childrenswear boutique with a "frank but delicate staff" offers a "carefully chosen selection of beautiful items" you don't "see anywhere else", from long lacy nightgowns and novelty robes to velvet peignoir sets and brazen bustiers; if you can tear yourself away from the unmentionables, take a peek at the "excellent mix of unusual" European clothing for infants and kids up to size 6.

BONPOINT **C**   27 | 26 | 19 | VE

1269 Madison Ave. (91st St.), 4/5/6 to 86th St., 212-722-7720
811 Madison Ave. (68th St.), 6 to 68th St., 212-879-0900

☑ "Classic and stylish (not trendy)", the "fabulous" French kids'
finery at these Upper East Side shops comes in "the most luxurious
textures and exquisite colors", all "nicely displayed" in Provençal-
style cases; it's "great for special occasions" if you want to spend
"a small fortune", but the sticker-shocked quip that "therapy might
be a better way to spend the cash" and find the vibe "stuffy."

Borealis **S** **C**   ▽ 22 | 22 | 19 | VE

229 Elizabeth St. (bet. Houston & Prince Sts.), B/D/F/S/V to B'way/
Lafayette St., 917-237-0152

☑ This Northern (as in NoLita) light shines with an "original",
"eclectic mix of jewelry", many pieces handcrafted by rising
stars and highlighting large, unfaceted, earthy stones; it's an
"interesting" array "for the Downtown crowd", but "be careful" –
despite the often-understated looks, it's "very expensive."

Borelli Boutique **S** **C**   25 | 23 | 20 | VE

16 E. 60th St. (bet. 5th & Madison Aves.), N/R/W to 5th Ave./59th St.,
212-644-9610

■ Millionaires may find nothing wrong with doling out top dollar
for "second to none" dress shirts at this small East 50s shop,
where made-to-measure merchandise is hand-stitched by Italian
seamstresses; close to 100 collar styles and over 1,500 fabric
choices allow you to create the "ultimate" in button-downs while
"heavenly" sweaters, pants and shoes complete the "must-see"
scenario; indeed "you'll pay" for the "great shopping experience" –
after all, "art has its price."

Boss, The **S**   25 | 23 | 20 | E

849 Flatbush Ave. (bet. Linden Blvd. & Martense St.), Brooklyn,
F to Church Ave., 718-287-4979

☑ Not to be confused with Hugo Boss, this specialty shop sports
a selection of "sleek stylish wear" with a Euro-Caribbean twist; a
"nice selection" of colorful Jean Mercius sport shirts, along with
the odd Armani, lines the long walls, while a vast assortment of
highly detailed dress trousers and colorful shoes fills the center
aisle; Flatbush fans appreciate the "wide cuts with good tailoring",
though the service sometimes seems on island time.

BOTTEGA VENETA **C**   28 | 26 | 22 | VE

635 Madison Ave. (bet. 59th & 60th Sts.), N/R/W to 5th Ave./59th St.,
212-371-5511; www.bottegaveneta.com

■ A "recent upgrade in style", courtesy of creative director Tomas
Maier, and an "excellent staff" create an "enjoyable shopping
experience" for fashionistas who zip over to this Madison Avenue
outpost for "unique Italian goods", including "soft and lovely"
shoes, accessories and status woven handbags, plus a luxe line of
apparel for men and women, all "priced for the elite"; kvetchers
quibble it's "not the same since Gucci" became a backer, but
supporters snap back "they still have it."

Botticelli **◐** **S** **C**   23 | 22 | 21 | E

666 Fifth Ave. (53rd St.), 6/E/V to 51st St./Lexington Ave., 212-586-7421
620 Fifth Ave. (49th St.), 6 to 51st St.; E/V to 53rd St./Lexington Ave.,
212-632-8300

(continued)
Botticelli
522 Fifth Ave. (bet. 43rd & 44th Sts.), 4/5/6/7/S to 42nd St./Grand Central, 212-768-1430
◪ From sexy kitten pumps to "chic" slingbacks to "contemporary" buckled boots, this "smart-looking" Fifth Avenue footwear phenom knows a thing or two about pampering patrons with "high-end", "quality Italian leather goods" "made to last"; the luxe collection includes "a terrific line of men's" shoes, "great accessories" and even shearling coats for guys and gals; still, a few price-sensitive assert "good for the feet, tough on the wallet."

Boucher [S] 22 | 22 | 20 | E
9 Ninth Ave. (Little W. 12th St.), A/C/E/L to 14th St./8th Ave., 212-206-3775; 866-623-9269; www.boucherjewelry.com
◪ Designer Laura Mady's "beautiful" "baubles and more" make this "friendly", aptly named ('*boucher*' means 'butcher') Meatpacking District jewelry shop the "perfect place" for wives-to-be "to pick out gifts for bridesmaids and friends"; "the storefront is tiny but it's loaded" with "colorful choices" like teardrop earrings and lariat necklaces declare devotees who also "delight at reasonable tabs"; still, a few beef it's "lovely, but overpriced – did they mine the stones themselves?"

Bowery Kitchen Supplies ◐ [S] [C] 21 | 12 | 14 | M
Chelsea Mkt., 75 Ninth Ave. (bet. 15th & 16th Sts.), A/C/E/L to 14th St./ 8th Ave., 212-376-4982; www.bowerykitchens.com
■ "If they don't have it, it doesn't exist" declare devotees of this commercial cooking equipment and supplies store in Chelsea Market that stocks a "wide-ranging selection" of all the "weird and wonderful" items "you'll ever need" – from convection ovens to cake rings – "if you love to cook or you just want to pretend to be a chef"; "good buys" abound, and there are also inexpensive glasses and dinner plates fit for frugal, first-time apartment-dwellers.

Bowery Lighting [S] [C] 21 | 13 | 15 | M
132 Bowery (bet. Broome & Grand Sts.), J/M/Z to Bowery, 212-941-8244
◪ "An extensive selection of lighting fixtures and lamps" in styles from art deco to contemporary is "crammed" into this "terrific" Lower East Side institution; "good prices" make it worth your while to sift through the "big jumble."

B. Oyama Homme [S] [C] – | – | – | E
2330 Seventh Ave. (bet. 136th & 137th Sts.), 2/3 to 135th St., 212-234-5128
Elegant gents satisfy their sartorial needs at this Seventh Avenue north, i.e. Harlem, boutique that specializes in high-end European-label suits, strikingly bold striped shirts, cashmere sweaters, ties and cufflinks like those worn by its well-turned-out owner Bernard Oyama; black-and-white photos from the days when men dressed to the nines, including shots of trendsetters like Duke Ellington and Nat King Cole, further enhance the bandbox vibe.

Boyd's of Madison Avenue ◐ [S] [C] 25 | 16 | 17 | E
655 Madison Ave. (bet. 60th & 61st Sts.), N/R/W to 5th Ave./59th St., 212-838-6558; 800-683-2693; www.boydsnyc.com
◪ "Everything imaginable for beauty", including makeovers, makeup, perfume, an "amazing" inventory of "hard-to-find

European items" and one of "the largest selections of hair accessories", keeps customers coming to this Upper East Side establishment – despite its "cluttered" setting and "overly attentive" salespeople; it started as an apothecary back in 1940, and today there is still a pharmacy in the back of the store.

Bra Smyth ◐[S][C] 25 | 16 | 23 | E

905 Madison Ave. (bet. 72nd & 73rd Sts.), 6 to 68th St., 212-772-9400; www.brasmyth.com

■ "The mother of lingerie stores", this "helpful", family-owned Upper Eastsider is one of the "only places where you can be assured of getting the exact fit" whether you're buying a "lacy, racy French bra-and-panty set" or a "beautiful nightgown"; the "professional" corsetieres and seamstresses "make sure you're securely hugged by their European" unmentionables and "alter in a flash"; P.S. they also have a "good selection" of bathing suits, activewear and kids PJs.

Brass Center, The ▽ 25 | 15 | 22 | E

248 E. 58th St. (bet. 2nd & 3rd Aves.), 4/5/6/F/N/R/W to 59th St./ Lexington Ave., 212-421-0090; www.thebrasscenter.com

■ It's a "great neighborhood store" in the East 50s, but it has a misleading moniker, since an array of materials, from chrome to porcelain, is used to produce the "quality" bathroom fixtures, plumbing, hardware and architectural fittings purveyed here; the "friendly" staff will help you select "imported items you won't find elsewhere" that are often "cheaper than mail-order" prices.

BREGUET 28 | 28 | 27 | VE

779 Madison Ave. (bet. 66th & 67th St.), 6 to 68th St., 212-288-4014; www.breguet.com

■ This Swiss luxury line may have been snapped up by the Swatch Group, but its East 60s time-keeping boutique featuring "flawless" watches that are "works of art" and "amazing" jewelry is still a miniature "Versailles"; enter the gates of "heaven" and follow in the footsteps of "upscale" clients Marie-Antoinette, Churchill and Napoleon – indeed, you'll receive the "royal" treatment from the "friendly" staff at this international chain, a presence since 1775 – just make sure you bring *beaucoup* bucks.

Breukelen [S][C] ▽ 21 | 22 | 17 | E

369 Atlantic Ave. (bet. Bonds & Hoyt Sts.), Brooklyn, A/C/G to Hoyt/ Schermerhorn Sts., 718-246-0024

■ While this hip Boerum Hill shop takes its name from the 17th-century Dutch appellation for the outer borough, the wares here are strictly contemporary – gorgeous two-tone glass by Japan-based Sugahara and cast-silver-and-gold jewelry by local artists – and are "great for gifts"; a tabletop-and-linen purveyor called Bark is located in the rear.

Bridal Atelier by Mark Ingram 26 | 23 | 27 | E

127 E. 56th St. (bet. Lexington & Park Aves.), 4/5/6/F/N/R/W to 59th St./ Lexington Ave., 212-319-6778; www.bridalatelier.com

■ "The perfect way to start and end your search" for an "elegant" bridal dress is with a stop at this "friendly", by-appointment-only East 50s townhouse where a "mellow atmosphere prevails"; the "knowledgeable" staff "listens to your taste and budget", bringing out "gowns that look wonderful on your particular body type" from a "large variety of designers", including Angel Sanchez, Domo

Adami and Wearkstatt; prices are "expensive, but they don't reach the exorbitant range."

Bridal Garden, The ●S | 13 | 8 | 13 | M |

54 W. 21st St., Ste. 907 (bet. 5th & 6th Aves.), R/W to 23rd St., 212-252-0661; www.bridalgarden.org

☑ You "gotta hit it just right" at this by-appointment-only, non-profit bridal store now in the Flatiron District, run by the Sheltering Arms Children's Services charity, but it's "worth a peek if you're on a budget"; the "wide selection" includes "used", worn-just-once creations, samples and extra inventory from designers like Vera Wang and Carolina Herrera; but critics caution "don't bother if you're not a model-size" "waif", plus gowns may "need to be altered elsewhere", bumping up the cost; N.B. a post-*Survey* relocation may outdate the above Presentation score.

Bridge Kitchenware C | 27 | 13 | 17 | M |

214 E. 52nd St. (bet. 2nd & 3rd Aves.), 6/E/V to 51st St./Lexington Ave., 212-688-4220; 800-274-3435; www.bridgekitchenware.com

■ It's the "best kitchenware store in the city" say supporters of this East 50s legend where "all the chefs shop"; the "astounding volume of merchandise" includes cutlery, "cake pans", copper pots and a "cornucopia of gizmos and gadgets" that could lead to "sensory overload"; you also may have to "blow the dust off" some items, but most maintain that's a small price to pay for "classic bargains" for the cook.

Brief Encounters S C   ∇ | 23 | 14 | 21 | E |

239 Columbus Ave. (71st St.), 1/2/3/9 to 72nd St., 212-496-5649

■ They've "always carried Cosabella" confide customers who gush over the "great selection" of European designer name undies and sleepwear at this "small", cramped Columbus Avenue corner shop stocked with "better stuff than it looks like they would have from their window displays"; service is equally uplifting thanks to a "very patient", "very knowledgeable staff" – "you can actually feel confident with a bra fitting here."

BRIONI C | 28 | 26 | 24 | VE |

55 E. 52nd St. (bet. Madison & Park Aves.), E/V to 5th Ave./53rd St., 212-355-1940
57 E. 57th St. (bet. Madison & Park Aves.), 4/5/6/F/N/R/W to 59th St./Lexington Ave., 212-376-5777
888-778-8775; www.brioni.com

■ "When price is not an issue", these Midtown representatives of the veteran fashion house are "unequalled" for their "fine men's clothing that's made to last a lifetime"; "discriminating buyers" salivate over the "eye-catching selection" that ranges from the "perfect Italian suit" to "flashy" "casual clothes", "great ties and beautiful shirts", all in a "Naples-in-New-York" setting; though "very knowledgeable", the service can be slightly "snooty" – but if "James Bond shops here, how can you go wrong?"; N.B. there's also a Brioni women's shop at 67 E. 57th St.

British American House S | 22 | 18 | 18 | E |

488 Madison Ave. (51st St.), 6/E/V to 51st St./Lexington Ave., 212-752-5880

☑ Those searching "for the continental look" can cast their eyes toward Midtown, where (despite the name) this 24-year-old retailer offers up an all-Italian range of men's clothing and accessories, arranged by color and designer; but while some applaud the "great quality" and "helpful service", skeptics sniff it's "nothing special."

Broadway Panhandler 🇸🇨 | 26 | 20 | 18 | M |

477 Broome St. (bet. Greene & Wooster Sts.), A/C/E to Canal St., 212-966-3434; 866-266-5927; www.broadwaypanhandler.com

■ Both "novice and experienced" types throng to this "Disneyland for cooks" in SoHo for "good deals" on a "plethora" of "everyday" pots and pans, "specialty bakeware", utensils and appliances from "low-end to high", all sold by a "knowledgeable staff" that doesn't "mind answering questions"; on weekends the expansive, columned space gets "crowded", but that doesn't keep wallet-watchers from the "not-to-be-missed" "annual yard sale" in June.

Brooklyn Museum Shop 🇸🇨 | 22 | 17 | 16 | M |

200 Eastern Pkwy. (Washington Ave.), Brooklyn, 2/3 to Eastern Pkwy., 718-638-5000; www.brooklynmuseum.org

■ Come on, "Manhattanites, Brooklyn isn't that far away", so hop the subway and get in on "the best-kept secret in town for gifts"; "the shop is like the museum – unpretentious, interesting, occasionally surprising", with a "nice blend of quality goods" "reflecting its strong collections in African, Asian and American art", as well as its borough identity; though "interestingly quirky" stuff is "jumbled together" with "fairly standard fare", brave the clutter and you're sure to find "excellent clearance-sale items."

BROOKS BROTHERS ◐🇸 | 22 | 21 | 20 | E |

666 Fifth Ave. (bet. 52nd & 53rd Sts.), E/V to 5th Ave./53rd St., 212-261-9440
1 Liberty Plaza (Broadway), R/W to Cortlandt St., 212-267-2400
346 Madison Ave. (44th St.), 4/5/6/7/S to 42nd St./Grand Central, 212-682-8800
800-274-1815; www.brooksbrothers.com

■ "Nine-to-fivers" insist this "granddaddy of preppy" "lives up to its reputation" for "conservative but stylish" business suits and "country club" duds that make even a "frumpy-looking guy into a GQ model in minutes"; society types "swear by" "timeless" blue blazers and "superb" "dress shirts", only regretting that women's apparel gets "a fraction of the floor space"; "unbeatable" service makes shopping "a pleasure", which is as it should be when these "razor-sharp clothes" "cut a big hole in your wallet."

Brookstone ◐🇸 | 21 | 21 | 19 | E |

Manhattan Mall, 901 Sixth Ave. (bet. 32nd & 33rd Sts.), B/D/F/N/Q/ R/V/W to 34th St./Herald Sq., 212-947-2144
South Street Seaport, 18 Fulton St. (bet. South & Water Sts.), 2/3/ 4/5/A/C/J/M/Z to Fulton St./Broadway/Nassau, 212-344-8108
16 W. 50th St. (bet. 5th & 6th Aves.), B/D/F/V to 47-50th Sts./ Rockefeller Ctr., 212-262-3237
20 W. 57th St. (bet. 5th & 6th Aves.), F to 57th St., 212-245-1405
JFK Int'l Airport, Concourse Level, Queens, 718-244-0192
LaGuardia Airport, Departure Level Concourse D, Queens, 718-505-2440
800-926-7000; www.brookstone.com

■ Stressed-out surveyors who stop at these "big playgrounds" for a "free massage" in their auto-reclining Shiatsu lounge chair "always find something irresistible" to buy; chockablock with "clever" "gizmos, widgets and tchotchkes" like voice-recording pens, talking thermometers and digital mini-camera keychains that "seem too gadgety to work well – but do", the chain is "good for impulse shopping" for "James Bond wanna-bes."

Bruce Frank Beads ●🅂🄲   ∇ 20 | 17 | 19 | M

215 W. 83rd St. (bet. Amsterdam Ave. & B'way), 1/9 to 86th St., 212-595-3746; 877-232-3775; www.brucefrankbeads.com

☑ They "take beaders seriously" at this retailer that offers "plenty of choice" among a "superior" assortment of new and vintage varieties "from around the world", with an especially "good selection of semi-precious" stones; but critics carp the "hip staff can be standoffish", particularly on "crowded weekends", and the "prices are high" – perhaps reflecting its "great location on the Upper West Side."

Bruno Magli   24 | 21 | 20 | VE

677 Fifth Ave. (bet. 53rd & 54th Sts.), 6/E/V to 51st St./Lexington Ave., 212-752-7900 🅂

789 Madison Ave. (bet. 67th & 68th Sts.), 6 to 68th St., 212-570-2776 www.brunomagli.it

☑ "What's not to love?"; "beautiful Italian leather and that classic look" make this Midtown shop's "quality" men's and women's shoes some of the "best and most comfortable ever worn" – "just don't look at the tag" – plus there's a "good selection" of leather goods and outerwear to fall for; but not everyone feels like a sole-mate – it's "boring" yawn the less-impressed, who find it "tailored for an older set", with "prices that make it into a gallery for many New Yorkers."

Bu and the Duck 🅂🄲   24 | 23 | 22 | E

106 Franklin St. (bet. Church St. & W. B'way), 1/9 to Franklin St., 212-431-9226; www.buandtheduck.com

■ "Slightly quirky", vintage-inspired kids' clothes and shoes "with a personal touch", cuddly rag dolls and antique children's furniture, that's what this "very fashionable" TriBeCa boutique has to offer; the selection is "completely original" – they even carry suspenders – and "service is very personal", but (gasp) be "prepared to break the bank."

BUCCELLATI   28 | 27 | 25 | VE

46 E. 57th St. (bet. Madison & Park Aves.), 4/5/6/F/N/R/W to 59th St./ Lexington Ave., 212-308-2900; www.buccellati.it

■ It "makes you feel like a Medici" to shop at this Italian "icon" in Midtown, a "class act" known for the "original, extraordinary workmanship" of its "signature pieces" of silverware and its "truly exclusive", Renaissance-inspired "exquisite jewels and settings"; the fittingly "elegant" surroundings and staff can be "intimidating", but it's a "feast for the eyes" – and if you're not careful, it can feast on your wallet too.

Built by Wendy 🅂🄲   23 | 19 | 19 | E

7 Centre Market Pl. (bet. Broome & Grand Sts.), 6 to Spring St., 212-925-6538; www.builtbywendy.com

■ On the SoHo-NoLita border, this "great little" boutique for chicks, and now dudes, too, "rocks" with a beige-and-white interior that provides backup for owner Wendy Mullin's "edgy" "urban cowgirl" and cowboy clothes and accessories, including the "coolest guitar straps" (a hint at the designer's beginnings – selling her wares in record stores).

BULGARI **G** 28 | 27 | 24 | VE

730 Fifth Ave. (57th St.), F to 57th St., 212-315-9000
783 Madison Ave. (bet. 66th & 67th Sts.), 6 to 68th St., 212-717-2300
800-285-4274; www.bulgari.com

◪ For those "over-the-top" moments, bauble-seekers with big budgets head toward this "luxe Italian goldsmith", whose Fifth and Madison Avenue venues provide "lovely showcases" for "stunning jewelry" and trendy watches ("great diamond settings"); "service is sometimes haughty", but "always helpful" and "prompt" (hint: be "dressed to kill when you walk in"); of course, "for the price, everything should be gorgeous – and it is."

Burberry **S** 25 | 24 | 21 | VE

131 Spring St. (Greene St.), 6 to Spring St., 212-925-9300
9 E. 57th St. (bet. 5th & Madison Aves.), 4/5/6/F/N/R/W to 59th St./ Lexington Ave., 212-371-5010
www.burberry.com

◪ Once known for its "classic" "famed trench coats" ("even one for your dog!"), this venerable Brit brand "reinvented" its image, stamping its familiar plaid on "super-expensive" his-and-hers clothes, "scarves, gloves, handbags and anything else your little English-loving heart desires" ("overexposed" sneer a few fashionistas); however, since everyone from "urban hipsters" to "the society set" now "stops 'n' shops" at the "well laid-out" Midtown and SoHo stores, at times the "excellent sales staff can get a little overwhelmed" and "arrogant" (too much plaid-itude)?

Burlington Coat Factory **◑SG** 14 | 8 | 7 | I

707 Sixth Ave. (bet. 22nd & 23rd Sts.), F/N/R/V to 23rd St., 212-229-2247; www.coat.com

◪ "When you're broke and need a gray wool skirt for an interview" or you otherwise "couldn't afford a coat", this "self-service" Chelsea flagship "offers a possibility" for "something basic", with the "occasional" chance of a discount designer "adventure"; citing garb ranging from "fantastic to phooey" and the "slowest cashiers in the Western hemisphere", "Bette Davis" wanna-bes pout "what a dump!"; N.B. the Baby Depot sells infants' clothing, gear and furniture.

Butter **◑SG** 24 | 22 | 20 | E

389 Atlantic Ave. (bet. Bond & Hoyt Sts.), Brooklyn, A/C/G to Hoyt/ Schermerhorn Sts., 718-858-8214

◼ Sister-owners Robin and Eva Weiss, progenitors of the "whole Atlantic Avenue revolution", recently folded their "subtly stylish girl's dream" of a womenswear shop into the gallerylike space formerly occupied by Jelly, their companion shoe store; loyalists "covet practically everything", satisfying cravings for "fine merchandise" from local and European labels, Rogan jeans and footwear from Gianni Barbato and Dries Van Noten; the "cleanly edited" collection is presented on spare racks and salespeople serve you selections in your size.

Butter and Eggs **S** ▽ 24 | 26 | 25 | M

83 W. Broadway (bet. Chambers & Warren Sts.), 1/2/3/9 to Chambers St., 212-676-0235; www.butterandeggs.com

◼ Located in TriBeCa's former wholesale dairy district, which inspired its name, this newcomer contains the 'ingredients to make a home', from "unusual" furniture, pillows and blankets to mirrors, candles and napkin rings; "enthusiastic owners" add to the "delightful" experience.

buybuy Baby ●🅂
23 | 20 | 17 | M

270 Seventh Ave. (bet. 25th & 26th Sts.), 1/9 to 23rd St.; 1/9 to 28th St., 917-344-1555; www.buybuybaby.com

■ "Finally!" A "bright", "wide open" "everything-for-baby store right here" in Chelsea cheer "parents and gift seekers" smitten by this two-floor "mecca's" "unbelievable selection" of newborn, infant and toddler "stuff" "well-presented" "under one roof"; "they've got all the basics, from Carters, Zutano and Little Me" clothing and layette items to "strollers, high chairs, car seats" and personalized furniture, plus "knowledgeable salespeople" to "ease pre-mommy fears" and an "excellent" "registry that makes shopping a breeze."

Cadeau ●🅂🄲
▽ 22 | 23 | 20 | VE

254 Elizabeth St. (bet. Houston & Prince Sts.), R/W to Prince St., 212-674-5747; 866-622-3322; www.cadeaumaternity.com

■ For "exquisitely made" maternity clothes with an urban attitude, head to this luxe NoLita boutique, the brainchild of former Barneys' execs turned designers; expecting fashionistas "flatter growing bellies" with Italian apparel, including hip workwear, casual funky options and even lingerie, plus all-natural prenatal skincare lines; there's also a made-for-impulse-purchasing lovely layette section – why resist?; N.B. pregnancy-related seminars are held monthly.

California Closets
21 | 16 | 21 | E

1625 York Ave. (86th St.), 4/5/6 to 86th St., 212-517-7877; 800-339-2567; www.calclosets.com

■ If you live in a typical NYC "small apartment", a complimentary "in-home consultation" from this "good" "custom-closet" pioneer on the Upper East Side specializing in space-saving designs will "make you want to start spring cleaning"; the company also comes up with storage solutions for garages and offices.

Calling All Pets 🅂🄲
▽ 23 | 17 | 24 | M

301 E. 76th St. (bet. 1st & 2nd Aves.), 6 to 77th St., 212-734-7051 1590 York Ave. (bet. 83rd & 84th Sts.), 4/5/6 to 86th St., 212-249-7387

■ "When you see the store cats", you know the "lovely" sister-owners and "helpful staff" "care" at these two Upper East Side pet shops that "cater to the many pooches and kitties in the area" with "gourmet food" and a "variety of treats and toys"; prices are "competitive", and though the interiors are "small", they "have everything you need."

Calvin Klein 🅂
25 | 25 | 19 | VE

654 Madison Ave. (60th St.), N/R/W to 5th Ave./59th St., 212-292-9000

☑ Less costs more at this Madison Avenue "minimalist mecca" designed by architect John Pawson, whose "sleek" all-white setting and concrete floors create a Calvinistic "fashion temple" for Klein's signature "tasteful, unadorned look" in his-and-hers "classic, elegant" apparel and accessories (high-end collection only – no CK here, ma'am) and "fabulous" home furnishings; some snipe the service can be "as cool as the design", but "if you love Calvin, this is the place to get it"; N.B. Klein recently turned the design reigns over to Francisco Costa.

Calypso 🆂🅲
21 | 21 | 17 | E

424 Broome St. (bet. Crosby & Lafayette Sts.), 6 to Spring St., 212-274-0449
935 Madison Ave. (74th St.), 6 to 77th St., 212-535-4100
280 Mott St. (bet. Houston & Prince Sts.), R/W to Prince St., 212-965-0990

🔳 "New Yorkers sick of black" make a beeline to Christiane Celle's "breezy, beachy" boutiques for "flirty, Caribbean-inspired" sarongs and "teeny bikinis", "floaty" "gypsy" skirts (some with bustles) and cotton tops, all "arranged by" "lush tropical color"; some pout that "prices could be lower", given that the "clothes are best suited for summer" or "trips to the tropics."

Calypso Bijoux 🆂🅲
22 | 22 | 18 | E

252 Mott St. (bet. Houston & Prince Sts.), R/W to Prince St., 212-334-9730

■ The folks behind the über-hot chain of island-ready clothing turn their hands to jewelry, augmented by a few accessories, with this "cute" little NoLita boutique, a "refreshing addition to any downtown shopping jaunt" down the block from one of their women's stores; the "fantastic" designers range from the ethereal Erickson Beamon to modern, sleek Morra Designs to Lyette, a line of romantic, Victorian-inspired pieces.

Calypso Enfant & Bebe ●🆂🅲
▽ 26 | 25 | 24 | E

426 Broome St. (bet. Crosby & Lafayette Sts.), 6 to Spring St., 212-966-3234

■ Laid-back and homey, this SoHo boutique is filled with "sweet", baby and kids' clothes "that are also hip" – and, in some instances, just like the "beautiful", colorful outfits mom buys herself at Calypso's women's shops around town; the "unique" apparel, including French-label goods, cashmere sweaters, hats and booties, is "not cheap, but it's so adorable you'll occasionally overlook the prices."

Calypso Homme 🆂🅲
21 | 17 | 17 | E

405 Broome St. (bet. Centre & Lafayette Sts.), 6 to Spring St., 212-343-0450

🔳 "Sensitive alpha-males can get their chick-magnet attire here", while wives and girlfriends "brighten up wardrobes" of "sartorially challenged companions" at this SoHo counterpart to Calypso's women's boutiques; this "interesting selection" of bright, "casual clothes" is also appealing if "you're looking for something different for vacations", plus the "nice", Continental-accented service gets you in a holiday mood; still, some resort to "window shopping" as it can be a "bit pricey."

Camera Land 🅲
▽ 23 | 16 | 22 | M

575 Lexington Ave. (bet. 51st & 52nd Sts.), 6/E/V to 51st St./ Lexington Ave., 212-753-5128; www.cameralandny.com

■ "Big-city selection and small-town service make a great combo" at this "solid local camera store" in the East 50s; the "excellent" offerings include all the latest gear, one of the East Coast's only do-it-yourself full-processing digital machines and a "great picture framing" department where homegrown mogul "Donald Trump gets his photos" matted.

Camouflage 🆂🅲
▽ 22 | 23 | 24 | E

141 Eighth Ave. (17th St.), A/C/E/L to 14th St./8th Ave., 212-741-5173
139 Eighth Ave. (17th St.), A/C/E/L to 14th St./8th Ave., 212-691-1750

■ Situated side-by-side in Chelsea, this "hip" pair "does a great job of interpreting trends with clothes that men want to wear", with labels that range from pattern-happy Etro to monochromatic

Helmut Lang; 139 Eighth Avenue carries outerwear and sporty styles, while 141 has dressier goods, but the "always chic" yet "conservative" merchandise, backed up by the "best service", makes each address a "favorite."

Camper ●⑤   25 | 25 | 17 | E
125 Prince St. (Wooster St.), R/W to Prince St., 212-358-1841; www.camper.com

◪ "European originality started" the bowling-shoe "craze", moving these "sassy" *zapatos* from "Spanish grandfather's closets to the runways", but it's the "comfort wrapped in" "adorable" looks that prompt patrons to profess their "love" and sigh, "wish they weren't so popular"; happy campers adore the brick-red SoHo shop's "minimalist" presentation of "cool colors", but cynics snipe they're "not as hip as they were years ago" and find the staff "über-snooty."

Canal Hi-Fi ⑤Ⓒ   19 | 11 | 13 | M
319 Canal St. (bet. B'way & Church St.), 6/J/M/N/Q/R/W/Z to Canal St., 212-925-6575; www.canalhifi.com

■ A Chinatown staple since 1977, this labyrinthine "hidden gem" is packed with a "hodgepodge" of home entertainment components, from the newest DVD players to turntables, microphones and other "DJ gear for pro-audio heads" as well as a staff that can help you negotiate all the tricky technical information; as for negotiating cost, some stereophiles say you "can haggle" to buy for less, while others feel it's already "priced like it fell out of a truck."

Canal Jean Company ⑤   19 | 13 | 11 | I
2236 Nostrand Ave. (bet. Aves. H & I), Brooklyn, 2/5 to Brooklyn College/ Flatbush Ave., 718-421-7590; www.canaljean.com

◪ Though smaller than its legendary but now-defunct SoHo sibling, this Flatbush "haven" still pulls in "starry-eyed" teens and twentysomethings with its "discount, baby, discount" jeans ("especially Levi's"), "off-the-wall" vintage threads, "funky club clothes" and lingerie; if you're willing to "dig into" "mounds of stuff", you may "be rewarded" with "spectacular deals."

Cantaloup ⑤Ⓒ   21 | 18 | 18 | E
1036 Lexington Ave. (74th St.), 6 to 77th St., 212-249-3566; www.cantaloup-nyc.com

◪ Offering "downtown attitude with uptown quality", this "hip" haunt done up with a chandelier and staffed with "adorable, ready-to-serve" salespeople is like a "breath of fresh air", bringing an "interesting" mix of "bohemian" yet sophisticated threads to "chic"-seekers; the racks and display table are "full of items from up-and-coming designers", plus "brands different for the neighborhood" and "fabulous for the fashion-minded"; but a few who stay out of the 'loup' find it too "expensive."

Capezio ⑤   19 | 14 | 17 | M
1650 Broadway (51st St.), 1/9 to 50th St., 212-245-2130
1776 Broadway, 2nd fl. (bet. 57th & 58th Sts.), 1/9/A/B/C/D to 59th St./ Columbus Circle, 212-586-5140
136 E. 61st St. (Lexington Ave.), 4/5/6/F/N/R/W to 59th St./Lexington Ave., 212-758-8833
1651 Third Ave. (bet. 92nd & 93rd Sts.), 6 to 96th St., 212-348-7210
877-532-6237; www.capeziodance.com

◪ "Good-quality" men's, women's and kids' "dancers' essentials from apparel to footwear" are the *pointe* of this chain that dates back to 1857; it's "not just for ballerinas", though, as it offers an "almost overwhelming selection" of "great work-out" gear as well, and though a few find the prices tutu "high", insiders divulge they "give discounts" to performers with appropriate ID; N.B. the Third Ave. branch is devoted to childrenswear.

Capitol Fishing Tackle Co. 🅒 | 25 | 18 | 23 | M |

218 W. 23rd St. (bet. 7th & 8th Aves.), 1/9 to 23rd St.; C/E to 23rd St., 212-929-6132; 800-528-0853
■ If the kitschy neon sign and "rustic-looking" bric-a-brac in the windows don't lure you into this 105-year-old "old-timer tackle shop", a 23rd Street fixture since 1969, perhaps the "knockout selection" will; aimed at novice and pro anglers alike, this "real treasure" stocks top-notch brand names in rods, reels and lines for freshwater, saltwater, surf casting and fly-fishing, plus the "knowledgeable staff" "knows their field very well" – they're determined not to have their customers tell the dreaded tale of 'the one that got away.'

Carlos Miele 🆂🅒 | ▽ 23 | 25 | 20 | E |

408 W. 14th St. (bet. 9th Ave. & Washington St.), A/C/E/L to 14th St./ 8th Ave., 646-336-6642; www.carlosmiele.com.br
■ It's not only Brazilian bombshells who slink into the Sao Paolo designer's first retail venture outside of his homeland, an architecturally "cutting-edge" shop/performance-art spot in the Meatpacking District done up in an icy palette and an otherworldly feel; Miele's "wearable and sexy", curve-hugging chiffon frocks, crocheted corsets, jackets, jeans and sensual suits in swanky colors is such "gorgeous stuff" it also attracts women svelte enough to show off toned bods in tantalizing ways.

Carlyle Custom Convertibles 🆂 | 23 | 18 | 19 | E |

1056 Third Ave. (bet. 62nd & 63rd Sts.), 4/5/6/F/N/R/W to 59th St./ Lexington Ave., 212-838-1525
122 W. 18th St. (bet. 6th & 7th Aves.), 1/2/3/9/F/L/V to 14th St./6th Ave., 212-675-3212
www.carlylesofa.com
■ "It's as comfortable as a bed", "but it's a beautiful couch" declare devotees of this duo's convertible sofas; you can choose from the stock available or use your own material and specs and have a "splendid" custom-made version constructed; it's "a little more expensive" than some others, but for the "very good quality", it's "worth it", and the 18th Street branch offers deep discounts on floor samples.

Carnegie Cards & Gifts 🌑🆂🅒 | ▽ 23 | 19 | 16 | M |

56 W. 57th St. (bet. 5th & 6th Aves.), F to 57th St., 212-977-2494
■ "Cluttered but cute" Midtown shop where you're likely to find everything from "lotions, potions and handbags" to "little home things"; it's "the perfect place for thoughtful presents", and there's a "great selection of cards" to accompany them.

Carole Stupell Ltd. | – | – | – | E |

29 E. 22nd St. (bet. B'way & Park Ave. S.), 6 to 23rd St., 212-260-3100
In business since 1929, the Stupell family has been selling primarily European china, crystal and silver plate, including their signature dishes shaped like lobsters and acorns, and continue to do so at this Gramercy Park venue; gift givers and trivia buffs take note: they claim to have created the bridal registry in 1931.

CAROLINA HERRERA
27 | 27 | 26 | VE

954 Madison Ave. (75th St.), 6 to 77th St., 212-249-6552;
www.carolinaherrera.com

■ Though the wedding dresses are "one-of-a-kind", brides-to-be aren't the only ones given "the most individualized attention in town" at this "beautifully furnished flagship" on the Upper East Side; a "wonderful, caring staff" epitomizes the "grace and style" of Herrera herself, making sure the "gorgeous, sexy gowns" and other "well-made" clothes are "discreetly displayed" in an "elegant" space with a "Guggenheim Museum–like" spiral staircase; N.B. Herrera's daughter Patricia Lansing recently joined the design staff.

Carol's Daughter ◐ S C
26 | 24 | 24 | M

1 South Elliot Pl. (DeKalb Ave.), Brooklyn, G to Fulton St.,
718-596-1862; www.carolsdaughter.com

■ "A wonderful little shop in the heart of Fort Greene" that "takes great pride in its merchandise", turning out "natural", homemade hair, bath and body products primarily geared to African-Americans, and "there's something for every skin type"; "friendly service" and "bargain" prices also make this sister shine.

Caron Boutique C
– | – | – | VE

675 Madison Ave. (bet. 61st & 62nd Sts.), 4/5/6/F/N/R/W to 59th St./
Lexington Ave., 212-319-4888

This nearly one-century-old French perfumery has opened its first New York boutique on Madison Avenue, bringing a tradition of luxurious, "rare fragrances", which are even available in limited edition Baccarat crystal bottles; the sumptuous space, accented in faux marble, glass and gold filigree, is a replica of the original on Avenue Montaigne in Paris.

CARTIER
29 | 28 | 24 | VE

653 Fifth Ave. (52nd St.), E/V to 5th Ave./53rd St., 212-753-0111;
www.cartier.com

■ When you crave the "*crème de la crème*", this "legendary" French jeweler is one of *les musts*; within its "magnificent townhouse" – a Fifth Avenue fixture since 1917 – lie "glittering display cases" full of "exquisite", "classy and understated" icons, like the "incomparable" Trinity rings and "the best tank watches", along with "younger, edgier" pieces; the staff is "well trained", "but the service department is truly extraordinary"; P.S. a recent "marvelous renovation" has created new space for the burgundy-colored leather goods and bridal registry.

Casa Amadeo Antigua
Casa Hernandez ◐
– | – | – | M

786 Prospect Ave. (bet. Longwood Ave. & 160th St.), Bronx, 2/5 to
Prospect Ave., 718-328-6896

An integral player in New York's music scene since 1927, when it first opened in East Harlem, this fabled phenom, now located in Longwood, Bronx, features a staggering collection of Puerto Rican and Latin titles on CD and vinyl; housed in a turn-of-the-century building, the store takes its name from its present owner, songwriter Mike Amadeo, and its original proprietor, Victoria Hernandez, sister of famed composer Rafael, and has long been a community hangout for performers, including Eddie Palmieri and Ray Barretto.

Cassina USA
27 **25** **21** **VE**

155 E. 56th St. (bet. Lexington & 3rd Aves.), 4/5/6/F/N/R/W to 59th St./Lexington Ave., 212-245-2121; www.cassinausa.com

■ "*Ciao, bella*" salute supporters of this East 50s furniture store showcasing the "best" "modern, sleek", "to-drool-over" designs by Piero Lissoni and Philippe Starck, as well as the cream of the classic crop, with seating, desks and tables by masters Frank Lloyd Wright, Le Corbusier, Charles Rennie Mackintosh and Gerrit Rietveld; dramatic Flos lighting by Jasper Morrison and a "surprisingly warm" staff are added turn-ons.

Castor & Pollux 🆂 🅲
– **–** **–** **E**

67½ Sixth Ave. (Bergen St.), Brooklyn, 2/3 to Bergen St., 718-398-4141; www.castorandpolluxstore.com

On an unlikely Prospect Heights block, Martha Stewart alum Kerrilyn Hunt runs up this cute-as-a-button boutique where many of the impeccably stylish goods – a "well-edited" mix of women's clothing, jewelry, handbags and beauty products – are crafted by the owner herself; a hipster-chick's best pal, this shop has been known to lure edgy Manhattanites with its one-of-a-kind wares.

Casual Male Big & Tall 🆂
15 **13** **19** **M**

291 Third Ave. (bet. 22nd & 23rd Sts.), 6 to 23rd St., 212-532-1415
527 86th St. (bet. 5th Ave. & Fort Hamilton Pkwy.), Brooklyn, R to 86th St., 718-921-9770
2435 Flatbush Ave. (bet. Aves. T & U), Brooklyn, 2/5 to Brooklyn College/Flatbush Ave., 718-252-1313 ●
1110 Pennsylvania Ave. (bet. Cozine & Flatlands Aves.), Brooklyn, L to Canarsie/Rockaway Pkwy., 718-649-2924
Bay Plaza, 2094 Bartow Ave. (CoOp City Blvd.), Bronx, 6 to Pelham Bay Park, 718-379-4148 ●
945 White Plains Rd. (bet. Bruckner Blvd. & Story Ave.), Bronx, 718-239-0761 ●
2295 Richmond Ave., Staten Island, 718-370-7767 ●
www.casualmale.com

☑ "Just when you thought you'd never find quality in your size – presto!" you come across "a whole store [actually, a whole chain] full of dressy, comfy stuff" made for men of stature; malcontents mutter about "some good fashions, some polyester nightmares", but most maintain the business and casualwear represent "the best buys for big guys" and laud the "affable help."

Caswell-Massey 🆂 🅲
24 **22** **22** **M**

518 Lexington Ave. (48th St.), 6/E/V to 51st St./Lexington Ave., 212-755-2254; www.caswell-massey.com

■ "Polished wooden counters" and chandeliers give this East 40s "classic" an "elegant ambiance from another age", and indeed the company claims to be America's oldest (1752) chemist/perfumer; "beauty products with a timeless appeal" like the popular Almond & Aloe line reside alongside "toiletries for babies and people with sensitive skin", shaving accessories and colognes that are said to have been favored by founding father George Washington.

Catherine Malandrino 🆂 🅲
26 **23** **19** **VE**

468 Broome St. (Greene St.), C/E to Spring St., 212-925-6765; www.catherinemalandrino.com

☑ SoHo "cool" merges with "frilly femininity" at this Broome Street boutique, a favorite of celebrities and hip stylists for its "fun, flirty" dresses and "well-cut" women's separates; while even disciples deplore the "limited selection" and the fact that the "floaty" "pieces are so heavy on the wallet", most praise the "friendly staff" and "neat artwork" on the "trademark" chartreuse walls.

Catherine Memmi 🆂🅲   – | – | – | VE

45 Greene St. (bet. Broome & Grand Sts.), R/W to Prince St., 212-226-8200; 212-226-8111; www.catherinememmi.com
Proponents of noted Parisian designer Catherine Memmi proclaim her first American outpost in SoHo showcasing her "clean", neo-minimalist "quality" furnishings in muted brown woods, pale leathers and "cool" neutral textiles one of the nabe's "best new stores"; her signature lighting, linens, scented candles and bath and beauty products are on hand here as well.

CATIMINI 🆂🅲   28 | 25 | 19 | VE

1284 Madison Ave. (bet. 91st & 92nd Sts.), 6 to 96th St., 212-987-0688; www.catimini.com
■ "This is where those kids who look like city kids shop" pronounce proponents who head to this Upper East boutique, the only U.S. branch of the French chain, for "adorable", "fun", "stylish" clothing "with a European flair"; the "beautiful but pricey", whimsical and colorful collection is "very cute" for "wee little ones" as well as children up to size 12.

Cécile et Jeanne ●🅹🆂🅲   ▽ 25 | 25 | 25 | M

311 Columbus Ave. (bet. 74th & 75th Sts.), B/C to 72nd St., 212-595-5907
1100 Madison Ave. (bet. 82nd & 83rd Sts.), 4/5/6 to 86th St., 212-535-5700
436 W. Broadway (bet. Prince & Spring Sts.), C/E to Spring St., 212-625-3535
www.cecilejeanne.com
■ "Satisfy any craving for whimsical jewelry" at this Uptown-Downtown trio from the "eye-catching", Paris-based designer, whose limited U.S. distribution makes the handmade "stunning" pieces – especially the signature doves – coveted by career women who like "truly enchanting" resin-studded baubles; a "choice find" with "wonderful service", "this store makes you feel like you're back in" the City of Lights.

Celine 🅲   25 | 23 | 21 | VE

667 Madison Ave. (bet. 60th & 61st Sts.), N/R/W to 5th Ave./59th St., 212-486-9700; www.celine.com
■ Marrying an American sensibility to a "tasteful", established French label, designer "Michael Kors delivers" creations that "dreams are made of" – constructed from the "best fabrics" with "unbeatable" tailoring – "for the pampered woman" who patronizes this "clean, sleek" Upper East Side boutique; complementing the "classy" clothes are "expensive accessories", perfume and leather goods, including the signature Inca loafer; N.B. at press time, Kors was slated to leave the company.

CELLINI   28 | 24 | 23 | VE

509 Madison Ave. (bet. 52nd & 53rd Sts.), E/V to 5th Ave./53rd St., 212-888-0505
Waldorf-Astoria, 301 Park Ave. (49th St.), 6 to 51st St., 212-751-9824
◪ Wristwatch worshipers say whether it's the Waldorf-Astoria location or the East 50s branch, "for pure selection, no one is better" than this establishment, a "fabulous" place for "hard-to-find" and "limited editions", especially of "luxury brands" like Franck

Müller; "prices are high", but it's possible to "get deals" from the "tough", yet highly "knowledgeable staff"; N.B. there's a strong selection of European jewelry as well.

CENTURY 21 ●S
22 10 9 I

22 Cortlandt St. (bet. B'way & Church St.), 2/3/4/5/A/C/J/M/Z to Fulton St./B'way/Nassau, 212-227-9092
472 86th St. (bet. 4th & 5th Aves.), Brooklyn, R to 86th St., 718-748-3266
www.c21stores.com

☑ "Support Downtown" by "bargain shopping" for "divine" "designer duds", "upscale" bed linens and cosmetics at this "madhouse" discount "goldmine" (with a branch in Brooklyn); women vie for space in the "scary" communal dressing rooms, "men can't try on clothes" at all and everyone "battles" "throngs" of "fashion hounds" "inspecting for flaws" in the aisles, but in the end, "who cares if the salespeople treat you like cows" and check-out takes a century? – it's all "sooo worth it", 'cause "when you hit, you hit big!"; N.B. the Bay Ridge store was renovated post-*Survey*.

CERAMICA S C
27 22 21 E

59 Thompson St. (bet. Broome & Spring Sts.), C/E to Spring St., 212-941-1307; 800-228-0858; www.ceramicadirect.com

■ Umbria and Tuscany come to the table with the 20 imported, hand-painted pottery patterns sold at this "crowded" SoHo ceramic shop; Italian craftsmen (mainly from the famed village of Deruta) employ ancient techniques to create "appealing" place settings, pasta bowls and platters that have a traditional look but are lead-free and dishwasher-safe to suit contemporary life.

Cesare Paciotti C
▽ 24 26 18 VE

833 Madison Ave. (bet. 69th & 70th Sts.), 6 to 68th St., 212-452-1222; www.cesare-paciotti.com

☑ Strut your stuff in these sexy stilettos and you'll "definitely find a sugar daddy" fawn femme fatales who hail Cesare on the Upper East Side for its "superb selection" of the "finest footwear with an edge" (certain to tempt the "splurge impulse in all of us") as well as its edgy menswear collection; still, a handful huff that "service has decreased over the years", shrugging "why bother?"

Champs ●S
16 13 13 M

1381 Sixth Ave. (56th St.), F to 57th St., 212-757-3634
1 W. 34th St. (5th Ave.), 6 to 33rd St., 212-239-3256
Staten Island Mall, 2655 Richmond Ave., Staten Island, 718-698-1560
www.champssports.com

☑ "Good-for-basics" chain where you can "pick up sneaks, Yanks jerseys, socks", activewear and "athletic gear" "in season" from "big-name sure sellers" like Adidas, Puma, Spalding, Vans, Louisville and the like; but those seeking high-end products jab at the "weak selection" and nix it as an "excuse for a full-service sporting-goods store."

Chanel
27 26 21 VE

15 E. 57th St. (bet. 5th & Madison Aves.), N/R/W to 5th Ave./59th St., 212-355-5050 S
139 Spring St. (Wooster St.), R/W to Prince St., 212-334-0055
800-550-0005; www.chanel.com

☑ "What tops Chanel?" – not much assert enthusiasts who call the 57th Street flagship and its newer SoHo sibling "the ultimate in luxury", giving high-fives to the "classic beauty and workmanship" of the women's apparel and accessories – now "modern and sexy" thanks to designer Karl Lagerfeld, who's taken "über-branding" to a whole new level; "label-conscious" ladies opt for those "timeless" quilted bags or the "always-in-fashion" suits, while others settle for lipstick, "perfume or a scarf"; still, even Coco would go loco at the "iffy service" ("intimidating" vs. "impeccable") and "elitist" prices.

Chanel Fine Jewelry

∇ 25 | 25 | 22 | VE

733 Madison Ave. (64th St.), F to Lexington Ave./63rd St., 212-535-5828; 800-550-0005; www.chanel.com

■ "Finally, the jewelry gets a store of its own" laud lovers of this new "luxe paradise" in the East 60s, designed by Peter Marino, with the fashion house's signature beige-and-black color scheme; the hedonistic baubles "exude the class and style" of Mlle. Coco's "original designs" (the signature matelassee pieces are quilted, just like the purses), as does the label-clad staff that "treats you like royalty"; P.S. walk through the adjoining bag-and-shoe boutique to check out "the ladies' room where Chanel perfumes are available for freshening up."

Charles Jourdan

23 | 23 | 20 | E

155 Spring St. (bet. W. B'way & Wooster St.), C/E to Spring St., 212-219-0490; www.charles-jourdan.com

☑ "My tootsies love this store" swoons a "made-it crowd" that coos over the "variety of styles from fancy-schmancy to basic everyday" to super-"sexy" at this SoHo boutique; these "shoes last" insist some surveyors who swear they "never go out of style", but a few beg to differ, asserting "they never change and we wish they did."

Charles P. Rogers ◗ⓢ

23 | 20 | 20 | E

55 W. 17th St. (bet. 5th & 6th Aves.), 4/5/6/L/N/Q/R/W to 14th St./ Union Sq., 212-675-4400; 800-582-6229; www.charlesprogers.com

■ This manufacturer began making "beautiful" brass, wrought-iron and wooden beds in the mid-19th-century and continues to sell a "fabulous" selection ranging from canopied to contemporary styles at "great prices" at its store in the Flatiron District; "excellent personalized service" also helps shoppers rest easy.

Charles Tyrwhitt ⓢ

22 | 21 | 20 | E

377 Madison Ave. (46th St.), 4/5/6/7/S to 42nd St./Grand Central, 212-286-8988; www.ctshirts.com

■ "Fine men's shirts in the English tradition are finally here in the U.S." applaud admirers of this Midtown yearling, perhaps "the most reasonable of the Jermyn Street" clothiers, specializing in "classy" styles not quite as "flashy as Thomas Pink's"; the black shelves brim with colorful cotton button-downs (both his and hers) with distinctive brass stays, silk ties and cuff links, and what's more, the "fab" staff harkens to higher-priced haberdashers; P.S. the "no-quibble mail-order service" offers "frequent discounts."

Charlotte Russe ⓢ

15 | 13 | 11 | I

Manhattan Mall, 1275 Broadway (bet. 32nd & 33rd Sts.), A/C/E to 34th St./Penn Station, 212-465-8425; www.charlotte-russe.com

☑ "Fabulous for the girl on a budget" is the mantra of "fashionably fickle" "teenyboppers" sweet on this newly arrived Manhattan Mall chain outpost; whether you're "looking for a cheap thrill", "fun, trendy" "last minute stuff to go out in" or "one store to buy a whole wardrobe", "this is the place"; still, dissenters tut that the threads are "trashy" and feel this outfit lacks "pizzazz."

Cheap Jack's ●S
17 | 10 | 11 | M

841 Broadway (bet. 13th & 14th Sts.), 4/5/6/L/N/Q/R/W to 14th St./ Union Sq., 212-777-9564; www.cheapjacks.com

☑ "If you have time to search the racks" (they stretch up to the ceiling), "you'll almost always find something to ring your chimes" at this Union Square used-clothing warehouse, crammed with "well-preserved winter coats", "vintage denim", Eisenhower-era dresses and tons of ties and T-shirts; but cons counter "this place should be called Overpriced Jack's", given the "ridiculous" tags.

Chelsea Garden Center Home S C
25 | 25 | 20 | E

435 Hudson St. (bet. Leroy & Morton Sts.), 1/9 to Canal St., 212-727-7100; www.chelseagardencenter.com

☑ "A veritable oasis in the city", this "huge loft space" in the West Village offers "high-quality" "gorgeous plants, pots and furniture", as well as "tinkling waterfalls", inspiring "lust" in even the most "die-hard urbanite"; though service is "attentive" and the "blooms are lovely and well cared for", many find the wares "overpriced."

Cherry ●S
∇ 20 | 16 | 16 | M

19 Eighth Ave. (bet. Jane & W. 12th Sts.), A/C/E/L to 14th St./8th Ave., 212-924-1410

☑ Nestled amid a row of boutiques, this small Villager offers an array of his-and-hers vintage apparel that looks "ultra-trendy", even though it dates from the 1950s–80s; mostly daywear, the "designer merch" includes early Calvin Klein and Anne Klein, plus glitzy footwear from shoemaker-to-the-stars Joseph LaRose; still, skeptics snap the stuff's "slightly overpriced."

Chico's S
18 | 19 | 20 | M

1310 Third Ave. (75th St.), 6 to 77th St., 212-249-9105
Bay Terrace, 23-60 Bell Blvd. (24th Ave.), Queens, 7 to Main St., 718-224-1256
888-669-4911; www.chicos.com

■ With its "big fan base among soccer moms", this "bit of Boca" chain with branches in Bayside and the East 70s delivers "funky", "flattering" and "travel-comfortable" apparel that "never wrinkles"; "reasonable" prices are "a boon to non-svelte" "boomers", but it's "too missy" for some; still, service is "low pressure" with discounts for passport members ("spend $500 and you're in").

Children's General Store ●S C
∇ 20 | 20 | 18 | M

Grand Central, 107 E. 42nd St., 4/5/6/7/S to 42nd St./Grand Central, 212-682-0004

☑ If you commute to Grand Central, "you can't avoid a stop" at this "nicely set up" toy store; the puzzles, books, educational games and sundry items are organized by category, and while the "selection is limited", it's well-edited so you may discover "stuff you won't find elsewhere" including "smaller less expensive items."

Children's Place, The ●S
17 | 16 | 14 | I

22 W. 34th St. (bet. 5th & 6th Aves.), B/D/F/N/Q/R/V/W to 34th St./ Herald Sq., 212-904-1190; 800-527-5355; www.childrensplace.com
Additional locations throughout the NY area

☑ "Inexpensive but real cute clothes" for little ones that "meet the need for trendy stuff" can be found at this chainster with locations in all five boroughs; "your dollar goes a long way here" – "the prices won't leave you wondering whether you can throw in a few socks" – plus "sales are frequent"; some shoppers find that "not the best quality materials are used, but for a little kid, it's not a big deal" – just "don't expect it to last more than two children."

Chloé C | 26 | 24 | 21 | VE |
850 Madison Ave. (70th St.), 6 to 68th St., 212-717-8220; www.chloe.com

■ Designer Phoebe Philo brings a "British cheekiness" to this 50-year-old French label, and her "cutting-edge" sensibility shows up in this Upper East Side boutique filled with "effortlessly chic" dresses and "flamboyant" T-shirts; "sophisticated shoppers" suggest that, since celebrities and "insiders get the pick of the fab stuff, get there pre-season" before everything (especially the "great-fitting pants") is gone.

CHOPARD C | 28 | 27 | 23 | VE |
725 Madison Ave. (bet. 63rd & 64th Sts.), 6 to 68th St., 212-218-7222; www.chopard.com

■ Fitted with mahogany and a marble fireplace, this East 60s jewel box of a "blinding gem" boutique is a veritable "candy store for big girls" whose sweet tooth runs to "nice, large-sized stones", "exquisitely intricate" designs and the "beautiful" signature Happy Diamond timepieces (the loose jewels float inside the face); this is a pretty "great spot for indulgence", though "not *everything* is prohibitively expensive."

CHRISTIAN LOUBOUTIN C | 28 | 26 | 21 | VE |
941 Madison Ave. (bet. 74th & 75th Sts.), 6 to 77th St., 212-396-1884

■ "The French certainly don't fail when it comes to shoes", and this "truly creative" designer is a prime example – he "knows how to take something fabulous and make it even better"; his "Parisian-style" Madison Avenue "super-chic boutique" "with a floor-to-ceiling chandelier in the alcove" showcases "elegant", "feminine" "sky-high heels" adorned with the "notorious" "scarlet sole" that "make you feel beautiful the moment you put them on" – "like a courtesan to Louis XIV."

CHRISTOFLE C | 28 | 26 | 22 | VE |
680 Madison Ave. (62nd St.), N/R/W to 5th Ave./59th St., 212-308-9390

■ For the "finest sterling place settings in the world" and "well-designed silver plate", tony types tout the Upper East Side branch of this über-upscale French silversmith whose flatware, though stratospherically priced, is "well worth" it; it also offers crystal, porcelain and table linens, making it a "great place to shop for weddings" or your own "elegant" entertaining.

Chrome Hearts C | 25 | 25 | 22 | E |
159 E. 64th St. (bet. Lexington & 3rd Aves.), 6 to 68th St., 212-327-0707

■ Calling all "billionaire bikers": on the Upper East Side, this "beyond expensive", very "hip spot" showcases "top-of-the-line silver" and the "most amazing leather" goods in "everything from belts to jewelry", much of it "custom-work for celebrities"; some say this "little hidden gem" is the "coolest retail space in NYC", but to properly reflect the prices, "there should be a VVE category."

Chuckies ●ⓈⒸ
1073 Third Ave. (bet. 63rd & 64th Sts.), F to Lexington Ave./63rd St., 212-593-9898

☑ "It's always a joy to see what's on the rack" at this "hip" slice of "heaven for shoe mavens" in the East 60s chockablock with "awesome" "designer" footwear "from Jimmy Choos" on down the line; the "high style" extends from the "crazy" setting (think velvet couches and chandeliers) to the attitude ("snobby staff" sigh the snubbed); P.S. "you better be a trust-fund baby to shop here" – unless you "stop by during sale" time for "bargains."

Church Shoes
689 Madison Ave. (62nd St.), 6 to 68th St., 212-758-5200; www.churchsshoes.com

■ Every banker worth his salt knows that "serious" British bench-crafted footwear hails from this East 60s boutique; the "right-wing wingtips", oxfords, loafers and "standard issue cap-toes that can't be beat" are "straight out of the preppy handbook" "with a touch of class"; "steep prices" may equal a "week's salary" but the shoes "wear like iron" and "repairs are hassle-free."

Circuit City ●Ⓢ
2232 Broadway (80th St.), 1/9 to 79th St., 212-362-9850
232 E. 86th St. (bet. 2nd & 3rd Aves.), 4/5/6 to 86th St., 212-734-1694
52 E. 14th St. (bet. 4th & 5th Aves.), 4/5/6/L/N/Q/R/W to 14th St./Union Sq., 212-387-0730
625 Atlantic Ave., 2nd fl. (Fort Greene Pl.), Brooklyn, 2/3/4/5/B/D/M/N/Q/R/W to Atlantic Ave., 718-399-2990
Gateway Ctr., 369 Gateway Dr. (Erskine St.), Brooklyn, A/C to Euclid Ave., 718-277-1611
96-05 Queens Blvd. (Junction Blvd.), Queens, G/R/V to 63rd Dr./Queens Blvd., 718-275-2077
136-03 20th Ave., Queens, 7 to Main St., 718-961-2090
2505 Richmond Ave., Staten Island, 718-982-1182
800-843-2489; www.circuitcity.com

☑ "If it requires an outlet, batteries or a player of any sort, they have it" at this national chain of "electronic wonderlands", and "the price is good, though you'd better find it yourself" – "they have few sales reps on the floors" and not enough folks behind the registers; instead of cooling your jets in the "frustratingly" "long checkout-line", try "ordering it online and picking it up right in the store whenever you want."

C.I.T.E. Design Ⓢ
108,120B Wooster St. (bet. Prince & Spring Sts.), 6 to Spring St.; R/W to Prince St., 212-431-7272; www.cite-design.com

☑ "Interesting" design duo in SoHo specializing in "groovy" mid-century furniture and accessories with a Danish bent; the selections "can be hit-or-miss", but most "keep going back."

City Opera Thrift Shop Ⓢ
222 E. 23rd St. (bet. 2nd & 3rd Aves.), 6 to 23rd St., 212-684-5344

☑ Boasting the "most pleasant atmosphere of any thrift shop in town" – and it's on a Gramercy Park "block loaded with 'em" – this store offers "unusual furniture", "designer duds" and "idiosyncratic items", like the once-happened-upon "occasional vintage opera costume"; some sigh over the "overpriced", "limited stock", but converts clap hands over their "classy finds."

City Quilter, The ◗⧅

27 | 25 | 27 | M

133 W. 25th St. (bet. 6th & 7th Aves.), 1/9 to 23rd St., 212-807-0390;
www.cityquilter.com

■ Twice the size of its original site, this recently relocated Chelsea "quilters' heaven" "does a great job of displaying" its 1,500 bolts of "special", contemporary cotton fabrics and "supplies such as books, notions" and "interesting patterns"; the nimble-fingered make a beeline for "wonderful" "classes that cover a variety of hand and machine techniques" and give a thumbs-up to the "friendly, funny crew."

City Sports ◗⧅

18 | 15 | 15 | M

153 E. 53rd St. (bet. Lexington & 3rd Aves.), 6/E/V to 51st St./
Lexington Ave., 212-317-0541; www.citysports.com

☑ There's "nothing fancy" at this Midtown athletic retreat, but you will find a "fair selection and fair prices" on "clothing specific to different sports", including "excellent work-out wear" for women, men and kids, "activity-related footwear" and sporting goods for every season; "check out their sale section for amazing deals on still current styles", but since the staff can be "invisible", you may have to be game to go it alone.

CK Bradley ⧅ⓒ

24 | 20 | 20 | E

146 E. 74th St. (Lexington Ave.), 6 to 77th St., 212-988-7999;
www.ckbradley.com

■ You'll feel you've "died and gone to Nantucket" in this cheerful pink, white and black Upper East Side shop where "country club chic" rules thanks to Camilla Bradley's "simple, elegant" dresses, separates, capes and toile totes; it's "a must for true prepsters" craving a colorful cummerbund or bow tie, plus it's "the only place to buy ribbon belts" for those days when you want to "add a splash of color to your outfit"; a post-*Survey* move may outdate the above Presentation score.

Claire's Accessories

12 | 11 | 11 | I

1385 Broadway (bet. 37th & 38th Sts.), B/D/F/N/Q/R/V/W to 34th St./
Herald Sq., 212-302-6616 ⧅
755 Broadway (bet. 8th St. & Waverly Pl.), R/W to 8th St.; 6 to Astor Pl.,
212-353-3980 ◗⧅
720 Lexington Ave. (58th St.), 4/5/6/F/N/R/W to 59th St./Lexington Ave.,
212-644-8665 ⧅
1381 Sixth Ave. (56th St.), F to 57th St., 212-977-9294 ◗⧅
2133 86th St. (Bay Pkwy.), Brooklyn, D/M to Bay Pkwy.,
718-333-9631 ◗
476 86th St. (bet. 4th & 5th Aves.), Brooklyn, R to 86th St.,
718-630-5895 ◗
Bay Terrace, 211-43 26th Ave. (212th St.), Queens, 7 to Main St.,
718-225-8392 ◗⧅
107-29 71st Ave. (Austin St.), Queens, E/F/G/R/V to Forest Hills/
71st Ave., 718-261-1680 ◗⧅
www.claires.com

☑ Anyone "who is or acts like a 12-year-old" enjoys indulging in the "dirt-cheap", "disposable jewelry" and "lots of hair thingies" displayed by this chain, aka the "goody-bag capital of the world"; fans find it the "perfect spot to shop for little sisters" or a "quick trend fix", but foes fume that the fads will outlast the merchandise and deplore the "indifferent service by gum-smacking teens."

Clarks England S
22 | 19 | 21 | M

363 Madison Ave. (45th St.), 4/5/6/7/S to 42nd St./Grand Central, 212-949-9545; www.clarksusa.com

■ The king of "comfort" has come a long way since peddling sheepskin slippers in the English countryside in 1825; today this East 40s shop is worth a hike for "solid", "dependable" men's and women's indoor, outdoor and "rugged shoes", all proffered by a "patient", "courteous" staff that helps customers find that "excellent fit" — in short, it's the kind of "reliability" you'd expect from the brains behind the Wallabee.

Classic Kicks S C
– | – | – | E

298 Elizabeth St. (bet. Bleecker & Houston Sts.), 6 to Bleecker St.; B/D/F/ S/V to B'way/Lafayette St., 212-979-9514; www.classickicks.com

The coolest in limited-edition, athletic and "classic" old-school sneakers sure to "bring back memories of childhood" from Nike, Vans and Puma, urban-meets-country-club activewear from the fashionable likes of Fred Perry, Lacoste, Tacchini and Le Coq Sportif, plus Hervé Chapelier totes are all aggregated under one roof at this snappy red-and-white candy box in NoLita, whose streets make a fitting playground for breaking in your new duds.

Classic Sofa ◗ S
▽ 24 | 16 | 18 | E

5 W. 22nd St. (bet. 5th & 6th Aves.), R/W to 23rd St., 212-620-0485; www.classicsofa.com

■ "If you want a good, comfortable sofa that doesn't look like every other one, shop here" say supporters of this Flatiron custom-couch company that offers hardwood frames, down-fill and a "great fabric selection" that ranges from suede to chenille and canvas; moreover, you can "have it your way", including "odd sizes and shapes", in as little as two weeks turnaround time.

Clay Pot ◗ S C
25 | 23 | 21 | E

162 Seventh Ave. (bet. 1st St. & Garfield Pl.), Brooklyn, B/Q to 7th Ave., 800-989-3579; www.clay-pot.com

◩ "Everyone loves getting gifts" from this 35-year-old "Park Slope staple", which carries a "bit pricey" "collection of works by artisans in all mediums", "from pottery and [handblown glass] to funky jewelry and elegant wedding bands"; "be prepared to fight a crowd on weekends" and holiday seasons, but the "helpful staff" makes waiting "worth it."

Clea Colet
24 | 22 | 22 | VE

960 Madison Ave. (bet. 75th & 76th Sts.), 6 to 77th St., 212-396-4608; www.cleacolet.com

■ "Feminine", "fanciful" "fairy princess dresses" await the betrothed at this by-appointment-only Madison Avenue bridal boutique where an "accommodating" staff (some of "the nicest people!") is on hand to complete the transformation; breathlessly "beautiful", these "excellent designs", ranging from the seductive to the majestic, are made from the highest quality silk and lace, with handcrafted beading and detailing completed in Europe.

Clio S C
– | – | – | M

92 Thompson St. (bet. Prince & Spring Sts.), C/E to Spring St., 212-966-8991; www.clio-home.com

Named after the Greek muse of history, this small SoHo shop inspires with an eclectic selection of home accessories that ranges from whimsical to worldly; horn salad servers, handblown glasses, cheese plates, colorful contemporary ceramics and clean cylindrical lighting are displayed on farm tables and in cupboards that are also for sale.

Cloisters Gift Shop, The 🅢🅒 | 21 | 20 | 18 | M |
The Cloisters, Fort Tryon Park, A to 190th St., 212-650-2277
■ "If you love Medieval" goodies, feed your Dungeons-and-Dragons fetish with "classy trinkets from the Dark Ages" at this "pleasant" boutique in the "beautiful" "castle"-like branch of the Met in Fort Tryon Park; it's "such a tiny space", its "limited selection" doesn't lure wanna-be knights and damsels "out of their way to shop", but if you're far Uptown, "it's worth a look-see."

CLUB MONACO 🅞🅢 | 20 | 20 | 16 | M |
2376 Broadway (87th St.), 1/9 to 86th St., 212-579-2587
520 Broadway (bet. Broome & Spring Sts.), C/E to Spring St., 212-941-1511
160 Fifth Ave. (21st St.), R/W to 23rd St., 212-352-0936
121 Prince St. (bet. Greene & Wooster Sts.), R/W to Prince St., 212-533-8930
1111 Third Ave. (65th St.), 6 to 68th St., 212-355-2949
888-580-5084; www.clubmonaco.com
◪ "For the budding fashionista" who isn't yet "so label conscious", this "minimal, chic" Canadian Club serves up everything from "clean, spare" (some say "bland") "black and white basics" to "smart Prada and Helmut Lang imitations" "from the latest runway", all at "an affordable price"; "inventory is switched monthly, so you never get bored", and their "absolutely fab" threads are "easy to wear", provided you're both hip and "hipless."

Clyde's 🅞🅢 | 26 | 22 | 22 | E |
926 Madison Ave. (74th St.), 6 to 77th St., 212-744-5050;
800-792-5933; www.clydesonmadison.com
■ "You can pick up your Joey New York Facial Scrub and your potassium iodide tablets in one trip" at this "boutiquey, little" Upper East Side pharmacy that also has an "outstanding selection of beauty products", along with other "pretty pricey notions" like Rigaud candles; if you need help, the "salesgirls know it all."

Coach 🅞🅢 | 24 | 23 | 20 | E |
2321 Broadway (bet. 84th & 85th Sts.), 1/9 to 86th St., 212-799-1624
35 E. 85th St. (Madison Ave.), 4/5/6 to 86th St., 212-879-9391
620 Fifth Ave. (50th St.), E/V to 5th Ave./53rd St., 212-245-4148
79 Fifth Ave. (16th St.), 4/5/6/L/N/Q/R/W to 14th St./Union Sq., 212-675-6403
595 Madison Ave. (57th St.), N/R/W to 5th Ave./59th St., 212-754-0041
342 Madison Ave. (44th St.), 4/5/6/7/S to 42nd St./Grand Central, 212-599-4777
143 Prince St. (bet. W. B'way & Wooster St.), R/W to Prince St., 212-473-6925
South Street Seaport, 193 Front St. (Water St.), 2/3/4/5/A/C/J/M/Z to Fulton St./B'way/Nassau, 212-425-4350
888-262-6224; www.coach.com
◪ "Always the gold standard for leather goods" chorus customers who canter over to this chain for "every kind of bag you could

want", "trendsetting accessories", belts and "indestructible" shoes, all of "unsurpassed quality" that "lasts for years"; the staff "treats you like royalty" plus they offer a "wonderful repair policy", but the less-impressed feel that it's "become too mainstream" – "it seems like everyone and their mother have one of their" purses; N.B. a new branch has opened in The Shops at Columbus Circle at Time Warner Center.

C.O. Bigelow Chemists ◗ S   27 | 22 | 20 | M

414 Sixth Ave. (bet. 8th & 9th Sts.), A/B/C/D/E/F/S/V to W. 4th St., 212-533-2700; 800-793-5433; www.bigelowchemists.com

■ "About as chic as a drugstore gets" sums up this "atmospheric" 1838 West Village classic where "old-time remedies and beauty products coexist with the latest New Age aromatherapy and herbal cures", "hard-to-find", "offbeat imported items", "terrific hair ornaments" and "cool cosmetics and trinkets" that make for nifty little stocking stuffers; just note that "while it exudes nostalgia, the prices are wholeheartedly 2004"; still, supporters are "happy it's still here" and proclaim "may it never fall to Duane Reade."

Coclico S C   – | – | – | E

275 Mott St. (bet. Houston & Prince Sts.), B/D/F/S/V to B'way/ Lafayette St., 212-965-5462; www.shopcoclico.com

For a "quirky selection" of shoes and boots "you won't find anyone else wearing" ("many from international designers you might not have heard of" such as the house label, Mosquitos, and Lisa Nadling), fashionistas hoof it to this lime-green nook in NoLita that also purveys handbags and jewelry; grab a cushion, groove to the ambient music and slip into a pair of the pricey "one-of-a-kind" finds.

Coconut Company   – | – | – | E

131 Greene St. (bet. Houston & Prince Sts.), R/W to Prince St., 212-539-1940

With an eclectic, albeit somewhat schizophrenic, mix of French antiques and Asian-inspired chairs and tables, this SoHo store strives for a kind of vague colonial elegance; one of the highlights here is Ian Mankin's collection of subtly striped fabrics.

Cog & Pearl S C   – | – | – | M

190 Fifth Ave. (Sackett St.), Brooklyn, M/R to Union St., 718-623-8200; www.cogandpearl.com

Artsy is the byword at Park Slope's Fifth Avenue phenom with a perky purple, green and stained-glass exterior and the feel of a funky gallery; the owners have a weakness for handmade items, exhibiting reworked vintage T-shirts, jewelry from a wide range of designers, including local favorite, Kiln Enamel, bags from Patch, upholstery fabric totes, decoupage ceramics from John Derian and bath products in accessible glass cases and casually stacked on tables.

Cohen's Fashion Optical ◗ S C   15 | 14 | 14 | M

767 Lexington Ave. (60th St.), 4/5/6/F/N/R/W to 59th St./ Lexington Ave., 212-751-6652; 800-393-7440; www.cohensfashionoptical.com
Additional locations throughout the NY area

◨ "Glasses for the masses" alongside "designer" numbers add up to an eyewear chain with "something for everyone"; but service that veers from "clueless" and "disinterested" to "very good" and "helpful" (with doctors on premises), and all the "wheeling and dealing" ("don't forget your coupon"), make a few feel framed.

Cole Haan S
| 23 | 22 | 20 | E |

620 Fifth Ave. (50th St.), B/D/F/V to 47-50th Sts./Rockefeller Ctr., 212-765-9747
667 Madison Ave. (61st St.), 4/5/6/F/N/R/W to 59th St./Lexington Ave., 212-421-8440
www.colehaan.com

■ "Treat your feet" to "butter soft", "solidly crafted shoes – you'll wear out before they do"; the "fabulous" range of "beautiful" footwear and "basic leather goods" is "stylish but conservative", plus the men's choices "have a nice edge", including Nike Airtech soles; "from free replacement laces to friendly smiles", the "pleasant atmosphere" makes this Fifth and Madison Avenue pair and its new sibling in The Shops at Columbus Circle at Time Warner Center "necessary stops" on any walking tour.

Colony Music ●S C
| 25 | 13 | 19 | E |

1619 Broadway (49th St.), 1/9 to 50th St., 212-265-2050; www.colonymusic.com

◪ Housed in the Brill building, "synonymous with American songwriting", this 50-plus-year-old "institution" is a "great" "source for music and memorabilia that's theatrical in nature"; it's "the place to go for sheet music", Broadway and pop and "tough-to-find stuff" even late at night, plus there's a "huge karaoke selection"; still, "they'll charge you for the convenience of having it" wail the wallet-pinched, who shriek at the "comically high prices."

COMME DES GARÇONS S C
| 24 | 26 | 20 | VE |

520 W. 22nd St. (bet. 10th & 11th Aves.), C/E to 23rd St., 212-604-9200

■ Even if you're "not destined to wear" Rei Kawakubo's "edgy" designs, visiting her "super space-age" "jewel" is "well worth the hike" to the edge of the Chelsea gallery district; from the brushed-aluminum entryway to the bright, white interior of steel booths, it seems "more museum than store" until you note the "outrageously expensive" prices on the "Japanese avant-garde clothing that could double as art."

Compact-Impact by TKNY ●S C
| – | – | – | M |

21 Ave. B (bet. 2nd & 3rd Sts.), F/V to Lower East Side/2nd Ave., 212-677-0500; www.compact-impact.com

Hip idea lab in the East Village where the digerati convene to check out the latest Japanese gadgets, like a device that can turn any surface into a speaker, a truly compact compact-disc player and a key-chain accessory that recharges cell phones; you can network with like-minded scensters and expats from Tokyo at the lounge in back, which serves Onigiri rice snacks and sake.

CompUSA ●S
| 20 | 16 | 11 | M |

1775 Broadway (57th St.), 1/9/A/B/C/D to 59th St./Columbus Circle, 212-262-9711
420 Fifth Ave. (37th St.), B/D/F/N/Q/R/V/W to 34th St./Herald Sq., 212-764-6224
97-77 Queens Blvd. (64th Rd.), Queens, G/R/V to 63rd Dr./Queens Blvd., 718-793-8663
800-653-3831; www.CompUSA.com

◪ A "comprehensive" selection of software, scanners, PCs, Macs and handhelds, as well as a "remarkable choice of games", is at your fingertips in these "busy" "warehouse" "musts for the computer geek" in you; "shabby service" might have you feeling you've "been through hell and back", but techies with "help-yourself attitude" find "all the minutiae" you and your desktop "could ever need."

Constança Basto ◗⑤⑥ | 23 | 24 | 20 | E |

573 Hudson St. (bet. Bank & 11th Sts.), A/C/E/L to 14th St./8th Ave., 212-645-3233; www.constancabasto.com

■ Known for her slithery, sky-high jeweled sandals and sleek, vibrant-colored heels – the barer, the better – "Brazilian socialite"-designer Constança Basto "storms New York", bringing a riot of Rio to her bright, boudoirlike West Village boutique; stiletto-seekers are "so in awe" of the "wonderful" "party shoes" they "almost don't notice" the "fun decor", a "gorgeous space" done up with hard-to-miss orange-and-white-striped wallpaper, orange ottomans and gilded mirrors.

Container Store, The ⑤ | – | – | – | M |

629 Sixth Ave. (bet. 18th & 19th Sts.), 1/9 to 18th St., 212-366-4200; 800-266-8246; www.containerstore.com

Certain space-deprived city dwellers can't contain themselves at the thought that this new, 25,000-sq.-ft. Chelsea store is stocked with 10,000 products for storage and organization – from wooden hangers to stacking drawers, shelving, photo albums and an abundance of bins, baskets and boxes; they also offer free closet-planning advice using their signature Elfa system.

Cooper-Hewitt National | 22 | 17 | 16 | M |
Design Museum Shop ⑤⑥

Cooper-Hewitt, 2 E. 91st St. (5th Ave.), 4/5/6 to 86th St., 212-849-8355; www.si.edu/ndm

■ "Don't let the old-school architecture" of the "gorgeous mansion it's housed in" "fool you" – this Upper East Side design "store has lots of cool, modern, funky items, from jewelry to wrapping paper to alarm clocks and ear-shaped paper clips"; the staff "does not rush you" as you browse the shelves "in Andrew Carnegie's library" for "a range of items you probably don't need at a range of prices you're willing to pay."

Cose Bella | – | – | – | VE |

7 E. 81st St. (bet. 5th & Madison Aves.), 6 to 77th St., 212-988-4210

"Beautiful" custom-made "designs and wonderful service that makes every bride feel like a princess" coo customers who throw the "wonderful" designer and staff at this by-appointment-only East 80s shop bouquets; there's more than walk-the-aisle-wear, discriminating shoppers also fall for the "couture" ready-to-wear "at semi-couture prices" (including "gorgeous dresses"), "with simple but elegant tailoring in an incredible array of beautiful silks" and sumptuous fabrics.

Cosmophonic Sound | ▽ 21 | 15 | 22 | E |

1622 First Ave. (84th St.), 4/5/6 to 86th St., 212-734-0459; www.cosmophonic.com

■ If you're looking for service on your large-screen TV projector, head to this "friendly", family-owned East 80s electronics store where "discriminating" shoppers "spend an arm and a leg" on the latest plasma TVs and customized remote controls and get "knowledgeable, attentive" guidance in planning their multiroom automation system.

COSTCO WHOLESALE ●Ⓢ   22 | 12 | 9 | I
976 Third Ave. (39th St.), Brooklyn, D/M/N/R to 36th St., 718-965-7603
32-50 Vernon Blvd. (B'way), Queens, N/W to Broadway,
718-267-3680
2975 Richmond Ave. (Staten Island Expwy.), Staten Island,
718-982-9000
www.costco.com

☒ For "one-stop" "bulk" "shopping like the Brady Bunch could've used", these outer borough, members-only "leviathans" sell "almost anything", from "massive tubs of condiments" to "clothes and electronics" – "they even do vacations and prescriptions"; if you have the patience for "insanely long lines", the "mandatory car" to cart the goods and "an extra apartment to hold it all", you can "stock up" on "great-deal" "quality brands" like Calvin Klein and Levi's, and if you're particularly "gluttonous", "you can have a [free] lunch with all the tastings they offer."

Costume National ●ⓈⒸ   24 | 24 | 17 | VE
108 Wooster St. (bet. Prince & Spring Sts.), R/W to Prince St.,
212-431-1530; www.costumenational.com
■ There's nothing costumey in this "austere", midnight-hued SoHo shop with its luminescent borders – just a "well-made, modern" collection by Italian designer Ennio Capasa of his-and-hers tailored jackets, separates and "some of the world's most beautiful" shoes; the "down-to-earth" staff keeps its distance as you traverse racks filled with "basic black", "streamlined-but-not-too-minimal" clothing that's "flattering if you have less than 3 percent body fat."

Council Thrift Shop   15 | 10 | 12 | I
246 E. 84th St. (bet. 2nd & 3rd Aves.), 4/5/6 to 86th St., 212-439-8373;
www.ncjwny.org
☒ "An occasional jewel can be found" among the "quality" designer clothes and "great household goods" at this Upper East Side thrift shop that benefits programs provided by the National Council of Jewish Women; though it's sometimes "a little more expensive than others", cognoscenti counsel there are "off-seasonal sales" that make it "worth a stop."

COUNTRY FLOORS   27 | 25 | 18 | VE
15 E. 16th St. (bet. 5th Ave. & Union Sq. W.), 4/5/6/L/N/Q/R/W to
14th St./Union Sq., 212-627-8300; www.countryfloors.com
■ "Definitely not your run-of-the-mill store", this "gorgeous" Union Square showroom sells a "beautiful" and "unique" "assortment" of "upper-end" floor and wall "tiles from all over the world", including handmade ones from Portugal, Provence and Morocco; the staff is "helpful" and "knowledgeable", but don't be floored by the prices.

Country Home & Comfort Ⓢ   ▽ 22 | 21 | 18 | E
43 W. 22nd St. (bet. 5th & 6th Aves.), R/W to 23rd St., 212-675-2705;
www.countryhomeandcomfort.com
☒ Not just for fans of the cozy country look, as the name implies, the styles of the "well-displayed" sofas, cupboards and tables at this Flatiron home-furnishings store range from contemporary to Asian-inspired and are imported from Indonesia, Holland and Hungary.

Crabtree & Evelyn C
21 | 22 | 19 | M

1310 Madison Ave. (bet. 92nd & 93rd Sts.), 6 to 96th St., 212-289-3923 S
520 Madison Ave. (bet. 53rd & 54th Sts.), E/V to 5th Ave./53rd St., 212-758-6419
Rockefeller Ctr., 620 Fifth Ave. (bet. 49th & 50th Sts.), B/D/F/V to 47-50th Sts./Rockefeller Ctr., 212-581-5022 S
Staten Island Mall, 2655 Richmond Ave., Staten Island, 718-982-8252
800-272-2873; www.crabtreeandevelyn.com

■ The Anglo-oriented amble over to this toiletries quartet to locate "lovely gifts for the hostess, grandma or mom" all at "reasonable prices"; a "friendly, helpful" staff will help you choose from a "great selection" of "good quality" bath oils, soaps and lotions and English-accented teas, cookies, lemon curd and chutney; N.B. a new branch has opened at The Shops at Columbus Circle at Time Warner Center.

Craft Caravan
∇ 24 | 23 | 22 | M

63 Greene St. (bet. Broome & Spring Sts.), R/W to Prince St., 212-431-6669

☑ A favorite haunt of fashion editors and stylists, this SoHo pioneer showcases a collection of cultures – from Japanese kimonos and African caftans to Native American cuffs – plus functions as a paradise for fabric and bead aficionados; the low-key staff is more than happy to describe the origin of each exquisitely crafted piece.

Crane & Co., Papermakers S
27 | 22 | 20 | E

Rockefeller Ctr., 59 W. 49th St. (bet. 5th & 6th Aves.), B/D/F/V to 47-50th Sts./Rockefeller Ctr., 212-582-6829; www.crane.com

■ For stationery that makes a simple "thank-you note seem like presidential correspondence", this Rockefeller Center store provides "possibly the most well-made paper on the planet" that's "perfect for any occasion"; though style mavens maintain the stock's "conservative", more insist that "new designs and colors" provide "arty" alternatives at prices that range from "reasonable" to "top-end."

CRATE & BARREL ●S
23 | 23 | 18 | M

Cable Bldg., 611 Broadway (Houston St.), B/D/F/S/V to B'way/Lafayette St., 212-780-0004
650 Madison Ave. (59th St.), N/R/W to 5th Ave./59th St., 212-308-0011
800-967-6696; www.crateandbarrel.com

■ "If you need to start from scratch", these SoHo and Midtown "musts for any Manhattan apartment" are "one-stop shops" whose "practical" housewares and handsome, "sturdy" furniture are "perfect for those on a budget who don't want to show it"; they're also the "place to stock up before a party" or for "wedding presents" (the "whole reason to get married is to register" here).

CREED & BOND NO. 9
29 | 28 | 22 | VE

9 Bond St. (bet. B'way & Lafayette St.), 6 to Bleecker St., 212-228-1732 ●S
897 Madison Ave. (72nd St.), 6 to 68th St., 212-794-4480
680 Madison Ave. (61st St.), N/R/W to 5th Ave./59th St., 212-838-2780

■ Since 1760, Creed has been making "the most luxurious" perfumes, which have come to be "relished" by the "rich and famous" – "Audrey Hepburn's" signature "Spring Flowers is a perennial favorite" and Grace Kelly and Natalie Wood were also fans; now its president, Laurice Rahmé, has come up with a new line, Bond No. 9 – a collection of 16 scents named after areas in the Big Apple – and housed it alongside the older Anglo-French front-runner.

C. Ronson 🆂🅲 | 14 | 14 | 12 | M |

269 Elizabeth St. (bet. Houston & Prince Sts.), B/D/F/S/V to B'way/ Lafayette St., 212-625-9074; 212-625-9075; www.cronson.com
🗷 Brainchild of DJ Charlotte Ronson, this closetlike NoLita shop puts the spin on designer undies (aka Tooshies), Shoshana swimsuits, Manon jewelry and the in-house wunderkind's flirty dresses, skirts and tube tops, plus rock 'n' roll tanks and tees "for the cute skateboarder chick in all of us"; still, a "not impressed" handful shout out it's "overpriced" "girlie stuff."

Crouch & Fitzgerald | 26 | 21 | 25 | E |

400 Madison Ave. (48th St.), B/D/F/V to 47-50th Sts./Rockefeller Ctr., 212-755-5888
■ Established in 1839, this "old-time leather store" on Madison Avenue still thrives thanks to "excellent quality" and a "wide selection" including "staples like Boyt, Longchamp and Hartmann" business cases, with "refined, old-world" "service to match"; the "products may not always have the highest styling, but classic and long lasting are better attributes anyway", and traditionalists take note: they carry "the gentleman's comb-and-file case for the breast pocket"; P.S. mark your calendar for their "super summer sale."

Crunch 🅓🆂 | ▽ | 18 | 14 | 12 | M |

404 Lafayette St. (bet. Astor Pl. & 4th St.), 6 to Astor Pl., 212-614-0120; 888-227-8624; www.crunch.com
Additional locations throughout the NY area
🗷 After your endorphin fix, you can get a shopper's high at this "nice" chain of urban gyms purveying "cool", "comfortable work-out wear" as well as yoga mats, candles, skincare products, videos and CDs; while critics carp about their "boring", "walking-billboard" branded gear, they carry other "funky" lines like Marika and Hardtail as well.

Custo Barcelona 🆂🅲 | – | – | – | E |

474 Broome St. (bet. Greene & Wooster Sts.), C/E to Spring St., 212-274-9700; www.custo-barcelona.com
Drivers en route to the Holland Tunnel may be distracted by the eye-catching women's clothing – and big-screen runway show – in this SoHo newcomer, decked out with contemporary art and filled with brothers Custo and David Dalmau's designs; it's an understatement to call these dresses, tees and jackets bold – they're blinding patchworks of bright and dark colors, Pop Art prints, geometric and abstract drawings and swirly portraits; men who dress to be noticed can adopt the riotous style too.

Cynthia Rowley 🆂🅲 | 23 | 21 | 22 | E |

376 Bleecker St. (bet. Charles & Perry Sts.), 1/9 to Christopher St./ Sheridan Sq., 212-242-3803
112 Wooster St. (bet. Prince & Spring Sts.), R/W to Prince St., 212-334-1144
■ Girls just wanna have fun in this "girlie-girl emporium", its quilted pastel walls a breath of "fresh air" in oh-so-boho SoHo; admirers applaud the store's "spunky vibe" with its rows of "whimsical", "flirty" clothing, accessories and cosmetics from the "queen of

swell", and laud the "low-pressure" sales staff that's "honest" with "helpful suggestions"; N.B. at press time, Cynthia opened a new shop on Bleecker Street steps away from Marc and Ralph.

DAFFY'S ●S — 16 | 9 | 8 | I

1775 Broadway (57th St.), 1/9/A/B/C/D to 59th St./Columbus Circle, 212-294-4477

1311 Broadway (34th St.), B/D/F/N/Q/R/V/W to 34th St./Herald Sq., 212-736-4477

462 Broadway (Grand St.), 6/J/M/N/Q/R/W/Z to Canal St., 212-334-7444

125 E. 57th St. (bet. Lexington & Park Aves.), 4/5/6/F/N/R/W to 59th St./ Lexington Ave., 212-376-4477

111 Fifth Ave. (18th St.), 4/5/6/L/N/Q/R/W to 14th St./Union Sq., 212-529-4477

335 Madison Ave. (44th St.), 4/5/6/7/S to 42nd St./Grand Central, 212-557-4422

88-01 Queens Blvd. (55th Rd.), Queens, G/R/V to Grand Ave., 718-760-7787

877-933-2339; www.daffys.com

☑ Bargain predators find it "impossible to resist" "regular" "fishing and hunting" expeditions at this "zoo" for "broke" fashion animals; "Daffaholics" say "the key is knowing when the new shipments come in" so you can "paw through" "stylish" "Italian clothing", "deep-discount designer underwear", the "greatest baby gifts", "adorable European children's" apparel, "occasional killer shoes" and other "treasures"; otherwise, you might find only a "hodgepodge" of "schlock" "picked over like a desert carcass."

Dana Buchman S — 24 | 22 | 21 | E

65 E. 57th St. (bet. Madison & Park Aves.), N/R/W to 5th Ave./59th St., 212-319-3257; 800-522-3262

■ For those fashionably attuned to the "corporate world" of "conservative" "outfit dressing", this Midtown boutique holds a bull market's worth of "businesswoman" clothing in fabrics that "feel much more expensive than they are"; their "perfect fit" pleases all sizes, including petites, while the service scores points for its "high-end" professionalism "without the pretension."

D & G ●S☐ — 23 | 24 | 19 | VE

434 W. Broadway (bet. Prince & Spring Sts.), C/E to Spring St., 212-965-8000; www.dolcegabbana.it

☑ An "outpost for the see-and-be-seen crowd" on SoHo's main drag, these "minimalist", "trippy" digs house "all the glitter and glam" that Domenico Dolce and Stefano Gabbana can capture in their "zany", "very Euro" designs, including "amazingly cut" jeans; but the parsimonious pout it's "way too expensive" for a diffusion line, claiming the goods are "more eye candy than real clothing."

Danskin ●S — 21 | 17 | 14 | M

159 Columbus Ave. (bet. 67th & 68th Sts.), 1/9 to 66th St./Lincoln Ctr., 212-724-2992; 800-288-6749; www.danskin.com

■ This "original", "old standby" in the West 60s sells "long-lasting", "high-quality gear" that's "designed for dancers, but wonderful for any workout", thanks to the "great textiles" used and the "beautiful" styles that the *jeté* set deems "good enough to wear to lunch"; with lines ranging from girls' to plus sizes, it's "for the ballerina in everyone."

Dante/Zeller Tuxedo

17 | 13 | 16 | M

459 Lexington Ave. (45th St.), 4/5/6/7/S to 42nd St./Grand Central, 212-286-9786; 800-464-0462; www.zellertuxedo.com

☑ Fans find this formalwear chain, with an East 40s flagship, the "first and only stop to pick up tuxedos" (either to buy or rent) given a collection that ranges from Joseph Abboud to Hugo Boss to Versace; but dissenters deem the digs "dingy" and warn "don't expect white-glove service at this black-tie event", especially during the month of June.

Darling 🆂🅲

– | – | – | E

1 Horatio St. (8th Ave.), A/C/E/L to 14th St./8th Ave., 646-336-6966

Former Broadway costume designer Ann French Emont scores big in her all-white West Village atelier, attracting a loyal following with a breath of fresh air (especially when its back garden is open) in the form of pretty retro-ish dresses she designs herself, a flirty lineup of well-edited women's wear from Cynthia Steffe, Poets Paint, plus Mary Green lingerie, darling accessories and some vintage shoes to boot; go on late-night Wednesdays for a sip of champagne while you shop.

Darryl's 🆂🅲

▽ 22 | 21 | 25 | M

492 Amsterdam Ave. (bet. 83rd & 84th Sts.), 1/9 to 86th St., 212-874-6677

■ "More than just a neighborhood place", this "sweet shop" in an Upper West Side area "without much choice in women's clothing" is "just the right size" to find fashionable, European-designed "items you've searched far and wide for" – from party clothes to work-out gear – thanks to the "great eye" of the eponymous owner.

DataVision ●🆂🅲

20 | 15 | 12 | M

445 Fifth Ave. (bet. 39th & 40th Sts.), 4/5/6/7/S to 42nd St./Grand Central, 212-689-1111; www.datavis.com

☑ "While the product range is good" at this branch of a chain store near Gramercy Park, the "crowded presentation" of computers, printers and projectors is "pushed" by an aggressive staff quoting "the highest ticket prices out there"; "however, savvy shoppers have the little-known option of haggling with sales reps" for "competitive" coin.

Daum 🅲

▽ 25 | 26 | 25 | VE

694 Madison Ave. (bet. 62nd & 63rd Sts.), N/R/W to 5th Ave./59th St., 212-355-2060; www.daum-france.com

■ "Even if you are not into glass", this "expensive" shop in the East 60s is "a must" declare devotees of its "wonderful workmanship", which consists primarily of *pate de verre* vases, candlesticks, stemware and such; while a few feel that some of the animal- and insect-bedecked designs from the long-standing French manufacturer are "over the top", "helpful salespeople" can assist you in "finding something simpler."

Dave's Army Navy ●🆂

21 | 12 | 17 | I

581 Sixth Ave. (bet. 16th & 17th Sts.), 1/2/3/9/F/L/V to 14th St./6th Ave., 212-989-6444; 800-543-8558

■ "Selling everything the working person (or person that wants to look like a working person) needs", from "Levi's to Carhart [clothes] to Red Wing shoes" along with army surplus, this Flatiron favorite is "a place every guy wants to shop at"; although there is "no floor plan" and the store's "not a lot to look at", a "friendly staff and almost unbeatable prices" ensure that most "don't leave empty-handed."

Davide Cenci
25 | **19** | **17** | **VE**

801 Madison Ave. (bet. 67th & 68th Sts.), 6 to 68th St., 212-628-5910; www.davidecenci.com

☑ "Wonderful Italian style" is well represented by the "great suits, jackets, slacks" and accessories ("the only place for silk socks") at this boutique in a Madison Avenue townhouse; it helps to "have the right body" for the "slim-fitting" wear, but if not, there's always the made-to-measure option; some mutter that "you could better afford to fly to Rome and buy from the source" – or simply "go during the sales"; P.S. ladies, don't overlook the "women's department on the fourth floor", especially the coats.

David's Bridal ●S
13 | **11** | **13** | **I**

35-00 48th St., Queens, G/R to Steinway St., 718-784-8200; 888-480-2743; www.davidsbridal.com

☑ "Cheap duds for the 'I dos'" and their wedding parties can be found at this Long Island City branch of the national chain where the "big array" of "gowns for all tastes" "makes you feel like you're sipping champagne from your bridal slippers, even though you're on a beer budget"; but the less-enthused declare the "bargain-basement prices come with" "mediocre help", particularly on "madhouse weekends", so make an appointment.

David Webb ☐
▽ **27** | **28** | **25** | **VE**

445 Park Ave. (bet. 56th & 57th Sts.), 4/5/6/F/N/R/W to 59th St./ Lexington Ave., 212-421-3030; www.davidwebb.com

■ Since 1948, this Park Avenue veteran has been satisfying the nature lover in all of us with its impressive array of animal-shaped fine jewelry in bold colors and enamels; though best known for its golden tiger brooches and sapphire-eyed horse clips, it also carries a collection of diamond-studded watches and Etruscan-inspired pieces.

David Yurman ☐
24 | **23** | **21** | **VE**

729 Madison Ave. (64th St.), 6 to 68th St., 212-752-4255; 877-226-1400; www.davidyurman.com

☑ "Cultish" describes the clientele of this modernistic "Madison Avenue boutique" that's "small in size but has lots of merchandise" from a "master jewelry designer"; loyalists "love the styling" of his "silver-and-gold combinations" adorned with "colorful stones", but skeptics snap the "trendsetting" two-toned pieces "are so everywhere that individuality is nonexistent."

David Z. ●S☐
21 | **16** | **15** | **M**

821 Broadway (12th St.), 4/5/6/L/N/Q/R/W to 14th St./Union Sq., 212-253-5511
556 Broadway (bet. Prince & Spring Sts.), 6 to Spring St.; R/W to Prince St., 212-431-5450
487 Broome St. (Broadway), R/W to Prince St.; 6 to Spring St., 212-625-9391
384 Fifth Ave. (bet. 35th & 36th Sts.), 6 to 33rd St., 917-351-1484
655 Sixth Ave. (21st St.), F/V to 23rd St., 212-807-8595

■ "Quick to move on fashion trends", this Manhattan chain is "the place" for his-and-her "casual, sporty", "urban footwear", including "new, hot sneaks for the hip-hop set"; it's a "sensible shoe paradise" with "choices galore" "in all the right flavors at the right price", plus "service is extremely helpful, not pushy"; but a few find fault with the "young sales force that keeps its distance" and sometimes "has a little attitude."

Davis & Warshow, Inc.
▽ 24 | 20 | 17 | E

A&D Building, 150 E. 58th St., 4th fl. (bet. Lexington & 3rd Aves.), 4/5/6/F/N/R/W to 59th St./Lexington Ave., 212-980-0966; www.daviswarshow.com
■ Since 1925, this showroom that's now located in the A&D Building has sold "quality" kitchen and bathroom fixtures (specializing in established American-made brands like Kohler), as well as plumbing and heating supplies; proponents praise the "good" merchandise and "long-standing reliability."

ddc domus design collections
25 | 24 | 18 | VE

181 Madison Ave. (34th St.), 6 to 33rd St., 212-685-0800; www.ddcnyc.com
■ Designed by the firm overseen by famed architect Philip Johnson, this airy, white space in Murray Hill boasts "spectaular window displays" and "amazing", albeit expensive, Italian furniture from masters like Massimo Vignelli and Achille Castiglioni; the leather futonlike sleeper sofa sells well, while the soaring suspended shelving that stretches from floor to ceiling by Carlos Scarpa catches the eye.

DDC Lab **S** **C**
22 | 23 | 17 | E

180 Orchard St. (bet. Houston & Stanton Sts.), F/V to Lower East Side/ 2nd Ave., 212-375-1647
427 W. 14th St. (bet. 9th & 10th Aves.), A/C/E/L to 14th St./8th Ave., 212-414-5801
www.ddclab.com
■ Lenny Kravitz and Maxwell are among the edgy dressers who experiment with designers Roberto Crivello and Savania Davies-Keiller's "fitted jeans", suede fatigues, cashmere coats with teflon coating and other high-tech "out-of-this world" creations; fashionistas of both sexes research and develop their look at the recently opened Meatpacking District flagship, a bright, white store with space-agey decor and arresting windows, and at the Lower East Side original, equipped with blood-red dressing rooms.

Dean & Deluca **◐** **S** **C**
26 | 23 | 19 | E

560 Broadway (Prince St.), R/W to Prince St., 212-226-6800; 800-781-4050; www.deandeluca.com
■ Loyalists love the "unusual" kitchen-oriented items, from caviar servers and Italian copper to sterling-silver salt cellars and top-of-the-line Laguiole knives, that are displayed in the rear of this statusy SoHo gourmet food mecca; but the miserly can only moan about "overpriced objects for those who obviously order in."

Debbie Fisher **S** **C**
– | – | – | E

233 Smith St. (bet. Butler & Douglass Sts.), Brooklyn, F/G to Bergen St., 718-625-6005; www.debbiefisher.com
Delicate, wispy jewelry constructed with semiprecious stones and beads is made by the eponymous artisan in a studio in back of this close-quartered Cobble Hill shop; perky shades of pink, orange, blue and green set off sleek, no-nonsense blond wood shelving that also displays a handful of ceramics and *objets* by other craftspeople.

Deco Jewels ◑ⓈⒸ
— | — | — | E

131 Thompson St. (bet. Houston & Prince Sts.), R/W to Prince St., 212-253-1222

"Specializing in vintage handbags made of Lucite", this "adorable little store" in SoHo is also "quite a find" for "well-curated costume jewelry" and "the best cuff links ever"; owner "Janice Berkson knows her stuff – and what looks best on you" too.

De La Espada Ⓢ
▽ 27 | 23 | 19 | VE

33 Greene St. (Grand St.), 6/J/M/N/Q/R/W/Z to Canal St., 212-625-1039; 212-625-1042; www.delaespada.com

■ For modernists "tired" of "cold minimalism", "warm woods" soften the hard-angled lines of the "beautifully handcrafted" benches, beds and coffee tables that fill this soaring SoHo space; since it's "far above a mere mortal home-furnishings store", expect equally elevated prices.

delfino ⓈⒸ
23 | 18 | 17 | E

1351 A Third Ave. (bet. 77th & 78th Sts.), 6 to 77th St., 212-517-5391
Rockefeller Ctr., 56 W. 50th St. (Rockefeller Plaza), B/D/F/V to 47-50th Sts./Rockefeller Ctr., 212-956-0868
www.delfinoshop.com

☑ "Jam-packed" with handbags, totes and wallets in a rainbow of shades and "creative, cutting-edge styles", this East 70s and West 50s duo offers a Longchamp, Mandarina Duck and Hervé Chapelier "addict's" fix as well as products from "their own terrific line"; though prices are as "expected for upscale" merch, "good sales" and an "excellent", "fun assortment" soften the blow.

DeMask ◑Ⓢ
23 | 22 | 17 | E

135 W. 22nd St. (bet. 6th & 7th Aves.), 1/9 to 23rd St., 212-352-2850; www.demask.com

■ "Personalized service compensates" for the skin sensation you may get from this shop's line of "well-made" collectibles; with stores in Europe and Chelsea, plus spreads in mainstream fashion mags, it's the "hottest place "for fetish lovers to buy sex-ellent clothes" to wear to "fun parties"; perch on the red round banquette while your lover wriggles into prospective purchases, including all things rubber, from ballroom gowns to hoods for the dungeon.

Demolition Depot/ Irreplaceable Artifacts ⌿
21 | 13 | 15 | E

216 E. 125th St. (bet. 2nd & 3rd Aves.), 4/5/6 to 125th St., 212-777-2900; www.demolitiondepot.com

■ Four floors of salvaged goods from mansions to Masonic lodges crowd this East Harlem warehouse whose architectural remnants range from church alters to entire wood-paneled rooms, making it the "best stop for that hard-to-find antique piece to complete your home"; the "adventurous" assert it's a "great way to spend some time unearthing treasures or trash."

DEMPSEY & CARROLL Ⓒ
29 | 25 | 26 | VE

1058 Madison Ave. (80th St.), 6 to 77th St., 212-249-6444; 800-444-4019; www.dempseyandcarroll.com

■ "One box of the embossed stationery" purveyed at this "*très* exclusive" East Side shop makes you "feel like *la crème de la crème* of NY"; its "beautifully done, traditional engraved" goods, voted No. 1 in this *Survey*'s Lifestyle category, are a "must-have" if you're "mailing to people who care" and are "nicely presented" in a "lovely" setting; customers "needing help with matters of etiquette" receive "excellent guidance" from the "incredible staff", and even though it's "verrry expensive", it's "worth it" at this "bastion of civilized living."

Dennis Basso S   – | – | – | VE

765 Madison Ave. (bet. 65th & 66th Sts.), 6 to 68th St., 212-794-4500
Furrier to the stratospheric class and bold-print glamour gals, this high-profile designer recently opened his first retail boutique on Madison Avenue's Saint-Honoré stretch after years in the Fur District; the spacious marble-clad salon is a subdued foil for the sumptuous pelts, and they come in a dazzling array of styles and shades; if nothing suits your specific fancy amid the coats, stoles and accessories, couture orders are accepted.

Dernier Cri S C   ∇ 20 | 20 | 16 | E

869 Washington St. (bet. 13th & 14th Sts.), A/C/E/L to 14th St./8th Ave., 212-242-6061
■ For chicks about to rock, owner Stacia Valle, MTV alum and former manager of the band Third Eye Blind, salutes you at her "über-cool", industrial-looking Meatpacking District boutique strewn with animal-skin rugs and packed with cult-fave labels like Gauge, Luella Bartley, Frost French and Twinkle; this slick music-minded mecca gets goth, alternative and punk princesses to walk this way with sexy blouses, minis and, of course, killer jeans and tees – get-down gear that says yeah baby, 'I'm with the band.'

Designer Resale S   22 | 20 | 17 | M

324 E. 81st St. (bet. 1st & 2nd Aves.), 6 to 77th St., 212-734-3639; www.resaleclothing.org
■ "Nothing like buying an Anna Sui suit for one-third the price" gloat groupies of this spacious consignment store that stretches across several brownstones' ground floors; "arranged in neat, well-edited racks", the "delectable items in all sizes" "range from Chanel and Armani to [relative] cheapies like Eileen Fisher and Ellen Tracy Company"; what with the affiliated Gentleman's Resale store adjacent and a Children's Resale shop just up the block, this concern threatens to "take up nearly all of East 81st Street."

Design Source By Dave Sanders C   ∇ 26 | 16 | 18 | E

115 Bowery (bet. Grand & Hester Sts.), 6/J/M/N/Q/R/W/Z to Canal St., 212-274-0022
■ Dave-otees tout the "great selection" of decorative hardware, tubs, sinks and plumbing fixtures at this Lower East Side bathroom source; "reliable" salespeople don't hesitate to "recommend reasonably priced" options, but hardworking folk might find the hours daunting, as it's open only till 5 PM on weekdays and 2:30 PM on Saturdays.

Design Within Reach S   25 | 22 | 19 | E

408 W. 14th St. (bet. 9th Ave. & Washington St.), A/C/E/L to 14th St./8th Ave., 212-242-9449 C
142 Wooster St. (bet. Houston & Prince Sts.), R/W to Prince St., 212-475-0001
76 Montague St. (Hicks St.), Brooklyn, 2/3 to Clark St., 718-643-1015 www.dwr.com
◪ This San-Francisco-based catalog and online outpost for "cool" furniture and accessories has "come to life" at new brick-and-

mortar locales in Manhattan and Brooklyn; a "sexy" selection of mid-century and contemporary designers like Maarten van Severen and Mies van der Rohe is the draw for some design devotees; but while some call it "affordable", others quickly counter "not much is within my wallet's reach" here.

Desiron 🅂🅲
▽ 21 | 21 | 17 | VE

151 Wooster St. (bet. Houston & Prince Sts.), R/W to Prince St., 212-353-2600; www.desiron.com

■ The Carfaro brothers custom-make "stylish", "user-friendly" mid-century–inspired furniture like bookcases, beds, bureaus and tables out of metal, wood and Lucite and showcase them in their expansive SoHo shop; minimalist-mavens maintain items are "expensive but worth it."

Destination ●🅂🅲
21 | 23 | 19 | E

32-36 Little W. 12th St. (bet. 9th Ave. & Washington St.), A/C/E/L to 14th St./8th Ave., 212-727-2031; www.destinationny.net

■ Accessories fiends saunter past the faux pigs standing guard outside this Meatpacking District "favorite" and into a huge, "luxurious yet spare" "art-meets-fashion" gallery-cum-showcase for "great unheralded designers" that "makes browsing fun"; "every woman needs to make a statement when she walks in a room" and with this handpicked selection of uniquely displayed "unusual" jewelry from Isabelle Puissant, European purses and shoes and select women's clothing, "you certainly will do so."

Details ●🅂🅲
22 | 17 | 12 | M

347 Bleecker St. (10th St.), 1/9 to Christopher St./Sheridan Sq., 212-414-0039
188 Columbus Ave. (bet. 68th & 69th Sts.), B/C to 72nd St., 212-362-7344
142 Eighth Ave. (17th St.), A/C/E/L to 14th St./8th Ave., 212-366-9498
57 Prince St. (Lafayette St.), R/W to Prince St., 212-965-9394

■ This "cute", "crowded" quartet of home-furnishings shops boasts more bathroom accessories (from shower curtains to toiletries), "scented candles" and "decorative kitchen accents" like "unique glassware" and placemats than "you can shake a stick at", making it a sensible source for "decorating and gifts."

Dialogica 🅂
23 | 20 | 20 | VE

59 Greene St. (bet. Broome & Spring Sts.), C/E to Spring St., 212-966-1934; www.dialogica.com

■ Cavernous, columned SoHo furniture store owned by a husband-and-wife design team that sells "high-priced" contemporary cabinets, beds and tables along with expansive sofas, chairs and chaises that can be upholstered in over 200 shades of chenille, velvet or faux suede.

Diana Kane 🅂🅲
– | – | – | E

229-B Fifth Ave. (bet. Carroll & President Sts.), Brooklyn, M/R to Union St., 718-638-6520; 718-230-4632; www.dianakane.com

Jewelry designer and lingerie lover Diana Kane brings some of her favorite things together in this boutique on Brooklyn's booming Fifth Avenue, selling handmade necklaces and earrings along with ultra-femme unmentionables from local and established designers like Samantha Chang, Eberjey, Cosabella and Petit Bateau; completing the dreamy picture: unusual skirts, handbags and bathing suits, plus Diptyque candles.

Diane T 🅂🅲   ▽ 23 | 18 | 18 | E

174 Court St. (bet. Amity & Bergen Sts.), Brooklyn, F/G to Bergen St., 718-923-5777

☑ A godsend for chic Cobble Hill chicks, this bright boutique owned by Diane Tkacz, "who knows her stock inside out", is "always packed with trendy shoppers" seeking "something a little funky", "fashionable, but accessible" in the color-coordinated, closetlike racks; acolytes who covet labels like Diane von Furstenberg, Juicy Couture and Katharine Hamnett profess they would "move back to Brooklyn just to be closer"; still, a handful harrumph service "fluctuates with how good you look."

DIANE VON FURSTENBERG 🅂🅲   27 | 24 | 22 | E

385 W. 12th St. (bet. Washington St. & West Side Hwy.), A/C/E/L to 14th St./8th Ave., 646-486-4800; www.dvf.com

■ It's a "labor of love" to get to this intimate, mirror-ceilinged boutique on a tree-lined street in the Meatpacking District, but DVF disciples declare it's "worth the trip" for the "sleek, sexy" wrap dresses in "distinct patterns" that look "flattering" whether you're "a 15-year-old girl or a 50-year-old woman"; no crowd-control problem here, so if it's "overwhelming personal attention" you want as you navigate the clothes, shoes and accessories, you got it.

Diesel Denim Gallery 🅂   25 | 24 | 19 | E

68 Greene St. (bet. Broome & Spring Sts.), 6 to Spring St.; R/W to Prince St., 212-966-5593; www.diesel.com

☑ "Not for the meek or mild", this "beautifully styled" jean "lover's paradise" offers a "myriad" of men's and women's "cuts, and washes" – enough to "drive you crazy"; "offering a semblance of exclusivity", this SoHo "outpost" is the only NYC store to carry Karl Lagerfeld's special collection, plus items you won't find at its sister stores; sure, the "denim bar" can "be quite intimidating", but "fear not" – the "knowledgeable staff" "helps you" search for "your perfect pair" of "pricey", "mmm . . . feel so good" blues.

Diesel Style Lab ◑🅂🅲   22 | 24 | 19 | E

416 W. Broadway (bet. Prince & Spring Sts.), R/W to Prince St., 212-343-3863; www.diesel.com

☑ In addition to "very hot" jeans, this "great-looking" SoHo "spin-off" of the "populist, avant-garde" denim label carries an edgier mix than its "counterparts", including a "wonderful selection of wild and fun urban night gear" for men and women; while devotees delight in the "cool stuff for Generation X", infidels indicate you have to be "Italian model" thin and "think it's normal to spend" oodles on "bizarre items" to shop here; a few crab about the Lab's staff that seems cast from "failed-actor central."

Diesel Superstore ◑🅂   23 | 22 | 17 | E

1 Union Sq. W. (14th St.), 4/5/6/L/N/Q/R/W to 14th St./Union Sq., 646-336-8552
770 Lexington Ave. (60th St.), 4/5/6/F/N/R/W to 59th St./Lexington Ave., 212-308-0055
www.diesel.com

■ A "postmodern superstore to overwhelm the senses", this dual Lex and Union Square "hypermarket" for "vintage-look" "Euro jeans" with a "flattering" fit and nearly all of the collections (including Style Lab and Diesel Kids) "pumps up the volume" –

literally – with a DJ booth; while "not as personal as the Denim Gallery", it's still where "scenesters and hippies live in peace", "coughing up the dough" for "trendy" "streetwear" "at trendy prices"; the "hip factor" extends to the "very helpful" staff.

Dimitri Nurseries S C ∇ | 21 | 14 | 18 | M |

1992 Second Ave. (bet. 102 & 103rd Sts.), 6 to 103rd St., 212-876-3996; www.dimitrisgardencenter.com

■ Fans are "perennial" at this Spanish Harlem greenhouse, nursery and "best-quality garden-service center" that's "worth the trek", since it's the only place in Manhattan that has 15,000 sq. ft. of "reasonably priced" plants and a vast variety of "outdoor trees" that come with "helpful advice" from a staff that's so friendly it makes up for the "inconvenience" of the long trip Uptown.

DINOSAUR HILL S C | 26 | 23 | 22 | M |

306 E. 9th St. (Second Ave.), 6 to Astor Pl., 212-473-5850; www.dinosaurhill.com

■ "A fanciful philosophy pervades" this East Village "wonderland" that feels like a "small town toy shop" yet offers an "amazingly large assortment", with "treasures tucked in every corner"; "delightful owner" Pamela Pier stocks "quirky" handmade "goodies" "for every child" (and "adults too"), from "unbelievable puppets" from Bali, Burma and Mexico to "classic" playthings and musical instruments, plus "unique baby and toddler clothes."

Dior Homme S C | – | – | – | VE |

17 E. 57th St. (bet. 5th & Madison Aves.), N/R/W to 5th Ave./59th St., 212-207-8448; www.dior.com

More jumpin' jack flash than Jean Paul Belmondo, this brand-new addition to the East 50s flagship boutique, housed in the former Dior Joaillerie space next door, features black slate floors and white laminated shelves, a dramatic backdrop that sets the slim cut suits, skinny ties and monogrammed "D" merchandise designed by the much *j'adored* Hedi Slimane in bold relief.

DIOR NEW YORK S C | 26 | 26 | 22 | VE |

21 E. 57th St. (bet. 5th & Madison Aves.), N/R/W to 5th Ave./59th St., 212-931-2950; www.dior.com

■ From perfume to purses, "the pleasures of Dior are many", and this "beautiful store for the beautiful people" on 57th Street carries most of 'em; the logo-obsessed love designer John Galliano's "cutting-edge glam" ("crazy, fun clothes" that the *Sex and the City* gals made "surprisingly wearable"), plus "of-the-moment" accessories and "good-quality makeup"; yes, it's "high-style at high prices", but "impeccable service that's never snotty" makes the expenditure worthwhile; N.B. Dior Joaillerie, also overseen by the British phenom, is now housed here on the first floor.

Disc-O-Rama Music World ● S C | 20 | 9 | 14 | I |

40 Union Sq. E. (bet. 16th & 17th Sts.), 4/5/6/L/N/Q/R/W to 14th St./ Union Sq., 212-260-8616
186 W. Fourth St. (bet. 6th & 7th Aves.), 1/9 to Christopher St./ Sheridan Sq.; A/B/C/D/E/F/S/V to W. 4th St., 212-206-8417
146 W. Fourth St. (6th Ave.), 1/9 to Christopher St./Sheridan Sq.; A/B/ C/D/E/F/S/V to W. 4th St., 212-477-9410
866-606-2614; www.discorama.com

■ "You won't find better deals" than at these three "extremely cramped" music stores, in the Village and Union Square, where "new releases", including DVDs, "Top 40 and popular radio hits", plus classical and "popular catalog items" "can be had very cheaply"; "while they may not have everything" and "the used rock selection varies greatly by location", the staff is "generally very friendly" and "if it isn't there, they'll get it for you"; N.B. the 186 W. Fourth Street location sells new merchandise only.

Disney ●S
20 | 23 | 18 | M

711 Fifth Ave. (55th St.), E/V to 5th Ave./53rd St., 212-702-0702
Kings Plaza, 5100 Kings Plaza, Brooklyn, 2/5 to Brooklyn College/
Flatbush Ave., 718-677-1860
800-328-0368; www.disneystore.com

☑ "If you love the Mouse, you must visit his house[s]", "where adults can be kids", "kids go wild" and "wallets get vacuumed"; the huge Fifth Avenue store, in particular, is like "a short trip to the Magic Kingdom", replete with an "animation gallery" and "multiple levels" "well stocked" with "everything Disney", plus the "lines and high prices that make it as much a headache as the theme park" itself; "it's a world of happiness" for Mickey junkies, but it can be a "nauseating typhoon of color and noise" for the "rodent"-phobic.

Disrespectacles S C
– | – | – | E

82 Christopher St. (bet. Bleecker St. & 7th Ave.), 1/9 to Christopher St./
Sheridan Sq., 212-741-9550
117 W. Broadway (bet. Duane & Reade Sts.), 1/2/3/9 to Chambers St.,
212-608-8892
www.disrespectacles.com

An "exceptional" staff offers "amazing" service, helping you select from the "sexy", "cool", "adventurous stock" of eyewear at this über-"hip" twosome; visit the West Village location (formerly Myoptics) with its "lovely atmosphere" or head to the more industrial TriBeCa branch to peruse the gallery of vintage specs collected by the owner.

DKNY ●S C
21 | 22 | 17 | E

655 Madison Ave. (60th St.), N/R/W to 5th Ave./59th St.,
212-223-3569
420 W. Broadway (bet. Prince & Spring Sts.), C/E to Spring St.,
646-613-1100
www.dkny.com

☑ Like the Big Apple itself, designer Donna Karan's "lower-end line" has "a little something for everyone" say natives and tourists "of different ages" and both genders who sail into the humongous "multifloor" Madison Avenue flagship store or its "spacious" SoHo sibling, "highly focused on their hunt" "for those staples with a modern edge" or "making a beeline for the housewares and accessories"; however, opponents opine it's "a bit overhyped", quipping that the quality of the apparel is just "DKOK".

Doggie-Do & Pussycats Too! C
23 | 23 | 22 | E

567 Third Ave. (bet. 37th & 38th Sts.), 4/5/6/7/S to 42nd St./Grand Central,
212-661-9111; www.doggiedo.com

☑ "Pampered" Murray Hill "pets with a Fifth Avenue complex" are gratified by the "unusual" "designer" accessories ("best outerwear for dogs in the city") supplied by this "cute" store; pooches having a bad-fur day can avail themselves of "great grooming" as owners "browse", assisted by the "friendly staff"; however, cat fanciers lament the "small selection" for felines, and penny-pinchers posit that "pricewise, it's way out of line."

Doggystyle [S] [C] 23 | 21 | 23 | E

100 Thompson St. (bet. Prince & Spring Sts.), C/E to Spring St.; R/W to Prince St., 212-431-9200; 212-431-5353; www.doggystylenyc.com

■ "For owners who love their dogs too much" (is that even possible?), this "adorable little" SoHo shop with a "very helpful" staff "has it all": doggy T-shirts and other "boutique-style attire", a "great selection of collars and leashes" and "outrageous gifts", like customized blankets, for "pampering" that furry bundle "in your life."

Dö Kham ◐ [S] [C] 25 | 19 | 20 | M

19 Christopher St. (bet. Greenwich Ave. & 7th Ave. S.), 1/9 to Christopher St./Sheridan Sq., 646-486-4064

304 E. Fifth St. (bet. 1st & 2nd Aves.), F/V to Lower East Side/2nd Ave., 212-358-1010

48 Greenwich Ave. (bet. Charles & Perry Sts.), 1/9 to Christopher St./Sheridan Sq., 212-255-9572

51 Prince St. (bet. Lafayette & Mulberry Sts.), 6 to Spring St., 212-966-2404

■ "Wear exotic flair, buy from this no-nonsense" outfit, that's the mantra of Kham cultists who ditch the Himalayas for this "lovely" Downtown quartet and its cache of "real"-deal Tibetan goods; customers cotton to the his and hers "ethereal" gauze and raw silk shirts in a wide range of "amazing" high-intensity colors and lengths, pashmina shawls, "beautiful fox- trimmed hats", ethnic jewelry and "intricately designed" bedspreads, concurring it's an appealing "addition to the vast world of fashion."

Dolce & Gabbana [C] 25 | 26 | 21 | VE

825 Madison Ave. (bet. 68th & 69th St.), 6 to 68th St., 212-249-4100; www.dolcegabbana.it

■ Step into *la dolce vita* at this airy Upper East Side boutique filled with the "body-flattering" men's and women's clothes that the D & G designers do so seductively well; all the irresistible trappings of the "Euro jet-set" are on display – "22nd-century jeans, the best sunglasses on the planet", "elegant, but not uptight" suits and the famed animal prints ("only they could make leopard spots and flowers on the same blouse work"); "crazy", perhaps, nevertheless, "it's hard to argue with such creativity" – so just say *arrivederci*, bank account.

Domain ◐ [S] [C] 21 | 22 | 18 | E

938 Broadway (22nd St.), R/W to 23rd St., 212-228-7450

Trump Palace, 1179 Third Ave. (69th St.), 6 to 68th St., 212-639-1101

101 West End Ave. (65th St.), 1/9 to 66th St./Lincoln Ctr., 917-441-2397

www.domain-home.com

■ "Plumper-than-plump" furniture like couches, chairs and chaises, along with "classic", "casually elegant", European-inspired dining tables and armoires, abounds at the Flatiron, East and West Side branches of this chain; most find the prices "fair", adding that there are "good sales" as well.

Domsey Express 🅂
16 | 7 | 7 | I

431 Broadway (bet. Hewes & Hooper Sts.), Brooklyn, J/M/Z to Hewes St., 718-384-6000
1609 Palmetto St. (Wyckoff Ave.), Queens, L/M to Myrtle/Wycoff Aves., 718-386-7661
www.domsey.com

☑ "Patience is a necessary virtue at this Downtown warehouse setting", a veritable "shopping mall of used clothes organized by type" or "sorted by the pound" – anything from "old (looking) jeans" to "Army/Navy" surplus to "vintage leather"; malcontents mutter the "ultracheap" merchandise is "now too picked-over by local Brooklyn hipsters", but fans find you can still "hit pay dirt" – just "be prepared to sift and sift and sift"; N.B. the Ridgewood, Queens, Express is somewhat smaller.

Donna Karan
23 | 25 | 21 | VE

819 Madison Ave. (bet. 68th & 69th Sts.), 6 to 68th St., 212-861-1001; www.donnakaran.com

■ Murmur "om" as you step inside this "serene oasis" on Madison Avenue, whose "Zen-like" setting (complete with Japanese sculptures and a bamboo garden) complements the "*crème de la crème*" collection clothing (no DKNY here) and extensive home furnishings; in keeping with the mood ("like a world-class spa when you walk in"), the "knowledgeable" sales staff guides males and females in pursuit of shopping nirvana, be it "beautifully sophisticated" basics or more "imaginative" garments.

Donzella
– | – | – | VE

17 White St. (bet. 6th Ave. & W. B'way), 1/9 to Franklin St., 212-965-8919; www.donzella.com

A mid-century modern collector's dream, this TriBeCa store sells stunning "rare pieces" by heavy-hitters like Paul Frankl, Edward Wormley, T.H. Robsjohn-Gibbings and Tommi Parzinger at "fair prices" for the quality; its selection of desks and cocktail tables is estimable, and custom-seating based on old European and American designs is also available.

Dooney & Bourke
22 | 22 | 18 | E

20 E. 60th St. (bet. Madison & Park Aves.), 4/5/6/F/N/R/W to 59th St./ Lexington Ave., 212-223-7444; 800-347-5000; www.dooney.com

☑ The "distinctive structured bags" "last for years" assert admirers who also frequent this chain's flagship on the Upper East Side for totes, luxury apparel, gloves, shoes and scarves; though the collection has expanded and "become current and relevant", critics consider it "too conservative" and "too expensive."

Door Store 🅂
16 | 15 | 16 | M

601 Amsterdam Ave. (89th St.), 1/9 to 86th St., 212-501-8699
1 Park Ave. (33rd St.), 6 to 33rd St., 212-679-9700
969 Third Ave. (bet. 58th & 59th Sts.), 4/5/6/F/N/R/W to 59th St./ Lexington Ave., 212-421-5273
123 W. 17th St. (bet. 6th & 7th Aves.), 1/9 to 18th St., 212-627-1515
www.doorstorefurniture.com

☑ "If you walk through the door of this store", you'll find "real furniture" – from dining and bedroom sets to bookcases – at "affordable prices"; frugal folks who are not looking for cutting-edge design make this long-standing East Coast chain their choice for "setting up a first household."

Dosa ◐ⓈⒸ
24 | 22 | 22 | E

107 Thompson St. (bet. Prince & Spring Sts.), C/E to Spring St., 212-431-1733

■ "Layering has never been so lightweight – or so beautiful" laud acolytes who alight at this "lovely" little SoHo haunt with bamboo fixtures for their seasonal dose of designer Christina Kim's "wonderful silks" and "well-made" cottons "with an ethnic feel"; whatever your destination, "be it St. Barths or Alphabet City", this "is your place" for "sexy, traveling and "comfort clothes", all style- and color-coordinated for "whimsical" mix-and-match options.

Douglas Cosmetics Ⓢ
21 | 20 | 20 | M

Grand Central, 27 Grand Central Terminal (Lexington Ave.), 4/5/6/7/S to 42nd St./Grand Central, 212-599-1776; 800-770-0081; www.douglascosmetics.com

☑ Its "convenient Grand Central location" makes this multibrand cosmetics and fragrance store a "great time saver" and perusing the "broad selection" of products is a pleasant "way to wait for a train"; "there are no discounts here" and some say there's a bit of a "supermarket feel", but who can complain when they generously "give away samples and free bonus gifts" with purchase.

Downtown Yarns Ⓒ
23 | 23 | 23 | M

45 Ave. A (bet. 3rd & 4th Sts.), F/V to Lower East Side/2nd Ave., 212-995-5991

■ "Homey" and "friendly", this "purl of a yarn store in the East Village" feels like it could be "in the Berkshires" with "a pet dog lying about", "a knitting guru to help with questions", a "super-helpful staff" and a "small but nice selection" of "funky, fun stuff"; P.S. there are "great classes for beginners as well as experts."

Drexel Heritage Ⓢ
25 | 21 | 19 | E

32 W. 18th St. (bet. 5th & 6th Aves.), 4/5/6/L/N/Q/R/W to 14th St./Union Sq., 212-463-0088; www.drexelheritage.com

■ Flatiron branch of a "reputable" 100-year-old manufacturer that sells "high-quality" "traditional furniture" along with more contemporary living room, dining room and bedroom sets inspired by everything from Californian to African influences; just be aware that part of the Heritage of this "fine old name" includes "expensive" price tags.

Drimmers Ⓢ
▽ 26 | 13 | 19 | M

1608 Coney Island Ave. (bet. L & M Aves.), Brooklyn, Q to Ave. M, 718-773-8483; www.drimmers.com

■ The folks at this "friendly" Coney Island "appliance heaven" won't take you for a ride when it comes to their "modest to high-end" merchandise, which is offered at "probably the cheapest price you can get"; you'll find the big stuff (Sub-Zero refrigerators and Thermador professional stoves) on the first floor and smaller items (Miele vacuum cleaners and Krups coffeemakers) on the second; delivery to the five boroughs is included in the sticker price.

Dr. Jay's ◐ⓈⒸ
17 | 13 | 11 | M

33 W. 34th St. (bet. 5th & 6th Aves.), B/D/F/N/Q/R/V/W to 34th St./Herald Sq., 212-695-3354; www.drjays.com
Additional locations throughout the NY area

☑ "Any DJ, hip-hop head or even Slick Rick would like" the "off da hook gear for any season", from streetwear to jerseys and team caps featured at this outfit with scores of stores throughout Bronx, Brooklyn, Queens and Manhattan; "it's a good source for name brands like" Outkast, Phat Farm, Puma and Timberland "without the department store hassle", plus it's "always reliable for urban kicks"; still, a few feel "patience helps" when it comes to service.

Duncan Quinn **S** **C**   – | – | – | E

8 Spring St. (bet. Bowery & Elizabeth St.), J/M/Z to Bowery, 212-226-7030; www.duncanquinn.com
Leave it to a Brit to bring together "top notch" tailoring and "one-of-a-kind designer sneakers" in a mod NoLita shop done up with antique fixtures and stocked with natty men's suits, shirts and impeccable extras like made-to-order bowler hats; the owner's "red hair matches the energy" of his high-end wares, translating into "very friendly service" and "expensive" prices."

Dune **C**   – | – | – | VE

88 Franklin St. (bet. B'way & Church St.), 1/9 to Franklin St., 212-925-6171; www.dune-ny.com
This stark TriBeCa space showcases sexy steel tables by graphics guru Fabien Baron, wood seating from David Khouri, Michael Solis' colorful storage units and rugs by Harry Allen and Richard Shemtov; everything is made-to-order, and all upholstered pieces are available in the store's award-winning textiles.

DUNHILL **S**   26 | 26 | 25 | VE

711 Fifth Ave. (bet. 55th & 56th Sts.), 6/E/V to 51st St./Lexington Ave., 212-753-9292
■ "Nothing like a cigar shop where you can also get custom-fitted suits and shirts" attest aficionados who enjoy this "oh-so-English" Midtown "temple of luxe" celebrated for its "great selection" of stogies and "upscale accoutrement" ("the Rolls-Royce of smoke" stores) as well as its "beautiful" clothes, watches and accessories; Anglophiles also admire the "fine service" at this century-old, two-floor "true gentleman's paradise" that "makes shopping fun, even for guys."

DYLAN'S CANDY BAR **⊘** **S** **C**   24 | 27 | 15 | E

1011 Third Ave. (60th St.), 4/5/6/F/N/R/W to 59th St./Lexington Ave., 646-735-0078; www.dylanscandybar.com
■ "A real-life Willy Wonka fantasy come true (minus the Oompa-Loompas)", Dylan (daughter of Ralph) Lauren's "whimsical" two-story East 60s "soda shop for the 21st century" has "something for kids of any age", from "not-sold-elsewhere M&M colors" to Swarovski crystal Pez dispensers, all "deliciously presented and dazzling in every way" – including the "designer price tags"; N.B. they host kids' birthday parties downstairs.

Earl Jean **S** **C**   24 | 21 | 18 | E

160 Mercer St. (bet. Houston & Prince Sts.), R/W to Prince St.; B/D/F/S/V to B'way/Lafayette St., 212-226-8709; www.earljean.com
■ The "down-to-earth" salespeople may give "you the once over" at this SoHo flagship that feels like a mod rec room, but they're just scoping out which "worth dieting for" jeans work for your big bad bod; this king of "low-riders" gets high-fives for "sexy, Western-style" denim and cords that "make anyone's butt look great" – indeed, combined with the "simply fab" shirts and jackets, it's the uniform of "hipsters, urban cowgirls and uptown well-to-do's"; N.B. there's now a men's collection too.

East Side Kids ▽ 20 | 18 | 19 | E
1298 Madison Ave. (92nd St.), 6 to 96th St., 212-360-5000

☑ Parents who find everything here from baby shoes to "real Mary Janes" to tween-friendly boots, plus even a variety of styles in adult sizes (and free popcorn) want to "tell everyone" about this Upper Eastsider that's also equipped with a stroller-friendly entrance; but don't dillydally during prime time, because the footwear "sells out early each season" (read: back-to-school and bound-for-camp) and may not be reordered.

E.A.T. Gifts 🅂🅲 21 | 18 | 15 | E
1062 Madison Ave. (80th & 81st Sts.), 6 to 77th St., 212-861-2544; www.elizabar.com

☑ "A wonderful place to pick up little knickknacks" and "silly whatnots" "for care packages, party favors", "stocking stuffers" or a "gift for yourself", this Upper Eastsider turns "everyone into a kid"; but cynics sound off that it's "small and crowded", adding they "can't stand Eli Zabar's *meshugge* prices."

E. Braun & Co. 🅲 25 | 22 | 25 | VE
717 Madison Ave. (bet. 63rd & 64th Sts.), F to Lexington Ave./63rd St., 212-838-0650

■ Loyalists who like luxe linens head to this Madison Avenue grande dame purveying "exquisite old-world" sheets, hand-embroidered tablecloths, napkins and placemats, plus towels and throws – all imported from Europe; a "wonderful staff" can also advise about custom-sizes and colors.

Ecco 🅂 23 | 20 | 20 | E
232 Seventh Ave. (4th St.), Brooklyn, F to 7th Ave., 718-788-1088

■ Small Park Slope seller of "offbeat home furnishings" that reverberates with "cool lamps", pillows, throws, "gorgeous" textiles and other "interesting" accessories that have a "one-of-a-kind feel."

Eddie Bauer ●🅂 17 | 16 | 16 | M
1976 Broadway (bet. 66th & 67th Sts.), 1/9 to 66th St./Lincoln Ctr., 212-877-7629
578 Broadway (bet. Houston & Prince Sts.), R/W to Prince St., 212-925-2179
1172 Third Ave. (bet. 68th & 69th Sts.), 6 to 68th St., 212-737-0002
711 Third Ave. (bet. 44th & 45th Sts.), 4/5/6/7/S to 42nd St./Grand Central, 212-808-0820
7000 Austin St. (69th Ave.), Queens, E/F/G/R/V to Forest Hills/71st Ave., 718-459-2270
800-426-8020; www.eddiebauer.com

☑ "Some things never change", but that doesn't bother "outdoorsy types" who "love" the "slow-down style" of "crunchy-granola staples" like "good weekend" chinos, "durable" polo shirts and "warm fleeces" at these "unisex" purveyors of "anti-Manhattan fashion"; stock up on "unique travel gadgets", backpacks and "camping doodads", but "Bauer beware" of "limited service."

Edith and Daha 🅂 – | – | – | E
104 Rivington St. (bet. Essex & Ludlow Sts.), F/J/M/Z to Delancey/Essex Sts., 212-979-9992

Vintage vixens get a "dizzying" dose of old and new in this shop on the "grungy Lower East Side" filled with "beautifully chosen" retro-femme pieces and "ultra-friendly owners" Edith Machinist and Sara Daha's own resurrected-for-today line of Holly Go Lightly frocks and hipper-than-thou separates; "possibly the best selection" of pumps, sandals, trainers and purses from the past fill out the "remember when?" inventory.

Edith Weber Antique Jewelry ─ | ─ | ─ | VE

994 Madison Ave. (77th St.), 6 to 77th St., 212-570-9668; www.antique-jewelry.com

Though tiny, this boutique offers "fantastic finds" in antique and vintage jewelry – anything from a Georgian mourning brooch to an Edwardian diamond tiara to an art deco wedding band; the tabs reflect the Upper East Side address, but the "friendly" mother-and-son owners, both known educators in the field, are discreetly "willing to adjust prices."

Edmundo Castillo S C ▽ 25 | 25 | 21 | VE

219 Mott St. (bet. Prince & Spring Sts.), 6 to Spring St., 212-431-5320

◪ Sleek, sophisticated and sliver-sized – think ultimate shoe closet – this acclaimed designer's NoLita shop vaunts its vampy wares with élan; vividly colored suede boots, sexy T-strap and bombshell-esque open-toed stilettos, all "works of art" exhibiting "spectacular workmanship", are made for negotiating cab rides, not pavement, and displayed in gray cubbyholes, with a few standouts reserved for the front window; curtains, retro-modern lamps and a friendly staff complete the uplifting experience; still, a handful find it too "expensive."

e. Harcourt's S C ─ | ─ | ─ | M

219 Mott St. (bet. Prince & Spring Sts.), 6 to Spring St., 212-226-8028

This little gem nestled on trendy Mott Street in NoLita might easily be overlooked if it weren't for the lit candles and fresh flowers floating in a pool in the front window; inside, a small selection of fragrance, soaps, incense and candles – all made in-house – should satisfy those in search of something different.

Eidolon S C ▽ 23 | 25 | 27 | M

233 Fifth Ave. (bet. Carroll & President Sts.), Brooklyn, M/R to Union St., 718-638-8194

■ 'Eidolon' means 'ideal image' in Greek, and that's the aim of this fashion-forward Park Slope boutique, a cooperative where local designers are given a pretty, petite pink-toned showcase for "eclectic", often "handmade" women's apparel and "unique accessories" (including hats, colorful print handbags and the "best shoes ever"); the "very friendly owners" ensure there's "always something fun" to try on.

Eileen Fisher S 23 | 22 | 21 | E

341 Columbus Ave. (bet. 76th & 77th Sts.), 1/9 to 79th St., 212-362-3000
314 E. Ninth St. (bet. 1st & 2nd Aves.), 6 to Astor Pl., 212-529-5715 ●
166 Fifth Ave. (bet. 21st & 22nd Sts.), R/W to 23rd St., 212-924-4777 ●
1039 Madison Ave. (bet. 79th & 80th Sts.), 6 to 77th St., 212-879-7799
521 Madison Ave. (bet. 53rd & 54th Sts.), E/V to 5th Ave./53rd St., 212-759-9888
395 W. Broadway (bet. Broome & Spring Sts.), C/E to Spring St., 212-431-4567
800-345-3362; www.eileenfisher.com

◪ "Over 40s" "get hooked" on the "beautiful simplicity" of this "comfortable" clothing in "understated tones" "typifying womanly elegance"; a "non-threatening" staff "stands ready to assist" at the SoHo flagship where "exemplary urban architecture relates Japanese principles to the designer's vision" of "timeless style" – "if you like the potato-sack look" sniff "slim figures"; N.B. a new branch has opened at The Shops at Columbus Circle at Time Warner Center.

Einstein-Moomjy **S**

25	20	20	E

141 E. 56th St. (bet. Lexington & 3rd Aves.), 4/5/6/F/N/R/W to 59th St./ Lexington Ave., 212-758-0900; 800-864-3633; www.einsteinmoomjy.com

■ From tribal to Tibetan and hand-knotted to broadloom, this "well-lit", "reliable" emporium in the East 50s stocks a "great selection" of "beautiful", "long-lived" "quality" rugs; if the "many one-of-a-kind" carpets don't suit your style, you can call your own shots with custom-made, and there are home furnishings as well.

Elgot

▽ 21	11	16	E

937 Lexington Ave. (bet. 68th & 69th Sts.), 6 to 68th St., 212-879-1200; www.elgotkitchens.com

☑ Upper Eastsiders who cry Wolf (as well as Sub-Zero, Miele and other "high-end kitchen appliances") call this "convenient" kitchen-and-bath showroom "the only place to go"; the staffers "know their merchandise" and can help design and install custom cabinetry, countertops and plumbing fixtures, but a few who've been burned warn of service ranging from "pushy" to indifferent.

Elie Tahari ◉

24	20	18	E

520 Fifth Ave., 2nd Fl. (bet. 43rd & 44th Sts.), 7/B/D/F/V to 42nd St./ 6th Ave., 212-398-2622; www.elietahari.com

■ Situated right up the block from the NY Public Library, this "well-stocked" "secret" appropriately carries "smart clothes for smart people" – specifically Elie Tahari's "last-forever", "worth-every-cent" sportswear, but all at 30 percent off retail; whether you seek suits that are "well tailored" for "the working girl" or "ultra-feminine", out-on-the-town dresses, "the salespeople are helpful, but not overbearing."

ELIZABETH LOCKE **C**

28	28	27	VE

968 Madison Ave. (bet. 75th & 76th Sts.), 6 to 77th St., 212-744-7878

■ This tiny, "superb" Upper East Side "jewel box" offers "a piece for every age" – and from every age, since the designer uses anything from ancient coins to 18th-century Chinese *objets* to 19th-century Venetian glass to fashion her "delicate", distinctive" and "timeless" wares, which are known for the "wonderful color of the 19 karat gold" she favors; the smitten also take a shine to the "very helpful, nice staff."

El Museo Del Barrio **S**

22	18	17	M

1230 Fifth Ave. (104th St.), 6 to 103rd St., 212-831-7272; www.elmuseo.org

■ At this "often-overlooked" shop at the top of Museum Mile, *amantes de las artes* can browse for books, CDs and posters by and about Puerto Rican, Caribbean and Latin American artists, plus "unusual" handmade crafts from the islands and Central and South America; the "wonderful" staff "explains the origins" of the "genuinely different" "items that express" "Hispanic life", ranging from "touch of the offbeat" esoterica like *fiestas patrones* masks to wooden *santos, mundillo* embroidery and porcelain figurines lodged inside *ajote* pods.

Emanuel Ungaro C
26 | 25 | 20 | VE

792 Madison Ave. (67th St.), 6 to 68th St., 212-249-4090;
www.emanuelungaro.fr
■ "Perfection" blooms as abundantly as the signature floral prints at this long-standing Madison Avenue boutique, home to the French designer's sensual collection of silk dresses, suits and separates; shoppers sum up its newly renovated interior (starring a fuchsia Plexiglas staircase) and sales staff in one word – "beautiful"; sure, everything is "extremely expensive", but "if you can afford it, you have no choice but to buy it" the pampered purr.

Emilio Pucci C
26 | 24 | 22 | VE

24 E. 64th St. (bet. 5th & Madison Aves.), 6 to 68th St., 212-752-4777;
www.emiliopucci.com
■ 'Let's do the time warp again' could be the motto of this legendary, "so retro" Upper East Side shop with its "psychedelic" prints beloved by Marilyn Monroe and Jackie O back then, and countless chic women right now (thanks to "seasonal updates" by Christian Lacroix); "if you aren't afraid of color, nothing beats" "splurging" on these "notoriously bright" "classics" – anything from g-strings to men's ties to "beach towels, a don't-miss for summer."

Emmelle S C
21 | 20 | 21 | E

123 E. 89th St. (bet. Lexington & Park Aves.), 4/5/6 to 86th St.,
212-289-5253
1042 Madison Ave. (bet. 79th & 80th Sts.), 6 to 77th St.,
212-570-6559
☑ Spacious and streamlined, these "great finds" on the Upper East Side offer "grown-up women" "wonderful service" and an "elegant selection" of "stylish, well-made" knits, suedelike tops, silky pant suits styled mostly in microfibers and even accessories; but the less-enthused deem the help "snooty" and snipe that the "loose-fitting clothing" is "geared toward middle-aged matrons."

Emporio Armani S
24 | 23 | 20 | E

110 Fifth Ave. (bet. 16th & 17th Sts.), 4/5/6/L/N/Q/R/W to 14th St./
Union Sq., 212-727-3240
601 Madison Ave. (bet. 57th & 58th Sts.), N/R/W to 5th Ave./59th St.,
212-317-0800
410 W. Broadway (Spring St.), C/E to Spring St., 646-613-8099
www.emporioarmani.com
■ Groupies go gaga over Giorgio's bridge-line emporia where both genders "can buy anything Armani, from underwear to shoes" to "timeless suits" and "comfy jeans", all bearing the trademark "good quality, details and elegant design" at "affordable prices" (well, compared with the designer's high-end collection, anyway); "personalized service" also helps "cultivate customers."

EMS (Eastern Mountain Sports) ● S
22 | 18 | 20 | M

591 Broadway (bet. Houston & Prince Sts.), R/W to Prince St.,
212-966-8730
20 W. 61st St. (B'way), 1/9/A/B/C/D to 59th St./Columbus Circle,
212-397-4860
888-463-6367; www.ems.com
■ "Heaven for outdoor junkies" and "crunchy urbanites who yearn" for valleys and streams, these SoHo and Upper West Side chain offshoots stock "high-quality" "hiking and more adventurous equipment" for sports like kayaking and mountaineering, plus some

of the "best wicking clothes", "fantastic backpacks" and bicycles; "they've got the goods" (much of it tested by the EMS Climbing School in Mount Washington), plus "they've got smart people behind the counter to help" "novices and the experienced alike."

Enchanted Forest 🆂🅲   24 | 27 | 22 | M

85 Mercer St. (bet. Broome & Spring Sts.), R/W to Prince St., 212-925-6677

■ "A tiny storybook land in itself", this "magical", "multilevel" gallery/toy boutique in SoHo is "truly an enchanted place for kids" and a "treat for adults" too; "you can happily get lost for hours" in the faux-forest setting (the "presentation alone is worth the trip"), plus there's a "friendly staff to help navigate the nooks and crannies packed with unusual stuffed animals" from around the world and other "fantasy stuff" like unique marionettes, soft sculptures, musical instruments and "creative little" craft kits.

Encore 🆂   22 | 15 | 14 | M

1132 Madison Ave. (bet. 84th & 85th Sts.), 4/5/6 to 86th St., 212-879-2850; www.encoreresale.com

☑ Since 1954, this Madison Avenue "grandmommy of resale shops" has kept the consignment-minded coming back encore and encore for its "ever-changing selection" of "current styles" ("very Uptown girl – lots of Chanel – but they cram in trendier labels too", plus some menswear); some hiss it's "a hit-or-miss place", but the majority rules it's "one of the best bets for finding a bargain."

Enelra ●🆂🅲   ▽ 22 | 17 | 16 | E

48 1/2 E. Seventh St. (bet. 1st & 2nd Aves.), 6 to Astor Pl., 212-473-2454

■ Sure, this "small" pink-and-red store stocked with "high-end lingerie, boas and robes" and owned by a "very funny East Villager" has "been around forever, but once you discover it, you wanna keep it secret" confide insiders; the "large selection of unique items and old standbys ranges from demure to" "kinky" to "beautiful, lacy and sexy"; the "knowledgeable" "employees even help lost boyfriends choose well."

Enzo Angiolini ●🆂   20 | 18 | 16 | M

551 Madison Ave. (55th St.), E/V to 5th Ave./53rd St., 212-339-8921
331 Madison Ave. (bet. 42nd & 43rd Sts.), 4/5/6/7/S to 42nd St./ Grand Central, 212-286-8726
Manhattan Mall, 901 Sixth Ave. (bet. 32nd & 33rd Sts.), B/D/F/N/Q/ R/W to 34th St./Herald Sq., 212-695-8903

■ For "finely crafted", "long-lasting" "treats for your feet" that "won't set you back a pretty penny" head to this national chain; the "leather is usually soft", and styles range from "sophisticated", "classic" and "work appropriate" ("good for climbing the corporate ladder") to "fashionable and comfortable at the same time"; but a few trendoids lament "it hasn't quite got today's chic" look and complain about "weird sizing."

Equinox Energy Wear 🆂🅲   21 | 15 | 15 | E

140 E. 63rd St. (Lexington Ave.), 4/5/6/F/N/R/W to 59th St./ Lexington Ave., 212-752-5360; www.equinoxnyc.com
Additional locations throughout the NY area

☑ "I will not sweat in these threads" vow vaunters of the "great work-out clothes" purveyed at these upscale gyms; "anyone who likes to exercise in style" wearing "stuff that'll take a beating" declares the duds "cute" and "fun", but jaded Gothamites gripe the designs are "too California" and the prices "outrageous."

ERES 🛇🖸   28 | 24 | 22 | VE

621 Madison Ave. (bet. 58th & 59th Sts.), 4/5/6/F/N/R/W to 59th St./ Lexington Ave., 212-223-3550
98 Wooster St. (Spring St.), C/E to Spring St., 212-431-7300 ●
800-340-6004; www.eresparis.com

■ Ooh-la-la – with "high-style" sleek shops on Madison Avenue and in SoHo, there's "no need to fly to Paris" for this French chain's "very chic" swimwear and intimate apparel that's "always sexy without being overt"; supporters tout the "superb quality, comfort" and "great fit" of these "upscale pieces", including some of the "simplest, well-made bathing suits" and "lovely, sheer" bras, panties and seamed stockings; *oui*, it's "expensive, but it's so beautiful" and "lasts forever."

Eric 🛇🖸   23 | 20 | 17 | E

1222 Madison Ave. (bet. 88th & 89th Sts.), 4/5/6 to 86th St., 212-289-5762
1333 Third Ave. (bet. 76th & 77th Sts.), 6 to 77th St., 212-288-8250

☑ "Watch out for the drool outside the windows" quip customers who skip over to this "expensive" Upper East Side shoe duo for a "right-on selection" of "the latest designerwear"; "Eric knows what NYC women want", from "the yummiest sandals" to house-label "upscale knockoffs", plus the "quality" "cannot be beat"; while a few find the "staff helpful", others opine they're full of "attitude"; N.B. sibling stores like Little Eric sell kids' footwear.

Erica Tanov 🛇🖸   ▽ 25 | 22 | 22 | E

204 Elizabeth St. (bet. Prince & Spring Sts.), 6 to Spring St.,
212-334-8020; www.ericatanov.com

■ With its white walls and hanging bulbs, a "peaceful", "soothing atmosphere" permeates this NoLita space; the designer's "crisp, fresh", "well-made ensembles", often trimmed with "great [vintage] fabrics", "make you feel like a girl", while the "adorable baby" outfits cater to your maternal side; the "charming sales help" ensures you will also "fall in love" with an assortment of jewelry, handbags, luxe undies and "epitome-of-cool" sneakers.

Erica Wilson Needle Works 🖸   22 | 19 | 16 | VE

717 Madison Ave. (bet. 63rd & 64th Sts.), 6 to 68th St., 212-832-7290;
800-973-7422

☑ Established in 1965 by Erica Wilson, the "British-trained" "grande dame of needlepoint", this Upper East Side stalwart is still one of "the best sources for high-quality canvases"; while it "stocks everything you need", worked-up stitchers say you "may need to take out a mortgage" to shop here and deem the "service snooty."

Ermenegildo Zegna 🛇   27 | 24 | 24 | VE

743 Fifth Ave. (bet. 57th & 58th Sts.), N/R/W to 5th Ave./59th St.,
212-421-4488; www.zegna.com

☑ Some may "have problems pronouncing the name, but [no one] questions" the quality at this Midtown haberdasher, known for the "best-fitting suits" in "gorgeous" wools, the "finest" ties and other "luxe looks", Italian style; perhaps the "beautiful things are sometimes buried" in the "small" space, but the service is as "impeccable" as the tailoring, making this "the place to buy all your clothes – right after you hit the Lotto"; N.B. at press time, plans were underway to relocate a few blocks down on Fifth Avenue.

Erwin Pearl [S] [C] 19 | 19 | 18 | M

677 Fifth Ave. (bet. 53rd & 54th Sts.), E/V to 5th Ave./53rd St., 212-207-3820
697 Madison Ave. (bet. 62nd & 63rd Sts.), 4/5/6/F/N/R/W to 59th St./ Lexington Ave., 212-753-3155
Rockefeller Ctr., 70 W. 50th St. (bet. 5th & 6th Aves.), B/D/F/V to 47-50th Sts./Rockefeller Ctr., 212-977-9088
800-379-4673; www.erwinpearl.com

◪ "Nothing like a fabulous fake to make your day" declare devotees who adore this Midtown mecca's "wonderful costume jewelry" ranging from "classic" to "kitschy"; these "great knockoffs" are "often mistaken for the real thing" – case in point: their 'Jackie O' three-strand necklace – so convincing are its concoctions of cubic zirconia and glass pearls; "if you can't afford Cartier, this is an alternative, still it's expensive for the average Joe."

Escada [S] 26 | 26 | 23 | VE

715 Fifth Ave. (56th St.), N/R/W to 5th Ave./59th St., 212-755-2200; www.escada.com

■ Fashionable *femmes fatales* keep tabs on the "drop-dead gorgeous" inventory at this "ultrachic" Fifth Avenue boutique, with its "curvaceous" clothing, "wonderful shoes" and tasteful accessories that are "oh, to dream" for; naturally, when buying such things as "beautifully hand-beaded gowns, you pay by the bead" – but the salespeople "treat you as if you matter whether [you purchase] full-price or on sale"; N.B. there's also a by-appointment-only Badgley Mischka Boutique on the first floor devoted to bridal gowns.

Estella ◐ [S] [C] – | – | – | E

493 Sixth Ave. (bet. 12th & 13th Sts.), 1/2/3/9/F/L/V to 14th St., 212-255-3553; www.estella-nyc.com

Brightly lit with stark white walls, an antique display table and a minimalist gallery feel, this Village yearling features a tight collection of finely made, pricey childrenswear from edgy European designers; while the handpicked selection is limited, with more of an emphasis on girls than boys, each piece is special and subtly offbeat, making it well worth exploring.

Etcetera [S] [C] 19 | 16 | 16 | M

1465 Second Ave. (bet. 76th & 77th Sts.), 6 to 77th St., 212-794-2704
489 Third Ave. (33rd St.), 6 to 33rd St., 212-481-6527

◪ There's "always something to buy" at this Upper East Side and Murray Hill duo, especially if you're looking for "quick", "creative gifts" you may not find "anywhere else"; "dorm-room decorators", "knickknack"-seekers and "housewarming" and shower attendees alike fall for the "funky" selection of jewelry and "beautiful, decorative" hand-painted pottery and glassware; while the "tight quarters" can inhibit easy "browsing", "just ask" the "helpful staff" for navigational assistance.

Ethan Allen [S] 22 | 22 | 19 | E

192 Lexington Ave. (32nd St.), 6 to 33rd St., 212-213-0600 ◐
1107 Third Ave. (65th St.), 4/5/6/F/N/R/W to 59th St./Lexington Ave., 212-308-7703
103 West End Ave. (bet. 64th & 65th Sts.), 1/9 to 66th St./Lincoln Ctr., 212-201-9840
112-33 Queens Blvd. (76th Rd.), Queens, F to 75th St., 718-575-3822

(continued)
Ethan Allen
*Heartland Shopping Ctr., 2275 Richmond Ave. (Nome Ave.),
Staten Island, 718-983-0100
888-324-3571; www.ethanallen.com*
■ Fans of this furniture company say it's "come a long way" since it started in 1932, since it's now offering not only "high-quality" "traditional" pieces and accessories but also more "modern" looks; there's also a "good design service" on hand to help "make decorating easy."

ETRO 🄲   27 | 27 | 23 | VE
720 Madison Ave. (bet. 63rd & 64th Sts.), F to Lexington Ave./63rd St., 212-317-9096; www.etro.it
■ Those seeking "true Milanese style" should Ferrari-it to the "sumptuous setting" of this East 60s outpost of the luxury-goods maker known for being "very forward colorwise"; its men's and women's clothing in "luxe fabrics" and "brilliant hues", including "nearly blinding shirts" and trademark paisleys, represents a "fine distillation of vibrant Italian" design, so "wear it with panache."

EUGENIA KIM ◑🅂   28 | 24 | 23 | E
203 E. Fourth St. (bet. Aves. A & B), F/V to Lower East Side/2nd Ave., 212-673-9787; www.eugeniakim.com
■ "Everyone who walks through the door" of this "hip" milliner's "intimate" red-and-blue-colored East Village shop is "treated like a star, even if they happen to be one" (she's "adorned the likes of J. Lo" and Janet Jackson); "super, super helpful", "with great taste" and "style", this hat honcho "clearly cares about" "what is right for your head" – no wonder the cap-tivated claim the "completely original designs" fashioned from felt, straw, fur or corduroy "are worth the price"; "Elsa Schiaparelli can rest easy now that Eugenia is around."

Eva ◑🅂🄲   ▽ 23 | 19 | 21 | E
227 Mulberry St. (bet. Prince & Spring Sts.), 6/J/M/N/Q/R/W/Z to Canal St., 212-925-3208
■ Rows of beautifully dressed mannequins line this NoLita boutique, its pale colors and neutral palette a subdued backdrop for the "fabulous quality" women's tops, jeans and dresses; the focus is on emerging stylemakers, so be open to new names.

Eve's Garden   22 | 18 | 23 | M
119 W. 57th St., Ste. 1201 (bet. 6th & 7th Aves.), N/Q/R/W to 57th St., 212-757-8651; 800-848-3837; www.evesgarden.com
☑ "Ladies, start your engines", 'cause this "great place for women, by women" has the tools to tune your gears, albeit discreetly; started 30 years ago as an "exercise in" "equality and freedom", the erotica store remains "hidden" "on the 12th floor of an office building" on 57th Street, and "shy" shoppers appreciate its "nice, quiet privacy", though it's "a little too timid" and "low on fun" for feistier fetishists.

Expo Design 🅂   23 | 22 | 16 | M
73-01 25th Ave. (Boody St.), Queens, N/W to Ditmars Blvd., 718-533-4600; 800-350-1481; www.expo.com
■ "You can get new towels or a new kitchen" at this "fancy version of Home Depot", which is the parent company of this Elmhurst monolith; browse through "well-designed displays" with

"everything possible for redecorating", from high-end Karastan rugs to refrigerators, ranges, lighting, bathroom fixtures and fans; "miles of aisles" make for "miles of possibilities in a variety of price ranges."

EXPRESS ●S

14 | 15 | 14 | I

584 Broadway (bet. Houston & Prince Sts.), R/W to Prince St.; B/D/F/S/V to B'way/Lafayette St., 212-625-0313;
www.expressfashion.com
Additional locations throughout the NY area

☑ "Upbeat" fashion chain where a "strange customer mix" of "high-schoolers to power-lunching corporate chicks" and, in some locations, "hip", "young" guys "can find almost anything" from "cute to sexy to glam to casual" in clothing and accessories "without a hefty tag", provided they "don't need it to last for more than one season"; the sales help is "nice", but "slower than it should be" for the "trend-driven" pace of a place called Express.

Express Men ●S

18 | 18 | 16 | M

(fka Structure)
901 Ave. of Americas (32nd St.), B/D/F/N/Q/R/V/W to 34th St./Herald Sq., 212-971-3807
89 South Street Seaport, Pier 17 (Fulton St.), 2/3/4/5/A/C/J/M/Z to Fulton St./Broadway/Nassau, 212-766-5709
7 W. 34th St. (bet. 5th & 6th Aves.), B/D/F/N/Q/R/V/W to 34th St./Herald Sq., 212-967-5093
Kings Plaza, 5350 Kings Plaza, Brooklyn, 2/5 to Brooklyn College/Flatbush Ave., 718-377-6334
www.expressfashion.com

☑ "Nice, fun", "safe clothes for safe boys" dominate this renamed chain where "decent", "durable" duds are "moderately priced"; Europhiles "disappointed" with a re-Structuring that "traded Italian-inspired tailoring" for "average Americana" yawn it's the "fashion equivalent of narcolepsy."

Eye Candy ●SC

20 | 19 | 18 | M

329 Lafayette St. (bet. Bleecker & Houston Sts.), 6 to Bleecker St.; B/D/F/S/V to B'way/Lafayette St., 212-343-4275;
www.eyecandystore.com

■ "You can always find something in this grandma's attic", a NoHo must-see that provides a "thoroughly enjoyable experience" thanks to the "great vintage handbags" and costume jewelry, including "cool-looking Lucite" and rhinestone numbers, along with "an eclectic collection" of "funky" eyewear, shoes and one-of-a-kind items; it's a "small shop", but with all the "tchotchkes galore", it definitely "lives up to its name."

Eye Man, The S

24 | 20 | 22 | E

2264 Broadway (bet. 81st & 82nd Sts.), 1/9 to 79th St., 212-873-4114;
www.eyeman.com

■ First-time customers become "lifelong customers" at this "homey, welcoming" Upper West Side optician that "has it all": a "fabulous selection" of "high-fashion" "spectacles with style" from names like Oliver Peoples, Paul Smith and Martine Sitbone "delivered with super service" from a "knowledgeable" staff with "expertise"; the "dedicated" optometrists show "meticulous concern for vision problems" and even kids' needs, offering "good cheer and jellybeans."

Fab 208 NYC ◐ [S] ▽ 17 | 14 | 18 | M

75 E. Seventh St. (bet. 1st & 2nd Aves.), F/V to Lower East Side/ 2nd Ave., 212-673-7581; www.fab208nyc.com

◪ "'70s retro fab" is always in at this "rocking and rolling" bubble-gum-pink-and-red East Villager, which specializes in "modified vintage" garb and T-shirts with logos we can't print in a family guide; some say the "one-of-a-kind items" "look better on the rack", but the owners "treat customers like friends", and "hey, you've got to get your leopard-print panties somewhere, right?"

FACE Stockholm [C] 20 | 22 | 16 | M

226 Columbus Ave. (bet. 70th & 71st Sts.), 1/2/3/9/B/C to 72nd St., 212-769-1420 [S]

1263 Madison Ave. (91st St.), 4/5/6 to 86th St., 212-987-1411

110 Prince St. (Greene St.), R/W to Prince St., 212-966-9110

www.facestockholm.com

◪ Swedish cosmetics company founded by a mother-and-daughter duo that's a "great place for colors and everything that glitters", as well as skincare and foundation products "with tones named after the months of the year"; prices are "reasonable", but some say, Face it, the "service varies" ("carry your Marc Jacobs bag with you if you want help"); N.B. a new branch has opened in The Shops at Columbus Circle at Time Warner Center.

Facets ◐ [S] [C] – | – | – | M

97A Seventh Ave. (bet. President & Union Sts.), Brooklyn, M/R to Union St., 718-638-3898

"In Park Slope, this gorgeous shop" lends diversity to the nabe's artisanal jewelry and watch options; the "small selection" of "uniquely crafted" pieces from independent designers "constantly changes", so "if you see it, you better grab it."

Facial Index [S] – | – | – | VE

104 Grand St. (bet. Greene & Mercer Sts.), 6/J/M/N/Q/R/W/Z to Canal St., 646-613-1055

A "great selection" of "edgy, hip, fab and funky" frames for fashionista faces are proffered at this SoHo eyewear boutique where the glasses are accessibly presented in a minimalist setting; the "fantastic" staff is "discreet" and "patient, even when they know you aren't going to buy anything", which makes it fun to "play" with the "pricey" wares.

Façonnable [S] 24 | – | 23 | E

636 Fifth Ave. (51st St.), E/V to 5th Ave./53rd St., 212-319-0111; www.faconnable.com

■ It's "tempting to keep" this recently relocated, plush-carpeted store "one of the best-kept secrets" in Midtown, but word is out about its "comfortable clothes" whose "bold patterns" and visible logo betray its Gallic roots (like a "French answer to Ralph Lauren"); gents enjoy the "fine neckwear" and "gorgeous shirts", while ladies sweep up the stairs to peruse the whole "classic" collection; for both sexes, the "unobtrusive" "service is everything."

Family Jewels, The [S] ▽ 23 | 19 | 17 | E

130 W. 23rd St. (bet. 6th & 7th Aves.), F/N/R/V to 23rd St., 212-633-6020; www.familyjewelsnyc.com

◪ "Alluring window displays" hint at the "fun browsing" that awaits within this long, low-ceilinged Chelsea vintage store; "if you dig, you can find the perfect item" among the men's and women's clothes, accessories and lingerie, with a "great selection of '50s cocktail dresses" and beaded bags particular standouts; some, however, huff "you'd have to hock the family jewels to buy here"; N.B. most of the merch is mid-century, but antique hounds should sniff out the stash of '20s gowns behind the counter.

FAO SCHWARZ 🅂🅲   27 | 27 | 18 | E
767 Fifth Ave. (bet. 58th & 59th Sts.), N/R/W to 5th Ave./59th St., 212-644-9400; www.fao.com

■ "Its wrapping paper is the little blue box of children's gifts" and like its Fifth Avenue neighborhood, it's "a New York experience", but more important, it's a "toy mecca" "for kids of all ages" with a baby boutique to boot; "who can resist the charm of Barbie world" and "giant stuffed bears to snuggle with"? plus, the "hands-on policy is a child's delight"; while the wide-eyed call it a "wonderland at Christmastime", cynics counsel "don't go over the holidays" "when it's a zoo" and "tourists move like snails"; N.B. at press time, the store was bought by New York investment firm D.E. Shaw & Co. and was closed for renovation with plans to reopen summer 2004.

Fat Beats ◑🅂   – | – | – | M
406 Sixth Ave. (bet. 8th & 9th Sts.), A/B/C/D/E/F/S/V to W. 4th St., 212-673-3883

If rap is your flava, this "legendary shop" in the Village is your crib; a "hip-hop DJ's mecca" "with retail stores in Amsterdam and LA" as well, "NYC's premier" spot for def sounds "continues to impress" with a phat selection of CDs, vinyl, videos, magazines and "T-shirts with their own logo"; the only beef you might have is with the "snotty clerks."

Federico De Vera 🅲   – | – | – | VE
1 Crosby St. (Howard St.), 6/J/M/N/Q/R/W/Z to Canal St., 212-625-0838; www.deveraobjects.com

After 13 years on the Left Coast, the gallery's namesake and owner has turned his discerning eye East, opening up shop in what's becoming the hottest little stretch in SoHo; high-end, in-house handmade jewelry like rose-cut diamond necklaces and carved Carnelian rings share space with equally expensive, one-of-a-kind finds such as antique Asian lacquer boxes, Indian bodhisattvas and bronze animal heads.

FELISSIMO DESIGN HOUSE   25 | 26 | 20 | E
10 W. 56th St. (5th Ave.), N/R/W to 5th Ave./59th St., 212-247-5656; www.felissimo.com

■ Puzzled patrons aren't quite sure if this "beautiful" space is "a store or a gallery" after its drastic refocusing a few years ago; to clarify the confusion, note that the top four floors of the stunning East Side townhouse are "serene" exhibition areas with ever-changing design displays of furniture and home furnishings, while the ground-floor gift shop offers a limited selection of "creative new products", kitchen gadgets and jewelry.

Fenaroli by Regalia 🅲   20 | 18 | 20 | E
501 Seventh Ave., Ste. 416 (37th St.), 1/2/3/9/A/C/E to 34th St./ Penn Station, 212-764-5924; www.fenarolinewyork.com

☑ Never mind the disenchanting Garment District location, just set your sights on the "little bitty" wedding day "things you simply must have" within; "from wonderful hair clips and sparkly" tiaras to "beautiful" veils, jewelry, handbags and "classy" "shoes that scream Cinderella", this appointments-suggested bridal accessories showroom, bolstered by a "helpful" staff, is a "novel, much needed concept"; sure, it's "expensive", but it's worth the "big splurge."

Fendi 🛇🄲 | 24 | 23 | 19 | VE |

720 Fifth Ave. (57th St.), N/R/W to 5th Ave./59th St., 212-767-0100
◩ Season after season, fashionistas feed their "Fendi-trendi" fetish with an "instantly recognizable" baguette, bauble or sable from this "impressive", "neatly organized" Fifth Avenue shop that "rocks" if you've got "attitude" and can afford the "skyscraper prices" for the "best leather goods", "amazing" accessories and "the furs, oh, the furs"; though you may have to fend for yourself, the "salespeople are friendlier than you might expect."

Fetch ◗🛇🄲 | 26 | 25 | 24 | E |

43 Greenwich Ave. (bet. 6th & 7th Aves.), A/B/C/D/E/F/S/V to W. 4th St., 212-352-8591; www.fetchpets.com
◼ For the "utmost in upper-crust pet accessories" without the "froufrou pretentiousness" of Uptown shops, this "decidedly Downtown" Greenwich Village store has "everything for the spoiled NYC" domestic companion, including an annual doggie "ice cream social"; the "helpful" staff is abetted by an owner who's "frequently on-site, as is Ali, the big Newfie that's often mistaken for a rug", and though "practical it's not", it's "perfect" for "gifts."

FILENE'S BASEMENT ◗🛇 | 15 | 8 | 8 | I |

2222 Broadway (79th St.), 1/9 to 79th St., 212-873-8000
620 Sixth Ave. (18th St.), F/L/V to 14th St./6th Ave., 212-620-3100
18704 Horace Harding Expwy. (188th St.), Queens, 718-479-7711
www.filenesbasement.com
◩ You may be "eternally grateful" for the "incredible buys" you dredge up here, but you "can't be shy about combing through" "mounds of clothing", and "you have to be lucky" to unearth "diamonds in the rough" like "sale Valentino and Bulgari ties" or "hand-embroidered designer sweaters", since the New York branches are "not up to snuff" with the "famed Boston bargain-center" flagship; spelunking insiders don't expect guidance from a "staff that's permanently on break."

Filth Mart 🛇 | 21 | 17 | 16 | M |

531 E. 13th St. (bet. A & B Aves.), L to 1st Ave., 212-387-0650
◼ It's "great digging" for dirt at this incense-scented, East Village vintage clothes and novelties store that "specializes in '60s, '70s and '80s" "finds of all kinds", including "tons of tees", "denim and leather jackets", plus rhinestones, "patches and iron-on" decals (this "is the birthplace of the bedazzled rock shirt"); "the owners make no bones about the fact that the merchandise is mostly used", but it's "perfectly priced."

Find Outlet 🛇 | 22 | 18 | 19 | M |

229 Mott St. (bet. Prince & Spring Sts.), B/D/F/S/V to B'way/Lafayette St.; 6 to Spring St., 212-226-5167
361 W. 17th St. (bet. 8th & 9th Aves.), A/C/E/L to 14th St./8th Ave., 212-243-3177
◼ There's "a sample sale every day" at this "appropriately named", "little" bargain "boutique" that makes "scrounging for designer discounts manageable" for its "edgier", "hip" clientele in Chelsea

and NoLita; since it's an outlet for overstocked items from the likes of Barneys and Fred Segal, the styles are "up-to-date", plus they're "arranged by color"; the sales help is "laid-back" and "friendly" and "e-mail notifications" keep you in on the "scoop."

Finyl Vinyl ◐ [S] [C] — | — | — | I

208 E. Sixth St. (Cooper Sq.), 6 to Astor Pl.; R/W to 8th St., 212-533-8007; www.finylvinyl.com

For that elusive '70s R&B album or folkie single, this East Village store might be the finyl spot; they specialize in obscure vinyl of all genres, including blues, funk, jazz, Latin, even spoken word; one caveat: day-trippers might find out that the Beatles riff on the door, 'Open Eight Days A Week', is a big teaser – hours are a bit more helter-skelter than that since it's open Tuesday–Sunday.

Fisch for the Hip [S] 25 | 22 | 19 | E

153 W. 18th St. (bet. 6th & 7th Aves.), 1/9 to 18th St., 212-633-9053; www.fischforthehip.com

◪ Wise men and women fish here at this Chelsea consignment store, with its "carefully selected inventory of hot designer garb" and "display cases bulging with Birkins, Kellys", Chanel, Vuitton and other status bags; a "friendly staff helps you unearth treasures" in the neatly ordered, burgundy-and-mustard setting; still, even some hipsters hiss "prices are high" by used-clothing standards.

Fishs Eddy ◐ [S] 21 | 20 | 16 | I

2176 Broadway (77th St.), 1/9 to 79th St., 212-873-8819
889 Broadway (19th St.), R/W to 23rd St., 212-420-9020
877-347-4733; www.fishseddy.com

◪ "Funky, fun" and "inexpensive kitchen and tableware" that's "good for starting out" "jam-pack" both these Upper West Side and Flatiron District locations where commercial-quality "vintage" china and glass "from cruise ships, boarding schools and defunct restaurants" along with new patterns by name designers like Cynthia Rowley are so "precariously stacked" you "sometimes feel like a bull" in a you-know-what shop; it can be "hit-or-miss", and you might have "to dig hard to find the good stuff."

Flight 001 ◐ [S] [C] 26 | 25 | 20 | E

96 Greenwich Ave. (bet. Jane & 12th Sts.), 1/2/3/9/F/L/V to 14th St./ 6th Ave., 212-691-1001; www.flight001.com

■ Even "non–jet setters" and "people who only fantasize" about making a getaway advise "don't leave the gate without" a visit to this "Bond-esque", "funky" "traveler's haven" in the West Village; the "clever, quirky selection" runs the gamut from "practical" "paraphernalia" like luggage and CD cases to "neat little doodads" "you didn't even know you needed", like Travel Scrabble, plus the "smart and informed" staff knows a thing or two about "creative gift wrap."

Flirt ◐ [S] [C] ▽ 16 | 20 | 22 | M

252 Smith St. (bet. DeGraw & Douglass Sts.), Brooklyn, F/G to Bergen St., 718-858-7931; www.flirtdesign.com

■ The "name says it all" at this "Smith Street star" that seduces with its "cute, offbeat" "girlie" wear in a "friendly environment"; a dizzyingly shabby-chic decor – pink-and-yellow checkerboard floors, silver-striped walls, old cabinets – is the backdrop for local designers' work, much of it in reworked vintage threads; they'll also artfully embellish old jeans.

Floris of London ▪ | 27 | 25 | 23 | E |

*703 Madison Ave. (bet. 62nd & 63rd Sts.), 4/5/6/F/N/R/W to 59th St./
Lexington Ave., 212-935-9100; 800-535-6747;
www.florisoflondon.com*

■ This "tiny" Madison Avenue outlet of the London perfumer
that's been purveying scents since 1730 offers "lovely gifts" like
"beautiful bath accessories" that evoke an "English garden",
men's toiletries, room sprays and candles, along with "potpourri
and pieces to put it in."

Florsheim Shoe Shops ▪ | 19 | 17 | 18 | M |

*444 Madison Ave. (50th St.), 6/E/V to 51st St./Lexington Ave.,
212-752-8017
101 W. 35th St. (6th Ave.), B/D/F/N/Q/R/V/W to 34th St./Herald Sq.,
212-594-8830 ●
www.florsheim.com*

◩ These "reliable" chain offshoots in the Garment District and
East 50s are "good for moderately priced nice shoes", especially
when you want "service instead of do-it-yourself shopping" say
a smattering of surveyors; but most find that "hit or miss" is more
the name of the game, convinced that the staff and quality are
"not the same as in days gone by."

Flou ▪ | – | – | – | E |

*42 Greene St. (bet. Broome & Grand Sts.), 6 to Spring St.,
212-941-9101; www.flou.com*

Stylish SoHo flagship of an Italian 'bedroom lifestyle' store that
carries everything to make that area more inviting – from ingenious
space-saving beds that lift up to reveal easily accessible storage
space underneath to luxe linens, leather furniture and sleek lighting.

Flying A ▪▪ | 21 | 19 | 17 | E |

*169 Spring St. (bet. Thompson St. & W. B'way), C/E to Spring St.,
212-965-9090; www.flyinga.net*

■ Zoom over to this "hip as hip can be" SoHo shop for an "instant
perk up" – guys and gals "can always find something" they "really
want to wear", plus the "staff is eager to help"; fly-savvy shoppers
scoop up "cute vintage pieces", plus au courant, "downtown
hipster" "stuff", including Fred Perry track suits, Blue Marlin
hoodies, DA-NANG cargo pants and Spitfire sunglasses; the red
tote shopping bags "alone are worth a purchase."

Fogal ▪▪ | 26 | 20 | 23 | VE |

*510 Madison Ave. (53rd St.), 6/E/V to 51st St./Lexington Ave.,
212-355-3254; www.fogal.com*

■ "Va-va-voom – a real head turner" exclaim enthusiasts of the
"exquisite beyond belief" French couture legwear and lingerie
sold at this Madison Avenue chain offshoot; while these "sheer
delights" "cost a fortune, they wear like iron" – indeed, "hosiery
does not have to be a disposable item" insist insiders who deem
the "amazing selection" "a lady's must in every color, and texture,
of the rainbow"; P.S. the staff is also "magnificent."

Foley & Corinna ●▪▪ | 25 | 20 | 23 | E |

*108 Stanton St. (bet. Essex & Ludlow Sts.), F/V to Lower East Side/
2nd Ave., 212-529-2338; www.foleyandcorinna.com*

■ If only we could "keep this one a secret" fawn fashionistas
over this Lower East Side women's boutique, convinced that it

offers some of "the best shopping on the planet"; its "exclusive" mix of Anna Corinna's "vintage finds" and Dana Foley's "genius" new designs "blends seamlessly" into a stew of "sexy, hip" dresses, tops and leather-belted trousers; salesgirls are "super-friendly", as are the owners, who are often "there to give advice"; N.B. Foley & Corinna Men opened post-*Survey* on Ludlow Street.

FOOTLIGHT RECORDS [S][C] 28 | 18 | 23 | M

113 E. 12th St. (bet. 3rd & 4th Aves.), 4/5/6/L/N/Q/R/W to 14th St./Union Sq., 212-533-1572; www.footlight.com

■ When you're "looking for an obscure Morricone soundtrack or a Japanese *Chorus Line*", "out-of-print cast albums" or "the best of the crooners (and croonerettes)" and pre-rock vocalists, sashay over to this Village "show-tune mecca", where a "fantastic selection" from "the world" of "theater, cabaret, television", Broadway "and more is on proud display"; a round of applause for the staff, please – they're "fellow fanatics of musicals" and "vintage music" and really "know their stuff."

Foot Locker ◐[S][C] 18 | 14 | 13 | M

120 W. 34th St. (bet. 6th & 7th Aves.), A/C/E to 34th St./Penn Station, 212-629-4419; 800-991-6815; www.footlocker.com

Additional locations throughout the NY area

◪ "Why go anywhere else" than this shoe-shop chain when you can track down the "largest selection" of "decent exercise gear" and "lots and lots" of "great cheap kicks" that may not "always be the coolest" but "can't be beat for sports"; still, some stomp on the "dodgy" service and "cluttered presentation", leaving cynics to conclude "when it comes to charm, these stores may as well be drive-thrus."

Forever 21 [S][C] 14 | 13 | 11 | I

5250 Kings Plaza (Flatbush Ave.), Brooklyn, 2/5 to Brooklyn College/Flatbush Ave., 718-434-9368

Queens Ctr., 90-15 Queens Blvd., Queens, G/R/V to Woodhaven Blvd., 718-595-0827

Staten Island Mall, 2655 Richmond Ave., Staten Island, 718-477-2121

800-966-1355; www.forever21.com

◪ "Cheap 'n' trendy", "teenie weenie", "wear 'em once and toss 'em" outfits that make you "look like a fashion model – from a safe distance" – draw droves of "teens and the twentysomething club crowd" to these outposts; "patient shoppers" who "need to be stylin'" insist it's worth "weeding through" the packed racks as "disorganized" as an adolescent's "bedroom" "to find real gems"; "you get no help, but who cares" – "you get what you pay for"; N.B. at press time, plans were afoot to open new branches in Midtown, Union Square and Downtown Brooklyn.

For Eyes [C] 21 | 18 | 16 | M

Graybar Bldg., 420 Lexington Ave. (bet. 43rd & 44th Sts.), 4/5/6/7/S to 42nd St./Grand Central, 212-697-8888; www.foreyes.com

■ "If you need to own multiple pairs and styles" of eyewear, this East 40s link of a chain sells a "great selection" of "designer frames" that are "inexpensive without looking cheap" (two pairs for $99 is the "best deal in NYC"); with "quick turnaround", it's a "godsend" for folks who "tend to lose their glass."

Forman's **S**
18 | 15 | 15 | M

145 E. 42nd St. (Lexington Ave.), 4/5/6/7/S to 42nd St./Grand Central, 212-681-9800 ◐
560 Fifth Ave. (bet. 45th & 46th Sts.), 4/5/6/7/S to 42nd St./Grand Central, 212-719-1000 ◐
59 John St. (bet. Dutch & William Sts.), 2/3/4/5/A/C/J/M/Z to Fulton St./ Broadway/Nassau, 212-791-4100
82 Orchard St. (bet. Broome & Grand Sts.), F/J/M/Z to Delancey/ Essex Sts., 212-228-2500

◪ It's "like shopping with your grandmother" at this "discounter worth visiting" where "everything looks good on you, dahlink", and you might be "pushed" into buying it; it's "not exactly bargain territory", and the "aggressive" help isn't for the faint of heart, but both "the plus-sized crowd" and "the petite businesswoman need look no further" for "work staples" "at a slightly lowered price."

Forréal **S C**
20 | 16 | 17 | E

1375 Third Ave. (bet. 78th & 79th Sts.), 6 to 77th St., 212-396-9535
1369 Third Ave. (bet. 78th & 79th Sts.), 6 to 77th St., 212-396-0563 ◐
1335 Third Ave. (bet. 76th & 77th Sts.), 6 to 77th St., 212-734-2105
www.forrealnyc.com

◪ "Take a peek to find out what the hot things are" suggest "free-spirited" fashionistas who bound over to this Third Avenue trio to scoop up denim and "hard-to-resist" weekend wear from "street hip" labels like Von Dutch and Miss Sixty; the new, "larger space" at 1375 also features "up-to-the-minute fashion imports" while the 1369 site is now an outlet – welcome news to the few who feel you need "Paris Hilton's allowance" to shop here.

Fortunoff **S**
23 | 19 | 18 | M

681 Fifth Ave. (54th St.), E/V to 5th Ave./53rd St., 212-758-6660; 800-367-8866; www.fortunoff.com

■ "Prices are fair" on the "massive selection" of silver, china and crystal at this "reliable" "New York institution" on Fifth Avenue, making it a "great place" for gifts; the "bridal registry is top-notch" and there's also an "excellent selection" of "quality" "high-end jewelry" at a "decent price."

42nd Street Photo ◐**S C**
19 | 10 | 12 | M

378 Fifth Ave. (bet. 35th & 36th Sts.), B/D/F/N/Q/R/V/W to 34th St./ Herald Sq., 212-594-6565; www.42photo.com

◪ It may "still be one of the best places to get new and used photo equipment after all these years", but – "oy" – you "better know what you're doing when you visit this store"; for starters, it's no longer on its eponymous thoroughfare, but in the West 30s, and though "these guys have the merchandise, they are very fast talkers"; but "don't be put off by their attitude", "don't settle" and you can get a "good price" on "many selections."

Fossil ◐**S**
19 | 18 | 16 | M

541 Broadway (bet. Prince & Spring Sts.), R/W to Prince St., 212-274-9579
530 Fifth Ave. (bet. 44th & 45th Sts.), 4/5/6/7/S to 42nd St./Grand Central, 212-997-3978
103 Fifth Ave. (bet. 17th & 18th), 4/5/6/L/N/Q/R/W to 14th St./Union Sq., 212-243-7296
www.fossil.com

■ Trendy watch chainlet offering a "fantastic way to find the latest fashion-magazine styles without the high prices"; the almost "overwhelming displays" of tickers range from classic to "colorful" to cutesy ("where else can you find a Felix the Cat" model?), but all are infinitely "wearable" and of "great quality" to boot; the SoHo store also carries womens- and menswear.

Fountain Pen Hospital 27 | 19 | 25 | M

10 Warren St. (bet. B'way & Church St.), R/W to City Hall, 212-964-0580; www.fountainpenhospital.com

■ "Everything you ever needed or wanted to know about pens" is contained in this "amazing" "sliver of a store" that's been in the Financial District since 1946; it's a "mecca" for belletrists, whether they prefer to use contemporary limited editions or vintage styluses, and the "approachable" staff is "terrific" and "knowledgeable", whether you're looking to "buy, sell or fix" a writing instrument.

Four Paws Club, The ◐ [S] [C] ▽ 25 | 23 | 25 | M

387 Bleecker St. (Perry St.), 1/9 to Christopher St./Sheridan Sq., 212-367-8265

■ The "super-helpful staff" knows "dogs by name" and "really cares about animals" at this West Village yearling that supplies "great snacks", a "wonderful selection of collars and unique" accessories as well as books and gifts for bipeds; though the store may be "small", it manages to accommodate a "friendly four-legged ambassador" in the form of a "huge cat" that's "worth checking out."

Fourteen Wall Street Jewelers ▽ 18 | 19 | 19 | M

14 Wall St. (bet. Broad St. & B'way), 2/3 to Wall St., 212-732-3788

■ Entering its third decade, this small, family-owned store is a typical mom-and-pop shop that Wall Streeters find "good for a gift" considering its inventory includes gold chains, birthstone jewelry and dress watches; the moderate prices are appreciated whether or not the market is bullish or bearish.

Fragments ◐ [S] [C] 27 | 24 | 16 | E

116 Prince St. (bet. Greene & Wooster Sts.), R/W to Prince St., 212-334-9588; 888-637-2463; www.fragments.com

◪ A "hipster's *Breakfast at Tiffany's*" shopping experience can be had at this SoHo showroom/retailer, that gives both "established" and "up-and-coming designers" space to show "one-of-a-kind" "jewelry treats" that "range from arty to dramatic to refined"; for over 20 years they've "set the trends" ("if Julia or J. Lo is wearing it, they sold it"), and if sometimes the staff "could not care less", well, at least that makes the browsing easy.

Fragrance Shop New York, The ◐ [S] ▽ 21 | 21 | 18 | M

21 E. 7th St. (bet. 2nd & 3rd Aves.), 6 to Astor Pl., 212-254-8950

■ If a stroll through the East Village leaves you craving some olfactory relief, you might want to pop into this pint-sized fragrance haven with an "amazing selection" of over 400 scents, which can be used to customize any oil, shampoo, lotion or cream that the shop carries.

Frank Stella Ltd. [S] 22 | 20 | 23 | E

440 Columbus Ave. (81st St.), B/C to 81st St., 212-877-5566 ◐

NY Athletic Club, 921 Seventh Ave. (58th St.), N/R/Q/W to 57th St., 212-957-1600

◪ Though founded in 1976, this haberdasher "constantly maintains its trendiness, even bringing back the horizontal-striped dress shirt" applaud advocates of its tailored garb, "nice choice of accessories" and "helpful, no-pressure service"; a few foes call it a fallen star ("used to be special"), but most feel it's still "worth the trip" either to the NY Athletic Club flagship or the Columbus Avenue branch.

Fratelli Rossetti S | 24 | 19 | 18 | VE

625 Madison Ave. (58th St.), 4/5/6/F/N/R/W to 59th St./Lexington Ave., 212-888-5107; www.rossetti.it

■ For "great Italian shoes" in "classic styles" with an unexpected fashion twist, "very beautiful leather bags", plus outerwear and accessories, make tracks to this East Side boutique; the "well-made" merchandise "never seems to wear out" – in fact it's played a wardrobe role in some stylesetters' lives "since forever"; while some surveyors insist that the "staff is always polite and helpful", a handful feels that service borders on "indifferent."

FRED LEIGHTON | 25 | 26 | 23 | VE

773 Madison Ave. (66th St.), 6 to 68th St., 212-288-1872

☑ Some of the "best window-shopping on Madison Avenue" can be had at this estate jeweler *par excellence,* "famous for loaning to Hollywood" stars his "spectacular selection" of "showstopping" sparklers; housed in an appropriately art deco–like setting (marble floors, exotic-wood cases and lacquered panels), "some [pieces] are antique, some are antique-style" (e.g. old stones in new settings), but all represent "glitz to the nth", albeit at "dazzling" prices; "lookyloos" beware, though – "they take jewelry seriously here and you better too."

French Connection S | 19 | 19 | 15 | M

700 Broadway (4th St.), 6 to Astor Pl.; R/W to 8th St., 212-473-4486
1270 Sixth Ave. (bet. 50th & 51st Sts.), B/D/F/V to 47-50th Sts./ Rockefeller Ctr., 212-262-6623
435 W. Broadway (Prince St.), R/W to Prince St., 212-219-1139 ●
888-741-3285; www.frenchconnection.com

☑ "Funky" fellas and femmes connect with "chic Euro" style in "durable" materials at this "sometimes innovative" British-based chain of "very clean" stores with "lovely displays"; "great basic tees" and "sleek" pants appeal to "young, nubile" "urbanites", but the "inflated price tags" don't, and the FCUK logo on T-shirts and shopping bags has prisses tsking "enough" – "who wants to wear what looks like a curse word?"

French Corner S C | ▽ 21 | 17 | 18 | E

464 W. Broadway (bet. Houston & Prince Sts.), R/W to Prince St., 212-505-1980

■ Ladies looking for that "killer look" love the chic, contemporary offerings at this "well-organized", spacious SoHo boutique, which corners the market on European lines like Moschino; it's possible to "pick up something hot for an [impromptu] night on the town" here including 7 For All Mankind jeans for men, as the "overeager, but honest" staff has "perfected the art of the quick sale."

French Sole S C | ▽ 18 | 17 | 22 | M

985 Lexington Ave. (71st St.), 6 to 68th St., 212-737-2859

■ "A real gem" purr patrons who pirouette over for "cute", "classic but stylish" "ballet flats in every color, texture" and "pattern"; from quilted leather numbers to suede or metallic must-haves; they're sure to leave you "speeding through the sidewalks of the

Upper East Side in comfort and European grace"; the "charming, old-world way to shop for shoes" ("wouldn't have it any other way") includes "hoping that your size will be stored way up high so you can watch the assistant climb to precarious heights on the pink ladder."

FRESH ◐ [S] [C] 27 | 27 | 22 | E

388 Bleecker St. (Perry St.), 1/9 to Christopher St./Sheridan Sq., 917-408-1850
57 Spring St. (bet. Lafayette & Mulberry Sts.), 6 to Spring St., 212-925-0099
800-373-7420; www.fresh.com

■ Head here "if you're on a diet, as you can inhale the divine scents of milk, sugar and chocolate without gaining a pound!" assert admirers about these West Village and NoLita toiletries stores with the "perfect name because that's how their products make you feel"; the beauty, bath and body lines, which rely mainly on natural home remedies whenever possible (like the best-selling Brown Sugar Body Polish), are "expensive" but "worth the splurge", and the "sweet" staff is "generous with free samples"; N.B. Gywneth Paltrow and Julianne Moore are among the celeb clientele.

FRETTE [C] 27 | 27 | 22 | VE

799 Madison Ave. (bet. 67th & 68th Sts.), 6 to 68th St., 212-988-5221; www.frette.com

■ "If Queen Elizabeth isn't sleeping on" "the Rolls-Royce" of sheets, she should be declare devotees of this "dreamland" on the Upper East Side selling "ultra-luxe bed and table linens from Italy" with "the highest thread count" to customers like the Vatican; those who Frette over "paying through the nose" should hit the store's "fabulous" 30–40 percent off sales in January and July.

Frick Collection [S] 20 | 18 | 19 | M

1 E. 70th St. (5th Ave.), 6 to 68th St., 212-288-0700; www.frick.org

◪ Housed in the "spectacular" 1914 Upper East Side digs of industrialist and avid collector Henry Clay Frick, this "real gem" of a museum's "pocket-size shop" has a "very fine selection of books", prints and "lovely" "mementos" "corresponding to the collection" of 15th- through 19th-century Western art; it's "staffed by polite people who will help if they can", and though it's a bit "limited" and "stodgy" for expansive Downtown tastes, it's "enough to satisfy those who love the Frick."

Frida's Closet [S] [C] 22 | 24 | 23 | M

296 Smith St. (bet. 2nd & Union Sts.), Brooklyn, F/G to Carroll St., 718-855-0311

■ Worshiped by Madonna and the subject of a Salma Hayek movie, Mexican artist Frida Kahlo inspires this "slightly bizarre concept" shop in Carroll Gardens showcasing a select few designers; inside the red-and-mustard-colored "tiny" space, adorned with the painter's portrait, each item is treated as a piece of art and each exclusive piece of "cute" clothing numbered, so you know you're getting something "unique" from the "low-key" staff.

Furla [S] [C] 24 | 23 | 17 | E

727 Madison Ave. (64th St.), 6 to 68th St., 212-755-8986
598 Madison Ave (57th St.), N/R/W to 5th Ave./59th St., 212-980-3208
www.furla.com

◪ Customers croon over the "outstanding selection" of "beautiful leather goods" at these Upper East side branches of the Bologna,

Italy–based chain, lauding the "stylish" bags done up in "clean lines and funky shapes" and "sophisticated" shoes and gloves at "semi-reasonable prices"; but critics sigh that the "snotty" staff can put a damper on their shopper's high; N.B. the 598 Madison Avenue branch opened post-*Survey.*

Furry Paws ● S C

22 | 17 | 19 | M

141 Amsterdam Ave. (66th St.), 1/9 to 66th St./Lincoln Ctr., 212-724-9321
120 E. 34th St. (bet. Lexington & Park Aves.), 6 to 33rd St., 212-725-1970
310 E. 23rd St. (bet. 1st & 2nd. Sts.), 6 to 23rd St., 212-979-0920
1039 Second Ave. (bet. 54th & 55th Sts.), 4/5/6/F/N/R/W to 59th St./Lexington Ave., 212-813-1388
1705 Third Ave. (bet. 95th & 96th Sts.), 6 to 96th St., 212-828-5308
■ A "good selection of merchandise" that includes "great stuff you can't find elsewhere" makes this chainlet a "one-stop shopping" destination for petaphiles; supporters also cite the "easy-to-browse" displays, a "helpful", "friendly" staff and "free delivery" that's "critical for a 20-pound bag of dog food" as factors that fuel their fur-vor for this "reliable" litter of "neighborhood stores."

Fye ● S C

19 | 17 | 14 | M

1290 Sixth Ave. (51st St.), N/R/W to 49th St., 212-581-1669; www.fye.com
Additional locations throughout the NY area
■ "Awesome! you can listen to some tracks before you buy" the CD – "gotta love that" gush tunesmiths who also applaud this chain's "pretty good selection of DVDs", games and videos, all at "better prices than Coconuts, its predecessor"; still, cynics are not entertained by this "typical" mega-outfit.

Gabay's Outlet S

16 | 9 | 13 | M

225 First Ave. (bet. 13th & 14th Sts.), L to 1st Ave., 212-254-3180;
www.gabaysoutlet.com
◪ "Not for the faint of heart", this "off-the-beaten-path", third-generation discounter in the East Village "can be a gold mine" for status goods, especially shoes (as in Choos) and handbags ("big name designers" Marc Jacobs, Fendi, Gucci); it's a "hit-or-miss situation" – "you never know what treasures" you'll "dig" up (like "Bergdorf's closeouts") "mixed in with the junk"; P.S. note to "bargain hunters turned off by its previous" "hodgepodge" state: a recent renovation may make it "worth" another "look."

Galileo ● S C

– | – | – | E

37 Seventh Ave. (13th St.), 1/9 to 18th St., 212-243-1629;
www.galileonyc.com
"Pricey but perfectly packaged" glassware – vessels, vases and Venetian varieties – populates shelf upon shelf of this Greenwich Village corner shop that also displays lamps, pillows and other home accessories; the "salespeople are helpful", and even the most persnickety person will "always find a gift here."

Gallery of Wearable Art

– | – | – | VE

34 E. 67th St. (bet. Madison & Park Aves.), 6 to 68th St., 212-570-2252;
www.galleryofwearableart.com
"One of the best-kept fashion secrets in NYC", this opulent East 60s boutique, lushly decorated to resemble a Parisian atelier, carries some of the "most glamorous, one-of-a-kind" bridal and evening gowns, fabulous couture-esque finds and lavishly embellished artisinal coats, all at stratospheric prices; made mostly from vintage textiles and embroidery, the unique creations channel spirits of

eras past, from siren-esque satin numbers à la Jean Harlow to regal Victorian-inspired knockouts.

Gallery Orrefors Kosta Boda **C**   26 | 23 | 22 | E

685 Madison Ave. (62nd St.), 4/5/6/F/N/R/W to 59th St./Lexington Ave., 212-752-1095; www.orrefors.com

■ "Beautiful art glass" from this over-100-year-old Swedish glassmaker can be had at its East 60s offshoot, where vases and votives, as well as one-of-a-kind, signed-and-limited-edition ornamental pieces make it an "excellent", albeit "pricey", "source for gifts."

Galo **S**   20 | 17 | 16 | M

825 Lexington Ave. (bet. 63rd & 64th Sts.), 6 to 68th St., 212-832-3922
895 Madison Ave. (72nd St.), 6 to 68th St., 212-744-7936
1296 Third Ave. (bet. 74th & 75th Sts.), 6 to 77th St., 212-288-3448

☑ "Dependability" is the operative word at this trio of women's and children's shoe stores offering a "large selection" of "classic", "comfortable", "finely crafted" "mainstays" for "dressy", professional and casual occasions; downtown girls may gripe about the "conservative" choices, but they're overruled by groupies of the "great" goods at "great prices."

Gant **S**   18 | 19 | 18 | E

645 Fifth Ave. (bet. 51st & 52nd Sts.), B/D/F/V to 47-50th Sts./ Rockefeller Ctr., 212-813-9170 ●
77 Wooster St. (bet. Broome & Spring Sts.), C/E to Spring St., 212-431-9610
www.gant.com

☑ Known as the "preppy" Ivy Leaguers' label from the 1950s on, this now-international brand, "cleanly presented" at the cherry-wood-accented Rockefeller Center flagship and its SoHo sibling, is still "rugby-oriented", but it's also evolved into an "updated" men's collection (after a "'guest' appearance on *Queer Eye for the Straight Guy,* what more do you need in the way of endorsement?"); but a handful gant get enthused, deeming it "overpriced"; N.B. at press time, plans were afoot to introduce a woman's line.

GAP ●**S**   16 | 16 | 15 | M

60 W. 34th St (B'way), B/D/F/N/Q/R/V/W to 34th St./Herald Sq., 212-760-1268; www.gap.com
Additional locations throughout the NY area

☑ "Diehards" return again and again to this "old reliable" for a "quick, basic fix" of "classic, clean", "all-American" attire for "the whole family", including "the best jeans", khakis, white tees, denim jackets and "no-nonsense" bras and undies "at good prices"; nevertheless, traditionalists lament "recent seasons'" "disco trends", while snobs "overwhelmed by blandness" coupled with a "significant" "gap" in service sniff that it might be "as convenient as the corner deli", but there's "always more promise than delivery."

GAPKIDS ●**S**   21 | 19 | 15 | M

60 W. 34th St. (B'way), B/D/F/N/Q/R/V/W to 34th St./Herald Sq., 212-760-1268; www.gap.com
Additional locations throughout the NY area

■ "You'll never leave empty-handed" from this "tried-and-true" chain that has "some of the cutest children's clothes around", with "designs that are a bit more adventurous and hipper than the adult" offerings ("this is how the cool kids dress"); both parents and tots "will be happy" with the "durable" clothing that "really takes the test of rough-and-tumble" boys and girls and "won't break the bank"; "sales are the way to go" say seasoned shoppers, who find that some items are "perfect for petite women too!"

Garden Shop at the Horticultural Society of New York, The ⊡

▽ | 21 | 22 | 21 | M |

128 W. 58th St. (bet. 6th & 7th Aves.), N/R/Q/W to 57th St., 212-757-0915; www.hsny.org
■ A "hidden gem" in Midtown, this century-old nonprofit provides a "great resource" for would-be horticulturalists with advice from its "helpful, knowledgeable staff"; it's also abloom with indoor and outdoor plants, an "interesting selection of bulbs" and "surprisingly nice gift items."

Gas Bijoux ⦿⬛⬛

| – | – | – | M |

238 Mott St. (Prince St.), 6 to Spring St., 212-334-7290
Owned by the folks behind Blue Bag, this tiny NoLita yearling (colored cotton-candy pink, with a huge chandelier) features jewelry handmade by designer André Gas; his clever, one-of-a-kind concoctions are characterized by semiprecious gems and beads in base-metal or silver settings.

Gateway Country ⬛⬛

| 19 | 20 | 16 | M |

200 Park Ave. S. (17th St.), 4/5/6/L/N/Q/R/W to 14th St./Union Sq., 212-982-4240; www.gateway.com
⬛ They phased out the bovine-and-silo theme at the Park Avenue offshoot of this computer company started on an Iowa farm, but customers "satisfied" with their "great PCs" and third-party printers, scanners and digital cameras still invoke the Holstein-print packaging, bellowing "mooove on over", you other chains; but critics counter bull and cite "poor service."

G.C. William ⬛⬛

| 23 | 17 | 17 | E |

1137 Madison Ave. (bet. 84th & 85th Sts.), 4/5/6 to 86th St., 212-396-3400
⬛ Tweens and "teenagers love" the "good selection of clothing" at this "friendly", funky-looking Madison Avenue "find" where "extremely trendy" labels du jour like Juicy Couture, Riley and Von Dutch are mixed with conservative duds that seemingly prove "preppy is alive and well"; it may "not always be what you want your daughter to wear, but she does", so buck up – then brace yourself for the "Upper East Side prices."

Generation Records ⦿⬛

| 25 | 18 | 15 | M |

210 Thompson St. (bet. Bleecker & W. 3rd Sts.), A/B/C/D/E/F/S/V to W. 4th St., 212-254-1100
■ New York's "funky", "fun" "punk headquarters" and "hideaway" in the Village is also a "Brit-pop and indie haunt" offering music "aficionados" everything from "avant-garde doom metal" to "rare imports"; while the resident "store cats are always happy to share their opinions on the music" and spin live records on their in-store system" so you can hear the sound quality, "don't expect warm and fuzzy service."

George Smith

▽ | 25 | 18 | 16 | VE |

75 Spring St. (Crosby St.), 6 to Spring St., 212-226-4747; www.georgesmith.com
■ Long-standing, statusy SoHo store whose "pricey", "beautiful" bespoke English furniture – the pieces are handmade to order,

from the birch or beech wood frame to the down-filled cushions – will "only get better" with wear; customers can choose from 70 styles of seating, including the signature sofa with turned wooden legs, and from a variety of fabrics that range from florals to solids and stripes.

Georg Jensen ☐   25 | 24 | 21 | VE
683 Madison Ave. (bet. 61st & 62nd Sts.), 4/5/6/F/N/R/W to 59th St./ Lexington Ave., 212-759-6457; www.georgjensen.com

■ This "upscale" Upper East Side branch of the 100-year-old Scandinavian silversmith showcases its "fabulous" clean-lined designs in cutlery, candlesticks and containers by mid-century masters like Arne Jacobsen and Henning Koppel; there's also jewelry that ranges from art-nouveau–inspired items to more modern takes on brooches and bracelets; N.B. it shares space with Royal Copenhagen Porcelain, which has been favored by Danish royalty ever since the company's kilns were first fired up in 1775.

Geppetto's Toy Box ☐☐   25 | 23 | 24 | M
10 Christopher St. (bet. Gay St. & Greenwich Ave.), A/B/C/D/E/F/S/ V to W. 4th St.; 1/9 to Christopher St./Sheridan Sq., 212-620-7511; 800-326-4566; www.nyctoys.com

■ "One smiles as one shops in this world of play", a "toy heaven" tucked away in the Village, where "the selection is true genius" (many "unique" offerings "nurture artistic expression") and the "knowledgeable, caring staff" "gives great gift-giving advice"; it's "fun to just browse", delighting in the spectacle of puppets surrounding their very own stage, and "adorable" marionettes mixing with jack-in-the-boxes and an enclave of enchanting dolls.

Geraldine ☐☐   23 | 23 | 20 | VE
246 Mott St. (bet. Houston & Prince Sts.), 6 to Spring St., 212-219-1620

■ Don't let the air-tight feel fool you – there are "true finds" at this "small, fun" minimalist NoLita boutique, home to a "cutting-edge selection" of cheeky sandals, revved-up pumps and mules that suit urban ladies just fine; come for well-known designs by the likes of Pierre Hardy, Narciso Rodriguez and Marc by Marc Jacobs and stay to discover "unique shoes" from up-and-coming young "European designers rarely seen elsewhere."

Gerry Cosby & Co. ●☐   23 | 13 | 16 | E
Madison Sq. Garden, 3 Penn Plaza (7th Ave. & 32nd St.), 1/2/3/9 to 34th St./Penn Station, 212-563-6464

☑ "Shopping here can be more exciting than the games at MSG" upstairs declare diehards who deem this "convenient" shop, stocked with one of the "best selections of sporting goods", a "must-go before events"; whether you're "tracking down that hard-to-find" "Rangers or Knicks jersey" or "real hockey equipment", this is the "place to go for the genuine article"; while some cynics would rather take a puck in the teeth than deal with the "intimidating service", fans shoot back it's a "venerable NYC experience."

Gerry's Menswear ●☐☐   24 | 22 | 20 | E
353 Bleecker St. (bet. Charles & 10th Sts.), 1/9 to Christopher St./ Sheridan Sq., 212-691-0636
110 Eighth Ave. (bet. 15th & 16th Sts.), A/C/E/L to 14th St./8th Ave., 212-243-9141

■ Can a store be "trendy and classic" at the same time? – this one can, thanks to its two locations: in Chelsea, sparse-yet-slick decor sets off a "reliably good selection", from Boss by Hugo Boss leather jackets and pants to cool contemporary threads from Nicole Fahri, Ted Baker, Ben Sherman and Fred Perry, "making shopping easy" for gay, modish men; the West Village branch caters to a more conservative clientele, with "European-oriented sportswear" from Armani and Pringle of Scotland sweaters.

Ghost ●⑤ⓒ   ▽ | 22 | 19 | 18 | E |
28 Bond St. (bet. Bowery & Lafayette St.), 6 to Bleecker St., 646-602-2891; www.ghost.co.uk

■ There's nothing scary here – except maybe "how much" this British brand's "light and glowy dresses" cost; nevertheless, this NoHo spot with a Parisian flea-market feel works "for society gals" and anyone else who craves the kind of "clothes that flow" "in a fantasy."

Ghurka   ▽ | 25 | 25 | 24 | VE |
41 E. 57th St. (Madison Ave.), N/R/W to 5th Ave./59th St., 212-826-8300; 800-587-1584; www.ghurka.com

■ "Some of the most beautifully tanned leather" comes "safari-style" at this Midtown mecca where you also find "top-notch help and presentation" ("only the finest for those with money"); disciples fall into line for the "durable, high-quality bags", "classic luggage" and trunks and lifestyle accessories inspired by the gear that Ghurkas, soldiers from Ghurka, Nepal who served in British and Indian military regiments, wore in the 1800s.

Gianfranco Ferré ⓒ   ▽ | 23 | 25 | 25 | VE |
845 Madison Ave. (bet. 70th & 71st Sts.), 6 to 68th St., 212-717-5430; www.gianfrancoferre.it

■ Once an architect, always an architect: this Italian-born designer has translated his first love into "beautifully constructed" men's and women's clothing, as well as precisely conceived accessories and fragrances ("great cologne!") at his sleek Upper East Side boutique; influenced by his early travels to India, even his tailored suits often possess a fluid drape.

Giorgio Armani ⑤ | 27 | 25 | 23 | VE |
760 Madison Ave. (65th St.), 6 to 68th St., 212-988-9191; www.giorgioarmani.com

■ *Grazie*, Giorgio! grin groupies who insist the Italian "master of design" "deserves his reputation" for his "ultimate-in-chic" couture, shown off in this Madison Avenue boutique; the exquisite ("are they real?") "employees glide across hushed, wide-open spaces" to assist with the rows of signature "sleek, minimalist" suits and separates, superb shoes and "stunning" eveningwear, a favorite of stars (both male and female) on award-show nights; these "casually elegant" threads, accessories and cosmetics can induce "sticker shock" – but for the "beautiful people", they're "the uniform for all occasions, except the gym."

Giraudon ●⑤ⓒ   ▽ | 23 | 20 | 22 | M |
152 Eighth Ave. (bet. 17th & 18th Sts.), 1/9 to 18th St., 212-633-0999; 800-278-1552; www.giraudonnewyork.com

☑ "If I designed shoes, they would look like this" gush ardent admirers of the French footwear at this small Chelsea shop; while fashion-forward fans flip for the "really nice selection" of "fun options" with a healthy dose of "attitude", gripers grouse they are simply "uncomfortable."

Girl Props ◐ S C
19 | 16 | 14 | I

33 E. Eighth St. (University Pl.), R/W to 8th St.; 6 to Astor Pl., 212-533-3159
153 Prince St. (bet. Thompson St. & W. B'way), R/W to Prince St.;
C/E to Spring St., 212-505-7615
www.girlprops.com

■ 'Inexpensive . . . we *never* say cheap' runs the slogan of this "urbanized" accessories pair in Greenwich Village and SoHo; "teens (and anyone else who likes to glitter)" enjoy the "best collection of cool-now, passé-in-an-hour jewelry", "funky, trendy trinkets" and wigs at "unbeatable prices" for costume parties or those "occasions when only a boa will do."

Giselle S C
23 | 17 | 16 | M

143 Orchard St. (bet. Delancey & Rivington Sts.), F/J/M/Z to Delancey/
Essex Sts., 212-673-1900; 877-447-3553; www.giselleny.com

■ "Keep the secret to yourself!" order admirers who adore this "Lower East Side classic", a four-floor discount emporium offering "good prices" on "high-end" European brands like Iceberg, Escada Sport, Laurel and Les Copains; the "well-organized", "beautiful selection of designer clothes" is "different from other stores", plus it's "always a deal", "especially at sale time."

GIUSEPPE ZANOTTI DESIGN C
27 | 26 | 22 | VE

806 Madison Ave. (bet. 67th & 68th Sts.), 6 to 68th St., 212-650-0455;
www.giuseppe-zanotti-design.com

■ "Don't expect to find the basics" at this "well laid-out" East 60s showcase for "totally off the hook", "super sexy", "high-concept", even "outlandish" women's sandals, stilettos and boots, some festooned with "fish scales, leather straps and Swarovski crystals", like "uniquely designed" "brooches for the feet"; there's just one caveat: "wear solid colors because your shoes will be the focus of everyone's attention!"

Givenchy S C
∇ 22 | 23 | 19 | VE

710 Madison Ave. (63rd St.), 4/5/6/F/N/R/W to 59th St./Lexington Ave.,
212-688-4338; www.givenchy.com

■ At its sleek East 60s outpost, this renowned Parisian house still offers "classic clothes", including "wonderful suits" that "will last a lifetime"; but in the hands of young designer Julien Macdonald, the collection has gained a more colorful edge, even as it retains the "tailored-to-fit" sophistication that makes each "elegant", "*très* expensive" piece "worth the money."

Global Table S C
∇ 27 | 25 | 18 | M

107 Sullivan St. (bet. Prince & Spring Sts.), C/E to Spring St.,
212-431-5839; www.globaltable.com

■ "You can always find something to buy" at Nathalie Smith's SoHo "tabletop heaven" where the "eclectic assortment of dishes", Capiz-shell bowls, tea sets and trays "from around the world" "are great pieces" that are elegant enough "to mix" with your "granny's china" without costing the family jewels; the space is "small", so watch that "huge tote bag" you're probably schlepping.

Goffredo Fantini S C
24 | 22 | 23 | E

248 Elizabeth St. (bet. Houston & Prince Sts.), B/D/F/S/V to B'way/
Lafayette St., 212-219-1501; www.goffredofantini.com

■ "Quirky Italian shoes for all occasions" are the draw at this "wonderful" NoLita boutique offering "modern", "beautiful" "well-made" footwear that's both "sexy and comfy" for men and women; the "hip" staff will "become your best friends" as you perch in a Plexiglas chair and slip into the "unique styles", many done up with rivets, buckles and other downtown details; thrifty sorts also recommend the "good sales" as well.

Goldin-Feldman — | — | — | E
150 W. 30th St., 5th fl. (7th Ave.), B/D/F/N/Q/R/V/W to 34th St./ Herald Sq., 212-239-0512
In a fifth-floor Garment District loft, this "well-established" third-generation furrier (a favorite with personal shoppers) prides itself on service, "asking what you want" in the way of "stylish" coats and, "if they don't have it, gladly making" your heart's desire; some say "don't be fooled" by the "showroom [atmosphere] – these are retail prices" (though less marked-up than those of the stores they sell to).

Good, the Bad and the Ugly, The S C 21 | 22 | 18 | M
437 E. Ninth St. (bet. Ave. A & 1st Ave.), L to 1st Ave., 212-473-3769; www.goodbaduglynyc.com
■ "Paging Chloë Sevigny" and all those "cool enough" to dig the Gertrude-Stein-meets-Wonder-Woman threads by owner-designer Judi Rosen, who "turns it out" in her "cute", forestlike East Village shop eccentrically decorated with "taxidermic animals" and retro mannequins; the "fun, funky", girly frocks, nipped-in jackets, "hip little tops", bottom-enhancing pants, "sexy" Howdy Doody undies and line of "adorable, vintage-looking accessories" called 'Miss Dater', all "warrant a stop", plus the "knee-highs rock."

Goodwill Industries ◑ S C 12 | 7 | 8 | I
220 E. 23rd St. (3rd Ave.), 6 to 23rd St., 212-447-7270
2196 Fifth Ave. (bet. 132nd & 135th Sts.), 2/3 to 135th St., 212-862-0020
514 W. 181st St. (Amsterdam Ave.), 1/9 to 181st St., 212-923-7910
217 W. 79th St. (Amsterdam Ave.), 1/9 to 79th St.; B/C to 81st St., 212-874-5050
258 Livingston St. (Bond St.), Brooklyn, A/C/G to Hoyt/ Schermerhorn Sts., 718-923-9037
52 W. Fordham Rd. (Davidson Ave.), Bronx, 4 to Fordham Rd., 718-733-2453
32-36 Steinway St. (Broadway), Queens, R/V to Steinway St., 718-932-0418
www.goodwill.org
◩ "From clothing to books to housewares, you never know what you may find" at this historic thrift-shop chain; naturally, "you're not going for a classy experience", and "you'll have to look hard" to find treasure, but who can resist when "a shirt may run you less than breakfast at Starbucks"?

Gotham Bikes S C ▽ 25 | 19 | 26 | M
112 W. Broadway (bet. Duane & Reade Sts.), 1/2/3/9 to Chambers St., 212-732-2453; www.gothambikes.com
◩ One of the "most courteous bike shops in town", this TriBeCan, owned by the same folks who run Toga Bikes, is staffed with avid, active, "very friendly" cyclists "without an air of snobbery", who are eager to help "bikers of all levels" (including Mayor Michael Bloomberg) choose the right vehicle from the "wide selection of prices and styles."

Gothic Cabinet Craft ●🄢🄒   15 | 8 | 14 | I

715 Ninth Ave. (49th St.), C/E to 50th St., 212-246-9525;
www.gothiccabinetcraft.com
Additional locations throughout the NY area

☑ "Budget-conscious folks" head to this multibranched seller of finished and unfinished wooden furniture for "basic stuff" like bookcases, beds, dressers and storage units, along with custom-built pieces; while the sophisticated sniff at the "so-so selection and quality", the frugal feel the "cheap" prices at this chain make it fine for furnishing a "first apartment."

Gotta Knit 🄢🄒   20 | 17 | 14 | E

498 Sixth Ave., 2nd fl. (bet. 12th & 13th Sts.), F/V to 14th St.; L to 6th Ave.,
212-989-3030; 800-898-6748

☑ A "very current", "colorful" selection of "pricey yet gorgeous yarns" awaits at this small, second-floor Greenwich Village knitting and crochet destination that's "always crowded" with hobbyists; while a smattering insist that the "knowledgeable staff" "holds your hand and helps you through whatever you need", many snarl that pals "of the house are treated well but unknowns" are "made to feel like intruders in an unfriendly knitting circle."

Gown Company, The   ▽ 15 | 12 | 19 | M

312 E. Ninth St. (bet. 1st & 2nd Aves.), L to First Ave.; 6 to Astor Pl.,
212-979-9000; www.thegowncompany.com

☑ "It's all about the service and the chance you'll luck out" at this "tiny", by-appointment-only East Village bridal shop where "if you can find" a sample dress from the likes of Lazaro or Helen Morley, or pull a one-off gown that never made it into production from the "off-the-rack rack, you've got yourself a steal"; it's "limited in sizes", so if you're pining for a "large selection, keep looking."

GRACIOUS HOME ●🄢   25 | 17 | 20 | E

1992 Broadway (67th St.), 1/9 to 66th St./Lincoln Ctr., 212-231-7800
1217 & 1220 Third Ave. (70th St.), 6 to 68th St., 212-517-6300
1201 Third Ave. (bet. 69th & 70th Sts.), 6 to 68th St., 212-517-6300
www.gracioushome.com

■ "From dimmers to doilies", these "bursting-at-the-seams" Lincoln Center and East Side stores make supporters "swoon" with an "amazing selection of everything for the home at all prices", including hardware, kitchenware, bedroom and bathroom accessories; the staff is "unbelievably knowledgeable" ("they have more and better answers than the Sears tool guy and constantly pull miracles from the ceiling-high shelves") and "free delivery is a nice added bonus"; N.B. the 1201 Third Avenue branch is devoted to lamps, lighting products and custom-made shades.

GRAFF   29 | 29 | 27 | VE

721 Madison Ave. (bet. 63rd & 64th Sts.), 6 to 68th St., 212-355-9292;
www.graffdiamonds.com

■ A dazzling array of "gems in every imaginable color and shape", including "drop-dead diamonds to drool over", makes this London-based outfit the "ultimate for jewelry"; many a passerby stops to gaze at the "most incredible window displays" on Madison Avenue, which — along with the "exquisite wood" interior — cause reviewers to vote the place No. 1 for Presentation; "prices are beyond expensive, they're astronomical", but the "courteous and helpful" staff "always wears a smile."

Grand Central Racquet **C**

22 | 15 | 20 | M

Grand Central, 45th St. Passageway (Vanderbilt Ave.), 4/5/6/7/S to 42nd St./Grand Central, 212-856-9647
341 Madison Ave. (44th St.), 4/5/6/7/S to 42nd St./Grand Central, 212-292-8851
www.grandcentralracquet.com

■ "Quality service on your racquet before you get on the train to the country club – what more could you want?" laud loyalists who head to this tiny, weekdays-only kiosk in Grand Central "by the Roosevelt Passageway" to get "favorites restrung" ("usually on the same day") and also "find great stuff"; the "excellent" Madison Avenue maven courts customers with a larger selection of squash and tennis equipment, shoes and accessories from hard-hitting brands like Head, Wilson and Prince.

Granny-Made **S** **C**

▽ 24 | 19 | 22 | E

381 Amsterdam Ave. (bet. 78th & 79th Sts.), 1/9 to 79th St., 212-496-1222; 877-472-6691; www.granny-made.com

◪ Stacks and stacks of imported handknit "stuff", plus a "nice selection" of "homemade" sweaters and hats for adults, children and babies inspired by a real grandmother can be found at this "small" Upper West Side boutique; while the choices "range from traditional to funky", the cost can be out of the loop for wallet-watchers who quip "hope some portion of the high prices is going to granny herself."

Great Feet **S** **C**

23 | 19 | 19 | M

1241 Lexington Ave. (84th St.), 4/5/6 to 86th St., 212-249-0551; www.striderite.com

■ "The place to go for your child's first pair" of Stride-Rites, this fun, large, "popular" Upper East Side store also offers one of the "best selections of kids' shoes, boots, sandals" and sneakers around; while it's "always crowded", you usually "don't have to wait long at off-times", since the "staff knows what they're doing" and can "handle the volume" – just "don't go on weekends, unless you're a masochist."

Green Onion, The **C**

26 | 20 | 23 | M

274 Smith St. (bet. DeGraw & Sackett Sts.), Brooklyn, F/G to Carroll St., 718-246-2804

■ "How cute is this store?" opine Onion-ites over the moon about the "local feel" and "unique, quality kids' stuff" stocked by this "wonderful" Cobble Hill shop on "hopping Smith Street"; "walk in, state the age and sex of child, and poof! they will help you find the perfect gift" – whatever you need, be it infants' or kids' clothing, toys or accessories, this "place has it all."

Greenstones **S** **C**

25 | 19 | 24 | E

442 Columbus Ave. (bet. 81st & 82nd Sts.), B/C to 81st St., 212-580-4322
1184 Madison Ave. (bet. 86th & 87th Sts.), 4/5/6 to 86th St., 212-427-1665

■ "Quality"-seekers "love to shop" for "beautiful European clothing and accessories" (primarily French lines like Catimini and Deux par Deux) for babies and children (up to age 10) at these stylish siblings, a lengthy stone's throw away on the Upper East and Upper West Sides; the "great" "staff helps you select your trendy kids' wardrobe" of "cute, playful but not overly sophisticated" clothing, and to top it off, you'll find one of "the best selections of hats in town."

Gringer & Sons 24 | 9 | 16 | M

29 First Ave. (2nd St.), F/V to Lower East Side/2nd Ave., 212-475-0600
◪ "Viking, Sub-Zero", Gaggenau and other choice kitchen-appliance manufacturers are found at this East Village storefront; the "crowded quarters" don't allow for "all models" to be "displayed on the floor", but they do carry a "large selection", so ask; while some sigh "it's easier to get a reservation at Nobu than get help" here, the staff does "know its stuff" once you do.

Gruen Optika 🆂 🅲 23 | 21 | 21 | E

2382 Broadway (87th St.), 1/9 to 86th St., 212-724-0850
2009 Broadway (bet. 68th & 69th Sts.), 1/9 to 66th St./Lincoln Ctr., 212-874-8749
1225 Lexington Ave. (83rd St.), 4/5/6 to 86th St., 212-628-2493
599 Lexington Ave. (52nd St.), 6/E/V to 51st St./Lexington Ave., 212-688-3580
1076 Third Ave. (64th St.), 6 to 68th St., 212-751-6177
◪ "For glasses you won't see everyone else wearing", this spec-tacular mini-chain offers a "wide selection" of "high-end", "off-the-radar brands as well as many of the biggies", making you a "gorgeous" "sight for classy eyes"; a few eye-dealists dis "indifferent service", but more maintain the "neighborly" staff "won't steer you wrong" and report a "wonderful experience picking out the right frames."

Gucci 🆂 27 | 26 | 21 | VE

685 Fifth Ave. (54th St.), 6/E/V to 51st St./Lexington Ave., 212-826-2600
840 Madison Ave. (bet. 69th & 70th Sts.), 6 to 68th St., 212-717-2619
www.gucci.com
◪ "Check your balance" (both financial and physical) before dipping into these Fifth and Madison Avenue dens of desire, where it's not if, but what, you want – and "everybody wants something" from the "flashy" luxury label; in Midtown, the multifloor, "sleek interior" is a "fun maze to explore" and the salespeople are "unpushy"; still, it's a "zoo", as logo-lovers and "tourists" "drool over" the "amazing purses", traditionalists embrace "status loafers" ("leather heaven on earth") and celebs and "super-trendies" storm the glam his-and-hers sportswear; N.B. at press time, designer Tom Ford was slated to bow out with Narcisco Rodriquez and Stella McCartney reportedly vying to fill his shoes.

Guess? 🌑🆂 19 | 20 | 17 | M

537 Broadway (bet. Prince & Spring Sts.), R/W to Prince St.; 6 to Spring St., 212-226-9545
South Street Seaport, 23-25 Fulton St. (Water St.), 2/3/4/5/A/C/J/ M/Z to Fulton St./B'way/Nassau, 212-385-0533
Kings Plaza, 5351 Kings Plaza, Brooklyn, 2/5 to Brooklyn College/ Flatbush Ave., 718-421-5075
2655 Richmond Ave. #209, Staten Island, 718-370-1594
800-394-8377; www.guess.com
◪ "No guesswork here" – this his-and-her chain hits the "what's hot, what's not" spot with "fantabulous" jeans, "sexy tops" and "party clothes" for "young New Yorkers"; while some question its currency – "reminds me of the '80s and Anna Nicole Smith" – defenders shoot back "these latest trends last longer than most."

Guggenheim Museum Store 🆂🅲   19 | 18 | 14 | E

Guggenheim Museum, 1071 Fifth Ave. (89th St.), 4/5/6 to 86th St.,
212-423-3615; 800-329-6109; www.guggenheimstore.org

◪ Architecture buffs "guess Frank Lloyd Wright didn't include a gift shop in his plans" because the "baubles", books, "art posters and postcards" at this Upper East Side museum are stuffed into a "cramped" space, though there's nothing "little" about the "high prices"; style snobs sniff that the "cool factor" on "Calderesque art mobiles", "funky magnets" and New York–themed date books "expired in the '80s", and if "those tourists from Iowa don't know that", it seems as though the "bored staff" does.

Gumbo 🆂🅲   – | – | – | M

493 Atlantic Ave. (bet. Nevins St. & 3rd Ave.), Brooklyn, 2/3/4/5/M/
N/Q/R/W to Atlantic Ave., 718-855-7808

A sumptuous stew of kids' and women's clothing, accessories and craft items from faraway lands draws customers to this cavernous Atlantic Avenue shop replete with African drums and an airy art gallery; options abound, from infants' apparel from labels like Zutano and Cotton Kidz to toddlers' and children's one-of-a-kind dresses, fleece pants and Peruvian sweaters for both little ones and fuzzy-loving adults; Saturday storytelling sessions and knitting classes for adults spice up the mix.

Gymboree 🆂   20 | 20 | 17 | M

2271 Broadway (81st St.), 1/9 to 79th St., 212-595-9071 ➊
2015 Broadway (69th St.), 1/9 to 68th St./Lincoln Ctr., 212-595-7662 ➊
1120 Madison Ave. (83rd St.), 4/5/6 to 86th St., 212-717-6702
1332 Third Ave. (bet. 76th & 77th Sts.), 6 to 77th St., 212-517-5548
1049 Third Ave. (62nd St.), 4/5/6/F/N/R/W to 59th St./Lexington Ave.,
212-688-4044
Staten Island Mall, 2655 Richmond Ave., Staten Island, 718-370-8679 ➊
877-449-6932; www.gymboree.com

■ Customers turn cartwheels for this "happy place to shop" and its "cute as a button", "color-themed" tots' clothing at "affordable prices"; the "adorable" collection driven selection is "great for coordinating a look", plus it's "generally durable" enough to "stand up through multiple washings" and maybe even "through siblings"; but less-adventurous shoppers pout that the "bright" shades are "flashy", concluding it's "better for babies and younger kids."

Gym Source 🆂   ▽ 27 | 21 | 22 | E

40 E. 52nd St. (bet. Madison & Park Aves.), 6 to 51st St., 212-688-4222;
888-496-7687; www.gymsource.com

■ The source indeed for the revolutionary Cybex ArcTrainer, plus "quality" cardio equipment from brands like Cybex, Nautilus and True, for the home, office or commercial gym, this two-floor Midtown offshoot of the East Coast chain also gets customers pumped with a "great selection" of free weights, benches, strength machines and accessories; the knowledgeable staff also provides "good service" – just ask Robert De Niro, said to be among the satisfied customers.

Hable Construction 🆂🅲   – | – | – | M

230 Elizabeth St. (bet. Houston & Prince Sts.), R/W to Prince St.,
212-343-8555; www.hableconstruction.com

The Hable sisters opened their NoLita boutique in a cozy space with tin ceilings and a garden out back, but their merch – bold-patterned felt-appliqué pillows and playful, printed placemats, runners and fabric – is of the moment; every fashionista needs one of their magazine bags – from demure ones, which hold this month's issues, to giant totes that can contain a year's worth.

Hammacher Schlemmer & Co. S | 24 | 23 | 20 | VE |

147 E. 57th St. (bet. Lexington & 3rd Aves.), 4/5/6/F/N/R/W to 59th St./ Lexington Ave., 212-421-9000; 800-421-9002; www.hammacher.com

■ "Techno geeks dream" of "clearing their first million to shop daily" at this "toy store for the rich and unconventional" in the East 50s, where "all the things you'll never need", including two-way radio wristwatches and mega-pixel picture-taking binoculars, are "tested for quality, presented with abundant information" and come with a "lifetime warranty"; "take visitors" and show them "what people are capable of inventing" – along with what they're "prepared to spend."

H&M ●S | 15 | 13 | 8 | I |

1328 Broadway (34th St.), B/D/F/N/Q/R/V/W to 34th St./Herald Sq., 646-473-1165

558 Broadway (bet. Prince & Spring Sts.), R/W to Prince St., 212-343-2722

515 Broadway (bet. Broome & Spring Sts.), R/W to Prince St.; 212-965-8975

640 Fifth Ave. (bet. 51st & 52nd Sts.), E/V to 5th Ave./53rd St., 212-489-0390

435 Seventh Ave. (34th St.), 1/2/3/9 to 34th St./Penn Station, 212-643-6955

125 W. 125th St. (Lenox Ave.), 2/3 to 125th St., 212-665-8300

Kings Plaza, 5100 Kings Plaza, Brooklyn, 2/5 to Brooklyn College/ Flatbush Ave., 718-252-5444

Queens Ctr., 90-15 Queens Blvd., Queens, G/R/V to Woodhaven Blvd., 718-592-4200

www.hm.com

❷ The "crazy throngs" and "horrendous lines" might make you "feel like you're at an *NSync concert" when you "jump into" this Swedish "madhouse" of fashion, but all the "disposable designer wanna-be clothing" is "trashy, flashy and so dirt cheap it doesn't matter"; avoid "peak" weekends, "buy in bulk" and indulge in a "guilt-free" "scavenger hunt" for all sizes of threads "du jour" for "punk rock clubs" and "last minute outfits" without "going broke" – translation: "$1.50 for earrings? I'm sold!"

Harris Levy S | 23 | 12 | 19 | M |

278 Grand St. (bet. Eldridge & Forsyth Sts.), B/D/S to Grand St., 212-226-3102; 800-221-7750; www.harrislevy.com

■ "Madison Avenue linens at less than Madison Avenue prices" is the mantra at this 1894 "Lower East Side landmark" where five "generations of [Levy] family pictures grace the walls"; savvy shoppers head here for a "beautiful selection of the best linens" – from 600-thread-count imported sheets to "special orders"; just don't let the queue at the counter or the "ask-for-it method of shopping" deter you.

Harry's Shoes S C | 23 | 17 | 20 | M |

2299 Broadway (83rd St.), 1/9 to 86th St., 212-874-2035; 866-442-7797; www.harrys-shoes.com

■ A "great example of a family shoe store", this "hectic" "Upper West Side institution" stocks a "multitude" of "premium brands", both domestic and imported, and a "good selection for the little ones"; the "amazingly old-school" "sassy" "salespeople seem to actually know something about footwear – what a concept!" and "just like when you were a kid" will even "measure your feet" ("if you have any fit or comfort issues these are the people to see"); just "avoid it on weekends", when it can be a "footloose" "madhouse" and "more crowded than Jones Beach in July."

HARRY WINSTON 29 | 29 | 26 | VE

718 Fifth Ave. (56th St.), E/V to 5th Ave./53rd St.; N/R/W to 5th Ave./ 59th St., 212-245-2000; 800-988-4110; www.harrywinston.com

■ "Jeweler to the stars", Academy Awards–night regular and the *Survey*'s No. 1 for Fashion/Beauty, this neo-classical Midtown icon's "name carries [as much] weight" as its celebrated sparklers ("who knew diamonds could be so big?") "that leave many speechless"; the "pinnacle of elegance" for the "elite, celebrities and moguls" may seem "a little snobbish" to mere mortals just looking, but "serious customers" who "have the money to spend" find "service impeccable."

Harry Zarin [S] 24 | 11 | 16 | M

318 Grand St. (bet. Allen & Orchard Sts.), F/J/M/Z to Delancey/ Essex Sts., 212-925-6112; www.harryzarin.com

■ This "nicely redone" "Lower East Side institution" purveys "rolls and rolls of discounted" home fabrics from bold-faced names and related hardware in a "new, organized presentation" encompassing three huge floors, including a custom design showroom at entry level; the "low-profile" staff can be "very generous with the scissors" ("lucky you if you sew"), plus it's hard to "beat them for price"; N.B. a post-*Survey* renovation may outdate the above Presentation score.

Harvey Electronics [S] 26 | 21 | 20 | VE

2 W. 45th St. (bet. 5th & 6th Aves.), B/D/F/V to 47-50th Sts./Rockefeller Ctr., 212-575-5000; 800-254-7836; www.harveyonline.com

◪ "Serious listeners" and those who "need hands-on guidance" through the full-frequency spectrum of 7.1 channel surround processors, integrated amplifiers and belt-driven turntables shop for the "ultimate gear" at this Midtown "high-end" "Disney World of flat-screen TVs", home theaters and "major stereo systems"; but since it's priced "for that wealthy electronics guy", it's "a great place" only "if you're Bill Gates."

HASTINGS TILE & IL BAGNO COLLECTION 26 | 27 | 20 | VE

230 Park Ave. S. (19th St.), 4/5/6/L/N/Q/R/W to 14th St./Union Sq., 212-674-9700; 800-351-0038; www.hastingstilebath.com

■ "Out-of-the-ordinary" and "up-to-the-moment" bathroom tiles as well as a "gorgeous selection" of sinks and fixtures attract "informed" customers to this "terrific" showroom off Union Square Park; the staff can "help you design your space", and the products are "nicely presented" in an "inspirational" fashion, but, alas, for wallet-watchers the prices are purely "aspirational."

Hat Shop, The [S][C] ▽ 25 | 25 | 25 | E

120 Thompson St. (bet. Prince & Spring Sts.), C/E to Spring St., 212-219-1445; www.hatsny.com

■ There's "something for everyone" at this Thompson Street atelier teeming with topper temptations; the "fantastic selection" from the owners' own line, plus 30 independent milliners, covers every nook and cranny and ranges from the practical to the all-out indulgent; the "amazing Linda" Pagan and her "terrific" staff will help you select the look that's right for your face, and don't forget: "hats can be made to measure."

Hattitude C ▽ 25 | 25 | 21 | E
93 Reade St. (bet. Church St. & W. B'way), 1/2/3/9 to Chambers St., 212-571-4558

■ "You can't walk out of" this "fun", ultra-feminine TriBeCa hat outpost "without buying something fabulous" fawn fans who fall for "the Emily Brontë heroine look" as well as deco-ish and "sassy, swinging" modern styles; owner Wendy Carrington's "unique" lids are made from "gorgeous" fabrics, many vintage, and they not only "fit and cover your ears", they also "pack wonderfully."

Hazel's House of Shoes S C 19 | 13 | 20 | M
35-16 Bell Blvd. (35th Ave.), Queens, 7 to Main St., 718-631-8412

☑ Set inside a converted house, Bayside's 26-year-old women's shoe emporium is "definitely a place to visit for bride and bridesmaid shoes" ("great dyeables" with "quick turnaround"), plus it also draws bargain hounds hunting for "evening slippers and handbags" at "outlet prices"; the selection can be "hit or miss" and varies by season, so you "gotta be lucky" or revisit often.

Heights Kids S – | – | – | E
85 Pineapple Walk (bet. Cadman Plaza & Henry St.), Brooklyn, 2/3 to Clark St., 718-222-4271

The height of convenience for mamas and papas, this Pineapple powerhouse carries everything but furniture for wee ones; parents praise the small but carefully chosen selection of strollers from brands like Bugaboo and Maclaren, car seats and baby gear that's the best of the best and also reach for the newborn–toddler apparel, from Catimini, Baby Dior and Zutano, as well as the huge array of wooden and educational toys from brands like Brio and Selecta; N.B. at press time, a new branch at 93 Pineapple Walk was slated to open.

Helene Arpels ▽ 28 | 25 | 25 | VE
470 Park Ave. (bet. 57th & 58th Sts.), 4/5/6/F/N/R/W to 59th St./ Lexington Ave., 212-755-1623

■ Proudly impervious to trends, this ladies' shoe salon of a certain age caters to the "well-heeled" "Park Avenue set" with a collection of "original" pumps, loafers and boots; no pointy toes or sky-high stilettos here – just "classic", colorful leather for day and jewel-encrusted satin and suede for night, along with a few suits and alligator purses; a plush gray-and-pale-blue showroom filled with Oriental rugs and tapestried chairs displays these emblems of elegant good taste.

Helmut Lang S C 24 | 25 | 16 | VE
80 Greene St. (bet. Broome & Spring Sts.), R/W to Prince St., 212-925-7214; www.helmutlang.com

■ Once you get the hang of Lang, admirers say, this is one of those SoHo stores that "justifies an expensive purchase", as "you'll be wearing it years later"; the immediate gratification lies in a "minimal interior" filled with "S&M-meets-career" suits, T-shirts and jeans for men and women – mostly black, white or neutrals – made in high-tech, stretchy "used-by-NASA materials" offset by luxe pieces in silk and cashmere; "prices are in outer space too"; N.B. a post-*Survey* refurb may outdate the above Presentation score.

Helmut Lang Parfums S · · · · · · · · · · · · · · 24 | 24 | 19 | E

81 Greene St. (bet. Broome & Spring Sts.), R/W to Prince St., 212-334-3921; 866-814-5264; www.helmutlang.com

■ The well-known designer opened this freestanding store directly across from his flagship boutique in SoHo as a showcase for his own line of "nice" perfumes, bath-and-body products and men's colognes; while the setting evokes the aesthetic of an old-world apothecary, performance artist Jenny Holzer's LED tribute to scent pulsing atop one of the walls adds an avant-garde element.

HENRI BENDEL S · · · · · · · · · · · · · · · · · · 24 | 24 | 20 | VE

712 Fifth Ave. (56th St.), E/V to 5th Ave./53rd St.; N/R/W to 5th Ave./ 59th St., 212-247-1100; 800-423-6335

☑ Enter the "extravagant" realm of this Fifth Avenue "jewel box" (complete with landmarked Lalique windows), which combines the "cachet" of a "small boutique" (with new concept shops opening 24/7) with the "selection of a large" emporium; it's famed for its "gold-standard cutting-edge beauty brands" on the main floor, and up the winding staircase lies an "eclectic mix" of jewelry, handbags and hats, plus the "latest and greatest" jeans and womenswear from emerging designers "high-styled for the young and the young-at-heart – and size"; however, some say the staff, though "helpful", can turn "hoity-toity" before handing over the "legendary" brown-and-white-striped shopping bag.

Henry Lehr S C · · · · · · · · · · · · · · · · · · 24 | 17 | 22 | E

268 Elizabeth St. (bet. Houston & Prince Sts.), B/D/F/S/V to B'way/ Lafayette St.; 6 to Spring St., 212-343-0567
232 Elizabeth St. (bet. Houston & Prince Sts.), B/D/F/S/V to B'way/ Lafayette St.; 6 to Spring St., 212-274-9921

■ These "cool and casual" NoLita lairs capture a lion's worth of "genuinely buyable stuff" for "young, slick shoppers", who like to browse among their "great selection of [designer] jeans", "hip boy/girl T-shirts and "cute gloves" to construct the ultimate more-in-the-know-than-thou uniform; P.S. bargain hunters wait for the "season's-end sale racks outdoors" (in summer).

Here Comes the Bridesmaid ● · · · · · · · · · 18 | 7 | 12 | M

238 W. 14th St. (bet. 7th & 8th Aves.), A/C/E/L to 14th St./8th Ave., 212-647-9686; www.bridesmaids.com

☑ "A bride looking to save her girls some money should visit" this Chelsea shop of "cheapie treasures" where bridesmaid dresses featured in "typical bridal magazines" await; but critics counter that the "sad presentation", "cast sloppily on racks", "looks like the backstage of a high school theater dressing room", adding that "appointments are overbooked."

HERMÈS C · 28 | 27 | 23 | VE

691 Madison Ave. (62nd St.), N/R/W to 5th Ave./59th St., 212-751-3181; 800-441-4488; www.hermes.com

■ For "posh" Parisian "perfection", nobody outdoes this "open and airy" Upper Eastsider (with an art gallery atelier) for "quality, style and status" goods, especially when it comes to "superbly made" scarves ("are eight too many?"), "ties that are the stuff of legend", the much-"lusted"-after Kelly and Birkin bags, and lesser known Plume and Constance purses; "don't be intimidated by the hype" – a doorman welcomes you in and salespeople are "approachable", if sometimes cobbled by the "crowds of tourists"; in the land of luxury, "this store is king", so prepare to "overpay at the palace"; N.B. at press time, Jean Paul Gaultier was slated to design a woman's ready-to-wear collection.

Hervé Leger [S] [C] 25 | 27 | 22 | VE

744 Madison Ave. (bet. 64th & 65th Sts.), 6 to 68th St., 212-794-7124

◪ The French designer behind the bandage dress – made famous by red-carpet star Kim Cattrall – fills up the lavender interior of his sleek two-story Madison Avenue boutique with curvaceous clothes, stilettos, handbags and seductive extras; even those wanting "more innovation, please" like being treated in a very European way with a glass of wine or champagne or a dab of his legendary perfume in the downstairs lounge before settling in to shop.

H. Herzfeld ▽ 25 | 18 | 21 | VE

507 Madison Ave. (bet. 52nd & 53rd Sts.), E/V to 5th Ave./53rd St., 212-753-6756; www.herzfeldonline.com

◪ Offering a "well-edited" selection of "high-end menswear" and accessories since 1890, this "reliable" Midtowner represents "one of the last of the classics, with European quality and tradition" (e.g. the custom-made shirt and suit service); perhaps its "fashion sense is a bit stuck in a rut" – "nothing purchased here will ever scare the horses" – but most "gottaluvit" for its "stuffy, timeless" appeal.

Hickey Freeman [S] 25 | 24 | 24 | VE

666 Fifth Ave. (bet. 52nd & 53rd Sts.), E/V to 5th Ave./53rd St., 212-586-6481; 888-603-8968; www.hickeyfreeman.com

■ In its "beautiful" two-year-old Fifth Avenue store, this "old standby" (since 1899) offers up "conservatively stylish", "well-constructed" "American tailored suits" "made from the finest material" and proffered by "expert help" who understands "that corporate look"; whether you opt for custom-made, off-the-rack or something from the "Bobby Jones collection of country-club lifestyle sportswear", the garments will "fit like a glove" (as indeed they should, given the "eye-popping prices"); P.S. suit buyers, "make sure to spring for the second pair of pants."

Hiponica ◐ [S] [C] – | – | – | E

238 Mott St. (bet. Prince & Spring Sts.), 6 to Spring St., 212-966-4388; www.hiponica.com

This "sweet", pastel-colored NoLita handbag spot is "chic, hip, mod and cool" all in one breath; the "cute" and clean-lined numbers by owner-designer Jem Filippi are done up with interesting details in felt, leather, flannel, velvet and nylon in offbeat color pairings that appeal to streamlined ladies with laptops and a well-honed sense of whimsy.

H.L. Purdy [C] 27 | 23 | 23 | VE

1195 Lexington Ave. (81st St.), 6 to 77th St., 212-737-0122
1171 Madison Ave. (86th St.), 4/5/6 to 86th St., 212-249-3997 [S]
971 Madison Ave. (76th St.), 6 to 77th St., 212-794-2020
501 Madison Ave. (52nd), E/V to 5th Ave./53rd St., 212-688-8050
www.hlpurdy.com

■ "Perfectionists in both designs and lenses", this "expensive but stylin'" Madison Avenue eyewear outfit (with a Lexington branch offering a children's center) is staffed with "meticulous" opticians offering "impeccable service"; "year after year", "this is the place to go if you need new specs" vow vision questers who are also purdy pleased that prescriptions can be filled for everything from "elegant" gold and jeweled frames to binoculars, opera glasses and even telescopes.

HMV ⊘S | 21 | 18 | 13 | M |

565 Fifth Ave. (46th St.), 4/5/6/7/S to 42nd St./Grand Central, 212-681-6700
308 W. 125th St., A/B/C/D to 125th St., 212-932-9619
www.hmv.com

☑ "More of an event than a music/video/book" emporium, with an "open layout and listening stations" where you can tune into "popular stuff", these chainsters stock "everything you might ever want to listen to or watch"; while fans find it a "favorite" source for "cool imports" with a "terrific" classical department too, mega-store cynics sniff it's "a bit pricey", offering "nothing special or different."

HOGAN SC | 23 | 26 | 23 | VE |

134 Spring St. (bet. Greene & Wooster Sts.), C/E to Spring St.,
212-343-7905; 888-604-6426

■ Bringing a "little boho to SoHo", this "interesting" shop (Tod's "exciting" sibling) dispenses "downtown conservative-hip chic" by way of "sublimely comfy" "funky footwear" and "terrific bags"; it's "always worth a visit" fawn fashionistas, who hotfoot it over for a host of "uncommon products" from "fabulous sneakers" to "great everyday loafers"; sure, the merchandise is "very expensive", but most insist it's "worth the money."

Hold Everything ⊘S | 19 | 19 | 16 | M |

1309 Second Ave. (69th St.), 6 to 68th St., 212-879-1450
104 Seventh Ave. (16th St.), 1/9 to 18th St., 212-633-1674
800-421-2264; www.holdeverything.com

☑ "Everything you need to get your ducks in order", and your closet, kitchen, bathroom and bookshelves too, is the point of these Chelsea and East Side stores providing "practical" "storage" "solutions" for "obsessive-compulsive people" and anyone living in a "cramped New York City apartment"; but penny-pinchers find them "pricey" and suggest you "use shoeboxes instead."

Holland & Holland | ▽ 28 | 27 | 24 | VE |

50 E. 57th St. (bet. Madison & Park Aves.), N/R/W to 5th Ave./59th St.,
212-752-7755; www.hollandandholland.com

■ Founded in 1835 as a firearms maker, this venerable British company aims "for the horsey set" (or "well-off wanna-be" men and women) who set their sights on "truly top-of-the-line" tweedy threads, "safari clothes" and "sporting books and accessories"; P.S. "even if you don't shoot, don't miss the bespoke guns on the top floor" of the East 50s townhouse.

HOLLYWOULD ⊘ | 27 | 25 | 23 | E |

198 Elizabeth St. (bet. Prince & Spring Sts.), 6 to Spring St.,
212-343-8344; www.ilovehollywould.com

■ "As the name suggests", designer Holly Dunlap's "NoLita treasure", decorated with blue walls, awning-striped benches and a luxe chandelier, is "all about glamour"; the "whimsical", brightly colored, "fun party shoes", "flashy heels" in "wild patterns" and "sexy" stilettos are not only "eye-catching, they're actually comfortable" to boot; the "to-die-for" selection appeals to "dollar-laden ladies with pooches as small as their purses" and celebs like Mena Suvari and Liv Tyler.

Home Depot ◐ [S] 22 | 13 | 15 | I

50-10 Northern Blvd. (bet. 49th & 50th Sts.), Queens, Q/R to Northern Blvd., 718-278-9031; 800-430-3376; www.homedepot.com

Additional locations throughout the NY area

◪ "Bigger is better" boast buffs of these "über-hardware stores" that are a "DIYer's dream", with "everything you could ever need", even "the little thingy that goes with the whatsit"; critics complain of "chaos" caused by "long lines at check-out" ("bring your overnight bag") and a staff that's adept at "playing deaf"; still, the "tremendous selection" and "great prices" lead many to plead "please come to Manhattan", and as we go to press, plans are afoot to do just that.

Homer – | – | – | VE

939 Madison Ave. (bet. 74th & 75th Sts.), 6 to 77th St., 212-744-7705; www.homerdesign.com

After hitting the Whitney, the design-driven can pop a few doors down to this East 70s contemporary furniture store where European and American pieces share space with the dark-stained chaises, shelves and beds designed by the owner, architect/designer Richard Mishaan.

Hooti Couture ◐ [S] [C] 22 | 23 | 25 | M

321 Flatbush Ave. (7th Ave.), Brooklyn, B/Q to 7th Ave., 718-857-1977

■ "Always a fun stop" when in Prospect Heights, this "delightful" antique-clothing store specializes in daytime and dressy duds from the 1940s on, with a "terrific selection of vintage bags" and "good furs"; the "live wire" "owner, who's got a great eye and the gift of gab", "refers to items as if they were people ('isn't she a beauty?')", and the sayings she scrawls on the garment tags (e.g. 'the dress I turned Ed down in') are, well, a hoot.

Hotel Venus by Patricia Field ◐ [S] [C] 20 | 23 | 17 | M

382 W. Broadway (bet. Broome & Spring Sts.), C/E to Spring St., 212-966-4066; www.patriciafield.com

■ Check into SoHo's "dominatrix-wear" dominion, owned by *Sex and the City* costumer Patricia Field; it's "like shopping at a circus" as you peruse the "eccentric, over-the-top club" and "drag queen" garb, (slightly) more sedate pieces from labels like Heatherette, House of Field and designers from around the world, plus lingerie, C. Ronson undies and menswear; other features include a Hello Kitty section and a beauty salon.

Hot Toddie [S] [C] – | – | – | E

741 Fulton St. (bet. S. Elliott Pl. & S. Portland St.), Brooklyn, C to Lafayette Ave., 718-858-7292; www.hottoddieonline.com

Cool styles for wee hipsters (infants through size 8) abound at this fairy-tale-esque boutique on the Clinton Hill/Fort Greene border aglow with chandeliers, gilt-framed mirrors and displays made from old French carriages; stylin' mamas coddle sons and daughters with Diesel, Marie Chantal and Dolce & Gabbana clothing and offbeat Paulina Quintana lap T-shirts and onesies; there's even a small selection of baby's first jewelry and a friendly staff to help stumped gift-givers; N.B. at press time, plans were underway to open a toy store nearby.

House of Oldies **C**
– | – | – | M

35 Carmine St. (bet. Bleecker St. & 6th Ave.), A/C/E/F/S/V to W. 4th St., 212-243-0500; www.houseofoldies.com

Your house would need a basement a city block long if you were storing 700,000 discs too; this thirtysomething labor of love hawks near-mint, mint and still-sealed vinyl of every conceivable non-classical genre, including out-of-print 45s, 78s and LPs (and no discs or tapes); if you've got a hankering for Elvis Presley's original Sun Studio singles or a *Sgt. Pepper* picture disc, they've got 'em, but you can only pick 'em up noon–5 PM Tuesday–Saturday, when they're open.

Housing Works Thrift Shop **S**
20 | 17 | 16 | I

306 Columbus Ave. (bet. 74th & 75th Sts.), 1/2/3/9/B/C to 72nd St., 212-579-7566
202 E. 77th St. (bet. 2nd & 3rd Aves.), 6 to 77th St., 212-772-8461
157 E. 23rd St. (bet. Lexington & 3rd Aves.), 6 to 23rd St., 212-529-5955
143 W. 17th St. (bet. 6th & 7th Aves.), 1/9 to 18th St., 212-366-0820
www.housingworks.org

■ If such a thing as a posh thrift is possible, this "quirky, mod" quartet certainly qualifies for its "great cross-section" of "high-quality merchandise" (particularly "cool picks" in furniture), often arrayed in "amusing window displays"; the seasoned say "for the best selection, shop early" in the day; N.B. a fifth branch is slated to open spring 2004.

Howard Kaplan Antiques & Bath Shop **C**
▽ 28 | 28 | 19 | VE

827 Broadway (bet. 12th & 13th Sts.), 4/5/6/L/N/Q/R/W to 14th St./Union Sq., 212-674-1000; www.howardkaplanantiques.com

◪ The beautiful facade of this Village store seems straight out of Paris' Left Bank, and inside, on its second floor, you'll find French antique and reproduction bathroom fixtures, plumbing, mirrors, lighting and accessories, from *grande* copper tubs to *petite* soap dishes; though its unique wares inspire *amour*, alas, it's "way too expensive" for many.

H. Stern **C**
24 | 24 | 22 | VE

645 Fifth Ave. (51st St.), E/V to 5th Ave./53rd St., 212-688-0300; 800-747-8376; www.hstern.net

■ Boasting over 150 stores worldwide, this Brazilian-based firm carries "classically creative", "artistic", timeless jewelry that "you can actually picture wearing"; the modern space makes it "comfortable to walk in and browse" among the precious and semiprecious stones, arranged by themes and the "passionate salespeople" are "customer-friendly"; while pieces can be pricey, many are "more reasonable than most Fifth Avenue jewelers."

H2O Plus **◗ S**
20 | 20 | 17 | M

650 Madison Ave. (60th St.), 4/5/6/F/N/R/W to 59th St./Lexington Ave., 212-750-8119
460 W. Broadway (bet. Houston & Prince Sts.), R/W to Prince St., 212-505-3223
800-242-2284; www.h2oplus.com

■ These white-and-blue Madison Avenue and SoHo toiletries stores feature a "sleek", mostly water-based line of bath and skincare products, along with perfumes, that "make you feel like you're on a tropical island"; reasonable prices also make them "great for gifts" for girls of all ages.

Hugo Boss S | 26 | 25 | 22 | VE |
717 Fifth Ave. (56th St.), N/R/W to 5th Ave./59th St., 212-485-1800; www.hugoboss.com

■ A recent "landmark on Fifth Avenue", this multifloor flagship with a striking facade and endless staircases invites you in for the "ultimate in cool men's [and women's] fashions"; some favor the "great suits" from the luxury Baldessarini line ("a grown-up brand for grown-up style"), while others say it's "the place to go for casual", avant-garde goods from the HUGO label; whichever, there's clearly a little bit of bad boy in every Boss ("so sexy I want to devour my boyfriend when he's wearing it!"); N.B. a new branch has opened in The Shops at Columbus Circle at Time Warner Center.

Hunting World S C | ▽ 18 | 18 | 20 | VE |
118 Greene St. (bet. Prince & Spring Sts.), R/W to Prince St., 212-431-0086; www.huntingworld.com

■ What started as the elite "safari look" in the '60s has since evolved into functional travel-worthy gear for a new generation of "urban gorillas" willing to shell out big bucks at this granite-walled SoHo shop; admirers snag bounty like "quality" Battue nylon handbags and luggage that meet the cold-weather challenge and durable canvas and leather duffles, totes and pouches; but a handful feel poached upon, opining "no reason to pay these prices."

Hyde Park Stationers | 23 | 19 | 21 | E |
1070 Madison Ave. (81st St.), 6 to 77th St., 212-861-5710

■ Established in 1943, this "friendly", "traditional stationery store" with a "professional" "staff that knows its stock" meets Upper East Siders' correspondence needs via shelves of "old favorite" notecard and invitation lines; the "top-notch merchandise" runs the gamut, from select office supplies and "nice wrapping paper" to an "array of unique toys and cards" at "fair prices."

Hyman Hendler & Sons | 25 | 10 | 13 | E |
67 W. 38th St. (bet. 5th & 6th Aves.), B/D/F/N/Q/R/V/W to 34th St./ Herald Sq., 212-840-8393; www.hymanhendler.com

■ "One of a vanishing breed", this 104-year-old Garment Center stalwart spanning three generations carries trimmings plus "all the ribbon you could ever imagine"; "tell them what you are looking for" and a "beautiful selection" ranging from lengths of grosgrain and velvet to novelty and vintage finds "starts to magically appear", in what feels like a "scene out of *Harry Potter*."

Ibiza ● S C | 25 | 23 | 21 | E |
56 University Pl. (10th St.), R/W to 8th St., 212-375-9984
46 University Pl. (bet. 9th & 10th Sts.), R/W to 8th St., 212-533-4614
42 University Pl. (bet. 9th & 10th Sts.), R/W to 8th St., 212-505-9907

■ Set between its two kids' satellites, this "fun" Village boutique is filled with "funky", "phenomenal" women's clothing that "works for all ages and occasions", with an emphasis on "luscious fabrics" and "hippie"-chick styles; Ibiza Kidz at 42 University is a "wonderful" spot to pick up "adorable prints" for tots, from Zutano separates to Petit Bateau T-shirts; and no. 56 a few doors down is "packed with toys" and "an amazing selection" of children's shoes from mostly European lines like Aster, Mod 8 and Primigi.

Ideal Tile
| 21 | 15 | 18 | M |

405 E. 51st St. (1st Ave.), 6/E/V to 51st St./Lexington Ave.,
212-759-2339; www.idealtileimporting.com

■ This outpost of a national franchise located in a small space in the East 50s packs a wallop with its "wonderful selection" of "fairly priced" granite, marble and ceramic kitchen-and-bath tiles that include the most current Italian designs; idealists also exult in the "helpful" staff.

IF S C
| 26 | 22 | 21 | VE |

94 Grand St. (bet. Greene & Mercer Sts.), 6/J/M/N/Q/R/W/Z to Canal St., 212-334-4964

☑ A pioneer (established 1979) in SoHo, this unadorned, loftlike "NYC treasure" keeps its "funky, cool", cutting-edge reputation firmly intact by offering a "terrific selection" for men and women from "avant-garde" European designers like Dries Van Noten, Veronique Branquinho and Martin Margiela that's "typically better than at larger" venues; while some insist the staff is "the best", a few find it iffy, sniffing it's a "bit snooty for no reason."

Il Bisonte S C
| ▽ 24 | 21 | 19 | E |

120 Sullivan St. (bet. Prince & Spring Sts.), C/E to Spring St.,
212-966-8773; 877-452-4766; www.ilbisonte.com

■ Antique fixtures and bison figurines set the tone for this "fabulous" Florence-based company's artisanal men's and women's leather handbags, briefcases, backpacks, totes and small leather goods, available in all shapes and sizes at this airy SoHo haven; ask for the "gorgeous" natural vegetable-tanned vacchetta leather – it starts out as a rich honeyed shade and gets deeper, darker and richer-looking with age; N.B. a new branch is planned for early 2004.

Illuminations
| 21 | 23 | 18 | M |

873 Broadway (18th St.), 4/5/6/L/N/Q/R/W to 14th St./Union Sq.,
212-777-1621; 800-226-3537; www.illuminations.com

■ "As trendy wax shops go, no one holds a candle to" this chain whose "beautifully lit", "tranquil" interiors "provide an excellent antidote to city craziness"; partisans are positively glowing about the "splendidly presented", "lovely displays" of merchandise and the "addictive", "amazing scents", and if your funds are tapering, "head to the sale items in the back for great deals."

Il Makiage S C
| 22 | 18 | 17 | M |

107 E. 60th St. (Park Ave.), 4/5/6/F/N/R/W to 59th St./Lexington Ave.,
212-371-0551; 800-722-1011; www.ilmakiage.com

■ Owner Ilana Harkavi opened this pioneering East Side cosmetics boutique back in 1972, and it's still a good destination for a "wide range" of colors – over 500 shades of nail polish, lipstick, eyeshadow and blush – textures and formulas, plus expert advice.

Il Papiro S C
| 25 | 23 | 21 | E |

1021 Lexington Ave. (bet. 73rd & 74th Sts.), 6 to 77th St., 212-288-9330

■ Fans of flame-stitched designs declare "very few stationery stores [match] the quality" of this Upper Eastside "haven" that makes you feel as if "you've been whisked" "to a shop in Florence"; "it's always nice to have or give a little Italian charm", evident in "a wide variety of guises", from "elegant, old-world writing supplies" and "high fashion papers", "desk blotters, picture frames" and hand-bound leather accessories to wastebaskets and tissue boxes, all awash in "marble mania", plus several prints, woodblock patterns and solids.

Ina 🅂   23 | 18 | 13 | E

208 E. 73rd St. (bet. 2nd & 3rd Aves.), 6 to 68th St., 212-249-0014
262 Mott St. (bet. Houston & Prince Sts.), 6 to Spring St., 212-334-2210
21 Prince St. (bet. Elizabeth & Mott Sts.), B/D/F/S/V to B'way/
Lafayette St., 212-334-9048
101 Thompson St. (bet. Prince & Spring Sts.), C/E to Spring St.,
212-941-4757
www.inanyc.com

☑ Clotheshorses who "really wanted, but couldn't afford, that Prada suit" last year head to these "high-end designer hideouts", consignment shops "well stocked" with "recent-season castoffs" that are "definitely still in style" (not much "funky fashion" here); loyalists laud the "attention to display" (especially for the "amazing shoes") and disregard "the unhelpful staff"; N.B. the Mott Street branch is men's only.

Industrial Plastic Supply Co.   23 | 11 | 14 | I

309 Canal St. (Mercer St.), 6/J/M/N/Q/R/W/Z to Canal St.,
212-226-2010; www.yourplasticsupermarket.com

■ The "funky interior designer", "nightclub" owner or "artist in you" "can find the weirdest things and get some creative ideas" at this "cool" Canal Street "mini-museum of plastic products" that also specializes in signage, point-of-purchase displays, decals and such services as etching and silk screening; the "cavernous", "worn-out" shop "is your place for pink duck cut-outs" and other "quirky but useful" "cheap, delightful crap" – just "make sure they" laser "cut to [your] specifications."

Infinity 🅂   22 | 11 | 16 | E

1116 Madison Ave. (83rd St.), 4/5/6 to 86th St., 212-517-4232

☑ "Trend central" for the "private school crowd", this Madison Avenue magnet draws throngs of "soon-to-be-teens" and full-fledged adolescents who "love" to burrow through the "hip clothing" from Juicy Couture and Miss Sixty, fancier finds that "fill the bill for bat mitzvahs" and "adorable accessories" in "oh-so-cramped" quarters; but a few parents find the layout "frustrating for adults", suggesting "wait outside for your girls" or choose "a quiet time to go."

Ingo Maurer Making Light 🅂   – | – | – | VE

89 Grand St. (Greene St.), A/C/E/ to Canal St., 212-965-8817;
www.ingo-maurer.com

This lighting store in a landmarked SoHo building showcases the eponymous German-born designer's lyrical creations like his signature 'Lucellino Lamp', a bulb with wings; the "intriguing concepts" and use of unusual materials and technology have led to collaborations with luminaries like Issey Miyake and exhibitions at MoMA and the Philadelphia Museum of Art.

Innovation Luggage ●🅂   19 | 13 | 14 | M

2001 Broadway (68th St.), 1/9 to 66th St./Lincoln Ctr., 212-721-3164
1755 Broadway (bet. 56th & 57th Sts.), 1/9/A/B/C/D to 59th St./
Columbus Circle, 212-582-2044
300 E. 42nd St. (2nd Ave.), 4/5/6/7/S to 42nd St./Grand Central,
212-599-2998

(continued)
Innovation Luggage
521 Fifth Ave. (bet. 43rd & 44th Sts.), B/D/F to 42nd St./6th Ave.; 4/5/6/7/S to 42nd St./Grand Central, 212-986-4689
670 Sixth Ave. (21st St.), 1/9 to 23rd St., 212-243-4720
1186 Third Ave. (69th St.), 6 to 68th St., 212-717-2740
866 Third Ave. (52nd St.), E/V to 5th Ave./53rd St., 212-832-1841
www.innovationluggage.com

◪ "Soft-sided, hard, inexpensive and expensive, there's something for everyone", from Kipling to Tumi to Victorinox, at this recently renovated Northeast chain of luggage emporiums; but the less-impressed can't handle the "cloying service" and carry on that it's "priced for businessmen", advising "look elsewhere" or wait for the "good buys on close-outs."

Innovative Audio 🖲🄲   ▽ 27 | 21 | 21 | VE
150 E. 58th St. (bet. Lexington & 3rd Aves.), 4/5/6/F/N/R/W to 59th St./Lexington Ave., 212-634-4444; www.innovativeaudiovideo.com

■ Now a solo act after closing its Brooklyn Heights branch, this East 50s home-entertainment source remains a "favorite", having sold the hottest devices via the "soft-sell approach" for 30 years; the "superlative" staff "just hooks up the equipment in a listening room and leaves you alone" for your date with "that special speaker", component or VCR/DVD combo.

Intérieurs 🄲   – | – | – | E
149-151 Franklin St. (bet. Hudson & Varick Sts.), 1/9 to Franklin St., 212-343-0800; www.interieurs.com

Beautiful exposed-brick TriBeCa store featuring plush upholstered contemporary furniture and lighting from the French company Modénature, along with Chinese antiques, Asian-inspired tables and furry flokatis.

INTERMIX 🖲🄲   24 | 20 | 16 | E
210 Columbus Ave. (bet. 69th & 70th Sts.), B/C to 72nd St., 212-769-9116
125 Fifth Ave. (bet. 19th & 20th Sts.), R/W to 23rd St., 212-533-9720
1003 Madison Ave. (bet. 77th & 78th Sts.), 6 to 77th St., 212-249-7858
www.intermixonline.com

◪ "Label-conscious" "FITs (fashionistas-in-training)" "won't go home empty-handed" from this "dangerously enticing" chain with its "discriminating", "well-edited" mix of "I-can't-believe-how-much-I-spent-but-I-had-to-have-it" women's clothing, shoes and accessories; an "easy-to-navigate" layout ("by color scheme") encourages you to "max out daddy's AmEx", but beware the "brutally honest" staffers, especially if you're "above a size 4."

International Center   22 | 19 | 18 | M
of Photography 🖲🄲
1133 Sixth Ave. (43rd St.), B/D/F/V to 47-50th Sts./Rockefeller Ctr., 212-857-9725; 800-688-8171; www.icp.org

■ "A photo lovers delight", ICP's Midtown shop is a "real resource" for shutterbugs; though it doesn't sell prints, "search and ye shall find the perfect postcard for collector friends", posters, videos and a "wonderfully extensive book collection" ("think of the coffee table potential!"), including limited editions autographed at Friday night signings; "buffs" snap up novelty cameras including the Pop 9, the Spy Cam and the Fry Cam, plus an "enticing array" of frames and albums to show off the results.

International Cutlery
▽ 23 | 21 | 19 | E

(fka Hoffritz)

367 Madison Ave. (bet. 45th & 46th Sts.), 4/5/6/7/S to 42nd St./ Grand Central, 212-924-7300; 866-487-6164; www.internationalcutlery.com

■ "There's no place like" this East 40s castle of cutlery sprawled over 15,000 sq. ft. with over 2,000 products, including 60 different pairs of scissors; though it's no longer affiliated with Hoffritz, it still carries "great knives" and other "good-quality" specialty items that are crafted in Germany.

Intrepid Sea-Air-Space Museum S
20 | 18 | 19 | M

Pier 86 (12th Ave. & 46th St.), C/E to 50th St.; A/C/E to 42nd St./ Port Authority, 212-957-7061; www.intrepidmuseum.org

■ The fleet is in – and now, so is the British Airways Concorde – with a cargo-hold full of "fun clothes" and "good trinkets for kids", "ex-Navy wives (they just love those hats)" and uniform fetishists at this "unbelievable" museum store for military-history paraphernalia; the duplex space is located in the Visitor's Center next to the Hudson River aircraft carrier, so landlubbers don't have to board ship to shop.

IS: Industries Stationery ●S C
▽ 22 | 23 | 20 | M

91 Crosby St. (bet. Prince & Spring Sts.), R/W to Prince St., 212-334-4447; www.industriesstationery.com

■ "If you are paper obsessed", update "your stationery wardrobe" with the "nice selection" of date books, journals, calendars and photo albums at this SoHo shop; you'll find a "streamlined" range, but one with a "specific color and print point of view" in designs featuring bold geometrics and "so cool" graphics that will make you want to "start writing immediately."

Isa S C
– | – | – | E

88 N. Sixth St. (bet. Berry & Whythe Sts.), Brooklyn, L to Bedford Ave., 718-387-3363

Guys and dolls responding to the word "hip" stock their closets at this Williamsburg shop–cum–gallery space that's frequently host to cool art exhibitions and music shows; sink into a comfy couch and contemplate the "unparalleled style" of clothing from the likes of Marc by Marc Jacobs, Missoni, YSL and United Bamboo, plus limited edition Nikes, all "excellent" enough to make Manhattanites "cross the bridge" at prices "not for the faint of cash."

ISSEY MIYAKE C
27 | 26 | 22 | VE

119 Hudson St. (bet. Franklin & N. Moore Sts.), 1/9 to Franklin St., 212-226-0100 S

992 Madison Ave. (77th St.), 6 to 77th St., 212-439-7822 www.isseymiyake.com

■ "Is it clothing or sculpture?" – a little bit of both insist acolytes of the "truly innovative", "immensely wearable" men's and women's garb by the boundary-breaking Japanese designer; whether it's displayed in the "art-world" setting of the TriBeCa flagship (a Frank Gehry–designed "21st-century" space that's a "wonder to behold") or the original Madison Avenue location, prices are "higher than the sun", but the "unpretentious" salespeople let you browse the "wild styles" and "eye-catching" accessories and are always "there if you need them."

Jacadi 🆂🅲　　　25 | 23 | 19 | VE
1296 Madison Ave. (92nd St.), 6 to 96th St., 212-369-1616
787 Madison Ave. (bet. 66th & 67th Sts.), 6 to 68th St., 212-535-3200
1260 Third Ave. (bet. 72nd & 73rd Sts.), 6 to 68th St., 212-717-9292
5005 16th Ave. (bet. 50th & 51st Sts.), Brooklyn, D/M to 50th St.,
718-871-9402
www.jacadiusa.com
◪ "Pretend you live in Paris and dress your child accordingly" at these "well-appointed" Upper East Side and Brooklyn chain links where it's a "delight to shop" for "classic", "European-style" baby and children's apparel (0-12 yrs.), "beautiful bedding, accessories" and playthings ("there are no softer soft toys in NYC"); while touters trumpet the "top-notch" togs as "worth every dime", scoffers rebel against the "fussy clothes", "hefty prices" and "snobby" staff.

Jack Spade 🆂🅲　　　22 | 23 | 20 | E
56 Greene St. (bet. Broome & Spring Sts.), C/E to Spring St.; R/W to
Prince St., 212-625-1820; www.jackspade.com
■ "More props than actual goods" make Andy Spade's "cool, but not contrived" SoHo "jewel box of updated schoolboy nostalgia" – think "model airplanes and hi-fis" – a "special place to visit"; the "manly hunks of leather and canvas" – "good-looking stuff, from bags and wallets" to luggage and briefcases – sport the "minimal" "look of a Kate" design, "but for dudes"; while ambiance-seekers swoon over the "overall aesthetic", modernists muse it should "move into the next century."

Jaded 🆂🅲　　　▽ 21 | 19 | 17 | M
1048 Madison Ave. (80th St.), 6 to 77th St., 212-288-6631;
www.jadedjewels.com
■ Jaded jewelry lovers may be rejuvenated by the "different items" at this Madison Avenue boutique, most of which are created by the owners; the handmade, "interesting semiprecious" works and "good copies of serious pieces" use 22 karat gold-plate and the historic lost-wax casting process to make meticulous replicas of antiquarian and Renaissance designs.

JAMES ROBINSON 🅲　　　28 | 27 | 25 | VE
480 Park Ave. (58th St.), 4/5/6/F/N/R/W to 59th St./Lexington Ave.,
212-752-6166; www.jrobinson.com
■ This "top-drawer", "museum"-like Midtown mecca for antique silver and jewelry is pricey but "worth it" for the privilege of owning a patrician piece of the past, be it belle epoque baubles by Cartier and Tiffany or historically inspired designs from Helen Woodhull; the "knowledgeable" staff can also show you "gorgeous" Georgian and Victorian porcelain dinner sets from Spode and Minton.

James II Galleries, Ltd. 🅲　　　26 | 22 | 23 | VE
11 E. 57th St., 4th fl. (bet. 5th & Madison Aves.), 4/5/6/F/N/R/W to
59th St./Lexington Ave., 212-355-7040; www.james2.com
■ Situated on the fourth floor of an East 57th Street building, this mirror- and needlepoint-adorned boutique aims for a British-townhouse feel and appeals to "English aristocrat" clients "or the equivalent" seeking something "unique", like a gold-mounted seal necklace; "when my dad doesn't know what my mom wants", these experts in 19th-century decorative arts, antiques and fine jewelry "know, offering the most personal service, but at a price – what a price!"

Jamie Ostrow C
24 | 23 | 20 | E

876 Madison Ave. (bet. 71st & 72nd Sts.), 6 to 68th St., 212-734-8890

☑ "If you're looking for paper with panache", including some of the "cutest invitations in town", tear over to this airy Madison Avenue stationer, a "classy", "costly" standby for celebs and matrons alike for over 20 years; bright colors, "tasteful" graphics and contemporary, "unique" typefaces seal the deal: "it's enough to make me give up e-mail and start writing letters again"; still, some say it's "overpriced" and wish the personnel were "more pleasant."

Jamin Puech S
– | – | – | E

247 Elizabeth St. (bet. Houston & Prince Sts.), 6 to Spring St., 212-431-5200

Old-world wooden showcases and a princely tufted couch set the tone for a dizzying array of super-groovy French purses festooned with finery like fringe, ruffles, topstitching and sequins, all tempered by a patchwork of understated, earthy hues; pricey it may be, but this little NoLita light, newly rekindled and relocated from its former Mott Street digs, gets extra credit for inspiration.

Jammyland ●S C
– | – | – | M

60 E. Third St. (bet. 1st & 2nd Aves.), F/V to Lower East Side/2nd Ave., 212-614-0185; 888-664-7369; www.jammyland.com

Hey mon, dis is de "real" 'ting for vintage reggae in the East Village, with fresh-off-the-boat British and Jamaican reissues in cassettes, CDs and platters from Marley to (Eek-a) Mouse, plus some new African and Latin sounds; the staff is "knowledgeable and always willing to help out", and you can pick up a T-shirt or sweatshirt for those cold nights in Jamaica (Queens).

Jam Paper & Envelope ●S
19 | 11 | 15 | I

611 Sixth Ave. (bet. 17th & 18th Sts.), F/L/V to 14th St./6th Ave.; 1/9 to 18th St., 212-255-4593
111 Third Ave. (bet. 13th & 14th Sts.), 4/5/6/L/N/Q/R/W to 14th St./ Union Sq.; L to 3rd Ave., 212-473-6666
www.jampaper.com

■ The "quirky selection" is the star at these East Village and Flatiron "no-frills" "warehouses for paper" where some "digging" through the "cluttered shelves" yields "beautiful" stationery, envelopes, bags and "fun office supplies" at "bargain" prices; the goods are "great for spurring creative ideas", particularly for "do-it-yourself" projects involving "neon colors."

J&R MUSIC & COMPUTER WORLD ●S
25 | 17 | 17 | M

15-23 Park Row (bet. Ann & Beekman Sts.), R/W to City Hall, 212-238-9000; 800-221-8180; www.jandr.com

■ This "fabulous" "family-owned" "institution" "has taken over Park Row" to become a "one-stop" "electronics nirvana" for "everything you need and want", including "all the newest gadgets" hawked by "knowledgeable" staffers who "won't take you to the cleaners"; a few steps out the door and around the corner you'll find "entertainment heaven" featuring a "vast selection" of CDs (including "straight-ahead jazz" and classical recordings), DVDs and videos at "decent prices"; the "crowds" "are not for the faint of heart", however, so "pick an off-time to go"; N.B. there's also a J&R Camera outlet down the block.

Janet Russo ⬛🅲　　　　　　▽ 20 | 19 | 19 | E

262 Mott St. (bet. Houston & Prince Sts.), 6 to Spring St.; N/R to Prince St., 212-625-3297; www.janetrusso.com

■ "100 percent girl" sums up this NoLita boutique whose mustard colored walls with dusty-rose paneling and crystal chandeliers light up the vintage-inspired "romantic", beaded, embroidered dresses and separates in "beautiful" silks and cottons that "fit very well", although some say there "aren't too many different cuts" to choose from; still, such whimsical extras as straw and velvet purses and Vietnamese good-luck dolls and shoes, hats and jewelry make up for any lack on the racks.

Jane Wilson-Marquis 🅲　　　　　　▽ 25 | 24 | 25 | E

130 E. 82nd St. (bet. Lexington & Park Aves.), 4/5/6 to 86th St., 212-452-5335
155 Prince St. (bet. Thompson St. & W. B'way), C/E to Spring St., 212-477-4408 ⬛
www.bridalgowns.net

■ "If you want something richly elegant", make an appointment at this English designer's SoHo and Upper East Side boutiques, "recommended for every bride-to-be" searching for the "dress of her dreams"; the "one-of-a-kind" silk "couture creations" are turned out in "exquisite designs", many in "Elizabethan and Renaissance-type" styles, and embellished with embroidery and appliquéd roses, plus there's also a ready-to-wear line offering simpler gowns, eveningwear and bridal party options; "everyone from the salespeople to the seamstress is helpful."

Janovic Plaza ⬛　　　　　　21 | 15 | 18 | M

1150 Third Ave. (67th St.), 6 to 68th St., 212-772-1400; 800-772-4381; www.janovic.com
Additional locations throughout the NY area

◩ "Go nowhere else" fawn followers of these paint, wallpaper and window-treatment stores that provide the "best places for decorating ideas", offering "easy, do-it-yourself" solutions, a "good selection" and "great value"; service, however, "ranges from pleasant and helpful to downright rude", and some dis the product display's "disorganization."

Jay Kos 🅲　　　　　　25 | 22 | 22 | VE

986 Lexington Ave. (bet. 71st & 72nd Sts.), 6 to 68th St., 212-327-2382
475 Park Ave. (bet. 57th & 58th Sts.), 4/5/6/F/N/R/W to 59th St./ Lexington Ave., 212-319-2770

◩ "The place to go for your inner dandy – and at these prices, your inner Rockefeller", this East 70s "classic" is one of "the most original New York men's stores" (and boy's, too, in this location); the "dapper owner" and his house brand's "original designs" offer a unique twist on traditional suits and shirts and to match, "great" Borsalino hats, Edward Green bespoke shoes and Brigg umbrellas; still, a few miffed sniff it's a mite "snooty"; N.B. the Park Avenue branch opened post-*Survey*.

Jazz Record Center　　　　　　– | – | – | M

236 W. 26th St., 8th fl. (bet. 7th & 8th Aves.), 1/9 to 28th St., 212-675-4480; www.jazzrecordcenter.com

Hidden in an eighth-floor Chelsea suite is a "jazz lover's paradise" thick with "unbelievable" vinyl, "unusual CDs", posters, books, magazines and such endangered species as musicians' one-sided, homemade acetate platters; the staff knows its stuff, riffing on inventory from compilations to Charlie Parker's *The Bird Blows the Blues*, said to be the very first LP he ever pressed.

J.CREW ●S
19 | 18 | 16 | M

91 Fifth Ave. (bet. 16th & 17th Sts.), 4/5/6/L/N/Q/R/W to 14th St./ Union Sq., 212-255-4848
347 Madison Ave. (45th St.), 4/5/6/7/S to 42nd St./Grand Central, 212-949-0570
99 Prince St. (bet. Greene & Mercer Sts.), R/W to Prince St., 212-966-2739
30 Rockefeller Plaza (bet. 5th & 6th Aves.), B/D/F/V to 47-50th Sts./ Rockefeller Ctr., 212-765-4227
South Street Seaport, 203 Front St. (bet. South & Water Sts.), 2/3/ 4/5/A/C/J/M/Z to Fulton St./B'way/Nassau, 212-385-3500
800-562-0258; www.jcrew.com

☑ "Conservatives" Crew-sing for the "perfect preppy fix" of "well-done", "white-bread" T-shirts, chinos, belts, sweaters, bathing suits and flip-flops gush "if I could die in a clothes store, it would be" in this "orderly, appealing" chain; "mellow colors" and "nice styles that stick around for more than one season" evoke "a drive through the country in a convertible with a dog in the backseat", a scenario that cosmopolitan style-mavens call a "snoozefest"; N.B. a new branch has opened in The Shops at Columbus Circle at Time Warner Center.

Jean Paul Gaultier ●
▽ 27 | 24 | 20 | VE

759 Madison Ave. (bet. 65th & 66th Sts.), 6 to 68th St., 212-249-0235; www.jeanpaul-gaultier.com

■ Fashion's original bad boy – he's the man who clad Madonna in her cone corset – favors the Starck (as in über-architect Philippe) approach in his Upper East Side shop (think crystal fixtures, quilted, flesh-toned taffeta walls and a movie-screen entrance flickering with exotic imagery 24/7); it all creates a sexy boudoir of "terrific" men's and women's clothing, accessories and JPG jeans, but some argue the selection doesn't represent "the best" of this "visionary."

Jeffrey New York ●S
24 | 23 | 20 | VE

449 W. 14th St. (bet. 9th & 10th Aves.), A/C/E/L to 14th St./8th Ave., 212-206-1272

☑ With its concrete floors and hip-hop music, this is clearly not your mother's department store, but an "ultra-mod" Meatpacking District pioneer that inspires raves for its "godlike" footwear (from Gucci to Prada, the "most comprehensive selection of high-fashion lines" in town) and "packed racks" of "unique", "slick" menswear; there's also a "carefully selected" array of women's designers, plus cosmetics and fine, contemporary jewelry for those "impulse purchases"; of course, "cool comes with a cost", but most pay up for the "best of the current season's best"; N.B. a new home-furnishings section features finds like Venini vases.

Jelena Behrend Studio
– | – | – | M

188 Orchard St. (bet. Houston & Stanton Sts.), F/V to Lower East Side/ 2nd Ave., 212-995-8497

This pioneering Lower Eastside designer dazzles her disciples (who range from retailers to rock stars) with "beautiful", intricate silver and gold bands, cuff and chain link bracelets, cocktail rings and pendants, which can be custom-engraved with messages, plus engagement rings made with diamonds, sapphires and emeralds; if it seems to have "little stock", be patient – the goods are being hand-hammered in the back room.

Jennifer Convertibles ●S 15 | 13 | 13 | M
902 Broadway (20th St.), R/W to 23rd St., 212-677-6862;
www.jenniferfurniture.com
Additional locations throughout the NY area
☑ "Functional furnishings at a reasonable price" is what supporters say about this sofa-bed chain that offers an "above-average selection of fabric choices" for hideaway beds that come in handy for "unexpected and expected quests" alike; but the unconverted complain about the lack of design "style", less than sterling service and the strict return policy – it's verboten.

Jensen-Lewis ●S 21 | 19 | 19 | M
89 Seventh Ave. (15th St.), 1/2/3/9 to 14th St., 212-929-4880;
www.jensen-lewis.com
■ Chelsea stalwart selling "funky", "very modern furniture and accessories" at "less-than-you-would-find-elsewhere" prices; design devotees dote on its American Leather Collection and "cool" tables and beds from Baronet and dub the "interesting", appropriately "apartment-sized" home furnishings here "New York living friendly."

Jewish Museum, The S 22 | 21 | 19 | M
1109 Fifth Ave. (92nd St.), 6 to 96th St., 212-423-3211
Jewish Community Center, 334 Amsterdam Ave. (76th St.), 1/9 to
79th St., 646-505-5730
www.jewishmuseum.org
■ The recently renovated shops at this Upper East Side museum perform "a mitzvah in themselves", "offering very special" "tchotchkes" and "gorgeous Judaica", from "books, housewares, decorations", music and toys to an expanded selection of "unusual jewelry" and "elegant, expensive religious items" just perfect for "bar mitzvah and wedding gifts"; N.B. the newly opened branch inside the J.C.C. in the West 70s has a funkier, more contemporary feeling.

Jill Platner SC – | – | – | E
113 Crosby St. (bet. Houston & Prince Sts.), R/W to Prince St.,
212-324-1298; www.jillplatner.com
Hidden behind blue doors on an oft-overlooked stretch of SoHo's Crosby Street lies a serene, utilitarian world where Platner's sculptural, organically shaped silver and gold jewelry is shown in wrought iron cases; she's "one to watch", as evidenced by the "amazing designs", which include necklaces and bracelets strung on colorful cords, hammered earrings and rings and dramatic leather cuffs; a slinky red bench and gigantic mobile signal you've arrived at the right place.

Jill Stuart SC ▽ 22 | 21 | 13 | E
100 Greene St. (bet. Prince & Spring Sts.), C/E to Spring St.; R/W to
Prince St., 212-343-2300; www.jillstuart.com
☑ This young NYC native's "feminine" style grabbed the spotlight in *Clueless,* but her "sexy" dresses, denims and doodads actually have an in-the-know twist; the two-story SoHo store, her only retail outlet, has lots of "funky" merchandise – though not much in

"real-people sizes" say regulars who avoid the "less-than-friendly" staff and tramp downstairs to the vintage collection below.

Jil Sander
25 | 25 | 21 | VE

11 E. 57th St. (bet. 5th & Madison Aves.), 6/E/V to 51st St./ Lexington Ave., 212-838-6100; 800-704-7317; www.jilsander.com

■ "Glad she came back to the fold" fawn fans who believe "Jil's return" this past spring to the Prada-owned German design house "adds freshness" to the "conservatively different" collection for men and women, displayed on floating racks in this "sleek", "beautiful" white-walled, limestone-floored, "easy-to-shop" East 57th Street flagship; "if streamlined is needed, this is the place" – "these minimalist yet timeless" "ultrachic" pieces offering an "exquisite fit" in "luxury fabrics" will live in "your wardrobe forever", plus the "competent staff knows the line well."

Jimmy Choo
27 | 25 | 19 | VE

645 Fifth Ave. (51st St.), 6/E/V to 51st St./Lexington Ave., 212-593-0800
716 Madison Ave. (bet. 63rd & 64th Sts.), 4/5/6/F/N/R/W to 59th St./ Lexington Ave., 212-759-7078
www.jimmychoo.com

■ For "hot, hot, hot, high-heeled high-end" stilettos that impart "an instant *Sex and the City* look", slither over to this Fifth Avenue "nirvana" and its new Madison Avenue flagship; the "drop-dead", "fabulous" "fairy-tale" "foot jewels" (created by Tamara Mellon and Sandra Choi) "aren't shoes, they're works of art" and so "coveted" that just "being seen in them is exhilarating"; while Choo-aholics claim these "must-haves" (including boots and handbags) are "worth a pinch or two on the foot" and the wallet, even they admit that "dealing with the snooty service" can bring you down to earth.

Jimmy Jazz ●⑤
▽ 19 | 17 | 12 | M

Fulton Mall, 442 Fulton St. (Bridge St.), Brooklyn, 2/3 to Hoyt St., 718-246-0427
Additional locations throughout the NY area

◙ Phat Farm, Sean Jean, Ecko Unltd. and Rocawear are some of the hot urban labels attracting jazz hounds to this borough-wide chain that's "great for jeans and other casual clothes that cost more elsewhere"; admirers applaud the extensive "range of sizes, in addition to a big-and-tall section" in most locations, along with name-brand athletic shoes; "that rap music has to go", though.

Jimmy's ⑤⑥
23 | 18 | 17 | VE

1226 Kings Hwy. (bet. 12th & 13th Sts.), Brooklyn, B/F/Q to Kings Hwy., 718-645-9685

■ It's out of the way for Manhattanites, but this boutique off Coney Island Avenue is not only "worth the trip", it ain't no sideshow to loyalists enticed by its "wide-ranging", well-edited inventory of "expensive, but pretty great" European designer clothes; the "nice", "good people selling" this top-of-the-line "stuff" are serious about high fashion, whether it's delivered in a cocktail dress, extravagant gown or men's jacket.

Jim Smiley ⑤
– | – | – | M

128 W. 23rd St., 2nd fl. (bet. 6th & 7th Aves.), 1/9/C/E to 23rd St., 212-741-1195; www.jimsmileyvintage.com

On the second floor of a Chelsea townhouse, a cozy living room–like setting surrounds an array of elegant women's (and some men's) vintage clothing – much of it bearing the original sales tags – mainly from the 1900s–1960s; mint-condition Norell and Balenciaga pieces fetch four figures, but most of the merch, from old-time emporiums like La Maison Blanche, costs under $200.

J.J. Hat Center **C** ▽ 24 | 19 | 25 | E
310 Fifth Ave. (bet. 31st & 32nd Sts.), B/D/F/N/Q/R/V/W to 34th St./ Herald Sq., 212-239-4368; 800-622-1911; www.jjhatcenter.com
■ "The real thing for classic men's" toppers with a few women's tossed in, this Garment Center favorite "keeps you well covered" (along with bigwigs like Pierce Brosnan and Ted Danson) with everything from "gangster styles" to "sexy Latin panamas"; this "old-timey" standby has been peddling hats since 1911, so it's no wonder the "experienced staff knows and loves" their *chapeaux.*

J. Leon Lascoff & Son 24 | 22 | 23 | E
1209 Lexington Ave. (82nd St.), 4/5/6 to 86th St., 212-288-9500; www.jleonlascoff.com
■ This "vintage" 1899 Upper East Side pharmacy "takes one back in time" to "the grandeur of the past", but carries "high-quality", contemporary beauty and bath products, "sophisticated European" imported items and "hard-to-find travel medications"; "civilized" service adds to the "classic, old-world" feel.

J. Lindeberg Stockholm **S C** ▽ 22 | 23 | 18 | E
126 Spring St. (Greene St.), C/E to Spring St.; R/W to Prince St., 212-625-9403
■ "Adventurous fashion types" find a "fantastic, sexy European line" at this "very trendy" 1970s-style store in SoHo, "primarily stocked with men's clothes" by a Swedish designer; devotees dig the "fairly tight-fitting" duds that are "way too hip for work, but good for the weekend", especially if you "want to be a rock star, baby!"

J. Mavec & Company **C** – | – | – | VE
946 Madison Ave. (74th & 75th Sts.), 6 to 77th St., 212-517-7665; www.jmavec.com
Small, serene Upper East Side boutique showcasing a dainty collection of precious pieces; though some think it offers "the most beautiful antique jewelry to be found" (mostly 19th- and early 20th-century), it also carries vintage-inspired works by Janet Mavec herself, plus designers Otto Jakob and Gabriella Kiss; N.B. at press time, plans were afoot to move to a still-to-be-determined location.

J. McLaughlin **S C** 20 | 20 | 17 | E
1311 Madison Ave. (bet. 92nd & 93rd Sts.), 6 to 96th St., 212-369-4830
1343 Third Ave. (77th St.), 6 to 77th St., 212-879-9565 ●
☑ No *"Preppy" Handbook* required when it comes to shopping at this warm, homey, "tasteful" 22-year-old Upper East Side standby; the button-down-and-khakis set asserts that it's "perfect for that business-casual" look and "good" "updated" "basics", plus they have "a ton of women's clothes too"; still, wallet-watchers wail that it's "wildly overpriced" "for the product offered."

J. Mendel **S C** ▽ 20 | 23 | 21 | VE
723 Madison Ave. (bet. 63rd & 64th Sts.), 4/5/6/F/N/R/W to 59th St./ Lexington Ave.; 6 to 68th St., 212-832-5830
■ "Ask your sugar daddy to buy you a present" at this "wonderful" East 60s fur salon with its champagne-colored walls, grand chandelier and mosaic floor; despite its "many years" in business,

this fifth generation company's coats and accessories (luxe hats, gloves and even purses) are "always cutting-edge" and they now even offer ready-to-wear and couture eveningwear; of course, "the prices are pure retail, but hey – it costs to look this stylish"; N.B. a post-*Survey* refurb may outdate the above Presentation score.

J.M. Weston C | 27 | 23 | 21 | VE |

812 Madison Ave. (68th St.), 6 to 68th St., 212-535-2100;
877-493-7866; www.jmweston.com

■ The "very well-made", "so comfortable" handcrafted footwear from this 111-year-old French line may set you back a pretty euro, but the men and women who pay homage at this Madison Avenue "shoe cathedral" find with proper care and costly resoling by expert in-store cobblers (who use materials from Limoges), "you'll keep them for life"; the timeless styles range from loafers to wing tips, and there's even a collection from designer Michel Perry.

Joan Michlin Gallery S C | 25 | 24 | 24 | E |

449 W. Broadway (bet. Houston & Prince Sts.), R/W to Prince St.,
212-475-6603; 800-331-1335; www.joanmichlin.com

■ Joan Michlin "goes back to the earliest Lincoln Center crafts fairs", but she "remains one of the best contemporary" jewelers, creating wearable "works of art" that are "impeccably" designed; manned by a "hard-selling, but very pleasant staff", her Victorian-style SoHo store's "a great place for gifts and peace offerings."

Joël Name Optique de Paris C | 24 | 23 | 24 | E |

65 W. Houston St. (Wooster St.), R/W to Prince St., 212-777-5888

■ Blonde and sleek, as in wood and lighting, this SoHo eyewear shop staffed with "helpful" optometrists is home to a "nice variety" of high-end, "well-made" designer frames; the "great glasses" – ah, "*now* I can see the price tag!" – come in out-of-sight styles like Judith Lieber's super-glam crystal-encrusted specs; P.S. "they also do repairs and lens replacement on vintage" numbers.

Joe's Fabrics and Trimmings S | ▽ 24 | 12 | 16 | I |

102-110 Orchard St. (Delancey St.), F/J/M/Z to Delancey/Essex Sts.,
212-674-7089; www.joesfabric.com

■ A "terrific selection" of designer fabrics for upholstery and draperies, plus trimmings on the first floor imported from France and Italy, all "at rock-bottom prices", abounds at this "super" store on the Lower East Side; "the help is really helpful" – and "if they don't have it, they'll get it" for you.

John Derian Company S C | ▽ 27 | 25 | 21 | E |

6 E. Second St. (Bowery), F/V to Lower East Side/2nd Ave.,
212-677-3917; www.johnderian.com

■ Decoupage devotees descend on the East Village on-site studio and shop of this eponymous owner for his "fabulous" vases, plates and paperweights decorated with vintage prints of flora, fauna and old letters; also adding to the atmosphere is a cache of charming Indian linens and French quilts, antique Chinese mirrors and carefully chosen odds and ends with "a twist on traditional style."

John Fluevog Shoes ● S | 23 | 21 | 19 | M |

250 Mulberry St. (Prince St.), R/W to Prince St., 212-431-4484;
800-381-3338; www.fluevog.com

■ Whether you're "a teen who hangs out" Downtown, "young at heart" or "bold and brazen" like Fluev-fans Marilyn Manson,

White Stripes drummer Meg White, Chlöe Sevigny and Gina Gershon, this Canadian mini-chain's NoLita offshoot is bound to help you "stand out from the crowd"; the "funkiest" "shoes with more personality than should be legal" are hawked by "tough, but amiable" sales folk, many sporting "different color hair every time" you pop by, in a cool setting that "makes you feel at home."

John Lobb 27 | 25 | 26 | VE

680 Madison Ave. (bet. 61st & 62nd Sts.), 4/5/6/F/N/R/W to 59th St./ Lexington Ave., 212-888-9797

■ "If you have to ask how much, don't even come" to this Madison Avenue "pinnacle" of "hands-down", the "best men's footwear available"; this longtime British subsidiary of Hermès offers handmade, ready-to-wear styles fashioned in England alongside bespoke Parisian-made versions created "the way shoes are supposed to be"; sure, they're "obscenely expensive", but they'll "make you look like a million bucks."

Johnston & Murphy [S] 22 | 19 | 20 | E

520 Madison Ave. (54th St.), E/V to 5th Ave./53rd St., 212-527-2342
345 Madison Ave. (44th St.), 4/5/6/7/S to 42nd St./Grand Central, 212-697-9375
888-324-6189; www.johnstonmurphy.com

◪ This grand East 40s and East 50s set of "standbys" offers a "solid, but unremarkable" range of "good basic material for your feet" that just may "satisfy the unadventurous"; the "durable", "well-made business" and dress shoes are doled out with "service that ranges from professional to pretentious."

John Varvatos [S] 24 | 25 | 23 | VE

149 Mercer St. (bet. Houston & Prince Sts.), R/W to Prince St., 212-965-0700; 800-689-0151; www.johnvarvatos.com

■ Rapidly rising toward the "top of the fashion food chain", this men's designer (whose résumé includes Ralph Lauren and Calvin Klein) offers "understated", "distinctly American" but decidedly stylish suitings, plus a "good selection of modern sportswear" and "must-have shoes" in his oak-and-blackened-steel "minimalist store" in SoHo; the "very friendly staff is willing to go the extra mile even if you're not" a celeb client like Hugh Jackman, Tom Cruise or Josh Hartnett.

Jo Malone ◐[S] 26 | 26 | 25 | E

Flatiron Bldg., 949 Broadway (23rd St.), R/W to 23rd St., 212-673-2220; 866-566-2566

■ "One whiff and you're hooked" at this "minimalist" Flatiron store with a "complex concept of layering fragrance" created by British scent-smith Jo Malone (but now under the Estée Lauder umbrella); "light", "natural" "fragrances are made from grocery-store items" like grapefruit and ginger and turned into "top-notch" products for the "body, face and home"; the "sleek" cream-and-black "packaging is also perfect for that special gift."

Jonathan Adler [S][C] 25 | – | 18 | E

47 Greene St. (bet. Broome & Grand Sts.), 6 to Spring St., 212-941-8950; 877-287-1910; www.jonathanadler.com

■ "Original" and "interesting" handcrafted ceramics and textiles have established the eponymous NYC owner/designer nationally (he also has stores in East Hampton and LA); while admirers "adore" his "simple" organic shapes and praise his Peruvian-inspired pillows as "cult items", wallet-watchers whine his star power inspires "astronomical prices"; N.B. a post-*Survey* move to a much larger Greene Street space accomodates more merch like mohair sofas and lacquer tables.

Joon ⓒ | 26 | 20 | 24 | E |

Grand Central, 107 E. 42nd St. (bet. Lexington & Vanderbilt Aves.), 4/5/6/7/S to 42nd St./Grand Central, 212-949-1700 ● ⓢ
782 Lexington Ave. (61st St.), 4/5/6/F/N/R/W to 59th St./Lexington Ave., 212-935-1007
Trump Tower, 725 Fifth Ave. (57th St.), 4/5/6/F/N/R/W to 59th St./ Lexington Ave., 212-317-8466
Winter Garden Atrium, 3 World Financial Ctr. (Vesey St.), 1/2/3/9/ A/C/E to Chambers St., 212-227-0557
800-782-5666; www.joon.com

■ "If it writes and it's beautiful, you'll find it here" say supporters of this mini-chain purveying a "great selection" of "pens as art"; "excellent service" from a "knowledgeable staff" ("if they don't have it, they'll order it") and prices set at "every budget" also get high marks; pen-sive surveyors insist they're "easy to overlook, but worth the effort to find."

Joovay ⓢ ⓒ | 27 | 16 | 24 | E |

436 W. Broadway (bet. Prince & Spring Sts.), C/E to Spring St., 212-431-6386

■ Shimmy into slinky slips, silk chemises, kimono-style vintage *haori* jackets, luxe pajamas and other "fantastic" siren-wear (à la celeb customers like Jennifer Lopez) at this "real lingerie store", a "tiny" top-drawer SoHo standby that offers high-end European and American lines like Cosabella, La Perla's Black Label and Christina Stott; "you feel special here" because the staff is "vested in making you look your sexiest for a night on the town or a night well-spent at home."

Jos. A. Bank ● ⓢ | 18 | 17 | 19 | M |

366 Madison Ave. (46th St.), 4/5/6/7/S to 42nd St./Grand Central, 212-370-0600; 800-285-2265; www.josabank.com

☑ Fondly known as the "poor man's Brooks Brothers", this Midtown outpost of a national chain specializes in "solid-quality, standard-issue business and business-casual" garb; but while "entry-level" executives applaud it as a "reliable source" and "good value", the more fashion-forward sniff the "selection's uninspiring" and chafe at extra costs ("you have to pay for cuffs" on pants); N.B. the first floor was renovated post-*Survey*, which may outdate the above Presentation score.

Joseph ⓢ ⓒ | 25 | 19 | 18 | E |

106 Greene St. (bet. Prince & Spring Sts.), C/E to Spring St.; R/W to Prince St., 212-343-7071 ●
816 Madison Ave. (bet. 68th & 69th Sts.), 6 to 68th St., 212-570-0077

☑ "Six-foot-tall supermodels" pack into the American outposts of this London-based brand, but don't be put off – although "long legs are encouraged", "you can always find a great fit" in the "exciting clothing", particularly the "pretty" "pants that can't be beat"; while the "quality and fabrics are gorgeous", critics complain about a "staff that doesn't offer much assistance"; N.B. the SoHo flagship carries womens- and menswear, but Madison Avenue is for ladies only.

Joseph Edwards 🇸🇨   ▽ 24 | 20 | 24 | M

*500 Fifth Ave. (42nd St.), 7 to 5th Ave.; 4/5/6/7/S to 42nd St./
Grand Central, 212-730-0612*

■ A Fifth Avenue fixture for over 20 years, this Midtowner offers an extensive selection of watches, ranging from Baume & Mercier and Breitling to TAG Heuer and Omega, all at very "fair prices"; but what really makes things tick is the "excellent customer service" and "superb repair" department.

Joyce Leslie 🇸   9 | 8 | 7 | I

20 University Pl. (8th St.), R/W to 8th St., 212-505-5419 ◐
*2147 86th St. (Bay Pkwy.-21st St.), Brooklyn, D/M to Bay Pkwy.,
718-266-0100* ◐
*Georgetown Shopping Center, 2109 Ralph Ave. (Ave. K), Brooklyn,
2/5 to Brooklyn College/Flatbush Ave., 718-251-3219* ◐
*Kings Plaza, 5100 Kings Plaza (Flatbush Ave.), Brooklyn, 2/5 to
Brooklyn College/Flatbush Ave., 718-252-6488* ◐
37-28 Main St. (38th Ave.), Queens, 7 to Main St., 718-353-8419 ◐
*56-48 Myrtle Ave. (bet. Catalpa & Hancock Sts.), Queens, L/M to
Myrtle/Wycoff Aves., 718-381-3031*
*Staten Island Mall, 2655 Richmond Ave., Staten Island,
718-370-1705* ◐
www.joyceleslie.com

☑ "If you want a one-off trashy dress to wear to that party", you'll find "funky runway look-alikes" galore at this "hootchie-wear" chain in the Village and the boroughs; "great for high-schoolers", "club kids" and "drag queens", the "slightly slutty" merchandise "won't even take a nibble of your wallet", though deeper pockets say it's "good for cheap but too cheap to be good."

J. Press   23 | 22 | 23 | E

*7 E. 44th St. (bet. 5th & Madison Aves.), 4/5/6/7/S to 42nd St./
Grand Central, 212-687-7642; 800-765-7737;
www.jpressonline.com*

■ "A classic" praise preppies who proclaim that this Midtown "store is like an alumni visit to your college campus", where you can find "the finest Wasp wear", from "madras jackets" to the "best Ivy League scarves"; seemingly, "the styles never change", so "if you buy a new wardrobe here, people will think you've had it forever."

Judith Leiber   26 | 25 | 23 | VE

*987 Madison Ave. (bet. 76th & 77th Sts.), 6 to 77th St., 212-327-4003;
866-542-7167; www.judithleiber.com*

■ When the Upper East Side status-minded need to make a "sparkling entrance", they're usually clutching one of these evening purses of hand-glued Austrian crystal, exotic- or animal-shaped "little jewels" that have represented the "epitome of accessories" for 40 years; "whimsical", "beautiful", "gaudy", "these bags are everything except practical", but "if money isn't an issue", why not indulge "the movie star in you" and while there, check out the newly introduced line of eyewear and shoes.

Judith Ripka 🇨   25 | 24 | 20 | VE

*673 Madison Ave. (61st St.), 4/5/6/F/N/R/W to 59th St./Lexington Ave.,
212-355-8300; 800-575-3935; www.judithripka.com*

☑ Fair warning – "you can't own just one piece" of the "addictive", "ultra-feminine jewelry" sold in this tiny East 60s boutique offshoot of a nationwide chainlet; all agree the "unique" pieces, especially the signature loop-and-toggle bracelets, convey "such status", but while some claim they "treat you like a queen", others say the approach is less than royal.

Julian & Sara ◐ [S] [C] ▽ 26 | 19 | 13 | VE

103 Mercer St. (bet. Prince & Spring Sts.), R/W to Prince St.; C/E to Spring St., 212-226-1989; www.julianandsara.com

◪ Small and sweet, this SoHo kids' boutique boasts a "wonderful selection" of "unique French and Italian clothing" that's to "be used daily, not just for special occasions"; but the jaded jab that it's just "another chance" for parents and grandparents "to spend too much on children's clothes."

Juno ◐ [S] [C] 19 | 19 | 18 | E

543 Broadway (bet. Prince & Spring Sts.), R/W to Prince St., 212-625-2560

426 W. Broadway (bet. Prince & Spring Sts.), C/E to Spring St., 212-219-8002

www.junoshoes.com

◪ Fashionable men and women snap up "very funky", "exciting" "European shoes" at these SoHo sister shops, including "nice nightlife styles", while hipster kids jet over for "unique" kicks; but not everyone jumps for Juno – the less-impressed find the collection "too clunky" and "expensive for what it is"; P.S. wallet-watchers "wait for the sales" and scoop 'em up by the armload.

Just Bulbs [S] 25 | 14 | 17 | M

5 E. 16th St. (5th Ave.), 4/5/6/L/N/Q/R/W to 14th St./Union Sq., 212-228-7820; www.justbulbs.net

◪ "The name says it all" – there's "every bulb under the sun" (possibly even "a few Edison models in the back") at this specialist once affectionately lampooned by Letterman; it's also "the place" for "odd-sized" incandescent items, LED's European fixtures and "fun, funky" stuff like novelty string lights; still, critics counter it's just "pricey"; N.B. a post-*Survey* move from the Flatiron District to Union Square puts this stalwart next door to its sibling, Superior Light & Fan, and may outdate the above Presentation score.

Just for Tykes [S] [C] 23 | 19 | 20 | E

83 Mercer St. (bet. Broome & Spring Sts.), R/W to Prince St., 212-274-9121; www.justfortykes.com

◪ Spacious and stylish, this "very cool" SoHo store stocks "all the upscale accessories and clothing a mom could ever want for her" offspring, arranged in colorful cubes and racks; aesthetes adore the "everyday casual chic" childrenswear from Catimini, Deux par Deux, Charabia, Kule and Quiksilver and fall for "amazing" nursery furniture lines like Casa Kids and Hic-cup, high-end bedding from Wendy Bellisimo and Nilaya, plus toys from Brio and gear like the Bugaboo stroller.

Just Shades [C] ▽ 20 | 14 | 18 | M

21 Spring St. (Elizabeth St.), 6 to Spring St., 212-966-2757; www.justshadesny.com

◪ This "reliable" NoLita store is "still the tops" to touters seeking toppers for their lamps; it supplies "plain, garden-variety" shades and will also custom-make versions for "hard-to-fit" fixtures or fashion them "from your own fabric"; however, a few doubters are left in the dark by a less than sparkling selection.

Jutta Neumann 🌓 C
▽ 26 | 17 | 22 | E

158 Allen St. (bet. Rivington & Stanton Sts.), F/V to Lower East Side/ 2nd Ave., 212-982-7048; www.juttaneumann-newyork.com

■ Craftsmanship is key to this "fantastic" Lower East Side leather guru who creates "great, original" couture sandals ("the perfect summer flats" that "last forever") in a vast range of colors and styles to your every specification – think Birkenstock meets Balenciaga for hipsters of all stripes – and even takes custom-orders for made-to-measure items; this designer also stitches up "amazing cuffs and bracelets" in leather and silver combinations and a colorful mix of "beautiful, modern bags, belts and wallets."

Kam Man 🌓 S
24 | 11 | 9 | I

200 Canal St. (bet. Mott & Mulberry Sts.), 6/J/M/N/Q/R/W/Z to Canal St., 212-571-0330; www.kammanfood.com

■ "It's an education just walking down the aisles" of this Chinatown supermarket with its cans of quail eggs and barrels of dehydrated fish, but the store's basement also offers "cool stuff" like the "largest selection of everyday Asian dinnerware, tea sets", woks and rice cookers "this side of Beijing", all at "inexpensive" prices.

Kangol S C
20 | 19 | 18 | E

196 Columbus Ave. (bet. 68th & 69th Sts.), 1/9 to 66th St./Lincoln Ctr., 212-724-1172

■ Since 1938, this men's and women's milliner has been topping us off, and now they've opened a "small", "super-cool" Upper West Side flagship that caters to the hip-hop crowd and scenesters alike; the red, white and blue labels on the "hot" selection of "all the hip items you need", including "excellent hats", eyewear, apparel and bags make it easy to go "all Kangol, all the time."

Karens for People + Pets C
21 | 20 | 16 | VE

1195 Lexington Ave. (bet. 81st & 82nd Sts.), 6 to 77th St.; 4/5/6 to 86th St., 212-472-9440; www.karensforpets.com

◪ "There's no place like Karens'" claim two-legged loyalists of this longtime pet shop and salon in the East 80s, where there's a "great selection" of "high-quality" accessories that include alligator and faux-fur clothes and carriers; but detractors deem it too dog-centric and caution "be prepared to spend."

Kar'ikter 🌓 S C
▽ 24 | 22 | 19 | M

19 Prince St. (bet. Elizabeth & Mott Sts.), R/W to Prince St.; C/E to Spring St., 212-274-1966; 888-484-6846; www.karikter.com

■ Sweetly schizophrenic NoLita store that aims at adults as well as *enfants*: the front of the shop sells grown-up amusements like fly swatters and gnome stools from Philippe Starck and "whimsical gadgets from Alessi", while the back features children's books, toys and merchandise inspired by the antics of fictional European characters like Babar, Tintin and Le Petit Prince.

Karkula C
▽ 21 | 22 | 17 | E

68 Gansevoort St. (bet. Greenwich & Washington Sts.), A/C/E/L to 14th St./8th Ave., 212-645-2216; www.karkula.com

■ One look at the leather and felt exterior of this home-furnishings shop in the Meatpacking District lets you know you're in for a "unique" experience; the "selection" of contemporary art, sculpture and porcelain lighting, along with seating and rugs from Paola Lenti, "feels very personal."

Kartell 🅂🅲   24 | 21 | 15 | M

39 Greene St. (bet. Broome & Grand Sts.), C/E to Spring St.,
212-966-6665; 866-854-8823; www.kartell.com
■ Get "chic", "cutting-edge plastic furniture" at "surprisingly low prices" given this store's SoHo location and its "hip", "well-designed products"; among the best-sellers here are Philippe Starck's stylish Ero and Ghost chairs, along with colorful storage from Piero Lissoni and shelving by Ron Arad; small-ticket items like desk accessories and bins also offer affordable splashes of color.

KATE SPADE 🅂🅲   23 | 24 | 19 | E

454 Broome St. (Mercer St.), R/W to Prince St., 212-274-1991;
www.katespade.com
☑ "Nothing says classic American girl" like this designer's "minimum-presentation-maximum-goods" SoHo "accessory museum"; "sweetly sophisticated" "Nantuckety" "classic bags with a kick" and "fabulous jewelry", shoes, paper, PJs and scents appeal to the "modern" woman "who still has time to handwrite a thank-you note" and keeps "spare change in the hundreds"; but patrons put off by the "aloof" service and "pricey stuff" pout "puh-lease, isn't everyone over the phenomenon by now?"; N.B. at press time, plans were afoot to introduce a new tabletop collection.

Kate Spade Travel 🅂🅲   23 | 22 | 18 | E

59 Thompson St. (bet. Broome & Spring Sts.), C/E to Spring St.,
212-965-8654; www.katespade.com
☑ "If you have to travel, why not do it in style" say Spade-philes who saunter over to this SoHo satellite store for satchels, duffels, wheeled suitcases and garment bags kitted out in "trendy" prints, solids and stripes; while aesthetes agree that the pieces are "so refined and expensive you'd be afraid to check them", cynics snap back they're "flimsy and faddish."

KATE'S PAPERIE 🅂   27 | 26 | 19 | E

561 Broadway (bet. Prince & Spring Sts.), R/W to Prince St.,
212-941-9816 ●
1282 Third Ave. (bet. 73rd & 74th Sts.), 6 to 77th St., 212-396-3670
140 W. 57th St. (bet. 6th & 7th Aves.), N/R/Q/W to 57th St., 212-459-0700
8 W. 13th St. (bet. 5th & 6th Aves.), F/V to 14th St., 212-633-0570
888-941-9169; www.katespaperie.com
☑ "E-mail? what e-mail" ask "serious scribes" of this "fabulous" quartet of stationers that the pulp faction calls a "spiritual awakening"; these "magnificent emporiums" abound with "stylish", "unique" goods for the "paper fetishist", as well as "beautiful journals", the "latest and greatest in invitations" and "cool stamps" – plus a gift-wrapping service; ranters ream "ridiculous" prices, but addicts aver "I'd like to send them a thank-you note"; N.B. the recently opened West 57th Street branch offers more high-end papeterie.

Kavanagh's   23 | 19 | 21 | VE

146 E. 49th St. (bet. Lexington & 3rd Aves.), 6 to 51st St.,
212-702-0152
■ "Blass, Beene, de la Renta" – only an "extremely well-heeled selection" of "top-shelf" "designer frocks", "previously owned Manolos", "carefully selected" Chanel and Hermès purses and "impeccable items in stellar condition" are "allowed to reside" at this antiques-furnished East 40s "Mercedes of Manhattan

resale shops"; "it's all fairly pricey, especially for consignment", but few match ex-director of Bergdorf Goodman "Mary Kavanagh's wonderful" personal shopping service and contacts ("she really does know every uptown girl in New York").

Kazuyo Nakano ⏹🇨   – | – | – | E

117 Crosby St. (bet. Houston & Prince Sts.), 6 to Spring St., 212-941-7093; www.kazuyonakano.com
"Everyday elegance with an angular touch" abounds at this simple white SoHo space with lilac and green touches where this Japanese designer, who learned the art of leathermaking from her father, creates an array of "luscious leather bags", totes and "perfect clutches" with more than a wink at the '70s; these industrial-ply skins "last a long time" – "wear it to death and it still looks great!"

KB Toys ⏹   16 | 9 | 9 | I

2411 Broadway (89th St.), 1/9 to 86th St., 212-595-4389 ●
Manhattan Mall, 901 Sixth Ave. (bet. 32nd & 33rd Sts.), B/D/F/N/Q/ R/V/W to 34th St./Herald Sq., 212-629-5386 ●
1411 St. Nicholas Ave. (bet. 180th & 181st Sts.), 1/9 to 181st St., 212-928-4816
877-552-8697; www.kbtoys.com
◪ The "basic" toy "selection is limited but the prices are great" at this national chain where you'll find "bargains all around" (they "tend to reduce the prices on slow-moving merchandise pretty quickly"); it helps to "go in here knowing what you want, since service is limited to ringing up purchases" lob the less game, who also find it "very cramped" and "messy."

KD Dance & Sport ●⏹🇨   ▽ 21 | 15 | 16 | M

339 Lafayette St. (Bleecker St.), 6 to Bleecker St., 212-533-1037; www.kddance.com
■ Designed by two former dancers, "the clothes here can make anyone feel like" a corps member declare devotees who dash over to this bright NoHo shop for "super comfy" wrap tops, jazz pants and fitted shorts in a variety of knit yarns and textures; the om-crowd oohs and ahs over the yoga collection of capris, camis, midriff tees and bodysuits in colors so calm they may send you into a Zen state; N.B. a post-*Survey* renovation may outdate the above Presentation score.

Keiko ⏹🇨   – | – | – | E

62 Greene St. (bet. Broome & Spring Sts.), 6 to Spring St., 212-226-6051; 888-534-5669; www.keikonewyork.com
Whether you want to make waves in a "custom-designed" or an "off-the-rack" directionally styled tankini, bikini or maillot done up in vibrant solids, stripes, mix 'n' match or Op-Art patterns, chances are this Japanese designer carries or can create "your perfect" suit at her SoHo boutique where men also get in the swim with trunks and so-brief bottoms in eye-popping shades; but looking like a bathing beauty "doesn't come cheap", so "be prepared" to shell out.

Kein ⏹   – | – | – | E

(fka La Maison Moderne)
144 W. 19th St. (bet. 6th & 7th Aves.), 4/5/6/L/N/Q/R/W to 14th St./ Union Sq., 212-691-9603; www.kein.com
Gone is the French name (fka La Maison Moderne) and the Gallic theme; now this Union Square lifestyle shop boasts two luxurious

in-house skin care lines as well as silk throws, stainless steel chairs, cabinetry and storage units suitable for sophisticates from any country.

Kelly Christy █C | – | – | – | E

235 Elizabeth St. (bet. Houston & Prince Sts.), R/W to Prince St.;
6 to Spring St., 212-965-0686; www.kellychristyhats.com
When milliner Kelly Christy makes magic behind the white curtain in her tiny NoLita atelier, the results include everything from updated cloches and elegant-shaped fedoras to fancier feathered numbers, custom-creations for a wedding day and men's toppers.

Kenjo C | ▽ 22 | 19 | 20 | E

40 W. 57th St. (bet. 5th & 6th Aves.), N/R/Q/W to 57th St., 212-333-7220
■ Though not well known by our voters, this West 57th store offers a "wonderful selection of watches" for fans of handmade mechanical chronographs or perpetual calendars, including "fine collectors' brands" such as Daniel Roth and Gerald Genta; "decent prices" and "personal service" keep the cognoscenti content.

Kenneth Cole New York ●S | 21 | 20 | 18 | E

597 Broadway (Houston St.), R/W to Prince St., 212-965-0283
353 Columbus Ave. (77th St.), B/C to 81st St., 212-873-2061
Grand Central, 107 E. 42nd St., 4/5/6/7/S to 42nd St./Grand Central,
212-949-8079
95 Fifth Ave. (17th St.), 4/5/6/L/N/Q/R/W to 14th St./Union Sq.,
212-675-2550
Rockefeller Ctr., 610 Fifth Ave. (49th St.), B/D/F/V to 47-50th Sts./
Rockefeller Ctr., 212-373-5800
800-536-2653; www.kennethcole.com
■ Best known for "trend-of-the-moment" footwear that "fits like a glove" ("no cruel shoes here"), this chain is also "a good stop" for "comfortable", "corporate casual" clothes ("black is always the default color of choice"); "granted, they won't win points for originality" – except for their "activist" ads – but "the ordinary chap [or chick] can find something" here; P.S. the "styles are a steal when on sale."

Kentshire Galleries ⊄C | 25 | 26 | 23 | VE

37 E. 12th St. (bet. B'way & University Pl.), 4/5/6/L/N/Q/R/W to
14th St./Union Sq., 212-673-6644; www.kentshire.com
■ It's "fun to just wander in and add to the wish list" at this British antiques-and-decorative-arts specialist in the Village offering a range of furniture, silver and porcelain – primarily Georgian and Regency – arranged in period room settings.

Kidding Around ●SC | ▽ 23 | 19 | 24 | M

60 W. 15th St. (bet. 5th & 6th Aves.), 1/2/3/9/F/L/V to 14th St./6th Ave.,
212-645-6337; www.kiddingaround.us
■ No kidding around, this expanded child-"friendly" Flatiron fun house is stocked with "imaginative toys for infants and up" "not found in department stores"; it's a "great place for gifts", and if you don't know what to buy, "the staff will work with you."

Kids Foot Locker S | 19 | 15 | 13 | M

120 W. 34th St. (bet. 6th & 7th Aves.), 1/2/3/9 to 34th St./Penn Station,
212-465-9041
226 E. Fordham Rd. (bet. Grand Concourse & Valentine Ave.), Bronx,
4/B/D to Fordham Rd., 718-561-4753

(continued)
Kids Foot Locker
5314 Fifth Ave. (bet. 53rd & 54th Sts.), Brooklyn, R to 53rd St., 718-439-4669
466 Fulton St. (Elm St.), Brooklyn, B/M/Q/R to DeKalb Ave., 718-422-7877
Kings Plaza, 5383 Kings Plaza, Brooklyn, 2/5 to Brooklyn College/ Flatbush Ave., 718-951-0710
90-15 Queens Blvd. (67th Ave.), Queens, F to Jamaica/179 St., 718-271-8115
Staten Island Mall, 2655 Richmond Ave., Staten Island, 718-477-1129
www.kidsfootlocker.com
☑ "A playful place", this chain is decorated with colorful displays and filled with "kids' shoes galore", from "basic sneakers" to "cool footwear" (and even athletic wear) from a "few trendy brands"; tots may "have a great time picking out favorites", however, the "uninformed" staff offers almost "no help" at all.

Kid's Supply Co. **S** ▽ | 24 | 24 | 21 | VE
1343 Madison Ave. (94th St.), 6 to 96th St., 212-426-1200;
www.kidssupplyco.com
☑ "If you've got the bucks", this Madison Avenue destination is "the place" to go for kids' bedding, lamps and furniture, which ranges from custom-made desks to solid cherry bunk beds; these investment pieces (for ages two and up) may "last post-college", and almost all of the merchandise can be custom-designed – including linens; still, a few pout it's "too pricey."

KIEHL'S ●**S** 27 | 21 | 24 | M
109 Third Ave. (13th St.), L to 3rd Ave.; 4/5/6/L/N/Q/R/W to 14th St./ Union Sq., 212-677-3171; 800-543-4571; www.kiehls.com
■ "Absolutely the best beauty products" make this "authentic" 1851 East Village "institution" a favorite of surveyors for skin, hair and body booty in "no-frills packaging", including the "world-famous" Lip Balm #1 and the Blue Astringent Herbal Lotion that's "guaranteed to make your zits vanish"; there's a generous "try-before-you-buy" policy, so an "incredibly knowledgeable staff" is "happy to hand out" "plentiful free samples"; N.B. a post-*Survey* expansion includes a new coffee and dessert bar.

Kieselstein-Cord 25 | 25 | 21 | VE
454 W. Broadway (bet. Houston & Prince Sts.), R/W to Prince St., 212-529-9361; 888-252-7009; www.kieselstein-cord.com
■ The gilded if not "gaudy" "array of precious and semiprecious stones", "exciting silver", gold and platinum jewelry, highly "ornamental" animal-themed "belts that make any outfit" and "timeless bags" – "only the best" baubles "from the legend" – can be found at this SoHo accessories "mecca"; "instantly recognizable for the work of art that it is", each "exorbitantly" priced piece can be "spotted a mile away", and for those with bucks to burn, make "impressive gifts."

Kimera **S** **C** – | – | – | M
366 Atlantic Ave. (bet. Bond & Hoyt Sts.), Brooklyn, A/C/G to Hoyt/ Schermerhorn Sts., 718-422-1147
274 Fifth Ave. (bet. 1st & Garfield Sts.), Brooklyn, M/R to Union St., 718-965-1313
www.kimeradesign.com
Back when Park Slope's Fifth Avenue was on the cusp, pioneering Yvonne Chu established a shoebox stuffed with her own Asian-

inspired line of raw-silk separates and special-occasion dresses, with some "gorgeous pieces" doubling as bridal wear, plus accessories from Brooklyn designers; with an additional larger, split-level shop, she's created a "charming" Moroccan-inspired world in Boerum Hill, bringing all of the above, plus furniture, pillows and throws from the Far East, to cutting-edge customers.

Kim's Mediapolis/Mondo/ Underground ◐ [S][C] 25 | 15 | 14 | M

85 Ave. A (bet. 5th & 6th Sts.), L to 1st Ave., 212-529-3410
144 Bleecker St. (bet. La Guardia Pl. & Thompson St.), A/B/C/D/E/F/S/V to W. 4th St., 212-260-1010
2906 Broadway (bet. 113th & 114th Sts.), 1/9 to 110th St., 212-864-5321
6 St. Marks Pl. (3rd Ave.), 6 to Astor Pl.; R/W to 8th St., 212-505-0311
www.kimsvideo.com

◪ On St. Marks Place and up in Morningside Heights are the "coolest" "CD and DVD meccas", where audiovisual "junkies" "fulfill their cravings" for "anything out of the ordinary in movies and music", scoring "gems in the used section" while fans of the other locales satisfy themselves with movie rentals; as for the "punker-than-thou" staff, who "will sneer at you no matter what you ask for", they should know that their "rude" schtick "has become a cliché by now."

Kirna Zabête [S][C] 25 | 24 | 20 | VE

96 Greene St. (bet. Prince & Spring Sts.), R/W to Prince St., 212-941-9656; www.kirnazabete.com

■ A candy-colored supermarket of SoHo style, this "brilliant", ever-evolving showcase for "the next big thing in fashion" is a "Downtown shopping must" proclaim cultists who praise the "devastatingly cool" offerings from Balenciaga, Rick Owens and scads of other "known-and-unknown" designers, as well as the "fun, bright, eclectic" baby and "dog stuff" and jewelry from Trish Becker, among others; walk downstairs to "buy gifts for girlfriends" (e.g. candles, Lulu Guiness cosmetic bags, Kala soaps), or check your e-mail at the in-house Macs.

Kiton [S][C] – | – | – | VE

4 E. 54th St. (bet. 5th & Madison Aves.), E/V to 5th Ave./53rd St., 212-813-0272; www.kiton.it

Made-to-measure menswear usually comes with a British accent but not so here at this Italian tailoring firm founded by Naples-born Ciro Paone, now fitting its signature high-sleeve jackets with puckered pleat shoulders in an elegant East 50s emporium taking up three floors in a classic landmark building.

Kiwi Design [S][C] ▽ 16 | 19 | 22 | E

78 Seventh Ave. (bet. Berkeley Pl. & Union St.), Brooklyn, 2/3/4 to Grand Army Plaza; Q to 7th Ave., 718-622-5551; www.kiwidesignco.com

■ Relocated at press time to a larger, more prominent Seventh Avenue site, this green-and-yellow "fashion outpost", owned by "lovely" Marlene Siegel, a seasoned retailer, and store namesake-designer Christine Alcalay, is "different from the usual" boutique; "it's worth the trip to look at" Kiwi's "beautiful" Audrey Hepburn–esque "creations", and while there, indulge in pants from Sanctuary, plus "easy, cozy" tees and sweaters from other tempting lines.

M | P | S | C

Kleinfeld ◐[S] 24 | 16 | 17 | E

8202 Fifth Ave. (82nd St.), Brooklyn, R to 86th St., 718-765-8500; www.kleinfeldbridal.com

◪ "If you can envision" your designer gown, "they've got it" at this "crazy busy", by-appointment-only Bay Ridge "bridal haven" where "helpful" consultants who know their merchandise "backwards and forwards" "bring the dresses in to you"; "go after you've gotten an education", "otherwise you'll be dazed and confused" by the "outstanding selection"; it's "not the fairy-tale mecca" expected pout the put-off, who proclaim the "pushy staff" may make you "run back to boutique-land"; N.B. there's now a fine jewelry and gift department too.

KMART ◐[S] 12 | 8 | 6 | I

770 Broadway (Astor Pl.), 6 to Astor Pl.; N/R to 8th St., 212-673-1540
250 W. 34th St. (bet. 7th & 8th Aves.), A/C/E to 34th St./Penn Station, 212-760-1188
1998 Bruckner Blvd. (bet. Pugsley Ave. & White Plains Rd.), Bronx, 6 to Parkchester/E. 177th St., then 36 bus to White Plains Rd., 718-430-9439
300 Baychester Ave. (bet. Bartow Ave. & Hutchinson River Pkwy.), Bronx, 6 to Pelham Bay Park, 718-671-5377
66-26 Metropolitan Ave. (bet. Audley St. & Grosvenor Rd.), Queens, M to Metropolitan Ave., 718-821-2412
2660 Hylan Blvd. (Lindbergh Ave.), Staten Island, 718-351-8500
2875 Richmond Ave. (Yukon Ave.), Staten Island, 718-698-0900
866-562-7844; www.kmart.com

◪ For "those on a budget", this "tacky-but-tolerable" "discount chain" provides a "giant" place to "spend a little, get a lot" of household staples and toiletries, "no-frills basics" apparel, "dirt-cheap" orchids and "DVD bargains"; for fans, the "nice range of appliances" and hardware and the Martha Stewart Collections can "actually make it a worthwhile shopping stop"; still, "service is lacking", as evidenced by often "poorly stocked" shelves, "messy" aisles and "unbearable" crowds at check-out.

Knits Incredible [S][C] 22 | 18 | 18 | E

971 Lexington Ave., 2nd fl. (bet. 70th & 71st Sts.), 6 to 68th St., 212-717-0477

■ Recently taken over by Ann Regis, former Gotta Knit owner, editor of *Vogue Knitting* and *Knitter's* magazine and creative director of Stacey Charles Inc., the past partner's company, this Upper East Side shop is still stocked with a "good selection" of "beautiful", "high-end", mostly natural fiber, hand-dyed and novelty yarns, "great buttons" and "creative designs" complete with customer-written directions; the skein-savvy say the "helpful staff" even offers "patient instructions for beginners."

KNITTING HANDS ◐[S][C] 26 | 21 | 23 | M

398 Atlantic Ave. (bet. Bond & Hoyt Sts.), Brooklyn, 2/3/4/5 to Nevins St., 718-858-5648; www.knittinghands.com

■ "Whether you're an experienced" yarnsmith or "just jumped on the bandwagon", this sprawling shop on edgy Atlantic Avenue has "all the goods you need to be a great knitter", as well as a "friendly staff" that helps you "navigate the world" of skeins and needles; "there's quite a bit to select from", in fact, it's one of the few "places to carry lower-end and higher-end" goods, from acrylics to cashmere; P.S. "classes of different levels" are held on the lower level.

Knitting 321 C
▽ 21 | 20 | 20 | E

321 E. 75th St. (bet. 1st & 2nd Aves.), 6 to 77th St., 212-772-2020
■ Stocked with a "beautiful selection of yarns", including natural fibers, plus European and fashion-forward skeins, books and supplies and decorated with a maple table made for gathering, this "friendly" Upper East Side knittery feels like a "secret discovery"; the "helpful owners" offer "hand-holding", making it worth a stop "for novices", plus now they also conduct crochet classes.

KNOLL
27 | 23 | 20 | VE

105 Wooster St. (bet. Prince & Spring Sts.), R/W to Prince St., 212-343-4000; www.knoll.com
■ "It doesn't get much bettter than this" SoHo showroom showing off some of the groundbreaking furniture designs it originally commissioned – Tulip chairs by Eero Saarinen, Cyclone tables from Isamu Noguchi and wire seating by artist Harry Bertoia – that have now become mid-century "classics", along with new contemporary pieces for the home and office.

Koh's Kids S C
26 | 20 | 19 | E

311 Greenwich St. (Chambers St.), 1/2/3/9 to Chambers St., 212-791-6915; www.kohskids.com
■ "Don't let the postage-stamp size fool you" be-Kohs this "gem of TriBeCa" "crams" a "small, but well-chosen selection" of "funky" and "unusual" American and European baby and children's clothing into its "tiny space"; the salespeople actually "help you find the perfect item after figuring out your kid's taste in clothes", ensuring that your offspring may "be the best dressed on the block."

Koos & Co.
– | – | – | VE

1283 Madison Ave., 2nd fl. (bet. 91st & 92nd Sts.), 6 to 96th St., 212-722-9855
As close to a couture atelier as you'll get on the Upper East Side, this unstuffy second-floor shop warmly welcomes both browsers and buyers to view veteran Dutch designer Koos van den Akker's one-of-a-kind, richly embellished, collaged wool and fur coats, jackets and dresses, a look beloved by devotees of (but costing much more than) his Koos of Course! collection seen on QVC.

KRAFT
26 | 21 | 18 | E

315 E. 62nd St. (bet. 1st & 2nd Aves.), 4/5/6/F/N/R/W to 59th St./ Lexington Ave., 212-838-2214; www.kraft-hardware.com
■ Since it opened in 1935, this purveyor of high-end plumbing fixtures, cabinet hardware and bathroom accessories in the East 60s has won a host of acolytes who "worship" the "exceptional custom" work that's delivered "on time"; the "great selection" ("if you can't find it, you aren't looking") and "informative staff" also elicit praise.

Kreiss Collection
▽ 23 | 22 | 20 | VE

215 E. 58th St. (bet. 2nd & 3rd Aves.), 4/5/6/F/N/R/W to 59th St./ Lexington Ave., 212-593-2005; www.kreiss.com
■ This very beige showroom near Bloomies features "ultraposh" upholstered furniture collections that range from European-elegant to California-casual, as well as luxe Italian bed linens; their "big" sectional sofas rival only the size of the "pocketbook" needed to buy them, but for smaller-scaled chairs, chaises and tables, there's the slimmer Sierra Towers Condo line.

Kremer Pigments
– | – | – | M

228 Elizabeth St. (bet. Houston & Prince Sts.), R/W to Prince St.,
212-219-2394; 800-995-5501; www.kremer-pigmente.com
Kremer is a scientist, but he isn't mad; while dry pigments of every hue make the "small" NoLita shop look "like a candy store for artists", the official U.S. outlet for the German doc's "excellent" powders is a sober place where "educated" staffers "give attention to each" painter, restorer, instrument or furniture maker in search of color concentrates, binders, brushes and other raw materials.

Krizia **C**
– | – | – | VE

769 Madison Ave. (bet. 65th & 66th Sts.), 6 to 68th St., 212-879-1211;
www.krizia.net
Think high-fashion Fellini, and you'll know what to expect at this East 60s boutique, home of high-end men's and women's collections designed by Mariuccia Mandelli – synonymous since 1957 with timeless classics with a twist; her embraceable style is reflected in the amiable salespeople, who make it a "pleasure to shop here."

Krups Kitchen & Bath, Ltd. **C**
24 | 11 | 16 | M

11 W. 18th St. (bet. 5th & 6th Aves.), 1/9 to 18th St., 212-243-5787
■ This "small", family-owned Flatiron shop is "stuffed to the ceiling" with such "top appliances" as Wolf and La Cornue stoves, along with bathroom fixtures from Kohler and Toto; "prices are very good for Manhattan", and they also offer a free design service.

La Belle Epoque **S** **C**
▽ 23 | 19 | 18 | E

280 Columbus Ave. (73rd St.), 1/2/3/9 to 72nd St., 212-362-1770;
www.vintageposters.us
■ If you've been seduced by the Paris flea-market look, you can replicate it by decorating your walls with "vintage" posters from this Upper West Side store purveying an "enormous selection" of "pricey but amazing" European advertising prints devoted to products ranging from champagne to chocolate.

La Boutique Resale **S**
21 | 15 | 13 | M

1045 Madison Ave., 2nd fl. (bet. 79th & 80th Sts.), 6 to 77th St.,
212-517-8099
160 W. 72nd St., 2nd fl. (bet. B'way & Columbus Ave.), 1/2/3/9 to
72nd St., 212-787-3098
www.laboutiqueresale.com
☑ Like many of its ilk, this second-floor shop offers recent-season clothes "for the classy woman", with labels like Alaïa and Plein Sud commingling with Chanel and St. John; however, it's "their collection of vintage wear" that makes them stand out among the "Madison Avenue resale crowd", though even fans find the staff *un peu* "pushy"; N.B. there's now a new sib in the West 70s.

La Brea **◐** **S** **C**
19 | 15 | 12 | M

Beacon Hotel, 2130 Broadway (bet. 74th & 75th Sts.), 1/2/3/9 to
72nd St., 212-873-7850
2440 Broadway (90th St.), 1/9 to 86th St., 212-724-2777
500 Lexington Ave. (47th St.), 6 to 51st St., 212-371-1482
1575 Second Ave. (bet 82nd & 83rd Sts.), 6 to 77th St., 212-772-2640
1321 Second Ave. (bet. 69th & 70th Sts.), 6 to 68th St., 212-879-4065
www.labrea.com
☑ "Last-minute" gift shoppers appreciate this mini-chain of "neat novelty shops" known for "unusual cards", "fun T-shirts" and

"gag items that are perfect for the person you sort of know"; though some sniff it's full of "middle-of-the-road tchotchkes", more insist "you can't find the same stuff anywhere else"; P.S. the fact that they're "open late is a plus."

La Cafetière ●S C
−|−|−| M

160 Ninth Ave. (bet. 19th & 20th Sts.), A/C/E/L to 14th St./8th Ave., 646-486-0667; www.la-cafetiere.com

The cheery "everyday household" wares like table linens, pitchers and bowls stocked at this Chelsea store recall sun-drenched days in France, which is where most of its home accessories are imported from; sheets and quilts are gorgeous and demand a pretty price to match.

Lace S C
−|−|−| E

223 Mott St. (bet. Prince & Spring Sts.), J/M/Z to Bowery, 212-941-0528

Don't let the Victorian atmosphere of this velveteened NoLita boutique fool you; amongst the floral wallpaper, antique furniture and gilded shelves lies a well-cultivated selection of women's shoes from the likes of Martine Sitbon and Vivienne Westwood that get sky-high scores for va-va-voom − so bring your smelling salts.

Lacoste S C
22 | 21 | 20 | E

608 Fifth Ave. (49th St.), E/V to 5th Ave./53rd St., 212-459-2300
543 Madison Ave. (bet. 54th & 55th Sts.), E/V to 5th Ave./53rd St., 212-750-8115
800-452-2678; www.lacoste.com

■ "Making a comeback − or has it always been in vogue?" ask "retro-preps" shopping this Madison Avenue boutique and its new Midtown flagship, who know the "classic" ("hasn't changed in years") polo shirt with "that little green gator" (actually, a crocodile) remains the "real" Wasp uniform; pick up a few in "all those beautiful colors", and try on some mocassins, sneakers, watches and perfumes too, before hitting the country club with Bootsie; N.B. the Fifth Avenue store opened post-*Survey*.

LaCrasia Gloves
22 | 18 | 21 | M

304 Fifth Ave. (31st St.), 6 to 33rd St., 212-803-1600; www.wegloveyou.com

■ "Gold can be found" among the dross at this "no frills" shop near the Empire State Building that "makes gloves more interesting"; boosters give the "beautiful, original accessories" a thumbs-up, applauding the "amazing collection" that ranges "from fancy to funky" and from cotton to calfskin, "providing perfect accents to any ensemble"; N.B. LaCrasia in Grand Central Terminal is separately owned but sells exclusive merchandise made by the Fifth Avenue hand honcho.

LaDuca Shoes C
−|−|−| E

534 Ninth Ave. (bet. 39th & 40th Sts.), A/C/E to 42nd St./Port Authority, 212-268-6751; www.laducashoes.com

A dancer who's worked with everyone from Twyla Tharp to Ann Reinking, choreographer/footwear guru Phil LaDuca offers a showstopping selection of character, jazz and tap numbers and custom-made designs in his tiny, tin-ceilinged shop in the shadow of Port Authority; while the colorful T-, X- and Y-strap shoes, can-can boots and platform sandals attract rockers like Björk and Aerosmith's Steven Tyler and Joe Perry, it's Broadway hoofers like *Hairspray* phenom Marissa Jaret Winokur who really like to strut the stage in these dramatic creations.

Lady Foot Locker ◐ [S] 19 | 16 | 13 | M

120 W. 34th St. (B'way), B/D/F/N/Q/R/V/W to 34th St./Herald Sq., 212-629-4626
5314 Fifth Ave. (bet. 53rd & 54th Sts.), Brooklyn, R to 53rd St., 718-439-4669
Kings Plaza, 5364 Kings Plaza, Brooklyn, 2/5 to Brooklyn College/ Flatbush Ave., 718-253-9631
Queens Ctr., 90-15 Queens Blvd., Queens, G/R/V to Woodhaven Blvd., 718-760-3271
Staten Island Mall, 2655 Richmond Ave., Staten Island, 718-370-0505
800-991-6815; www.ladyfootlocker.com

◪ "Know your stuff before you set foot in" this chain and you just may find a winning combination of "fitness and casual" "shoes from Adidas, New Balance and Converse to walk, run, hop, skip and jump in", plus a "modest selection" of athletic apparel from national brands like Reebok and Nike; but naysayers nix this "nothing special" outfit, deeming the "variety and sizes too limited" and the "frazzled" staff "poorly informed."

Laina Jane ◐ [S] [C] 25 | 21 | 23 | E

416 Amsterdam Ave. (80th St.), 1/9 to 79th St., 212-875-9168
45 Christopher St. (bet. 7th Ave. & Waverly Pl.), 1/9 to Christopher St./ Sheridan Sq., 212-807-8077

■ When your significant other prefers you in states of undress, head to this "lovely little" lingerie twosome in the Village and the Upper West Side to uncover the "cutest bras, thongs, hot pants and sleepwear", "including the latest in Cosabella" and "very pretty" unmentionables from labels like Eberjey and Hanky Panky; N.B. the original site at 35 Christopher Street is now closed.

Lalaounis [C] ▽ 28 | 26 | 20 | VE

739 Madison Ave. (bet. 64th & 65th Sts.), 6 to 68th St., 212-439-9400; www.lalaounis.gr

■ "You'll feel like a goddess [wearing] a piece" of "unique Greek- and Roman-style jewelry" as well as designs inspired by the Byzantine era, American Indians and a host of other civilizations, all available at this Upper East Side boutique, whose light-wood setting showcases its "extensive collections" of highly stylized, hand-hammered 18 and 22 karat gold pieces; admirers attest this is craftsmanship "to rival the Ancients" – even if prices rival airfare to the Mediterranean.

La Layette et Plus Ltd. [C] ▽ 26 | 19 | 19 | VE

170 E. 61st St. (bet. Lexington & 3rd Aves.), 4/5/6/F/N/R/W to 59th St./ Lexington Ave., 212-688-7072

◪ "When your mother-in-law is buying your layette" make a beeline for this "outrageously expensive" East 60s baby emporium; stocked with "beautiful", "fantastic quality" linens, clothing and furniture for precious bundles up to 18 months, it's "truly a wonderful experience for any mom-to-be"; still, a few are put off by the "snooty service" and find the "cramped" quarters make browsing near "impossible."

Lâle [S] – | – | – | E

200 Mott St. (bet. Kenmare & Spring Sts.), 6 to Spring St., 212-941-7641; www.lalenyc.com

New NoLita boutique where you can browse through classic and contemporary Istanbul-inspired home accessories without being in a frenetic bazaar setting; white walls serve as the serene backdrop for colorful ceramic plates, intricately patterned tiles, vibrant vases and rich kilim rugs, all handmade in Turkey; just don't expect to bargain about the prices.

LALIQUE ☒
28 | 27 | 21 | VE

712 Madison Ave. (bet. 63rd & 64th Sts.), 6 to 68th St., 212-355-6550; 800-214-2738; www.lalique.com

■ If you're going for "gorgeous", you'll clearly find it at this sliver of Parisian posh transplanted to Madison Avenue, where the famed French crystal maker displays designs that range from perfume bottles and paperweights to "beautiful" museum-quality bowls, vases, sconces and screens, many with the company's signature satin finish; if you're looking for something less fragile, they also offer jewelry and leather goods like belts and briefcases.

Lana Marks ☒
27 | 26 | 25 | VE

645 Madison Ave. (bet. 59th & 60th Sts.), N/R/W to 5th Ave./59th St., 212-355-6135; www.lanamarks.com

☒ Luxury knows no bounds at this Madison Avenue boutique where 150 ladylike styles of Italian-made alligator, crocodile, ostrich and lizard handbags are offered in over 100 vibrant shades; sure, "prices are out of this world", but you "must own at least one" declare devotees; this Palm Beach–based designer certainly keeps good company – popular namesakes include the Farrah Fawcett tote and the Princess Diana handbag, and she counts Julianne Moore, Sarah Jessica Parker, Sharon Osbourne and Britney Spears among her celeb clients.

Language ☒☒
26 | 23 | 19 | VE

238 Mulberry St. (bet. Prince & Spring Sts.), R/W to Prince St.; 6 to Spring St., 212-431-5566; 888-474-5566; www.language-nyc.com

☒ "Beautifully combining art, fashion and beauty" in one space, this "NoLita original" speaks volumes with its "so-cool" designer threads ("all the Chloé you want", a Language house label created by Brazilian owner Ana Abdul and several other collections), plus jewelry, housewares and "the latest copy of *Visionaire*; "hot" goods translate into "flaming prices" ("ouch"), so "shop with your sugar daddy."

LA PERLA ☒☒
27 | 24 | 20 | VE

93 Greene St. (bet. Prince & Spring Sts.), C/E to Spring St., 212-219-0999
777 Madison Ave. (bet. 66th & 67th Sts.), 6 to 68th St., 212-570-0050
866-527-3752; www.laperla.com

■ Even "if you don't look like Marilyn Monroe, you certainly will feel like her" after the "unpretentious staff" "gets through with you" at this Madison Avenue outpost and its spacious, sleek SoHo sibling; "how can you not feel sexy" when you "splurge" on "the best in luxury lingerie" (as well as "beautiful bathing suits, clothing", hosiery and perfume)?; "oh, that I could afford to wear" these "exquisite" "delicates" "every day" wail the wistful, to which pragmatists retort "get your boyfriend to buy it" – plus now he can even pick up underwear here for himself.

La Petite Coquette ◐☒☒
27 | – | 20 | VE

51 University Pl. (bet. 9th & 10th Sts.), 6 to Astor Pl., 212-473-2478; 800-240-0308; www.thelittleflirt.com

■ "You could spend hours pawing the lacy next-to-nothings" from "crème de la crème" labels like Chantal Thomass and Lise Charmel and "still not be bored" at Rebecca Apsan's "*très* feminine" "lingerie classic" on University Place that's double the size of its original space; "this is where stars" like Sarah Jessica Parker shop for "really nice scanties" – indeed "you'll find" everything from "reasonably priced thongs to $400 and up merry widows" to an extensive line of swimwear that's certain "to make someone's heart beat faster" to jewelry from local artists.

La Petite Princesse S C   – | – | – | M
203 Lafayette St. (bet. Broome & Spring Sts.), 6 to Spring St., 212-965-0535; www.sohoprincess.com
At this NoLita insider's secret, French clothing and jewelry designer Carole Le Bris sells celebrities like Penélope Cruz and Liv Tyler a wide selection of one-of-a-kind costume pieces studded with semi-precious stones, Italian glass, Swarovski crystals, cubic zirconia or colorful enamels – plus some apparel – at prices that let even the parsimonious feel like princesses.

Laundry by Shelli Segal S C   23 | 21 | 19 | E
97 Wooster St. (bet. Prince & Spring Sts.), C/E to Spring St.; R/W to Prince St., 212-334-9433
■ Sure, "the label is available at department stores", but this streamlined SoHo shop often carries creations you won't "see elsewhere"; meant for the "young or young at heart", the laundry list of temptations includes "romantic, cutting-edge" dresses and "well put-together" separates that go from "basics that fit normal women" to "very foo-foo" to "NYC nightlife" looks "you won't regret in the morning", plus jewelry and accessories.

Layla S C   – | – | – | E
86 Hoyt St. (bet. Atlantic Ave. & State St.), Brooklyn, A/C/G to Hoyt/ Schermerhorn Sts., 718-222-1933
Light and lovely, with flowing curtains in the windows, pristine white walls and a stark black floor, this Hoyt Street shrine to the home boasts shelves jammed with quilted silk coverlets, pillows and soft embroidered throws in brilliant colors, most imported from India, Turkey and Morocco; for those who prefer to wear their ethnic exotica, there's a selection of embellished shirts, vibrant skirts and fine gold jewelry.

Laytner's Linen & Home ● S   20 | 14 | 14 | M
2270 Broadway (82nd St.), 1/9 to 79th St., 212-724-0180
237 E. 86th St. (bet. 2nd & 3rd Aves.), 4/5/6 to 86th St., 212-996-4439
800-690-7200; www.laytners.com
☑ Fans of these Uptown home-furnishings emporiums pronounce them a "reliable" "place to find baskets, shower curtains", "300–600-thread-count sheets" and French Country-, Mission- and Shaker-style furniture at "moderate" prices; but critics carp about the "limited selection" of "pretty basic merchandise" that can be a "little dated."

LEATHER MAN, THE ● S   28 | 20 | 23 | E
111 Christoper St. (bet. Bleecker & Hudson Sts.), 1/9 to Christopher St./Sheridan Sq., 212-243-5339; 800-243-5330; www.theleatherman.com
■ "Breathe in" swoon skin enthusiasts dizzy over the aromatic, "excellent assortment" of "custom and off-the-rack" "fine leather goods" at this Christopher Street boutique; there are "no lingerie, boas and the like" here – just loads of high-end hides tailored on-

site, plus a "vast selection of toys and implements" to feed your "fetish"; "the shaved-head staff" might look "scary", but "they're so friendly and knowledgeable, you'll find yourself recommending the place", that is if you're not "bound and gagged."

Le Chien Pet Salon 🇸🇨 ▽ 18 | 23 | 12 | VE
Trump Plaza, 1044 Third Ave. (bet. 61st & 62nd Sts.), 4/5/6/F/N/R/W to 59th St./Lexington Ave., 212-861-8100; 800-532-4436; www.lechiennyc.com
◪ Located in the Trump Plaza in the East 60s, this pet salon and boutique will "make even the most affluent person wish they were a dog for a day"; the selection, from rhinestone collars to poochy perfume, is supplied by "the finest designers" on the furry fashion scene; however, it's "way overpriced" to some, and others growl about the staff's "snobbery."

Le Corset by Selima 🇸🇨 ▽ 25 | 20 | 24 | E
80 Thompson St. (bet. Broome & Spring Sts.), C/E to Spring St., 212-334-4936
◼ If Selima Salaun's "tiny little" charmer in SoHo "isn't your favorite lingerie store, it should be" insist insiders who fall for her own "hip and slinky" wares, as well as a "wonderful mix" of "contemporary designer items" from ooh-la-la labels like Aubade, Fifi Chachnil and Chloé; retro-babes also cinch up "unique vintage" corsets, bras, girdles, baby dolls and gowns and even a few Pucci numbers; N.B. Salaun also owns Bond 07 by Selima and Selima Optique and co-owns Lunettes et Chocolat.

Le Décor Français 🇨 – | – | – | VE
1006 Lexington Ave. (bet. 72nd & 73rd Sts.), 6 to 68th St., 212-734-0032; www.ledecorfrancais.com
Though known for its colorful fabrics, ranging from silks and taffetas to cottons and horsehair, this "very small, elegant" Upper East Side shop also sells some select home furnishings; pillows, exotic candles, vintage table lamps, retro-inspired upholstered furniture and custom-made pieces help transform city pads into *pieds-à-terre.*

Lederer de Paris 🇨 24 | 22 | 20 | VE
457 Madison Ave. (51st St.), 6/E/V to 51st St./Lexington Ave., 212-355-5515; 888-537-6921; www.ledererdeparis.com
◪ "To own a bag from here is special" coo customers who canter over to this tony boutique, a Madison Avenue presence since the 1940s; "if you want a treat" that's "not ostentatious" and "a nice change from those yawn-worthy" bold-faced names, the "beautiful selection" of "very expensive", "top-of-the-line" handbags, attachés and small leather goods fit the bill; get ready to pony up big bucks – or "watch for the great sales."

Lee's Art Shop ●🇸🇨 23 | – | 17 | E
220 W. 57th St. (bet. B'way & 7th Ave.), N/Q/R/W to 57th St./7th Ave.; 1/9/A/B/C/D to 59th St./Columbus Circle, 212-247-0110; www.leesartshop.com
◪ "Tony Bennett" and other West 50s "art-supply junkies" "can kill an hour or more browsing" through this "greatly expanded", "almost gallerylike store" that's grown to four floors; "though they stock professional supplies, they're also for the hobbyist", as "they carry beautiful journals, stationery, photo albums", "frames of all sizes" and some genuine "oddball things"; N.B. Lee's Studio,

which features lighting and home furnishings, has moved to the top three floors here.

Lee's Studio ◖ S C
`23 | – | 16 | E`

1069 Third Ave. (63rd St.), 4/5/6/F/N/R/W to 59th St./Lexington Ave., 212-371-1122
220 W. 57th St. (bet. B'way & 7th Ave.), N/Q/R/W to 57th St./7th Ave.; 1/9/A/B/C/D to 59th St./Columbus Circle, 212-581-4400
www.leesstudio.com

■ There's an extensive collection of furniture (from sofas to coffee tables), along with fixtures, fans and a "varied and robust" imported and domestic lighting collection ranging from "funky" to contemporary to Mission- and Tiffany-styles, so there's "something for every home" at this duo; still, shoppers are split on the staff, with some giving glowing reports about "knowledgeable" service, but others taking a dimmer view; N.B. post-*Survey*, it moved into expansive new digs with its sibling, Lee's Art Shop on West 57th Street, and the Third Avenue branch reopened after a fire.

Le Fanion C
`– | – | – | E`

299 W. Fourth St. (Bank St.), 1/9 to Christopher St./Sheridan Sq., 212-463-8760; 800-258-8760; www.lefanion.com

Sweet little slip of a West Village tabletop shop showcasing "beautiful" pottery and earthenware ranging from *café au lait* cups to pitchers glazed in the warm colors of the south of France; adding to the atmosphere are antique armoires and fanciful contemporary chandeliers cascading with colored crystal fruit.

Legacy S C
`– | – | – | E`

109 Thompson St. (bet. Prince & Spring Sts.), C/E to Spring St., 212-966-4827
362 Atlantic Ave. (bet. Bond & Hoyt Sts.), Brooklyn, A/C/G to Hoyt/ Schermerhorn Sts., 718-403-0090
www.legacy-nyc.com

Abiding by the philosophy of mixing the old with the new, this SoHo standby and new Boerum Hill offshoot offer a pristine, handpicked selection of women's vintage apparel, shoes and accessories along with owner Rita Brookoff's own womenswear created from retro and retro-style fabrics, plus au courant lines like Ben Sherman, Cocokliks and M.R.S.; the Thompson Street shop tends to carry more expensive and esoteric designer garb from days gone by.

Legs Beautiful Hosiery
`20 | 16 | 16 | M`

Citicorp Bldg., 153 E. 53rd St. (bet. Lexington & 3rd Aves.), 6/E/V to 51st St./Lexington Ave., 212-688-9599
MetLife Bldg., 200 Park Ave. (45th St.), 4/5/6/7/S to 42nd St./ Grand Central, 212-949-2270 ◖
2 World Financial Ctr. (Vesey St.), E to World Trade Center, 212-945-2858

☑ "The place to buy everything you need for your legs (and then some)", these gam-havens about town always update their "nice selection of designer hosiery" and shapewear and are "great for socks and undies too"; while it's "not exciting" and can feel "cramped", most admit they're darn "convenient."

Leonard Opticians C
`26 | 21 | 25 | E`

1264 Third Ave. (bet. 72nd & 73rd Sts.), 6 to 68th St., 212-535-1222
40 W. 55th St. (bet. 5th & 6th Aves.), F to 57th St., 212-246-4452

☑ With over 6,000 "really unique frames" to choose from, patrons can't help but anoint this Eastside-Westside duo (fka Leonard Poll) a "godsend"; the "friendly" staff is "good at fashion consultation" and "they work wonders" with "complicated prescriptions" – it's almost a "throwback to old-fashioned artisanal opticians" – with licensed professionals "grinding lenses on-premises"; still, wallet-watchers wince "it's very good, but very expensive"; N.B. a post-*Survey* renovation of the 55th Street shop may outdate the above Presentation score.

LÉRON
27 | 23 | 23 | VE

750 Madison Ave. (65th St.), 6 to 68th St., 212-753-6700; 800-954-6369; www.leron.com

■ Since 1910, this tony, family-owned East Side shop has been selling "sublime" bed-, bath- and table linens and lingerie; there's a choice of over 5,000 designs, and they can custom-make anything, like putting your favorite pooch's picture on pillows or sheets; just be aware that such "amazing personalization" and "spectacular workmanship" comes at a "heart-pounding price."

Les Copains **C**
22 | 22 | 20 | VE

807 Madison Ave. (bet. 67th & 68th Sts.), 6 to 68th St., 212-327-3014

■ Though the parent company's in Italy, a "very French" sensibility permeates this "elegant" East 60s women's boutique, whose signature sweater sets and "pretty" dresses are "a little on the grown-up side"; *les amis* actually have three collections at three different price ranges to choose from and what's more the staff "couldn't be nicer."

Les Migrateurs **S** **C**
– | – | – | E

188 Duane St. (bet. Greenwich & Hudson Sts.), 1/2/3/9 to Chambers St., 212-966-8208; www.lesmigrateurs.com

Gallic owner Henri Personnaz designs most of the colorful furniture and accessories sold at his TriBeCa store, like leather-topped game tables and stunning colored-glass consoles, which are all made back home; curvaceous vases from fellow Frenchman Christian Tortu can be found downstairs, along with Personnaz's ingenious table lights.

LeSportsac **○** **S** **C**
19 | 18 | 19 | M

1065 Madison Ave. (81st St.), 6 to 77th St., 212-988-6200
176 Spring St. (bet. Thompson St. & W. B'way), C/E to Spring St., 212-625-2626
877-397-6597; www.lesportsac.com

■ If "lightweight is the criteria", then these signature ripstop parachute-nylon goods all done up in "cool designs" with fun patterns updated every four-to-six weeks are "the best travel bags around"; the modern Upper East Side and SoHo chain branches are lined with "inexpensive, sporty little fashion statements" "you gotta have", from totes to wallets, as well as pricier newbies like Gwen Stefani's new line, L.A.M.B., which even includes clothing.

Lestan Bridal **S**
20 | 11 | 13 | M

1902 Ralph Ave. (bet. Ave. U & Flatlands Ave.), Brooklyn, L to Canarsie/Rockaway Pkwy., 718-531-0800; www.lestanbridals.com

☒ "One step into" this "busy" Canarsie store and you've "entered the bridal zone" as to-be's and "their mothers consult with saleswomen downstairs to uncover the perfect gown" while "bridal parties compete upstairs to find a dress they can agree on"; the staff can be alternately "personal" and "slightly aggressive" and you may "wait forever", but given the selection and over 30 year's experience, "you can probably find something" "splendid."

Lester's S C   22 | 17 | 21 | E

1534 Second Ave. (80th St.), 6 to 77th St., 212-734-9292
2411 Coney Island Ave. (Ave. U), Brooklyn, Q to Ave. U, 718-645-4501
■ "Sure to please the most picky child", this Gravesend stalwart and Upper East Side sibling carry a "cutting-edge" "selection of what's trendy this week for kids", including "some European labels" and layette items, dressing everyone from babies to teens; "the shoe department is always busy" (and stocks labels like Aster and Shoe Be Do), but the "friendly" "staff handles the chaos well"; while a few fume it's "crowded" with "pushy moms", supporters retort "why go elsewhere?"

Levi's Store, The ⦿ S C   21 | 18 | 18 | M

536 Broadway (bet. Prince & Spring Sts.), R/W to Prince St., 646-613-1847
750 Lexington Ave. (59th St.), 4/5/6/F/N/R/W to 59th St./Lexington Ave., 212-826-5957
800-872-5384; www.levis.com
■ Go "back to basics" at this "trusty" denim giant on Lex and its newer sibling in SoHo; worshipers "love the low-riders", the "classic Red Tab" line and the "made-to-order option" for "hard-to-fit bodies", plus, guess what, a pair of jeans here doesn't "require all of your food money for a week"; but while some praise the "polite" staff, others opine they need a 911 to fetch the 501s.

Lexington Gardens C   ▽ 26 | 25 | 19 | E

1011 Lexington Ave. (bet. 72nd & 73rd Sts.), 6 to 68th St., 212-861-4390
■ "Beautiful items" can be found at this cozy Lexington Avenue "shop for decorative accessories for the garden" (fountains, tables, benches), along with antiques for the home and "custom-made dried floral arrangements."

Lexington Luggage S C   22 | – | 21 | M

(fka Jobson's Luggage)
666 Lexington Ave. (bet. 55th & 56th Sts.), 6/E/V to 51st St./Lexington Ave., 212-355-6846
■ "Anything you need to go anywhere" can be had at this recently renamed and relocated Lexington Avenue luggage establishment boasting a "huge selection" of "high-quality", "mid-market" suitcases and garment bags; thanks to its new three-floor quarters, it's no longer "cramped", plus you're still rewarded with "helpful", "knowledgeable" salespeople who go the extra mile; N.B. the shop moved post-*Survey* and also begat a new sibling called Carnegie Luggage in the West 50s.

Lightforms S C   ▽ 21 | 18 | 12 | M

509 Amsterdam Ave. (bet. 84th & 85th Sts.), 1/9 to 86th St., 212-875-0407
168 Eighth Ave. (bet. 18th & 19th Sts.), A/C/E/L to 14th St./8th Ave., 212-255-4664
■ "From traditional to contemporary to funky", these Upper West Side and Chelsea lighting stores "carry it all", from European and American designs to period reproductions, along with bulbs and household accessories; the "good selection and prices" please partisans, but a few detect an "attitude" from the staff.

Lighting By Gregory **S** **C**   24 | 16 | 14 | M
158 Bowery (bet. Broome & Delancey Sts.), J/M/Z to Bowery; 6 to Spring St., 212-226-1276; 888-811-3267; www.lightingbygregory.com

🔲 Gregorians chant that this "mack-daddy of generic lighting" boasts "the best selection in the city", with over 150 different product lines at "prices that can't be beat"; however, the service at this "vast" Lower East Side "destination" fluctuates from "knowledgeable" and "helpful" to "impatient" and "ungracious."

Lighting Center, The **C**   ∇ 22 | 17 | 15 | E
240 E. 59th St. (2nd Ave.), 4/5/6/F/N/R/W to 59th St./Lexington Ave., 212-888-8383; www.lightingcenter-ny.com

🔲 On the fringe of the design district in the East 50s, this lighting store specializes in "nicely presented", high-end contemporary fixtures from European manufacturers, as well as dimmers and gizmos; but while the space "looks great", foes are left in the dark by service that's "lacking."

Ligne Roset **S**   24 | 25 | 20 | VE
250 Park Ave. S. (20th St.), 6 to 23rd St., 212-375-1036
1090 Third Ave. (64th St.), 6 to 68th St., 212-794-2903
155 Wooster St. (bet. Houston & Prince Sts.), R/W to Prince St., 212-253-5629
www.ligne-roset-usa.com

■ "Ooh, who wouldn't want to live in these spaces?" ask acolytes about these French furniture showrooms filled with the company's "sleek", "modern" sofas, chaises and tables – the epitome of "form and function"; you'll need "a fat wallet", but the lauded delivery service and "approachable staff" may ease the separation anxiety.

Liliblue **S** **C**   – | – | – | M
955 Madison Ave. (75th St.), 6 to 77th St., 212-249-5356; www.liliblue.com
An Upper East Side magnet, the store offers a "fun", selective collection of "fabulous-looking" costume jewelry – primarily from Parisian designers – including some "real showstopper pieces" at such "reasonable prices" you won't mind if they last only a season; accessories mavens also gravitate toward the "very cute" bags and hats and scarves, mostly from France; "gracious service" leaves a lingering afterglow.

Lilliput **S** **C**   ∇ 29 | 22 | 19 | E
265 Lafayette St. (bet. Prince & Spring Sts.), 6 to Spring St., 212-965-9567
240 Lafayette St. (bet. Prince & Spring Sts.), 6 to Spring St., 212-965-9201
www.lilliputsoho.com

■ Set less than a block apart, these SoHo havens for hip Lilliputians stock an exciting mix of dressy outfits, fantasy dress-up options and punchy play clothes from the likes of Diesel and Lili Gaufrette, plus fun footwear, from rubber boots to ruby slippers; the smaller original shop at 265 Lafayette focuses on newborn through eight years while its larger sib dresses babies through tweens and teens (up to size 18), with a limited but interesting toy selection in both.

Lincoln Stationers **◑** **S**   25 | 19 | 17 | E
1889 Broadway (63rd St.), 1/9 to 66th St./Lincoln Ctr., 212-459-3500; 800-298-7367; www.lincolnstationers.com

■ "One of the only stationery stores left on the Upper West Side", this "well-stocked" two-floor shop elicits bravos from boosters of its "personalized" writing paper and other "great stuff" like "floral-patterned file folders" that "make you want to open a home office"; it's "a bit cluttered", and service can be "negligent, if pleasant", but the "fabulous selection" of "fine merchandise" pleases loyalists; N.B. a post-*Survey* renovation may impact the above Presentation score.

Linda Dresner
▽ 21 | 20 | 24 | VE

484 Park Ave. (bet. 58th & 59th Sts.), 4/5/6/F/N/R/W to 59th St./ Lexington Ave., 212-308-3177

☑ You may have to "work up the courage" to enter this spacious, marble-floored Park Avenue women's boutique, whose spare, "understated" looks seem "a bit sterile" to some; but once inside, the reward is an "unusual selection" of "upscale" European and Japanese notables – including a large Jil Sander collection – chosen by the eponymous owner, a much-respected style maven; the highly rated, "helpful" staff reflects the "taste and quality" of the boss' picks.

Lingerie on Lex 🆂🅲
▽ 21 | 15 | 19 | E

831 Lexington Ave. (bet. 63rd & 64th Sts.), 6 to 68th St., 212-755-3312

■ An "excellent stop for the bridal bound" as well as seekers of sensuous scanties, this "lovely" "little gem near Bloomies" has a great selection of color-coordinated, "top-of-the-line lingerie" including "all the best" labels, from "Cosabella to Hanky Panky" to Lise Charmel to La Perla, plus loungewear, pjs, robes, sleepwear and pantyhose, with many items from Europe; the staff is not only "very helpful and knowledgeable", they're also "husband-friendly."

Links of London 🅲
24 | 23 | 20 | E

535 Madison Ave. (bet. 54th & 55th Sts.), 6/E/V to 51st St./ Lexington Ave., 212-588-1177
MetLife Bldg., 200 Park Ave. (45th St.), 4/5/6/7/S to 42nd St./ Grand Central, 212-867-0258
800-210-0079; www.linksoflondon.com

☑ With their woody, eggshell-colored interiors, this "visually pleasing" Midtown duo is a "wonderful place to pick up silver gifts with pizzazz" (check out the cuff links in particular) plus even gold and diamond jewelry; fans are unfazed by the platinum prices for the sterling items, but "personnel who are a bit snobby" tarnish the experience a tad.

Lion & The Lamb 🅲
18 | 18 | 13 | E

1460 Lexington Ave. (bet. 94th & 95th Sts.), 6 to 96th St., 212-876-4303; www.lionandlambshop.com

☑ The "selection shines" at this "little shop in an unlikely neighborhood" on the Upper East Side, which carries needlepoint, embroidery, beads and yarn – "everything you need for a knitting project"; while acolytes adore the "excellent service and classes", others opine the owner should tame his woolly ways – "smoking in the store? not cool!"

Lisa Shaub 🆂🅲
▽ 23 | 20 | 20 | E

232 Mulberry St. (bet. Prince & Spring Sts.), R/W to Prince St., 212-965-9176; www.lisashaub.com

■ "So chic, but not pretentious" sums up this natty NoLita hat haven where owner "Lisa is often" on hand "giving the place a mom-and-pop-shop feel"; whether made from soft felt, wool or polar fleece, this designer's "unique styles" for women, men and babies offset "high-fashion ensembles" and are "lovely for every season", plus she will "custom-make anything to fit your color, material or size preference" and also offers scarves and gloves.

LITTLE ERIC 🆂🅲   28 | 22 | 18 | VE

1118 Madison Ave. (bet. 83rd & 84th Sts.), 4/5/6 to 86th St., 212-717-1513
1331 Third Ave. (bet. 76th & 77th Sts.), 6 to 77th St., 212-288-8987

■ Decorated with paintings and pictures of children, these "fabulous", brightly colored Upper East Side footwear siblings carry an "excellent assortment" of "upscale kids'" loafers, Mary Janes, boots and Nike and Superga sneakers, most "made in Italy"; "they stand by their product", including their own "adorable" collection; while most items are "both stylish and age-appropriate", some offerings may be more for "special occasions" "unless your little one is a lady who lunches"; N.B. at press time, the Third Avenue store was closed for renovation and planned to reopen early 2004.

Little Folk Art 🆂🅲   ▽ 26 | 24 | 23 | VE

159 Duane St. (bet. Hudson St. & W. B'way), 1/2/3/9 to Chambers St., 212-267-1500

■ Treasure trove in TriBeCa for hand-painted nursery and kid-room furniture, plus decorative items with a distressed country look and beautiful bedding from companies like Nilaya; shower-bound shoppers seeking the ultimate gift and parents of means also swoon over the very special layette pieces, those all-important first books for a baby's library and other charming cherishables.

Little Folks 🆂   19 | 9 | 14 | M

123 E. 23rd St. (bet. Lexington & Park Aves.), 6 to 23rd St., 212-982-9669

■ It may "look like dreck from the outside", but parents "can pretty much find whatever it is they need" at this "handy", one-stop "good Gramercy kids' shop" stocked with everything from "baby supplies, strollers and related accessories" to "high quality" name brand children's apparel at "very reasonable" prices; a few folks feel "if they were open on Saturdays they would be even more convenient."

Lively Set, The 🆂🅲   – | – | – | E

33 Bedford St. (bet. Carmine & Downing Sts.), 1/9 to Houston St., 212-807-8417

Don't mind the bit of rust and dust in this charming West Village home-and-garden-furniture shop; the vintage merchandise – from metal chairs and tables to dressers, mirrors, chandeliers, lighting and Italian garden tools – is "always a surprise" and "never boring."

Livi's Lingerie 🆂   ▽ 21 | 8 | 25 | M

1456 Third Ave. (bet. 82nd & 83rd Sts.), 4/5/6 to 86th St., 212-879-2050

■ A "good old-fashioned bra store" offering "old-world service", this "New York treasure" on the Upper East Side carries an "interesting assortment" of "unique items", including bridal bustiers and lingerie, plus loungewear and cotton undies; the "genuinely helpful" "mavens" "fit you personally" "to a tee" – indeed, they "know what they're doing", and what's more, they're "honest with you."

Liz Lange Maternity 🅢🅒

26 | 25 | 23 | E

958 Madison Ave. (bet. 75th & 76th Sts.), 6 to 77th St., 212-879-2191;
888-616-5777; www.lizlange.com

■ "Fashionable" females "who want to maintain" "their sleek New York look even though they're pregnant" head to this Upper East Side designer boutique for "chic" mix-and-match looks a "world away from blah maternity wear"; the "stretch jeans rock" and the "elegant trousers show how beautiful pregnant women can be", plus for active moms-to-be, there's even a Liz Lange for Nike line of athletic wear; it's "costly, but worth it" – especially "if the grandparents are paying."

Liz O'Brien 🅒

– | – | – | VE

800A Fifth Ave. (61st St.), N/R/W to 5th Ave./59th St., 212-755-3800;
www.lizobrien.com

Aficionados of this Upper East Side shop trust the eponymous owner's "wonderful eye" for "fabulous" American and French mid-century furniture, mainly from the 1940–1970s, so they "shop here often" to get first dibs on coveted, costly pieces by such masters as Billy Haines, James Mont, Jean Royère and Maison Jansen.

L'Occitane ◗🅢

25 | 24 | 21 | E

2303 Broadway (83rd St.), 1/9 to 86th St., 212-496-1967;
888-623-2880; www.loccitane.com
Additional locations throughout the NY area

■ Francophiles seeking a "little bit of Provence in New York" head for these "sweet retreats" where they are "transported by the scents of lavender and verbena wafting around them"; the chain's "pricey" but "wonderful skin products" include "luxurious" soaps, fragrances, cosmetics and lotions, as well as what some consider "the best men's grooming toiletries", all "beautifully packaged" for you or a friend; N.B. a new branch has opened in The Shops at Columbus Circle at Time Warner Center.

LOEHMANN'S ◗🅢

19 | 10 | 8 | M

101 Seventh Ave. (bet. 16th & 17th Sts.), 1/9 to 18th St., 212-352-0856
5740 Broadway (236th St.), Bronx, 1/9 to 238th St., 718-543-6420
2807 21st St. (Emmons Ave.), Brooklyn, Q to Sheepshead Bay,
718-368-1256
www.loehmanns.com

☑ "Look like a countess but spend like a clerk", "just as your mom and grandma" did, at the city's "original" designer discounter, where "women of all walks" "dig through the racks" in the Back Room for "steals and deals" on "up-to-the-minute" "catwalk" garb, "from Prada to Nicole Miller"; the Insider Club "loyalty program is nice", but "oy", "it can be stressful" "climbing over" the "unorganized" merchandise while clerks "yell at you to hang clothes back up" and the oldsters tut it "ain't what it used to be."

Lo-Fi 🅢🅒

– | – | – | M

162 W. 84th St. (Amsterdam Ave.), 1/9 to 86th St., 212-579-2144;
www.lo-fi-nyc.com

"Lo-Fi is definitely hi-fi in my book" laud acolytes who appreciate the niche filled by this modern, sophisticated West 80s menswear newcomer; stylin' guys in tune with the collectible, must-have labels, including jeans from Seven and Paper Denim & Cloth and cool threads from Ben Sherman and Von Dutch, sigh "awesome", thankful for a convenient spot to satisfy that fashion fix.

Loftworks 🆂🅲

16 | 15 | 15 | M

100 Lafayette St. (Canal St.), A/C/E to Canal St., 212-343-8088;
212-431-3335; www.loftworkslafayette.com

☑ "Slowly building a rep", this "easy-to-shop", three-level discounter on the TriBeCa-Chinatown border offers a "nice selection" of men's, women's and children's brand name and designer apparel "perfect for the fashion conscious on a tight budget"; ranging from Burberry to Hugo Boss to Tommy Hilfiger, "the merchandise changes on a regular basis" with a "much better presentation than most" of its kind; still, a few with loftier aspirations deem it a "mixed bag."

London Jewelers 🆂🅲

26 | 24 | 21 | VE

37-15 Junction Blvd. (bet. Roosevelt & 37th Aves.), Queens, 7 to
Junction Blvd., 718-639-7636

☑ Cuban-link chains and gold medallions are just some of the "gorgeous but extremely expensive jewelry" on offer at this Corona specialist "with class" (no relation to the East Hampton outfit of the same name) and now double the space; the ample glass-case displays of diamonds and gemstones make browsing easy – it's a "luxury experience when buying luxury goods" – but dress "well-to-do" if you want them to "pay attention to you"; N.B. a recent renovation may outdate the above Presentation score.

Longchamp

24 | 20 | 18 | E

713 Madison Ave. (63rd St.), 6 to 68th St., 212-223-1500;
866-566-4242; www.longchamp.com

■ These "super-lightweight" nylon French bags, available in "every color of the rainbow", are "perfect for traveling, lugging gym clothes and books" or just "schlepping around"; Long-lovers also champion this Madison Avenue shop's "wonderfully styled and well-made" luggage, leather goods and backpacks, all well priced for what they are.

Loom 🆂🅲

23 | 22 | 20 | M

115 Seventh Ave. (bet. Carroll & President Sts.), Brooklyn, B/F/Q to
7th Ave., 718-789-0061

■ "There's something funky-cool for all types" of Park Slopers at this "sleek, Zen-like" "local favorite" offering a "varied selection" of "unique jewelry" from Park Slope designer Mieko Takahashi, "fun accessories" ("awesome bags" from Marimekko) and "well-priced gift items ranging from elegant to cheeky"; the "interesting vases, candles", Thomas Paul pillows, "soaps and products not found elsewhere in the area" keep this "beautiful" shop humming with Loom-ites who muse the neighborhood "needs more boutiques" like this.

LORD & TAYLOR ⬤🆂

21 | 17 | 17 | M

424 Fifth Ave. (bet. 38th & 39th Sts.), 4/5/6/7/S to 42nd St./Grand Central,
212-391-3344; 800-348-6940; www.lordandtaylor.com

☑ "Orderly, organized and quiet", this "good, classic department store" remains an "old-time favorite" for many a Murray Hiller, who applaud the "consistent quality" and "reasonable prices" of its "fancy and practical" "real woman's clothes", menswear, a "wide selection of kid stuff" and accessories; however, while it's "trying to escape the grandma stigma with new designers", modernists find it "kind of frumpy", with "uneven service"; still, "since it's not a tourist attraction" (except for the "terrific

Christmas windows"), there are "no long register lines" – and oh, those "bargains on coupon days!"

Lord of the Fleas **C**
16 | 12 | 13 | I

2142 Broadway (75th St.), 1/2/3/9/B/C to 72nd St., 212-875-8815 **S**
305 E. 9th St. (bet. 1st & 2nd Aves.), 6 to Astor Pl., 212-260-9130 **S**
437 E. 12th St. (bet. Ave. A & 1st Ave.), L to 1st Ave., 212-843-3269
▪ Bringing "a little bit of St. Marks Place to the Upper West Side" and, well, the East Village, this trio is not only "the ultimate for 12-year-olds" – ladies also laud this Lord's "fresh" selection of "slightly rebellious", "bohemian" and "trendy clothing" sure to "spices up wardrobes"; sure the "somewhat cramped" quarters are a royal pain and "you really have to search, but it's worth it for" the "gypsy bargains."

LORO PIANA **S** **C**
28 | 25 | 23 | VE

821 Madison Ave. (bet. 68th & 69th Sts.), 6 to 68th St., 212-980-7961
■ Enter "cashmere heaven" at this Upper East Side retailer, home of a 19th-century Italian purveyor of "conservative, high-quality knitwear" and custom-made clothing for men, women and children; go ahead, "spoil yourself" with the "touch and feel" of "awesome" wool scarves, robes or throws; the staff makes the "extra effort to find articles", as "not everything is on display."

Louis Féraud
26 | 25 | 22 | VE

3 W. 56th St. (bet. 5th & 6th Aves.), N/Q/R/W to 57th St./7th Ave., 212-956-7010
■ Just off Fifth Avenue in the West 50s, this "heavenly", flatteringly lit boutique keeps its sophisticated clientele of ladies who lunch supplied with just the right amount of rich colors, ooh-able fabrics and "elegant, elegant, elegant, elegant" softly tailored classics ("the quality is amazing and the fit is fabulous"); polished and pretty salespeople are willing and able to assist.

Louis Vuitton **S**
27 | 25 | 20 | VE

116 Greene St. (bet. Prince & Spring Sts.), 6 to Spring St.; R/W to Prince St., 212-274-9090; 866-884-8866; www.vuitton.com
▪ The "snob factor", "little thank-you notes for shopping", the logo bags that "last forever" and the "ultimate luggage indulgence" ("where else can a girl purchase a steamer trunk?") – ah, the list of why folks "love Louis" goes on, which is about how long you'll wait for this luxury firm's most-desirables, and sometimes service too; still, the Marc Jacobs–designed mens- and womenswear is "top quality and beautiful to boot" (especially the boots), so shop the SoHo location ("less inundated with tourists") or the 57th Street mega-store – the world's largest LV store – which opened as we were going to press.

Lounge, The **S** **C**
21 | 23 | 17 | E

593 Broadway (bet. Houston & Prince Sts.), R/W to Prince St., 212-226-7585
■ "You look so fine just walking into" this "cool newcomer" – in fact, the whopping 16,000-sq.-ft., two-level store featuring "funky, of-the-moment" men's and women's apparel, from "affordable to more expensive" names like Von Dutch, James Perse, Roberto Cavalli and Katharine Hamnett, is "just what SoHo needed"; the high-tech setting, DJ booth and basement filled with edgy footwear and score-worthy jeans complete the "nightclub" feel; shoppers can also 'lounge' in Angelina's, an in-house Italian cafe.

Love Saves The Day ◗⧈
20 | 19 | 14 | M

119 Second Ave. (7th St.), 6 to Astor Pl., 212-228-3802

■ "Kitsch rules" at this "East Village vintage shop", "full of novelty items galore" – "that old, now-defunct board game you loved as a child, collectible action figures, unopened packages of baseball cards"; the colorful, "crowded" premises also contain old "records to sift through", plus a "clothing section" of casualwear including dresses, shirts and skirts and new, libidinous gag gifts that'll titillate "out-of-town friends."

Lowell/Edwards
– | – | – | VE

979 Third Ave., 5th fl. (bet. 58th & 59th Sts.), 4/5/6/F/N/R/W to 59th St./Lexington Ave., 212-980-2862; 800-778-7249; www.lowelledwards.com

As every interior decorator knows, the Upper East Side's D&D Building is stuffed to its gilded gills with high-end showrooms, and this store is one of the sexiest, displaying remote-controlled, custom home-entertainment systems, including Runco cabinets that magically open onto Denon plasma TVs, or KEF stereo speakers that descend from the ceiling on cue; if you don't have a bring-your-own, they'll set you up with an in-house designer.

Luca Luca ⧈⧇
22 | 23 | 22 | VE

1011 Madison Ave. (78th St.), 6 to 77th St., 212-288-9285
690 Madison Ave. (62nd St.), 4/5/6/F/N/R/W to 59th St./Lexington Ave., 212-753-2444

◪ Strap on the stilettos for trawling these Upper East Side shops, home to the "hottest" cashmeres, shearlings and shiny, slinky separates that go from daytime to evening for oh-so-"sexy" "matrons"; some won't Luca twice at the "trashy-flashy" threads (too "way out"), but for most, the "ridiculously great service" ("in-store alterations" and free, same-day delivery) outweighs the "ridiculously priced" frocks.

Lucky Brand Jeans ⧈
21 | 20 | 21 | M

260 Columbus Ave. (70th St.), 1/2/3/9 to 72nd St., 212-579-1760 ◗
172 Fifth Ave. (22nd St.), R/W to 23rd St., 917-606-1418 ◗
38 Greene St. (Grand St.), A/C/E to Canal St., 212-625-0707
1151 Third Ave. (67th St.), 6 to 68th St., 646-422-1192 ◗
800-964-5777; www.luckybrandjeans.com

■ Even the "most picky of jean connoisseurs" feels 'lucky' at this "retro" yet "streetwise" denim "mecca" where the "cool" "consistent-for-fit" jeans slither over "teenyboppers of all ages" and "don't cost as much as some other trendy" brands; sure there are "thousands of options", but it's not like looking for a needle in a haystack – the "service with a smile" "demystifies the art of buying" and helps "you find that perfect pair."

Lucky Wang ⧈⧇
– | – | – | M

799 Broadway (bet. 10th & 11th Sts.), 4/5/6/L/N/Q/R/W to 14th St./Union Sq., 212-353-2850; 866-353-2850; www.luckywang.com

"Come here" to this Greenwich Villager for "adorable" pint-sized baby kimonos – "a must for the urban baby" – plus "whimsical" "Asian-inspired children's" cardigans, skivvies, T-shirts and bibs, all displayed in a white, modern, "open, inviting space that belies its small" dimensions; grown-ups also strike it lucky for themselves, scooping up fuzzy creations like bags, coin purses, pillows and lamps made from colorful tinsel; another bit of kismet: "the staff is a treat."

Lucy Barnes ◑ⓈⒸ   ▽ 23 | 21 | 23 | E

117 Perry St. (bet. Greenwich & Hudson Sts.), 1/9 to Christopher St./ Sheridan Sq., 212-647-0149; www.lucybarnes.com

■ It's refreshing to see a romantic rebel, and that's just the spirit of this cozy boutique in the heart of the Village; whitewashed brick walls and a simple tin ceiling set the stage for "floaty, fancy, fabulous threads" for women and brides-to-be, in "eclectic" floral prints and embroidered vintage cottons – all embodying "deliciously new ideas"; N.B. at press time, the shop was slated to move to 320 West 14th Street in early 2004.

Lulu Guinness ◑ⓈⒸ   ▽ 23 | 26 | 19 | E

394 Bleecker St. (bet. W. 11th & Perry Sts.), 1/9 to Christopher St./ Sheridan Sq., 212-367-2120; www.luluguinness.com

■ Burgeoning Bleecker Street is more "adorable" than ever thanks to this "quaint" girlie shop that "beams with personality" and "whimsical" murals "splashed across the walls"; "you feel like you're across the pond with Lulu herself", and the "crazy", "colorful", "clever designs and shapes" of the handbags, cosmetic cases and, now, footwear, scarves, eyewear and fragrance "put a smile on your face"; indeed, "the roses on the black satin purse are so red you want to water them."

Lunettes et Chocolat ◑ⓈⒸ   26 | 24 | 22 | E

25 Prince St. (bet. Elizabeth & Mott Sts.), 6 to Spring St.; R/W to Prince St., 212-925-8800; 866-925-8800; www.maribelle.com

■ "Even if you're not in the market" for eyewear, this "quirky" "little shop" embodies an "interesting concept" – an oh-so-French marriage of "cool" Selima Salaun glasses and "divine" MarieBelle chocolates – that's worth a "stop-in" when you're cruising NoLita; it also purveys "chic hats", and if the "minimal" selection of goods "isn't earth-shattering", the "cute" decor and "to-die-for" cocoa keeps a lunettic fringe coming back.

L'Uomo ◑ⓈⒸ   ▽ 20 | 23 | 22 | E

383 Bleecker St. (Perry St.), 1/9 to Christopher St./Sheridan Sq., 212-206-1844

☑ Male clients claim you "can't miss" with this veteran Villager, which blends a comprehensive collection of Stone Island and Hugo Boss with exclusive Orlando casual clothing, Moreno Martini de Firenze spread-collar sport shirts and uncommon leather outerwear plus soon-to-come, Michael Kors – all displayed in an easy-to-shop space staffed by "exceptional" salespeople; if the labels seem too "pricey", just "wait until the goods go on sale."

Luxury Brand Outlet ◑ⓈⒸ   12 | 5 | 9 | M

355 E. 78th St. (bet. 1st & 2nd Aves.), 6 to 77th St., 212-988-5603
1222 Second Ave. (64th St.), F to Lexington Ave./63rd St., 212-734-2505
866-645-8987; www.luxurybrandoutlet.com

☑ "Hey, you never know" what "chic brands" of "designer clothes" you'll find "lurking under all the mess" at this Upper Eastside discount duo; "patient" burrowers "especially love the shoes", bags and belts, but pout that the "poor selection" and "expensive" prices keep this duo from "rising to its potential."

Lyd **S** **C**

| – | – | – | E |

405 W. 44th St. (9th Ave.), A/C/E to 42nd St./Port Authority,
212-246-8041; www.lydnyc.com

You may need to put a lid on your spending once you step inside this Hell's Kitchen boutique, a contemporary, white-walled, gallerylike shop done up with turquoise accents and mod, globe-shaped pendant light; owner Mia Gonzalez edits a tasteful selection of cool threads from young New York, London and LA designers, complimented by offbeat handbags, shoes and accessories and soon plans to add her own collection to the delightful mix.

Lyric Hi-Fi, Inc. **C**

| 26 | 20 | 18 | VE |

1221 Lexington Ave. (bet. 82nd & 83rd Sts.), 4/5/6 to 86th St.,
212-439-1900; www.lyricusa.com

☑ "Whether you're stopping in to chat about budget phono pre-amp options or to audition some serious stereo equipment", the goods at this sound-and-vision specialty store are "stellar"; the folks on the floor at the East 80s flagship of the country's first high-end audio/video retailer are highly informed and seasoned, but antagonists argue that "snooty doesn't begin to describe them."

M.A.C. Cosmetics **S**

| 24 | 23 | 19 | M |

Flatiron Bldg., 1 E. 22nd St. (B'way), R/W to 23rd St.,
212-677-6611 ◑
113 Spring St. (bet. Greene & Mercer Sts.), 6 to Spring St., 212-334-4641
202 W. 125th St. (bet. Adam Clayton Powell Jr. &
Frederick Douglass Blvds.), A/B/C/D to 125th St., 212-665-0676
152 Montague St. (bet. Clinton & Henry Sts.), Brooklyn, A/C/F to
Jay St./Borough Hall, 718-596-2028
800-387-6707; www.maccosmetics.com

☑ A long-standing "beauty staple" for professionals, this cosmetics company showcases a "wide variety of colors and shades", particularly when it comes to lipstick, "can't-live-without-it" Lipglass and eyeshadow, to "bring out your inner drag queen", "glam girl" or "grown-up"; while "reasonable prices" make it "a bargain next to other comparable lines", it can be "hit-or-miss with the salespeople" 'cause "it's kind of cool but also kind of scary that the entire staff wears makeup – including the men."

MacKenzie-Childs **S**

| 23 | 23 | 18 | VE |

14 W. 57th St. (bet. 5th & 6th Aves.), N/R/W to 5th Ave./59th St.,
212-570-6050; 888-665-1999; www.mackenzie-childs.com

■ "Alice in Wonderland is in there somewhere" assert observers of this home-furnishings shop whose "unique" and "eccentric" items range from "incredibly colored" "hand-painted ceramics" to "whimsical" furniture like fish-shaped chairs and candy-striped tuffets; but while pros praise the "sensory overload" here, a few find the "busy" merch and "expensive" prices make them "dizzy"; N.B. a post-*Survey* move from Madison Avenue to West 57th Street may outdate the above Presentation score.

MACY'S ◑ **S**

| 18 | 13 | 9 | M |

151 W. 34th St. (bet. Broadway & 7th Ave.), 1/2/3/9 to 34th St./
Penn Station, 212-695-4400; 800-343-0121; www.macys.com

☑ This 102-year-old "king of the department stores" can be "hard to navigate" (the Herald Square flagship "spans a full city block"), but if you "have a compass and the patience", you'll find an "impressive variety" of merchandise, including "high-energy" cosmetics counters with funkier lines like Anna Sui, an expanded jewelry area, a "canyon" of appliances ("the Cellar is stellar!") and an "expansive" shoe selection; critics claim it's a "miracle on 34th Street" if the "disgruntled" salespeople don't "scare you away"; still, for sheer "variety" you "can't beat the behemoth" – and besides, who else would sponsor Thanksgiving Day parades and July 4th fireworks?; N.B. a post-*Survey* renovation may outdate the above Presentation score.

Magic Windows 🆂🅲 | 23 | 20 | 21 | E |
1186 Madison Ave. (87th St.), 4/5/6 to 86th St., 212-289-0028; www.magic-windows.com
☑ "Worth a trip Uptown for beautiful" domestic and imported children's clothing that spans the ages, this Madison Avenue boutique offers a "varied selection" ranging from layette to "top-quality classics" for boys and girls to "inviting dresses" and "gorgeous prom gowns"; styles tend to be "very conservative for younger kids, but more fashion-forward into the pre-teen years"; still, the less spellbound sigh that the merchandise tends to be "too girlie."

Magry Knits 🆂 | – | – | – | E |
80 E. Seventh St. (bet. 1st & 2nd Aves.), F/V to Lower East Side/ 2nd Ave., 212-674-6753; www.magryknits.com
The "very friendly and approachable" owner of this "great little find" in the East Village not only "dyes and hand-spins" her own skeins, turning out some of the "most varied" and "creative yarn in the city", she also "carries "hand-knit garments that are stylish and hip", drawing celebs like Patti LaBelle and Tracee Ross; "personalized classes" are also offered (the proprietor's "patience" with newbies "is a virtue"), and "weekly stitch parties round out the fun."

Make Up For Ever 🆂 | ▽ 26 | 21 | 25 | M |
409 W. Broadway (bet. Prince & Spring Sts.), R/W to Prince St.; C/E to Spring St., 212-941-9337; 877-757-5175; www.makeupforever.fr
■ Paris-based cosmetics company that started in 1984 as a line of professional theatrical makeup, whose SoHo branch draws civilians as well with "everything you could ever need", including a "huge variety" of "great, custom colors" with a "massive amount of pigmentation" and moderate prices.

Malia Mills Swimwear 🆂🅲 | 26 | 20 | 25 | E |
960 Madison Ave., 2nd fl. (bet. 75th & 76th Sts.), 6 to 77th St., 212-517-7485
199 Mulberry St. (Spring St.), 6 to Spring St., 212-625-2311
800-685-3479; www.maliamills.com
■ Savvy swimmers set a course for these NoLita and now Madison Avenue bikinilands of "mix-and-match sizes" for "every shape" in silky solids or cool prints; a "super-knowledgeable" staff (including the designer herself on weekends) knows how to make you "feel comfortable about your body", and if you need an even more Malia-ble moment, have your "sexy, figure-flattering" (and, yes, "pricey") suit custom-adorned with Swarovski crystals; N.B. the East 70s branch opened post-*Survey*.

Malo | ▽ 27 | 22 | 23 | VE |
814 Madison Ave. (68th St.), 6 to 68th St., 212-396-4721; www.malo.it
■ There's nothing shallow about Malo – on the contrary, the Italian designer's East 60s boutique specializes in ultrathick, four-ply

"classic cashmere" for men and women that "lasts a lifetime"; a "most wonderful" staff "really takes the time to help you" with your "pricey" purchase, be it a "beautiful sweater" or a leather bomber jacket, and now, wallets and accessories.

M&J Trimming   27 | 19 | 17 | M

1000-1008 Sixth Ave. (bet. 37th & 38th Sts.), B/D/F/N/Q/R/V/W to 34th St./Herald Sq., 212-204-9595; 800-965-8746; www.mjtrim.com

■ "Wow!" – this 67-year-old Garment District trimming emporium is "like crawling into a cool granny's knitting basket" say handy hobbyists with a "DIY bent"; "prepare to be dazzled" by the "floor-to-high-ceiling array of ribbons, fringe, lace" and "other doodads" – you'll think you've "died and gone to button-and-trim heaven"; it's "inspiring and overwhelming" – "whatever madness you want to indulge" "you'll find it here"; N.B. at press time, plans were underway to expand and renovate into one huge store.

Manfredi C   26 | 25 | 22 | VE

702 Madison Ave. (bet. 62nd & 63rd Sts.), 4/5/6/F/N/R/W to 59th St./Lexington Ave., 212-734-8710

■ In the East 60s, this Italian maestro creates "masterpieces", from "fun watches" to light, "lovely", "wonderfully designed fine jewelry" that emphasizes the reflective nature of the gold and makes "amazing use" of colorful gemstones; some of his creations, like the single jewels suspended between lariatlike chokers, "you won't see anywhere else" devotees declare, making it "worth the trip."

Manhattan Doll House Shop, The S C   25 | 23 | 21 | E

428 Second Ave. (bet. 24th & 25th Sts.), 6 to 23rd St., 212-725-4520; www.manhattandollhouse.com

■ A "dream destination for girls from ages three to 83", this "lovely" Gramercy Park shop, recently relocated from Third to Second Avenue, boasts over 100 different types of "beautiful, intricate doll houses" you can construct yourself or buy complete, plus every 'home' "accessory you can think of"; for a full-on fantasy, scope out the "excellent selection of the finest" dollies like the Madame Alexander collection; N.B. there's even a hospital for antique playthings in need of TLC.

Manhattan Portage S C   22 | 17 | 18 | M

333 E. 9th St. (bet. 1st & 2nd Aves.), 6 to Astor Pl., 212-995-5490
301 W. Broadway (Canal St.), A/C/E to Canal St., 212-226-4557
www.manhattanportage.com

■ "Make your chiropractor happy" by wearing a "super-durable" canvas or nylon messenger, laptop or utility bag from this set of pint-sized East Village and SoHo shops; "practical, functional" and boasting a ubiquitous Manhattan skyline logo, these "must-have" "city staples" for "college kids and up-and-comers travel smoothly "from office to park", and seem to "last forever."

MANOLO BLAHNIK C   28 | 26 | 21 | VE

31 W. 54th St. (bet. 5th & 6th Aves.), E/V to 5th Ave./53rd St., 212-582-3007

■ "Dip into your trust fund" before heading over to Midtown's "holy grail" of "ultimate high heels" made even more "famous by Sarah Jessica Parker in *Sex and the City*"; this "chichi" "shrine" seduces "fashionistas" with "divine", "beautifully crafted" "masterpieces", in other words, "definitely cab shoes – no walking allowed, unless you're making your way from bar to table, then sashay away"; while a handful hails service as "good", many maintain it's nearly "nonexistent unless the salesperson recognizes you or your handbag."

Marc by Marc Jacobs ◐[S][C] 26 | 24 | 20 | E

403-5 Bleecker St. (W. 11th St.), 1/9 to Christopher St./Sheridan Sq., 212-924-0026; www.marcjacobs.com

■ "What a treat to have on Bleecker Street" gush "Marc believers" smitten by the "absolutely delicious" retro yet "youthful", "modern looks" "nicely displayed" ("makes for easy window shopping") in these "simple, yet unique" connected men's and women's boutiques; "editors, celebrities" and their ilk "like his imagination", not to mention his "fab sweaters" and "wonderful leather jackets", so "expect to see" plenty of bold-faced names in these "hassle-free" "hot" shops 'cause this is "where anyone who has any fashion clue" gravitates.

Marc Jacobs [S][C] 26 | 23 | 20 | VE

163 Mercer St. (bet. Houston & Prince Sts.), R/W to Prince St., 212-343-1490; www.marcjacobs.com

◪ New Yorkers of all sexes worship Marc "major-splurge" Jacobs, long a design wunderkind on Seventh Avenue and now a veritable force of fashion-forward fancies that fans "can't get enough of"; at his spare SoHo boutique, he's "cornered the market" on "fresh, uncomplicated, cool" clothing – half-"Minnie Mouse, half-Edie Sedgwick" – and reinvented classic shoes and bags into "hot, hot, hot" must-haves that make up for some staff "attitude, attitude."

Marc Jacobs Accessories ◐[S][C] 26 | 25 | 19 | VE

385 Bleecker St. (Perry St.), 1/9 to Christopher St./Sheridan Sq.; A/C/E/L to 14th St./8th Ave., 212-924-6126; www.marcjacobs.com

■ "A must on every Downtown hipster's shopping list", this "adorable" corner boutique "brightens up Bleecker Street" with "beautiful people behind and around the counter" and "lovely" accessories bound to "make any outfit", "all well laid-out and easy to find"; "you can't go wrong" with the "retro" "cool shoes", plus the "soft, luscious" "trendy handbags" "toted on the arms of everyone from young starlets to baby socialites" "are to die for" – "who knew the kooky school-girl look could be so chic?"

Mare ◐[S] ▽ 23 | 21 | 20 | E

426 W. Broadway (bet. Prince & Spring Sts.), C/E to Spring St., 212-343-1110; www.mare.com

◪ With its curvy surfaces and "beautiful Italian shoes", this little bit of the Mediterranean in SoHo is always "worth a stop", especially if you're on the prowl for "high-fashion" "Downtown" footwear including some of the "most comfortable stiletto-heel boots ever made"; while a smattering of sidesteppers demur at "designs that shy away from being too original", sole-mates maintain "you never know what you'll find."

Mariko [C] ▽ 21 | 18 | 20 | E

998 Madison Ave. (77th St.), 6 to 77th St., 212-472-1176

■ Ladies who lunch and socialite wanna-bes alike shop at this cluttered, beige-and-cream-colored Upper Eastside jeweler, a "great choice for fabulous fakes", whether one's taste runs to of-the-moment styles or timeless looks, like a copy of the three-strand pearl choker made popular by Jackie O.

Marimekko [S] ▽ 22 | – | 20 | E

1262 Third Ave. (bet. 72nd & 73rd Sts.), 6 to 68th St., 212-628-8400; 800-527-0624; www.kiitosmarimekko.com

■ "Bold, graphic stripes" and designs infused with a "little bit of Finland", like the "wonderful, splashy" prints "we knew in the '70s" and '60s can still be found at this Upper Eastsider, which moved to this space last November; the "timeless stuff", including textiles, tablecloths, bedding, "great totes" and accessories, plus "beautiful cotton" apparel for adults and kids, is "still great after all these years."

Marithé & François Girbaud [S][C] 23 | 24 | 19 | E

47 Wooster St. (bet. Broome & Grand Sts.), A/C/E to Canal St., 212-625-0066; www.girbaud.com

■ The original French 'jeanologists' famous in the '80s for their signature baggy pleated pants house their "unique" urban-wear in this modern, bright SoHo store, a sprawling, "very arty" tree-filled space worthy of their "to-swoon-for" collection; for chic femmes and hommes with euros to spare, "this is a place to treat yourself" to the designers' higher-end, European "quality" denim, tops, jackets, coats and more – a style that's very much alive for the "young at heart."

Market NYC – | – | – | M

268 Mulberry St. (bet. Houston & Prince Sts.), B/D/F/S/V to B'way/ Lafayette St., 917-750-6918; www.themarketnyc.com

This Saturdays-only showcase for a rotating roster of emerging talent in a NoLita school gym feels like a "modern-day church bazaar" filled with booths of "uniquely crafted accessories", jewelry and apparel; there are "great deals to be had since you're not buying the goods direct" from the "young designers" who pay a pittance to sell their wares here; still, a handful feel it's "expensive for clothing" from "wanna-bes."

Marni [S][C] ▽ 28 | 26 | 23 | VE

161 Mercer St. (bet. Houston & Prince Sts.), R/W to Prince St., 212-343-3912

■ Fashion purists scoop up "lovely" designs at this distinctively "beautiful" SoHo boutique, furnished with a milky-glass floor and chrome 'tree-limb' fixtures, knowing they'll surely be one season ahead of the pack in Consuelo Castiglioni's trendsetting creations; using rich fabrics and unexpected colors, this acclaimed Italian designer cultivates a heady "combination of ease, romance and toughness" that keeps her brand of "feminine" chic from being "too girlie"; P.S. there's some "great stuff" for guys too, but "be ready to spend."

Marsha D.D. [S][C] ▽ 23 | 17 | 20 | E

1574 Third Ave. (bet. 88th & 89th Sts.), 4/5/6 to 86th St., 212-831-2422

■ "*The* place" for tween clothing and accessories, this large Upper East Side "kids' favorite from age 10 on" exudes a "very hip" vibe with a red rubber floor, rad snowboard benches and zebra-striped carpeting in the dressing rooms; the owner is "on top of the trends", so the "stuff is way-cool" – "mostly jeans, T-shirts" and sweaters from "hot" labels like Diesel, Juicy and Quiksilver; yeah, it's "expensive", but they have "everything" this age group wants.

Marshalls ◑ⓈⒸ
16 | 8 | 8 | I

105 W. 125th St. (Lenox Ave.), 1/9 to 125th St., 212-866-3963
625 Atlantic Ave. (Hanson Pl.), Brooklyn, 2/3/4/5/B/D/M/N/Q/R/W to Atlantic Ave., 718-398-5254
1832 86th St. (Iaunton Ave.), Brooklyn, N to 86th St., 718-621-3434
48-18 Northern Blvd., Queens, Q/R to Northern Blvd., 718-626-4700
888-627-7425; www.marshallsonline.com

☑ "Scavenger hunters" go "diving for pearls" at this "shopper's paradise" with branches in Brooklyn, Queens and Harlem, digging up brand names "at frugal prices"; "there are lots of surprises on every trip" – just "get in early before the vultures circle the fresh stock" and "when you're done rooting through" the contemporary "designer handbags, shoes" and apparel, scout out the "great stash of household" "goodies"; sure there's "much schlock", but "you're not here for the neatness – or customer service."

Martin ◑ⓈⒸ
▽ 26 | 21 | 26 | M

206 E. Sixth St. (bet. 2nd & 3rd Aves.), 6 to Astor Pl., 212-358-0011

■ Behind an East Village storefront lies a "tiny" shop with a tin ceiling, "kind of like a friend's bedroom", filled with much-raved-over pants and jeans ("the be-all and end-all for anyone tall") and "offbeat, but not too weird" jackets, tops and dresses with an edgy rock 'n' roll energy (to match the collage of musicians on the wall).

Mary Adams The Dress Ⓢ
– | – | – | E

138 Ludlow St. (bet. Rivington & Stanton Sts.), F/V to Lower East Side/ 2nd Ave., 212-473-0237; www.maryadamsthedress.com

"*Très* funky" separates, plus custom-made and off-the-rack party frocks and wedding dresses for the "not-so-typical bride" are this Lower East Side designer's raison d'être; this is the "stuff that dreams are made of", with "original" girlie getups turned out in vibrant shades or white with a burst of bright detailing, offset by romantic ruffles, flouncy layers or "baroque" bustle-backs; N.B. the shop maintains regular store hours and also takes appointments.

Mary Arnold Toys
24 | 20 | 24 | E

1010 Lexington Ave. (bet. 72nd & 73rd Sts.), 6 to 68th St., 212-744-8510

■ "Recommending gifts for specific ages" may be a "lost art" elsewhere, but not at this "cute toy shop" on the Upper East Side, where the "staff is helpful" and "knowledgeable"; the "very nice selection" includes dolls, crafts and early-development choices and even special "things you can't find in other larger chain stores."

Mary Quant Colour Concept
21 | 25 | 20 | M

520 Madison Ave. (bet. 53rd & 54th Sts.), E/V to 5th Ave./53rd St., 212-980-7577; www.maryquantamericas.com

■ The creator of the mini-skirt and the Mother of Mod also puts her flower-power daisy imprint on this East 50s makeup shop; the young at heart will groove to this "Twiggy acolytes' paradise" of cosmetics in "every color you could imagine", along with a skincare line and small selection of women's clothing; "low prices" also make for a swinging time.

Mason's Tennis Mart Ⓢized Ⓒ
21 | 18 | 18 | E

56 E. 53rd St. (bet. Madison & Park Aves.), 6/E/V to 51st St./ Lexington Ave., 212-755-5805

☑ A popular stop for U.S. Open attendees, this "been-around-forever" Midtown shop "always has the latest tennis stuff", including designer attire from the likes of Ellesse and Fila, a "great selection of equipment" and a "staff that has great patience" to help you score what you need; while they certainly "know" their game here, "they sure do charge you for the knowledge" declare the price conscious, but even they say the "deals are terrific" if you "catch the 50 percent off sale" twice a year.

Maternity Works ◐[S][C] 17 | 11 | 16 | I

16 W. 57th St. (bet. 5th & 6th Aves.), F to 57th St., 212-399-9840; www.maternitymall.com

■ "From cheapo to primo, there are great" bargains "to be found" at this Midtown maternity mecca where "high-end brand names" such as Mimi Maternity and Pea in the Pod (all owned by the same parent company) are sold "at a fraction of the price"; there's "not much ambiance", the "space is small and the merchandise crammed" together, but "you'll feel like you're searching for hidden treasure and you'll be rewarded . . . sometimes."

Maurice Villency 26 | 25 | 22 | VE

200 E. 57th St. (3rd Ave.), 4/5/6/F/N/R/W to 59th St./Lexington Ave., 212-725-4840; www.villency.com

■ This 71-year-old company's blocklong, glass-fronted flagship on East 57th Street is the backdrop for "well-constructed", "pricey" contemporary custom-made furniture – some fabricated in "leather like butter"; the store has also made its first foray into home accessories ranging from sheets to lamps and pillows.

Mavi Jean ◐[S][C] 20 | 18 | 18 | M

832 Broadway (bet. 12th & 13th Sts.), 4/5/6/L/N/Q/R/W to 14th St./ Union Sq., 866-628-4575; www.mavi.com

■ For "total denim immersion", all "body types", from "tall, long-legged girls" to "little people" "with J-Lo's booty" to guys who want to be "fashionable without being slaves to fashion" plunge into this new Union Square jean-aria, an "interesting concept" flagship with "big imaginative windows", a "warehouse feel" and a staff that "rocks"; the "extensive selection" of "trendy" blues-wear offers a "stylish alternative to other hip brands, plus they're softer", more "affordable" and come in "lots of washes and styles."

Maxilla & Mandible [S][C] ▽ 24 | 23 | 18 | E

451 Columbus Ave. (bet. 81st & 82nd Sts.), B/C to 81st St., 212-724-6173; www.maxillaandmandible.com

■ "If you're dying to buy junior a trilobite for his birthday", "putter around" this Upper West Side osteological shop "after the Museum of Natural History" – "for the kid" or even the photographer, collector or naturalist "interested in skulls and skeletons, there is no where else like it."

MaxMara [S][C] 25 | 24 | 21 | VE

813 Madison Ave. (68th St.), 6 to 68th St., 212-879-6100
450 W. Broadway (bet. Houston & Prince Sts.), R/W to Prince St.; C/E to Spring St., 212-674-1817

■ Why "hop" around "to get a complete look" when these Madison Avenue and SoHo "palaces" for "very classy" Italian merchandise" "have it all", from "the most divine coats" to "sumptuous" separates and "businesswear"; loyalists "love" the "long racks filled with delicious", "luxurious" covetables and laud service that's a "pleasure", "whether you're rich or not", concluding it's "shopping heaven with prices to match, but aren't you worth it?";

N.B. at press time, Proenza Schouler was reportedly being courted to design the sportier collection.

Max Studio 🅂 | 22 | 20 | 18 | E |
415 W. Broadway (bet. Prince & Spring Sts.), R/W to Prince St.; C/E to Spring St., 212-941-1141; www.maxstudio.com
■ "Defines my closet" assert the Studio savvy who "never leave empty-handed" from this "friendly, bright" two-floor SoHo boutique; the "well-thought out" "good quality simple separates" in neutrals and subtle prints have a "flirty flair" that "verge on trendy" but are "actually designed for everyday women" in "realistic sizes"; "prices are reasonable" for the hood ("it's all relative, right?") plus there are always "ongoing sales" on the "fun lower level."

Mayle 🅂🅲 | 24 | 23 | 19 | E |
242 Elizabeth St. (bet. Houston & Prince Sts.), B/D/F/S/V to B'way/ Lafayette St., 212-625-0406
■ Set up to feel like designer Jane Mayle's closet, the "adorable atmosphere" of this NoLita boutique "draws you in, but the clothes make you stay" sigh stalwarts who save up for the "vintage-inspired" femme-fatale sheaths, signature cotton T-shirts and "whimsical" wares; fans feel it's "what shopping should be – fun, relaxed and beautiful."

Me & Ro 🅂 | 24 | 25 | 19 | E |
241 Elizabeth St. (bet. Houston & Prince Sts.), 6 to Spring St., 917-237-9215; www.meandrojewelry.com
☑ Designed by the architects ShoP with a red plaster wall and a floating flower pond in the window, this "tiny" NoLita space aims to be "spiritually stylish" to reflect the East-meets-West feel of its dangling, beaded jewelry that often carries "Sanskrit-inscribed" "messages of peace, fearlessness and love"; "everything here is delicate – except for the prices" and perhaps the "laissez-faire" staff (maybe they should study the inscriptions).

Mecox Gardens 🅂🅲 | 22 | 21 | 15 | VE |
962 Lexington Ave. (bet. 70th & 71st Sts.), 6 to 68th St., 212-249-5301; www.mecoxgardens.com
■ It's an indoor/outdoor haute hodgepodge at this Upper East Side offshoot of a Southampton house and garden shop; from global scavenger hunts, these folks bring back and artfully arrange an eclectic collection of modern pieces, "beautiful" antiques and reproductions into object lessons for clientele, in which a fin-de-siècle Chinese demi-lune table might be topped with a contemporary ceramic lamp.

Medici ❶🅂🅲 | 18 | 17 | 18 | M |
420 Columbus Ave. (bet. 80th & 81st Sts.), B/C to 81st St., 212-712-9342
24 W. 23rd St. (bet. 5th & 6th Aves.), F/V to 23rd St., 212-604-0888
☑ Worth checking into now and again, this footwear outfit is known for colorful "fashionable shoes, at good prices", that oftentimes sport "very inventive" heels and detailing, as well as "cute" handbags and accessories; but stylesetters scoff that they're either "a few seasons ago" or just plain "wanna-be."

Meg ❶🅂🅲 | ▽ 22 | 20 | 25 | M |
312 E. Ninth St. (bet. 1st & 2nd Sts.), 6 to Astor Pl., 212-260-6329
■ "Made for real women, not dolls" marvel mavens about designer Meghan Kinney's modus operandi, the results of which are

displayed in her East Village boutique; her "totally wearable" womenswear may be Downtown hip, but it's always flattering with its unusual textiles and sexy, siren necklines.

Memorial Sloan-Kettering Cancer Center Thrift Shop
17 | 15 | 14 | M |

1440 Third Ave. (bet. 81st & 82nd Sts.), 4/5/6 to 86th St., 212-535-1250

⚉ "My friends would faint if they knew it's where I get my gorgeous clothes" confide the "cheapskate ladies who lunch" and shop at this "spacious" Upper East Side thrift store that's the beneficiary of "the highest-quality donations", including "great home furnishings"; even opponents who opine it's "overpriced" admit "there are bargains to be had."

Mendel Goldberg Fabrics **S C**
▽ 25 | 13 | 20 | E |

72 Hester St. (bet. Ludlow & Orchard Sts.), F/J/M/Z to Delancey/ Essex Sts., 212-925-9110

⚉ The fabric selection, while limited, is "great", and the Lower East Side store is so small if you blink you may miss it, but the service is huge – "they remember your name, and everything you ever bought"; no wonder it's a must-stop for serious sewing circles.

Men's Wearhouse ●**S**
19 | 19 | 21 | M |

115 Broadway (Cedar St.), 2/3/4/5/A/C/J/M/Z to Fulton St./ Broadway/Nassau, 212-233-0675
380 Madison Ave. (46th St.), 4/5/6/7/S to 42nd St./Grand Central, 212-856-9008
655 Sixth Ave. (20th St.), F/N/R/V to 23rd St., 212-243-3517
2021 Bartow Ave. (Ash Loop), Bronx, 6 to Pelham Bay Park, 718-320-8347
2535 Richmond Ave. (bet. Platinum Ave. & Richmond Hill Rd.), Staten Island, 718-982-5751
www.menswearhouse.com

⚉ "Men who hate to shop" can get "a whole wardrobe", including rented formalwear, in "one easy day" at this "inexpensive" fashion chain, with a branch (aptly enough) in the Financial District and other office-accessible sites; "good tailoring" and "helpful" service make it "worth a visit" for most, though a few kvetch it's "not the classy store it promotes."

Metro Bicycles **S C**
21 | 15 | 21 | M |

417 Canal St. (6th Ave.), 1/9 to Canal St., 212-334-8000
332 E. 14th St. (bet. 1st & 2nd Aves.), 4/5/6/L/N/Q/R/W to 14th St./ Union Sq., 212-228-4344
1311 Lexington Ave. (88th St.), 4/5/6 to 86th St., 212-427-4450
546 Sixth Ave. (14th St.), A/C/E/L to 14th St./8th Ave., 212-255-5100
231 W. 96th St. (B'way), 1/2/3/9 to 96th St., 212-663-7531
360 W. 47th St. (9th Ave.), A/C/E to 42nd St./Port Authority, 212-581-4500
www.metrobicycles.com

⚉ "They stand behind their" "excellent selection" of accessories, parts and "bikes for all members of the family" at this chainlet throughout Manhattan; the "helpful" staff "really knows its stuff" and is "willing to lend a hand" to steer you toward a bevy of brands including Trek, Raleigh and Klein – "the only thing they won't do is take you for a ride."

Metropolitan Lumber & Hardware 🅂   21 | 11 | 18 | M

617 11th Ave. (bet. 45th & 46th Sts.), A/C/E to 42nd St./Port Authority, 212-246-9090
175 Spring St. (bet. Thompson St. & W. B'way), C/E to Spring St., 212-966-3466
108-20 Merrick Blvd. (109th Ave.), Queens, E/J/Z to Jamaica Ctr. Parsons/Archer, 718-657-0100
108-56 Roosevelt Ave. (108th St.), Queens, 7 to 111th St., 718-898-2100
34-35 Steinway St. (bet. 34th & 35th Aves.), Queens, R to Steinway St., 718-392-4441

◪ "Great selection" is the draw at these "local" hardware standbys purveying "high-quality tools, specialty parts" and "lumber to go" for "minor to major construction projects"; service fluctuates from "the most helpful on the planet" to "lacking" ("you'd better know what you're looking for"), but home improvers appreciate that these "solid" stores are "close" by.

METROPOLITAN MUSEUM OF ART GIFT SHOP 🅂   25 | 23 | 18 | M

The Cloisters, Fort Tryon Park, A to 190th St., 212-923-3700
1000 Fifth Ave. (81st St.), 6 to 77th St., 212-570-3894
Macy's Herald Sq., 151 W. 34th St. (bet. 6th & 7th Aves.), B/D/F/N/Q/R/V/W to 34th St./Herald Sq., 212-268-7266 🌑
113 Prince St. (bet. Greene & Wooster Sts.), R/W to Prince St., 212-614-3000 🌑
Rockefeller Ctr., 15 W. 49th St. (5th Ave.), B/D/F/V to 47-50th Sts./Rockefeller Ctr., 212-332-1360 🌑
South Street Seaport, 14 Fulton St., 2/3/4/5/A/C/J/M/Z to Fulton St./Broadway/Nassau, 212-248-0954
www.metmuseum.org

■ What "could be amazing individual jewelry, art print, stationery and book stores", as well as an "educational children's" boutique, gets "rolled into one" at the "granddaddy of museum shops" scattered all over town; you can "do most of your holiday shopping" amid a "treasure trove" "covering all prices and tastes" from "cerebral" and "expensive" to "cute" and on "clearance"; "the only problem is fighting the crowds" of "tourists with fanny packs."

Mexx 🅂   – | – | – | M

650 Fifth Ave. (52nd St.), E/V to 5th Ave./53rd St., 212-956-6505
19 Union Sq. West (15th St.), 4/5/6/L/N/Q/R/W to 14th St./Union Sq., 646-486-1302
866-444-1344; www.mexx.com

Style-seekers searching for a quick fix turn to this Dutch fast-fashion chain newly arrived in Union Square and on Fifth Avenue; the high-tech-looking, two-floor outposts may not be as jam-packed (yet) as H&M (or as cheap, either), but much like its competitor, they're filled with desirable trends that turn on a dime; guys and gals scoop up cool-as-cool-can-be threads ranging from casual workwear to edgy activewear and streetwear, all designed with Euro flair for mexx-imum effect.

Michael Anchin Glass Co. 🅂🅲   – | – | – | M

245 Elizabeth St. (bet. Houston & Prince Sts.), 6 to Spring St., 212-925-1470; www.michaelanchin.com

Some of the "most exciting glass in New York" and a "kaleidoscope of shimmering color" light up this little NoLita gallery whose owner, Michael Anchin, blows all the "beautiful pieces" that crowd the shelves himself; his long-necked vases and orb lamps are one-of-a-kind items "you'll never find anywhere else."

Michael Ashton C | – | – | – | VE |
933 Madison Ave. (74th St.), 6 to 77th St., 212-517-6655
This small Upper Eastsider positively glitters with the grandiose estate and period jewelry filling its cases; it's elegantly adorned with antique furniture, the better to get you in the mood to blow a bundle on an early 20th-century parure or an art deco watch.

Michael C. Fina ◗S | 25 | 22 | 19 | E |
545 Fifth Ave. (45th St.), 4/5/6/7/S to 42nd St./Grand Central, 212-557-2500; 800-289-3462; www.michaelcfina.com
■ "Wend your way past the newly engaged couples registering" at this Midtown emporium and you'll find "fantastic prices" on an "amazing assortment" of china, crystal, silver, stainless steel and giftware in styles that "range from traditional to trendy" (i.e. from Spode to Calvin Klein); since "they have everything under the sun", it's a "wonderful source" for "wedding presents" and "baby gifts."

Michael Dawkins C | 27 | 27 | 24 | E |
33 E. 65th St. (Madison Ave.), 6 to 68th St., 212-639-1540; www.michaeldawkins.com
■ Darling of the department stores, Michael Dawkins has a "great eye" and it shows in his "very wearable, very chic" "original" jewelry in which the "design excels"; his gallerylike East 60s boutique shines with "arty and interesting" pieces demonstrating his signature silver granulation technique (affixing miniscule spheres in patterns onto a metal surface).

Michael Eigen C | 24 | 21 | 21 | E |
Grand Central, Lexington Passage, 4/5/6/7/S to 42nd St./Grand Central, 212-949-0170 S
1200 Madison Ave. (bet. 87th & 88th Sts.), 4/5/6 to 86th St., 212-996-0281 800-780-3861; www.michaeleigen.com
■ "If you forgot that tomorrow is your anniversary, go see Michael" and his "wonderful selection of contemporary fine jewelry" well-displayed at his shops on Upper Madison Avenue and in Grand Central; he offers more than "a few lovely things" from the dainty Erica Courtney line and Indian-inspired Me & Ro as well as other "innovative designers"; watches, wedding bands and traditional fine diamond pendants are on hand too.

Michael Kors | 26 | 23 | 24 | VE |
974 Madison Ave. (76th St.), 6 to 77th St., 212-452-4685
■ There's something deliciously over-the-top about the fabrics, cut and (sigh) cost of Kors' carefree classics, "designed with love for women" (and men too); the "great location" (the East 70s) of his subtly colored flagship boutique – the work of architect Dan Rowen – and "personal service" ensure the return of regulars who devour the "oh, yum" sportswear.

Michael's | 22 | 17 | 17 | M |
1041 Madison Ave. (bet. 79th & 80th Sts.), 6 to 77th St., 212-737-7273; www.michaelsconsignment.com
■ Even those who think "consignment shops aren't all they're cracked up to be" are game to go on a "treasure hunt for couture" at this spacious duplex with large dressing rooms, established in 1954; "Upper East Side ladies with taste" "snag" "jewels" from

the "well-organized" "host of mint condition haute fashion names crowding the racks" while the betrothed believe the wedding-gown section "could be your last stop on the bridal train."

Michele Varian 🆂
– | – | – | E

33 Crosby St. (bet. Broome & Grand Sts.), 6 to Spring St., 212-343-0033; www.michelevarian.com

Michele Varian's namesake bedding shop in SoHo specializes in dreamy felt pillows with appliquéd flowers and birds, gorgeous quilts and velvet-and-silk throws; it may be located in the little-traversed southern end of Crosby Street, but that doesn't keep the celebs residing in the swank apartment building nearby from heading here for elegant, Eastern-influenced accessories.

Michelle Roth
26 | 25 | 23 | VE

24 W. 57th St. (bet. 5th & 6th Aves.), F to 57th St., 212-245-3390; www.michelleroth.com

■ It's a "Cinderella experience" at this Midtown "bridal dream" thanks to "charming" brother and sister co-owners Michelle Roth and Henry Weinreich and their "super-friendly staff", who "treat you like the belle of the ball"; the "beautifully crafted gowns", "ranging from simple and elegant to nontraditional", are presented in an "environment that's very comfortable for an overwhelming task" – "a real treat" for the aisle-bound; N.B. by appointment only, Tuesday, Thursday and Friday.

Michel Perry 🇨
∇ 26 | 26 | 25 | VE

320 Park Ave. (51st St.), 6/E/V to 51st St./Lexington Ave., 212-688-4968

■ Whether he makes them ruched, pointy or spike-heeled, this Frenchman knows a few things about creating come-hither shoes; nestled in his girlie pink Park Avenue "salon" decorated with 18th-century mirrors and modern art is a "drool-worthy" selection for the fairy-tale day you decide that you "already have enough Manolos."

Miele 🆂🇨
– | – | – | E

159½ Ludlow St. (bet. Rivington & Stanton Sts.), F/J/M/Z to Delancey/Essex Sts., 212-475-9240

On the Lower East Side, nothing fancier than two small rooms connected by a narrow hallway constitutes a hip store and in this one, cult labels like Frost French and Christopher Deane provide the way-cool lineup of clothes, footwear (including slouchy Kägi boots), accessories and sweet nothings; the sleek silhouettes are definitely not for "appliance-sized women."

Mika Inatome
– | – | – | VE

11 Worth St. (bet. Hudson St. & W. B'way), 1/9 to Franklin St., 212-966-7777; www.mikainatome.com

"You feel as if you're getting your money's worth" at this TriBeCa by-appointment-only bridal shop where Mika Inatome and her designers "work with you to" custom-"make a dress that fits your personality"; the contemporary styles, like an elegant silk jacquard gown, an adventurous one-shoulder number and made-for-the-red-carpet satin crêpe confection, can all be adjusted to taste.

MIKIMOTO 🇨
28 | 25 | 23 | VE

730 Fifth Ave. (bet. 56th & 57th Sts.), N/R/W to 5th Ave./59th St., 212-457-4600; 888-701-2323; www.mikimoto.com

■ "Pearl people" profess the "only place to buy" "the definitive necklace" is at this Japanese master, credited with creating the first cultured strands in 1893; at this light-wood, contemporary Midtown site, the "classic beauties" – "some so big they could be gumballs" – are "beautifully displayed", and a "knowledgeable" staff describes how they're "exquisitely made"; "you'll have them for life, and be paying for them that long as well."

Mimi Maternity [S] [C] 21 | 18 | 21 | M

2005 Broadway (69th St.), 1/2/3/9 to 72nd St., 212-721-1999 ◐
1125 Madison Ave. (84th St.), 4/5/6 to 86th St., 212-737-3784
1021 Third Ave. (bet. 60th & 61st Sts.), 4/5/6/F/N/R/W to 59th St./ Lexington Ave., 212-832-2667
Winter Garden Atrium, 225 Liberty St., 2nd level (South End Ave.), R/W to Rector St., 212-566-1382
Staten Island Mall, 2655 Richmond Ave., Staten Island, 718-761-0097 ◐
877-646-4666; www.mimimaternity.com

◪ "What a relief!" sigh expectant moms – "you can buy your pregnancy wardrobe" at this chain "without breaking the bank"; "the styles are fun", and the staff helps you find "great basics" that "fit and wear well"; the "only downside is the price" retort the budget conscious – "how long are you gonna wear these" items?

Mini Mini Market ◐ [S] [C] ▽ 20 | 21 | 20 | M

218 Bedford Ave. (bet. N. 4th & 5th Sts.), Brooklyn, L to Bedford Ave., 718-302-9337; www.miniminimarket.com

■ A "Brooklyn girl's dream", especially for "Williamsburg hipsters", this "fantastic find" is loaded with a "cute selection of fashionable" accessories, apparel, shoes, body products and gifts from local talents as well as designers from afar; "good prices", a "varied selection" and a decidedly cool retro vibe (pink-and-red floors) all make it "worth the trip" on the L train.

Mish – | – | – | VE

131 E. 70th St. (bet. Lexington & Park Aves.), 6 to 68th St., 212-734-3500

"Where all the bright young things shop" for all the bright things they can don is this East 70s jewel box for exclusive designs by bow tie–bedecked namesake Mish Tworkowski (ex Sotheby's); whimsy, color and craftsmanship combine in limited-edition and unique multi-hued sapphire and diamond briolette necklaces, 18 karat cuff bracelets, chokers and button earrings in bamboo motifs, and gold-and-semiprecious-stone signature pagoda brooches, all of which go like hotcakes.

Miss Lou's Herbs and Tings ◐ [S] – | – | – | E

436 E. Ninth St. (bet. Ave. A & First Ave.), L to First Ave., 212-260-4085

"Tiny but fabulous" shop "tucked away on East Ninth Street" whose concept is to take care of the inside of the body as well as the outside; accordingly, there's a selection of 120 herbal teas along with an assortment of natural-based, "high-end" makeup and skincare products from the likes of Jurlique and Korres, along with perfume and candles; owner Jacqueline Gaussen manages to be "helpful yet unobtrusive."

Missoni [C] 23 | 23 | 21 | VE

1009 Madison Ave. (78th St.), 6 to 77th St., 212-517-9339; www.missoni.com

■ In this understated Upper East Side boutique, the well-respected Italian knitwear-maker known for "colorful beauty" "stays fresh" year after year by coming up with lively and "highly original" textured patterns in men's, women's and accessories collections; so if you feel "dizzy" with desire, dig deep into your pocket for "one or two pieces to jazz up your Calvins and Armanis."

Miss Sixty ☉ | 21 | 20 | 17 | E |

246 Mulberry St. (bet. Prince & Spring Sts.), B/D/F/S/V to B'way/ Lafayette St., 212-431-6040 ◑⬛
386 W. Broadway (bet. Broome & Spring Sts.), C/E to Spring St., 212-334-9772
www.misssixty.com

■ "Poke around" these SoHo and NoLita '70s-flashback emporia "especially known" for "cheeky", "radical" Italian jeans (the "tightest, sexiest" around); accessories like denim backpacks and suitcases may be "teenager-ish", but if you groove on "casual-with-a-kick" tops and bottoms, go with the flow and "shell out some bucks for a good-quality item" or two.

Miu Miu ☉ | 22 | 22 | 18 | E |

831 Madison Ave. (bet. 69th & 70th Sts.), 6 to 68th St., 212-249-9660
100 Prince St. (bet. Greene & Mercer Sts.), R/W to Prince St., 212-334-5156 ⬛

⬛ The Madison Avenue and flagship SoHo locations of this line for women and "rich teens" feel much like any "typical space", but just "browsing" the "sexy, see-through, stylish" sheaths and separates makes you feel like an "ever-cute" "hipster"; however, while "less pricey than [parent] Prada, it still puts pressure on the pocketbook" – too much for basically "playful" purses and shoes, some sniff.

Mixona ◑⬛☉ | ▽ 26 | 26 | 23 | E |

262 Mott St. (bet. Houston & Prince Sts.), 6 to Spring St., 646-613-0100; www.mixona.com

■ "A nice airy shop with friendly service" and "beautifully displayed merchandise", this "fun" "fave" in NoLita coaxes coquettes to come hither with its "unique collection" of "gorgeous gossamer little things" "for every taste, from basic Hanro and wacky leather items" to lust-worthy lacy bras and panties from Leigh Bantivolgio; "sexy and wearable", this "great selection" of unmentionables "should be at the top of any girl's drawer."

Modell's ◑⬛ | 17 | 12 | 11 | I |

1293 Broadway (34th St.), B/D/F/N/Q/R/V/W to 34th St./Herald Sq., 212-244-4544; 800-275-6633; www.modells.com
Additional locations throughout the NY area

⬛A "New York institution" since 1889, this "basic, no-frills", "all-purpose sporting goods" chain "aims to please" with a "good" "mix" of "exercise clothing and gear", "team paraphernalia", "great buys on equipment" and "bargains on athletic shoes" – "if you can't find it here, give up"; but bashers boo at the "cramped" quarters and cite "disinterested" and "inexperienced" service.

Modernica ☉ | 24 | 22 | 20 | E |

57 Greene St. (bet. Broome & Spring Sts.), 6 to Spring St., 212-219-1303; www.modernica.net

■ For those "doing the mid-century thing", this SoHo showroom is a "must-see", since its reissues of modern furniture classics by Charles and Ray Eames and Herman Miller, as well as George Nelson's bubble lamps, are offered at "great value" "compared with other neighborhood stores" with the same aesthetic.

Modern Stone Age 🆂🅲   ▽ 22 | 20 | 20 | E
54 Greene St. (Broome St.), R/W to Prince St., 212-219-0383;
www.modernstone.com

■ Step off the crowded SoHo sidewalks and into this "soothing, Zen-like store" where "beautiful" babbling fountains form a "serene" backdrop for "unusual" furniture and bath-and-kitchen accessories made out of stone, such as "stunning" fireplaces, sinks, frames and otherworldly onyx lamps; the owners, a former conceptual artist and an ex-interior architect, will also custom-make pieces for any room in the house.

MOMA DESIGN STORE 🆂🅲   26 | 23 | 17 | E
81 Spring St. (Crosby St.), 6 to Spring St., 646-613-1367 ◑
44 W. 53rd St. (bet. 5th & 6th Aves.), E/V to 5th Ave./53rd St., 212-708-9669
www.momastore.org

☑ "A fabulous place to spend money" on "have-it-all" pals is this destination for "cutting-edge design"; amid the "authorized Corbu and Eames reproductions", "minimalist housewares", ergonomic gizmos, "offbeat jewelry", "graphically arresting" stationery and "funky" art books, "you won't see yourself coming and going" (and neither will the "ditzy" staff), but "the look in people's eyes when you give them a gift from MoMA" says "groovy, baby" – "you're the coolest cat in town."

Mommy Chic ◑🆂🅲   24 | 22 | 22 | E
2449 Broadway (bet. 90th & 91st Sts.), 1/2/3/9 to 96th St.,
212-769-9099; 866-244-2666; www.mommychic.com

■ Designer/co-owner Angela Chew recently moved her boutique from NoLita to the West 90s where she showcases her "great selection" of "fun, fabulous" maternity fashions; "everything fits", from the "yummy" knits and "sophisticated" hand-beaded evening gowns to more casual weekend wear and denim pieces, plus the "staff is sympathetic to hormonal women"; parents also adore the baby-and-children's line (newborns through age six), made from fine European cottons, as well as luxe satins.

Montblanc 🆂🅲   25 | 25 | 22 | VE
120 Greene St. (bet. Prince & Spring Sts.), R/W to Prince St.,
212-680-1300; 866-828-4810
598 Madison Ave. (bet. 57th & 58th Sts.), N/R/W to 5th Ave./59th St.,
212-223-8888; 800-581-4810
www.montblanc.com

■ "For those who demand the best", these "quiet" shops in SoHo and on Madison Avenue are the peak of "self-pampering", providing the "ultimate writing instrument" ("everyone wants one, two . . . and then there are the collector's editions"), as well as "great cuff links", watches, leather goods and stationery; the "friendly staff" provides "outstanding service" that matches the "excellent quality" of the merchandise; N.B. the Midtown store's post-*Survey* relocation may outdate the above Presentation score.

Montmartre 🆂🅲   21 | 18 | 14 | E
2212 Broadway (79th St.), 1/9 to 79th St., 212-875-8430 ◑
247 Columbus Ave. (71st St.), B/C to 72nd St., 212-721-7760 ◑
225 Liberty St. (S. End Ave.), R/W to Rector St., 212-945-7858
1157 Madison Ave. (85th St.), 4/5/6 to 86th St., 212-988-8962 ◑

☑ "Need something for a night out tonight?" "you'll find it" at these "friendly" boutiques, "stuffed" with "classy clothing with a touch of girlyness"; the Upper West side locations have been fixtures for over 20 years and they're still "great for seasonal staples" and the "latest in fashion" from "always-hip designers" like Nanette Lepore, Theory and Rebecca Taylor; still, a few find the staff "a bit snooty" and the merchandise "somewhat overpriced"; N.B. at press time, a huge branch was set to open in The Shops at Columbus Circle at Time Warner Center.

MOOD FABRICS INC. C | 28 | 15 | 20 | M |

225 W. 37th St., 3rd fl. (7th Ave.), 1/2/3 to 34th St./Penn Station, 212-730-5003

■ A "fabric-aholic's heaven" staffed with "helpful" salespeople, this third-floor textile titan in the Garment Center is a "must for the fashion student or creative soul"; the "overwhelming number of options" include everything from "Astroturf to silk shantung" to "faux fur" to "new, exotic" offerings from high-end and up-and-coming designers at "prices that can't be beat" so "be prepared to rummage" – "and let your imagination run rampant."

Mood Indigo S C | 25 | 19 | 16 | E |

181 Prince St. (bet. Sullivan & Thompson Sts.), C/E to Spring St., 212-254-1176

◪ Take "a trip back in time" at this "salt-and-pepper-shaker heaven" in SoHo, where the "kitschy" array of "retro items" also includes colorful Fiestaware, Russel Wright dinnerware, whimsical barware and vintage glass plates and bowls; still, the moody muse it's "way overpriced."

Moon River Chattel S C | – | – | – | M |

62 Grand St. (bet. Kent & Wyeth Aves.), Brooklyn, L to Bedford Ave., 718-388-1121

Williamsburg home-furnishings shop where you can wax nostalgic over weathered farm tables and vintage table linens, along with mostly reproduction toys and enamelware; in an annex across the street, the owners offer architectural salvage from old buildings and signage from long-gone carnivals.

Morgane Le Fay S C | 26 | 25 | 23 | VE |

746 Madison Ave. (bet. 64th & 65th Sts.), N/R/W to 5th Ave./59th St., 212-879-9700
67 Wooster St. (bet. Grand & Spring Sts.), C/E to Spring St., 212-219-7672

■ Walking into these East 60s or SoHo stores feels like visiting a chic cathedral, with their "architectural" dresses and "ethereal" gowns lending a magical air to the high-ceilinged rooms; the "ever-unique", "fantasy" clothing "makes you wish you had a ball to attend every night", but chances are you'll need a fairy godmother to afford it.

Morgan Library Shop S C | 22 | 19 | 19 | M |

29 E. 36th St. (Madison Ave.), 6 to 33rd St., 212-590-0390;
www.morganlibrary.org/shop

■ Amid the workaday bustle in Murray Hill, one of NY's "most underrated museums" is "an oasis of calm" for "discerning" bibliophiles, and its "nicely designed" shop follows suit; "laid out as if Mr. Morgan planned it as well as he planned his exquisite library", it offers "tasteful" "little gifts" and "excellent-quality" cards and books "you can't find elsewhere", all mirroring the rare printed matter and drawings on display; the staff is "personable", "maybe because few people" browse this "well-kept secret."

MORGENTHAL FREDERICS S   28 | 26 | 23 | VE

*944 Madison Ave. (bet. 74th & 75th Sts.), 6 to 77th St.,
212-744-9444*
*699 Madison Ave. (bet. 62nd & 63rd Sts.), 4/5/6/F/N/R/W to 59th St./
Lexington Ave., 212-838-3090*
399 W. Broadway (Spring St.), C/E to Spring St., 212-966-0099 ◐
www.morgenthal-fredericsny.com

■ "The Rolls-Royce" of opticians sports three NYC locations, all
with "great" David Rockwell–designed interiors, a backdrop for
"traffic-stopping" eyewear designs that combine a "molto-trendy"
look with the "latest technology"; the "wonderfully seasoned staff"
is "genuinely interested in helping you find suitable frames" and
create an "unusually un-stressful shopping experience"; the only
catch: "you'll really think you need glasses when you see the
prices"; N.B. a new branch has opened in The Shops at Columbus
Circle at Time Warner Center.

Morris Brothers S   22 | 15 | 18 | M

2322 Broadway (84th St.), 1/9 to 86th St., 212-724-9000

■ "A mainstay for the camping set" for generations, this Upper
Westsider is also an "old standby" for "anything and everything
for kids" and teens, from "pajamas and gym clothes to sporting
clothes" to all of the "trendy" "essentials" (think Juicy Couture
and Mavi); but the less-enthralled pout that the "presentation
could use a boost."

MOSS S C   26 | 27 | 21 | VE

*146 Greene St. (bet. Houston & Prince Sts.), R/W to Prince St.,
212-226-2190; 866-888-6677; www.mossonline.com*

■ All hail Murray Moss and his "cutting-edge" SoHo "shrine to
good design", a "pristine citadel of modern taste" with "unusual,
museum-quality merchandise"; everything – from "drop-dead
beautiful" Moser crystal and Nymphenburg porcelain to vases by
Hella Jongerius and "clever" lighting by Droog – is "preciously
priced" and "strikingly" displayed behind glass in a "gorgeous
white-walled space" where salespeople serve as well-versed
curators of what's "cool."

Motherhood Maternity S   17 | 12 | 16 | I

1449 Third Ave. (82nd St.), 6 to 77th St., 212-734-5984
*36 W. 34th St. (bet. 5th & 6th Aves.), B/D/F/N/Q/R/V/W to 34th St./
Herald Sq., 212-695-9106 ◐*
www.motherhood.com

◪ "Nice for the price", this nationwide maternity chain comes in
handy for "casual, utilitarian" "inexpensive basics like T-shirts
and jeans" – in short, "not too hip clothes at reasonable prices";
though you can "save a lot of money" initially, many miffed moms
moan that the styles are "frumpy."

Movado ◐ S C   25 | 23 | 22 | E

*Rockefeller Ctr., 610 Fifth Ave., ground level (bet. 49th & 50th Sts.),
B/D/F/V to 47-50th Sts./Rockefeller Ctr., 212-218-7555*
138 Spring St. (Wooster St.), C/E to Spring St., 212-431-0249
www.movado.com

◪ Known for the "sleek, simple designs" of its oft-imitated "classic
timepieces", this venerable company keeps on ticking amid the
"welcoming atmosphere" of its Rockefeller Center and SoHo
homes; the "service is somewhat snobbish but helpful", however

even fans find the "watches are more creatively styled than the [newer] jewelry" and housewares lines.

Mrs. John L. Strong S
25 | 22 | 19 | VE

Barneys, 699 Madison Ave., 2nd. fl. (bet. 62nd & 63rd Sts.), 4/5/6/F/N/R/W to 59th St./Lexington Ave., 212-838-3848

■ What insiders insist is the "Bentley of the society stationers" may have changed hands, but the previous owner stayed on as president to ensure the "high-end", "traditional" letter paper and invitations remain "some of the best in the world"; tucked away on the second floor of Barney's, it still purveys the same "gorgeous", "classic" products, and if some whisper the "service is less than friendly", more "love it for the fact that it represents seven decades of moneyed Manhattan."

Munder-Skiles
– | – | – | E

799 Madison Ave., 3rd fl. (bet. 67th & 68th Sts.), 6 to 68th St., 212-717-0150
"Garden furniture takes on a new elegance" at this "Hamptons-crowd choice" in the East 60s where designer John Danzer offers unique outdoor (and some indoor) chairs, tables and accessories; many items are based on originals from Monticello and Edith Wharton's home, The Mount, for which he has the exclusive license, and others display modern influences; N.B. consultation is also available.

Museum of Arts & Design Shop S C
– | – | – | E

(fka American Craft Museum Shop)
40 W. 53rd St. (bet. 5th & 6th Aves.), E/V to 5th Ave./53rd St., 212-956-3535; www.madmuseum.org
No longer solely devoted to artisans' work, this recently renamed and reconceptualized Midtown museum now boasts a shop that's also an expression of its new direction; creative souls can't help but be bowled over by the colorfully stocked windows and the trove of merchandise, an integrated treatment of art, design and crafts, featuring jewelry, ceramics, glassware, furniture, unusual gift items by current artists and even handiwork like hats and scarves.

Museum of the City of New York, The S
22 | 20 | 17 | M

1220 Fifth Ave. (103rd St.), 6 to 103rd St., 212-534-1672, ext. #227; www.mcny.org
■ Offering "a little taste of the Big Apple", especially for "old-school NYC lovers", this "well put-together" store is "where you should buy all those cool" Gotham gifts; "from tomes to trinkets" to "period-style toys" to pricey, framed Bernice Abbott reproductions, this "nostalgia trip" is filled with "all sorts of New York knickknacks" that "have substance and depth, and reflect your museum experience perfectly" – plus it might be the only place in the five boroughs where you can still buy a spaldeen and a stickball bat.

Mxyplyzyk S C
24 | 20 | 14 | M

125 Greenwich Ave. (bet. Horatio & 13th Sts.), A/C/E/L to 14th St./8th Ave., 212-989-4300; www.mxyplyzyk.com
◪ "Cool, cool, cool" West Village "boutique of fun and fancy" featuring hip tabletop, kitchen and bath items with a "high-design quotient" for almost low-rent prices; a rather "brusque" staff presides over the "crowded" space "crammed" with "random" and "funky gift" ideas – see-through scales and doggie banks – "that you won't find anywhere else."

Myoptics 🅢🅒   25 | 23 | 22 | E

123 Prince St. (bet. Greene & Wooster Sts.), R/W to Prince St.,
212-598-9306
96 Seventh Ave. (bet. 15th & 16th Sts.), 1/2/3/9/F/L/V to 14th St./
6th Ave., 212-633-6014
42 St. Marks Pl. (bet. 1st & 2nd Aves.), 6 to Astor Pl., 212-533-1577
www.myoptics.com

■ "Edgy glasses for the urban-chic geek" are the trademark of this "funky" outfit where a "fabulous selection" of "wonderful" frames is matched by "impeccable workmanship"; the salespeople "really like their jobs" and "have a great eye – no pun intended – for what looks best on you", and though a few warn that "some locations are better than others", most are satisfied with the "mix of style and quality"; N.B. at press time, plans were underway to open a new TriBeCa branch.

M Z Wallace 🅢🅒   ▽ 21 | 20 | 18 | E

93 Crosby St. (bet. Prince & Spring Sts.), 6 to Spring St.,
212-431-8252; www.mzwallace.com

■ Cement floors, white exposed brick and an airy atmosphere drive home the point of this SoHo shop's "tasteful" merchandise: organization; "sturdy in structure, snappy in style", these "fashionable bags" and totes, turned out in canvas and leather in "great color combos", are "very 'in' with the times", sporting surprising details like "cell phone pockets and MetroCard holders" that bear "New Yorkers in mind"; P.S. zip one open and check out the "fun", brilliant interior.

Nalunyc 🅢🅒   – | – | – | E

10 Little W. 12th St. (9th Ave.), A/C/E/L to 14th St./8th Ave.,
212-675-7873; www.nalunyc.com

"A surfer's paradise" in the Meatpacking District? "damn straight!"; a reminder that Oahu and Manhattan have something in common, geographically speaking, this tiny shop rides the nabe's wave as a shopping destination, offering boards from T&C in various lengths, wet suits, itsy bikinis, Billabong shorts and flip-flops, as well as splashy videos, all displayed in a no-frills, hang-loose atmosphere.

Nancy & Co. 🅢🅒   20 | 17 | 16 | E

1242 Madison Ave. (89th St.), 4/5/6 to 86th St., 212-427-0770

▨ Women seeking an "interesting selection" of tasteful, "classy" sportswear, "gorgeous knits" and "unusual" accessories find this Upper Eastsider "worth a visit" when "in the neighborhood"; but malcontents mutter over the "frumpy", "overpriced basics" and suggest the staff isn't such great company, either.

Nancy Geist 🅢🅒   ▽ 24 | 23 | 21 | E

107 Spring St. (Mercer St.), R/W to Prince St.; 6 to Spring St.,
212-925-7192

■ "Strategically plan your walk home" so you can "pass by the windows" of this gallery-esque SoHo footwear shop with curvy, cushy benches and "ogle" the "gorgeous" creations within; the "stylish" handmade Italian sandals and shoes come in lots of "cute" colors, and they're so "lovely" they make you "want to maintain your pedicure"; while the wistful "wish I could afford more" (they're a "bit pricey"), others opine the tags are "right for the quality."

Nancy Koltes at Home ◗Ⓢ

25 | 22 | 20 | VE

31 Spring St. (bet. Mott & Mulberry Sts.), 6 to Spring St.,
212-219-2271; www.nancykoltes.com

■ This "lovely, little" "find" on Spring Street sells "gorgeous stuff" like "beautiful bedding" (600-thread-count) made in Italy, "luxurious" table linens, towels and comforters (including an exclusive on Scandia Down); it's molto "expensive" but that doesn't keep converts from "coveting" the covers here.

Nanette Lepore ⓈⒸ

25 | 21 | 22 | E

423 Broome St. (bet. Crosby & Lafayette Sts.), 6 to Spring St.,
212-219-8265; www.nanettelepore.com

■ "On a skinny day", stop by this "pretty" SoHo boutique with its "bright" pink floor, birdcages and chandelier to try on "crisp, colorful", "delicate and beautifully patterned" dresses or one of the "well-made", "flirty" separates; converts "swoon" about the "relatively light price tag" (compared with other designers), calling this "a sure winner for extremely feminine clothing."

National Wholesale Liquidators ◗Ⓢ

15 | 7 | 7 | I

632 Broadway (Houston St.), B/D/F/S/V to B'way/Lafayette St.,
212-979-2400
691 Co-Op City Blvd. (bet. Carver Loop & Peartree Ave.), Bronx, 6 to
Pelham Bay Park, 718-320-7771
2201 59th St. (Bay Pkwy.), Brooklyn, N to 23rd Ave., 718-621-3993
4802-22 New Utrecht Ave. (48th St.), Brooklyn, D/M to 50th St.,
718-438-2604
71-01 Kissena Blvd. (71st Ave.), Queens, 7 to Main St., 718-591-3900
www.nationalwholesaleliquidators.com

◪ "For this and that from here and there", it's a "riot to shop in" this "dollar store on steroids" in NoHo and the boroughs; "students moving in for the semester" "fill carts up quickly" with "candles, cleaning products, picture frames, salted mixed nuts, batteries, face wash, sponges" and other "dorm-room chic" "essentials", some with "brand names"; it's "sloppy, dumpy" and the staff is "rude", but "do you really care when the prices are this cheap?"

Natuzzi ⓈⒸ

21 | 21 | 18 | E

101 Greene St. (bet. Prince & Spring Sts.), R/W to Prince St.,
212-334-4335; www.natuzzi.com

■ This is "the place if you're into leather" – furniture that is, say supporters of this airy SoHo showroom for "comfortable" imported Italian seating in a "great assortment of colors and styles", which are also offered in easy-to-clean, less expensive microfiber; "unless you're on a tight budget", the fairly priced pieces are right on the money.

Nautica ◗ⓈⒸ

19 | 20 | 18 | E

Rockefeller Ctr., 50 Rockefeller Plaza (bet. 5th & 6th Aves.), B/D/F/
V to 47-50th Sts./Rockefeller Ctr., 212-664-9594; 877-628-8422;
www.nautica.com

◪ "More Cape Cod than Ocean City", the "something-white" "classics" at this West 50s chainster service men and women who've sailed "above and beyond the J. Crew yacht wanna-bes and Tommy Hilfiger preppy" set; if the merchandise is similar to everything else "you already have in your closet", at least it's "good quality", though money-wise mates say "save money" and stay on the lookout "until they have a sale."

NBA Store ◖◗ⓈⒸ
23 | 25 | 16 | E

666 Fifth Ave. (52nd St.), 6/E/V to 51st St./Lexington Ave.,
212-515-6221

☑ "Your one-stop shop for all your NBA gear" is this East 50s store that's "great for gifts for the basketball aficionados" on your list; sportswear includes jerseys, T-shirts, warm-up jackets and the interior's a "playland for kids of all ages", with a "great court inside"; the service, however, gets a penalty for "indifference", and others cry foul over the "expensive" merchandise.

Nellie M. Boutique ⓈⒸ
21 | 17 | 17 | E

1309 Lexington Ave. (88th St.), 4/5/6 to 86th St., 212-996-4410;
www.nelliem.com

■ "Beware of a major splurge upon entering" this "bastion of funky chic", a "surprise find" "conveniently located on the Upper East Side"; "the "wonderful selection" of "everything from Lilly Pulitzer to Juicy Couture" to "lesser known European" and American "contemporary lines", "plus some twists", "can make anyone light up", especially when shopping for "party- and casual wear"; the staff offers "good personal service", and bridal parties get full-on attention.

Nemo Tile Company
23 | 19 | 19 | M

48 E. 21st St. (bet. B'way & Park Ave. S.), 6 to 23rd St.,
212-505-0009
177-02 Jamaica Ave. (Liberty Ave.), Queens, F to Hillside,
718-291-5969
800-636-6845; www.nemotile.com

■ These family-owned "low-key stores" in the Flatiron District and Jamaica are "the places" to go for tile, offering the "full range, from basics to luxury styles", as well as plumbing and bathroom accessories; the "helpful service" ("if you get the right salesperson, the advice is golden") and "great prices" make this pair among the "best" resources for budget-minded DIYers.

Nest Ⓢ
– | – | – | M

396A Seventh Ave. (bet. 12th & 13th Sts.), Brooklyn, F to 7th Ave.,
718-965-3491; 866-231-1900

Perched in the South Slope, this home-furnishings shop, owned by two former graphic designers, aims to feather the nests of fellow dwellers; the orange store sign and perky blue exterior feel like an urban welcome wagon, inviting customers to enter and explore the Japanese stoneware, retro-modern lamps, Indian bedspreads, fuzzy throws and colorful terry-cloth towels, all arranged in cool cubes.

Neue Galerie ⓈⒸ
23 | 23 | 20 | E

1048 Fifth Ave. (86th St.), 4/5/6 to 86th St., 212-628-6200;
www.neuegalerie.org

☑ Upper Fifth Avenue's "museum jewel", set in a Beaux Arts mansion, boasts Ronald Lauder's collection of "great" German and Austrian works from the 19th and 20th centuries offset by this "clearly top-class shop"; "book treasures", "fabulously designed" repros of jewelry and tableware are featured along with *objets d'art* "you just saw in the galleries" inspired by artists like Hoffmann and Loos; the "stunning, if pricey merchandise" "may be your cup of tea, but if not, just enjoy a cup of chocolate *mit schlage*" in downstairs Café Sabarsky that "feels just like Vienna."

New Balance S
`23 | 17 | 19 | M`

821 Third Ave. (50th St.), 6/E/V to 51st St./Lexington Ave., 212-421-4444
51 W. 42nd St. (bet. 5th & 6th Aves.), 7/B/D/F/V to 42nd St./6th Ave., 212-997-9112
www.newbalance.com

■ Perhaps they're "not as flashy" as some of the other sneaker stores, but these "cool" emporiums in the East 50s and West 40s sell "the greatest shoes on the planet" according to admirers (chief among them "runners"); the "seasoned staff" will "help you find the best pair for your foot type", with lots of options for "odd sizes", and they "always carry the latest models before anyone else."

New Museum of
Contemporary Art Store S C
`22 | 21 | 19 | M`

583 Broadway (bet. Houston & Prince Sts.), R/W to Prince St., 212-219-1222; www.newmuseum.org

■ For "cool stuff in cool digs", hip culture-vultures go underground to this recently renamed, ample SoHo museum shop filled with edgy postmodern items and lit ranging from "kitsch to intriguing" and an "excellent array of up-to-date art books" from "just about every contemporary artist"; fans "feel arty" just "browsing" at "neat gifts" like a Keith Haring domino set or a Yoshitomo Nara snow globe, praising the "unique" goods with a resoundingly positive "snap!"; N.B. at press time, plans were afoot to move to the Bowery.

New York & Co.
`17 | 16 | 15 | M`

4261 Broadway (181st St.), 1/9 to 181st St., 212-927-3624 S
83 Nassau St. (bet. Fulton & John Sts.), 2/3/4/5/A/C/J/M/Z to Fulton St./Broadway/Nassau, 212-964-2864
515-521 86th St. (Shore Rd.), Brooklyn, R to 86th St., 718-680-2252 S
5308 Fifth Ave. (53rd St.), Brooklyn, R to 53rd St., 718-492-9292 S
Kings Plaza, 5335 Kings Plaza, Brooklyn, 2/5 to Brooklyn College/ Flatbush Ave., 718-338-7373 S
8603 21st Ave. (86th St.), Brooklyn, D/M to Bay Pkwy., 718-996-0734 S
30-37 Steinway St. (bet. 30th & 31st Aves.), Queens, G/R/V to Steinway St., 718-204-0117 S
Staten Island Mall, 2655 Richmond Ave. (Platinum Ave.), Staten Island, 718-698-8060 S
www.nyandco.com

◪ "Walk in and walk out" in "good basics" with "urban flair" that are "not showstoppers but nice enough to wear to the office"; fans find the "true sizes flattering" for the "everyday woman no matter her size or shape" and praise pieces that offer "hints of trends" at "moderate prices"; but those who'd rather not join this company pout it's "always a step behind" in "style" and find the staff "pushy, pushy, pushy."

New York Central Art Supply C
`25 | 15 | 21 | M`

62 Third Ave. (11th St.), 4/5/6/L/N/Q/R/W to 14th St./Union Sq., 212-473-7705; 800-950-6111

■ The "encyclopedic assortment" of "quality" paper and "general printmaking supplies" gives bookmakers the "shivers" at this "old-school" "king of art-supply" stores in the East Village; the family-run sixtysomething joint is "cramped and ugly", but their stock is "beautiful", "the staff knows what they're doing" and "you can't go wrong with the place where Andy Warhol bought his supplies."

New York Doll Hospital ♥ C
23 | 18 | 24 | E

787 Lexington Ave., 2nd fl. (bet. 61st & 62nd Sts.), 4/5/6/F/N/R/W to 59th St./Lexington Ave., 212-838-7527

■ "For generations", "adults and children alike have needed to believe that caring nurses in crisp white uniforms tend to" "cherished dolls and teddy bears" at this second-floor, 101-year-old "true New York institution" on Lex, but it's owner Irving Chais who's likely to "fix up" "these important members of the family" so they look "brand new"; sure, the space is "messy, with parts strewn about, but that's why you feel comfortable", plus while there you can purchase a new friend from a selection of antique moppets.

New York Elegant Fabric
▽ 25 | 19 | 19 | M

222 W. 40th St. (bet. 7th & 8th Aves.), 1/2/3/7/9/N/Q/R/S/W to 42nd St./Times Sq., 212-302-4980

■ Though its "excellent selection" may be "on the expensive side for the district", this West 40s stop is worth investigating, as it "always has some very unique fabric" finds on hand that you "don't seem to see anywhere else", particularly piece goods for men's suits.

New York Golf Center ● S C
26 | 22 | 17 | E

Golf Club at Chelsea Piers, Pier 59 (18th St. & West Side Hwy.), A/C/E/L to 14th St./8th Ave., 212-242-8899
131 W. 35th St. (bet. B'way & 7th Ave.), B/D/F/N/Q/R/V/W to 34th St./Herald Sq., 212-564-2255
www.newyorkgolf.com

■ Covering 9,000 sq. ft., this "huge" Garment Center chain offshoot "feels like you're in the clubhouse of a really nice" golf facility; the "helpful staff" guides you through the "great selection" of "single clubs and full sets", apparel, shoes and accessories at a cost that's "par for the course"; its smaller sibling on the main floor of the Golf Club at Chelsea Piers also has "excellent equipment" from brands like Callaway and Cobra, but wallet-watchers warn about "Pebble Beach prices on the Hudson", advising "just go to hit golf balls."

New York Look, The C
21 | 16 | 13 | E

2030 Broadway (69th St.), 1/2/3/9 to 72nd St., 212-362-8650 ● S
551 Fifth Ave. (45th St.), 4/5/6/7/S to 42nd St./Grand Central, 212-557-0909 ● S
30 Lincoln Plaza (bet. B'way & 62nd St.), 1/9/A/B/C/D to 59th St./Columbus Circle, 212-245-6511 ● S
570 Seventh Ave. (41st St.), 1/2/3/7/9/N/Q/R/S/W to 42nd St./Times Sq., 212-382-2760
468 W. Broadway (Houston St.), C/E to Spring St., 212-598-9988 ● S

◪ "Ignore the cheesy name" say fans of this women's apparel chain, whose branches "look like tourist marts from the outside" but on the inside contain "decent-quality" contemporary "career and dress-up" threads, "well-made shoes" and "stunning costume jewelry" by "small designers from all over the world"; "good sales" mitigate the "extortionate prices", but wear "armor to fend off" the "overbearing" staff, "legendary for being pushy."

New York Public Library Shop
21 | 18 | 17 | M

455 Fifth Ave. (40th St.), 4/5/6/7/S to 42nd St./Grand Central, 212-340-0839 S
42nd St. & Fifth Ave., 7 to 5th Ave., 212-930-0641

(continued)

New York Public Library Shop
Schomburg Ctr., 515 Malcolm X Blvd. (135th St.), 2/3 to 135th St.,
212-491-2206 **S**
www.thelibraryshop.org
■ Take a study break at the Library shops to "find the perfect
gift for that fussy aunt in Wisconsin", particularly if she's of a
"scholarly" bent; "lovely books", "good kids'" stuff and "fun NY
memorabilia" are "expertly presented and reasonably priced";
N.B. the Schomburg Center's boutique specializes in African
handicrafts and literature by and about African-American writers.

New York Replacement Parts Corp.   ▽ 22 | 5 | 17 | M
1456 Lexington Ave. (bet. 94th & 95th Sts.), 6 to 96th St.,
212-534-0818; 800-228-4718; www.nyrp.com
■ What some boast is the "best plumbing supply house around"
may be this "reliable" East 90s store, with a "fine showroom for
bath fixtures" and a general store "next door that has everything";
the staff is "incredibly knowledgeable" and the "prices are great",
and though you should "prepare to wait", if you're "patient", you
"can get what you want."

New York Transit Museum ◗ **S** **C**   19 | 17 | 16 | M
Grand Central, Main Concourse, 4/5/6/7/S to 42nd St./Grand Central,
212-878-0106; www.mta.nyc.ny.us/museum
◪ Next stop, Grand Central for an underground spree at "the
deepest store you'll ever visit", "selling everything subway-
related"; "token cuff links, transit-map ties" and "MetroCard tote
bags" are part of the "fun, weird stuff" the city is made of, but the
shop does "need a better selection of merchandise."

Nice Price **S** **C**   19 | 10 | 14 | I
493 Columbus Ave. (bet. 83rd & 84th Sts.), 1/9 to 86th St., 212-362-1020;
www.clothingline.com
◪ Stylish skinflints say this "bare-bones" Upper Westsider is a
"sure thing" for huge "savings" on duds "you drooled over"
elsewhere, including Diane von Furstenberg and Cynthia Rowley
"finds"; though "bargains" for "every bodytype" still "end up
triaged here", the "disarray" has nostalgists waxing "18 years ago,
this place was wonderful – or was I much poorer and less fussy?"

Nicole Farhi **S** **C**   23 | 25 | 19 | VE
10 E. 60th St. (bet. 5th & Madison Aves.), N/R/W to 5th Ave./59th St.,
212-223-8811
■ When London's calling, *au courant* Anglophiles head to this hip,
East 60s lifestyle shop, whose floors – a stylish series of floating
glass, walnut and bluestone platforms – display male and female
"classic" clothes, accessories and "especially well-done leather"
goods, plus "wonderful home furnishings" and antique trifles;
those hungry for more hit the "excellent restaurant" downstairs,
open for lunch only.

Nicole Miller **S** **C**   22 | 20 | 20 | E
780 Madison Ave. (bet. 66th & 67th Sts.), 6 to 68th St., 212-288-9779
134 Prince St. (bet. W. B'way & Wooster St.), R/W to Prince St.,
212-343-1362
www.nicolemiller.com
■ Play "dress up" at these small SoHo and Upper East Side
boutiques where "from the [scarf] to the purse, they get it right

every time", whether your ideal "special-occasion outfit" is "that little black dress you've been looking for forever" or something in the designer's signature "wild patterns and colors"; the fun is enhanced by "helpful employees", particularly on Prince Street.

Niketown ◐ [S] 23 | 24 | 17 | M

6 E. 57th St. (bet. 5th & Madison Aves.), 4/5/6/F/N/R/W to 59th St./ Lexington Ave., 212-891-6453; www.niketown.com

◪ The "Shangri-la of Nike-ness" may be this "mega-store" in the East 50s that's a "wonderland for fans" of the swoosh-buckling brand; the "presentation is mind-blowing", with five floors filled with "up-to-the-minute merchandise", including the "newest" sneakers and the "best work-out clothes"; though a few feel it's "a little light on the women's selection" and the "service is harried", more maintain it provides a "great shopping experience."

1950 ⊭ ▽ 25 | 25 | 17 | E

440 Lafayette St. (bet. Astor Pl. & E. 4th St.), 6 to Astor Pl., 212-995-1950

■ Airy, expansive and expensive East Village furniture store offering "beautiful", hard-to-find mid-century French pieces like Jean Prouvé desks and Charlotte Perriand bookshelves, along with tables and chairs by George Nakashima, the Japanese-American craftsman whose graceful, organic wood furniture is rarely spotted for sale outside his home state of Pennsylvania.

99X ◐ [S] [C] 23 | 19 | 18 | M

84 E. 10th St. (bet. 3rd & 4th Aves.), R/W to 8th St.; 6 to Astor Pl., 212-460-8599; www.99xny.com

■ "Anglophile heaven", whether you're a "mod, a punk or just your regular indie kid", this "super-friendly" British-owned East Village boutique "rocks" one step beyond with its "not for poseurs" "funky footwear" like Tredair UK creepers, "hard-to-find Doc Martens" and "old-school Pumas" and hipster clothing with "retro charm" from labels like Ben Sherman and Fred Perry; scenesters also dig the pork-pie hats and oh-so-New-Wave skinny ties.

NINE WEST ◐ [S] 18 | 17 | 14 | M

675 Fifth Ave. (bet. 53rd & 54th Sts.), 6/E/V to 51st St./Lexington Ave., 212-319-6893; www.ninewest.com

Additional locations throughout the NY area

◪ "Go West – you can't go wrong" at this "jam-packed" "safe bet" if you need "attractive" "everyday workhorse" shoes "at everyday prices" or the "latest runway knockoffs"; "a perfect combo of style and comfort", the "fashionable footwear" inspires "average Janes" "all across America" to "follow the trends while going easy on the pocketbook"; but the less enthused point to "spotty service" that "takes a lifetime" and conclude this "generic" chain is "for those who miss suburban malls."

Noir et Blanc...Bis [C] ▽ 19 | 17 | 19 | M

19 W. 23rd St. (bet. 5th & 6th Aves.), R/W to 23rd St., 212-627-1750

■ Despite the name, not everything is 'black and white' in this Flatiron store – *au contraire,* insiders who "come for undiscovered gems" confide that the goods are arranged by color, the jewel-like tones sparking up the women's tailored separates (plus a beaded top or two) from a range of U.S., European and British designers like Ghost; semiprecious jewelry, velvety scarves and purses round out the ensembles.

Nom de Guerre [S][C] — | – | – | E

640 Broadway (Bleecker St.), 6 to Bleecker St., 212-253-2891
There's no sign outside, but NoHo scenesters still manage to find this minimalist, industrial feeling shop with a hip, rec-room vibe in the basement below Swatch; owned by Isa Saalabi and Holly Harnsongkarm of Brooklyn's Isa, there's no attitude here, just a fun, let's groove atmosphere thanks to collectible sneakers, denim from Levi's vintage and Red Label and Rogan, plus offbeat tees by Devon Ojas; translated, its name means 'alias', or in this case, another name for underground cool.

Noose, The ◐[S][C] 23 | 19 | 17 | E

261 W. 19th St. (bet. 7th & 8th Aves.), 1/9 to 18th St., 212-807-1789
■ For 20 years, all walks of New Yorkers have been fit to be tied at this hard-core Chelsea boutique that "whips" the competition "into submission" with its custom-made and European sex toys, body-stimulating P.E.S. electrical systems and other less shocking accoutrement, all proffered by a staff that's "helpful if you're in the market to try something new"; "prices are sometimes a smack on the rear" – latex bondage suits run up to $2,000 – "but it's worth the pain" (and "awesome fun for everyone").

Norman's Sound & Vision ◐[S][C] 20 | 12 | 16 | I

67 Cooper Sq. (bet. 7th & 8th Sts.), 6 to Astor Pl., 212-473-6599
33 St. Marks Pl. (bet. 2nd & 3rd Aves.), 6 to Astor Pl., 212-253-6162
■ The "excellent stock" of CDs, vinyl, videos and DVDs at these sibs in the East Village reflects proprietor "Norman's encyclopedic knowledge" and his connections – "he often gets discs before they're released"; the goods are "jammed into the displays so tight, it takes an effort to pull them out", but when you do, you too might boast "I love paying $10 for the same brand-new item my friends bought for $18 at HMV."

North Face, The [S] 25 | 21 | 19 | E

2101 Broadway (73rd St.), 1/2/3/9 to 72nd St., 212-362-1000; 800-362-4963; www.thenorthface.com
■ You can "'face' any mountain" – or Central Park "molehill" – armed with "high-tech" "goodies" from the "Hummer" of "extreme weather" wear with a "beautiful" new outpost in the Upper West Side's Ansonia building; "performance-designed" to "keep you toasty", these "classic" "puffy jackets", sweaters, hats, mittens and ski pants are "a must for crunchy granola types", "urban" adventurers and, of course, outdoorsy types "answering the call of the wild."

N. Peal [C] 25 | 22 | 21 | VE

5 W. 56th St. (5th Ave.), N/R/W to 5th Ave./59th St., 212-333-3500; www.npeal.com
■ Peel off that merino crewneck and slip into one of the "whisper soft" plush puppies proferred by a "lovely" staff in this West 50s boutique; sweater girls and guys cozy up to the "incredible selection of fine", "fabulous cashmere" and stacks of scarves (say 'pashmina, please') displayed on curvy blonde wood; "the price is right if you figure the airfare you save by buying it here" instead of ye olde Scotland, plus it's one investment that "you'll have for years."

Nursery Lines C   ▽ 26 | 22 | 23 | VE
1034 Lexington Ave. (74th St.), 6 to 77th St., 212-396-4445

■ Moms furnishing nurseries and gift-givers intent on spoiling junior converge at this sweet shop on the Upper East Side offering a "well-edited" selection of "custom-made" and "trendy linens", unique bedroom accessories, plus "traditional European" clothing for kids up to age four; but the cost of these luxurious goods just may rock your cradle – in fact, you may want to "get a second mortgage" before setting out.

NYCD ◐S   ▽ 21 | 15 | 22 | I
173 W. 81st St. (bet. Amsterdam & Columbus Aves.), 1/9 to 79th St., 212-724-4466; www.nycd-online.com

■ "Reminiscent of Village stores", this recently relocated "mom-and-pop shop" is "legendary on the Upper West Side" as "the best place for cheap" new and used CDs, with an "excellent mix" of rock, jazz, soundtracks, "hard-to-find" and import titles; you can also go gridlock surfing through the über-bargain boxes; N.B. the new location may outdate the above Presentation score.

Oculus 20/20 ◐S   – | – | – | E
189 Bedford Ave. (bet. N. 6th & 7th Sts.), Brooklyn, L to Bedford Ave., 718-666-0040
552 Henry St. (Carroll St.), Brooklyn, F/G to Carroll St., 718-852-9871

"Great glasses" from tight collections of high-end designers like Lunor and Frances Klein are the focus at these Brooklyn siblings where the chic goods are displayed in bright "jewel-box spaces"; eyewear isn't the only "find" – during the holiday season the stores also stock a small selection of fashionable hats and necklaces; much like the neighborhood, the Williamsburg shop is a bit funkier.

Oilily SC   24 | 23 | 20 | E
820 Madison Ave. (bet. 70th & 71st Sts.), 6 to 68th St., 212-628-0100; www.oililyusa.com

☑ "Pippi Longstocking lives!" exclaim enthusiasts who head to the Upper East Side branch of this Netherlands-based chain for "cute", "funky" infants', children's and women's "clothes with bright, fun, happy dispositions" in a "kaleidoscope of colors" and patterns; the styles are so "unique", with "amazingly high prices", that some surveyors say it's "just not my bag" – "considering how fast kids grow you may be better off investing in college."

O'Lampia Studio SC   ▽ 27 | 20 | 23 | E
155 Bowery (bet. Broome & Delancey Sts.), 6 to Spring St., 212-925-1660; www.olampia.com

■ It's "the best on the Bowery" brag boosters of this lighting store that shines with its "simple", "beautiful", custom-made designs that are "well crafted" by folks who "know how to handle their materials"; all this "great style" is "worth the price", especially when you factor in the "strong service" that "goes the extra mile."

Olatz   – | – | – | VE
43 Clarkson St. (bet. Greenwich & Hudson Sts.), 1/9 to Houston St., 212-255-8627; www.olatz.com

This new West Village shop's namesake and owner is the wife of painter Julian Schnabel, so guess whose art works are up on the walls?; they may not be for sale but the designer's pricey linens –

some with delicate hand embroidery and others with bold bands of color – along with towels, robes and pajamas are.

Olde Good Things 🅂🅲
23 | 13 | 18 | M

19 Greenwich Ave. (W. 10th St.), A/B/C/D/E/F/S/V to W. 4th St., 212-229-0850
124 W. 24th St. (bet. 6th & 7th Aves.), F/N/R/V to 23rd St., 212-989-8401
400 Atlantic Ave. (Bond St.), Brooklyn, B/M/Q/R to DeKalb Ave., 718-935-9742
888-551-7333; www.oldegoodthings.com

☑ "Prepare to dig in and get your hands dirty" at this four-floor Chelsea warehouse, a "hit-or-miss" "treasure trove of salvaged past grandeur" ranging from sconces to mirrors, marble mantels, huge iron gates and every pediment and ornament in between; vintage building materials like tin ceilings and wood beams are also part of the pickings; N.B. the Brooklyn branch is slowly being phased out, while the Greenwich Avenue offshoot is relatively new.

Olden Camera ●🅲
21 | 9 | 16 | M

1265 Broadway (32nd St.), B/D/F/N/Q/R/V/W to 34th St./Herald Sq., 212-725-1234

☑ This "leftover from the old camera neighborhood" near Herald Square sells just that – old cameras as well as new ones too; "hard-to-find gear" including antique folding types, '50s Brownies and 8 and 16mm film equipment make for "interesting" rummaging, and it might be the "best place to go for used Leicas and accessories" on the cheap, but with an "aged" setting and "gruff staff", it's "surely a pale reflection of its once-glorious self."

OLD NAVY ●🅂
15 | 14 | 14 | I

149-150 W. 34th St. (bet. 6th & 7th Aves.), B/D/F/N/Q/R/V/W to 34th St./Herald Sq., 212-594-0115; 800-653-6289; www.oldnavy.com
Additional locations throughout the NY area

☑ Its crew of fans insists there's "no better place" to scoop up "super-duper", "cheap" but "durable", "casual" "necessities like tanks, sweats, pajamas", jeans, jackets and flip-flops "for the whole family" than this "fast-food" fashion chain; its fleet of foes feel "rock-bottom pricing" doesn't make up for "old styles no sailor would ever wear" and "service that sometimes stinks."

Olive and Bette's 🅲
22 | 17 | 17 | E

252 Columbus Ave. (72nd St.), 1/2/3/9 to 72nd St., 212-579-2178
1070 Madison Ave. (bet. 80th & 81st Sts.), 6 to 77th St., 212-717-9655
158 Spring St. (bet. W. B'way & Wooster St.), C/E to Spring St., 646-613-8772 🅂
www.oliveandbettes.com

☑ "Trendy teenyboppers" beat a fast track to these "adorable" boutiques, tempted by their "quintessential tops shop" reputation ("keep the cute T-shirts coming!") and "fresh", "super-fun" attitude; prices are "awfully steep", but "girl power" prevails thanks to a "knowledgeable" staff "always full of suggestions"; N.B. at press time, plans were afoot to renovate the SoHo shop.

Oliver Peoples 🅲
26 | 24 | 22 | VE

755 Madison Ave. (bet. 65th & 66th Sts.), 6 to 68th St., 212-585-3433 🅂
366 W. Broadway (Broome St.), R/W to Prince St., 212-925-5400
888-568-1655; www.oliverpeoples.com

■ "The originator of the modern 'cool glasses' scene" presents a "huge" selection of "gorgeous" frames that are "cutting-edge trendy, but not to the point that they'll be out of style next season"; the SoHo and Upper East Side branches are "beautifully designed", the staff is "helpful" and the "quality" of the eyewear "makes it easier to see your empty wallet after you pay their prices."

OM Boutique **S** **C**   – – – VE

134 E. 27th St. (Lexington Ave.), 6 to 28th St., 212-532-5620 ❶
100 Lexington Ave. (27th St.), 6 to 28th St., 212-684-5194
Film buffs bowled over by Bollywood, the thrillingly over-the-top cinema from India, and enthusiasts of ethnic goods covet the colorful striking wares at this Lexington Avenue shop filled with gorgeous silk saris, sarongs, men's *kurtas,* patterned bedspreads, statues of deities and Indian CDs; venture around the corner to OM Saree Palace on East 27th Street for more treasures or to be fitted by a staff tailor in the warm, enveloping atmosphere.

OMO Norma Kamali **C**   20 22 16 E

11 W. 56th St. (bet. 5th & 6th Aves.), N/Q/R/W to 57th St.,
212-957-9797; 800-852-6254; www.normakamalicollection.com
☑ The designer who "brought shoulder pads and sneakers into fashion" is still going strong in her cool, museumlike West 50s boutique, all of whose rooms (and you, when you leave) "smell like her fantastic fragrance"; citing the "beautiful swimwear" and "eclectic vintage pieces", supporters say "her stuff never goes out of style", but critics counter there's "little innovation here" – the "best characteristic is the store itself"; P.S. OMO stands for 'On My Own.'

OM Yoga ❶ **S** **C**   ▽ 23 17 18 M

826 Broadway, 6th fl. (12th St.), 4/5/6/L/N/Q/R/W to 14th St./Union Sq.,
212-254-9642; www.omyoga.com
☑ "Zen in a store" sigh a smitten handful who head to this handy nook in the popular yoga destination, now located above the Strand, for colorful logoed T-shirts, strike-a-pose yoga pants (some made of hemp blends), mats and books and kits by owner Cyndi Lee; but not everyone is flexible about the cost, claiming it's "expensive for paraphernalia you can find elsewhere at better prices."

Only Hearts ❶ **S** **C**   21 21 19 M

386 Columbus Ave. (bet. 78th & 79th Sts.), 1/9 to 79th St.; B/C to
81st St., 212-724-5608
230 Mott St. (bet. Prince & Spring Sts.), 6 to Spring St., 212-431-3694
www.onlyhearts.com
■ "Lingerie that's comfy and sexy – who knew?" coo coquettes aquiver over these "cute little shops" on the Upper West Side and NoLita; it's "fun to browse" through the jewelry cases and the "crowded racks" filled with "good basic" "staples" and "lots of sassy", lace-trimmed "colorful" camis and chemises "you can even wear out clubbing"; P.S. the Mott Street site stocks a broader selection of innerwear-inspired "adorable clothes" plus lounge- and yoga-oriented casualwear.

On Stage Dance Shop **C**   – – – M

197 Madison Ave. (bet 34th & 35th Sts.), 6 to 33rd St.,
212-725-1174
The no-frills ambiance at this compact Murray Hill shop may not prompt rounds of applause, but the neatly organized dancewear from labels like Capezio, Danskin and Danza may elicit encore visits; it's a bonanza for basics as well as hip, street-inspired looks, with

loads of leggings, camis, tights and jazz pants underscored by ballet slippers, dance shoes and kids' tutus.

On Your Toes Dancewear C
| – | – | – | **M** |

2090 Hylan Blvd. (bet. Hamden & Hunter Aves.), Staten Island, 718-980-4880

One of the "best stores on Staten Island for dancewear" hail a handful of hoofers who head to this accessible shop for leotards, activewear and tights from top brands like Capezio and Danskin balanced by a showstopping selection of jazz, tap and pointe shoes; would-be performers and center-stagers who like to test the goods first can pivot and *relevé* away on the wood floor.

Opening Ceremony S C
| – | – | – | **E** |

35 Howard St. (bet. Broadway & Crosby St.), N/R to Canal St., 212-219-2688; www.openingceremony.us

A "very cool concept" drives this "new generation store" for men and women in NoLita, which every season introduces "unique, original" "designers from different parts of the world" (be it "Brazil or Hong Kong"), a tempting proposition that keeps acolytes "going back to check out the new stuff"; it's like the Olympics of fashion, so if you carry a torch for "avant-garde fashion", bear in mind that the prices and international togs are strictly gold medal.

Orchard Corset S C
| 22 | 6 | 20 | **M** |

157 Orchard St. (bet. Rivington & Stanton Sts.), F/J/M/Z to Delancey/ Essex Sts., 212-674-0786; 877-267-2427; www.orchardcorset.com

☑ "No naughty nighties here, just good everyday lingerie" and "spot-on fitting" from a "family of pros" "right out of central casting" opine patrons who "come on down" to this 73-year-old Lower East Side institution for "great deals"; "oy!", it's a "totally bra-zarre experience", from the "owners who guess your size with a look" to the "cramped", "chaotic" "closetlike" digs ("not for browsing"), nevertheless it's "a real slice of New York" that's "worth the trip"; N.B. closes at 2 PM on Fridays.

Oriental Lamp Shade Co. C
| ∇ 27 | 19 | 21 | **E** |

816 Lexington Ave. (bet. 62nd & 63rd Sts.), 4/5/6/F/N/R/W to 59th St./ Lexington Ave., 212-832-8190
223 W. 79th St. (bet. Amsterdam Ave. & B'way), 1/9 to 79th St., 212-873-0812
www.orientallampshade.com

■ "Try the silk" lampshades at these "friendly neighborhood merchants" in the East 60s and West 70s, and "you'll never go back to poly" posit proponents, who include the "finest designers"; "they make anything" "you could possibly imagine", and the "helpful" staff can rewire and repair your treasures as well; the enlightened insist the "good quality" is "worth the price."

Original Leather Store ◐ S
| 17 | 14 | 17 | **E** |

256 Columbus Ave. (72nd St.), 1/2/3/9 to 72nd St., 212-595-7051
1100 Madison Ave. (bet. 82nd & 83rd Sts.), 4/5/6 to 86th St., 212-585-4200
176 Spring St. (Thompson St.), C/E to Spring St., 212-219-8210
171 W. Fourth St. (bet. 6th & 7th Aves.), A/B/C/D/E/F/S/V to W. 4th St., 212-675-2303
800-872-5384; www.originalleather.com

☑ Beauty is skin deep at this chainlet of Manhattan hide houses where a menagerie of "good quality leathers" from basic lambskin to genuine python is fashioned into "classic pieces" and ready-to-wear cuts; 'destroyed' leather flight jackets for him share racks with low-waisted bell-bottoms for her, plus shearlings and sheddings from Seraphin and other high-end European manufacturers; still a handful huff you rarely find "anything unexpected" plus it's "somewhat expensive."

Original Penguin [S] – | – | – | M

1077 Sixth Ave. (41st St.), 7/B/D/F/V to 42nd St./6th Ave., 646-443-3520; www.originalpenguin.com

The crocodile's not the only logo game in town for hip prepsters now that the Penguin has arrived in Midtown, steps away from Bryant Park; these vintage-inspired menswear classics with attitude, ranging from velour shirts, rugby striped sweaters and pullovers, tees and khakis to leather jackets, are all presented in a shop reminiscent of a '60s-style rec room, complete with trophy murals, mid-century furniture and a wall covered with collegiate photos.

Origins ◐ [S] 22 | 22 | 21 | M

2327 Broadway (bet. 84th & 85th Sts.), 1/9 to 86th St., 212-769-0970
Flatiron Bldg., 175 Fifth Ave. (22nd St.), R/W to 23rd St., 212-677-9100
Grand Central, 75 Grand Central Terminal (42nd St. & Vanderbilt Ave.), 4/5/6/7/S to 42nd St./Grand Central, 212-808-4141
Rockefeller Ctr., 44 W. 50th St. (bet. 5th & 6th Aves.), B/D/F/V to 47-50th Sts./Rockefeller Ctr., 212-698-2323
402 W. Broadway (Spring St.), C/E to Spring St., 212-219-9764
800-674-4467; www.origins.com

■ "What's better than looking good, smelling great" and being environmentally friendly at the same time? ask acolytes of this chain that's "an oasis from the concrete jungle"; fans "love" the "East-meets-West, Zen-type scents" and the "great range" of plant-based skincare and bath-and-body products ("Oprah's endorsement of the Ginger Soufflé Whipped Body Cream" didn't hurt either); a "great, no-pressure sales staff" and moderate prices help make "you feel like you're doing yourself a favor by shopping here."

Orvis Company [S] 21 | 23 | 19 | E

522 Fifth Ave. (44th St.), 4/5/6/7/S to 42nd St./Grand Central, 212-827-0698; 888-235-9763; www.orvis.com

■ Track down "country bumpkin clothing" for men and women, including "sporting wear for the well-heeled" "trout fisherman and his Labrador retriever" and "everything anyone could want for fly-fishing" and hunting, from rods and reels to traps and clays, at this Midtown offshoot of this 147-year-old Vermont-based chain; while you may want to "take up" angling or shooting "just to shop here", armchair outdoorsmen opine "it's fun to just look around."

Oshkosh B'Gosh ◐ [S] [C] 22 | 19 | 18 | M

586 Fifth Ave. (bet. 47th & 48th Sts.), B/D/F/V to 47-50th Sts./Rockefeller Ctr., 212-827-0098; www.oshkoshbgosh.com

■ "Every kid needs a pair of overalls" from this "good source of staples" that also "sets the standard" for "sturdy", "everyday" baby and children's clothes, as well as shoes and plush toys for infants; head to the Midtown branch of this chainster to shop for "excellent quality" "tough stuff" little ones will "wear again and again", all at "reasonable prices."

Other Music ●🅂🅲
25 **20** **21** **M**

15 E. Fourth St. (bet. B'way & Lafayette St.), 6 to Astor Pl.,
212-477-8150; www.othermusic.com
■ Opposite Tower Records (geographically and philosophically) is the Village's "adventurous music-lover's paradise", specializing in "ultra-obscure" indie and underground sounds on CD and vinyl hawked by staffers "who actually know something about what they're selling"; a customer base representing the "highest concentration of DJs per square foot" in the city means "you won't find any of that teenybopper mall crap here."

Otte 🅂🅲
24 **23** **17** **E**

121 Greenwich Ave. (13th St.), A/C/E/L to 14th St./8th Ave.,
212-229-9424
132 N. Fifth St. (bet. Bedford Ave. & Berry St.), Brooklyn, L to
Bedford Ave., 718-302-5001
■ "Sweetly tempting girly things" aptly describes the inventory of this romantic, yet edgy Williamsburg shop (*otte* means "clothing" in Korean) with its pink walls and antique furniture; its newer West Village offshoot, an "instant favorite", has equally "tantalizing" items from labels like Lu Lu Lamé, Rebecca Taylor and Mon Petit Oiseau "so tasty" your "heart practically breaks"; it's hard not to succumb to "some of the best fashion names, even if it is a bit on the pricey side."

Otter, The 🅂🅲
– **–** **–** **E**

361 Bleecker St. (bet. Charles & W. 10th Sts.), 1/9 to Christopher St./
Sheridan Sq., 212-243-0284
When "you need something in a pinch", this West Villager has it all and will satisfy your compulsion for "the next trendy jeans, bag or little dress long before you" "see them everywhere else"; a few feel prices can be "a bit high", but thanks to its "good choices" of covetable, contemporary New York and LA designers, this boutique once known as Sleek makes cost seem like no biggie.

Otto Tootsi Plohound ●🅂🅲
26 **23** **17** **E**

38 E. 57th St. (Madison Ave.), N/R/W to 5th Ave./59th St.,
212-231-3199
137 Fifth Ave. (bet. 20th & 21st Sts.), R/W to 23rd St.,
212-460-8650
273 Lafayette St. (Prince St.), F/S/V to B'way/Lafayette; R/W to
Prince St., 212-431-7299
413 W. Broadway (bet. Prince & Spring Sts.), R/W to Prince St.,
212-925-8931
■ "If you've got a shoe fetish", this "fab" foursome, overflowing with a "dizzying selection" of "what's next" – "all designer, all the time" – is a "lovely place to drool"; the "just-so gal" and her guy swoon for "swanky", "offbeat", "fancy schmancy", "Downtown footwear" from labels like Costume National, Freelance and Prada, as well as lesser-known "hip, chic European" names; sure, the staff can be "indifferent", but few "fashion-forward" fans seem to care, as this "temple" has some of the "most stylish kicks around."

Out of the Closet Thrift Shop ⌿
▽ 16 **11** **12** **E**

220 E. 81st St. (bet. 2nd & 3rd Aves.), 6 to 77th St., 212-472-3573
☑ Set in an 1838 farmhouse on the Upper East Side, "this is no ordinary thrift shop", but one that offers 10,000 books, Meissen and Flora Danica porcelain and the occasional Rodin watercolor,

as well as clothes and records; as could be expected, "these knickknacks cost a paddy-whack and a half", but it all goes to a "great cause" (direct services for AIDS patients) and there are frequent sales of "up to 90 percent off – honest!"

Oxxford Clothes S | 27 | 24 | 25 | VE

36 E. 57th St. (bet. Madison & Park Aves.), 4/5/6/F/N/R/W to 59th St./ Lexington Ave., 212-593-0204; www.oxxfordclothes.com

■ Although it opened in 1998, this 57th Street haberdasher bears an "older, distinguished look" befitting its historic label, since 1916 a synonym for traditional but "fashionable" menswear; privileged patriots pursuing "perfection" prefer it for selling "completely handmade American suits", "custom-made" to their physiques ("off-the-peg" is available too); prices for the clothing and "top-notch shoes" are "in the stratosphere", but high-fliers insist this is "the best the U.S. has to offer."

PA (Personal Affairs) S C | – | – | – | M

102 E. 7th St. (bet. Ave. A & 1st Ave.), L to 1st Ave., 212-420-7778
335 Lafayette St. (Bleecker St.), 6 to Bleecker St., 212-966-1004
www.pa212.com

East Village and NoHo sophisticates flock to this dynamic duo to refresh nine-to-five wardrobes with high-end tweeds, knits and denims "European cut" with an edgy twist "you won't find in department stores"; the tailored, rather than trendy shapes "always get compliments", plus the "charming" staff is "always willing to help with a bigger size or suggest a good pairing"; "decor is minimal" (read: generic) to "keep prices low."

Palma S C | – | – | – | E

521 Broome St. (bet. Sullivan & Thompson Sts.), C/E to Spring St., 212-966-1722

On the outskirts of Soho, this "lovely family-owned" shop with "extremely friendly service" has been selling its "beautiful", feminine classics long before (some 28 years) the big brands moved in, plus they now boast a recently expanded menswear selection, all showcased in a vast, amber-colored space augmented by glass and bamboo; much of the merchandise is "handmade", and some pieces are so "totally unique" they may elicit "huge compliments", even years after purchase.

Palmer Pharmacy S | 22 | 23 | 20 | E

2395 Broadway (88th St.), 1/9 to 86th St., 212-724-4800

■ "It's an asset to the neighborhood" is what local loyalists say about this 46-year-old pharmacy that's "a breath of fresh air on the Upper West Side"; in addition to "esoteric cosmetics brands" and toiletries like Lafco Portuguese soaps, "there are always new, unusual gifts, especially for children", from wooden toys to baby blankets.

Pan Aqua Diving S C | ▽ 25 | 19 | 24 | E

460 W. 43rd St. (bet. 9th & 10th Aves.), A/C/E to 42nd St./Port Authority, 212-736-3483; 800-434-0884; www.panaqua.com

■ For "a wonderful selection" of scuba diving and snorkeling gear and "expert servicing on the premises", paddle over to this Hell's Kitchen shop; fans flip for "great classes" at Manhattan health clubs and group trips and also give the "friendly, helpful staff" a fins-up; sure, "top quality isn't cheap, but if you are 100 feet underwater you might ask yourself, what is your life worth?"

P&S Fabrics S
23 | 12 | 18 | I

355 Broadway (bet. Franklin & Leonard Sts.), 1/9 to Franklin St., 212-226-1534; www.psfabrics.com
■ Tucked in TriBeCa, this "huge" "favorite" is "filled with every fabric you could possibly want" for "clothing and home" (you'll "want to reupholster everything!"), plus "lots of notions, craft supplies", a "good selection of patterns" and "great yarns"; the "owners are very pleasant" and so is the "friendly, helpful" staff; P.S. "rummage through the basement" for deals "on a rainy day."

Paparazzi S C
21 | 21 | 17 | M

379 Third Ave. (bet. 27th & 28th Sts.), 6 to 28th St., 212-448-1231
■ "A dangerous impulse-shopping location", this "cute" Gramercy Park spot is the "perfect place to find" a "hodgepodge" of "last-minute gifts", "wrapping paper, cards", "unique" "picture frames and other trinkets", plus it's also a "good stop" for "novel ideas" to "spice up your contribution to that company-party" grab bag; the "space is small", but the merchandise is "nicely presented" in a "colorful" and "inviting" way.

Paper Presentation ◗ S
25 | 20 | 16 | M

(fka Paper Access)
23 W. 18th St. (bet. 5th & 6th Aves.), 1/9 to 18th St., 212-463-7035; 800-727-3701; www.paperpresentation.com
■ "Tons and tons of paper" "as far as the eye can see" fills this Flatiron "one-stop shop" that fulfills "all your stationery needs" with a "wide variety of invitations and cards" and "great craft supplies" that are an "artist's delight"; it's "better-priced" than much of the competition, and "you can always find what you need" amid the "seemingly mile-long" shelves.

Papyrus
23 | 22 | 17 | M

2157 Broadway (bet. 75th & 76th Sts.), 1/2/3/9 to 72nd St., 212-501-0102 S
Grand Central, 107 E. 42nd St. (Lexington Ave.), 4/5/6/7/S to 42nd St./ Grand Central, 212-490-9894 S
852 Lexington Ave. (bet. 64th & 65th Sts.), 6 to 68th St., 212-717-0002 S
600 Lexington Ave. (bet. 52nd & 53rd Sts.), E/V to 5th Ave./53rd St., 212-355-6200
1270 Third Ave. (73rd St.), 6 to 77th St., 212-717-1060 S
www.papyrusonline.com
◪ For scribes who prize the "lost art" of hard-copy correspondence and "can't settle for plain white paper", this "cheery" chain ("dig" the "convenient" Grand Central branch) purveys a "clever" collection" of "quality" stationery and cards ranging from "tasteful to whimsical to beautiful"; equally appealing are the "rich wrapping papers", "tchotchkes galore" and "lovely gifts"; if a few pout that it's "pretty pricey" for a papyrus ("who knew trees cost so much?"), most note it's "worth every penny."

PARAGON SPORTING GOODS ◗ S
25 | 18 | 16 | M

867 Broadway (18th St.), 4/5/6/L/N/Q/R/W to 14th St./Union Sq., 212-255-8036; 800-961-3030; www.paragonsports.com
◪ "A four-season sporting goods" "adventureland", this three-floor Union Square "Shangri-La" offers a "complete inventory" of "the highest-quality equipment for whatever sport takes your fancy", from skiing and tennis to rock climbing and kayaking, "and

the clothing to go with it"; "it's athletically inspiring just to be" in this "virtual playground" that makes you feel "like a kid in a really expensive candy store" – "you could spend days browsing the merchandise"; but the less-enthused gripe that "service may be hard to find", especially on weekends, when it's "as crowded as a World Cup soccer match."

Park Avenue Audio 🆂🅲

| 24 | 20 | 20 | E |

425 Park Ave. S. (29th St.), 6 to 28th St., 212-685-8101

■ "Listen up:" "this is not your average electronics store" assert audiophiles who head to this Gramercy Park establishment run by three generations of hi-fi enthusiasts for "an excellent selection" of "high-end equipment" with "premium prices" "to match"; the "knowledgeable", "low pressure sales" staff is ready to work with you or your interior designer to customize and install your "top-of-the-line" audio or home-theater setup, in fact they "really seem to want to match the customer to the right system."

Parke & Ronen ●🆂🅲

| – | – | – | E |

176 Ninth Ave. (21st St.), C/E to 23rd St., 212-989-4245; www.parkeandronen.com

Chelsea-ites love to roam this charmingly sleek boutique that pays equal attention to men and women with neatly tailored pants and jackets in wool, leather or Ultrasuede, stand-out-in-a-crowd print shirts and love-thy-body T-shirts, all designed by Parke Lutter and Ronen Jehezkel; sweet staffers amiably attend customers.

Paron Fabrics

| 23 | 15 | 17 | M |

206 W. 40th St. (bet. 7th & 8th Aves.), A/C/E to 42nd St./Port Authority, 212-768-3266; www.paronfabrics.com

■ "Anything you could want in fashion fabrics" for apparel is here at this recently relocated Midtown shop, that's also now a solo act; it's the "first place to go" for "discounted bargains" thanks to its "terrific half-price section", plus it also stocks "great designer fabrics", from Anne Klein to Bill Blass, and a "beautiful" choice of other textiles; P.S. "if they don't have it, they'll get it."

Patagonia ●🆂

| 26 | 22 | 22 | E |

426 Columbus Ave. (81st St.), B/C to 81st St., 917-441-0011
101 Wooster St. (bet. Prince & Spring Sts.), R/W to Prince St.; C/E to Spring St., 212-343-1776
800-638-6464; www.patagonia.com

■ Whether you're taking an "adventure trip" or "keeping warm on the subway", these "great" Upper West Side and SoHo stores provide "the world's best outdoor clothing", including "cool baby" and kids' stuff, according to the fleece police, who also rave about the chain's "environmentally conscious" corporate mission; the "classic styling" means the "long-lasting products" "never become outdated", and the staff makes it a "pleasure to shop."

Patch NYC 🆂🅲

| 22 | 24 | 18 | E |

17 Eighth Ave. (bet. Jane & W. 12th Sts.), A/C/E/L to 14th St./8th Ave., 212-807-1060; www.patchnyc.com

■ "Quirky" with "a patch of whimsy", this Village accessories boutique with attentive service is "perfect for the girl-next-door hoping to add something kitschy to her solid colors"; "animal lovers can wear their favorite pals" on their tote bags and also scoop up "adorable" clutches shaped like deer and dachshunds, plus knit hats and scarves.

Paterson Silks   14 | 7 | 9 | M
300 E. 90th St. (2nd Ave.), 4/5/6 to 86th St., 212-722-4098
151 W. 72nd St. (bet. Amsterdam & Columbus Aves.), 1/2/3/9 to
72nd St., 212-874-9510
215-22 73rd Ave. (Bell Blvd.), Queens, Q 75 Bus, 718-776-5225
☑ A "neighborhood necessity", this textile trio on the Upper West Side, Upper East Side and Queens can be "convenient for fabric for a children's school project", notions, apparel and upholstery purposes; but most patrons are put off by the "surly service" and "high prices", advising "compare, and you'll go elsewhere."

Patina 🅂   – | – | – | M
451 Broome St. (bet. B'way & Mercer St.), 6 to Spring St., 212-625-3375
Situated on a SoHo side street, this pink space seems less a store than a room filled with someone's favorite things – if one's favorites were a 1930s Shalimar perfume bottle, a 1940s crocodile purse or a 1960s Yves Saint Laurent car coat; despite the tiny digs, the accessories and housewares are neatly displayed in wall-unit cubicles; though not bargain-basement, prices are reasonable given the unique nature of the period pieces.

Paul & Shark 🅂🄲   24 | 24 | 22 | VE
772 Madison Ave. (66th St.), 6 to 68th St., 212-452-9868; www.paulshark.it
■ "Before that yachting weekend", savvy sailors set course for the Madison Avenue member of this global fleet, which specializes in "great outdoor apparel" made in Italy; yes, the water-repellent knits, coats and shoes cost "stratospheric" amounts – but given their high-tech quality, most don't find them "overpriced."

Paul Frank Store 🅂🄲   20 | 22 | 19 | M
195 Mulberry St. (Spring St.), 6 to Spring St., 212-965-5079;
www.paulfrank.com
☑ "There's plenty of monkeying around" at this NoLita "bastion of kitschy", "happy" clothing where "middle school" and "skater grrls, cute gay boys" and "those who don't take life too seriously" "can't get enough of Julius", the wide-mouthed primate, and his "whimsical" cartoon character friends that enliven these "fun to wear" accessories and "adorable" T-shirts, PJs and hoodies; but those who don't go ape scratch their heads: "why aren't people tired of these animal faces yet?"

Paul Smith 🅂🄲   27 | 23 | 18 | VE
108 Fifth Ave. (bet. 15th & 16th Sts.), 4/5/6/L/N/Q/R/W to 14th St./
Union Sq., 212-627-9770; www.paulsmith.co.uk
■ A Flatiron hot spot for "snappy" menswear, this British import with bubble-gum pink walls relies on a sly sense of color and "eye-catching" stripes to create "quirky takes on classic silhouettes"; the staff is "dandy" at helping, and "though you will pay the price for looking so cool", most say it's worth it for a "shirt with a little something special" or some "irreverent" accessories ("who thought cuff links could be fun?").

Paul Stuart 🅂🄲   26 | 25 | 24 | VE
45th St. & Madison Ave., 4/5/6/7/S to 42nd St./Grand Central,
212-682-0320; 800-678-8278; www.paulstuart.com
■ "For the classic English look, look no further" than this family-owned Midtown haberdasher – "one of the few full-service men's stores left in NYC" – where the "great colors, workmanship" and

"lofty quality" of the clothes and furnishings "round out a traditional wardrobe with flair and style"; advocates also applaud the "retro-modern interiors" patrolled by a "helpful sales staff"; it's all pretty "pricey", but why not splurge, "if you've got the jack"; P.S. they offer similarly "distinguished" womenswear on the mezzanine.

Payless Shoe Source ⦿S

| 11 | 10 | 9 | I |

1 Herald Sq., 1293 Broadway (34th St.), B/D/F/N/Q/R/V/W to 34th St./ Herald Sq., 212-947-0306; www.payless.com
Additional locations throughout the NY area

☑ "If you're looking for knockoff styles at inexpensive prices", "you can find some real deals" on "footwear for the entire family" at this national chain with branches in all five boroughs; it's a "great place to get" "trendy, summer stuff" "you'll trash on vacation" and kids' shoes, since they'll grow out of them so fast", but critics quickly counter "pay less . . . get less."

P.C. Richard & Son ⦿S

| 16 | 12 | 12 | M |

120 E. 14th St. (bet. 3rd & 4th Aves.), 4/5/6/L/N/Q/R/W to 14th St./ Union Sq., 212-979-2600; 800-369-7915; www.pcrichard.com
Additional locations throughout the NY area

☑ This family-run giant with stores in most of the boroughs is known for its "good prices" and broad selection, but it "sabotages itself with horrendous service" and "bad presentation" of electronics "scattered on shelves"; many reviewers relate that it's more of a "source for basic household appliances like stoves, refrigerators and air conditioners" than for monitors, scanners and PCs.

Peanutbutter & Jane SC

| 22 | 14 | 21 | M |

617 Hudson St. (bet. Jane & W. 12th Sts.), A/C/E/L to 14th St./8th Ave., 212-620-7952

■ "Crammed" to the "rafters", like a "very, very nice attic" with "offbeat" togs "for Village kids", infants and toddlers "(read: funky, fun, one-of-a-kind clothes)", "great accessories" like sequined Mary Janes and "unique toys", this "tiny" tot shop with a "mom and pop feel" has "lots to offer"; "there's not much you don't want to take home, including the babies in strollers", plus the "wonderful owner helps you make sense of it all."

Pearldaddy ⦿SC

| – | – | – | M |

202A Mott St. (bet. Kenmare & Spring Sts.), 6 to Spring St., 212-219-7727
At this NoLita insider's secret, the world is your oyster, since every item in the narrow, exposed-brick space is made from freshwater pearls; the large, varied selection ranges from simple, traditional pearl studs to the best-selling multistrand necklaces dyed bronze or baby-blue, while pearl-hungry daddies can choose from a variety of cuff links.

PEARL PAINT S

| 27 | 16 | 16 | I |

308 Canal St. (bet. B'way & Church St.), A/C/E to Canal St.; 6/J/M/ N/Q/R/W/Z to Canal St., 212-431-7932
207 E. 23rd St. (bet. 2nd & 3rd Aves.), 6 to 23rd St., 212-592-2179
www.pearlpaint.com

☑ "Could you ever beat" the "enormous stock" at this "Pearl in the oyster bed of art supplies"?; a "crazy" six-story "walk-up tenement" on Canal Street "organized like a rabbit warren" "jammed with people and excellent merchandise", it's "cheap and nasty", "joyful" and "inspiring"; the "stairs'll kill ya", as "the elevator never comes", and "the staff can be helpful or condescending depending on the moon's rotation", but you'll "thank the Lord it's around" because "if it ain't here, it ain't"; N.B. Gramercy is home to a smaller sibling.

Pearl River Mart ●ⓈⒸ

`19` `10` `9` `I`

477 Broadway (bet. Broome & Grand Sts.), 6/J/M/N/Q/R/W/Z to Canal St., 212-431-4770
200 Grand St. (bet. Mott & Mulberry Sts.), 6/J/M/N/Q/R/W/Z to Canal St., 212-966-1010
800-878-2446; www.pearlriver.com

■ "Exotic fun" is yours for the taking at this recently relocated SoHo department store and its Chinatown sibling, two "treasure troves" of "fun, funky and functional" items you "suddenly, desperately need"; what it "lacks in presentation", it "makes up for in quantity" with an "astonishing" "grab bag" of "all things Asian-inspired", much like what's in "rarified NoLita boutiques" – only at "dirt-cheap" prices; sure, "the staff has attitude", but cool fashionistas know its "exquisite" embroidered slippers, silk "Suzy Wong" cheongsams and "subtle ceramics" make it a no-brainer for bargain-priced styling; N.B. the post-*Survey* move may outdate the above Presentation score.

P.E. Guerin

`–` `–` `–` `VE`

23 Jane St. (bet. 8th & Greenwich Aves.), A/C/E/L to 14th St./8th Ave., 212-243-5270; www.peguerin.com

Since 1857, the Guerin family has provided metalwork for public buildings and parks as well as residences all over the country; plated brass hinges, knobs and plumbing and lighting fixtures are made either at the company's Valencia, Spain, foundry or on-site in the West Village, and its artisans can reproduce period pieces; N.B. by appointment only.

PENHALIGON'S Ⓢ

`26` `26` `25` `E`

870 Madison Ave. (71st St.), 6 to 68th St., 212-249-1771;
877-736-4254; www.penhaligons.com

■ Founded in 1870, this British bastion of toiletries has been making pricey perfumes and "long-lasting" colognes for the likes of Winston Churchill, and its tiny Madison Avenue offshoot continues the tradition with the "finest fragrances", along with shaving sets, silver scent bottles, soaps and candles.

Penny Whistle ⓈⒸ

`23` `20` `19` `M`

448 Columbus Ave. (bet. 81st & 82nd Sts.), B/C to 81st St., 212-873-9090 ●
1283 Madison Ave. (bet. 91st & 92nd Sts.), 6 to 96th St., 212-369-3868

■ "The bear blowing bubbles outside is a giveaway" – there are "great little things for little hands" at this "charming" Upper West Side toy store, and a smaller selection of "unique, intelligent" merchandise at its Upper East Side sibling; full of "clever gifts", like marionettes and choo-choo accessories, "these lovely boutiques" are "fun for kids and adults"; while it "may not have the best selection in town, it's always worth a visit."

Perfumania ●ⓈⒸ

`18` `12` `12` `I`

Empire State Bldg., 20 W. 34th St. (bet. 5th & 6th Aves.), B/D/F/N/ Q/R/V/W to 34th St./Herald Sq., 212-736-0414; 866-557-2368; www.perfumania.com
Additional locations throughout the NY area

☑ It's the "large selection" of "discounted" "designer and drugstore perfumes" and men's colognes that's the draw at this chain of "no-frills stores" located throughout the city; they claim to guarantee the lowest price or they pay you.

Perlier Kelemata 🅂🅲   ▽ 25 | 25 | 22 | E

436 W. Broadway (bet. Prince & Spring Sts.), R/W to Prince St., 212-925-9999; 877-737-5353; www.perlier.com
■ Little, light-filled SoHo space that's the serene setting for five all-natural Italian and French bath-and-body collections from Perlier, Kelemata, Cerealia, Imaginez and Victor; fragrances like Honey and White Almond, Orange Blossom and Vetiver fill the air, inspiring some weary shoppers to head straight home for a warm scented bath.

Petco   21 | 17 | 14 | M

2475 Broadway (95th St.), 1/2/3/9 to 96th St., 212-877-1270
860 Broadway (17th St.), 4/5/6/L/N/Q/R/W to 14th St./Union Sq., 212-358-0692 ◑🅂
147 E. 86th St. (bet. Lexington & 3rd Aves.), 4/5/6/to 86th St., 212-831-8001 ◑🅂
560 Second Ave. (bet. 31st & 32nd Sts.), 6 to 33rd St., 212-779-4550 ◑🅂
157-20 Cross Bay Blvd. (157th Ave.), Queens, A to Howard Beach/ JFK Airport, 718-845-3331 ◑🅂
1756 Forest Ave. (Morningstar Rd.), Staten Island, 718-370-8820 ◑🅂
800-571-2952; www.petco.com
☑ A "one-stop shop for all pet needs", this superstore chain carries "most major brands of food", a "large variety of accessories and gifts" and "staple" "supplies for every critter imaginable"; alas, "what it gains in size, it loses in personal service", and there are oftentimes "long lines at check-out" – still, there's praise for the "good prices" ("don't forget to apply" for 'Pals', its "frequent-buyer's card").

Peter Elliot 🅂   23 | 20 | 19 | VE

1070 Madison Ave. (81st St.), 6 to 77th St., 212-570-2300
1067 Madison Ave. (81st St.), 6 to 77th St., 212-570-5747
☑ "Still tweedy after all these years", this "small but exquisite" East 80s haberdasher offers a "focused selection of some of the best men's fashion"; critics cry "cool it on the markups", but most feel warmly about a staff that "turns the most hopeless into respectable citizens"; P.S. for "great preppy stuff when you feel like splurging on the kids" there's Peter Elliot Jr. at 1067 Madison while the women's store at 1071 Madison is "fab too" as is the newly opened Barbour by Peter Elliot.

Peter Fox Shoes ◑🅂🅲   24 | 22 | 22 | VE

105 Thompson St. (bet. Prince & Spring Sts.), C/E to Spring St., 212-431-7426; www.peterfox.com
■ "Unusual" "wedding shoes" "you won't scoff at" for "brides who would like something other than the typical" fare, plus "funky" footwear for off-the-aisle occasions, some with "Victorian flair", are all in store at this small, girlish SoHo shop; the "friendly" staff ensures a "pleasant shopping experience."

Peter Hermann 🅂🅲   – | – | – | M

118 Thompson St. (Prince St.), C/E to Spring St., 212-966-9050
As tightly packed as a Jamin Puech purse, since 1987 this small SoHo store's been a must-stop for his-and-hers accessories – from bags and backpacks to scarves, gloves, sunglasses and billfolds –

in leather, vinyl or rubber; Mandarina Duck and Strenesse and Orla Kiely are other big brands.

Peters Necessities for Pets [S] [C] ▽ 18 | 15 | 19 | M

236 E. 75th St. (bet. 2nd & 3rd Aves.), 6 to 77th St., 212-988-0769

■ "These guys are great" – "especially Pete, who runs the show" rave regulars of this East 70s pet shop where the "good service" extends to "free treats" for furry noshers; the selection's "not terribly big", but it carries a few items you "won't find elsewhere."

Petit Bateau [S] [C] 25 | 21 | 19 | E

1094 Madison Ave. (82nd St.), 4/5/6 to 86th St., 212-988-8884; www.petit-bateau.com

■ "The perfect tee is hard to find, but the French have done it right", coming up with "arguably the most comfortable" ones "in the world", or at least the "best darn T-shirt this side of Madison Avenue"; though intended for babies, children and teens up to 18 (check out the "lovely cotton pajamas and onesies" as well), the "little" tops are also "cult favorites" for "small women"; P.S. the Europe-bound "wait to shop for them in Paris" "for a fraction of the price."

Petland Discounts ◐ [S] 17 | 12 | 14 | I

7 E. 14th St. (bet. 5th Ave. & University Pl.), 4/5/6/L/N/Q/R/W to 14th St./ Union Sq., 212-675-4102; www.petlanddiscounts.com

Additional locations throughout the NY area

◪ "If you're on a budget, your pet won't be able to tell you shop" at this large discount chain that's "well stocked" with "everything you need for your little beasties" at "dirt-cheap prices"; however, while the staff at some locations is "friendly", others are so "surly, they should be whacked with a rolled-up newspaper."

Pet Stop ◐ [S] [C] 21 | 16 | 17 | M

564 Columbus Ave. (bet. 87th & 88th Sts.), 1/9/B/C to 86th St., 212-580-2400

■ "Everyone's helpful" at this "very decent neighborhood pet store" in the West 80s, where an "excellent selection of dog food", all kinds of animal supplies and "reliable delivery service" keep both local canines and their humans happy.

Pharma [S] – | – | – | E

17 Clinton St. (bet. Houston & Stanton Sts.), F/J/M/Z to Delancey/ Essex Sts., 212-505-3505; www.pharmanyc.com

This newcomer to the ultrahot Lower East Side seduces with a heady mix of "delicious products for skin and body" displayed in a sleek, clean modern setting that perfectly compliments the all-natural lineup of balms, lotions and potions from names like Dr. Hauschka, Pacifica and even locally made goods like salves, sprays and bath salts from Budda Nose.

Phat Farm [S] 19 | 20 | 14 | E

129 Prince St. (bet. W. B'way & Wooster St.), R/W to Prince St., 212-533-7428; www.phatfarmstore.com; www.babyphat.com

◪ "Great hip" apparel that's "pfine pfor" "young people" jonesing for "Wasp clothes three sizes too big" can be found at this SoHo shop done up with marble floors, cherry cabinets and leather walls; this "perfect locale" showcases hip-hop entrepreneur Russell Simmons' line of threads and sneakers and also spotlights his wife Kimora Lee's hot Baby Phat collection; better bring along a phat wallet – a phew phind it a "little overpriced"; N.B. a post-*Survey* renovation may outdate the above Presentation score.

Philosophy di Alberta Ferretti S C | 24 | 23 | 19 | VE |

452 W. Broadway (bet. Houston & Prince Sts.), C/E to Spring St., 212-460-5500; www.aeffeusa.com

■ Despite the name, there are no bookish babes here; on the contrary, a "Ferretti fox can be seen from miles away" in "dreamy clothes" from this "dreamy store" on SoHo's main drag that's dedicated to the Italian designer's hip line of "richly woven" women's jackets and ethereal dresses; water cascades under the floor of this museumlike interior, a lush, shimmery accent to the luxe space with its "twentysomething staff."

PIAGET C | 28 | 27 | 27 | VE |

730 Fifth Ave. (bet. 56th & 57th Sts.), N/R/W to 5th Ave./59th St., 212-246-5555; 800-359-4538; www.piaget.com

■ "Many a favorite dress watch" has come from this longtime Geneva concern, whose Midtown outpost bears a striking look with gray walls and white wood display cases; timepieces that some call "the best in the world" complement the "painstakingly crafted" fine jewelry; just "watch out" (pun intended) for "high-end luxury" price tags as well; N.B. a post-*Survey* refurb may outdate the above Presentation score.

Pieces ● S | – | – | – | E |

671 Vanderbilt Ave. (Park Pl.), Brooklyn, B/Q to 7th Ave.; 3 to Grand Army Plaza, 718-857-7211; www.piecesofbklyn.com

Sporting new, white modern decor, the better to show off the sexy separates for women within (with a few slamming items for men), this happening Prospect Heights boutique owned by a retail-schooled married couple also buzzes with a friendly coffee klatch vibe; the strut-your-stuff wear includes lines like Eva Fortune, Pinko and Chip & Pepper, unusual labels like Ya-Ya and Timosi, plus a few fabulous hats, accessories and shoes – hey, what's a 'piece' without a head-to-toe look?

Pier 1 Imports ● S | 18 | 18 | 14 | I |

461 Fifth Ave. (40th St.), 4/5/6/7/S to 42nd St./Grand Central, 212-447-1610
71 Fifth Ave. (15th St.), 4/5/6/L/N/Q/R/W to 14th St./Union Sq., 212-206-1911
1550 Third Ave. (87th St.), 4/5/6 to 86th St., 212-987-1746
www.pier1.com

◪ The "budget-minded" make a beeline for these "jam-packed" branches of a chain brimming with "practical" wicker, rattan and bamboo baskets and furniture, "funky candleholders", "place mats and plates", "colorful" pillows and "odd knickknacks"; the stylish may sniff at the store's "basic", "cookie-cutter" merchandise, but pros praise its "cost-effective home-decor solutions."

Pierre Deux S | 24 | – | 18 | E |

625 Madison Ave. (bet. 58th & 59th Sts.), 4/5/6/F/N/R/W to 59th St./Lexington Ave., 212-521-8012; www.pierredeux.com

■ "Toile, toile and more toile" – Madison Avenue's "ultimate source of French country style" appeals to "the Francophile in all of us"; the famous "pretty prints" turn up in "*très* beautiful fabrics", "soft, sturdy carryalls", "colorful tablecloths" and upholstered furniture, plus there are plenty of "lovely touches for the home", from pewter and glassware to rugs; the "ever-expanding" selection of "goods doesn't come cheap" but "it's nice to browse"; N.B. the store moved to larger quarters 12 blocks down Madison post-*Survey*.

Pilar Rossi **C**

▽ 25 | 21 | 24 | E

784 Madison Ave. (bet. 66th & 67th Sts.), 6 to 68th St., 212-288-2469
■ When it's knock-'em-dead time, many a femme fatale turns to this "elegant" Spanish specialist in sequins and chiffon; inside her minimalist jewel box in the East 60s lies a perfectly edited collection of dramatic, well-cut suits and beautifully embellished special-occasion and evening wear; so go with a gala in mind, and the obliging staff will offer one-on-one service plus they even do custom order.

Pink Pussycat ● **S**

19 | 16 | 17 | M

355 Fifth Ave. (bet. 4th & 5th Sts.), Brooklyn, F/M/R to 4th Ave./9th St., 718-369-0088
167 W. Fourth St. (bet. 6th & 7th Aves.), A/B/C/D/E/F/S/V to W. 4th St., 212-243-0077
www.pinkpussycat.com
☑ "Tourists, drag queens" and "pimply" "first-time buyers" "come together" at a "naughty", "entertaining" "pit stop for props", from house-made whips and bondage gear to lubes and oils, at West Fourth Street's "famed" "landmark" of "smut" that's also "valued for its people-watching potential"; design fetishists fret the "decor is clinical, but how much can you do with vibrators and plastic butts?", despite connoisseurs' critique that "the inventory" "isn't living up to its illustrious" 38-year rep; N.B. the tamer Park Slope branch carries mostly lingerie.

Pink Slip ● **S**

22 | 14 | 19 | M

Grand Central, 107 E. 42nd St. (bet. Lexington & Park Aves.), 4/5/6/ 7/S to 42nd St./Grand Central, 212-949-9037; 866-816-7465; www.thepinkslip.com
☑ "Definitely the place to go to add spice to your bedroom", "this little store" carries an "amazing selection" of come-hither wear, from cami-corsets by Arianne to "beautiful" chemises and bra sets from Mary Green; while it's "surprisingly classy considering its Grand Central location", shy flowers give it the slip, claiming "it's a little embarrassing trying on lingerie in the train station."

Pintchik **S**

23 | 15 | 17 | M

478 Bergen St. (Flatbush Ave.), Brooklyn, 2/3 to Bergen St., 718-783-3333
■ "You can buy your items, go home and complete the entire job before you can even get out of" the bigger chain stores maintain mavens of this "true neighborhood" hardware purveyor in Park Slope; it's "tough to beat for paint and supplies", the "salespeople are knowledgeable and friendly", and if the layout feels a "bit cramped", the fact that it has "everything you could possibly want" more than compensates.

P.J. Huntsman & Co.

– | – | – | M

36 W. 44th St. (bet. 5th & 6th Aves.), 7/B/D/F/V to 42nd St./6th Ave., 212-302-2463; 800-968-3418; www.pjhuntsman.com
Entering this mini-sporting shop, surrounded by Midtown university clubs, is like visiting a cozy gentlemen's study filled with country casual coats, trousers and sweaters, gear and gifts for the gentry (or those aspiring); owner/manager Pat Colombo provides personal attention for patrons perusing his properly priced 'performance' articles made in the U.S., U.K. and Italy.

Planet Kids ●S
21 14 14 M
2688 Broadway (103rd St.), 1/9 to 103rd St., 212-864-8705
247 E. 86th St. (bet. 2nd & 3rd Aves.), 4/5/6 to 86th St.,
212-426-2040
■ "A must for baby shopping", these two Uptown boys' and girls'
galaxies offer a "great selection" of a "wide range of items" at
"reasonable" prices; the original Upper East Side shop sells toys,
furniture, strollers, swings, high chairs and clothing from labels
like Polo, Carter and Phat Farm for layette to age two, while the
newer, smaller satellite on the Upper West Side carries apparel
for ages right up through the teens.

Pleasure Chest ●S C
20 19 18 M
156 Seventh Ave. S. (bet. Charles & Perry Sts.), 1/9 to Christopher St./
Sheridan Sq., 212-242-2158; 800-316-9222; www.adulttoyexpress.com
☑ It's "porn for the masses" at this Village "pleasure" purveyor
that's "as essential as Costco" for all your "bridal shower gag gift"
needs, including that popular little dynamo, the Pocket Rocket;
"the nice thing about the place is that they have the toys out so
you can handle them, turn them on" and "giggle away"; you might
find the "prices high" and the sales help hit-or-miss, but you'll
"always want to rush home afterward" to give the goods a whirl;
N.B. the store was remodeled post-*Survey* and now features smoky
wood paneling and a modern interior.

Pleats Please S C
▽ 25 25 18 E
128 Wooster St. (Prince St.), R/W to Prince St., 212-226-3600;
www.pleatsplease.com
■ Patrons will be pleat-ing for more when they enter this glass-
encased SoHo shop designed by architect Toshiko Mori with its
"admirably bold" line of high-tech, super-pleated polyester pieces
imbued with "Issey Miyake's artistry"; somewhat "cheaper" than
the designer's main line, the easy-to-pack dresses, tops and witty
accessories – such as the best-selling, felt fortune-cookie bag –
shine in "lovely colors and textures" sure to "stop traffic."

Plein Sud S C
▽ 26 24 19 VE
70 Greene St. (bet. Broome & Spring Sts.), C/E to Spring St.,
212-431-8800
■ Join the colorful caravan at this SoHo boutique, a true hot spot
for "gorgeous", "very sexy, special-occasion dresses" and other
clingy, "out-there-but-lots-of-fun" and ultra-wearable garments
from a Moroccan-French designer whose heritage influences the
store interior as well as the clothing; just make sure your camel
is carrying buckets of gold to cover the cost of these silk, fur
and leather creations.

POGGENPOHL U.S. INC.
26 25 19 VE
150 E. 58th St. (bet. Lexington & 3rd Aves.), 4/5/6/F/N/R/W to 59th St./
Lexington Ave., 212-355-3666
230 Park Ave. S. (19th St.), 4/5/6/L/N/Q/R/W to 14th St./Union Sq.,
212-228-3334
www.poggenpohl-usa.com
☑ Europe's oldest kitchen manufacturer proffers "exquisite"
"modern" style and high-tech innovations that incorporates tinted
glass, stainless steel, aluminum and wood, plus on-site designers
at its East 50s and Flatiron showrooms can help customize its
ergonomically correct cabinetry and appliances; but "bring along

a bucket of water and a friend to throw it in your face, because you're going to need reviving when you see their prices."

Pokemon Center, The 🅂🅒   16 | 22 | 17 | M

10 Rockefeller Plaza (48th St.), B/D/F/V to 47-50th Sts./Rockefeller Ctr., 212-307-0900; www.pokemoncenter.com

☑ "Pikachu lives in New York", specifically in a "magic kingdom" in Rockefeller Plaza that's "more of a playground than a store" where "avid followers" also find a "definitive assortment" of all 251 cartoon characters fashioned into action figures, Game Boys and trading cards – "what a Poke scene!"; but "all the yellow and zingy-ness is enough to drive you mad" declare the disenchanted who also feel these toys have "peaked in popularity."

Poli Fabrics   25 | 17 | 22 | M

227 W. 40th St. (bet. 7th & 8th Aves.), A/C/E to 42nd St./Port Authority, 212-768-4555; www.polifabrics.com

■ "Beautiful fabrics for reasonable prices" and a "frank" staff make this "reliable, accommodating" Garment District retail/wholesale "old standby" a "favorite" for those in-the- know; "check it out often because those special designer fabrics" from American and European couture houses "get snapped up fast."

Poltrona Frau 🅂   – | – | – | VE

145 Wooster St. (bet. Houston & Prince Sts.), R/W to Prince St., 212-777-7592; www.frauusa.com

SoHo outpost of a 92-year-old Italian manufacturer that offers a more rounded and colorful take than some of its competitors on luxe leather home furnishings like its sofas and Vanity Fair chair; thank god their seating is so soft (it also turns up in Mercedes and Ferrari interiors) that it will comfortably cushion your fall after you see the ultraexpensive ticket prices.

Pompanoosuc Mills 🅂   24 | 21 | 20 | E

124 Hudson St. (Ericsson Pl.), 1/9 to Franklin St., 212-226-5960; www.pompy.com

☑ Every simple, "well-constructed" piece of wood furniture sold at this long-standing TriBeCa store is made to order in Vermont; most of the tables, sofas, consoles, chairs, bookshelves and beds are available in a wide choice of hardwoods, but critics simply shrug at the "boring" styles.

Pondicherri ◗🅂🅒   19 | 18 | 17 | M

454 Columbus Ave. (bet. 81st & 82nd Sts.), 1/9 to 79th St.; B/C to 81st St., 212-875-1609; www.pondicherrionline.com

■ For 35 years the owners of this West 80s emporium have been producing hand-blocked textiles in New Delhi; when it comes to clothing, there are some "good, basic Indian imports", but it's the reasonably priced traditional Shahjahan table linens and embroidered silk pillows that outshine all else.

Pookie & Sebastian ◗🅂🅒   ▽ 26 | 19 | 24 | M

249 E. 77th St. (bet. 2nd & 3rd Aves.), 6 to 77th St., 212-717-1076
531 Third Ave. (36th St.), 6 to 33rd St., 212-951-7110

■ It's "worth fighting through the crowd" at this "top-notch" boutique (an increasingly less "well-kept secret on the Upper East Side") that allows shoppers to "stay hip without spending a fortune" on up-to-the-minute styles and looks, including the "first wave of mania" for the jeans *du jour*; the "very-much-on-top-of-things" salespeople are "kind enough to call" when new shipments arrive; N.B. the new Murray Hill branch opened post-*Survey*.

Porthault 🄲   ▽ 28 | 24 | 23 | VE

18 E. 69th St. (Madison Ave.), 6 to 68th St., 212-688-1660;
www.dporthault.fr

■ "These are sheets you'll want to pass down from generation to generation – after you frame them", of course, sigh sybarites about these "ultimate-in-luxury" "linens from France" housed in a charming Upper East Side townhouse; this "wonderland" of pretty prints also offers beautiful bath towels and a "lovely" selection of "gifts" like children's clothing, candles and china.

Portico 🅂   23 | 22 | 16 | E

903 Broadway (20th St.), R/W to 23rd St., 212-473-6662
Chelsea Mkt., 75 Ninth Ave. (bet. 15th & 16th Sts.), A/C/E/L to 14th St./
8th Ave., 212-243-8515 ◗
450 Columbus Ave. (bet. 81st & 82nd Sts.), B/C to 81st St., 212-579-9500
72 Spring St. (bet. Crosby & Lafayette Sts.), 6 to Spring St., 212-941-7800
www.porticohome.com

◪ Home-furnishings shops featuring a "limited" but "stylish" selection of beds, "chic towels", luxe Egyptian cotton linens and "lovely scented things" for those who want to live like "kings and queens"; minimalists maintain that the "clean"-looking merch isn't "overdesigned", making it "perfect for real city life", but wallet-watchers whine about the "expensive" big-city prices; N.B. the Chelsea Market outlet offers discounts on overstocked or slightly damaged items.

Pottery Barn ◗🅂   21 | 22 | 17 | M

1965 Broadway (67th St.), 1/9 to 66th St./Lincoln Ctr., 212-579-8477
600 Broadway (Houston St.), N/R to Prince St.; B/D/F/S/V to
B'way/Lafayette St.; 6 to Bleecker St., 212-219-2420
127 E. 59th St. (Lexington Ave.), 4/5/6/F/N/R/W to 59th St./
Lexington Ave., 917-369-0050
www.potterybarn.com

■ "Every apartment in New York has something" from this home-furnishings "staple" offering "mainstream chic" and a "mix" of "stylish" "quality goods" that "will work with any decor"; "don't expect to be unique if you shop here", but the more conventional claim that "moderate prices" make it a "great place for gifts" and "seasonal items to perk up your home."

Prada 🄲   25 | 25 | 18 | VE

575 Broadway (Prince St.), R/W to Prince St., 212-334-8888 ◗🅂
45 E. 57th St. (bet. Madison & Park Aves.), 4/5/6/F/N/R/W to 59th St./
Lexington Ave., 212-308-2332
724 Fifth Ave. (bet. 56th & 57th Sts.), N/R/W to 5th Ave./59th St.,
212-664-0010 🅂
841 Madison Ave. (70th St.), 6 to 68th St., 212-327-4200
www.prada.com

◪ This "ultracool" line "still has bite" for "die-hard designer fans", and although it's found in several "shopping destinations", its "epicenter" lies in the "electrifying" Rem Koolhaas–designed SoHo flagship – a "masterpiece" to many, a "well-dressed amusement park" to others; still, you "can't miss" a trip, if only to ogle the "awesome sloping ramp" interior, "classic-yet-edgy" and vintage-inspired fashions, skincare lines and much-ado-about-Miuccia

Prada footwear and purses; service veers from "businesslike" to "hard-to-get", and "black nylon has never sold for so much", but neither gives pause to the patrons who pant "Prada, please"; N.B. the 57th Street store sells shoes and bags only.

PRATESI C   29 | 24 | 21 | VE

829 Madison Ave. (69th St.), 6 to 68th St., 212-288-2315; www.pratesi.com
■ For "beautiful Italian linens and towels" "without flying to Italy", hedonists head to this long-standing Upper East Side specialty shop purveying additional "high-end" items "you could just melt in", like "yummy bathrobes"; "there's nothing like sleeping in a bed" made with their sheets – it's just the prices that will give you nightmares.

Prato Fine Men's Wear Outlets   ▽ 16 | 11 | 14 | I

122 Nassau St., 1st fl. (Ann St.), 2/3/4/5/A/C/J/M/Z to Fulton St./ B'way/Nassau, 212-349-4150 S
492 Seventh Ave. (bet. 36th & 37th Sts.), 1/2/3/9 to 34th St./Penn Station, 212-564-9683 ◑
28 W. 34th St. (bet. B'way & 5th Ave.), B/D/F/N/Q/R/V/W to 34th St./ Herald Sq., 212-629-4730 ◑ S
8508 Fifth Ave. (85th St.), Brooklyn, R to 86th St., 718-491-1234 S
30-48 Steinway St. (bet. 30th & 31st Aves.), Queens, G/R/V to Steinway St., 718-274-2990 ◑ S
888-467-7286; www.pratooutlets.com
☑ Scattered throughout the city, this men's discount clothing chain can be a "good enough place for cheap stuff" – more specifically, "bargain"-priced brand names, including leather jackets, shirts, pants, coats and "decent suits" that can often be "tailored in a day"; but critics claim "you get what you pay for, and not one bit more."

Premium Goods S C   – | – | – | E

694 Fulton St. (St. Felix St.), Brooklyn, C to Lafayette Ave., 718-403-9348; www.premiumgoods.net
Fly folk who don't like to see their footwear coming and going head to this funky Fort Greene sneaker specialist that traffics in high-style, limited production and sometimes startlingly priced Nike and Adidas models, as well as must-haves from Tokyo's hip Bathing Ape line, which are scarcely seen stateside; befitting their collectible status, the super-edgy goods are displayed in a minimal, sleek setting reminiscent of an art gallery.

Princeton Ski Shop ◑ S   18 | 15 | 14 | M

21 E. 22nd St. (bet. B'way & Park Ave. S.), R/W to 23rd St., 212-228-4400; www.princetonski.com
■ "If you're a winter freak", slalom over to this Flatiron sporting-goods store and "stock up on ski essentials"; the "nice selection" "may not be large, but they can seriously outfit" the slope bound in outerwear and equipment from brand names like Columbia, Salomon, K-2, Head, Fisher and Rossignol; insiders confide there are "great late-season bargains" – in fact you may want to "hold out until their sales" come New Year's, Labor Day and other times of the year; N.B. they also offer ski and snowboard tune-ups.

Print Icon ◑ S   22 | 17 | 16 | M

7 W. 18th St. (bet. 5th & 6th Aves.), 4/5/6/L/N/Q/R/W to 14th St./ Union Sq., 212-255-4489; www.printicon.com
■ This "nice, big", airy, three-floor Flatiron phenom is reaching for iconic status as a combination print shop and paperie; pick up

"great gift wrapping", "unique" pre-made cards and "beautiful" personalized stationery and invitations "in an ample selection of colors" and "any kind of paper you need" from over a thousand high-quality choices from the likes of Strathmore and Saint-Armand for your custom letter-press, offset and computer-produced creations; N.B. as we were going to press, plans were afoot to move to two new locations.

Puma ●S
24 | 21 | 15 | M

521 Broadway (bet. Broome & Spring Sts.), 6 to Spring St.; R/W to Prince St., 212-334-7861; www.puma.com

■ "Very cool and fresh in that 'I'm-so-funky-Euro-sporty' way", this "trendy yet athletic" brand boasts a "new attitude" at this spacious two-floor SoHo "museum" that's a "lot of fun to shop"; "start collecting your" edgy and "old-school Pumas here" advise "fashion concious" sneaker diehards, who track down "phat" "hard-to-find models" downstairs before moving up to street level for the "great lookin'" "retro-hip work-out and go-out wear" and limited-edition apparel; N.B. at press time, plans were reportedly afoot to open a branch in the Meatpacking District, with another offshoot to follow.

Pumpkin Maternity S C
▽ 23 | 22 | 21 | M

407 Broome St. (bet. Centre & Lafayette Sts.), R/W to Prince St.; 6 to Spring St., 212-334-1809; 800-460-0337; www.pumpkinmaternity.com

■ "The funkiest pregnancy store on the planet" rave fans who give "thanks to Pumpkin" Wentzel, a jack-o'-many-trades indie rocker turned designer and SoHo boutique owner for her "comfortable, fun" maternity clothes "geared toward downtown sensibilities"; in addition to her signature shirred little black dress with an expanding waistline, moms and moms-to-be scoop up beauty products and nursing items.

Purdy Girl ●S C
21 | 18 | 22 | M

540 LaGuardia Pl. (bet. Bleecker & W. 3rd Sts.), 6 to Bleecker St.; A/B/C/D/E/F/S/V to W. 4th St., 646-654-6751
220 Thompson St. (bet. Bleecker & W. 3rd Sts.), A/C/E/F/S/V to W. 4th St., 212-529-8385

■ For "frilly", "flirty" dresses and "girlie gear" that's "as feminine as can be", this Village duo is "a find" indeed; absolutely "darling collections" "at fair prices" guarantee a teenage, twentysomething and youthful-in-spirit clientele, drawn to the mix of "mainstay designers like Nanette Lepore", Trina Turk, Bianca Nero and "lesser-knowns", all presented by salespeople who exude a "super-friendly" vibe.

Purl S C
25 | 23 | 20 | E

137 Sullivan St. (bet. Houston & Prince Sts.), C/E to Spring St., 212-420-8796; www.purlsoho.com

☑ "Trendy downtowners" and "experienced" "grannies" alike "jam into" this "darling" SoHo yarn shop with a "cozy" vibe "conducive to sitting and knitting awhile"; "what makes this store" is the "friendly, helpful staff" "as well as the great selection" of "natural fibers in fantastic colors", plus the "lovely", "touchable collection" of basic wools, luxury cashmeres and hand-painted options, antique needles, crochet hooks and pattern books; still, some are purl-plexed by the "pricey basics", suggesting stick to "high-end" stuff.

Purple Passion/DV8 S C
23 | 18 | 19 | E

211 W. 20th St. (bet. 7th & 8th Aves.), C/E to 23rd St., 212-807-0486; www.purplepassion.com

■ "Damn good fun" "for all your fetish needs", this ample duplex in Chelsea stocks "a wide selection of latex (hoods, catsuits and the like) for your next walk on the slippery side", "sexy underwear" and dominatrix gear, over 500 corsets, plus all the gadgets "you have to see to believe"; downstairs, the bigger hardware shares its showroom with an erotic art gallery; "no need to be shy – the staff is pretty knowledgeable and can help you on your way."

Push S C
▽ 23 | 27 | 25 | E

240 Mulberry St. (bet. Prince & Spring Sts.), 6 to Spring St.; B/D/F/S/V to B'way/Lafayette St., 212-965-9699; www.pushnewyork.com

■ Owner-designer Karen Karch operates this "treasure" of a NoLita shop, which clients coo is "the coolest" for its jewelry "displayed on dollhouse furniture" or hollowed-out radios in a setting that also features a carved-wood facade, cabinets with art deco hardware, crystal chandelier and exposed pipes; the "accommodating" staff doesn't have to push to sell her "fantastic, hip designs" to happy couples (the braided, bejeweled wedding and engagement rings are particularly big-sellers); N.B. a post-*Survey* renovation may outdate the above Presentation score.

Quiksilver Boardriders Club S
19 | 20 | 14 | M

109-111 Spring St. (Mercer St.), R/W to Prince St., 212-334-4500
3 Times Sq. (bet. 6th & 7th Aves.), 7/B/D/F/V to 42nd St./6th Ave., 212-840-8111 ❿
800-576-4004; www.quiksilver.com

☑ "Surf's up, dude" declare devotees who get stoked at this "colorful" SoHo shop with red boards slung on the sidewalk and the "feel of a resort" within; surfers, snowboarders and skaters make waves for the "cool stuff" including awesome board shorts, T-shirts, "good comfy jeans" and the Roxy line for women; the staff sometimes "works at its own pace", so the time-pressed may find it a wipeout; N.B. the Times Square flagship, which opened post-*Survey*, boasts TVs, all broadcasting ocean waves.

Radio Shack ❿ S
14 | 11 | 14 | M

50 E. 42nd St. (bet. Madison & Park Aves.), 4/5/6/7/S to 42nd St./ Grand Central, 212-953-6050; www.radioshack.com
Additional locations throughout the NY area

☑ With 7,200 Shacks throughout the nation, this "oldie but goodie" has been "reliable, cheap" and expanding since 1919; though its "inept" staff "may not be classy" and "you can do better elsewhere" on big-ticket items, its multiple locations serve up parts, cables, digital cameras, MP3 players and other "small" bytes for "various electronic needs"; besides, "some of this stuff you just can't get anywhere else."

Rafe S C
23 | 22 | 20 | E

1 Bleecker St. (Bowery), F/V to Lower East Side/2nd Ave., 212-780-9739; 800-486-9544; www.rafe.com

■ Against a signature blue backdrop, this vast NoHo shop owned by "nice guy" designer Ramon Felix (nickname: Rafe) overflows with "fa-bu-lous" "fun-to-carry" shoulder bags, clutches, totes and footwear for up-to-date girls (like Björk and Parker Posey) plus "fantastic" luggage for guys; "designed like artwork", the ante of classic handbag shape is upped by a mega-dose of retro-detailing, eye-catching colors and durable craftsmanship; the "cool" covetables are so "interesting" you may "buy the opposite of what you came for!"

R.A.G. | 15 | 16 | 14 | M |

1501 Broadway (43rd St.), 1/2/3/7/9/N/Q/R/S/W to 42nd St./Times Sq., 212-768-8751 ◗ Ⓢ
Grand Central, 105 E. 42nd St. (Lexington Ave.), 4/5/6/7/S to 42nd St./ Grand Central, 212-682-3831
Port Authority, subway mezzanine (42nd St.), A/C/E to 42nd St./ Port Authority, 212-279-1829 ◗ Ⓢ
225 W. 34th St. (bet. 7th & 8th Aves.), 1/2/3/9/A/C/E to 34th St./ Penn Station, 212-971-0338 ◗ Ⓢ

☑ At this men's mini-chain, "classic rags anyone would be proud of", including the best-selling American flag sweater, "informal" knitwear, shirts and pants with designer flair (but low prices) are displayed in compact spaces throughout Midtown, including the Port Authority; while some say the staff "can sell headphones to the deaf", others find service "rude" and say there's little to "wow you"; N.B. the Grand Central branch opened at press time.

Rags-A-Go-Go Ⓒ | 17 | 14 | 15 | I |

218 W. 14th St. (bet. 7th & 8th Aves.), A/C/E/L to 14th St./8th Ave.; 1/2/3/9 to 14th St., 646-486-4011

☑ On 14th Street, a bare-bones "vintage must" is enlivened by stuffed animals on the walls and a "rainbow" of "fun stuff"; "if you want cowboy boots, tracksuits, T-shirts" and cords, "this is your Eden", all "organized by color" and by price points; still, a handful fret this "truly used clothing" is "not as cheap as I would like."

Ralph Lauren Ⓢ | 24 | 24 | 19 | VE |

380 Bleecker St. (bet. Charles & Perry Sts.), 1/9 to Christopher St./ Sheridan Sq., 212-645-5513 ◗
888 Madison Ave. (72nd St.), 6 to 68th St., 212-434-8000
867 Madison Ave. (72nd St.), 6 to 68th St., 212-606-2100
271 Mulberry St. (bet. Houston & Prince Sts.), 6 to Bleecker St., 212-343-0841
381 W. Broadway (bet. Broome & Spring Sts.), C/E to Spring St., 212-625-1660 ◗
800-475-7674; www.polo.com

■ Welcome to "American Classics" 101, a "monument" to a "middle-class [ideal of] haute couture" for every member of the family that gets an "A+ for window" displays; though "each store has its own vibe", most kudos go to the "gorgeous" Rhinelander Mansion flagship (867 Madison Avenue), which makes you feel "you've entered someone's private" estate, with its "portrait-lined staircases", seemingly "million-dollar-a-year flower budget" and "exquisite" antique jewelry; the "helpful staff" makes it easy to navigate the "timeless" apparel, "crisp accessories" and housewares collections; N.B. the Mulberry Street branch, called RRL, carries only that line and the new Bleecker Street boutique, which opened post-*Survey*, focuses on casual women's clothing.

Ralph Lauren Baby Ⓢ Ⓒ | 26 | 27 | 22 | VE |

872 Madison Ave. (71st St.), 6 to 68th St., 212-434-8099; www.polo.com
■ "Special tiny tots" "born with a silver spoon" (and perhaps a "country club mom") "finally get their own store" "from the man

himself" who recently unveiled this "very sweet", "frighteningly expensive" white-linen walled clothing emporium, complete with a cashmere bar, next to his Madison Avenue flagship; it's "pretty spectacular" – every infant and toddler "deserves to be dressed by Ralph" in "simply adorable", "stylish", "classic, preppy wear" and those "beautiful sweaters."

Rampage ●S   15 | 14 | 14 | I
127 Prince St. (Wooster St.), R/W to Prince St., 212-995-9569
Staten Island Mall, 2655 Richmond Ave., Staten Island,
718-697-0130
www.rampage.com
☑ "When you need to look hot" "without breaking your piggy bank", make tracks to these "trend central" SoHo and Staten Island offshoots of the national chain; fans fall for the "fun", "cute cheapies", including body-hugging tops and "sexy" jeans and minis "good for clubbing" or a "night on the town" and the "cutting-edge" "knockoffs" and accessories; still, the less-impressed snipe these "truly throwaway" "for one-season-only" pieces are "strictly for the teeny-bopper set."

Ray Beauty Supply ☐   23 | 8 | 14 | I
721 Eighth Ave. (bet. 45th & 46th Sts.), A/C/E to 42nd St./Port Authority,
212-757-0175; 800-253-0993; www.raybeauty.com
☑ "Don't expect service or atmosphere" at this "hidden secret of the haircare industry", a "mecca for glamour girls and drag queens alike", located in the West 40s; it's all about "incredible bargains" on "hard-to-find items" and "serious, professional quality" hair and beauty supplies, from straighteners, shampoos and scissors to "high-end appliances" (like the touted SuperSolano hair-dryer).

RCS Computer Experience S☐   20 | 18 | 13 | E
575 Madison Ave. (56th St.), E/V to 5th Ave./53rd St., 212-949-6935;
www.rcsnet.com
☑ "Be sure to try out whatever you are buying first", and you too might think that the "selection of current technology products" at this East 50s "hands-on" outlet "blows other electronics stores away"; the staff gives consultations in-store and will help install at home for a fee, still some say their "hard sell" approach doesn't compute; N.B. a post-*Survey* renovation may outdate the above Presentation score.

Reaction by Kenneth Cole ●S   18 | 18 | 16 | M
130 E. 57th St. (Lexington Ave.), 4/5/6/F/N/R/W to 59th St./Lexington Ave.,
212-688-1670; www.kennethcole.com
■ East 57th Street is home to the "hip, young" "more reasonable cousin" of the signature collection, which gets favorable reactions for "good-quality", "wearable" his-and-hers clothing plus men's suits; for those seeking "basics", including "comfy, trendy" shoes and "affordable leather goods", these are the "designer duds" for you; N.B. the store was redecorated post-*Survey* with a toned down color palette.

Really Great Things S☐   ▽ 25 | 25 | 25 | VE
300 Columbus Ave. (74th St.), B/C to 72nd St., 212-787-5868
284 Columbus Ave. (bet. 73rd & 74th Sts.), B/C to 72nd St., 212-787-5354
☑ Upper Westsiders know the "masters of temptation" at this "spa-like shop" include "hard-to-find" European and Japanese women's (and a little men's) wear, and even "better shoes" ("the real winner

here") – in short, offerings that are more couture-oriented than at its new sibling at 300 Columbus Avenue, which carries mostly hard-to-find ready-to-wear; while it lives up to its name and has "attentive salespeople" who aim to please, wags wager "with those tags, it should be renamed Really Expensive Things."

Rebecca Moss Ltd. C

▽ | 25 | 19 | 19 | E

510 Madison Ave. (53rd St.), E/V to 5th Ave./53rd St., 212-832-7671; 800-465-7367; www.rebeccamoss.com

■ Owner-designer Sam Zagoory named this "little gem" of a Madison Avenue shop after his grandmother, but his line of "unique" pens and "colorful leather goods" (from agendas to condom holders) is anything but old-fashioned; the store also carries other brands of writing instruments, as well as "great cards and stationery."

Rebel Rebel ● S

| 24 | 16 | 21 | M

319 Bleecker St. (bet. Christopher & Grove Sts.), 1/9 to Christopher St./ Sheridan Sq., 212-989-0770

■ "When you have the money to buy that prized David Bowie on vinyl", pop on down to Bleecker Street and "dig, dig, dig" through the "British imports (and a little Irish), music magazines and memorabilia" at this "small" CD and LP shop; manager/"hottie" David and his "knowledgeable staff make great suggestions", it's one of "the best record stores for celeb sightings", and now that she's Mrs. Guy Ritchie, the "Anglophilic" shop's "Madonna fixation" isn't so "inexplicable."

Redberi S C

– | – | – | E

339 Flatbush Ave. (Park Pl.), Brooklyn, B/Q to 7th Ave., 718-622-1964

A tin ceiling, varnished wood floors and reupholstered chairs form the tasteful backdrop for this ultra-femme newbie in Prospect Heights; the handpicked womenswear is full of surprises like retooled vintage finds, juiced up by the stylish proprietess herself, fresh pieces from cult faves Zero 4 Wendy, Petro Zillia and James Perse, undie sets from C. Ronson and ripe-for-the-plucking jewelry and accessories; there's also a beauty corner stocked with natural products sure to rejuvenate spirits.

RedLipstick S C

– | – | – | M

64 Sixth Ave. (bet. Bergen & Dean Sts.), Brooklyn, 3/4 to Bergen St., 718-857-9534; www.redlipstick.net/shop

Knitwear whiz, women's clothing and jewelry designer and Web producer Staceyjoy Elkin has turned this former Prospect Heights ice cream shop (checkerboard floor intact) into a tiny, offbeat venue for her own creations, plus unique finds from local and LA designers, at prices that range from dirt cheap to stratospheric; the no-frills tables and racks boast everything from 22 karat jewelry to edgy womenswear.

Reebok Store ● S

| 18 | – | 15 | M

160 Columbus Ave. (bet. 67th & 68th Sts.), 1/9 to 66th St./Lincoln Ctr., 212-595-1480; www.reebok.com

☑ "Stylish and functional" his-and-her's active- and casualwear, including everything from tennis outfits to training tops and shorts to NFL- and NBA-licensed jerseys and products fill this mammoth Upper West Side outpost downstairs from the "celebrity hot spot Sports Club"; the footwear is just as wide-ranging, running the gamut from sneakers to yoga shoes; prices can be "too expensive", but insiders confide it's a "great deal if you get the gym-membership discount"; N.B. a post-*Survey* remodelling created two separate spaces for men and women.

REEM ACRA
28 | 26 | 26 | VE

14 E. 60th St. (bet. 5th & Madison Aves.), 4/5/6/F/N/R/W to 59th St./ Lexington Ave., 212-308-8760; 888-933-9474; www.reemacra.com
■ This "top-flight", "exclusive" bridal and eveningwear boutique a stone's throw from Barneys insures "dreams come true" for the betrothed and babes alike; what woman doesn't want to "feel like royalty" in "to-die-for" "mind-boggling designs" boasting "exquisite" details like gold threadwork and lace and beading?; the staff is "helpful and calming" to jittery brides, but "get ready to leave your inhibitions (and wallet) behind" at this wedding "heaven."

Refinery S C
▽ 27 | 23 | 26 | M

254 Smith St. (DeGraw St.), Brooklyn, F/G to Bergen St., 718-643-7861
■ "Every local needs a 718 T-shirt" ("they shouldn't let you over the Brooklyn Bridge without one") and a bag to boot from this "friendly" Carroll Gardens boutique, one of the original shops to spring up on happening Smith Street; owner-designer Suzanne Bagdade's "hip", "personalized" handbags and totes created from "extra special" vintage ties and hand-me-down fabrics are displayed on lean tables built by her husband for this airy, modern space.

REINSTEIN/ROSS C
28 | 27 | 22 | VE

29 E. 73rd St. (bet. 5th & Madison Aves.), 6 to 68th St., 212-772-1901
122 Prince St. (bet. Greene & Wooster Sts.), R/W to Prince St., 212-226-4513 S
www.reinstein.com
■ "Small" all-white jewelry store on the Upper East Side, with a SoHo branch, that showcases "beautiful Byzantine-like designs" in "unique shades" of "brushed gold" and "incredible fancy-colored sapphires" and other gemstones; "handmade in homage to ancient goldsmiths", the "intricate" pieces can also be made-to-order in your honor for a particularly precious, "expensive delight."

Religious Sex ⊘ S C
20 | 16 | 14 | M

7 St. Marks Pl. (bet. 2nd & 3rd Aves.), 6 to Astor Pl.; R/W to 8th St., 212-477-9037; www.religioussex.com
☑ "Perfect for when you want to let the little punk girl inside you scream out", with a cache of "goth treasures for males", this "just plain cool" "veritable St. Marks institution" "jam-packed" with "semi-naughty" lingerie, clothing and fantasy wear meets "all your fetish needs"; "corsets, anyone?" this "kinky underwear" "you can wear out", plus "stunning" "medieval-Renaissance-style" standouts and bondage pieces are "not for the faint of heart"; still some Sex addicts fail to put faith into "claustrophic" quarters and a staff with "attitude."

Reminiscence ⊘ S
17 | 18 | 15 | M

50 W. 23rd St. (bet. 5th & 6th Aves.), F/N/R/V to 23rd St., 212-243-2292; www.reminiscence.com
■ "Step into a shopping time warp" when you enter this "pop-culture" paradise that offers an "eclectic" "mix of seasonal '60s and '70s [casualwear] and new retro-style clothing" from the store's own label; up front, "the perfect party favors, inappropriate gag gifts" and other novelties nestle alongside lunchboxes and "kitschy

toys"; despite the name, there's "not much real vintage" here, but it's definitely "worth a gander" if you're cruising Chelsea.

Repertoire ☐ | – | – | – | E |
75 Grand St. (bet. Greene & Wooster Sts.), A/C/E to Canal St., 212-219-8159; www.repertoire.com
The repertoire of home furnishings at this pricey SoHo store ranges from chairs from Italian maker Gervasoni to daybeds from Dominic Gasparoly and tables from Tomas Frenes.

Replay ●S☐ | 19 | 20 | 17 | E |
109 Prince St. (Greene St.), R/W to Prince St.; B/D/F/S/V to B'way/ Lafayette St., 212-673-6300; www.replay.it
◪ "If you're looking for jeans for your guy", yourself or your kids, plus "good novelty knits" and casual "hip shirts", "check out" this "cool" two-floor SoHo shop with a "really neat setup" featuring brick and straw display cubes; "favored by Europeans", this Italian collection offers "a fresh alternative" with "fashionable silhouettes" that make it "worth the extra expense"; still, some assert "prices are out of sight"; N.B. a post-*Survey* renovation may outdate the above Presentation score.

Restoration Hardware ●S | 22 | 23 | 18 | M |
935 Broadway (bet. 21st & 22nd Sts.), R/W to 23rd St., 212-260-9479; 800-762-1005; www.restorationhardware.com
◪ "Doorknobs, furniture polish and leather sofas" along with lighting, "clever kitsch" like "retro" "gadgets" (e.g. a 1955 hand warmer) and other "vintage-looking stuff" are sold at this Flatiron branch of the home-furnishings-and-hardware chain; "nostalgia"-obsessed fans feel the "weird mix works" and makes for "old-fashioned" "fun", but critics counter it's a "pricey" "mixed bag."

Resurrection S | 24 | 21 | 16 | E |
217 Mott St. (bet. Prince & Spring Sts.), R/W to Prince St.; 6 to Spring St., 212-625-1374; www.resurrectionvintage.com
■ If "Pucci's your thing" or you think "Courrèges is to die for", this NoLita specialist in '60s and '70s "high-quality couture" "in very good condition" will provide "the perfect piece to cause a buzz"; appropriately decorated with Space Age–style chandeliers, round blue chairs and blood-red walls, the "nice digs" make for pleasant browsing, "but be ready to drop some major cash" for the "collectible" goods (e.g. $125 for period Levi's).

Reva Mivasagar S | ▽ 25 | 25 | 23 | E |
28 Wooster St. (bet. Canal & Grand Sts.), A/C/E to Canal St., 212-334-3860; www.revadesigns.com
■ "Very chic", "but still festive enough" for the big day, these retro-inspired yet modern, ivory or colored custom-made creations are fashioned "for the not-too-bridey bride" who "can't stand the sugary-sweetness of the wedding industry"; "a pleasure to work with", the "very talented" Singapore-born designer is often at his SoHo shop, where he also turns out eveningwear that "delivers consistently classy looks."

Richard Metz Golf ☐ | ▽ 21 | 19 | 19 | E |
12 E. 46th St. (Madison Ave.), 4/5/6/7/S to 42nd St./Grand Central, 212-599-7252; 888-737-4659; www.richardmetzgolf.com
◪ Go on, "take a mulligan" – the high ceilings at this 34-year-old family-owned "golfer's dreamworld" tucked into a second-floor

Midtown location are made for swinging; while some applaud the "nice selection of woods and irons", apparel, shoes and bags, a few find it "limited", particularly the putters and balls.

Ricky's ●ⓢ   24 | 15 | 12 | I
718 Broadway (bet. Astor Pl. & Washington St.), 6 to Astor Pl., 212-979-5232; www.rickys-nyc.com
Additional locations throughout the NY area
■ "Duane Reade meets the Pink Pussycat" sums up this "naughty" but nice chain "crammed full of kitsch and beauty booty", from "the great selection" of hair products and makeup to "novelty items" like "fake tattoos", "pink wigs and vibrators with kangaroos on them"; be prepared for a "totally New York experience", right down to the salespeople who sometimes seem to "see customers as an annoying distraction from figuring out what club to go to that night"; P.S. if you're feeling "funky" and looking for a costume "on Halloween, this is the place to be."

Rico ⓈⒸ   – | – | – | E
384 Atlantic Ave. (bet. Bond & Hoyt Sts.), Brooklyn, A/C/G to Hoyt/Schermerhorn Sts., 718-797-2077; www.shoprico.com
Owner Rico Espinet showcases his lamps and lighting solutions as well as furniture from Mitchell Gold, Maria Yee and Dellarobia at this Boerum Hill studio and store; originally a sculptor and a stage-lighting professional, the designer taps into both retro and modern inspirations, using materials like hand-blown frosted glass and polished chrome to create his line.

Rita's Needlepoint Ⓒ   22 | 19 | 23 | E
150 E. 79th St., 2nd fl. (bet. Lexington & 3rd Aves.), 6 to 77th St., 212-737-8613
■ "An unpretentious shop" that "feels like a little club with constant coffee klatches", this Upper East Side boutique tempts with a "good merchandise mix" ranging from "cute, simple and inexpensive to grand, gorgeous projects" that may call for one of Rita's and other artists' "fabulous custom-painted" canvases; the "sage owners" and their "knowledgeable staff" lend "superior advice", making it "a joy to shop here."

Ritz Furs   ▽ 17 | 15 | 13 | E
107 W. 57th St. (bet. 6th & 7th Aves.), N/Q/R/W to 57th St., 212-265-4559; www.ritzfurs.com
■ For "those who know furs", there are "excellent bargains" to be had at this West 50s salon, which showcases "gently used designer" and a few new coats and accessories; by pelt standards, "prices are for plebeians" – especially in the everything-under-$1,000 basement – whether you're getting a "sumptuous" sable, a mink bikini or a fox cell-phone holder.

RK Bridal Ⓢ   19 | 9 | 13 | M
318 W. 39th St. (bet. 8th & 9th Aves.), A/C/E to 42nd St./Port Authority, 212-947-1155; 800-929-9512; www.rkbridal.com
☑ "You want to get married twice so you can buy two dresses instead of one" at this "no-frills" Garment District "supermarket of bridalwear" "crammed" with over 1,000 "gems" that are "worth a trip for the thrifty bride", plus bridesmaid, flower girl and even prom dresses and accessories; "bring your armor to fight the crowds" on weekends carp critics who find the "help too snooty for the factory outlet" environs, hissing "not for the couture girl."

Ro ▣ⓒ   – | – | – | E

267 E. 10th St. (bet. Ave. A & 1st Ave.), L to 1st Ave., 212-477-1595;
www.gotoro.com

The East Village collaboration between architect Gene Miao and
fashion designer Yvonne Roe, on display in a utilitarian showroom
space, is all about form – black and brown (with the occasional
white, red or baby blue) leathers meet clean, uncluttered lines
in messenger, computer, tote, duffel and attaché shapes with
interesting details; an oversized artists' portfolio boasts transparent
outer pockets for tape measures and loose foreign coins.

Roberta's Lingerie ⓒ   ▽ 22 | 18 | 19 | E

1252 Madison Ave. (90th St.), 4/5/6 to 86th St., 212-860-8366

☑ Whether you go to this "lovely" peach-colored "neighborhood
shop" on Madison for "your first bra", a bathrobe and slippers or
"your honeymoon outfit", "make sure you check in with the experts
to get the right fit" and cup size; while boosters big on little
nothings claim the choices from imported and domestic designers, plus
bathing suits, are "wonderful", "with a broad price range" to
boot, a handful shrug that they've "never understood the appeal
of this store."

Robert Clergerie ▣   25 | 22 | 21 | VE

681 Madison Ave. (bet. 61st & 62nd Sts.), N/R/W to 5th Ave./59th St.,
212-207-8600; www.robertclergerie.com

■ "Comfort reigns" and "wonderful quality" rules at this Madison
Avenue outpost where some of the "best" shoes "the French have
to offer" can be found, along with handbags and accessories;
the "great styles", including the "popular" wedgie, range from
"chunky" to "out there" to just plain "fab" – little wonder loyalists
"want more and more"; service is "friendly", prompting patrons
to opine "every store in the world should be run as well."

Robert Lee Morris ▣ⓒ   22 | 22 | 17 | E

400 W. Broadway (bet. Broome & Spring Sts.), C/E to Spring St.,
212-431-9405; 800-829-8444; www.robertleemorris.com

■ The "standard bearer for high-end", "serious, modern" sterling-
silver jewelry since the '70s is still going strong at his SoHo
boutique, turning out "statement-making" designs, like the
signature Knuckle rings, that are "not for the meek" (but are often
in 18 karat gold nowadays).

Robert Marc   27 | 25 | 25 | VE

436 Broadway (Prince St.), R/W to Prince St., 212-343-8300 ◗▣
190 Columbus Ave. (bet. 68th & 69th Sts.), 1/9 to 66th St./Lincoln Ctr.,
212-799-4600 ◗▣
1300 Madison Ave. (bet. 92nd & 93rd Sts.), 6 to 96th St., 212-722-1600 ▣
1046 Madison Ave. (bet. 78th & 79th Sts.), 6 to 77th St.,
212-988-9600 ▣
782 Madison Ave. (bet. 66th & 67th Sts.), 6 to 68th St.,
212-737-6000 ▣
551 Madison Ave. (bet. 55th & 56th Sts.), N/R/W to 5th Ave./59th St.,
212-319-2000 ▣
400 Madison Ave. (bet. 47th & 48th Sts.), E/V to 5th Ave./53rd St.,
212-319-2900
www.robertmarc.com

■ La "crème de la crème" of spectacle shops may well be this
Downtown-Midtown-Uptown Manhattan chain that purveys

products that help you "get over bad memories of those big plastic frames you had to wear in the fourth grade"; the "unbelievable selection" of "beautiful", "up-to-the-minute" eyewear is "well organized" and "presented", and the "discerning", "talented" staff "helps you find flattering" glasses that give "you a new outlook on life" that's "worth the price."

Roberto Cavalli [S][C] 25 | 23 | 22 | VE

711 Madison Ave. (bet. 63rd & 64th Sts.), 4/5/6/F/N/R/W to 59th St./ Lexington Ave., 212-755-7722; www.robertocavalli.it

■ "Prepare to be pampered" by the "accommodating, friendly staff" at this East 60s boutique, whose namesake designer "knows how to flatter the female form" with "gorgeously bold", "big-bucks" dresses, coats and "sexy" jeans; body-hugging and bedecked with furs, feathers and silk appliqués, his "top-notch hippie chic" is "not made for a shy person" but is "so right for a *Sex and the City* night", plus he now also offers fragrances for women and men.

ROBERT TALBOTT [C] 27 | 26 | 25 | VE

680 Madison Ave. (bet. 61st & 62nd Sts.), N/R/W to 5th Ave./59th St., 212-751-1200; 800-747-8778; www.roberttalbott.com

■ "The only place for shirts and neckwear" ("they actually have bow ties!") swoon supporters about this compact but "lovely Madison Avenue store", an "upper-class gem" for its "gorgeous" garb in "fab colors" ranging from men's formalwear to women's blouses, scarves and shearling jackets; "although the prices are steep", "where else can one find a seven-fold necktie, at least outside of Italy?"

Roche Bobois [S] 25 | 25 | 20 | VE

200 Madison Ave. (35th St.), 6 to 33rd St., 212-725-5513; www.rochebobois.com

■ At this East 30s furniture standby, the "good-quality", "modern" and sleek sofas, beds, tables and wall systems "wear well", especially the seating upholstered in luxe leather that feels almost "like buttah."

Rochester Big & Tall 25 | 23 | 24 | E

1301 Sixth Ave. (52nd St.), B/D/F/V to 47-50th Sts./Rockefeller Ctr., 212-247-7500; 800-282-8200; www.rochesterclothing.com

■ Jolly in-the-green giants "love" the fact that "large men have a place to go where they don't have to settle on something" they don't really want; "one of the few plus-size men's shops in Manhattan", this "upscale" Midtowner carries all the best-known designer brands, and their salespeople, who "remember you and the size you wear", are "unsurpassed"; however, the skinny on the "hefty prices" is "your wallet better be as big as your waistline."

Rocks in your Head ◐[S] ▽ 22 | 17 | 21 | I

157 Prince St. (bet. Thompson St. & W. B'way), R/W to Prince St., 212-475-6729; www.rocksinyourhead.com

■ "Lord knows how they afford the rent" given the "good prices" on new and used selections, but somehow this SoHo "sleeper" manages; a "friendly" "indie-record haven" "behind whose doors are some of the hardest-to-find albums in the city", it's "fun, eclectic and you'll likely see a rock star" cruising for a rare CD – it's so hip, "the guys from *High Fidelity* would look like Michael Bolton in here."

Room
▽ 21 | 21 | 18 | E

182 Duane St. (bet. Greenwich & Hudson Sts.), 1/2/3/9 to Chambers St., 212-226-1045; 888-420-7666; www.roomonline.com

■ What began life as a stylish magalog is now a "smart" TriBeCa purveyor of "fresh"-looking minimalist furnishings mostly designed in-house and displayed in a sparse loft setting.

Rooms & Gardens
– | – | – | VE

7 Mercer St. (bet. Canal & Grand Sts.), 6/J/M/N/Q/R/W/Z to Canal St., 212-431-1297; www.roomsandgardens.net

Even if you weren't to the manor born, this SoHo purveyor of vintage furniture and European antiques (mostly French) from the 18th to mid-20th century lets you live like you were by providing the proper trappings like ornate garden urns and mercury-glass mirrors; new shipments arrive every three or four months, so don't give up on that 19th-century oak convent table you've always wanted.

Rosen & Chadick Textiles
▽ 27 | 21 | 19 | M

246 W. 40th St. (bet. 7th & 8th Aves.), A/C/E to 42nd St./Port Authority, 212-869-0142; 800-225-3838

■ Heralded as one of the "top fabric suppliers to Broadway and the entertainment industry", this "all-purpose" two-floor textile shop "in the heart of the Garment District" also offers the home-sewing set an "impressive selection of top-quality" goods, particularly "great menswear" options.

Roslyn S C
22 | 19 | 19 | E

276 Columbus Ave. (73rd St.), 1/2/3/9 to 72nd St., 212-496-5050

■ "Whether it is the latest fad or a classic piece" of estate or reproduction jewelry, an "antique ring", kicky, "adorable" hats and bags, this boutique – "one of the best finds on the Upper West Side" – is "sure to have it"; the eclectic mix of fine collectibles from owner Roslyn Grent as well as other talented designers is matched by "salespeople who accommodate special requests."

Rothman's S
20 | 18 | 19 | M

200 Park Ave. S. (17th St.), 4/5/6/L/N/Q/R/W to 14th St./Union Sq., 212-777-7400; www.rothmansny.com

■ Those who "seek value for name-brand quality" head to the top of Union Square, where they can "get designer men's clothes at discount prices" – both tailored togs (Hickey Freeman, Hugo Boss, etc.) and casual separates from Tommy Bahama, Ted Baker and Ben Sherman, plus coats, shoes and accessories; the "informed, friendly staff" is geared toward "guys who don't like to shop."

Rubin Chapelle S C
– | – | – | E

410 W. 14th St. (bet. 9th Ave. & Washington St.), A/C/E/L to 14th St./ 8th Ave., 212-647-8636; www.rubinchapelle.com

On West 14th Street's designer row, this spare, sleek arrival holds its own with a thin Lucite-paneled 'curtain' and curvy white racks that showcase Sonja Rubin's and Kip Chapelle's intriguing blend of masculine-feminine tailoring; the asymmetrical separates and leather jackets for both sexes have avant-garde 'look-at-me' details that ensure everyone will.

Rue St. Denis ● S
▽ 23 | 19 | 18 | M

174 Ave. B (11th St.), L to 1st Ave., 212-260-3388; www.vintagenyc.com

■ From European label and designer name vintage dresses and outerwear to men's suits, there are "great finds every time" at this spacious store, which specializes in leather biker gear from England and unusually patterned clothes, primarily from the 1940s–1980s, for him, her and baby; East Village seekers also note that "every item is in excellent condition" – naturally, since most have never been worn.

Rug Company, The 🆂🅲
– | – | – | VE

88 Wooster St. (bet. Broome & Spring Sts.), C/E to Spring St.; 212-274-0444; www.therugcompany.info

The British have landed at this SoHo offshoot of a London-based firm featuring an extensive collection of carpets – from hand-knotted Nepalese ones to classic wovens and a designer collection from well-known English names like Marni, Paul Smith, Lulu Guinness and Nina Campbell; but whatever you want you're covered, since the rugs can be made to any size.

Ruzzetti & Gow 🅲
– | – | – | M

22 East 72nd St., 3rd fl. (bet. 5th & Madison Aves.), 6 to 68th St., 212-327-4281; www.ruzzettiandgow.com

They may not sell their silver-coated seashells down by the seashore, but they do sell them at their Upper East Side, third-floor home-accessories shop; joining the artfully embellished conchological crowd gathered here are silvered vegetables and fruits, decorative coral for the table, rock-crystal votives and semiprecious stone bowls and boxes; the price is rather reasonable considering nature's gifts have been given such a glam gilding.

Sacco 🌑🆂
21 | 18 | 18 | M

324 Columbus Ave. (75th St.), 1/2/3/9/B/C to 72nd St., 212-799-5229
118 E. 59th St. (bet. Lexington & Park Aves.), 4/5/6/F/N/R/W to 59th St./ Lexington Ave., 212-207-3151
14 E. 17th St. (5th Ave.), 4/5/6/L/N/Q/R/W to 14th St./Union Sq., 212-243-2070
94 Seventh Ave. (bet. 15th & 16th Sts.), 1/9 to 18th St., 212-675-5180
111 Thompson St. (Prince St.), R/W to Prince St., 212-925-8010
www.saccoshoes.com

■ Offering a "fashionable" "comfort line" that's one of the "best" for "pounding the pavement" "in style" "without making you look like a school nurse", this chainlet stalwart also stocks an "extensive range" of "sensibly creative" high heels, "beautifully crafted" in Italy; prices are "reasonable", and take heed: insiders confide "they have very good sales."

Safavieh Carpets 🆂
▽ 24 | 20 | 22 | E

902 Broadway (bet. 20th & 21st Sts.), R/W to 23rd St., 212-477-1234
238 E. 59th St. (bet. 2nd & 3rd Aves.), 4/5/6/F/N/R/W to 59th St./ Lexington Ave., 212-888-0626
153 Madison Ave. (32nd St.), 6 to 33rd St., 212 683-8399
866-422-9070; www.safavieh.com

■ These "destinations for Oriental rugs" carry carpeting from all over the world, ranging from India to Turkey and China; while the antique-oriented have lots to choose from, the Hampton and SoHo collections are colorful experiences for contemporary types.

Saigoniste 🆂🅲
– | – | – | M

239 Mulberry St. (bet. Prince & Spring Sts.), 6 to Spring St., 212-925-4610; www.saigoniste.com

"Eye-catching window displays" attract shoppers drawn to the "fashion-forward", "Vietnamese-inspired" home accessories at this packed NoLita purveyor; "sleek" and "colorful" lacquer bowls, trays, vases and sushi sets make Asian-appreciators "want to jet off" to Saigon "or at least order some noodles when they get home."

Saint Laurie Merchant Tailors

| 21 | 17 | 20 | E |

22 W. 32nd St., 5th fl. (bet. B'way & 5th Ave.), B/D/F/N/Q/R/V/W to 34th St./Herald Sq., 212-643-1916; www.saintlaurie.com

■ "Everyone needs at least one custom-made" or "semi-custom-made suit" and this "strong option for classic men's clothing" in the Garment District "is the place to get it"; a broad selection of fabrics and "excellent craftsmanship" characterizes the experience and the made-to-measure goods are "worth the longer wait", since these tailors who are "in touch with customers' needs" "clothe your mediocre midsection magnificently"; finance types swear by all the saints that "good deals" can be had.

SAKS FIFTH AVENUE S

| 26 | 24 | 20 | E |

611 Fifth Ave. (bet. 49th & 50th Sts.), B/D/F/V to 47-50th Sts./Rockefeller Ctr., 212-753-4000; www.saks.com

■ The "old-world elegance" and "open, airy" atmosphere of this Midtown "landmark" make it a "pleasure to shop" its "top-drawer" women's collections, "ultracivilized" menswear and "a nice mix" of "serious and stylish shoes" for both ("sales are to run for"); "eager makeup artists abound" among the "varied" cosmetics counters, and "kudos" also go to bridal-salon trunk shows, "lovely leather goods" and "lust-inducing" accessories, especially the lingerie department ("best bra-fitting in town"); a "splendid" restaurant, an "A+ return policy" and a staff that's "happy to find merchandise at another location" help "uphold its reputation" for service; and at year's end, "you can feel the holiday spirit the minute" you walk in.

Salon Moderne C

| – | – | – | E |

281 Lafayette St. (bet. Houston & Prince Sts.), R/W to Prince St., 212-219-3439

This SoHo home-furnishings store's Italian imports include plush modern sofas, mirrors, luscious pillows, throws and a few well-chosen vintage pieces; the showroom also offers custom-work.

Salvation Army

| 13 | 6 | 8 | I |

536 W. 46th St. (bet. 10th & 11th Aves.), A/C/E to 42nd St./Port Authority, 212-757-2311; www.salvationarmy.org
Additional locations throughout the NY area

☑ "If you've time to sort through the mayhem, then dive on in" to "the old standby of secondhand shops", which "carries everything donate-able" at low "prices, regardless of brand or era"; among the army of branches, the "Grand Kahuna" on 46th Street is "interesting for clothing and cheap furniture"; the staff, however, needs to do some KP.

Salvatore Ferragamo S

| 27 | 25 | 23 | VE |

655 Fifth Ave. (bet. 52nd & 53rd Sts.), E/V to 5th Ave./53rd St., 212-759-3822
124 Spring St. (Greene St.), C/E to Spring St., 212-226-4330
800-628-8916; www.salvatoreferragamo.it

☑ When in need of "shopping therapy", "treat yourself" to the "comfort and status" of this Italian brand in its revamped Fifth Avenue flagship and SoHo sibling; though they carry his-and-hers clothes, "quality scarves" and the "best ties in the world", most say "nothing else matters" but the "hardworking" yet "soft-as-butter shoes" that come in "sizes for everyone" and actually are "a great value", given they "wear like iron"; some sigh "styles are a bit staid", but an "inviting staff" keeps the footwear a "favorite"; N.B. the Midtown mecca relocated post-*Survey*, which may outdate the above Presentation score.

Sam & Seb 🇸🇨   – | – | – | M
208 Bedford Ave. (bet. N. 5th & 6th Sts.), Brooklyn, L to Bedford Ave., 718-486-8300; www.samandseb.com
Done up in bright pink and orange, this hard-to-miss Williamsburg boutique for newborns to six-year-olds offers an arty selection that's keyed into neighborhood demands; the cool collections include European labels as well as local Brooklyn designers, bright Oink! baby apparel and whimsical rain boots, plus Black Sabbath, Bob Marley, Beastie Boys and Jimi Hendrix T-shirts as well as Blondie and Billy Idol onesies for budding superstars who just want to rock on, at least through the night.

Sam Flax   23 | 20 | 16 | E
425 Park Ave. (55th St.), 4/5/6/F/N/R/W to 59th St./Lexington Ave., 212-935-5353
12 W. 20th St. (bet. 5th & 6th Aves.), F/V to 23rd St., 212-620-3038 🇸
www.samflax.com
☑ "Treat yourself" at this "overstuffed" Flatironist and Park Avenue sibling where "everything is quality" and "to the point in style and function", from "beautiful" Aeron chairs to "writing implements you never knew you needed"; budding Picassos say it's "really a high-end office supply" place, so "skip the art materials, since you can find a better, cheaper selection elsewhere", and "go straight to the gifts, furniture" and custom frames.

Sam Goody   14 | 13 | 10 | M
390 Sixth Ave. (8th St.), A/B/C/D/E/F/S/V to W. 4th St., 212-674-7131 ◑🇸
5100-47 Kings Plaza (bet. Flatbush Ave. & Ave. U), Brooklyn, 2/5 to Brooklyn College/Flatbush Ave., 718-253-6701 ◑🇸
66-26 Metropolitan Ave., Queens, M to Middle Vlg./Metropolitan Ave., 718-456-0085
Queens Ctr., 90-15 Queens Blvd., Queens, G/R/V to Woodhaven Blvd., 718-592-2268 ◑🇸
Staten Island Mall, 2655 Richmond Ave., Staten Island, 718-698-7070 ◑🇸
www.samgoody.com
☑ "Need Britney at full retail?" – this "not-so-Goody" of a veteran chain with just one branch left in the Village and a few in the boroughs has "got it"; it sure is convenient, and the staff is up on "current hits" and "hip-hop, but good luck finding anyone who knows anything about another genre", and though the "excellent loyalty program" can pay off in long-term savings, the everyday "ridiculous prices" have even the "teenybopper crowd" grumbling "this is why they invented Napster."

Sample 🇸🇨   – | – | – | M
268 Elizabeth St. (bet. Houston & Prince Sts.), B/D/F/S/V to B'way/Lafayette St., 212-431-7866; 866-239-6779; www.samplestudio.com
Tucked into a tiny red-awninged shop in NoLita is designer Tu Ly's austere sweater bar, filled with distinctive knitwear that "will work with everything else in your closet;" "cute" "sweater basics",

many with an edgy twist, come in fine gauge silks, mercerized cotton, angora, and chunky wool yarns in a host of styles, from retro cardigans to chic hoodies; delicate jewelry and quirky print handbags fill out the sampling of goodies.

Samuel Jackson Design Company ●◒S   – | – | – | E

31 Crosby St. (bet. Broome & Grand Sts.), R/W to Prince St., 646-613-9379; www.samueljacksondesigns.com

It may be hard to spot from the street, but this moody basement SoHo shop with exposed-brick walls and abstract paintings is filled with lushly knit accessories, slouchy leather and suede bags in funky and whimsical shapes and swinging, '70s-style knitwear that make it worth seeking out; you may not run into Samuel L. behind the counter – the actor has nothin' to do with these groovy goods – but more than a few rockers have been known to bop by.

S&W   21 | 9 | 11 | M

165 W. 26th St. (bet. 6th & 7th Aves.), 1/9 to 28th St., 718-431-2800 S C
4217 13th Ave. (43rd St.), Brooklyn, D/M to Fort Hamilton Pkwy., 718-431-2800 ●S C
4209 13th Ave. (bet. 42nd & 43rd Sts.), Brooklyn, D/M to Fort Hamilton Pkwy., 718-431-2800

☑ You must "go early in the season" for "best buys" on "top-quality" "designer coats, shoes and bags" at this "little place for the odd treasure" that's been in Chelsea and Brooklyn "for eons"; "purses are their strong suit", but cheapsters with a "memory of the past" say "their clothing selection has suffered in recent years" while the saleswomen are as "high pressure" as ever, but not on Friday evening or Saturday, when they're closed "since they are Shomer Shabbat."

Sanrio ●◒S   22 | 21 | 16 | M

(aka Hello Kitty Store)
233 W. 42nd St. (bet. 7th & 8th Aves.), 1/2/3/7/9/N/Q/R/S/W to 42nd St./ Times Sq., 212-840-6011; www.sanrio.com

■ "Meow!" "happiness reigns" at this now larger "dream store for children of any age" in Times Square where droves of "kids, club kids, girly girls" and tween "tourists" alike shop for "everything Kitty" plus "oh-so-cute" items plastered with cartoon icons like "bad boy penguin" Batz-Maru and "Chococat too"; cuddle up to the "fun Japanese pop" adorableness with "loads of tiny trinkets" and other "fun products", from pencil cases, waffle irons and pink TVs to towels, shower curtains, alarm clocks and even boom boxes.

Sansha S   – | – | – | M

1717 Broadway, 2nd fl. (bet. 54th & 55th Sts.), N/Q/R/W to 57th St., 212-246-6212; 800-398-9562; www.sansha.com

Twinkle-toed customers of all ages and sexes hotfoot it up the steps to this Midtown dancer's delight for stage-worthy footwear, such as handcrafted "good-quality" split-sole ballet slippers and pointe, jazz, flamenco, tap and character shoes; the *grande* selection of leotards and legwear, ranging from unitards to *All That Jazz*–esque fishnets, is enough to make any trouper *jeté* for joy.

SANTA MARIA NOVELLA S C   27 | 27 | 25 | E

285 Lafayette St. (bet. Houston & Prince Sts.), 6 to Spring St., 212-925-0001; www.smnovella.com

■ "There's a scented hush to the place, as if you were entering a sort of retail cathedral", which is appropriate given that this

NoLita newcomer is a branch of the famous Florence *farmacia* founded by monks in 1612; billing itself as the world's oldest body-care line, the company offers "gorgeous, albeit, pricey" natural-ingredient soaps, skin lotions, eau de colognes and pure essences like Mimosa and Magnolia; all that "bliss in a bottle" makes for "pure heaven for beauty product junkies."

Satellite Records ●S
– | – | – | M

259 Bowery (bet. Houston & Prince Sts.), F/V to Lower East Side/ 2nd Ave., 212-995-1744; www.satellite-records.com
The place to beat for dance music, with numerous vinyl and a few CD listening stations, this "true club-life superstore" on the Bowery (with branches in Atlanta and Boston) has one of "the best selections for trance, house", jungle, hip-hop and drum 'n' bass; the "help is pretty knowledgeable and responsive", and they definitely can tell you where the party is – check out the rack of invites near the album cases up front.

Scandinavian Ski & Sport Shop ●SC
23 | 18 | 16 | VE

40 W. 57th St. (bet. 5th & 6th Aves.), F to 57th St., 212-757-8524; www.skishop.com
☑ Steep yourself in "top-of-the-line" skis, ski boots, snowboards and some of the "best Norwegian sweaters in New York", plus parkas and jackets from Bogna and Nils, Ugg boots, mountain bikes, sporting goods, tennis gear and apparel at this retail chalet, a Midtown fixture since 1948; still, some bad sports scoff the selection is "limited", adding "how do you say overpriced in Swedish?"

Scarlet Ginger SC
– | – | – | M

376 Atlantic Ave. (bet. Bond & Hoyt Sts.), Brooklyn, A/C/G to Hoyt/ Schermerhorn Sts., 718-852-8205
London-born designer Charlie Smith brings a fresh *Fantasia* feel to Boerum Hill with her cool, cheery new womenswear boutique; the front area is filled with an eclectic mix of Australian, British and Brazilian goods, with many pieces punk-inspired and/or reworked vintage-wear, all complemented by the proprietor's own flirty handknit scarves and hats; red carpet divas short on cash take note: you can rent the handpicked garb stashed to the rear.

Scarpe Diem SC
▽ 21 | 21 | 21 | E

2286 Broadway (bet. 81st & 82nd Sts.), 1/9 to 79th St., 212-362-5070
☑ "Very downtown for its uptown" West 80s address, this chic red-and-white boutique offers an upscale mix of "good chick shoes" and handbags from the likes of Lulu Guinness and Nakano; the stock "changes quite often", a coup for fashion hounds always looking for the next stylin' thing, plus "the staff is helpful and friendly and keeps great hours"; still, a few pout it's not for "conservative" types.

Schneider's C
▽ 22 | 11 | 15 | M

20 Ave. A (2nd St.), F/V to Lower East Side/2nd Ave., 212-228-3540; www.schneidersbaby.com
■ It may be a "schlep to get to" this Alphabet City children's supply store, "but where else are you going to buy your Maclaren stroller in the East Village?", plus other major brands of car seats, walkers, cribs and the like; this is "the place for all baby needs", from furniture to gifts and toys to footwear.

Scholastic Store, The ●S
22 | 22 | 20 | M

557 Broadway (bet. Prince & Spring Sts.), R/W to Prince St.,
212-343-6166; www.scholasticstore.com

■ This "merrily colorful" SoHo store staffed with "knowledgeable, friendly" folk "expands children's imaginations" with its "interesting toys and games that coordinate" with best-sellers like "*Harry Potter* and other beloved characters"; the "nice, open space" encourages kids to "play and explore" while its "new book smell reminds you of your childhood"; it's a "very bonding experience" for parents and little ones alike who "linger and interact with the compelling contents"; P.S. the "storytelling can't be beat."

School Products Co. C
21 | 14 | 20 | M

1201 Broadway, 3rd fl. (bet. 28th & 29th Sts.), R/W to 23rd St.,
212-679-3516; 800-847-4127; www.schoolproducts.com

■ A "bargain-basement atmosphere" reigns at this 56-year-old on the fringes of the Flatiron District, and that's why it's a "favorite", with oceans of yarns on skeins and "on cones – a delight for machine knitters" and weavers – and "terrific buys on cashmere and upscale yarns" for hand-knitters; it's "truly a place for those who love their craft", and it's all finished off with a "really helpful, low-key staff."

Schweitzer Linen C
26 | 14 | 14 | E

457 Columbus Ave. (bet. 81st & 82nd Sts.), B/C to 81st St., 212-799-9642 S
1053 Lexington Ave. (bet. 74th & 75th Sts.), 6 to 77th St., 212-570-0236
1132 Madison Ave. (bet. 84th & 85th Sts.), 4/5/6 to 86th St., 212-249-8361
800-554-6367; www.schweitzerlinen.com

■ "Gorgeous", "sophisticated" European linens at "great prices" and scallop-edged Egyptian-cotton towels that are Porthault look-alikes for less are the draws at this trio of specialty shops; they have a "terrific" mail-order catalog that offers other bed-and-bath-oriented items like tapestry pillows and will also produce fully customized bedding from customers' color schemes and design ideas.

SCO S C
– | – | – | E

230 Mulberry St. (bet. Prince & Spring Sts.), 6 to Spring St.,
212-966-3011; 866-966-7268; www.scocare.com

The name of this "great, little" NoLita shop stands for Skin Care Options, and flexible, "custom-made products" are just what they offer: clients choose from the line of existing cleansers, toners, creams and scrubs, then elect to have them infused with natural ingredients (ranging from papaya to parsley) based on the specific needs of their skin; converts leave with containers labeled with their name, the product's expiration date – and a little less money in the bank.

Scoop Men's ●S C
23 | 22 | 17 | E

1273 Third Ave. (bet. 73rd & 74th Sts.), 6 to 77th St., 212-535-5577;
www.scoopnyc.com

☑ "Long overdue, baby", this East 70s adjunct connected to the "trendy" women's boutique next door has "everything the stylish metrosexual male needs"; the "mix of uptown and downtown styles" puts customers who like to "be the first on their block" to scoop up that "cool guy T-shirt", "hard-to-find" Prada vest, John Varvatos shearling or Paul Smith shirt and "high-end yummy denim" "at the top of the fashion times"; "it ain't cheap and service can be snooty" "unless you're Ben Affleck", but perhaps "that's the cost of hip."

SCOOP NYC ◐ [S] [C] 23 | 21 | 13 | VE

532 Broadway (bet. Prince & Spring Sts.), R/W to Prince St., 212-925-2886
1275 & 1277 Third Ave. (bet. 73rd & 74th Sts.), 6 to 77th St., 212-535-5577
873 Washington St. (bet. 13th & 14th Sts.), A/C/E/L to 14th St./8th Ave., 212-929-1244
www.scoopnyc.com

◪ It's like a "trip around the Downtown boutiques all in one place" exclaim enthusiasts of these "high-energy" spots pulsating with the "hottest" "high-end brands" – a "great selection of shoes, separates and going-out clothes" from the likes of Paper Denim & Cloth, Marc by Marc Jacobs and Theory – all familiar to "fashion-forward" "It girls"; the thrifty sniff it's "expensive considering it's all trendy stuff", but if you can "splurge, go for it" and overlook the "self-congratulatory" salespeople; N.B. the Meatpacking District branch also sells menswear.

Scott Jordan Furniture [S] 25 | 22 | 26 | E

137 Varick St. (Spring St.), 1/9 to Canal St.; C/E to Spring St., 212-620-4682; www.scottjordan.com

■ "If you like solid cherry furniture, start here first" profess proponents of this two-story SoHo space selling "supremely beautiful", "handcrafted", "heirloom-quality" Mission-style chairs, tables, sofas and beds, which are produced in the former Brooklyn Navy Yard; "reasonable prices" for the quality and a "very patient" staff make shopping here a pleasure.

Screaming Mimi's ◐ [S] 21 | 20 | 17 | M

382 Lafayette St. (E. 4th St.), 6 to Astor Pl.; R/W to 8th St., 212-677-6464; www.screamingmimis.com

◪ "Funkadelic possibilities" abound at this NoHo store "catering to the kids from NYU and neighboring high schools" plus scores of adults with its "large selection of '60s, '70s" and '80s vintage pieces, including cocktail and prom dresses, "crazy shoes" and costume jewelry; but while groupies groove on the "glitzy" pink-and-gold decor, skeptics scream the scene is strictly "for browsing rather than buying", since the "merchandise is expensive for what it is."

Scrips Elixers [S] – | – | – | E

215 Mulberry St. (Spring St.), 6 to Spring St., 212-941-4600; www.scripselixers.com

Swanky NoLita emporium offering upscale versions of ordinary household items and products – an Italian art deco toothbrush, lavender ironing spray – along with every beauty elixer a woman could want and more Nickel grooming goops for men than you'll find on TV's *Queer Eye for the Straight Guy*.

Scuba Network ◐ 23 | 18 | 22 | M

669 Lexington Ave. (bet. 55th & 56th Sts.), 4/5/6/F/N/R/W to 59th St./Lexington Ave., 212-750-9160 [S]
655 Sixth Ave. (bet. 20th & 21st Sts.), F/N/R/V to 23rd St., 212-243-2988 [S]
290 Atlantic Ave. (Smith St.), Brooklyn, F/G to Bergen St., 718-802-0700
800-688-3483; www.scubanetwork.com

■ Divers go off the deep end for the "varied selection" of "good scuba stuff" plus goggles, fins and kayaks for other water activities, all from "most of the best brands" at these "convenient" Manhattan and Brooklyn offshoots of the 25-year-old chain; "the knowledgeable staff" really "knows how to swim" and how to outfit enthusiasts of all ages with equipment that "fits correctly", while instructors provide "good training" for certification and help you plan your next excursion below sea level.

Scully & Scully   27 | 25 | 21 | VE

504 Park Ave. (59th St.), 4/5/6/F/N/R/W to 59th St./Lexington Ave., 212-755-2590; 800-223-3717; www.scullyandscully.com
■ "Aristocratic" Park Avenue home-furnishings grande dame that has been catering since 1934 to collectors of Herend porcelain, repro Chippendale- and Sheraton-style chairs, animal figurines and velvet bed steps; if your tastes tend toward the "traditional" (some say "stuffy"), it's an "ideal", albeit very expensive, place for adding "final touches to a room or for house presents."

Seaman Schepps ⓒ   ▽ 26 | 26 | 24 | VE

485 Park Ave. (58th St.), 4/5/6/F/N/R/W to 59th St./Lexington Ave., 212-753-9520
■ Since the early '20s, the "rich and elite" of New York, Palm Beach and Nantucket have supported this Park Avenue jeweler; as the founder's name implies, the house specialty is diamond-studded, coral pieces designed in the shape of shells, starfish or other creatures of the sea (opal, chalcedony and other cabochon stones are "fabulous" too); each creation is signed and numbered – an exclusive, artistic touch that alleviates the heavy price points.

Sean ◐ⓈⒸ   ▽ 22 | 19 | 16 | M

224 Columbus Ave. (bet. 70th & 71st Sts.), 1/2/3/9/B/C to 72nd St., 212-769-1489
132 Thompson St. (bet. Houston & Prince Sts.), C/E to Spring St., 212-598-5980
www.seanstore.com
■ Known for its "great selection of cotton shirts in a myriad of colors", this brown-and-orange-hued West 70s and SoHo duo also offers European-made "good-quality coats, shirts and pullovers without being *très cher*", all from French designer Emile Lafaurie; styles manage to be "mod" *sans* changing drastically from year to year.

Searle Ⓢ   24 | 22 | 19 | E

156 Fifth Ave. (bet. 20th & 21st Sts.), R/W to 23rd St., 212-924-4330 ◗
1124 Madison Ave. (84th St.), 4/5/6 to 86th St., 212-988-7318
1035 Madison Ave. (79th St.), 6 to 77th St., 212-717-4022
805 Madison Ave. (68th St.), 6 to 68th St., 212-628-6665
609 Madison Ave. (E. 58th St.), 4/5/6/F/N/R/W to 59th St./Lexington Ave., 212-753-9021
1296 Third Ave. (bet. 73rd & 74th Sts.), 6 to 77th St., 212-717-5200
1051 Third Ave. (62nd St.), 4/5/6/F/N/R/W to 59th St./Lexington Ave., 212-838-5990
www.searlenyc.com
◪ Though known for its own line of "good-investment" raincoats and "legendary shearlings", there's "a lot more than coats" at this mini-chain nowadays – specifically, "a mix of classic and trendy" womenswear, including some "sexy tops and dresses that make men look twice" from labels like Trina Turk and Milly; however, even those who "love the clothes, hate the price tags",

while a "personable" staff that "does not leave you alone" is a plus for some, a minus for others; N.B. a few branches also carry casual men's pants, shirts and sneakers.

Seigo 🅂🄲   21 | 22 | 21 | E

1248 Madison Ave. (90th St.), 4/5/6 to 86th St., 212-987-0191

■ This East 90s haberdasher can spice up even the most workaday of suits, offering nearly twice as many "wonderful ties" as days in the year, including a "wide variety" of woven and print bow ties; if the super-delicious "kimono-quality" silks loomed in Japanese mills don't have you fit to be tied in no time, the "different designs" certainly will.

Seize sur Vingt 🅂🄲   ▽ 25 | 20 | 22 | E

243 Elizabeth St. (bet. Houston & Prince Sts.), R/W to Prince St., 212-343-0476; www.16sur20.com

■ Owners James and Gwendolyn Jurney are "some of the nicest neighbors on the block", with a "spacious, lovely" NoLita shop specializing in "elegant hip", "hand-tailored" shirts with a "fabulous fit" for men and women in "exquisite" Egyptian cotton that's "far beyond one's imagination"; the "good-looking" button-downs, bolstered by a small selection of suits and coats, can be made to measure at the rear of the shop or bought "off-the-rack" (rolling racks, that is) for a little less.

Selia Yang 🅂🄲   27 | 20 | 22 | E

328 E. Ninth St. (bet. 1st & 2nd Aves.), 6 to Astor Pl.; R/W to 8th St., 212-254-9073 ●

324 E. Ninth St. (bet. 1st & 2nd Aves.), 6 to Astor Pl., 212-254-8980

www.seliayang.com

■ No blushing brides at this clean, white-walled East Village shop staffed wth "friendly" folk – just hip and happening gals who adore this "incredible designer's" "simple, classic", made-to-order wedding dress designs, available in an array of textures and styles, each revealing her flair for "cutting clothes for real women"; the shop next door at 324 E. Ninth Street is stocked with "beautiful high-style" organza bridesmaid dresses, evening gowns and bridal samples.

SELIMA OPTIQUE 🅂🄲   28 | 25 | 23 | E

84 E. Seventh St. (bet. 1st & 2nd Aves.), F/V to Lower East Side/2nd Ave., 212-260-2495

899 Madison Ave. (bet. 72nd & 73rd Sts.), 6 to 77th St., 212-988-6690

59 Wooster St. (Broome St.), C/E to Spring St., 212-343-9490

www.selimaoptique.com

■ "Fantastic, funky, flirty", "wonderfully made" and "boldly" hued eyeglasses as well as "gorgeous shades" that "you won't see on every Joe on the street" attract admirers to Selima Salaun's mini-chain of boutiques; service "varies by location" ("excellent" to "friendly" to "unhelpful"), but regardless of the staff, the "cool merchandise" means "addicts" have "difficulty walking out without" making a purchase or two.

Selvedge 🅂   ▽ 22 | 24 | 21 | E

250 Mulberry St. (Prince St.), R/W to Prince St.; 6 to Spring St., 212-219-0994

☑ A "hot space" for a "cool collection", this NoLita boutique displays "high-end" Levi's (including the Red collection), that's "not your basic stuff", with photos of hipsters and Native Americans standing watch; collaborations with artists result in jeans boasting unique renderings for individualists who also indulge in the "one-of-a-kind" limited edition collectibles; "too many wanna-bes" wail a few, fearful they'll detract from this "great store."

SEPHORA ◐ [S] 26 | 24 | 18 | M

2103 Broadway (bet. 73rd & 74th Sts.), 1/2/3/9 to 72nd St., 212-362-1500
1500 Broadway (bet. 43rd & 44th Sts.), 1/2/3/7/9/N/Q/R/S/W to 42nd St./Times Sq., 212-944-6789
555 Broadway (bet. Prince & Spring Sts.), R/W to Prince St., 212-625-1309
119 Fifth Ave. (19th St.), 4/5/6/L/N/Q/R/W to 14th St./Union Sq., 212-674-3570
1149 Third Ave. (67th St.), 6 to 68th St., 212-452-3336
130 W. 34th St. (bet. 6th & 7th Aves.), 1/2/3/9 to 34th St./Penn Station, 212-629-9135
71-30 Austin St. (Continental Ave.), Queens, 718-544-0009
Staten Island Mall, 2655 Richmond Ave., Staten Island, 718-761-7724
www.sephora.com

■ "Great one-stop-shopping" "beauty supermarkets", with almost "every brand" of cosmetics, body products and fragrance "under the sun", that have changed the lives of "makeup junkies", who love the "freedom" to "smudge, dab and spritz" with testers "without encountering the dreaded overeager department-store help"; "if you know what you want", it's "the ultimate candy shop for every lip-gloss-loving girl"; N.B. a new branch has opened in The Shops at Columbus Circle at Time Warner Center.

SERGIO ROSSI [S] [C] 27 | 23 | 21 | VE

772 Madison Ave. (66th St.), 6 to 68th St., 212-327-4288; www.sergiorossi.com

■ "Hot, hot, hot" chorus stylesetters who sizzle in the "drop-dead gorgeous Italian" "shoes of the gods" (think "rhinestone evening sandals and "sexy" stiletto boots) they scoop up at this "chic" Madison Avenue shop along with swanky handbags; men get a foot up on fashion here too with "beautiful", "impeccably made" footwear that's also indulgently "expensive"; while enthusiasts exult in the "exceptional" staff, the put-off pout about "snobby salespeople" who don't "seem interested in selling" their wares.

Seven New York [S] [C] 24 | 22 | 19 | E

180 Orchard St. (bet. Houston & Stanton Sts.), F/V to Lower East Side/ 2nd Ave., 646-654-0156; www.sevennewyork.com

■ "A bit out of the way", and locked within a steel-door-and-concrete exterior, this Lower Eastsider measures its cool in "established and emerging avant-garde designers" (Bernhard Willhelm, Boudicca, Raf Simons, Preen), plus accessories from the likes of As Four, all on offer for the male and female "hipster who doesn't want to look like every other" trendoid in NYC; the "service-oriented" staff provides almost "too much information" on the inventory.

17 at 17 Thrift Shop 19 | 16 | 15 | M

17 W. 17th St. (5th Ave.), 4/5/6/L/N/Q/R/W to 14th St./Union Sq., 212-727-7516; www.ujafedny.org

■ "If you catch them at the right time", there are "high-quality bargains to be had" at this Flatiron "treasure hunt" of a thrift store, "especially on furniture" (including a steady supply of pianos) and "surprising designer clothing" finds, "particularly when they get the society donations"; "you feel good buying" here, as proceeds go to owner UJA-Federation of NY and Gilda's Club.

S. Feldman Housewares 🖪   24 | 16 | 22 | E

1304 Madison Ave. (92nd St.), 6 to 96th St., 212-289-3961; 800-359-8558; www.wares2u.com

■ "From tacks to espresso machines", you'll find "anything you need in the way of housewares" and "gadgetries" at this 75-year-old store on the Upper East Side; locals who shop here for Miele vacuums, Oxo utensils and a colorful "selection of Alessi products" "pay full price" but get a "great choice" of unusual, often trendy, merchandise and "excellent service."

Shabby Chic 🖪🄲   21 | 24 | 16 | E

83 Wooster St. (bet. Broome & Spring Sts.), R/W to Prince St., 212-274-9842; www.shabbychic.com

■ Those who "love the cozy, comfy, country" style evoked by oversized, slipcovered chairs, ottomans and sofas in solids and faded florals flock to this SoHo fabric and home-furnishings shop inspired by designer Rachel Ashwell; while a few fume that her "original" "pricey" flea-market look has been "knocked off by all" and is getting a "bit worn", most maintain it remains among the "prettiest stuff in the world."

Shanghai Tang 🖪   22 | 24 | 18 | E

714 Madison Ave. (bet. 63rd & 64th Sts.), N/R/W to 5th Ave./59th St., 212-888-0111; 888-252-8264; www.shanghaitang.com

☑ "Stimulating" "jolts of color" give shoppers the sense of traveling "in the Orient" "without the jet lag" when they visit the Upper East Side outpost of this Chinese conglomerate; "vibrant", "authentic" Asian ready-to-wear and custom-made clothing for adults and kids in "fabulous fabrics" (especially the "exquisite silk pajamas") and "unique gifts" help create an atmosphere of "feng shui at its finest" for fans; but critics carp it'd be "cheaper to go to Hong Kong" – not to mention NY's Chinatown.

Sharper Image 🖪   21 | 22 | 18 | E

98 Greene St. (bet. Prince & Spring Sts.), R/W to Prince St, 917-237-0221
900 Madison Ave. (bet. 72nd & 73rd Sts.), 6 to 68th St., 212-794-4974
50 Rockefeller Plaza (bet. 5th & 6th Aves.), B/D/F/V to 47-50th Sts./ Rockefeller Ctr., 646-557-0861 ◐
South Street Seaport, 89 South Street, Pier 17, 2/3/4/5/A/C/J/M/Z to Fulton St./Broadway/Nassau, 212-693-0477
10 W. 57th St. (bet. 5th & 6th Aves.), F to 57th St., 212-265-2550
800-344-4444; www.sharperimage.com

☑ The multiple locations of this "whimsical", "high-tech" "FAO Schwarz for adults" represent a "slicker-than-slick" "gadgeteer's heaven" full of things you "don't really need, but can't resist", like "massage chairs they may have to evict you from"; sober shoppers say "justifying these prices" for "shine-over-substance", "battery-operated things" like a toy Beetle/CD alarm clock or the world's smallest handheld color TV "requires some fuzzy logic."

SHERLE WAGNER INTERNATIONAL, INC.   28 | 26 | 20 | VE

60 E. 57th St. (Park Ave.), 4/5/6/F/N/R/W to 59th St./Lexington Ave., 212-758-3300; www.sherlewagner.com

■ Flaunting a "bit of Palm Beach" decadence in "the heart of Gotham", this East 50s bathroom shrine caters to the Park Avenue set and Sun King wanna-bes seeking "ultra-sumptuous" gold-plated swan-head fixtures, hand-painted basins and tiles and taps encrusted with semiprecious stones; it also purveys lighting accessories, linens and wallpaper; just be flush enough to not flinch at the tremendous tabs.

Shin Choi **C**
26 | **22** | **20** | **E**

119 Mercer St. (bet. Prince & Spring Sts.), R/W to Prince St., 212-625-9202; www.shinchoi.com

■ Large and modern, this "SoHo treasure" with a calm, earthy vibe houses this Korean designer's "sleek, simple clothes"; Choi, who's made her mark with "good taste" and "beautiful lines on all of her" pieces, turns out tailored coats, suits and separates in feel-good-on-the-body, "interesting fabrics" like cashmere, soft lace and plush double-faced wool, oftentimes adding unexpected "funky" touches; celeb customers are said to include Helen Hunt, Julia Roberts and Susan Sarandon.

Shirt Store, The
20 | **17** | **21** | **E**

51 E. 44th St. (Vanderbilt Ave.), 4/5/6/7/S to 42nd St./Grand Central, 212-557-8040; 800-289-2744; www.shirtstore.com

☑ Suit-and-tie guys confirm there are "some sharp", "reliable tailored shirts for the everyday man" at this small, unassuming store near Grand Central, "but the real lift here is the custom factor" and the "informed staff"; it feels "like an old-fashioned haberdasher", with "wonderful handmade" button-downs available with fine stitching in a "wide range of colors" and sizes (from 14/32 to 18.5/37); but a few fret about prices ("not for bargain hunters") and feel its offerings are "not stylish" enough.

Shiseido **S** **C**
25 | **24** | **21** | **E**

298 Fifth Ave. (31st St.), R/W to 28th St., 212-629-9090

■ This over-a-century-old Japanese cosmetics giant is far less well known in America, but its small, understated Fifth Avenue outpost offers the opportunity to try its sleekly packaged makeup and "high-quality" skincare products, particularly creams designed to counter signs of sun damage and age spots.

Shoe **S** **C**
▽ **22** | **20** | **18** | **E**

197 Mulberry St. (bet. Kenmare & Spring Sts.), 6 to Spring St., 212-941-0205

■ Passport covers, coin purses and bright leather bags galore line this crafty NoLita shop, but the Cydwoq shoes for men and women, offering a "very specific look", are what shoppers are having a "love, love, love affair with", enthusing "bring it on!"; there's "always something surprising" to scoop up among the "wonderful, handmade" styles with leather cord shoelaces and a '70s-era Berkeley bent, and it's all nestled atop "organic, original" wooden displays.

Shoe Biz **◐** **S** **C**
19 | **10** | **13** | **M**

2315 Broadway (84th St.), 1/9 to 86th St., 212-799-4221

■ "Upper West Side moms and girlie-girls alike flock to this addictive emporium" owned by shoe mogul Steve Madden for "stylish" kicks, "kitten heels and glammed-up thongs to wear tomorrow and forget next year"; the "varied selection of current trends", represented by lines like Puma and David Aaron, leads most mavens to conclude you "usually find what you're looking for"; N.B. there's also a small selection of trendy men's footwear.

Shoofly 🅂🅲
26 | 23 | 16 | E

*42 Hudson St. (bet. Duane & Thomas Sts.), 1/2/3/9 to Chambers St.,
212-406-3270; www.shooflynyc.com*

■ "If you have a daughter who is an arty version of Imelda Marcos" and/or a style-savvy son, head to this "*très* adorable" children's and teen's shop in TriBeCa; what's in-store: "cute European shoes" "from the funkiest casualwear to gorgeous galoshes" to classic Mary Janes from labels like Aster, Babybotte, Mod 8 and Minibel, plus accessories and some of the "best hats around", all "imaginatively presented" in a cabinlike setting.

Shop 🅂🅲
▽ 26 | 24 | 22 | E

*105 Stanton St. (Ludlow St.), F/V to Lower East Side/2nd Ave.,
212-375-0304*

■ "Favorite shopping hideaway" for those in-the-know that focuses on the "feminine" – a point of view that's rather "unexpected" for the Lower East Side; "whimsical" pink painted-tile floors and cream walls lend "adorable" atmosphere to the "cute clothes" and shoes, and even "cuter" patrons and the "nice salespeople", creating an "awesome experience."

Shu Uemura Beauty Boutique 🅂
24 | 23 | 20 | E

*121 Greene St. (bet. Houston & Prince Sts.), R/W to Prince St.,
212-979-5500; 888-540-8181; www.shuuemura-usa.com*

■ A "beautiful, sparse" SoHo space is a suitably Zen setting for this line of "high-end" Japanese cosmetics, featuring "unique colors", "the best brushes on the market" and of course its award-winning eyelash curler; "superb service" and the surprising absence of NY crowds enhance the experience.

Sid's 🅂
▽ 21 | 16 | 19 | M

*345 Jay St. (Willoughby St.), Brooklyn, A/C/F to Jay St./Borough Hall,
718-875-2259*

◪ "There's no one in Brooklyn Heights who hasn't walked the aisles" of this "essential" "classic", with "endless rooms" full of hardware, lumber and paint in a "labyrinthine building" that its "brethren" believe is "absolute paradise"; penny-pinchers profess there are "no bargains" and the service can be "quirky" but admit that "most times you can find what you need."

Sigerson Morrison 🅂🅲
27 | 23 | 18 | VE

*28 Prince St. (Mott St.), 6 to Spring St., 212-219-3893;
www.sigersonmorrison.com*

■ "Always an outfit maker" chorus "chic career girls" and stylish night-owls who flock to this "hip" NoLita destination for an "amazing array" of "happy little shoes" in a "rainbow of colors" ranging from "detailed and feminine" "strappy sandals and winter heels" to "pointy shapes" "with a bit more edge"; "granted", these "little masterpieces" "for the well heeled" are "not cheap, but good footwear never is"; as for service – "they know they don't have to sell you."

Sigerson Morrison Bags 🅂🅲
25 | 23 | 20 | VE

*242 Mott St. (bet. Houston & Prince Sts.), 6 to Spring St., 212-941-5404;
www.sigersonmorrison.com*

■ Small and sparsely appointed, this NoLita hot spot is "chock-full of fabulous", "fun, nontraditional", "beautiful leather" handbags, totes and wallets to "go with their perfect-for-the-neighborhood shoes", sold at their larger sister shop around the corner; "there's a reason why" these "splurge"-worthy carryables "that fit everyone's needs" are so "popular": it's the snappy shades and clean, clever "girlie" styling designers Kari Sigerson and Miranda Morrison have made their own.

Simon Pearce **S**   26 | 25 | 23 | E

500 Park Ave. (59th St.), 4/5/6/F/N/R/W to 59th St./Lexington Ave., 212-421-8801

120 Wooster St. (bet. Prince & Spring Sts.), R/W to Prince St., 212-334-2393
www.simonpearceglass.com

■ "Once you start, you can't stop" buying some of the "beautiful" "handcrafted" "classic glass" stemware, bowls, vases and lamps at these "addictive" Midtown and SoHo stores that also purvey pottery and customized etched or inscribed items; while prices are "surprisingly low for what you get", the "real value is the seconds merchandise", which is offered "at a discount", making it a "great place to get a wedding present" or register for one.

Simon's Hardware & Bath   26 | 20 | 17 | E

421 Third Ave. (bet. 29th & 30th Sts.), 6 to 28th St., 212-532-9220; 888-274-6667; www.simons-hardware.com

☑ "For knobs, hinges and hardware", this Gramercy Park shop "has the best selection in the city", offering a "vast", "eye-popping" assortment ("nice knockers!"); sadder-but-wiser types sigh the "gold-mine" goods come at "gold-mine prices" and add the service can be "aggravating", but most agree that it's all "worth it" for the "fantastic" and otherwise "hard-to-find" fixtures and plumbing on offer.

Skechers **◑S**   18 | 18 | 16 | M

2169 Broadway (76th St.), 1/9 to 79th St., 212-712-0539
530 Broadway (Spring St.), C/E to Spring St.; R/W to Prince St., 212-431-8803
150 Fifth Ave. (W. 20th St.), R/W to 23rd St., 212-627-9420
3 Times Square (42nd St. bet. B'way & 6th Ave.), 1/2/3/7/9/N/Q/R/ S/W to 42nd St./Times Sq., 212-869-9550
140 W. 34th St. (bet. 6th & 7th Aves.), B/D/F/N/Q/R/V/W to 34th St./ Herald Sq., 646-473-0490
800-678-5019; www.skechers.com

■ "Really cool shoes at affordable prices" that "promise to get you noticed with their high heels and fun looks", plus "comfy sneaks" that "hold up to heavy wear", draw guys and girls of all ages to this chain with "lots of energy"; but a smattering of sophisticates swipes it's "fun if you're 12" and like "hitting the mall and talking on your pink cell phone all day."

Small Change **C**   23 | 13 | 19 | VE

1196 Lexington Ave. (bet. 81st & 82nd Sts.), 4/5/6 to 86th St., 212-472-7613
964 Lexington Ave. (70th St.), 6 to 68th St., 212-772-6455

☑ "Worth the trip Uptown" insist insiders who fall for the "adorable kids' clothes" at this "wonderful" East 70s boutique; there are "plenty of" "great quality", "elegant" "European classics" "with a twist", plus the "lovely owner" and "helpful staff" make you feel like they're "your personal shoppers"; but forget small change – "you need a big wallet" to shop here, which is why many suggest "check out their end of season sales."

Smiley's ⊞   22 | 16 | 20 | I

92-06 Jamaica Ave. (bet. 92nd St. & Woodhaven Blvd.), Queens, J/Z to Woodhaven Blvd., 718-849-9873; www.smileysyarns.com

■ Though "nothing exotic or high fashion" awaits at this wool-filled Woodhaven shop, it's "worth the subway ride" to enthusiasts, who rejoice in the "bags and bags of wonderful yarns" at "bargain prices", pattern books and "helpful" service; some items are sold online, plus every fall this "avid knitter's" haven hosts a "once-a-year sale" featuring bulk skeins in select hotels in the NYC area.

Smith & Hawken ●Ⓢ   24 | 24 | 21 | E

394 W. Broadway (bet. Broome & Spring Sts.), C/E to Spring St., 212-925-1190; 800-940-1170; www.smithandhawken.com

■ "The place for English gardening tools" is this SoHo store that's also hailed for its "great teak furniture", "healthy plants" and "equipment from around the world"; its "pretty", "well-maintained" setting makes it a "fun place to hang out", and the "salespeople seem to love what they do"; despite quibbles that it's "a bit pricey", the "quality" merchandise adds up to "good value" for green thumbs.

SMYTHSON OF BOND STREET   27 | 27 | 22 | VE

4 W. 57th St. (5th Ave.), F to 57th St., 212-265-4573; 866-769-8476; www.smythson.com

■ "If it's good enough for the Queen, it's good enough for me" say loyal subjects of this "darling" British import on West 57th Street, with its "addictive", "luxurious" selection of "classic, elegant" stationery, "little leather notebooks and diaries in eye-popping colors" that "are a pleasure to use" and new line of luxe handbags; though a few yell "yikes" over the prices, most insist it's "truly worth it" for the "high quality."

SOCCER SPORT SUPPLY   26 | 15 | 24 | M

1745 First Ave. (bet. 90th & 91st Sts.), 4/5/6 to 86th St., 212-427-6050; 800-223-1010; www.homeofsoccer.com

■ Drenched in history, as evidenced by the memorabilia display, this Upper East Side "soccer player's heaven" has been kicking it since 1933; "the staff knows their topic since they live it, and breathe it", helping players score "state-of-the-art equipment and apparel", from Diadora balls, Adidas shoes, Puma King Pro shin guards and Reusch goalkeeper apparel to Official International Club Team wear, Official World Cup Replica clothing and much more; N.B. at press time, plans were afoot to expand.

SoHo Baby Ⓢ Ⓒ   – | – | – | E

251 Elizabeth St. (bet. Houston & Prince Sts.), B/D/F/S/V to B'way/Lafayette St., 212-625-8538

The name may say 'SoHo', but the location is actually NoLita for this specialty shop stocked with lots of "cute things" to "spoil your kids", like "very unique baby clothes from France, Japan and Korea", ranging from casual to special-occasion attire, plus a selection of layettes, sheets, hand-stitched books and toys; N.B. you may even spot a model and/or celeb while browsing.

Sole Kitchen   – | – | – | VE

236 W. 135th St., A/B/C/D to 125th St., 212-281-6940

"They are doing some cool things up in Harlem" say hipsters of footwear and accessory designer Etu Evan's boutique, where women and men fall for his funky styles, ranging from severe stilettos to kickin' boots, made to measure and paired with a unique handbag.

Sol Moscot [S] 20 | 12 | 19 | M

118 Orchard St. (Delancey St.), F/J/M/Z to Delancey/Essex Sts., 212-477-3796
69 W. 14th St. (6th Ave.), F/L/V to 14th St./6th Ave., 212-647-1550
107-20 Continental Ave. (bet. Austin St. & Queens Blvd.), Queens, E/F/G/R/V to Forest Hills/71st Ave., 718-544-2200
www.solmoscotopticians.com

■ Envision decades past from one of the original seats in the octogenarian Orchard Street or Queens branch of this "friendly", family-run "New York favorite" optician that also boasts a Flatiron sibling; old-timey discounts meet newfangled "top-of-the-line" frames from Calvin, Giorgio, Christian, Alain (Mikli) and the rest of the designer gang at "prices too low to believe"; even the "energetic staff" is a throwback: you're "treated like a valued friend here", in fact they "know what you want better than you do."

Some Odd Rubies [S][C] – | – | – | M

151 Ludlow St. (bet. Rivington & Stanton Sts.), F/V to Lower East Side/2nd Ave., 212-353-1736; www.someoddrubies.com

"Fluffy and frilly" describes this Lower East Side vintage newcomer run by actress Summer Phoenix and pals Odessa Whitmire and Ruby Canner, who "will alter" or refashion their gorgeous retro finds, "whatever it takes to make it work for you on the spot"; there's nothing *odd* about the "great atmosphere", which includes a huge dressing room, the perfect forum to check out your look.

Sonia Rykiel [C] 25 | 25 | 22 | VE

849 Madison Ave. (bet. 70th & 71st Sts.), 6 to 68th St., 212-396-3060; www.soniarykiel.com

■ This "great visionary's" "clothes make you feel so French you just want to want to yell out 'ooh-la-la' when wearing them" fawn fans of the veteran Parisian designer who file over to her East 70s "showcase for that Sonia look", or to just gaze at the "creative windows"; her "wonderful knits" and "unique dresses" flaunt "innovative twists", ensuring they'll "be favorites for ages" and she even offers "beautiful black clothes for color-phobic New Yorkers."

Sonic Groove ◐[S][C] – | – | – | M

206 Ave. B (bet. 12th & 13th Sts.), L to 1st Ave., 646-602-2943; www.sonicgroove.com

When you crave rave, "the godfathers of the techno scene are chilling it out and playing records behind the counter" in the East Village at this "legendary shop" (now in a new home) with a house label co-owned by mega-DJs Frankie Bones, Adam X and Heather Heart; it opens at 1 PM, just in time for the all-night partyers to stumble out of the clubs and score that new "hard house" hit or electro classic they just finished dancing to.

Sony Style [S] 22 | 23 | 15 | E

550 Madison Ave. (bet. 55th & 56th Sts.), E/V to 5th Ave./53rd St., 212-833-8800; www.sonystyle.com

◪ If you're one of those "tech-happy people" who's infatuated with Sony WEGA TVs and DVD Dream Systems, this East 50s store, connected to the "museumlike", interactive Wonder Technology Lab, is "a great place to look at products" and "keep abreast of developments"; though the staff "truly knows" its stuff, gearheads argue that their "fine mass-market merchandise" is "more fun to play with than buy" at "prices that are beatable" by others; N.B. the lower level was redesigned post-*Survey* and now features custom furniture for home entertainment systems.

Sorelle Firenze C

| – | – | – | E |

139½ Reade St. (bet. Greenwich & Hudson Sts.), 1/2/3/9 to Chambers St., 212-528-7816; www.sorellefirenze.com

"Feel like a princess" at this inviting TriBeCa boutique where the super-feminine chic of Florentine co-owners Monica and Barbara Abbatemaggio comes across in a cozy little world filled with Italian fashions (some made by the sisters' mama), custom-made bridal dresses and eveningwear, plus accessories, sexy lingerie and adorably detailed childrenswear.

SOUND BY SINGER S

| 28 | 21 | 15 | VE |

18 E. 16th St. (bet. 5th Ave. & Union Sq. W.), 4/5/6/L/N/Q/R/W to 14th St./Union Sq., 212-924-8600; www.soundbysinger.com

☑ "Hard-core audio nerds" will feel at home in this Union Square boutique where the 10 extensively, expensively adorned demo rooms allow buyers to evaluate the "mega-buck systems" including Burmster, Crestron and Krell, among others; "if it's worth owning, they have it", admirers attest, but sensitive shoppers shudder the "extreme attitude" that permeates the place reflects a staff that has "egos to match" the prices.

Sound City

| 18 | 13 | 13 | M |

58 W. 45th St. (bet. 5th & 6th Aves.), B/D/F/V to 47-50th Sts./ Rockefeller Ctr., 212-575-0210; 800-326-1677; www.soundcityny.com

☑ Whether you are looking for a new FireWire to download your digital pictures or just need to upgrade to a better-integrated amplifier for your stereo, this West 40s retailer "will get you what you want"; serving the community since 1978, the "friendly" staff "knows their stuff" and can guide you through the audio bells and whistles as well as the computer basics; still, a few sound off about "impatient sales"-people; N.B. a post-*Survey* renovation may outdate the above Presentation score.

Space Kiddets C

| ▽ 25 | 13 | 15 | E |

46 E. 21st St. (bet. B'way & Park Ave.), 6/N/R to 23rd St., 212-420-9878; www.spacekiddets.com

■ "Trendy" parents and their offspring are over the moon about this "tiny", brightly colored Gramercy Park destination packed with "a great selection of unusual, fun, urban fashions", "party stuff", plus an assortment of eclectic toys, "European clothing lines" and shoes from newborn sizes to pre-teen; sure, "your breath will be taken away by the exorbitant prices", but remember, "the sales are great."

Speedo Authentic Fitness

| 18 | 13 | 15 | M |

150 Columbus Ave. (bet. 66th & 67th Sts.), 1/9 to 66th St./Lincoln Ctr., 212-501-8140 ●S
500 Fifth Ave. (42nd St.), 4/5/6/7/S to 42nd St./Grand Central, 212-768-7737 S
90 Park Ave. (39th St.), 4/5/6/7/S to 42nd St./Grand Central, 212-682-3830
www.speedousa.com

☑ "If you swim for fitness, these are the stores" for "good, basic bathing suits" that have a "bit of pizzazz", as well as "great gym bags", all kept afloat by a "helpful" staff; work-out wear, however, draws a split decision: "fun and functional" vs. "hit-or-miss", but the "reasonable prices" for "professional"-grade gear make a big splash.

Spence-Chapin Thrift Shops **S**   17 | 14 | 15 | M

1473 Third Ave. (bet. 83rd & 84th Sts.), 4/5/6 to 86th St., 212-737-8448
1850 Second Ave. (bet. 95th & 96th Sts.), 6 to 96th St., 212-426-7643
www.spence-chapin.org

✓ "Many well-heeled New Yorkers seem to bless" these Upper East Side thrift shops "with their designer clothes", "vintage sweaters" and "excellent secondhand furniture"; the merchandise is "well organized", and though some sniff prices are "inflated", "it's worth it when one scores" at this adoption services charity; N.B. the Third Avenue shop stocks more upscale goods than its sibling.

Spoiled Brats ❶ **S** **C**   20 | 18 | 21 | M

340 W. 49th St. (bet. 8th & 9th Aves.), C/E to 50th St., 212-459-1615;
www.spoiledbratsnyc.com

■ "One of my dog's favorite places to shop" quip customers of this "sweet little" Hell's Kitchen "pet parlor", "one of the few places where you can get raw organic meat and other healthy things" like Burt's Bees body products "for special critters"; there are also "lots of fun toys", odor-masking candles and "treats for pooch" and kitty alike, plus the "gracious owners" and staff are "true animal lovers" – they even "rescue strays" and offer cat adoption and shelter services.

Sports Authority ❶ **S**   18 | 13 | 10 | M

636 Sixth Ave. (19th St.), 1/9 to 18th St.; F/V to 23rd St., 212-929-8971
845 Third Ave. (51st St.), 6/E/V to 51st St./Lexington Ave., 212-355-9725
57 W. 57th St. (6th Ave.), F to 57th St., 212-355-6430
www.thesportsauthority.com

✓ Fans fawn that these three branches of a national chain are "one-stop-shopping" headquarters for sports galore, including fishing, basketball and yoga apparel and gear, but the less impressed pummel the "middle-of-the-road selection" – it's "not the best place for specialty gear" – and sound off about "no visible help."

Spring Flowers **C**   27 | 21 | 20 | VE

905 Madison Ave. (72nd St.), 6 to 68th St., 212-717-8182 **S**
538 Madison Ave. (55th St.), E/V to 5th Ave./53rd St., 212-207-4606
1050 Third Ave. (62nd St.), 6 to 68th St., 212-758-2669

✓ "Be prepared to drop a bundle", in fact, "bring your Donald" because this European-esque, Upper East Side children's wear trumps others in the "glorious" "special-occasion dress" and suit department; the selection of "absolutely beautiful", "dreamy clothing", which also includes "hard-to-find Italian knit cardigans", "top-of-the-line" separates and "fancy shoes", completes the rosy picture.

Stacia **S** **C**   ▽ 21 | 19 | 16 | E

267 Smith St. (DeGraw St.), Brooklyn, F/G to Carroll St., 718-237-0078;
www.staciany.com

■ Young designer Stacy Johnson (a Cynthia Rowley vet) invites basics-weary, color-starved fashionistas to her cozy Carroll Gardens boutique, which has a vintage feel with its turquoise walls, chandeliers and wrought-iron accents; "hip with a dash of old-world charm", her whimsically named collections (Boudoir Satin,

Edwardian Cord) are heavy on va-va-voom dresses, suits and separates in silks, tweeds and other "amazing textiles"; knitwear, lingerie and the best-selling duffel bags round out the inventory.

Stackhouse ◐ [S] [C] – | – | – | E

282 Lafayette St. (bet. Houston & Prince Sts.), R/W to Prince St.; B/D/F/S/V to B'way/Lafayette St., 646-613-0687
276 Lafayette St. (bet. Houston & Prince Sts.), R/W to Prince St.; B/D/F/S/V to B'way/Lafayette St., 212-925-6931

Snowboard and skate rats and just plain hipsters air down to this Lafayette Street destination for urban-cool sweaters, hoodies, trainers and accessories from labels like Blue Marlin, Analog, Obey, Hurley and Spiewak that look as rad in motion as they do hanging out; the chill vibe extends to a kick-back area with a coffee table littered with magazines, an art gallery downstairs and a new shop for women a few doors down at 282 filled with edgy streetwear.

Staples 19 | 14 | 11 | M

1065 Sixth Ave. (40th St.), 1/2/3/7/9/N/Q/R/S/W to 42nd St./Times Sq., 212-997-4446; 800-378-2753; www.staples.com
Additional locations throughout the NY area

◪ With the "convenience" of more branches than you can shake a scanner at, this "office supply" "supermarket" chain is perfect "for a quick work-related emergency", as "you can slip in and pick up" "peripherals and accessories" from PDAs to printers, toners to telephone cables; true, the "messy" presentation and sales associates who play "hard-to-get" might have you crying "bring back the mom-and-pop stationery store" – until you get a load of the "efficient online shopping" and "wonderful delivery policy."

Starting Line, The ◐ [S] [C] ▽ 21 | 16 | 18 | M

180 Eighth Ave. (bet. 19th & 20th Sts.), A/C/E/L to 14th St./8th Ave.; 1/9 to 18th St., 212-691-4729; www.thestartinglinenyc.com

■ . . . And they're off, to this busy Chelsea boutique with lime-green walls and aisles filled with a "hot potluck" of casual clothes, including Puma activewear and sport shoes as well as après-gym garb from NYBased, Itsus T-shirts and trendy bags; goal-oriented guys appreciate the "no-frills" atmosphere and "helpful staff."

Steinlauf & Stoller ▽ 24 | 13 | 16 | M

239 W. 39th St. (bet. 7th & 8th Aves.), A/C/E to 42nd St./Port Authority; 1/2/3/7/N/Q/R/S/W to 42nd St./Times Sq., 212-869-0321; www.steinlaufandstoller.com

■ From shears and steel pins to cording, shoulder pads, zippers and thread, all the "wonderful things that used to be in Woolworth's can still be found" at this 56-year-old Garment Center sewing notions stalwart; "if you want it, it's probably there, but you may have to ask for help" as you "dodge stray elbows" and "mix with designers and dressmakers matching swatches."

Stella [C] – | – | – | VE

138 W. Broadway (bet. Duane & Thomas Sts.), 1/2/3/9 to Chambers St., 212-233-9610; www.stellastore.com

Lust-worthy must-haves for the bedroom and bathroom beckon browsers to this TriBeCa haven, owned by two decorating pros; set against mustard-colored walls, the displays are as inviting as the merchandise, with custom drapes hanging from the high ceiling, antique beds (yes, they're for sale) boasting handmade coverlets and towering cabinets crammed with luxurious linens.

Stella Dallas [S] ▽ 21 | 16 | 19 | M

218 Thompson St. (bet. Bleecker & W. 3rd Sts.), A/B/C/D/E/F/S/V to W. 4th St., 212-674-0447

■ "A nice selection of dresses", primarily from the '40s and '50s, coexists with a collection of mid-century sweaters, '30s lingerie, scarves, "skinny ties" and even kids' clothes at this veteran Village vintage shop; it's a "massive amount for such a small space", but given that everything's "in good condition", "in decent sizes and at uninflated prices", most love to dally here.

Stella McCartney [S] [C] 25 | 25 | 20 | VE

429 W. 14th St. (bet. 9th Ave. & Washington St.), A/C/E/L to 14th St./8th Ave., 212-255-1556; www.stellamccartney.com

◪ "Stella's found her groove" in her pink-walled Meatpacking District destination for the "younger, hipper set", offering "enough edge to be cool"; "once inside" you're "transported to a place of class and beauty" as "every detail is thought out, from the dressing rooms" to the mannequins walking on water in a reflecting pool "showing her designs to great effect" to the "non-fawning" staff; you may "need to be one of the Beatles to afford" her coveted collection, including, "sexy stilettos", lingerie and now fragrance.

Stephane Kélian [S] [C] 25 | 25 | 21 | VE

717 Madison Ave. (bet. 63rd & 64th Sts.), N/R/W to 5th Ave./59th St., 212-980-1919

158 Mercer St. (bet. Houston & Prince Sts.), R/W to Prince St., 212-925-3077

www.kelian.fr

■ Using the "best woven leathers and comfortable lasts", this "innovative" designer, "a master at staying true to his heart", handcrafts "fabulous French footwear" with a "twist of the latest trend built in", as well as handbags, wallets and accessories; the "professional" service at his Madison Avenue and SoHo boutiques caters to men and "women who really have style", a clientele that realizes that "when these shoes are good, they're very, very good", and though they're "pricey, they're worth every penny"; N.B. the Madison Avenue store is open only on Sundays during wintertime.

Stephen Russell [C] – | – | – | VE

962 Madison Ave. (bet. 75th & 76th Sts.), 6 to 77th St., 212-570-6900

"If you need a 19th-century diamond tiara, this is the place to go" attest antique-jewelry acolytes of this petite Upper East Side shop, which prides itself on museum-quality merchandise; the wares include new pieces as well, but whatever the date of origin, the goods are "high class."

Stereo Exchange ◐ [S] [C] 23 | 14 | 17 | E

627 Broadway (bet. Bleecker & Houston Sts.), R/W to Prince St., 212-505-1111; www.stereoexchange.com

■ With all those audiovisual animals "drooling" over an inventory that includes "everything under the sun in higher-end merch", this "superior" NoHo store "can be a zoo"; the "knowledgeable staff" is, thankfully, more concerned with "guiding you to the right" plasma TV or performing a multiroom, multisource installation than giving the "hard sell", and while "most of what they carry isn't cheap", the "value is always excellent"; N.B. a post-*Survey* redesign may outdate the above Presentation score.

STEUBEN C

29	28	23	VE

667 Madison Ave. (61st St.), N/R/W to 5th Ave./59th St., 212-752-1441; 800-783-8236; www.steuben.com

■ A "glass-lover's paradise" where "stunning merchandise" – voted Tops in our Home/Garden category – is "beautifully showcased" in a soaring, three-story Madison Avenue space that serves as the flagship of this 100-year-old "premier" American company; crystal animals, apples, bowls, sculptures and engraved and etched objects are offered at shattering prices, but it's "worth every penny" for a "gift to show appreciation" or seal the deal.

Steve Madden ●S

16	16	14	M

540 Broadway (Spring St.), R/W to Prince St., 212-343-1800
105 E. 86th St. (bet. Lexington & 3rd Aves.), 4/5/6 to 86th St., 212-426-0538
41 W. 34th St., B/D/F/N/Q/R/V/W to 34th St./Herald Sq., 212-736-3283
5380 Kings Plaza (Farragut Rd.), Brooklyn, 2/5 to Brooklyn College/ Flatbush Ave., 718-677-3985
Staten Island Mall, 2655 Richmond Ave. (bet. Platinum Ave. & Ring Rd.), Staten Island, 718-494-6459
800-747-6233; www.stevemadden.com

☑ From "platform sandals to Frankenstein-esque boots", to a new line of higher-end, more sophisticated styles, every "modern man" and "trendy" "girl has to have a pair" of this "omnipresent" chain's "funky", "reasonably priced shoes" that are "easier to walk in than they look"; but the less impressed aren't mad for the "clunky look – so late '90s" – and find it "truly an uncomfortable experience, from sales clerks" "too hip to help" to footwear that you "get to wear for only one season."

Steven ●S

20	18	16	M

(fka David Aaron)
529 Broadway (bet. Prince & Spring Sts.), R/W to Prince St., 212-431-6022

☑ When you "can't afford Gucci and Prada but still want to look fashionable", slip into some "fantastic", "high-quality knockoff" shoes from Steve Madden's "bustling" SoHo "store for grown-ups"; while mavens are mad for the "cool", "stylish" selection that's "tamer" than his teen line, the less-impressed pout they're "too trendy to be carried past a couple of seasons" and lace into the "lackadaisical help."

Steven Alan S C

22	–	18	E

103 Franklin St. (bet. Church St. & W. B'way), 1/9 to Canal St., 212-343-0692
60 Wooster St. (bet. Broome & Spring Sts.), C/E to Spring St.; R/W to Prince St., 212-334-6354
www.stevenalan.com

■ For the "younger, fashion-savvy set" whose taste runs "left of center", this spacious TriBeCa haunt showcases "edgy", "small designer lines from NY, LA and Tokyo" for men and women, with "price points that aren't too bad" for "cool labels"; still, "this ain't H&M", so bring the bucks for basics that "can't be found" elsewhere; N.B. the original smaller SoHo location was recently renovated and reopened following a fire.

STICKLEY, AUDI & CO. S C

26	23	22	E

160 Fifth Ave., 4th fl. (bet. 20th & 21st Sts.), R/W to 23rd St., 212-337-0700; www.stickley.com

■ Named in part after Gustave and Leopold Stickley, who were synonymous with the American Arts and Crafts movement, this three-floor Flatiron District showroom features reissues of their Mission Style sofas, chairs, cabinets, beds and tables, along with other lines like Baker; the made-to-order pieces aren't "cheap, but they are beautifully made" and there are "great" "periodic sales."

Stitches East **C**   22 | 20 | 14 | E
Park Ave. Plaza, 55 E. 52nd St. (bet. Madison & Park Aves.), E/V to 5th Ave./53rd St.; 6 to 51st St., 212-421-0112
✒ "If you're looking for" "intriguing", "high-end yarns, needlepoint canvases and supplies", head to this "refined environment", "tucked into the lobby of a Midtown office building"; but put-out patrons point to a "snooty" "sales staff that barely registers customers' presence", adding "dilettantes, beware."

ST. JOHN **S**   26 | 26 | 24 | VE
665 Fifth Ave. (bet. 52nd & 53rd Sts.), E/V to 5th Ave./53rd St., 212-755-5252; www.stjohnknits.com
■ When the need arises to "dress like the wife of a congressman", this East 50s boutique beckons with Marie St. John's "ladies-who-lunch" suits ("unbelievable what they can do with knits") and "glitzy" evening confections, "as well as matching accessories"; the "gracious" service and "environment befit a queen", a "senior investment banker" or any "discerning" customer who doesn't mind the "very pricey" tags.

St. Marks Sounds **◗S⇄**   ▽ 25 | 15 | 15 | I
20 St. Marks Pl. (bet. 2nd & 3rd Aves.), 6 to Astor Pl., 212-677-3444
16 St. Marks Pl. (bet. 2nd & 3rd Aves.), 6 to Astor Pl., 212-677-2727
■ "Maybe the best used sections in the whole world" are found a couple of doors down from each other on the East Village's most honky-tonk block; the street-level store also "has fair prices" on "breaking bands" and other "new stuff", "but if you're bargain hunting, go to the upstairs location", where the goods are mostly previously played CDs and "promos in great condition."

Straight from the Crate **◗S**   14 | 6 | 13 | I
1114 First Ave. (61st St.), 4/5/6/F/N/R/W to 59th St./Lexington Ave., 212-838-8486
1251 Lexington Ave. (bet. 84th & 85th Sts.), 4/5/6 to 86th St., 212-717-4227
261 Madison Ave. (38th St.), 4/5/6/7/S to 42nd St./Grand Central, 212-867-4050
464 Park Ave. S. (bet. 31st & 32nd Sts.), 6 to 33rd St., 212-725-5383
161 W. 72nd St. (B'way), 1/2/3/9 to 72nd St., 212-579-6494
50 W. 23rd St. (bet. 5th & 6th Aves.), R/W to 23rd St., 212-243-1844
www.straightfromthecrate.com
✒ These "cramped" furniture stores are more akin to "storage rooms" than "showrooms", but for "twentysomething" "dorm"-dwellers or those furnishing a "first apartment", that's a "small price to pay" for affordable desks, dressers, bookcases and shelving units; still, snobs sniff the stuff "looks like it was made from a crate rather than taken out of one" and shrug "you get what you pay for."

Strawberry **◗S**   9 | 9 | 8 | I
129 E. 42nd St. (Lexington Ave.), 4/5/6/7/S to 42nd St./Grand Central, 212-986-7030
Additional locations throughout the NY area
✒ "Stylish" "teenyboppers" "who aren't millionaires" "keep up with short-lived trends" in "cheeky" "club gear", sportswear,

costume jewelry, "fun shoes" and other "flashy" "throwaways" at this "fad"-meister; like Velveeta is to cheese, this chain is to designer boutiques, churning out "knockoffs galore" for "dirt cheap"; still, some sniff "stay away unless" you're "at work, get a horrible stain" on your outfit and "need something to change into."

Strider Records
– | – | – | E

22 Jones St. (bet. Bleecker & W. 4th Sts.), 1/9 to Christopher St./ Sheridan Sq.; A/B/C/D/E/F/S/V to W. 4th St., 212-675-3040; www.striderrecords.com

Connie Francis cohabitates with Jimi Hendrix at this Village veteran stocking thousands upon thousands of 45s, LPs and even 78s of tunes from the '40s to the '70s; these oldies experts buy collections and have been known to broker heady deals, such as the consignment sale of the rarest rock album ever: a version of Bob Dylan's 1963 *Freewheelin'* – including four tracks deleted shortly after release.

String 🆂🅲
25 | 21 | 16 | E

1015 Madison Ave. (bet 78th & 79th Sts.), 6 to 77th St., 212-288-9276; www.stringyarns.com

☑ "This is not your granny's yarn store" assert skeinsmiths who head to this "elegant", "tiny space on Madison" for "very posh" finds in "astounding color palettes", hand-painted varieties and textures, plus scads of supplies; "Upper East Side matrons and world travelers bustle in and out" while others join the "welcoming" knitting circle and work with the in-house designer on custom patterns; but a handful are needled by the "pricey" goods and find the "atmosphere snobby."

STUART MOORE 🆂
28 | 26 | 21 | VE

128 Prince St. (Wooster St.), R/W to Prince St., 212-941-1023

☑ A "cool vibe" emanates from this SoHo "emporium of gems that excites the heart" with its "unique styles and extremely creative use of metals" from European and American designers; it's best known for its own namesake "modern" line of engagement and wedding rings, so "amazing" they'll "make you want to get married"; P.S. "they'll even do custom designs."

Stuart Weitzman 🆂
24 | 22 | 21 | E

625 Madison Ave. (bet. 58th & 59th Sts.), N/R/W to 5th Ave./59th St., 212-750-2555; www.stuartweitzman.com

■ "Luxury meets comfort and sophistication meets sass" at this "attractive" Madison Avenue "source" that tempts would-be Cinderellas with "creative, daring window displays"; the "lovely" staff helps "event-going ladies" select footwear ranging from "perfect choices" for "dressy" "occasions" "you can dance in all night" to "practical and funky styles" that last "season after season" to "great wedding shoes" ("a must for brides"); P.S. check out the "fantastic scarves and accessories" and the new branch in The Shops at Columbus Circle at Time Warner Center.

Stubbs & Wootton 🅲
23 | 24 | 21 | E

22 E. 72nd St. (bet. 5th & Madison Aves.), 6 to 68th St., 212-249-5200; 877-478-8227; www.stubbsandwootton.com

■ "Popular among the Palm Beach"–"South Hampton society set", and "perfect for that Waspy look", the "super-preppy" slippers and heels sold at this "hidden gem" on the second floor of an East 70s townhouse keep "Muffy, Buffy and Tuffy" "happy"; "oh what fun it is" to choose from the classic and whimsical "over-the-top" patterns in needlepoint, velvet and suede, plus you can even get them monogrammed; traditionalists of all stripes also swear by the shoes for junior – and the ribbon belts.

Studio Museum in Harlem Gift Shop S
`22` `20` `21` `M`

144 W. 125th St. (bet. Lenox & 7th Aves.), 2/3/A/B/C/D to 125th St., 212-864-0014; www.studiomuseum.org

◪ Take the A train to this Harlem museum showcasing artists of African and African-American descent where the "staff goes out of their way to help" you and R&B, jazz and neo-soul plays on the sound system; a separate street-side entrance leads to an ample, airy shop with a well-displayed selection of "culturally awake" literature, children's books, posters, postcards, jewelry, T-shirts, "picture frames and accessories for your house", merchandise so "unique it's tempting to stock up for gifts."

Stussy NYC S C
`20` `19` `15` `M`

140 Wooster St. (bet. Houston & Prince Sts.), R/W to Prince St., 212-995-8787; www.stussy.com

◪ "Awesome for 20 years" swear supporters of this "stylin'" surfer-dude label, as they slide into the skylit SoHo shop (now boasting murals from graffiti artist Kawz) to update their casual wardrobes with a new "T-shirt or hat or key chain" ("nice bags" of nylon from Head Porter too); but cynics say it's "losing ground to newer brands" – or "maybe there's just not a lot there for us thirtysomethings anymore."

Style by Annick de Lorme S C
`–` `–` `–` `E`

120 Wooster St. (bet. Prince & Spring Sts.), R/W to Prince St., 212-219-0447

Annick de Lorme, who formerly owned SoHo's Cap Sud, has shuttered that home-furnishings shop and opened this much larger venue on Wooster Street; she's brought along her two most popular lines – classic hand-woven rattan bistro chairs from Maison Gatti and linear lighting and furniture from contemporary Parisian designer Julie Prisca – but this time around she's added French and Chinese antiques to her aesthetic mix.

Suarez
`25` `23` `23` `E`

450 Park Ave. (57th St.), 4/5/6/F/N/R/W to 59th St./Lexington Ave., 212-753-3758

■ "New York bag ladies feel like they've died and gone to heaven" at this Park Avenue boutique offering "third-generation family service with a smile" along with "top-quality luxury" handbags, plus "beautiful accessories" and shoes "in styles and prices for all pocketbooks"; "devoted clients" make it their "first stop in any shopping quest" for the "fabulous designer knockoffs" made by the same Italian "craftsmen" who create the status purses, but without the "brand sticker shock" or "someone else's initials."

Sublime American Design S
`–` `–` `–` `VE`

26 Varick St. (Beach St.), 1/9 to Franklin St., 212-941-8888; www.sublimeamericandesign.com

Occupying a three-level space in TriBeCa, this expansive and expensive new store showcases the furniture and accessories of established American talent – from the Boyms and Harry Allen to Vladimir Kagan and Roy McMakin – as well as emerging designers who previously had little or no outlet for their work; about 50 names are represented, while the store's lower level is devoted to rotating exhibits.

Sude ●◐S◐ ▽ 20 | 18 | 26 | M
2472 Broadway (91st St.), 1/2/3/9 to 96th St.; 1/9 to 86th St., 212-721-5721
829 Ninth Ave. (bet. 54th & 55th Sts.), 1/9/A/B/C/D to 59th St./ Columbus Circle, 212-397-2347
■ Located in a Hell's Kitchen hood not known for super-femme boutiques, and now in the West 90s too, this much-"needed" duo is the "perfect place to stop when you need that little something for a first date" – or a fashionable pick-me-up; the color-coordinated selection of "trendy, reasonably priced items" includes labels like Plenty, Poleci and Juicy Couture, as well as lesser-known edgy lines, plus the eponymous owner "writes a description on each tag" with styling suggestions, a helpful approach that sudes disciples to a tee.

Suncoast Motion Picture Co. ●S◐ 16 | 14 | 12 | M
Manhattan Mall, 901 Sixth Ave. (bet. 32nd & 33rd Sts.), B/D/F/N/Q/ R/V/W to 34th St./Herald Sq., 212-268-2171
5402 Kings Plaza (Ralph Ave.), Brooklyn, 2/5 to Brooklyn College/ Flatbush Ave., 718-951-0076
www.suncoast.com
■ "Different from other chain video stores", these Manhattan and Queens siblings offer "corporate movie" posters and novelty items on the bill as well; despite mediocre marks, vocal critics applaud the "decent" price and selection.

Super Runners Shop S 25 | 18 | 25 | M
360 Amsterdam Ave. (77th St.), 1/9 to 79th St., 212-787-7665
Grand Central, Main Concourse, 4/5/6/7/S to 42nd St./Grand Central, 646-487-1120 ●
1337 Lexington Ave. (89th St.), 4/5/6 to 86th St., 212-369-6010
1246 Third Ave. (72nd St.), 6 to 68th St., 212-249-2133
www.superrunnersshop.com
■ "Geared toward active people", this "must-see" outfit will "keep you running back again and again for their fine prices" and "excellent selection of sneakers, apparel and gadgets" from big-name brands like New Balance, Brooks, Adidas, Hind and Saucony; the "extremely knowledgeable staff of avid" athletes is full of "insight and enthusiasm" and will not only "hand you" the "proper shoe" that "your gait requires", but offer "marathon advice you can bank on."

Supreme S◐ – | – | – | E
274 Lafayette St. (bet. Houston & Prince Sts.), R/W to Prince St., 212-966-7799
Skate rats – or those just aspiring to the rad, rakish aesthetic – can suit up and get a new set of wheels at this outpost located on a stretch of Lafayette Street devoted to other like-minded shops; way-cool labels include Rookie, Good Enough and the house brand's own line of hoodies, tees, hats and, of course, skateboards.

Surprise! Surprise! S 16 | 9 | 10 | I
91 Third Ave. (12th St.), L to 3rd Ave., 212-777-0990;
www.surprisesurprise.com
◪ "Very crowded" East Village home-furnishings store that's "stuffed to the gills" with a "hodgepodge" of "good" "inexpensive"

stuff, from small appliances to "folding furniture", shelving systems, "knickknacks" and "trendy" "decor items" by Umbra; with low "prices like these, the dollar-store presentation is no surprise", but the attitude sure might be.

Suzanne Couture Millinery ▽ 28 | 27 | 25 | VE

27 E. 61st St. (bet. Madison & Park Aves.), 4/5/6/F/N/R/W to 59th St./ Lexington Ave., 212-593-3232; www.suzannemillinery.com
■ "Expensive" couture toppers and bridal headpieces engage single sophisticates and the betrothed alike at this Upper East Side brownstone – and now, so do designer-owner Suzanne Newman's new collection of handbags; elegant veils are festooned with silk roses or floppy satin bows, while tiaras are encrusted with pretty pearls, plus there's also a diverse mix of close-up-worthy cocktail hats, fedoras and newsboy caps that appeal to ladies who lunch and celebs of all stripes.

Suzette Sundae Ⓢ ▽ 19 | 21 | 20 | M

182 Ave. B (bet. 11th & 12th Sts.), L to 1st Ave., 212-777-7870; www.suzettesundae.com
■ Put a cherry on top of this "artistic" Alphabet City yearling with its impressive array of vintage shoes, "one-of-a-kind jewelry" and racks of "amazing" inventive women's clothing by emerging designers "mixed with reworked vintage" beauties; it's "not for everyone", but "you'll have fun browsing" even if you don't buy any of the seriously "great finds."

Swarovski Ⓢ 21 | 25 | 20 | E

625 Madison Ave. (bet. 58th & 59th Sts.), N/R/W to 5th Ave./59th St., 212-308-1710; www.swarovski.com
■ Once known mainly for its little faceted figurines, this Austrian crystal palace has recently started to shine as the fashion crowd's favorite supplier of sparkly tattoos and high-quality costume jewelry; with its honey-colored wood floors and red-and-blue setting, the Midtown store features such "sparkling treasures", plus a "fine selection of small gifts" and tabletop accessories "for every taste and budget."

Swatch ⦵Ⓢ 19 | 21 | 19 | I

1528 Broadway (45th St.), 1/2/3/7/9/N/Q/R/S/W to 42nd St./Times Sq., 212-764-5541
640 Broadway (Bleecker St.), 6 to Bleecker St., 212-777-1002
5 E. 57th St. (5th Ave.), N/R/W to 5th Ave./59th St., 212-317-1100
438 W. Broadway (Prince St.), R/W to Prince St., 646-613-0160
100 W. 72nd St. (Columbus Ave.), 1/2/3/9 to 72nd St., 212-595-9640
888-800-1021; www.swatch.com
▨ "You can always find new designs at these now-classic" watch "candy shops" whose "cheap", "casual", plastic timepieces "truly do last"; but while the "staff's super" (especially the "'doctor' at the 57th Street main store") and the styles are still "fun for Swatch addicts" and "the younger generation", foes find the appeal's all "a little '80s"; N.B. there's now also a jewelry collection called Bijoux made from "cool" materials like silicon, resin and stainless steel.

Swiss Army ⦵Ⓢ 24 | 21 | 20 | M

136 Prince St. (bet. W. B'way & Wooster St.), C/E to Spring St., 212-965-5714; 866-997-9477; www.swissarmybrands.com
■ The requisitely sporty, cement-floored SoHo outpost of the famed Swiss brand stocks "not just knives" – although there are

blades aplenty ("and everyone needs one") – but also "top quality" "precision" watches and "sleek gadgets", plus wallets and luggage emblazoned with the signature "neat logo" and a "cool" line of Victorinox men's clothing; it's "the antithesis of army navy supply" style – and "a must for the well-equipped urban warrior."

SYMS ◐🅂   16 | 10 | 11 | I

400 Park Ave. (54th St.), 6/E/V to 51st St./Lexington Ave., 212-317-8200
42 Trinity Pl. (Rector St.), R/W to Rector St., 212-797-1199
www.syms.com

☑ Browsing "here is like going on a safari" – you practically have to "bring your machete to sort through" the hordes of "stock on hand", "but the finds can be rather spectacular at low prices" boast "bargain hunters" who love to "save money" at this popular discounter in the East 50s and the Financial District; "gambling shoppers" "play the waiting game", since "prices go down as time goes by", while "educated consumers" "stick to menswear", as it's "more classic" than the "gaudy" women's collection.

TAG Heuer 🅂🄲   26 | 23 | 21 | VE

422 W. Broadway (bet. Prince & Spring Sts.), C to Spring St.; R/W to Prince St., 212-965-5304; 800-321-4832; www.tagheuer.com

■ Boasting an entire wall carved from an old maple tree, this SoHo store is the U.S.'s sole company-owned source for the stainless steel, high-performance, multifunctional watches that have sports fanatics salivating; these "top-of-the-line timepieces with top-of-the-line prices" "last forever" and work "for every occasion", since they now come in a variety of styles including dressier options in rose gold with diamonds or rubies and styles inspired by designs from the '20s, '30s and '40s; N.B. there's also a sleek new line of sunglasses.

Tah-Poozie ◐🄲   19 | 18 | 17 | I

50 Greenwich Ave. (bet. 6th & 7th Aves.), 1/9 to Christopher St./ Sheridan Sq., 212-647-0668 🅂
78A Seventh Ave. (15th St.), 1/2/3/9 to 14th St., 646-638-0750

■ These "fun", "funky" Downtown holes-in-the-wall are crammed with "low-priced" "gag gifts", toys, tchotchkes, trinkets, tarot cards, yoga and massage gizmos and postcards – just the sort of "cool", "cute" stuff that "never fails to delight" "kids or kidlike adults"; the "salesperson will inform you" the name means 'orange-y' in Hebrew (and will also let you "try before you buy" from out-of-package samples).

TAKASHIMAYA   25 | 28 | 22 | VE

693 Fifth Ave. (bet. 54th & 55th Sts.), E/V to 5th Ave./53rd St., 212-350-0100; 800-753-2038

■ A "good example of less is more", this "feel-the-Zen" "hybrid department store/boutique" from Japan is a "serene" "culture trip" in Midtown; the "haunting displays" encourage enthusiasts to "just stop by to see the flowers" or finger the "elegant" clothing for adults (including the new NOW department) and kids, "rare cosmetics brands", "exquisite" linens, "design museum"–quality housewares or "gifts for a finicky friend" all from around the world; it may be "a tad overpriced", but fans "buy anything just to get it wrapped" in the distinctive triangular box; P.S. "no visit is complete" without a trip to its tearoom.

Talbots 19 | 19 | 20 | M

2289-2291 Broadway (bet. 82nd & 83rd Sts.), 1/9 to 79th St., 212-875-8753 ◐
525 Madison Ave. (bet. 53rd & 54th Sts.), E/V to 5th Ave./53th St., 212-838-8811 [S]
South Street Seaport, 189 Front St. (bet. South & Water Sts.), 2/3/4/5/A/C/J/M/Z to Fulton St./B'way/Nassau, 212-425-0166 ◐
1251-1255 Third Ave. (72nd St.), 6 to 68th St., 212-988-8585
800-825-2687; www.talbots.com

■ Shoppers "know what to expect" at this fashion chain "where tradition reigns" in "classic" "career" and "casual" wear that "epitomizes American taste" for "conservative young business women", "mature" "suburbanite" "moms" and all shapes and sizes of "wanna-be Wasps"; "this is not the store to go to if you want to look hot", but if you need to dress "like a lady" "to fool the future in-laws", you can do it here "at an affordable price."

Talbots Kids and Babies [S] 22 | 21 | 22 | M

527 Madison Ave. (54th St.), E/V to 5th Ave./53rd St., 212-758-4152
1523 Second Ave. (79th St.), 6 to 77th St., 212-570-1630
800-992-9010; www.talbots.com

■ For "classic" clothes that are "more preppy/traditional than trendy", make tracks to these Upper East Side and new East 50s chain offshoots; it's "good" for "well-made" "basics like shorts, cardigans, blouses and T-shirts" and prices are "reasonable"; still, a few taunters tut that the togs are "a little too luxe for everyday", quipping it's "very Connecticut – pass my daughter her pearls", please; N.B. the men's shop is also housed in this Madison Avenue location.

T. Anthony Ltd. 26 | 25 | 25 | VE

445 Park Ave. (56th St.), 4/5/6/F/N/R/W to 59th St./Lexington Ave., 212-750-9797; www.tanthony.com

■ "Guaranteed to turn heads at the airport", the "movie-star–quality luggage" (owned by Marilyn Monroe) and new collection of wheeled duffels at this "very upper-class", "very Madison Avenue" boutique conveys "understated wealth"; the "wide variety" of wares, including handbags, photo albums, jewel boxes and leather goods, comes in "classic lines and stand-out colors that never fail to please"; once tried, "you cannot return to anything else" – and why would you, when it's such a "pleasure to shop" here, though you may "feel like you need to get dressed up" first.

Target ◐[S] 20 | 17 | 14 | I

519 Gateway Dr. (Erskine St.), Brooklyn, L to Canarsie/Rockaway Pkwy., 718-235-6032
88-01 Queens Blvd. (55th Rd.), Queens, G/R/V to Grand Ave., 718-760-5656
135-05 20th Ave. (Whitestone Expwy.), Queens, 718-661-4346
www.target.com

■ "Making big-box stores cool", this "cheap chic mecca" "hits" the "bull's-eye" with "everything from doorknobs" to "suede jackets"; "recent (or not so recent) college grads spiffy up" pads with "great versions of mundane household stuff" from limited-edition Michael Graves or Todd Oldham collections and "spruce up" wardrobes with "stylish" Cynthia Rowley or Isaac Mizrahi garb ("no wonder it's known as Tar-Jay"); the "uncluttered aisles are as wide as the midwest prairie – with salespeople about as scarce"; at press time, plans were afoot to open a Bronx branch.

Tarzian True Value **S**

▽ | 20 | 14 | 22 | M

193 Seventh Ave. (bet. 2nd & 3rd Sts.), Brooklyn, F to 9th St.,
718-788-4120; www.tarzianhardware.com

☑ This "Park Slope gem" satisfies "all your hardware desires" with a "good selection" ranging from gardening and plumbing supplies to "esoteric accessories"; locals rave about the "knowledgeable", "friendly", "first-rate" staff and "not-bad-at-all prices" that "differentiate" this store, but deplore the "crammed"-in goods set in a "rabbit-warren layout" that's "difficult" to maneuver.

Tarzian West **S C**

▽ | 21 | 15 | 17 | M

194 Seventh Ave. (2nd St.), Brooklyn, F to 7th Ave., 718-788-4213;
www.tarzianwest.com

■ "Cramped" "little store" that's been selling what locals "need for the kitchen and bath" in the Park Slope neighborhood for three generations, long before the status-stroller set moved in; the stock includes everything from "spoon rests and bath mats" to gadgets and cookware, making it "Brooklyn's answer to Gracious Home."

Tatiana

18 | 16 | 18 | M

767 Lexington Ave. (bet. 60th & 61st.), 4/5/6/F/N/R/W to 59th St./
Lexington Ave., 212-755-7744; www.tatianas.com

■ "Be sure not to miss this unassuming upstairs" corner space of an East 60s office building, a "thrill-a-minute" consignment shop "stocked with gently used" vintage couture "treasures" and "lovely items with tags still attached"; it's a "great place for designer duds" – "a bit of everything from Chanel" suits to Moschino jeans to "party-style goods" and "incredible" accessories – "Hermès shoes for $95? who'da thunk it?", plus the staff "isn't too pushy."

Ted Baker **S C**

24 | 21 | 19 | E

107 Grand St. (Mercer St.), 6/J/M/N/Q/R/W/Z to Canal St.,
212-343-8989; www.tedbaker.co.uk

■ You too "can now look like a Brit" – and a "hip" one at that – at this "cool SoHo store" for men (and women too) decorated with rough-hewn wooden display tables, murals and a mechanical dog; comprised of "nifty patterns" and "the best materials", the "modern stylings" are "edgy enough to be interesting, but conservative enough" for work – especially the crease-resistant suits, and microfiber and no-iron cotton shirts that "always look crisp."

Ted Muehling **C**

▽ | 29 | 28 | 27 | E

27 Howard St. (bet. B'way & Lafayette St.), 6/J/M/N/Q/R/W/Z to
Canal St., 212-431-3825

■ Some say NYC "can be divided into those who wear Ted Muehling earrings and those who don't"; indeed, when it comes to "perfectly simple", "original and ethereal" work, this artisan "reigns" (and "don't miss the ceramics" and decorative objects "he's now making" too); the earthy atmosphere of his SoHo shop, which also carries Gabriella Kiss' line, offers an "amazing respite from the ordinary shopping experience", so in between that, the "gorgeous jewelry and the impeccable service, what more could you want?"

Tekserve **S**

25 | 22 | 26 | M

119 W. 23rd St. (bet. 6th & 7th Sts.), F/N/R/V to 23rd St.,
212-929-3645; www.tekserve.com

■ In a "new, bigger" space featuring an "interesting waiting area with a 10-cent Coke machine", this "Mac paradise" in Chelsea is "very in among the cognoscenti" for all things Apple, as well as repairs, upgrades and custom video and audio configurations; the "extremely knowledgeable" and "caring" staff will "almost bring tears to your eyes", despite the odd "long wait" and "retail" prices.

TENDER BUTTONS ⊄ C   28 | 22 | 20 | E |
143 E. 62nd St. (bet. Lexington & 3rd Aves.), 4/5/6/F/N/R/W to 59th St./ Lexington Ave., 212-758-7004
■ An "Upper East Side must", this "charming" "little paradise" "raises button selection to an art form" – "who knew there were so many on the planet, let alone in one store?"; the "glorious selection" of "unique adornments", many imported from France and Italy, ranging from the "wild and wacky" to "everyday replacements" to antique cuff links offers fasten-ating "fun" for all – little wonder you "bump into everyone from fashion designers to teenagers" here.

Tent and Trails S   27 | 7 | 20 | M |
21 Park Pl. (bet. B'way & Church St.), 1/2/3/9/A/C/E to Chambers St., 212-227-1760; 800-237-1760; www.tenttrails.com
☑ Camping is the only game at this "beloved hideaway" in the Financial District that stocks a "wide variety at various price levels" of "anything you could want for the outdoors" from tents, stoves and backpacks to Patagonia and The North Face apparel to day hiking gear; expect an "extremely knowledgeable and personable staff", though take heed: bread crumbs and "patience may be needed to hack through the jungle of merchandise."

Ten Thousand Things C   24 | 21 | 19 | E |
137 W. 19th St. (bet. 6th & 7th Aves.), 1/9 to 18th St., 212-352-1333
■ Converts claim this Chelsea temple, set among "graffiti covered warehouses" and boasting hand-blown glass sconces and display cases made with 15 kinds of wood, is "the place to go for" David Rees and Ron Anderson's "super-delicate, wispy-looking" "Zen jewelry" (the store name comes from a Tao quote) made of oxidized silver, "unique stones" and more precious substances; "prices can be high, but often you're paying for" the "cool little" designs "profiled in so many fashion mags."

Terence Conran Shop, The ● S   24 | 25 | 17 | E |
407 E. 59th St. (1st Ave.), 4/5/6/F/N/R/W to 59th St./Lexington Ave., 212-755-9079; www.conran.com
■ Located in a "must-see", albeit "out-of-the-way", location beside the Queensboro Bridge is this "modern, clean" home-furnishings emporium named after its knighted English owner; two floors of "slightly edgy" furniture by hot, young designers like Christophe Pillet and Jasper Morrison, along with "unusual" accessories for the tabletop, kitchen and bath are part of a "limited" "tasteful selection" that's "beautifully presented."

TG-170 ● S C   22 | 17 | 20 | E |
170 Ludlow St. (bet. Houston & Stanton Sts.), F/V to Lower East Side/ 2nd Ave., 212-995-8660; www.tg170.com
■ The pop feel of this Lower East Side boutique, "one of the first" to bring style to the area, underscores the "Downtown hip" goodies you find courtesy of owner Terri Gillis, whose "slightly alternative yet womanly personality" shows in her "nice cross-section" of "cool li'l finds" from small lines of clothes (Mercy, Karen Walker, Lauren Moffitt) and accessories, including the best-selling Freitag

bags and now jewelry from Bing-Bang and other NYC designers; N.B. at press time, plans were underway to double the space size.

Theory S   25 | 22 | 19 | E
230 Columbus Ave. (bet. 70th & 71st Sts.), 1/2/3/9 to 72nd St., 212-362-3676

■ "Clean, simple, elegant" is the theory behind this "young, hip working woman's" line, and its new West 70s flagship conveys all that and more in a modern, "minimalist" store staffed with "attentive" salespeople; the "very flattering", "sexy, sleek" pieces – the "foundation" of "many a wardrobe" – make an "easy transition from office to cocktails" and can "transform anyone into a New Yorker"; P.S. "get ready to shell out more than a couple of bucks for the look."

37=1 S C   – | – | – | E
37 Crosby St. (bet. Broome & Grand Sts.), R/W to Prince St., 212-226-0067; www.jeanyu.com

Long, narrow and gallerylike, with wispy little nothings hanging from wall pegs like delicate pieces of art, Jean Yu's peachy sliver of a by-appointment-only store in SoHo caters to coquettes who prefer garter belts and sultry stockings to pantyhose, and dresses and luxurious lingerie on the silky side; for fashionistas who like their fit just so, she also creates custom-made undies.

30 Vandam S C   – | – | – | M
30 Vandam St. (bet. Sixth Ave. & Varick St.), C/E to Spring St., 212-929-6454; www.30vandam.com

This spacious 'incubator' on the SoHo border offers edgy young clothing and accessory designers a hospitable showcase for their wares as well as business support to help grow their reputations; creative types who enjoy speculating on Seventh Avenue's next marquee name, or just appreciate small-production, handcrafted garments, jewelry, shoes and hats, pop in for a dose of cool, plus a snack at the in-house chocolate bar and cafe; at press time, plans were afoot to add housewares.

Thomas Pink S   25 | 24 | 21 | VE
520 Madison Ave. (53rd. St.), E/V to 5th Ave./53rd St., 212-838-1928
1155 Sixth Ave. (44th St.), 1/2/3/7/9/N/Q/R/S/W to 42nd St./Times Sq., 212-840-9663
888-336-1192; www.thomaspink.co.uk

☑ "Every banker worth a bonus" gets bewitched by these British stores in Midtown, with their "fabulous presentation" of "top-of-the-line shirts" and "great office blouses" in "fantastic colors" and "superb fabrics" ("nice cuff links" and ties too); negatives natter "no way these [goods] are worth these prices", but the scores side with those who say for the "ultimate in Jermyn Street" style, "think Pink"; N.B. a new branch has opened in The Shops at Columbus Circle at Time Warner Center.

Thomasville S   23 | 22 | 20 | E
91 Seventh Ave. (16th St.), 1/2/3/9 to 14th St., 212-924-7862
217-04 Northern Blvd. (217th St.), Queens, 7 to Main St., 718-224-2715
www.thomasville.com

☑ For nearly 100 years, this manufacturer of "beautiful furniture" has crafted "high-quality" "traditional styles" for the living room, bedroom and dining room, and its Chelsea and Queens showrooms carry a selection ranging from rococo to Mission styles; but whether you feel helped or "hounded" by the sales staff will have to be your call.

THOS. MOSER CABINETMAKERS 🖪 28 | 26 | 25 | VE |
699 Madison Ave., 2nd fl. (bet. 62nd & 63rd Sts.), F to Lexington Ave./ 63rd St., 212-753-7005; 800-708-9016; www.thosmoser.com
■ Each "glorious" piece of "handcrafted" furniture is signed and dated in the company's workshop in Maine then shipped to this Madison Avenue showroom; enthusiasts exclaim that the "clean-lined", black-cherry chairs, cabinets and tables are "absolutely to die for" and worthy of "passing down to your grandchildren", which is fortunate "because it will take several generations to pay for them."

TIFFANY & CO. 🖪🄲 27 | 27 | 21 | VE |
727 Fifth Ave. (57th St.), N/R/W to 5th Ave./59th St., 212-755-8000; 800-843-3269; www.tiffany.com
☑ Fifth Avenue's "quintessential NYC landmark", this "mammoth emporium" is a multifloored "sight to behold", carrying all things of "classic" luxury that "make you feel so glam" – "breathtaking" diamond solitaires, "silver baby rattles", "beautiful china and crystal" and "designer jewelry from Elsa Peretti and Paloma Picasso"; on weekends, when you need to "duck around" the "fanny-pack–clad tourists", the "well-trained staff" that "treats Trumps and tramps" alike can be "hard to get to", and critics carp that with "mass-marketing" "the institution is becoming a factory", but most will still gladly "buy something here – if only to get that famous robin's egg–blue box."

Timberland 🖪 21 | 18 | 16 | M |
709 Madison Ave. (63rd St.), F to Lexington Ave./63rd St., 212-754-0436; 888-802-9947; www.timberland.com
☑ Urban rangers find a "nice presentation" of "excellent rugged clothing and shoes", including the signature waterproof leather boot, at this "ubiquitous chain's" "woodsy Madison Avenue" outpost; still, a few skeptics sniff the stuff's strictly "for taking the SUV out of the city."

Tip Top Shoes 🖪 22 | 14 | 21 | M |
149-155 W. 72nd St. (bet. B'way & Columbus Ave.), 1/2/3/9 to 72nd St., 212-787-4960; 800-925-5464; www.tiptopshoes.com; www.workshoes.com
■ A "classic family", "service-oriented" footwear store "with actual" "experienced salespeople" who "unhurriedly" "help you find the right size and style" "like in the old days", this Upper West Side stalwart is "a shoe-lover's dream"; the "amazing variety" of "excellent", "high-quality brand names" like Clarks, Ecco, Frye, Merrell and Rockport are the "comfiest" – "my feet really thanked me"; N.B. Tip Top Kids two doors down carries brands like Puma, Birkenstock and Elefanten for girls, boys and infants.

T.J. MAXX ◑🖪🄲 16 | 9 | 7 | I |
620 Sixth Ave. (bet. 18th & 19th Sts.), 1/9 to 18th St., 212-229-0875
1509 Forest Ave. (Marianne St.), Staten Island, 718-876-1995
2530 Hylan Blvd. (New Dorp Ln.), Staten Island, 718-980-4150
800-285-6299; www.tjmaxx.com
☑ "Decorate your whole apartment in Ralph Lauren" and the like for "dirt cheap", and "no one will ever believe you got it" all at this

discount "chain store" with Chelsea and borough branches that are also "wonderful" for "plus sizes" and "children's clothes and toys"; still, "digging's required" to "strike it lucky" amid "last season's name brands" that are "jammed together" by a "surly staff."

TLA Video ◐ [S] 27 | 19 | 23 | I

52 W. Eighth St. (bet. 5th & 6th Aves.), A/B/C/D/E/F/S/V to W. 4th St., 212-228-8282; www.tlavideo.com

■ "Believe it or not, we have Philadelphia to thank for this fine movie store" sans "attitude" in Greenwich Village; the "excellent, eclectic", "large selection" of "foreign and alternative" titles, including a "not-quite-Disney" kiddie section, is perhaps the "best in NYC", if not "in the world"; "films organized by actor or theme" "make for pleasant browsing and interesting discoveries of what stars would prefer to keep the lesser-knowns of their oeuvre."

Todd Hase [S] ▽ 27 | 24 | 22 | VE

261 Spring St. (bet. Hudson & Varick Sts.), C/E to Spring St., 212-871-9075; www.toddhase.com

■ Sophisticated SoHo furniture store specializing in the eponymous interior designer/owner's handcrafted, pared-down contemporary pieces with classic lines made the old-world way – hand-tied springs support upholstered mohair or silk seating, and hand-fitted marquetry patterns top some of the tables; "great lamps" made of leather and wood are apt accents for the chic sofas, settees and chairs that have a celebrity and fashion following.

Tod's [S] [C] 26 | 25 | 20 | VE

650 Madison Ave. (bet. 59th & 60th Sts.), N/R/W to 5th Ave./59th St., 212-644-5945; www.tods.com

■ "Once you wear a pair" of these "preppy", "princely slippers" "there's no turning back" confides a "certain Upper East Side set"; the "ultimate in loafers", these "unbelievably comfortable" "instant classics are in a class by themselves" – "don't buy the driving moccasins unless you drive a Mercedes"; "bright, airy and perfectly minimalist", "everything about this shop shines, from the shoes" to the small leather goods, handbags and women's jackets "to the clerks' smiles to the entertaining doormen", though a handful feels the "salespeople could use some fine-tuning."

Toga Bikes [S] [C] 24 | 19 | 21 | E

110 West End Ave. (64th St.), 1/9 to 66th St./Lincoln Ctr., 212-799-9625; www.togabikes.com

◪ "They have everything, know everything" and "will get you on the bike that's right for you" exclaim enthusiasts of this "clean, well-organized" "ultimate high-end" Upper Westsider that's "almost a bicycle boutique"; as at Gotham, its sibling Downtown, the stock now includes wet suits and running apparel, plus the "helpful" staff takes "tremendous time" with customers, offering "fantastic" services like triathlon-specific tips and free lifetime tune-ups with major purchases and appointments for time-pressed cyclists.

Tokio 7 ◐ [S] 22 | 14 | 14 | M

64 E. Seventh St. (bet. 1st & 2nd Aves.), 6 to Astor Pl., 212-353-8443

◪ "At this East Village consignment shop", an ever-changing, "reasonably priced" "hodgepodge" of "vintage and off-season designer wear" ("from no-names to big names") keeps the low-ceilinged setting hopping with "young NYU students", entry-level executives and "hip fashionistas on a budget"; there's "not much to speak of servicewise – but the merchandise is why we're here, so who cares?"

Tokyo Joe ◐ 🅢　　　22 | 12 | 16 | M

334 E. 11th St. (bet. 1st & 2nd Aves.), L to 1st Ave., 212-473-0724

☑ Though now a solo act thanks to the closing of the Gramercy Park branch, this used-clothing East Villager is still a "closet of wonders" (and scarcely bigger than a walk-in) say the Joes and Janes who "pop in to check out" the "high-profile designer brands" – "anything from Marc Jacobs skirts to Coach straw-and-leather totes", plus shoes and accessories – at "perfect prices" and in "very decent condition"; "just don't expect ambiance, as there is none."

Tommy Hilfiger ◐ 🅢　　　17 | 18 | 16 | E

372 W. Broadway (Broome St.), C/E to Spring St., 917-237-0983;
www.tommyhilfiger.com

☑ A neon American flag presides outside this multilevel SoHo store, chock-full of the designer's "faux-prep" classics for both sexes, as well as all of his rah-rah accoutrement – belts, hats, ties, watches and fragrances – for this born-in-the-USA brand; however, cynics sneer you "look like a walking ad" in the logo-laden clothes.

TOTEM DESIGN GROUP 🅒　　　26 | 22 | 21 | E

71 Franklin St. (bet. B'way & Church St.), 1/9 to Franklin St.,
212-925-5506; www.totemdesign.com

■ "Drool-worthy wonders for lovers of contemporary" home furnishings are found at this "cutting-edge" TriBeCa hot spot showcasing a "fab selection" of about 30 American and European designers; the "colorful merchandise" with a high style quotient includes chairs and desk accessories from Karim Rashid and rugs by Verner Panton.

Tourneau 🅢🅒　　　26 | 22 | 19 | E

12 E. 57th St. (Madison Ave.), N/R/W to 5th Ave./59th St., 212-758-7300
500 Madison Ave. (52nd St.), E/V to 5th Ave./53rd St., 212-758-6098
200 W. 34th St. (7th Ave.), 1/2/3/9 to 34th St./Penn Station,
212-563-6880
www.tourneau.com

☑ "If it ticks they have it" at this timepiece chain, "arguably the most complete watch store in NYC", which also offers "terrific" (if "overpriced") repair service; while the "well-organized" "vast displays" are "great for browsing", some shoppers compare the "knowledgeable staff" to "used-car salesmen", meaning "be prepared to bargain"; N.B. a new branch has opened in The Shops at Columbus Circle at Time Warner Center.

TOWER RECORDS/VIDEO ◐ 🅢🅒　　　24 | 19 | 14 | M

1961 Broadway (66th St.), 1/9 to 66th St./Lincoln Ctr., 212-799-2500
692 Broadway (E. 4th St.), 6 to Astor Pl., 212-505-1500
20 E. Fourth St. (Lafayette St.), B/D/F/S/V to B'way/Lafayette St.; 6 to
Astor Pl., 212-505-1500
383 Lafayette St. (bet. E. 4th & Great Jones Sts.), 6 to Astor Pl.,
212-505-1166
Trump Tower, 725 Fifth Ave. (57th St.), N/R/W to 5th Ave./59th St.,
212-838-8110
www.towerrecords.com

■ It can be "overwhelming", but this "sprawling", "stacked to the gills"chain "always has what you want if you can figure out where it is"; don't expect much help from the "aloof" staff, but do know that the DVD/video store faces the world music/record annex on Lafayette, Lincoln Center is the "last bastion of broad classical selections" and the NoHo flagship has some of "the best jazz and Broadway" offerings around; N.B. at press time, the company filed for bankruptcy protection.

Town Shop 🅂   24 | 10 | 20 | M

2273 Broadway (bet. 81st & 82nd Sts.), 1/9 to 79th St., 212-787-2762
■ "An Upper West Side institution" done up in pink retro-style decor, this "real neighborhood store" not only stocks "all of the basic and some higher-end lingerie labels", it's also one of the "best places to get truly fitted for a bra" or a bathing suit; "it might be crowded at times, but that's because everyone knows" that the owners (the late Mrs. Koch's sons Peter and Danny), along with the staff "have the magic touch."

Toys In Babeland ◑🅂   26 | 24 | 28 | M

43 Mercer St. (bet. Broome & Grand Sts.), 6/J/M/N/Q/R/W/Z to Canal St., 212-966-2120
94 Rivington St. (bet. Ludlow & Orchard Sts.), F/J/M/Z to Delancey/Essex Sts., 212-375-1701
800-658-9119; www.babeland.com
■ The staff at this "woman-centered", "super sex" store on the Lower East Side and its new SoHo sidekick makes everyone "feel comfortable" – gals "can shop here without feeling leered at, and couples can get frank advice on the relative merits of battery versus plug-in" stuff; with "help books" and "classes to teach you how to get the most out of" "the superb selection" of "tools", "a potentially embarrassing trip" becomes a "pleasurable" "education."

Toys R Us ◑🅂   23 | 19 | 13 | M

1514 Broadway (44th St.), 1/2/3/7/9/N/Q/R/S/W to 42nd St./Times Sq., 800-869-7787; www.toysrus.com
Additional locations throughout the NY area
■ Bound to leave "any kid in total awe" (including "your husband – aka kid for a day"), this "must-stop" Times Square flagship, the "big boy in discount toys", is like a "mini-amusement park"; while mavens are over the moon about the "massive selection" and "huge" Barbie Dream House larger than many NYC apartments, it's the "delightful" "Ferris wheel that takes the cake"; but killjoys growl that it's "all glitz for tourists – I can find the same merchandise without the chaos", "pushy parents and wailing children."

Toy Tokyo 🅂🅲   ▽ 25 | 18 | 17 | M

121 Second Ave. (bet. 7th & 8th Sts.), R/W to 8th St.; 6 to Astor Pl., 212-673-5424; www.toytokyo.com
■ "If Anime and robots are your bag, check out this second-floor" East Village shop stuffed with modern-day and decades-past "eclectic, eccentric collectibles from A to Z", "imported from Japan" and "all over the world"; the "He-Man, My Little Pony and Smurf" stuff may "bring you back to your youth", and if you have a yen for wind-ups, Transformers, Star Wars and Star Trek action figures, grab a "big kid" and jet on over.

Tracy Feith 🅂🅲   ▽ 21 | 25 | 20 | E

209 Mulberry St. (bet. Kenmare & Spring Sts.), 6 to Spring St., 212-334-3097
■ "It's dangerous, but so much fun" to dip into this small shop, where the onetime surfer-dude designer offers up his "rich-girl

garb" alongside actual surfboards; the vibe is as "relaxed and beachy" as you get in NoLita, affording ample time to play among the "decadently beautiful" dresses, "sparkly shoes", jewelry and "fab handbags" with a "one-of-a-kind feel."

Transit ◗ⓈⒸ   20 | 18 | 12 | M

665 Broadway (bet. Bleecker & Bond Sts.), 6 to Bleecker St.; B/D/ F/S/V to B'way/Lafayette St., 212-358-8726; www.transitnyc.com
☑ "Old-school to new-school" urbanites get on track at this multilevel mass-transit-themed NoHo store, where "trendy, sporty streetwear" and kicks from labels like Adidas, Nike, ENYCE and Sean Jean are "well presented" (the sneaker wall resembles a makeshift train); while fans are down with the "phat threads", most dis the "clueless" workers, confiding "be prepared to wait" as the "Jay-Z wanna-bes" "think their attitude will help sell clothes" – not!

Trash and Vaudeville ◗ⓈⒸ   21 | 19 | 17 | M

4 St. Marks Pl. (bet. 2nd & 3rd Aves.), R/W to 8th St.; 6 to Astor Pl., 212-982-3590
■ The name "says it all" – the "rock 'n' roll gear" and "punk, goth" and "just bad taste" clothing make this "famous" 28-year-old East Village legend "super-wonderful" to teens and twentysomethings, who can't wait to "upset mom at the next family dinner" and to middle-aged scenesters, too; fans fall for the "excellent selection of British shoes (Doc Martens, etc.)", "tons" of "huge platforms" and yes, even "fetish wear" ("bondage pants", anyone?); at times the staff may be "too cool to help you."

Treasure Chest, The ◗ⓈⒸ   – | – | – | M

171 Seventh Ave. (bet. 1st St. & Garfield Pl.), Brooklyn, F to 7th Ave., 718-768-6292
Crammed with handcrafted jewelry from local designers, unusual picture frames and tchotchkes, this wee, "wonderful" Park Slope standby lives up to its name and then some; the helpful staff happily shows you whatever takes your fancy, from Skagan watches to unique novelty necklaces and earrings to art deco rings; N.B. it's owned by the same folks who run Facets.

Treillage Ⓒ   ▽ 25 | 23 | 19 | VE

418 E. 75th St. (bet. 1st & York Aves.), 6 to 77th St., 212-535-2288; www.treillageonline.com
■ Interior design luminary Bunny Williams and antique dealer John Rosselli showcase their "beautiful" garden-related vintage finds – chandeliers, Parisian benches, *faux-bois* tables, stone sculptures and such – at this picturesque Upper East Side store; alas, it's "very expensive", so wags suggest heading here for inspiration, "then traveling to France to buy."

Triple Five Soul ⓈⒸ   21 | 21 | 16 | M

290 Lafayette St. (bet. Houston & Prince Sts.), R/W to Prince St.; B/D/F/S/V to B'way/Lafayette St., 212-431-2404
145 Bedford Ave. (N. 9th St.), Brooklyn, L to Bedford Ave., 718-599-5971
www.triple5soul.com
■ This recently expanded SoHo gallery-shop and newly opened Williamsburg branch are where "break dancers, graffiti artists", "every hip-hop lover" and "all the hipsters" come to "get a dose of the latest" *trés* cool" "urbanwear"; Soul-seekers say this is "the place to purchase" "trendy as hell" denim, T-shirts, sweaters and "comfy sweatpants" or "that special" "fetish-worthy bag

with more zippers than you could ever need", plus rolling DJ cases with pouches for headphones and records.

TROY 🆂🅲   28 | 26 | 21 | VE

138 Greene St. (bet. Houston & Prince Sts.), R/W to Prince St., 212-941-4777; www.troysoho.com

■ Since Troy Halterman opened his "tony" SoHo furniture store eight years ago, the soaring space has been home to classic repro pieces as well as "cool" contemporary designs by Living Devani, e15 and other hip manufacturers; just note that "great taste" comes with a big price tag.

TSE   24 | 22 | 18 | VE

827 Madison Ave. (bet 68th & 69th Sts.), 6 to 68th St., 212-472-7790

■ Tse-lovers say this East 60s store is a "great place to lust after" luxurious, "softer-than-your-kitty" knitwear for men, women and children; "treat yourself at least once" to the "simple, modern" styles in "gorgeous" colors, all the while remembering that "cashmere doesn't have C-A-S-H in its name for nothing."

Tucker Robbins 🅲   – | – | – | E

139 E. 57th St., 4th fl. (Lexington Ave.), 4/5/6/F/N/R/W to 59th St./ Lexington Ave., 212-355-3383
33-02 Skillman Ave. (33rd St.), Queens, 7 to 33rd St., 718-764-0222 888-880-6442; www.tuckerrobbins.com

MoMA QNS isn't the only newish stop in Long Island City – designer Tucker Robbins transplanted himself here from Chelsea and brought his signature Asian and African finds, which range from Philippine Capiz-shell screens to Yoruba ladders, along with his own line of contemporary wooden furniture, with him; N.B. he's also opened a new branch on East 57th Street.

Tumi 🆂🅲   27 | 21 | 22 | VE

Grand Central, 64 Grand Central Terminal (42nd St.), 4/5/6/7/S to 42nd St./Grand Central, 212-973-0015
520 Madison Ave. (54th St.), E/V to 5th Ave./53rd St., 212-813-0545
Rockefeller Ctr., 53 W. 49th St. (bet. 5th & 6th Aves.), B/D/F/V to 47- 50th Sts./Rockefeller Ctr., 212-245-7460
www.tumi.com

■ "If you actually use your luggage", "save your money" for these "top-of-the-line" travel bags and leather goods that "endure all that wear and tear"; the staff offers "superior service" and "stands by the warranty"; sure, the suitcases may be "hard to pick out on airport carousels", but just the sight of one may "speed your check-in at hotels"; N.B. a new branch has opened in The Shops at Columbus Circle at Time Warner Center.

TURNBULL & ASSER 🅲   29 | 28 | 28 | VE

42 E. 57th St. (bet. Madison & Park Aves.), 4/5/6/F/N/R/W to 59th St./ Lexington Ave., 212-752-5700; 877-887-6285;
www.turnbullandasser.com

■ Pray, sir, step into the "old-gentlemen's-club" atmosphere of this East 57th Street "prestige" British haberdasher set in a three-floor restored townhouse; the outfitter of "important male dressers from Prince Charles" to James Bond cossets customers with "wonderful service" (voted the *Survey*'s No. 1) – indeed, you can "always please a guy by buying him a silk tie", pjs, an overcoat or a "stylishly colored", "custom-made shirt" in fine Egyptian or Sea Island cotton from here (women get this royal treatment too).

Umkarna 🅢🅒   – | – | – | E

69 Fifth Ave. (Prospect Pl.), Brooklyn, D/M/N/R to Pacific St., 718-398-5888; www.umkarna.com

Owner Luisa Giugliano transports the spirit of a Middle Eastern bazaar to Park Slope's Fifth Avenue, offering ethnic exotica enthusiasts antique and modern wearables and housewares from Turkey, India, Russia and Central and Eastern Asia; textiles from Uzbekistan and caftans with a casbah feel complement Bollywood-esque jewelry, while the back room boasts unique furniture and impulse items, from Moroccan tea glasses (made in Italy!) to slippers made for Arabian Nights.

Union 🅢🅒   ▽ 23 | 20 | 19 | E

172 Spring St. (bet. Thompson St. & W. B'way), C/E to Spring St., 212-226-8493

☑ Supporters say this SoHo shoebox seems a streetwise "staple" thanks to its mix of local, British and Japanese designers from Cooperstown Authentic reissued baseball jerseys to "their own original-logo T-shirt that'll be on display at MoMA one day"; but skeptics sniff "skate on" – the menswear here is too "pricey."

Unis 🅢🅒   – | – | – | E

226 Elizabeth St. (Prince St.), 6 to Spring St., 212-431-5533; www.unisnewyork.com

Glam gals can join hipster boys at this small, spare-looking, white-walled NoLita hot spot where "designer worth watching" DKNY alum Eunice Lee outfits downtowners in her relaxed cotton jersey and canvas sportswear offset by sexy details and ubiquitous zippers; camouflage, stripes and shots of bright color spark the otherwise muted shades of her unbuttoned-cool styles.

Unisa 🅢🅒   19 | 18 | 17 | M

701 Madison Ave. (bet. 62nd & 63rd Sts.), 4/5/6/F/N/R/W to 59th St./ Lexington Ave., 212-753-7474; www.unisa.com

■ "Cute", "delicately shaped shoes that knock off designer looks convincingly" at "reasonable" prices draw stylish bargain-hunters to this minimally designed Madison Avenue standby done up with leather benches; it's "a good source for footwear" "you need after you've spent your spending money on the outfit" and "great for trendy" options too.

United Colors of Benetton 🅢   16 | 17 | 15 | M

2308 Broadway (bet. 83rd & 84th Sts.), 1/9 to 86th St., 212-769-0121 ◗
749 Broadway (bet. 8th St. & Waverly Pl.), 6 to Astor Pl., 212-533-0230 ◗
555 Broadway (bet. Prince & Spring Sts.), R/W to Prince St., 212-941-8010 ◗
188 E. 78th St. (3rd Ave.), 6 to 77th St., 212-327-1035 ◗
601 Fifth Ave. (bet. 48th & 49th Sts.), E/V to 5th Ave./53rd St., 212-317-2501 ◗
120 Seventh Ave. (17th St.), 1/9 to 18th St., 646-638-1086
South Street Seaport, 10 Fulton St. (bet. South & Water Sts.), 2/3/ 4/5/A/C/J/M/Z to Fulton St./Broadway/Nassau, 212-509-3999
666 Third Ave. (42nd St.), 4/5/6/7/S to 42nd St./Grand Central, 212-818-0449 ◗
www.benetton.com

☑ "They're not just sweaters anymore", but the "rebirth" of the people's place for "classic Italian cool" still has shoppers asking if it's "evolved enough" to deliver "sharp, simple" essentials at "decent prices"; some are "pleasantly surprised" by "bright" cotton tops and suits for "working girls with style", while those who say "controversial ads are no substitute for good clothes" cite "larges that fit like smalls" and "complete lack of service."

Untitled ●ⓈⒸ
21 | 19 | 18 | E

26 W. Eighth St. (bet. 5th & 6th Aves.), A/B/C/D/E/F/S/V to W. 4th St., 212-505-9725

■ "In a little nook on Eighth Street", this two-floor boutique has "been around serving up high-fashion before anyone else" (since the mid-'80s, anyway); the relaxed atmosphere features "fun, helpful" clerks who ease male and female customers – many of them music biz insiders, "rock star wanna-bes and real rockers too" – into "sexy, trendy, hipster" threads from bold-faced names like Jean Paul Gaultier, just right for Big Apple nights; N.B. there are now also designer clothes for kids from the likes of D&G.

Upland Trading
24 | 18 | 23 | M

236 E. 13th St. (bet. 2nd & 3rd Aves.), 4/5/6/L/N/Q/R/W to 14th St./ Union Sq., 212-673-4994

■ Tucked away on East 13th Street is this "nice, little", woodsy shop chock-full of quality outerwear, handcrafted Italian bags, Irish scarves by Inis Meàin and "a great collection of the safari/ rugged look"; male and female cosmopolites stop by "before going on a foreign adventure" or just "come for traditional", "hard-to-find fine casualwear" "with a twist"; owner/manager Armando Nagron is such "a truly elegant, laid-back kind of guy" that you "can't go into the store and not buy anything."

Uproar Home Ⓒ
▽ 22 | 17 | 18 | E

121 Greene St. (bet. Houston & Prince Sts.), R/W to Prince St., 212-614-8580; www.uproarhome.com

■ Expansive upholstered sofas (available as sleepers) and chairs and sturdy, handmade wooden cabinets are the focus of this SoHo store housed in a cast-iron building with beautiful interior columns; smaller-scale home accessories include throws, trays, mirrors and handblown glass lamps.

Urban Angler Ⓒ
23 | 21 | 21 | E

206 Fifth Ave., 3rd Fl. (bet. 25th & 26th Sts.), 6 to 23rd St., 212-979-7600; 800-255-5488; www.urbanangler.com

■ One of the "top fishing emporiums in the country", this "charming, idiosyncratic" anglers haven near Madison Square Park is a "great place to explore, dream" and shop; whether "you need high-end flyrods" or "great stuff" like reels, lines, tackle, vises, technical clothing or luggage, "this is the place to go", plus it all comes with "expert advice"; while you're docked, you may want to catch casting lessons and book signings; a post-*Survey* relocation may outdate the above Presentation score.

Urban Archaeology Ⓒ
27 | 25 | 21 | VE

239 E. 58th St. (bet. 2nd & 3rd. Aves.), 4/5/6/F/N/R/W to 59th St./ Lexington Ave., 212-371-4646
143 Franklin St. (bet. Hudson & Varick Sts.), 1/9 to Franklin St., 212-431-4646
www.urbanarchaeology.com

■ "A must if you're renovating a home", these "amazing stores" in TriBeCa and the East 50s provide a "one-of-a-kind shopping" experience with a "grand selection" of "unique" fixtures and fittings salvaged from "old buildings", "absolutely gorgeous tiles" and reproductions of "antique" plumbing and lighting; the "pleasant staff" is "knowledgeable", but the "prices are outrageous" for anyone who's not a "millionaire."

Urban Monster 🟦🟥   – | – | – | M

396 Atlantic Ave. (bet. Bond & Hoyt Sts.), Brooklyn, F/G to Bergen St.; A/C/G to Hoyt/Schermerhorn Sts., 718-855-6400; www.urbanmonster.com

Vibrant and kid-friendly, with Jolly Roger apple-green and grape-soda-colored floors, this Boerum Hill yearling fills the needs of babies and moms with a retail emporium and romper room for classes galore, from Mommy & Me to pilates; the merchandise runs the gamut from hip children's clothing from labels like Zutano and Cotton Caboodle to baby essentials like Combi Activity Rockers and Maclaren strollers to maternity apparel, nursing gear, Petunia Picklebottom diaper bags and bath toys.

Urban Optical 🟦🟥   ▽ 22 | 18 | 22 | M

152 Bedford Ave. (bet. N. 8th & 9th Sts.), Brooklyn, L to Bedford Ave., 718-388-5078 ●
330 Seventh Ave. (9th St.), Brooklyn, F to 7th Ave., 718-832-3513

■ "A nice selection of fashionable frames" from hot properties like Alain Mikli, Oliver Peoples, Chanel, Prada, Gucci, DKNY and Ralph Lauren pack the windows and vitrines of these small yet appealing Williamsburg and Park Slope siblings; owner "Dr. Adam Friedland is the best" believe boosters – "he is so accommodating and has great taste too", plus his staff is "knowledgeable and friendly"; little wonder these eyewear havens usually brim with browsers and buyers.

Urban Outfitters ●🟦   18 | 18 | 11 | M

2081 Broadway (72nd St.), 1/2/3/9 to 72nd St., 212-579-3912
628 Broadway (Bleecker St.), B/D/F/V to B'way/Lafayette St.; 6 to Bleecker St., 212-475-0009
162 Second Ave. (bet. 10th & 11th Sts.), 6 to Astor Pl.; L to 3rd Ave., 212-375-1277
526 Sixth Ave. (14th St.), F/L/V to 14th St./6th Ave., 646-638-1646
374 Sixth Ave. (bet. Washington & Waverly Pls.), A/B/C/D/E/F/S/V to W. 4th St., 212-677-9350
800-282-2200; www.urbn.com

◪ "Downtown" goes "all around town" with this "poseur-cool" chain of "duds" for "dudes and chicks"; "funky-punky" clothes for the "fast and furious" sit alongside "wacky", "kitschy" knickknacks and home accessories for apartment- and dorm-dwellers, making it "a fun place to wander" ("where else can you get a cool scarf and penis pasta" at the same time?), despite the "overly inflated" price tags and "intimidating", "multi-pierced" "alterna-teen" staff.

Utrecht 🟦   22 | 17 | 17 | M

111 Fourth Ave. (bet. 11th & 12th Sts.), 4/5/6/L/N/Q/R/W to 14th St./ Union Sq., 212-777-5353; www.utrecht.com

◪ East Village "all-purpose" "clean, serene, art-selling machine" offering a "good selection" of paint, easels, canvas and graphic arts supplies from name brands like Old Holland, Gamblin and Winsor & Newton for painters with promise and professionals too; prices are "reasonable", especially on the "house brand's" acrylics, oils and brushes, and the staff is "student-friendly"; but the less-impressed paint another picture, pouting that the choices "are not as wide" as some competitors.

Valentino C
26 | 25 | 25 | VE

747 Madison Ave. (bet. 64th & 65th Sts.), 6 to 68th St., 212-772-6969; www.valentino.it
■ "High-end" refinement meets "friendly and knowledgeable" service at this limestone-floored East 60s boutique – a "beautiful space to shop in" – "catering to wealthy Upper Eastsiders" and bi-coastal celebrities (e.g. Julia Roberts, Ashley Judd), who love the legendary Italian designer's "classic" "stunning eveningwear, shoes and accessories"; P.S. gents, "great clothes of the most European style" await you too.

VAN CLEEF & ARPELS
29 | 28 | 27 | VE

744 Fifth Ave. (57th St.), N/R/W to 5th Ave./59th St., 212-644-9500; www.vancleef.com
■ Located next to Bergdorf Goodman, this venerable French house is the "friendliest of the big-name jewelers" profess fans of the "incredible designs" – especially the familiar clover and other exquisitely updated art nouveau fauna and flora creations – executed with invisibly set gems; though there's lots of "nice ice", it's the "surprisingly warm" staff that makes it "a dream to shop" in the intimate lime-green-and-lavender environs.

Varda
24 | 21 | 18 | E

*2080 Broadway (71st St.), 1/2/3/9 to 72nd St., 212-873-6910 **S***
786 Madison Ave. (67th St.), 6 to 68th St., 212-472-7552
*118 Spring St. (bet. Greene & Mercer Sts.), 6 to Spring St., 212-343-9575 **S***
■ A "dream come true" proclaim those taken by the "timeless", "beautifully crafted", "quality leather shoes and boots" and "good service" at this "classic" trio; while the "comfortable, conservative" styles may "not be for the hipster, trendy crowd, they're dependable when you need a break from dancing all night in *Sex and the City* heels."

Variazioni ●SC
20 | 18 | 15 | E

309 Columbus Ave. (bet. 74th & 75th Sts.), 1/2/3/9 to 72nd St., 212-874-7474
71 Spring St. (bet. Lafayette & Crosby Sts.), R/W to Prince St.; B/D/F/S/V to B'way/Lafayette St., 212-941-1000
1376 Third Ave. (bet. 78th & 79th Sts.), 6 to 77th St., 212-744-9200
◪ For a good *variazioni* of "out-of-the-ordinary" options in "breezy" separates and "great eveningwear", everyone from "the struggling actress to the Wall Street banker" would do well to "check out" this chainlet; however, critics claim the clothes "walk the walk, but can't talk the talk" (quality control is "not the greatest") and warn the "pushy salespeople" "won't let you leave empty-handed."

Ventilo C
26 | 25 | 23 | E

*69 Greene St. (bet. Broome & Spring Sts.), R/W to Prince St., 212-625-3660 **S***
810 Madison Ave. (68th St.), 6 to 68th St., 212-535-9362
www.ventilo.fr
■ Rich SoHo gypsies and Madison Avenue acolytes who "don't want to look like every other" woman scoop up "lovely clothing that's just a bit exotic (you can tell it's French)", plus hand-painted floral purses, fringed silk shawls and poetically named perfumes

at these inviting old-world boutiques with a beaded, bohemian vibe; "everything is flattering", with "gorgeous textures, colors and cuts", indeed these pieces "will become standards you keep for years."

Venture Stationers ◐[S] 24 | 16 | 16 | E

1156 Madison Ave. (bet. 85th & 86th Sts.), 4/5/6 to 86th St., 212-288-7235; 888-388-2727

■ Upper Eastsiders have ventured to this "great neighborhood place" for over 30 years for "lovely and varied merchandise" from engraved stationery and "pens galore" to Longchamp bags to Halian desk and home accessories to "cute little notebooks" and "colored paper clips" (it's an "office supply hoarder's paradise"); in fact, it's so "well stocked", it's "easy to spend money here whether you plan to or not."

Vera Wang Bridal Salon 26 | 25 | 20 | VE

980 Madison Ave., 3rd fl. (bet. 76th & 77th Sts.), 6 to 77th St., 212-628-9898

991 Madison Ave. (77th St.), 6 to 77th St., 212-628-3400

www.verawang.com

◪ "The place to call the minute you get engaged" rhapsodize romantics who love "the queen of bridal gowns'" "always tasteful" designs (as well as her shoes and china) at this Upper East Side by-appointment-only salon; the "lovely staff" proffers "the royal treatment", presenting the "superlative" "dreams on a hanger, inviting you to be a star" for a day; while the less-rapturous retort "if attitude is your thing, it's here, along with the cost", even they rationalize that "it's a rite of passage"; N.B. Wang's Maids Salon at 980 Madison specializes in bridesmaid and flower girl dresses.

Vercesi Hardware [S] 23 | 14 | 25 | I

152 E. 23rd St. (bet. Lexington & 3rd Aves.), 6 to 23rd St., 212-475-1883

■ "Service is key" at this "great, old-fashioned" Gramercy Park hardware store, where the "excellent", "funny", "no-attitude" staff provides a "deep repository of advice on all home fix-it projects" and can help you identify "any widget you need"; the shop stocks a "large variety" of goods at "reasonable prices", and even though it's a "madhouse on Saturdays", its devotees deem it "worth the wait."

Verdura [C] 27 | 26 | 26 | VE

745 Fifth Ave., Ste. 1205 (bet. 57th & 58th Sts.), N/R/W to 5th Ave./ 59th St., 212-758-3388; www.verdura.com

■ "For the best in jewelry" with an "excellent" idiosyncratic flair, "it doesn't get better than Verdura" declare the cultlike cognoscenti who patronize this showroom high above 57th Street, also known for its "experienced staff"; using the original, oft-imitated designs of its legendary namesake (whose signature Maltese-cross cuff bracelets adorned the wrists of Chanel and Diana Vreeland), the firm turns out witty, glamorous pieces – precious and semiprecious "stones, the enamel, the settings!" – they all dazzle.

Veronique [S][C] ▽ 20 | 20 | 20 | VE

1321 Madison Ave. (93rd St.), 6 to 96th St., 212-831-7800; 888-265-5848; www.veroniquematernity.com

■ "The answer for the sexy pregnant woman", this sleek, newly renovated Upper East Side boutique offers "unique merchandise" from Italy, France and America; it's "expensive, but worth it for the flattering clothes" from labels like Earl, Diane von Furstenburg and Citizens for Humanity and "friendly", "knowledgeable staff" (plus personal shoppers) "who help find what will be the gems of your maternity wardrobe", including "womanly bathing suits"; N.B. they now also carry a small line of infants wear.

Versace 🄲   23 | 25 | 21 | VE

647 Fifth Ave. (bet. 51st & 52nd Sts.), E/V to 5th Ave./53rd St.; 6 to 51st St., 212-317-0224 🆂

815 Madison Ave. (68th St.), 6 to 68th St., 212-744-6868

www.versace.com

☑ "You gotta say wow" as you glide through the "imposing" entry of the Fifth Avenue flagship or the "modern" Madison Avenue branch of the late Italian maestro, whose "big-budget" womens- and menswear is now designed by sister Donatella; the "staff can seem standoffish at first, but they warm up" and become "extremely helpful", especially with the "wonderful selection of accessories"; but while fans find "fun" in the "fashion-first" clothes, the "bold looks" are deemed "too bizarre" for others.

Verve ●🄢🄲   24 | 18 | 20 | E

353 Bleecker St. (bet. Charles & W. 10th Sts.), 1/9 to Christopher St./ Sheridan Sq., 212-691-6516

336 Bleecker St. (bet. Christopher & W. 10th Sts.), 1/9 to Christopher St./Sheridan Sq., 212-675-6693

282 Columbus Ave. (bet. 73rd & 74th Sts.), 1/2/3/9 to 72nd St., 212-580-7150

■ "Can't walk by without lightening my wallet" declare devotees delighted by the "eclectic mix of items" sure to "spice up your wardrobe" at this "friendly" trio; the "mini bazaar"-like Upper West Side and the 353 Bleecker Street shops are "attractively strewn with colorful", "Verve-acious handbags" ("helps feed the fetish"), "fun, funky hats" and the "cutest scarves and jewelry" – "no boring cookie cutter pieces here" – while the shoe boutique, now at 336 Bleecker Street, is "always worth checking out."

Vespa 🄢🄲   25 | 21 | 19 | VE

13 Crosby St. (bet. Grand & Howard Sts.), 6/J/M/N/Q/R/W/Z to Canal St., 212-226-4410; www.vespasoho.com

■ "*Viva Italia!*" symbolizing "quintessential cool" since Jean-Paul Belmondo's day, the updated classic motor scooters showcased at this SoHo offshoot of Piaggio USA's revitalized Tuscany-based chain come in vibrant va-va-vroom colors with customized suede seats ("there is no other brand my bum deserves more"), hot-hued helmets, riding apparel and a battery of accessories to match; the minimalist, garagelike shop "embodies the legend" while the staff nurtures it, assisting new bikers with the licensing and driving school process.

Via Spiga 🄢🄲   23 | 21 | 20 | E

692 Madison Ave. (bet. 62nd & 63rd Sts.), 6 to 68th St., 212-988-4877

390 W. Broadway (bet. Broome & Spring Sts.), R/W to Prince St., 212-431-7007

800-557-0250; www.viaspiga.com

■ "They usually hit fashion right on the head" at these SoHo and newly relocated Madison Avenue "meccas" maintain mavens, who take a shine to the "friendly service" as well as the "wonderfully styled shoes" that not only "stand out", but "also withstand wear and tear and are – gasp – comfortable"; fence-straddlers feel it "bounces between a little too out there and a little too boring, but when they find the middle ground – yum"; N.B. they also carry outerwear, cashmere sweaters, accessories and men's footwear.

Victoria's Secret S
17 | 20 | 17 | M

1328 Broadway (34th St.), B/D/F/N/Q/R/V/W to 34th St./Herald Sq., 212-356-8383; 800-888-1500; www.victoriassecret.com
Additional locations throughout the NY area

☑ It's "like walking into a" cream-and-black "boudoir" with marble floors breathe brevity-boosters – "once you shop" at this "wonderland of intimate apparel" "you're hooked"; "the formula works" thanks to a "great presentation" of "perpetually sexy stuff", from "trendy little nighties" to "everyday undies" to girlie cosmetics, but patrons put off by the "cloying salespeople" and "so-so quality" pout "her secret is that these undergarments belong in the mall, not Midtown"; N.B. the 34th Street flagship also offers personalized bra fittings.

Vilebrequin S C
25 | 24 | 21 | VE

1070 Madison Ave. (81st St.), 6 to 77th St., 212-650-0353
436 W. Broadway (Prince St.), C/E to Spring St., 212-431-0673
888-458-0051; www.vilebrequin.com

■ The search for "wonderful, creative bathing suits for men and adorable ones for little boys" terminates at these Upper East Side and SoHo boutiques where the spirit of Saint-Tropez reigns; the "unique" "European styling", executed in colorful prints and stretch fabrics, offers a "very flattering fit"; "granted, the prices are prohibitive, but one can get a lot of mileage out of swimming trunks", plus now they also offer summery linen pants and shirts.

Villeroy & Boch S
24 | 25 | 23 | E

901 Broadway (20th St.), R/W to 23rd St., 212-505-1090;
800-845-5376; www.villeroy-boch.com

■ Flatiron purveyor of the 1748 Luxembourg-based company's "classy" dinnerware and serving pieces that are a "perennial hit at housewarmings" and "great for wedding gifts"; there are "lots of lovely" "classic" patterns, but an "attentive" and "helpful" staff can guide the china-challenged when it comes to creating more contemporary "mix-and-match" looks; N.B. in addition, the space also serves as a showroom for the company's tiles, bathroom fixtures and ceramic kitchen sinks.

V.I.M. ● S
14 | 8 | 8 | I

16 W. 14th St. (6th Ave.), F/L/V to 14th St./6th Ave., 212-255-2262;
www.vim.com
Additional locations throughout the NY area

☑ "More jeans than you will ever know what to do with" reside at this convenient mega-chain of "good-for-hanging-out" labels like Fubu, Phat Farm and Mudd, plus "lots of cheap basics", from urban streetwear, boots from Timberland and must-have activewear to sneakers galore from major brands, including Adidas, Puma, Nike and Skechers; while "prices are decent", the less-impressed opine there are "better alternatives" to be found.

Vinylmania ●
– | – | – | M

60 Carmine St. (bet. Bedford St. & 7th Ave. S), 1/9 to Houston St., 212-924-7223; www.vinylmania.com

"For vinyl junkies", this Carmine Street ol' reliable is "the place to get your" dance music; wax enthusiasts groove to the wide selection of popular and hard-to-find acid jazz, progressive house, trance and Eurodance LPs that includes everyone from Ashanti to the Thievery Corp; "breakbeats, imports and CDs are on the menu" too, and so are DJ accessories; P.S. the "staff knows what they're talking about", plus "special orders don't upset 'em."

VIRGIN MEGASTORE ◐ [S] 25 | 22 | 14 | M

1540 Broadway (bet. 45th & 46th Sts.), 1/2/3/7/9/N/Q/R/S/W to 42nd St./Times Sq., 212-921-1020
52 E. 14th St. (Broadway), 4/5/6/L/N/Q/R/W to 14th St./Union Sq., 212-598-4666
www.virginmegamagazine.com

■ These "big, scary" Times Square and Union Square "FAO Schwarzes for music fans" "saturate the senses", boasting a "huge selection of imports and other genres" "you can spend all day listening to on headphones" "before you buy"; "like New York City itself, it offers the extreme of everything" – in fact, you might join the chorus of shoppers "over 14 years old" who plead "turn down the volume" on the piped-in tunes.

Vitra [S] [C] ▽ 28 | 24 | 20 | VE

29 Ninth Ave. (bet. 13th & 14th Sts.), A/C/E/L to 14th St./8th Ave., 212-929-3626; www.vitra.com

■ This Meatpacking District showroom for the Swiss furniture maker was designed by buzz-generating young architect Lindy Roy; a molded walnut staircase connects the two-storied space, which features conveyer-belt-like displays of iconic pieces from 20th-century masters like Jean Prouvé, Verner Panton and Frank Gehry for the home and office.

Vivienne Tam [S] [C] 24 | 23 | 17 | E

99 Greene St. (bet. Prince & Spring Sts.), R/W to Prince St., 212-966-2398; www.viviennetam.com

■ There's a whole lotta "daring" going on at this SoHo boutique, and it's not just the red walls with a painted dragon; the vibe also lies in the "unique Asian-inspired" womenswear; "although it can be an ego-kicker" for those not sleek enough for "skin-tight T-shirts and skirts", "you won't see yourself coming and going in these outfits."

Viv Pickle [S] – | – | – | E

238 W. 10th St. (bet. Bleecker & Hudson St.), 1/9 to Christopher St./ Sheridan Sq., 212-924-0444; www.vivpickle.com

Tired of picking through other folks' handbag designs? – so was corporate VP (aka Vivacious Pickle) Susan Murphy until she ditched it all to open this huge, uncluttered West Village shop where you can create your own tour de force; inspired enthusiasts can select a shape, fabric, lining and handles to compose the purse of their dreams, plus the Philadelphia-based owner-designer also purveys a line of riotously colored ready-made bags and totes.

Walter Steiger 23 | 22 | 18 | VE

417 Park Ave. (55th St.), 6/E/V to 51st St./Lexington Ave., 212-826-7171; www.walter-steiger.com

■ "Comfortable and luxurious at the same time – who knew you could get that in a high-end, high-heeled shoe?" crow customers who flock to this Park Avenue designer boutique; the footwear "with flair", ranging from stiletto boots to fashionable flats, and the "beautiful bags" are made from unusual and über-soft leathers – little wonder that Walter-ites whine "expensive."

Warren Edwards
∇ 24 | 19 | 18 | VE

107 E. 60th St. (Park Ave.), 4/5/6/F/N/R/W to 59th St./Lexington Ave., 212-223-4374; www.warrenedwards.com

■ This pricey East 60s shop caters to cab-riding women and nattily dressed men with "true couture" footwear that can be "customized to your exact details" or bought off the shelf, plus coordinating handbags, leather goods and belts; twice a year this "living legend" designer – half of the famed 1980s Susan Bennis Warren Edwards label – rolls out ultra-femme collections of sexy heels, sling-backs and mules spiced with a little leopard print or the like and fabulous footwear for guys made from all kinds of skins.

Watch World **S**
∇ 17 | 15 | 16 | M

649 Broadway (Bleecker St.), 6 to Bleecker St., 212-475-6090; www.sunglasshut.com
Additional locations throughout the NY area

■ Part of the Sunglass Hut chain, with several "convenient locations" around town, this well-equipped NoHo outpost offers what fans find are the "best prices" on "basic watches" (plus new batteries); it's the sort of place where you can "get a great deal on a Swiss Army watch" or a Revo chronograph.

WATERWORKS
28 | 28 | 19 | VE

475 Broome St. (Greene St.), R/W to Prince St., 212-274-8800 **S**
225 E. 57th St. (bet. 2nd & 3rd Aves.), 4/5/6/F/N/R/W to 59th St./ Lexington Ave., 212-371-9266
www.waterworks.com

☑ "Wish I had more bathrooms" sigh staunch supporters of these "beautiful" SoHo and East 50s stores selling "wonderful fixtures", the "chicest supplies" and an "amazing array of decorative tiles"; it's a "pleasure to walk around the showrooms", and the "helpful staff" "doesn't hound you", but bashers bemoan the "ridiculous prices" that make it all too easy to "get soaked."

Wedding Day Details **C**
– | – | – | M

328 E. 9th St. (bet. 1st & 2nd Aves.), 6 to Astor Pl.; R/W to 8th St., 212-979-7060; www.thegowncompany.com

Everything but the bridal dress (which you can find across the street at its sister shop, the Gown Company) is available at this inviting, *très* feminine East Village salonette decorated to feel like a woman's bedroom; all of the accessories necessary to complete a wedding day ensemble are here, from shoes and bras to veils and jewelry, plus the aisle-bound can bring in their own dresses to give their look a trial run; N.B. they also do alterations.

Wedding Library **◑C**
∇ 17 | 19 | 16 | E

50 E. 81st St. (bet. Madison & Park Aves.), 6 to 77th St.; 4/5/6 to 86th St., 212-327-0100
29 E. 73rd St. (bet. 5th & Madison Aves.), 6 to 77th St., 212-249-2050
www.theweddinglibrary.com

☑ An "information gathering spot" for brides that's "extremely helpful in resourcing reception venues, photographers, musicians", DJs and invitations, this East 80s townhouse and its new East 70s offshoot are the "places to come" for "gorgeous headpieces", accessories and bridesmaid shoes, dresses and favors; but naysayers file the research-end under "unimaginative", opining "if you've read even one magazine, chances are you know as much as the 'librarians.'"

Wempe C
27 | 24 | 23 | VE

*700 Fifth Ave. (55th St.), E/V to 5th Ave./53rd St., 212-397-9000;
800-513-1131; www.wempe.com*

■ Although this Midtowner "looks like nothing from the outside", the interior is a treasure trove for timepieces of a "high-end" nature from such makers as Cartier, IWC, Patek Philippe and Rolex, plus fine jewelry clocks; the staff's "butlerlike service" makes shopping here "a real joy", and while a "my-watch-cost-more-than-your-car ambiance" fills the air, regulars report that "price cuts come with the asking"; N.B. a post-*Survey* expansion may outdate the above Presentation score.

West Elm S
– | – | – | M

*75 Front St. (Main St.), Brooklyn, F to York St., 718-875-7757;
866-westelm; www.westelm.com*

The Williams-Sonoma-owned home furnishings catalogue comes to life in this 5,000-sq.-ft., industrial-looking, loftlike store in up-and-coming Dumbo; the moderately priced modern pieces include dark-wood platform beds and bedding, clean-lined couches, acrylic nesting tables, galvanized steel storage cubes, modular seating, floor-length curtains and shimmering pillows; N.B. same-day delivery is available.

West Side Kids S C
22 | 17 | 19 | M

498 Amsterdam Ave. (84th St.), 1/9 to 86th St., 212-496-7282

■ You "can always find a rainy-day game that's engaging", "good educational" and "handcrafted toys" from brands like Lego and Playmobil for ages 0-14, plus "inexpensive stocking stuffers" and Zutano clothing at this jam-packed Upper West Side staple where the "staff is very knowledgeable" and will help you "through any birthday" gift dilemma.

Wet Seal ● S
13 | 15 | 12 | I

*670 Broadway (Bond St.), 6 to Bleecker St., 212-253-2470
65 E. Eighth St. (B'way), R/W to 8th St., 212-228-6188
901 Sixth Ave. (34th St.), B/D/F/N/Q/R/V/W to 34th St./Herald Sq.,
212-216-0622
www.wetseal.com*

☑ "Tanned Britney wanna-bes" "stuff themselves into" "trendy" tube, tank and T-shirts, cords, minis and other "post-Contempo Casuals" at this "juniors'" fashion chain for "prom queens" still wet behind the ears; the service is less than sterling, but the "one-season" "girlie" wear is so "cheap", you won't have to blow all your "babysitting money" at once.

What Comes Around Goes Around ● S
25 | 21 | 18 | E

*351 W. Broadway (bet. Grand & Broome Sts.), A/C/E to Canal St.,
212-343-9303; www.nyvintage.com*

☑ "Western wear never went out" at this dang-good SoHo store, whose dude-ranch decor makes for a "world-class collection of collectible denim"; the "knowledgeable staff" helps navigate among the "great vintage" items ranging from late 1800s finds to 1980s concert tees to the store's own line of reconstructed pieces; however, those unwilling to spend bucks on buckskin banter the place "should be named What Comes Around Goes Up In Price"; N.B. a new deco-inspired addition features high-end womenswear dating back to the 1900s.

White on White C 23 | 25 | 20 | E

888 Lexington Ave. (66th St.), 6 to 68th St., 212-288-0909;
www.whiteonwhiteny.com

■ It's the owner's Swedish sensibility that brings serenity and "style" to this "pretty" East 60s home-furnishings shop where the namesake color turns up on "exquisitely presented" and painted Gustavian furniture, ceramics, bedding, embroidered textiles and children's wear; "it's a pleasure to shop here" but it's pricey.

Whitney Museum Store S C 18 | 15 | 15 | M

945 Madison Ave. (75th St.), 6 to 77th St., 212-570-3614;
www.whitney.org

✔ "Richard Avedon waited for me to buy his books and signed them: what more do you want?" – well, how about "geometric-patterned mini-umbrellas, giant-hand salad scoopers" and other "unique", "modern" "Americana" "at moderate prices" from this Upper East Side museum shop; unfortunately, being banished to the basement "between the staircase and the bathroom", it's "more of a counter than a full-fledged store."

Wicker Garden C ▽ 26 | 22 | 21 | VE

1327 Madison Ave. (bet. 93rd & 94th Sts.), 6 to 96th St., 212-410-7001;
www.wickergarden.com

■ The mom of "Eloise probably shopped here" quip fans who head to this Victorian-style Upper East Side spot to pore over the "storybook" infants' clothes for babes up to 15 months; there's also a "large selection" of "unique baby" items to choose from, including "beautiful" wicker furniture designed by the owner, bassinets and layette essentials; sure, it can be "over-the-top in price", but hey, browsing never hurt anyone.

William Barthman C 24 | 21 | 22 | E

174 Broadway (Maiden Ln.), 4/5/6 to Fulton St., 212-732-0890
1118 Kings Hwy. (Coney Island Ave.), Brooklyn, N to Kings Hwy.,
718-375-1818 S
800-727-9725; www.williambarthman.com

■ Like the "old-time jeweler back home", this "historical place" (founded in 1884) is a "great spot to drop a wad of cash" on "good, classic watches and jewelry" (from Aaron Basha to David Yurman) and Montblanc pens; the "repair service is stellar", as are the "appraisers on-site", all of which makes this vet a "favorite in the Financial District" and Sheepshead Bay too.

Williams-Sonoma ● S 25 | 24 | 20 | E

121 E. 59th St. (Lexington Ave.), 4/5/6/F/N/R/W to 59th St./
Lexington Ave., 917-369-1131
1175 Madison Ave. (86th St.), 4/5/6 to 86th St., 212-289-6832
110 Seventh Ave. (bet. 16th & 17th Sts.), 1/9 to 18th St.,
212-633-2203
800-541-2233; www.williams-sonoma.com

■ This national chain has "the best of everything" – from All-Clad cookware and German knives to always-cool KitchenAid mixers and Cuisinart food processors – a status-loving cook or bride-to-be could want; there are "no bargains, but it's a pleasure shopping here" because the "helpful" staff and "well-organized", "beautifully presented" merchandise "make you want to buy"; N.B. as we go to press, a new branch has opened in The Shops at Columbus Circle at Time Warner Center.

William-Wayne & Company
40 University Pl. (9th St.), R/W to 212-533-4711 **S**
846-850 Lexington Ave. (bet. 64th & 6
800-318-3435; www.william-wayn(
■ Could there possibly be "too ma
"fun" home-furnishings stores in G
East 60s, where ceramic garden sea
topped honey jars share space with ......ι-οι-pearl-handled
servers, tinware and "monkey-themed things"?; the owners have
"really got an eye", so "it's a great place" "to find an unusual gift,
even if it's for yourself."

Willoughby's ●S
`19 15 14 M`
136 W. 32nd St. (bet. 6th & 7th Aves.), 1/2/3/9 to 34th St./Penn Station,
212-564-1600; 800-378-1898; www.willoughbys.com
☑ Beyond the cell phones, wristwatches and blood-pressure
machines lurk "cameras, cameras, cameras", new and old, at
this centenarian "granddaddy" in the Garment District; with a
"good selection" of "prices as low as you can get without really
shopping around", it remains a "safe place to buy", though
shutter snobs dis the "once-proud" place for employing "staffers
who are ignorant of even the most basic rules of photography";
N.B. closed on Saturdays.

Wolford
`26 21 21 VE`
122 Greene St. (Prince St.), R/W to Prince St., 212-343-0808 **S**
996 Madison Ave. (bet. 77th & 78th Sts.), 6 to 77th St., 212-327-1000
619 Madison Ave. (bet. 58th & 59th Sts.), 4/5/6/F/N/R/W to 59th St./
Lexington Ave., 212-688-4850
800-965-3673; www.wolford.com
■ "Steep prices indeed, but these are no ordinary undies" assert
fans who consider this Austrian "luxe" line of unmentionables "the
gold standard"; "nothing looks sleeker under a jacket than their
[string] bodysuits", the "fishnets, stay-up stockings and everyday
hose", available in "patterns, textures" and seasonal colors, are
"sublime", plus "the salespeople, from SoHo to Madison, are
happy to help find your size and style"; P.S. collaborative efforts
include limited-edition collections from Vivienne Westwood (it's a
"little wild") and Playboy.

Wool Gathering **S C**
`21 18 15 E`
318 E. 84th St. (bet. 1st & 2nd Aves.), 4/5/6 to 86th St., 212-734-4747;
www.thewoolgathering.com
☑ "Beautiful buttons and wools" abound in this "charming little"
Yorkville shop where the purl-and-stitch set find a "good range
of yarn" and supplies, including skeins that are "excellent for
children's" wear, plus needlepoint materials too; one catch: knit-
pickers pout that you may "get a chilly reception from the staff."

World of Golf, The **C**
`25 15 23 E`
189 Broadway (Dey St.), 4/5/6 to Fulton St.; N/R to Cortlandt St.,
212-385-1246
147 E. 47th St. (bet. Lexington & 3rd Aves.), 6 to 51st St., 212-755-9398 **S**
800-499-7491; www.theworldofgolf.com
☑ "The name says it all" – these huge "candy stores for avid
golfers" in Midtown and the Financial District showcase "all the
fine brands" of equipment, from Callaway to Odyssey, including one

selections in the city" and tee-time apparel, plus
club fitting; fans find the "staff knowledgeable
", but critics wonder whether "anything ever goes on
re; N.B. at the Broadway branch's studio, professionals
analysis technology to diagnose your swing.

X-Large **S** **C** | 19 | 18 | 15 | M |

267 Lafayette St. (bet. Prince & Spring Sts.), R/W to Prince St.,
212-334-4480; www.xlarge.com

■ "Glad there's an X-Large around for people who don't fit into
the mold" muse admirers of this urban NoLita shop, founded over
a decade ago by Beastie Boy Mike D; "after all these years, it's
kept its cool" offering "funky", ramped-up streetwear, jeans,
beanies, accessories, Vans sneakers and graphic "T-shirts for
the Downtown crowd" that's "going for that skater look", plus a
like-minded mini women's line that's "really cute."

Xukuma **S** | – | – | – | M |

183 Lenox Ave. (bet. 119th & 120th Sts.), 2/3 to 116th St.,
212-222-0490; www.xukuma.com

On the parlor floor of a Harlem rowhouse, this hip lifestyles store
brings a little of everything that's Downtown to Uptown, from
chandeliers to bath products to original design T-shirts and
jewelry; Sia candles, frames and vases, Wonderfully Delicious
gourmet edibles and Torre and Tajus clocks are perfect fillers for
the shop's unique twist on the gift basket.

Yarn Co., The **C** | 25 | 18 | 14 | E |

2274 Broadway, 2nd fl. (bet. 81st & 82nd Sts.), 1/9 to 79th St.,
212-787-7878; 888-927-6261; www.theyarnco.com

☑ "It's all here, including top-shelf knitters to remedy beginner
blues" and teach classes, stacks of high-end and "novelty yarns"
plus pattern books, chorus the crafty who congregate on the
second-floor of this Upper Westsider; but critics are in a snit, saying
"being a friend of the house gets you good service, otherwise
expect to be ignored."

Yarn Connection, The **C** | 22 | 14 | 22 | M |

218 Madison Ave. (bet. 36th & 37th Sts.), 6 to 33rd St.,
212-684-5099

■ "About the size of a small closet", this Murray Hill knitting and
needlework shop "feels like a hidden jewel", offering "a great
selection of smashing yarn" and flosses as well as "good patterns
and books"; the "absolute angel" of an owner and her staff
"embody the knitting grandmother" most "never had" and make you
feel "welcome", "even if you're not known or not planning to spend
a bundle" and they even offer beginning and advanced classes.

Yellow Door **S** **C** | 23 | 21 | 21 | E |

1308 Ave. M (bet. 13th & 14th Sts.), Brooklyn, Q to Ave. M,
718-998-7382; www.theyellowdoor.com

■ "Madison Avenue in Midwood" describes this "savvy shoppers'
mecca" that's "not just for jewelry or watches" from names like
SeidenGang and Christian Dior – "real Brooklynites know" it's
also the door to step through for "unique, tasteful" home-design
collectibles, Herend dinnerware from Hungary and wedding gifts
from Baccarat, Lalique, MacKenzie-Childs and Waterford; some
of the "lovely things are equally as off-the-beaten-track" as this
"convenient", "surprising find", staffed with "quality sales help."

Yellow Rat Bastard 🅂🄲 | 18 | 15 | 12 | M |

478 Broadway (bet. Broome & Grand Sts.), 6/J/M/N/Q/R/W/Z to Canal St., 212-334-2150; 877-935-5728; www.yellowratbastard.com

☑ "A haven of imperfection in the glossy world of SoHo", yeah, "this Bastard's alright" agree "ravers", "flygirls, B-boys", "teen punk wanna-bes" and "anyone searching for an edgy" "skater chic", "hip streetwear" look; "loud, funky music" and an "anything but chic" graffiti-walled decor resembling the streets and sights of NYC set the tone to shop for "lots of Paul Frank", Ecko, Diesel, Ben Sherman, Hurley and Dickies; still, some find the "crowded" quarters "hard to navigate."

Yigal Azrouel 🅂🄲 | 24 | 22 | 19 | VE |

408 W. 14th St. (bet. 9th Ave. & Washington St.), A/C/E/L to 14th St./8th Ave., 212-929-7525; www.yigal-azrouel.com

☑ Befitting its Meatpacking District locale, this pricey boutique has gritty chic down pat with brick walls, chandeliers and plush couches to sit on and contemplate this Israeli designer's "sexy, colorful" curvaceous dresses; groupies gush that these "beautifully done" creations are not your run-of-the-mill stuff – they're more "like canvases of expressionistic artwork" – and even fashion-forward guys (rock star Lenny Kravitz is said to be a fan) find the "fab menswear" rules.

Yohji Yamamoto 🅂🄲 | 27 | 24 | 22 | VE |

103 Grand St. (Mercer St.), R/W to Prince St., 212-966-9066

■ Away from the madding SoHo crowd, this boutique – "more a museum than a store" – is a quiet "treasure" for "true aficionados" (male and female) of this "creative, thoughtful" Japanese designer; the "surprisingly low-pressure" staff lets shoppers browse the predominantly black collection and "innovative" goods, or just gaze at the "interesting artwork."

Yumi Katsura | 26 | 25 | 21 | VE |

907 Madison Ave. (bet. 72nd & 73rd Sts.), 6 to 77th St., 212-772-3760; www.yumikatsura.com

☑ If you "want to live out every girl's fantasy, get a dreamy" made-to-order "gown with a twist of originality" at this "calm" Upper East Side by-appointment-only bridal boutique – "you'll spend a lot of money, but you get a top-quality dress with personality", plus "personalized service" from designer Erisa Katsura, Yumi's niece and her "very helpful", "attentive" consultants; but a few underwhelmed customers "expected a little more glamour" to "justify such high prices."

Yves Saint Laurent Rive Gauche | 26 | 25 | 24 | VE |

3 E. 57th St. (bet. 5th & Madison Aves.), N/R/W to 5th Ave./59th St., 212-980-2970
855 Madison Ave. (bet. 70th & 71st Sts.), 6 to 68th St., 212-988-3821
www.ysl.com

■ "Brilliant, classic, forever" fawn fashionistas over this legendary Left Bank house, transplanted to the "stylish environment" of his-and-hers boutiques on the Upper East Side; the highly acclaimed collections, designed by Tom Ford (until his departure this spring), create a frenzy among fans like Demi Moore and Sarah Jessica Parker, from the Nadja flower bags to the slim-cut tuxedos to the elegant eveningwear; N.B. the sleek, new black-and-white shop set in an East 57th Street tower, offers cosmetics and accessories, with men's and women's ready-to-wear on the second floor.

ZABAR'S ●⑤ⓒ
26 | 16 | 15 | M

2245 Broadway (80th St.), 1/9 to 79th St., 212-787-2000;
800-697-6301; www.zabars.com

■ "Look here before you buy housewares anywhere else" because the "quality and prices" at this "densely stocked" West Side "institution", which was voted the No. 1 Major Gourmet Market in our *NYC Marketplace Survey*, are "hard to beat" and the "eclectic" cookware and appliances, plus "every imaginable gadget", will "make you want to refurnish your kitchen every time you visit"; be prepared for "crowds and chaos" on the weekends, but take comfort in the fact that "you can pick up dinner while you're here."

Zales Jewelers ●⑤
14 | 16 | 15 | M

535 Broadway (bet. Prince & Spring Sts.), R/W to Prince St., 212-625-0998
170 Fifth Ave. (22nd St.), R/W to 23rd St., 917-606-1406
1187 Third Ave. (69th St.), 6 to 68th St., 212-717-7871
Kings Plaza, 5176 Kings Plaza, Brooklyn, 2/5 to Brooklyn College/
Flatbush Ave., 718-338-9527
Queens Ctr., 90-15 Queens Blvd., Queens, G/R/V to Woodhaven Blvd.,
718-760-3702
Staten Island Mall, 2655 Richmond Ave., Staten Island, 718-982-6562
800-311-5393; www.zales.com

☑ This nationally known retailer is ok for "high-school, first-love type of gifts" like "affordable" diamond rings, pendants and bracelets; Manhattanites may mutter it's all "mall jewelry", but hey, "it's a chain, for God's sake."

Zara ●⑤
19 | 19 | 13 | M

580 Broadway (bet. Houston & Prince Sts.), R/W to Prince St.,
212-343-1725
101 Fifth Ave. (bet 17th & 18th Sts.), 4/5/6/L/N/Q/R/W to 14th St./
Union Sq., 212-741-0555
750 Lexington Ave. (59th St.), 4/5/6/F/N/R/W to 59th St./Lexington Ave.,
212-754-1120
39 W. 34th St. (bet. 5th & 6th Aves.), B/D/F/N/Q/R/V/W to 34th St./
Herald Sq., 212-868-6551
www.zara.com

■ There's no need to "pawn the TiVo" to "inject verve" into your wardrobe – this "hot label" from Spain dishes out "shockingly affordable" "runway-inspired" looks for men and women; on the "pulse" of "what's new", the chain's "sexy" stylings give "great bang for the buck", though "sizing can be a bit tricky" since the garments are "European cut."

Z'Baby Company ⑤ⓒ
24 | 18 | 17 | VE

996 Lexington Ave. (72nd St.), 6 to 68th St., 212-472-2229
100 W. 72nd St. (Columbus Ave.), 1/2/3/9/B/C to 72nd St., 212-579-2229 ●
www.zbabycompany.com

■ "For a special outfit" for the kids, layette items or a "unique baby gift" for newborn–12 months, zip over to these "crazy-expensive" but "chic, upscale" bookend stores on the Upper East and Upper West Sides; while devotees declare the selection of "trendy, fashionable" childrenswear is "unbeatable" and "even the boys' clothes are cute", conservatives archly counter "shop here" "if you want your kid to dress like Britney Spears."

Zero/Maria Cornejo ◐⬛◖

▽ 19 | 21 | 15 | E

225 Mott St. (bet. Prince & Spring Sts.), 6 to Spring St., 212-925-3849
■ If you're one of those fashionistas who likes to display your art on your back instead of your wall, this NoLita "half-boutique, half-gallery" is an "ultra-esoteric" rite of passage; Maria Cornejo creates her "original, well-crafted" women's garments with an "avant-garde" "twist" behind the "frosted-glass wall in the back", so meet the designer before the contents of your wallet become less than zero.

Zitomer ◐⬛

24 | 17 | 17 | VE

969 Madison Ave. (bet. 75th & 76th Sts.), 6 to 77th St., 212-737-5560;
888-219-2888; www.zitomer.com
▣ "You can buy a tube of toothpaste or a $300 party dress for a little girl" at this "if-you-need-it-they-got-it" Upper East Side drugstore and "beauty mecca" "packed" with high-end cosmetics, skincare and toiletries, "every hair accessory you can imagine", an assortment of "odds and ends" like hosiery, plus a pet boutique dubbed Z Spot and an entire toy floor called Zittles; of course, such "convenience comes at a price" (somebody's got to pay for those "friendly doormen").

Indexes

STORE TYPE
LOCATIONS
MAPS
MERCHANDISE
SPECIAL FEATURES

STORE TYPE

LOCATIONS

Where necessary, we've noted merchandise type.

MANHATTAN

Chelsea

(30th to 24th Sts., west of 5th Ave., and 24th to 14th Sts., west of 6th Ave.)

AFNY, *Bath Fixtures*
Alcone, *Grooming/Toiletries*
Angel Street Thrift Shop
Balenciaga, *Designer*
Barking Zoo, *Pet*
Barneys Co-op, *Dept. Store*
Bed Bath & Beyond, *Home*
Best Buy, *Electronics*
Blades Board and Skate
Bowery Kitchen Supplies
Burlington Coat Factory, *Discount*
buybuy Baby
Camouflage, *Men's Clothing*
Capitol Fishing Tackle Co.
Carlyle Convertibles, *Home*
City Quilter, *Fabrics/Notions*
Comme des Garçons, *Designer*
Container Store, *Home*
DeMask, *Sex Shops*
Details, *Home*
Door Store, *Home*
Family Jewels, *Vintage*
Find Outlet, *Discount*
Fisch for the Hip, *Consignment*
Gerry's Menswear
Giraudon, *Shoes*
Here Comes the Bridesmaid
Hold Everything, *Home*
Housing Works Thrift Shop
Innovation Luggage
Jazz Record Center
Jensen-Lewis, *Home*
Jim Smiley, *Vintage*
La Cafetière, *Home*
Lightforms
Loehmann's, *Discount*
Men's Wearhouse, *Fashion Chain*
Metro Bicycles
Myoptics, *Eyewear*
New York Golf Center
Noose, The, *Sex Shops*
Olde Good Things, *Home*

Parke & Ronen, *Men's & Women's Clothing*
Portico, *Home*
Purple Passion/DV8, *Sex Shops*
Sacco, *Shoes*
S&W, *Discount*
Scuba Network
Sports Authority
Starting Line, *Men's Clothing*
Tah-Poozie, *Gifts/Novelties*
Tekserve, *Computers*
Ten Thousand Things, *Jewelry*
Thomasville, *Home*
T.J. Maxx, *Discount*
United Colors of Benetton, *Fashion Chain*
Urban Outfitters, *Fashion Chain*
V.I.M., *Jeans*
Williams-Sonoma, *Home*

Chinatown

(South of Hester St. & north of Pearl St., bet. Bowery & B'way)

Canal Hi-Fi, *Electronics*
Kam Man, *Home*
Loftworks, *Discount*
Pearl Paint, *Art Supplies*
Pearl River Mart, *Dept. Store*

East Village

(14th to Houston Sts., east of B'way)

Academy Records & CDs
a.cheng, *Women's Clothing*
Air Market , *Accessories*
Alan Moss, *Home*
Alpana Bawa, *Men's & Women's Clothing*
Alphabets, *Gifts/Novelties*
Amarcord Vintage Fashion
Angela's Vintage Boutique
Anna, *Women's Clothing*
Arche, *Shoes*
Azaleas, *Hosiery/Lingerie*
Barbara Feinman Millinery
Barbara Shaum, *Shoes*
Blue, *Women's Clothing*
Body Shop

Compact-Impact by TKNY, *Electronics*
Crunch, *Activewear*
Dinosaur Hill, *Toys*
Dö Kham, *Accessories*
Downtown Yarns
Eileen Fisher, *Fashion Chain*
Enelra, *Hosiery/Lingerie*
Eugenia Kim, *Accessories*
Fab 208 NYC, *Women's Clothing*
Filth Mart, *Thrift*
Finyl Vinyl, *Record*
Footlight Records
Fragrance Shop New York
Gabay's Outlet, *Discount*
Good, the Bad and the Ugly, *Women's Clothing*
Gown Company, *Bridal*
Gringer & Sons, *Appliances*
Jammyland, *CD/Record*
Jam Paper & Envelope
John Derian, *Home*
Kiehl's, *Cosmetics/Toiletries*
Kim's Mediapolis, *CD/DVD/Video*
Lord of the Fleas, *Tween/Teen*
Love Saves The Day, *Vintage*
Magry Knits, *Knitting*
Manhattan Portage
Martin, *Women's Clothing*
Mavi Jean
Meg, *Women's Clothing*
Metro Bicycles
Miss Lou's Herbs and Tings, *Cosmetics/Toiletries*
Myoptics, *Eyewear*
New York Central Art Supply
1950, *Home*
99X, *Clothing*
Norman's Sound & Vision, *CD/DVD/Record/Video*
PA (Personal Affairs), *Women's Clothing*
Religious Sex, *Hosiery/Lingerie*
Ro , *Luggage*
Rue St. Denis, *Vintage*
Schneider's, *Children's*
Selia Yang, *Bridal*
Selima Optique, *Eyewear*
St. Marks Sounds, *CD/Record*
Surprise! Surprise!, *Home*
Suzette Sundae, *Women's Clothing*
Tokio 7, *Consignment*
Tokyo Joe, *Consignment*
Toy Tokyo

Trash and Vaudeville, *Men's & Women's Clothing*
Upland Trading, *Men's Clothing*
Urban Outfitters, *Fashion Chain*
Utrecht, *Art Supplies*
Wedding Day Details, *Bridal*

East 40s

Airline Stationery
Allen Edmonds, *Shoes*
American Girl Place, *Toys*
Ann Taylor Loft, *Fashion Chain*
Barami Studio, *Women's Clothing*
Biscuits & Baths Doggy Village
Bloom, *Jewelry*
Bombalulus, *Children's*
Botticelli, *Shoes*
Brooks Brothers, *Fashion Chain*
Caswell-Massey, *Cosmetics/Toiletries*
Cellini, *Jewelry/Watches*
Charles Tyrwhitt, *Men's & Women's Clothing*
Children's General Store, *Toys*
Clarks England, *Shoes*
Coach, *Handbags*
Crabtree & Evelyn, *Cosmetics/Toiletries*
Crouch & Fitzgerald, *Luggage*
Daffy's, *Discount*
Dante/Zeller Tuxedo
Douglas Cosmetics
Eddie Bauer, *Fashion Chain*
Elie Tahari, *Designer*
Enzo Angiolini, *Shoes*
For Eyes, *Eyewear*
Forman's, *Discount*
Fossil, *Watches*
Grand Central Racquet
HMV, *CD/DVD/Video*
Innovation Luggage
International Cutlery
J.Crew, *Fashion Chain*
Johnston & Murphy, *Shoes*
Joon, *Stationery*
Jos. A. Bank, *Men's Clothing*
Joseph Edwards, *Watches*
J. Press, *Men's Clothing*
Kavanagh's, *Consignment/Vintage*
Kenneth Cole NY, *Designer*
La Brea, *Gifts/Novelties*
Lacoste, *Designer*
Legs Beautiful Hosiery
Links of London, *Jewelry*

Location Index

Location Index

Judith Leiber, *Accessories*
Kate's Paperie, *Stationery*
Knits Incredible
Knitting 321
La Boutique Resale, *Consignment*
Le Décor Français, *Home*
Leonard Opticians, *Eyewear*
Lexington Gardens
Liliblue, *Jewelry*
Little Eric, *Children's*
Liz Lange Maternity
Luca Luca, *Women's Clothing*
Luxury Brand Outlet, *Discount*
Malia Mills Swimwear
Mariko, *Jewelry*
Marimekko, *Home*
Mary Arnold Toys
Mecox Gardens, *Home*
Michael Ashton, *Jewelry*
Michael Kors, *Designer*
Michael's, *Consignment/Vintage*
Mish, *Jewelry*
Missoni, *Designer*
Morgenthal Frederics, *Eyewear*
Nursery Lines, *Children's*
Oilily, *Children's*
Papyrus, *Gifts/Novelties*
Penhaligon's, *Cosmetics/Toiletries*
Peters Necessities for Pets
Pookie & Sebastian, *Women's Clothing*
Prada, *Designer*
Ralph Lauren, *Designer*
Ralph Lauren Baby
Reinstein/Ross, *Jewelry*
Rita's Needlepoint
Robert Marc, *Eyewear*
Ruzzetti & Gow, *Home*
Schweitzer Linen
Scoop Men's, *Men's Clothing*
Scoop NYC, *Women's Clothing*
Searle, *Women's Clothing*
Selima Optique, *Eyewear*
Sharper Image, *Electronics*
Small Change, *Children's*
Sonia Rykiel, *Designer*
Spring Flowers, *Children's*
Stephen Russell, *Jewelry*
String, *Knitting*
Stubbs & Wootton, *Shoes*
Super Runners Shop
Talbots, *Fashion Chain*
Talbots Kids/Babies
Treillage, *Home*

United Colors of Benetton, *Fashion Chain*
Variazioni, *Women's Clothing*
Vera Wang Bridal Salon
Wedding Library
Whitney Museum Store
Wolford, *Hosiery/Lingerie*
Yumi Katsura, *Bridal*
Yves Saint Laurent Rive Gauche, *Designer*
Z'Baby Company
Zitomer, *Cosmetics/Toiletries*

East 80s

Agnès B., *Designer*
A la Maison, *Home*
Anik, *Women's Clothing*
Art and Tapisserie, *Toys*
Artbag, *Handbags*
Au Chat Botte, *Children's*
Bambini, *Children's*
Barbour by Peter Elliot, *Men's & Women's Clothing*
Bebe Thompson, *Children's*
Best Buy, *Electronics*
Betsey Johnson, *Designer*
Biscuits & Baths Doggy Village
Bis Designer Resale, *Consignment*
Blacker & Kooby, *Stationery*
Bombay Company, *Home*
California Closets, *Home*
Calling All Pets
Cécile et Jeanne, *Jewelry*
Circuit City, *Electronics*
Coach, *Handbags*
Cose Bella, *Bridal*
Cosmophonic Sound, *Electronics*
Council Thrift Shop
Dempsey & Carroll, *Stationery*
Designer Resale, *Consignment*
E.A.T. Gifts
Emmelle, *Women's Clothing*
Encore, *Consignment*
Eric, *Shoes*
G.C. William, *Children's*
Great Feet, *Children's*
Greenstones, *Children's*
Gruen Optika, *Eyewear*
Guggenheim Museum Store
Gymboree, *Children's*
H.L. Purdy, *Eyewear*
Hyde Park Stationers
Infinity, *Children's*
Jaded, *Jewelry*
Jane Wilson-Marquis, *Bridal*

Location Index

J. Leon Lascoff & Son, *Cosmetics/Toiletries*
Karens for People + Pets
La Brea, *Gifts/Novelties*
Laytner's Linen & Home
LeSportsac, *Handbags*
Lester's, *Children's*
Little Eric, *Children's*
Livi's Lingerie
Lyric Hi-Fi, Inc., *Electronics*
Magic Windows, *Children's*
Marsha D.D., *Children's*
Memorial Sloan-Kettering Shop, *Thrift*
Metro Bicycles
Met. Museum of Art Shop
Michael Eigen, *Jewelry*
Mimi Maternity
Montmartre, *Women's Clothing*
Motherhood Maternity
Nancy & Co., *Women's Clothing*
Nellie M. Boutique, *Women's Clothing*
Neue Galerie, *Museum Shops*
Olive and Bette's, *Women's Clothing*
Original Leather Store, *Men's & Women's Clothing*
Out of the Closet Thrift Shop
Petco
Peter Elliot, *Men's Clothing*
Petit Bateau, *Children's*
Pier 1 Imports, *Home*
Planet Kids
Schweitzer Linen
Searle, *Women's Clothing*
Small Change, *Children's*
Spence-Chapin Thrift Shops
Steve Madden, *Shoes*
Straight from the Crate, *Home*
Super Runners Shop
Venture Stationers
Vilebrequin, *Men's Clothing*
Wedding Library
Williams-Sonoma, *Home*
Wool Gathering, *Knitting/Needlepoint*

East 90s & Up

Adrien Linford, *Home*
Ann Crabtree, *Women's Clothing*
Annie & Company Needlepoint
Bonpoint, *Children's*

Capezio, *Activewear*
Catimini, *Children's*
Cooper-Hewitt Shop, *Museum Shops*
Crabtree & Evelyn, *Cosmetics/Toiletries*
Dimitri Nurseries, *Garden*
East Side Kids
El Museo Del Barrio, *Museum Shops*
FACE Stockholm, *Cosmetics/Toiletries*
Furry Paws, *Pet Supplies*
Jacadi, *Children's*
Jewish Museum
J. McLaughlin, *Men's & Women's Clothing*
Kid's Supply Co., *Children's/Home Furnishings*
Koos & Co., *Designer*
Lion & The Lamb, *Knitting/Needlepoint*
Museum/City of New York
New York Replacement, *Bath Fixtures*
Paterson Silks, *Fabrics/Notions*
Penny Whistle, *Toys*
Roberta's Lingerie
Robert Marc, *Eyewear*
Seigo, *Accessories*
S. Feldman Housewares
Soccer Sport Supply
Spence-Chapin Thrift Shops
Veronique, *Maternity*
Wicker Garden, *Children's*

Financial District

(South of Chambers St.)
Century 21, *Discount*
Forman's, *Discount*
Fountain Pen Hospital, *Stationery*
Fourteen Wall Street Jewelers
J&R Music/Computer
Joon, *Stationery*
Legs Beautiful Hosiery
Men's Wearhouse, *Fashion Chain*
Mimi Maternity
Montmartre, *Women's Clothing*
New York & Co., *Fashion Chain*
Prato Fine Men's Wear
Syms, *Discount*
Tent and Trails, *Sporting Goods*
William Barthman, *Jewelry*
World of Golf

Flatiron District

(Bounded by 24th & 14th Sts., bet. 6th Ave. & Park Ave. S., excluding Union Sq.)

ABC Carpet & Home
ABC Carpet
Abracadabra, *Toys*
Academy Records & CDs
Adorama Camera
A.I. Friedman, *Art Supplies*
Alkit Pro Camera
Ann Sacks, *Tile*
Anthropologie, *Fashion Chain*
Apartment 48, *Home*
Arden B. , *Fashion Chain*
Artistic Tile
Aveda, *Cosmetics/Toiletries*
A/X Armani Exchange, *Designer*
Banana Republic Men's, *Fashion Chain*
Bang & Olufsen, *Electronics*
Bath & Body Works
Beads of Paradise, *Jewelry*
Bebe, *Fashion Chain*
Beckenstein Fabrics
Birnbaum & Bullock, *Bridal*
Bombay Company, *Home*
Bridal Garden
Charles P. Rogers, *Home*
Classic Sofa
Club Monaco, *Fashion Chain*
Coach, *Handbags*
Country Home & Comfort
Daffy's, *Discount*
Dave's Army Navy
David Z., *Shoes*
Domain, *Home*
Drexel Heritage, *Home*
Eileen Fisher, *Fashion Chain*
Emporio Armani, *Designer*
Filene's Basement, *Discount*
Fishs Eddy, *Home*
Fossil, *Watches*
Hastings Tile & Il Bagno
Illuminations, *Home*
Intermix, *Women's Clothing*
Jam Paper & Envelope
J.Crew, *Fashion Chain*
Jennifer Convertibles, *Home*
Jo Malone, *Cosmetics/Toiletries*
Just Bulbs
Kenneth Cole NY, *Designer*
Kidding Around, *Toys*
Krups Kitchen & Bath, Ltd.
Ligne Roset, *Home*

Lucky Brand Jeans
M.A.C. Cosmetics
Medici, *Shoes*
Nemo Tile
Noir et Blanc...Bis, *Women's Clothing*
Origins, *Cosmetics/Toiletries*
Otto Tootsi Plohound, *Shoes*
Paper Presentation, *Stationery*
Paul Smith, *Designer*
Pier 1 Imports, *Home*
Portico, *Home*
Princeton Ski Shop
Print Icon, *Stationery*
Reminiscence, *Vintage*
Restoration Hardware, *Home*
Sacco, *Shoes*
Safavieh Carpets
Sam Flax, *Art Supplies*
School Products, *Knitting/Needlepoint*
Searle, *Women's Clothing*
Sephora, *Cosmetics/Toiletries*
17 at 17 Thrift Shop
Skechers, *Shoes*
Sol Moscot, *Eyewear*
Space Kiddets, *Children's*
Stickley, Audi & Co., *Home*
Straight from the Crate, *Home*
Villeroy & Boch, *Home*
Zales Jewelers
Zara, *Fashion Chain*

Garment District

(40th to 30th Sts., west of 5th Ave.)

Aldo, *Shoes*
BabyGap, *Children's*
B&H Photo-Video Pro Audio
B&J Fabrics
Barami Studio, *Women's Clothing*
Beckenstein Men's Fabrics
Blades Board and Skate
Brookstone, *Electronics*
Champs, *Sporting Goods*
Charlotte Russe, *Fashion Chain*
Children's Place
Claire's Accessories
CompUSA
Daffy's, *Discount*
Dr. Jay's, *Activewear*
Enzo Angiolini, *Shoes*
Express Men, *Fashion Chain*
Fenaroli by Regalia, *Bridal*
Florsheim Shoe Shops
Foot Locker, *Sneakers*

Purdy Girl, *Women's Clothing*
Ricky's, *Cosmetics/Toiletries*
Sam Goody, *CD/DVD/Video*
Sonic Groove, *CD/Record*
Stella Dallas, *Vintage*
Strider Records
Tah-Poozie, *Gifts/Novelties*
TLA Video
United Colors of Benetton, *Fashion Chain*
Untitled, *Women's Clothing*
Urban Outfitters, *Fashion Chain*
Vinylmania, *CDs/DVDs/Records/Videos*
Wet Seal, *Fashion Chain*
William-Wayne, *Home*

Harlem/East Harlem
(West of Morningside Ave., bet. 125th & 157th Sts.; bet. 5th & Morningside Aves., bet. 110th & 157th Sts.; east of 5th Ave., north of 100th St.)
B. Oyama Homme, *Men's Clothing*
Demolition Depot, *Home*
Goodwill Industries, *Thrift*
H&M, *Fashion Chain*
HMV, *CD/DVD/Video*
M.A.C. Cosmetics
New York Public Library Shop
Sole Kitchen, *Shoes*
Studio Museum/Harlem
Xukuma, *Home*

Little Italy
(South of Delancey St. & north of Canal St., bet. Bowery & Lafayette St.)
Pearl River Mart, *Dept. Store*

Lower East Side
(Houston to Canal Sts., east of Bowery)
Alife Rivington Club, *Sneakers*
Altman Luggage
A.W. Kaufman, *Hosiery/Lingerie*
Bowery Lighting
DDC Lab, *Men's & Women's Clothing*
Design Source/Dave Sanders, *Bathroom Fixtures*
Edith and Daha, *Women's Clothing*

Foley & Corinna, *Women's Clothing*
Forman's, *Discount*
Giselle, *Discount*
Harris Levy, *Home*
Harry Zarin, *Fabrics/Notions*
Jelena Behrend, *Jewelry*
Joe's Fabrics and Trimmings
Jutta Neumann, *Shoes*
Lighting By Gregory
Mary Adams The Dress, *Bridal*
Mendel Goldberg Fabrics
Miele, *Women's Clothing*
O'Lampia Studio, *Lighting*
Orchard Corset
Pharma, *Cosmetics/Toiletries*
Seven New York, *Women's Clothing*
Shop, *Women's Clothing*
Sol Moscot, *Eyewear*
Some Odd Rubies , *Vintage*
TG-170, *Women's Clothing*
Toys In Babeland, *Sex Shop*

Meatpacking District
(Gansevoort to W. 15th Sts., west of 9th Ave.)
Alexander McQueen, *Designer*
Artsee, *Eyewear*
auto, *Home*
Bodum, *Home*
Boucher, *Jewelry*
Carlos Miele, *Designer*
DDC Lab, *Men's & Women's Clothing*
Dernier Cri, *Women's Clothing*
Design Within Reach, *Home*
Destination, *Accessories*
Diane von Furstenberg, *Designer*
Jeffrey New York, *Dept. Store*
Karkula, *Home*
Nalunyc, *Sporting Goods*
Rubin Chapelle, *Designer*
Scoop NYC, *Men's & Women's Clothing*
Stella McCartney, *Designer*
Vitra, *Home*
Yigal Azrouel, *Designer*

Murray Hill
(40th to 30th Sts., east of 5th Ave.)
Aerosoles, *Shoes*
Barton-Sharpe Ltd., *Home*

Location Index

Location Index

J.Crew, *Fashion Chain*
Met. Museum of Art Shop
Sharper Image, *Electronics*
Talbots, *Fashion Chain*
United Colors of Benetton,
   Fashion Chain

TriBeCa

(South of Canal St. & north of
Chambers St., west of B'way)
Archipelago, *Home*
Assets London, *Women's
   Clothing*
A-Uno, *Women's Clothing*
Baker Tribeca, *Home*
Brooks Brothers, *Fashion Chain*
Bu and the Duck, *Children's*
Butter and Eggs, *Home*
Disrespectacles, *Eyewear*
Donzella, *Home*
Dune, *Home*
Gotham Bikes
Hattitude, *Accessories*
Intérieurs, *Home*
Issey Miyake, *Designer*
Koh's Kids
Les Migrateurs, *Home*
Little Folk Art, *Children's/Home
   Furnishings*
Metro Bicycles
Mika Inatome, *Bridal*
P&S Fabrics
Pompanoosuc Mills, *Home*
Room, *Home*
Shoofly, *Children's*
Sorelle Firenze, *Women's
   Clothing*
Stella, *Home*
Steven Alan, *Men's & Women's
   Clothing*
Sublime American Design,
   Home
Totem Design Group, *Home*
Urban Archaeology, *Home*

Union Square

(Bounded by 17th & 14th Sts.,
bet. Union Sq. E. &
Union Sq. W.)
Agnès B., *Designer*
Cheap Jack's, *Thrift*
Circuit City, *Electronics*
Country Floors, *Bathroom
   Fixtures & Tiles*
Diesel Superstore, *Jeans*
Disc-O-Rama Music World
Gateway Country, *Electronics*

Kein, *Cosmetics/Toiletries*
Mexx, *Fashion Chain*
Paragon Sporting Goods
P.C. Richard & Son, *Electronics*
Petco
Petland Discounts
Poggenpohl U.S., *Home*
Rothman's, *Men's Clothing*
Sound by Singer, *Electronics*
Virgin Megastore, *CD/DVD/
   Video*

Washington Hts. & Up

(North of W. 157th St.)
Cloisters Gift Shop, *Museum
   Shops*
Goodwill Industries, *Thrift*
KB Toys
Met. Museum of Art Shop
New York & Co., *Fashion Chain*

West Village

(14th to Houston Sts., west of
7th Ave. S., excluding
Meatpacking District)
Albertine, *Women's Clothing*
Annelore, *Designer*
Beasty Feast, *Pet*
Betwixt, *Children's*
Beyul, *Home*
blush, *Women's Clothing*
Chelsea Garden Center Home
Cherry, *Vintage*
Constança Basto, *Shoes*
Cynthia Rowley, *Designer*
Darling, *Women's Clothing*
Details, *Home*
Disrespectacles, *Eyewear*
Flight 001, *Luggage*
Four Paws Club, *Pet*
Fresh, *Cosmetics/Toiletries*
Galileo, *Home*
Gerry's Menswear
Leather Man, *Sex Shops*
Lively Set, *Home*
Lucy Barnes, *Designer*
Lulu Guinness, *Handbags*
L'Uomo, *Men's Clothing*
Marc by Marc Jacobs,
   Designer
Marc Jacobs Accessories
Mxyplyzyk, *Home*
Olatz, *Home*
Otte, *Women's Clothing*
Otter, The, *Women's Clothing*
Patch NYC, *Accessories*
Peanutbutter & Jane, *Children's*

Location Index

West 60s

Agatha Paris, *Jewelry*
American Folk Art Museum
Bonne Nuit, *Hosiery/Lingerie*
Danskin, *Activewear*
Details, *Home*
Domain, *Home*
Eddie Bauer, *Fashion Chain*
EMS, *Sporting Goods*
Ethan Allen, *Home*
Furry Paws, *Pet Supplies*
Gracious Home
Gruen Optika, *Eyewear*
Gymboree, *Children's*
Innovation Luggage
Intermix, *Women's Clothing*
Kangol, *Accessories*
Lincoln Stationers
Mimi Maternity
New York Look, *Women's Clothing*
Pottery Barn, *Home*
Reebok Store, *Activewear*
Robert Marc, *Eyewear*
Speedo Authentic Fitness
Toga Bikes
Tower Records/Video

Montmartre, *Women's Clothing*
North Face, *Activewear*
Olive and Bette's, *Women's Clothing*
Only Hearts, *Hosiery/Lingerie*
Oriental Lamp Shade Co.
Original Leather Store, *Men's & Women's Clothing*
Papyrus, *Gifts/Novelties*
Paterson Silks, *Fabrics/Notions*
Really Great Things, *Women's Clothing*
Roslyn, *Accessories*
Sacco, *Shoes*
Sean, *Men's Clothing*
Sephora, *Cosmetics/Toiletries*
Skechers, *Shoes*
Straight from the Crate, *Home*
Super Runners Shop
Swatch, *Watches*
Theory, *Designer*
Tip Top Shoes
Urban Outfitters, *Fashion Chain*
Varda, *Shoes*
Variazioni, *Women's Clothing*
Verve, *Handbags/Shoes*
Z'Baby Company

West 70s

American Museum/Nat. History
Bang & Olufsen, *Electronics*
Berkley Girl, *Tween/Teen*
Betsey Johnson, *Designer*
Blades Board and Skate
Bloch, *Activewear*
Brief Encounters, *Hosiery/Lingerie*
Cécile et Jeanne, *Jewelry*
Eileen Fisher, *Fashion Chain*
FACE Stockholm, *Cosmetics/Toiletries*
Filene's Basement, *Discount*
Fishs Eddy, *Home*
Goodwill Industries, *Thrift*
Granny-Made, *Children's*
Housing Works Thrift Shop
Jewish Museum
Kenneth Cole NY, *Designer*
La Belle Epoque, *Home*
La Boutique Resale, *Consignment*
La Brea, *Gifts/Novelties*
Lord of the Fleas, *Tween/Teen*
Lucky Brand Jeans

West 80s

Allan & Suzi, *Consignment/Vintage*
Alphabets, *Gifts/Novelties*
April Cornell, *Designer*
Assets London, *Women's Clothing*
Avventura, *Home*
Bath Island, *Cosmetics/Toiletries*
Bicycle Renaissance
Bombay Company, *Home*
Bruce Frank Beads, *Jewelry*
Circuit City, *Electronics*
Club Monaco, *Fashion Chain*
Coach, *Handbags*
Darryl's, *Women's Clothing*
Door Store, *Home*
Eye Man, *Eyewear*
Frank Stella Ltd., *Men's Clothing*
Greenstones, *Children's*
Gruen Optika, *Eyewear*
Gymboree, *Children's*
Harry's Shoes
KB Toys
Laina Jane, *Hosiery/Lingerie*
Laytner's Linen & Home
Lightforms

L'Occitane, *Cosmetics/ Toiletries*
Lo-Fi, *Men's Clothing*
Maxilla & Mandible, *Toys*
Medici, *Shoes*
Morris Brothers, *Children's*
Nice Price, *Discount*
NYCD, *CD/DVD*
Origins, *Cosmetics/Toiletries*
Palmer Pharmacy
Patagonia, *Activewear*
Penny Whistle, *Toys*
Pet Stop
Pondicherri, *Home*
Portico, *Home*
Scarpe Diem, *Shoes*
Schweitzer Linen
Shoe Biz
Talbots, *Fashion Chain*
Town Shop, *Hosiery/Lingerie*

United Colors of Benetton, *Fashion Chain*
West Side Kids, *Toys*
Yarn Co., The, *Knitting*
Zabar's, *Cookware*

West 90s
Albee Baby Carriage Co.
La Brea, *Gifts/Novelties*
Metro Bicycles
Mommy Chic, *Maternity*
Petco
Sude, *Women's Clothing*

West 100s
(West of Morningside Ave.)
Kim's Mediapolis, *CD/DVD/ Video*
Marshalls, *Discount*
Planet Kids

BRONX

ABC Carpet & Home Warehse.
Casa Amadeo, *CDs/Records*
Casual Male Big & Tall, *Men's Clothing*
Goodwill Industries, *Thrift*
Kids Foot Locker

Kmart, *Discount*
Loehmann's, *Discount*
Men's Wearhouse, *Fashion Chain*
Nat'l Wholesale Liquidators, *Discount*

BROOKLYN

Bay Ridge
Century 21, *Discount*
Claire's Accessories
Joyce Leslie, *Fashion Chain*
Kleinfeld, *Bridal*
New York & Co., *Fashion Chain*

Bensonhurst
Best Buy, *Electronics*
Claire's Accessories
Marshalls
Nat'l Wholesale Liquidators, *Discount*
New York & Co., *Fashion Chain*

Boerum Hill
Bark, *Home*
Breukelen, *Home*
Butter, *Women's Clothing*
Gumbo, *Children's*
Kimera, *Women's Clothing*
Knitting Hands
Layla, *Home*
Legacy , *Vintage*

Olde Good Things, *Home*
Rico, *Home*
Scarlet Ginger, *Women's Clothing*
Scuba Network
Urban Monster, *Children's*

Borough Park
Jacadi, *Children's*
Nat'l Wholesale Liquidators, *Discount*
S&W, *Discount*

Brooklyn Heights
American Houseware
Design Within Reach, *Home*
Heights Kids
M.A.C. Cosmetics
Sid's, *Hardware*

Canarsie
Casual Male Big & Tall, *Men's Clothing*
Lestan Bridal

Sunset Park
Kids Foot Locker
Lady Foot Locker
New York & Co., *Fashion Chain*

Williamsburg
Amarcord Vintage Fashion
Beacon's Closet, *Consignment/
    Thrift/Vintage*

Isa, *Men's & Women's Clothing*
Mini Mini Market, *Accessories*
Moon River Chattel, *Home*
Oculus 20/20, *Eyewear*
Otte, *Women's Clothing*
Sam & Seb, *Children's*
Triple Five Soul, *Men's &
    Women's Clothing*
Urban Optical, *Eyewear*

QUEENS

Astoria
Goodwill Industries, *Thrift*
Metropolitan Lumber
New York & Co., *Fashion Chain*
Prato Fine Men's Wear

Bayside
Bombay Company, *Home*
Chico's, *Fashion Chain*
Claire's Accessories
Hazel's House of Shoes
Paterson Silks, *Fabrics/Notions*
Thomasville, *Home*

College Point
Babies "R" Us
Circuit City, *Electronics*
Target, *Dept. Store*

Corona
London Jewelers
Metropolitan Lumber

Elmhurst
Best Buy, *Electronics*
Daffy's, *Discount*
Expo Design , *Home*
Forever 21, *Fashion Chain*
H&M, *Fashion Chain*
Kids Foot Locker
Lady Foot Locker
Sam Goody, *CD/DVD/Video*
Target, *Dept. Store*
Zales Jewelers

Flushing
Best Buy, *Electronics*
Brookstone, *Electronics*
Filene's Basement, *Discount*
Joyce Leslie, *Fashion Chain*
Nat'l Wholesale Liquidators,
    Discount

Forest Hills
Claire's Accessories
Eddie Bauer, *Fashion Chain*
Ethan Allen, *Home*
Sephora, *Cosmetics/Toiletries*
Sol Moscot, *Eyewear*

Howard Beach
Petco

Jamaica
Brookstone, *Electronics*
Metropolitan Lumber
Nemo Tile

Long Island City
Costco Wholesale, *Discount*
David's Bridal
Home Depot, *Hardware*
Marshalls, *Discount*
Tucker Robbins, *Home*

Middle Village
Kmart, *Discount*

Rego Park
Bed Bath & Beyond, *Home*
Circuit City, *Electronics*
CompUSA, *Electronics*

Ridgewood
Domsey Express, *Thrift*
Joyce Leslie, *Fashion Chain*

Rockaway Beach
Sam Goody, *CD/DVD/Video*

Woodhaven
Smiley's, *Knitting/Needlepoint*

STATEN ISLAND

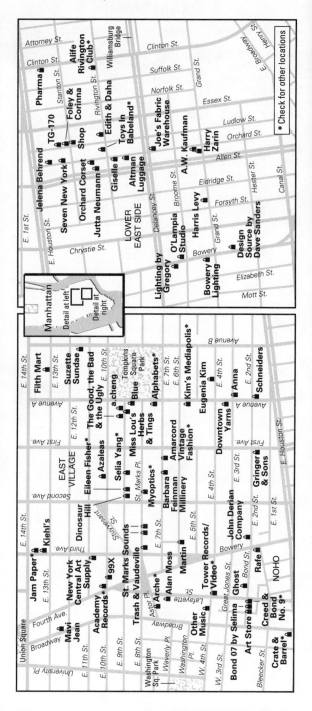

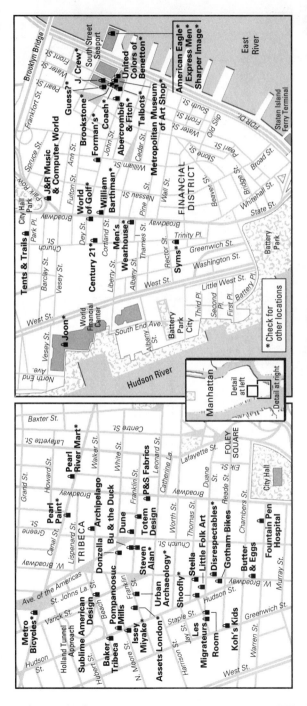

* Check for other locations

Manhattan

Area of detail

Second Ave.

E. 21st St.

E. 20th St.

E. 19th St.

E. 18th St.

Third Ave.

E. 17th St.

E. 16th St.

E. 15th St.

E. 14th St.

Lexington Ave.

Gramercy Park

E. 23rd St.

E. 22nd St.

Park Ave. S.

Irving Pl.

Union Sq. E.

Space Kiddets

Nemo Tile*

Ligne Roset

Hastings Tile & Il Bagno

Poggenpohl U.S. Inc.

Paragon Sporting Goods

Rothman's

Illuminations*

Ann Sacks

Petco*

Virgin Megastore*

Fourth Ave.

Union Square Park

Mexx*

Union Sq. W.

Sound by Singer

Country Floors

Agnès B.

ABC Carpet & Home (Carpets & Rugs)

ABC Carpet & Home

Daffy's*

Sacco*

Just Bulbs

Anthropologie*

Diesel Superstore*

Flatiron Building

Jo Malone

Origins*

M.A.C. Cosmetics*

Lucky Brand Jeans*

Restoration Hardware*

Domain*

Eileen Fisher

Bang & Olufsen*

Broadway

Otto Tootsi Plohound*

Safavieh Carpets

Portico*

Fishs Eddy*

Aveda*

Zara*

Fifth Ave.

Club Monaco*

Abracadabra

Stickley, Audi & Co.

Searle*

Sam Flax*

Intermix*

Sephora*

Krups

Academy Records*

Kenneth Cole*

J. Crew

Emporio Armani*

Paul Smith

Artistic Tile*

Arden B.*

Bebe*

Paper Presentation*

Adorama Camera

Drexel Heritage

Ave. of the Americas

W. 23rd St.

W. 22nd St.

W. 21st St.

W. 20th St.

W. 19th St.

W. 18th St.

W. 17th St.

W. 16th St.

W. 15th St.

W. 14th St.

Filene's Basement*

T.J. Maxx*

A.I. Friedman

Charles P. Rodgers

Bed, Bath & Beyond

Dave's Army Navy

Metro Bicycles*

Urban Outfitters*

Seventh Ave.

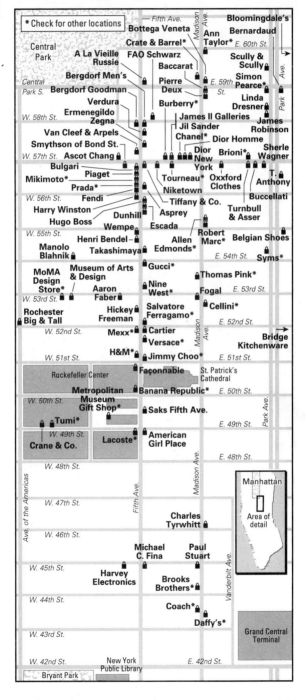

* Check for other locations

Central Park

Central Park S.

W. 58th St.

W. 57th St.

W. 56th St.

W. 55th St.

W. 53rd St.

W. 52nd St.

W. 51st St.

W. 50th St.

W. 49th St.

W. 48th St.

W. 47th St.

W. 46th St.

W. 45th St.

W. 44th St.

W. 43rd St.

W. 42nd St.

Ave. of the Americas

Fifth Ave.

Madison Ave.

Vanderbilt Ave.

Park Ave.

— Fifth Ave.

Bloomingdale's
Bernardaud
Bottega Veneta
Ann Taylor*
E. 60th St.
Crate & Barrel*
Scully & Scully
A La Vieille Russie
FAO Schwarz
Baccarat
E. 59th St.
Simon Pearce*
Bergdorf Men's
Pierre Deux
Linda Dresner
Bergdorf Goodman
Burberry*
James Robinson
Verdura
James II Galleries
Ermenegildo Zegna
Jil Sander
Van Cleef & Arpels
Chanel*
Dior Homme
Smythson of Bond St.
Dior New York
Brioni*
Sherle Wagner
Ascot Chang
Bulgari
Tourneau*
Oxxford Clothes
T. Anthony
Mikimoto*
Piaget
Niketown
Buccellati
Prada*
Tiffany & Co.
Fendi
Harry Winston
Dunhill
Turnbull & Asser
Hugo Boss
Wempe
Asprey
Escada
Robert Marc*
Belgian Shoes
Henri Bendel
Allen Edmonds*
E. 54th St.
Manolo Blahnik
Takashimaya
Syms*
MoMA Design Store*
Museum of Arts & Design
Gucci*
Thomas Pink*
Aaron Faber
Nine West*
Fogal
E. 53rd St.
Rochester Big & Tall
Hickey Freeman
Salvatore Ferragamo*
Cellini*
E. 52nd St.
Mexx*
Cartier
H&M*
Versace*
Bridge Kitchenware
Jimmy Choo*
E. 51st St.
Rockefeller Center
Façonnable
St. Patrick's Cathedral
Metropolitan Museum Gift Shop*
Banana Republic*
E. 50th St.
Saks Fifth Ave.
E. 49th St.
Tumi*
American Girl Place
Crane & Co.
Lacoste*
E. 48th St.
Manhattan
Area of detail
Charles Tyrwhitt
Michael C. Fina
Paul Stuart
Harvey Electronics
Brooks Brothers*
Coach*
Daffy's*
Grand Central Terminal
New York Public Library
Bryant Park

E. 59th St.

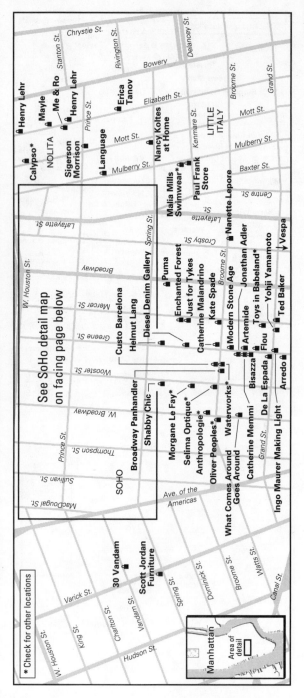

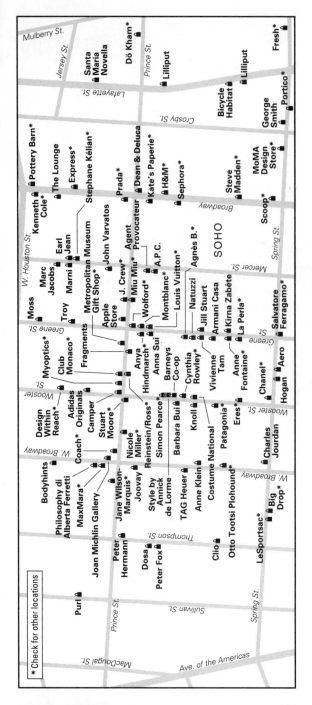

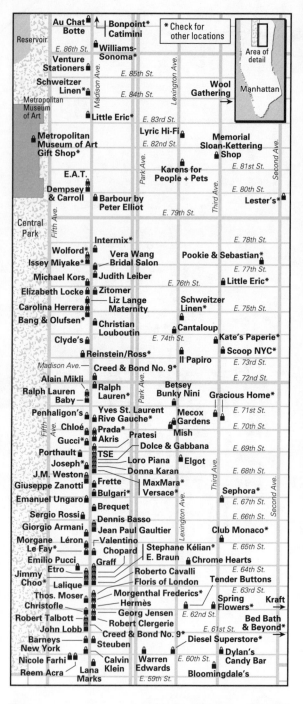

Reservoir

Au Chat Botte

Bonpoint*
Catimini

*Check for other locations

E. 86th St.

Williams-Sonoma*

Venture Stationers

E. 85th St.

Schweitzer Linen*

E. 84th St.

Wool Gathering

Area of detail

Manhattan

Metropolitan Museum of Art

Little Eric*

E. 83rd St.

Lyric Hi-Fi

Memorial Sloan-Kettering Shop

Metropolitan Museum of Art Gift Shop*

E. 82nd St.

E.A.T.

Karens for People + Pets

E. 81st St.

Dempsey & Carroll

Barbour by Peter Elliot

E. 80th St.

Lester's*

E. 79th St.

Central Park

Intermix*

E. 78th St.

Wolford*
Issey Miyake*

Vera Wang Bridal Salon

Pookie & Sebastian*

E. 77th St.

Michael Kors

Judith Leiber

E. 76th St.

Little Eric*

Elizabeth Locke

Zitomer

Schweitzer Linen*

E. 75th St.

Carolina Herrera

Liz Lange Maternity

Bang & Olufsen*

Christian Louboutin

Cantaloup

Clyde's

E. 74th St.

Kate's Paperie*

Reinstein/Ross*

Il Papiro

Scoop NYC*

E. 73rd St.

Creed & Bond No. 9*

Madison Ave.

E. 72nd St.

Alain Mikli

Ralph Lauren Baby

Ralph Lauren*

Betsey Bunky Nini

Gracious Home*

E. 71st St.

Penhaligon's

Yves St. Laurent Rive Gauche*

Mecox Gardens

Chloé*

Prada*

Mish

E. 70th St.

Gucci*

Akris

Pratesi

Porthault

TSE

Dolce & Gabbana

E. 69th St.

Joseph*

Loro Piana

Elgot

J.M. Weston

Donna Karan

E. 68th St.

Giuseppe Zanotti

Frette

MaxMara*

Sephora*

Emanuel Ungaro

Bulgari*

Versace*

E. 67th St.

Brequet

Sergio Rossi

Dennis Basso

E. 66th St.

Giorgio Armani

Jean Paul Gaultier

Club Monaco*

Morgane Léron

Valentino

E. 65th St.

Le Fay*

Chopard

Stephane Kélian*

Emilio Pucci

Graff

E. Braun

Chrome Hearts

E. 64th St.

Jimmy Choo*

Etro

Roberto Cavalli

Floris of London

Tender Buttons

Lalique

E. 63rd St.

Thos. Moser

Morgenthal Frederics*

Spring Flowers*

Kraft

Christofle

Hermès

Georg Jensen

Robert Talbott

Robert Clergerie

E. 62nd St.

Bed Bath & Beyond*

John Lobb

Creed & Bond No. 9*

E. 61st St.

Barneys New York

Steuben

Diesel Superstore*

Nicole Farhi

Calvin Klein

Warren Edwards

Dylan's Candy Bar

Reem Acra

Lana Marks

E. 60th St.

Bloomingdale's

E. 59th St.

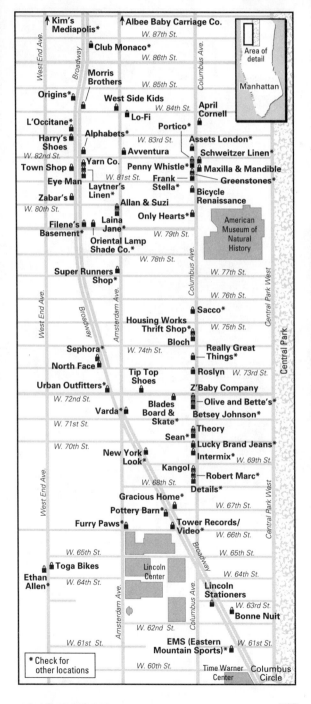

↑ Kim's Mediapolis*

↑ Albee Baby Carriage Co.

W. 87th St.

Club Monaco*

W. 86th St.

Morris Brothers

W. 85th St.

Origins*

West Side Kids

W. 84th St.

April Cornell

Lo-Fi

L'Occitane*

Portico*

Assets London*

Alphabets*

W. 83rd St.

Schweitzer Linen*

Harry's Shoes

Avventura

W. 82nd St.

Yarn Co.

Penny Whistle*

Maxilla & Mandible

Town Shop

Eye Man

Frank Stella*

Greenstones*

Zabar's

Laytner's Linen*

Bicycle Renaissance

W. 80th St.

Allan & Suzi

Only Hearts*

Filene's Basement*

Laina Jane*

American Museum of Natural History

Oriental Lamp Shade Co.*

W. 79th St.

W. 78th St.

Super Runners Shop*

W. 77th St.

W. 76th St.

Sacco*

Housing Works Thrift Shop*

W. 75th St.

Bloch

Sephora*

Really Great Things*

North Face

W. 74th St.

Roslyn   W. 73rd St.

Urban Outfitters*

Tip Top Shoes

Z'Baby Company

W. 72nd St.

Olive and Bette's*

Varda*

Blades Board & Skate*

Betsey Johnson*

W. 71st St.

Theory

Sean*

Lucky Brand Jeans*

New York Look*

Intermix*   W. 69th St.

Kangol

W. 70th St.

Robert Marc*

W. 68th St.

Details*

Gracious Home*

W. 67th St.

Pottery Barn*

Furry Paws*

Tower Records/ Video*

W. 66th St.

W. 65th St.

W. 65th St.

Toga Bikes

Lincoln Center

W. 64th St.

Ethan Allen*

W. 64th St.

Lincoln Stationers

W. 63rd St.

Bonne Nuit

W. 62nd St.

EMS (Eastern Mountain Sports)*   W. 61st St.

W. 61st St.

* Check for other locations

W. 60th St.

Time Warner Center

Columbus Circle

West End Ave. / *Broadway* / *Amsterdam Ave.* / *Columbus Ave.* / *Central Park West* / *Central Park*

Area of detail

Manhattan

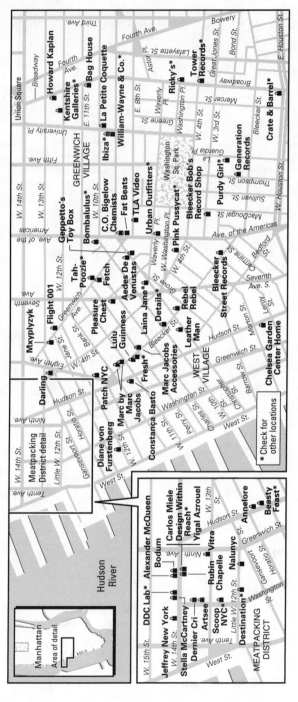

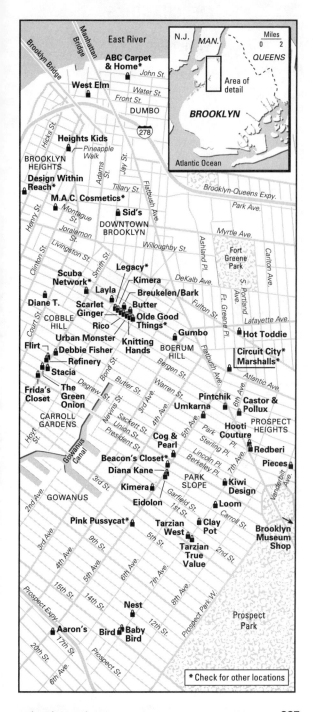

MERCHANDISE

FASHION/BEAUTY

Accessories

Add
Air Market
Alexia Crawford
Ann Crabtree
Anya Hindmarch
Asprey
Barbara Feinman Millinery
Barneys Co-op
Barneys New York
Bergdorf Goodman
Bergdorf Men's
Bird
Bloom
Bloomingdale's
Blue Bag
Bond 07 by Selima
B. Oyama Homme
Cantaloup
CK Bradley
Claire's Accessories
Coach
Cog & Pearl
Destination
Diane T
Dior Homme
Dunhill
Edith and Daha
Eugenia Kim
Eye Candy
Flying A
Girl Props
Giuseppe Zanotti Design
Good, the Bad and the Ugly
Hat Shop
Hattitude
Henri Bendel
Hermès
Hervé Leger
Intermix
Jack Spade
Jamin Puech
Jeffrey New York
J.J. Hat Center
Jutta Neumann
Kangol
Kate Spade
Kelly Christy
Kieselstein-Cord
LaCrasia Gloves
Liliblue
Lisa Shaub

Loom
Lord & Taylor
Lyd
Macy's
Marc Jacobs Accessories
Market NYC
Marsha D.D.
Mexx
Miele
Mini Mini Market
New York & Co.
Patch NYC
Paul Frank Store
Pearl River Mart
Peter Hermann
Redberi
Roslyn
Ruzzetti & Gow
Saks Fifth Avenue
Salvatore Ferragamo
Scarlet Ginger
Seigo
Some Odd Rubies
Suarez
Suzette Sundae
Swiss Army
Takashimaya
30 Vandam
Urban Outfitters
Verve
Viv Pickle
Wedding Day Details

Activewear

Active Wearhouse
Adidas Originals
Avirex
Bloch
Capezio
Champs
Classic Kicks
Crunch
Danskin
Dr. Jay's
Equinox Energy Wear
KD Dance & Sport
Keiko
Lacoste
Malia Mills Swimwear
Nalunyc
NBA Store
New Balance

Niketown
North Face
OM Yoga
On Stage Dance Shop
On Your Toes Dancewear
Paragon Sporting Goods
Patagonia
Premium Goods
Princeton Ski Shop
Puma
Quiksilver
Reebok Store
Sansha
Scandinavian Ski & Sport Shop
Speedo Authentic Fitness
Sports Authority
Stackhouse
Starting Line
Super Runners Shop
Supreme

Bridal

Amsale
Barneys New York
Bergdorf Goodman
Birnbaum & Bullock
Blue
Bridal Atelier by Mark Ingram
Bridal Garden
Clea Colet
Cose Bella
David's Bridal
Fenaroli by Regalia
Gallery of Wearable Art
Gown Company
Hazel's House of Shoes
Here Comes the Bridesmaid
Jane Wilson-Marquis
Kimera
Kleinfeld
Lestan Bridal
Macy's
Manolo Blahnik
Mary Adams The Dress
Michael's
Michelle Roth
Mika Inatome
Pilar Rossi
Reem Acra
Reva Mivasagar
RK Bridal
Saks Fifth Avenue
Selia Yang
Stuart Weitzman
Suzanne Couture Millinery
Vera Wang Bridal Salon
Wedding Day Details

Wedding Library
Yumi Katsura

Clothing: Designer

Agnès B.
Agnès B. Homme
Akris
Alexander McQueen
Alpana Bawa
Anna Sui
Anne Fontaine
Anne Klein
Annelore
April Cornell
A/X Armani Exchange
Balenciaga
Barbara Bui
BCBG Max Azria
Betsey Bunky Nini
Betsey Johnson
Built by Wendy
Burberry
Calvin Klein
Carlos Miele
Carolina Herrera
Catherine Malandrino
Celine
Chanel
Charles Tyrwhitt
Chloé
Comme des Garçons
Costume National
C. Ronson
Cynthia Rowley
Dana Buchman
D & G
Diane von Furstenberg
Dior New York
DKNY
Dolce & Gabbana
Donna Karan
Dosa
Duncan Quinn
Elie Tahari
Emanuel Ungaro
Emilio Pucci
Emporio Armani
Ermenegildo Zegna
Escada
Etro
Fendi
Ghost
Gianfranco Ferré
Giorgio Armani
Givenchy
Gucci
Helmut Lang

Henry Lehr
Hermès
Hervé Leger
Hugo Boss
Issey Miyake
Janet Russo
Jean Paul Gaultier
Jill Stuart
Jil Sander
John Varvatos
Joseph
Kenneth Cole NY
Koos & Co.
Krizia
Lacoste
Laundry/Shelli Segal
Loro Piana
Louis Féraud
Louis Vuitton
Lucy Barnes
Malia Mills Swimwear
Malo
Marc by Marc Jacobs
Marc Jacobs
Marithé + François Girbaud
Marni
MaxMara
Max Studio
Mayle
Michael Kors
Missoni
Miu Miu
Morgane Le Fay
Nanette Lepore
Nicole Farhi
Nicole Miller
N. Peal
OMO Norma Kamali
Paul Smith
Philosophy di Alberta Ferretti
Pleats Please
Plein Sud
Prada
Ralph Lauren
Reaction by Kenneth Cole
Reem Acra
Roberto Cavalli
Rubin Chapelle
Salvatore Ferragamo
Shin Choi
Sonia Rykiel
Stacia
Stella McCartney
St. John
Theory
Tommy Hilfiger
Tracy Feith

TSE
Unis
Valentino
Ventilo
Versace
Vivienne Tam
Yigal Azrouel
Yohji Yamamoto
Yves Saint Laurent Rive Gauche
Zero/Maria Cornejo

Clothing: Men's

A.
Abercrombie & Fitch
Active Wearhouse
Addison on Madison
Agnès B. Homme
Air Market
Alice Underground
Alpana Bawa
American Eagle Outfitters
Andy's Chee-Pees
A.P.C.
Ascot Chang
Asprey
A/X Armani Exchange
Bagutta Life
Ballantyne Cashmere
Banana Republic
Banana Republic Men's
Barbour by Peter Elliot
Barneys Co-op
Barneys New York
Beacon's Closet
Beau Brummel
Bergdorf Men's
Billy Martin's Western
Bloomingdale's
Borelli Boutique
Boss, The
B. Oyama Homme
Brioni
British American House
Brooks Brothers
Burberry
Burlington Coat Factory
Calvin Klein
Calypso Homme
Camouflage
Canal Jean Co.
Carlos Miele
Casual Male Big & Tall
Century 21
Charles Tyrwhitt
Cherry
Club Monaco
Comme des Garçons

Robert Talbott
Rochester Big & Tall
Rothman's
Rubin Chapelle
Rue St. Denis
Saint Laurie Merchant Tailors
Saks Fifth Avenue
Salvatore Ferragamo
Scoop Men's
Sean
Seize sur Vingt
Selvedge
Shirt Store
Starting Line
Steven Alan
Stussy NYC
Takashimaya
Target
Ted Baker
Thomas Pink
Timberland
T.J. Maxx
Tokio 7
Tommy Hilfiger
Transit
Trash and Vaudeville
Triple Five Soul
Turnbull & Asser
Union
Unis
United Colors of Benetton
Urban Outfitters
Valentino
Versace
Vilebrequin
V.I.M.
What Comes/Goes Around
X-Large
Yigal Azrouel
Yohji Yamamoto
Yves Saint Laurent Rive Gauche
Zara

Clothing: Men's/Women's

(Stores carrying both)
Abercrombie & Fitch
Active Wearhouse
Air Market
Alice Underground
Alpana Bawa
American Eagle Outfitters
Andy's Chee-Pees
A.P.C.
Asprey
Atrium
A/X Armani Exchange
Bagutta Life

Ballantyne Cashmere
Banana Republic
Barbour by Peter Elliot
Barneys Co-op
Barneys New York
Beacon's Closet
Billy Martin's Western
Bloomingdale's
Brooks Brothers
Burberry
Burlington Coat Factory
Calvin Klein
Canal Jean Co.
Carlos Miele
Century 21
Charles Tyrwhitt
Cherry
Club Monaco
Comme des Garçons
Costume National
Custo Barcelona
Daffy's
D & G
DDC Lab
DeMask
Designer Resale
Diesel Denim Gallery
Diesel Style Lab
Diesel Superstore
DKNY
Dö Kham
Dolce & Gabbana
Domsey Express
Donna Karan
Earl Jean
Eddie Bauer
Emporio Armani
Encore
Ermenegildo Zegna
Etro
Façonnable
Family Jewels
Filene's Basement
Fisch for the Hip
Flying A
French Connection
Gabay's Outlet
Gap
Gianfranco Ferré
Giorgio Armani
Gucci
Guess?
H&M
Helmut Lang
Henry Lehr
Hermès
Holland & Holland

Hugo Boss
Ina
Isa
Issey Miyake
J.Crew
Jean Paul Gaultier
Jeffrey New York
Jil Sander
J. McLaughlin
Kenneth Cole NY
Kmart
Krizia
Lacoste
Levi's Store
Loehmann's
Loftworks
Lord & Taylor
Lord of the Fleas
Loro Piana
Louis Vuitton
Lounge, The
Lucky Brand Jeans
Macy's
Malo
Marc by Marc Jacobs
Marc Jacobs
Marni
Marshalls
Mavi Jean
Mexx
Nautica
Nicole Farhi
99X
Nom de Guerre
North Face
N. Peal
Old Navy
OM Boutique
Opening Ceremony
Original Leather Store
Palma
Parke & Ronen
Paul Frank Store
Paul Stuart
Phat Farm
Pieces
Prada
Quiksilver
Rags-A-GoGo
Ralph Lauren
Reaction by Kenneth Cole
Reminiscence
Replay
Roberto Cavalli
Rubin Chapelle
Rue St. Denis
Saks Fifth Avenue

Salvatore Ferragamo
Seize sur Vingt
Selvedge
Shanghai Tang
Takashimaya
Target
Thomas Pink
T.J. Maxx
Tokio 7
Tommy Hilfiger
Transit
Trash and Vaudeville
Triple Five Soul
Turnbull & Asser
Unis
United Colors of Benetton
Upland Trading
Urban Outfitters
Valentino
Versace
V.I.M.
What Comes/Goes Around
X-Large
Yellow Rat Bastard
Yigal Azrouel
Yohji Yamamoto
Yves Saint Laurent Rive Gauche
Zara

Clothing: Women's

Abercrombie & Fitch
a.cheng
Active Wearhouse
Agnès B.
Akris
Albertine
Alexander McQueen
Alice Underground
Alpana Bawa
American Eagle Outfitters
Amy Chan
Andy's Chee-Pees
Anik
Anna
Anna Sui
Ann Crabtree
Anne Fontaine
Anne Klein
Annelore
Anthropologie
A.P.C.
April Cornell
Arden B.
Asprey
Assets London
A-Uno
A/X Armani Exchange

Azaleas
Ballantyne Cashmere
Banana Republic
Barami Studio
Barbara Bui
Barbour by Peter Elliot
Barneys Co-op
Barneys New York
BCBG Max Azria
Beacon's Closet
Bergdorf Goodman
Betsey Bunky Nini
Betsey Johnson
Big Drop
Billy Martin's Western
Bird
Bloomingdale's
Blue
blush
Bond 07 by Selima
Brooks Brothers
Built by Wendy
Burberry
Burlington Coat Factory
Butter
Calvin Klein
Calypso
Canal Jean Co.
Cantaloup
Carlos Miele
Carolina Herrera
Castor & Pollux
Catherine Malandrino
Celine
Century 21
Chanel
Charles Tyrwhitt
Charlotte Russe
Cherry
Chico's
Chloé
CK Bradley
Club Monaco
Comme des Garçons
Costume National
C. Ronson
Custo Barcelona
Cynthia Rowley
Daffy's
Dana Buchman
D & G
Darling
Darryl's
DDC Lab
DeMask
Dernier Cri
Designer Resale

Destination
Diane T
Diane von Furstenberg
Diesel Denim Gallery
Diesel Superstore
Dior New York
DKNY
Dolce & Gabbana
Domsey Express
Donna Karan
Dosa
Earl Jean
Eddie Bauer
Edith and Daha
Eidolon
Elie Tahari
Emanuel Ungaro
Emilio Pucci
Emmelle
Emporio Armani
Encore
Erica Tanov
Ermenegildo Zegna
Escada
Etro
Eva
Express
Fab 208 NYC
Façonnable
Family Jewels
Fendi
Filene's Basement
Fisch for the Hip
Flirt
Flying A
Foley & Corinna
Forréal
French Connection
French Corner
Frida's Closet
Gabay's Outlet
Gap
Ghost
Gianfranco Ferré
Giorgio Armani
Giselle
Givenchy
Good, the Bad and the Ugly
Gucci
Guess?
H&M
Helmut Lang
Henri Bendel
Henry Lehr
Hermès
Hotel Venus/Patricia Field
Hugo Boss

Merchandise Index

Clothing/Shoes: Children's

Reminiscence
Resurrection
Ritz Furs
Rue St. Denis
Salvation Army
Screaming Mimi's
17 at 17 Thrift Shop
Some Odd Rubies
Spence-Chapin Thrift Shops
Stella Dallas
Tatiana
Tokio 7
Tokyo Joe
What Comes/Goes Around

Cosmetics/Toiletries

Aedes De Venustas
Alcone
Anna Sui
Aveda
Barneys Co-op
Barneys New York
Bath & Body Works
Bath Island
Bergdorf Goodman
Bergdorf Men's
Bloomingdale's
Body Shop
Boyd's of Madison Avenue
Calvin Klein
Carol's Daughter
Caron Boutique
Caswell-Massey
Chanel
Clyde's
C.O. Bigelow Chemists
Crabtree & Evelyn
Creed & Bond No. 9
Diane von Furstenberg
Dior New York
Douglas Cosmetics
e. Harcourt's
FACE Stockholm
Floris of London
Fragrance Shop New York
Fresh
Giorgio Armani
Helmut Lang Parfums
Henri Bendel
H2O Plus
Il Makiage
J. Leon Lascoff & Son
Jo Malone
Kein
Kiehl's
L'Occitane
Lord & Taylor

M.A.C. Cosmetics
Macy's
Make Up For Ever
Mary Quant Colour
Miss Lou's Herbs and Tings
OMO Norma Kamali
Origins
Palmer Pharmacy
Penhaligon's
Perfumania
Perlier Kelemata
Pharma
Prada
Ray Beauty Supply
Ricky's
Saks Fifth Avenue
Santa Maria Novella
SCO
Scrips Elixers
Sephora
Shiseido
Shu Uemura
Takashimaya
Yves Saint Laurent Rive Gauche
Zitomer

Eyewear

Alain Mikli
Artsee
Cohen's Fashion Optical
Disrespectacles
Eye Man
Facial Index
For Eyes
Gruen Optika
H.L. Purdy
Joël Name Optique de Paris
Leonard Opticians
Lunettes et Chocolat
Morgenthal Frederics
Myoptics
Oculus 20/20
Oliver Peoples
Robert Marc
Selima Optique
Sol Moscot
Urban Optical

Furs

Bergdorf Goodman
Bloomingdale's
Dennis Basso
Fendi
Goldin-Feldman
J. Mendel
Ritz Furs
Saks Fifth Avenue

Handbags

Add
Amy Chan
Anya Hindmarch
Artbag
Balenciaga
Bally
Barneys Co-op
Barneys New York
Bergdorf Goodman
Bloomingdale's
Blue Bag
Bottega Veneta
Botticelli
Celine
Chanel
Charles Jourdan
Coach
Cole Haan
Crouch & Fitzgerald
Custo Barcelona
D & G
Deco Jewels
delfino
Destination
Dior New York
Dolce & Gabbana
Dooney & Bourke
Express
Fendi
Fratelli Rossetti
Furla
Gabay's Outlet
Ghurka
Gianfranco Ferré
Gucci
Hazel's House of Shoes
Henri Bendel
Hermès
Hiponica
Hogan
Holland & Holland
Il Bisonte
Jamin Puech
Jeffrey New York
Judith Leiber
Jutta Neumann
Kate Spade
Kazuyo Nakano
Lana Marks
Lederer de Paris
LeSportsac
Longchamp
Loom
Lord & Taylor
Louis Vuitton
Lulu Guinness

Macy's
Manhattan Portage
Marc Jacobs Accessories
Missoni
Miu Miu
M Z Wallace
Nine West
Patch NYC
Peter Hermann
Prada
Rafe
Refinery
Ro
Robert Clergerie
Saks Fifth Avenue
Salvatore Ferragamo
Samuel Jackson
Scarpe Diem
Sergio Rossi
Sigerson Morrison Bags
Steve Madden
Suarez
T. Anthony Ltd.
Triple Five Soul
Verve
Via Spiga
Viv Pickle
Walter Steiger
Yves Saint Laurent Rive Gauche

Hosiery/Lingerie

ABH Design
Agent Provocateur
Anthropologie
A.W. Kaufman
Azaleas
Barneys New York
Bergdorf Goodman
Bloomingdale's
Bodyhints
Bonne Nuit
Bra Smyth
Brief Encounters
Burlington Coat Factory
Century 21
Daffy's
Diana Kane
Enelra
Eres
Filene's Basement
Fogal
H&M
Henri Bendel
Joovay
Laina Jane
La Perla
La Petite Coquette

HOME/GARDEN

Cookware
Bed Bath & Beyond
Bloomingdale's
Bodum
Bowery Kitchen Supplies
Bridge Kitchenware
Broadway Panhandler
Crate & Barrel
Dean & Deluca
Gracious Home
International Cutlery
Kam Man
Kmart
Macy's
Moss
Pearl River Mart
S. Feldman Housewares
Tarzian West
Williams-Sonoma
Zabar's

Fine China/Crystal
Avventura
Baccarat
Bardith
Barneys New York
Bergdorf Goodman
Bernardaud
Bloomingdale's
Carole Stupell
Christofle
Daum
Fortunoff
Gallery Orrefors
Georg Jensen
James Robinson
James II Galleries
Lalique
Macy's
Michael C. Fina
Moss
Saks Fifth Avenue
Simon Pearce
Steuben
Swarovski
Takashimaya
Tiffany & Co.
Vera Wang Bridal Salon
Villeroy & Boch

Furniture/Home Furnishings
Babies'/Children's
ABC Carpet & Home
Albee Baby Carriage Co.
Au Chat Botte
Bear's Place, A

Bellini
Bombay Company
buybuy Baby
Drexel Heritage
Ethan Allen
Gracious Home
Just for Tykes
Kid's Supply Co.
La Layette et Plus
Little Folk Art
Little Folks
Planet Kids
Schneider's
Shabby Chic
White on White
Wicker Garden

General
ABC Carpet & Home
ABC Carpet (Carpets/Rugs)
ABC Carpet & Home Warehse.
ABH Design
Adrien Linford
Aero
A la Maison
Alan Moss
American Folk Art Museum
An American Craftsman
Anthropologie
Apartment 48
April Cornell
Archipelago
Armani Casa
Arredo
AsiaStore/Asia Society
auto
Baker Tribeca
Banana Republic
B&B Italia
Bark
Barneys New York
Barton-Sharpe Ltd.
BDDW
Bed Bath & Beyond
Bergdorf Goodman
Beyul
Bloomingdale's
BoConcept
Bodum
Bombay Company
Breukelen
Brooklyn Museum Shop
Butter and Eggs
California Closets
Calvin Klein
Carlyle Convertibles
Carole Stupell
Cassina USA

Poggenpohl U.S.
S. Feldman Housewares
Target
Tarzian West
Williams-Sonoma
Zabar's

Silver

A La Vieille Russie
Asprey
Barneys New York
Bergdorf Goodman
Bloomingdale's
Buccellati

Carole Stupell
Cartier
Christofle
Fortunoff
Georg Jensen
James Robinson
James II Galleries
Macy's
Michael C. Fina
Moss
Saks Fifth Avenue
Scully & Scully
Tiffany & Co.

LIFESTYLE

Art Supplies

A.I. Friedman
Art Store
Industrial Plastic
Kremer Pigments
Lee's Art Shop
New York Central Art Supply
Pearl Paint
Sam Flax
Utrecht

Baby Gear

Albee Baby Carriage Co.
Babies "R" Us
Bellini
Bloomingdale's
buybuy Baby
Heights Kids
Just for Tykes
Kmart
Little Folks
Macy's
Planet Kids
Schneider's
Target
Urban Monster

Cameras/Video Equipment

Adorama Camera
Alkit Pro Camera
B&H Photo-Video Pro Audio
Best Buy
Camera Land
Circuit City
42nd Street Photo
Olden Camera
Sony Style
Willoughby's

CDs/Videos/Records/DVDs

Academy Records & CDs
Best Buy
Bleecker Bob's Golden Oldies
Bleecker Street Records
Blockbuster Video
Casa Amadeo
Colony Music
Disc-O-Rama Music World
Fat Beats
Finyl Vinyl
Footlight Records
Fye
Generation Records
HMV
House of Oldies
Jammyland
J&R Music/Computer
Jazz Record Center
Kim's Mediapolis
Norman's Sound & Vision
NYCD
Other Music
Rebel Rebel
Rocks in your Head
Sam Goody
Satellite Records
Sonic Groove
St. Marks Sounds
Strider Records
Suncoast Motion Picture Co.
TLA Video
Tower Records/Video
Vinylmania
Virgin Megastore

Electronics

Apple Store SoHo
Bang & Olufsen
Best Buy

Merchandise Index

Brookstone
Canal Hi-Fi
Circuit City
Compact-Impact by TKNY
CompUSA
Cosmophonic Sound
DataVision
Gateway Country
Hammacher Schlemmer
Harvey Electronics
Innovative Audio
J&R Music/Computer
Lyric Hi-Fi, Inc.
Park Ave. Audio
P.C. Richard & Son
Radio Shack
RCS Computer Experience
Sharper Image
Sony Style
Sound by Singer
Sound City
Staples
Stereo Exchange
Tekserve

Fabrics/Notions

ABH Design
B&J Fabrics
Beckenstein Fabrics
Beckenstein Men's Fabrics
City Quilter
Harry Zarin
Hyman Hendler & Sons
Joe's Fabrics and Trimmings
Le Décor Français
M&J Trimming
Marimekko
Mendel Goldberg Fabrics
Mood Fabrics
New York Elegant Fabric
P&S Fabrics
Paron Fabrics
Paterson Silks
Pierre Deux
Poli Fabrics
Rosen & Chadick Textiles
Steinlauf & Stoller
Tender Buttons

Gifts/Novelties

Alphabets
American Folk Art Museum
American Museum/Nat. History
AsiaStore/Asia Society
Bloom
Brooklyn Museum Shop
Carnegie Cards/Gifts

Cloisters Gift Shop
Cooper-Hewitt Shop
Disney
Dylan's Candy Bar
E.A.T. Gifts
El Museo Del Barrio
Etcetera
Frick Collection
Guggenheim Museum Store
Illuminations
International Ctr. Photography
Intrepid Sea-Air-Space
Jewish Museum
Kar'ikter
La Brea
Met. Museum of Art Shop
MoMA Design
Morgan Library Shop
Museum/Arts & Design Shop
Museum/City of New York
Neue Galerie
New Museum/Contemp. Art
New York Public Library Shop
New York Transit Museum
Paparazzi
Papyrus
Sanrio
Studio Museum/Harlem
Tah-Poozie
Whitney Museum Store

Knitting/Needlepoint

Annie & Company Needlepoint
Downtown Yarns
Erica Wilson Needle Works
Gotta Knit
Knits Incredible
Knitting Hands
Knitting 321
Lion & The Lamb
Magry Knits
Purl
Rita's Needlepoint
School Products
Smiley's
Stitches East
String
Wool Gathering
Yarn Co., The
Yarn Connection, The

Luggage

Altman Luggage
Bag House
Bloomingdale's
Bottega Veneta
Crouch & Fitzgerald

SPECIAL FEATURES

(Indexes list the best of many within each category.)

Additions
(Properties added since the last edition of the book)

Airline Stationery
Air Market
Akris
A la Maison
Albertine
Alcone
American Girl Place
American Houseware
Anna
Ann Crabtree
Annelore
Archipelago
Arden B.
Arredo
Artsee
Art Store
Atrium
Azaleas
Babies "R" Us
Balenciaga
Bambini
Barbara Shaum
Barbour by Peter Elliot
Betwixt
Bisazza
Bloch
blush
BoConcept
Borelli Boutique
B. Oyama Homme
Breguet
Butter and Eggs
Cantaloup
Carlos Miele
Carole Stupell
Carol's Daughter
Catherine Memmi
Charlotte Russe
Chico's
Church Shoes
CK Bradley
Clarks England
Classic Kicks
Coclico
Cog & Pearl
Container Store
C. Ronson
Custo Barcelona

Darling
Debbie Fisher
De La Espada
delfino
Dennis Basso
Design Within Reach
Diana Kane
Diane T
Dinosaur Hill
Dior Homme
Disrespectacles
Doggystyle
Douglas Cosmetics
Duncan Quinn
Ecco
Edith and Daha
Emmelle
Etcetera
Expo Design
Federico De Vera
Flying A
Forever 21
Fragrance Shop New York
Gabay's Outlet
Galo
G.C. William
Giselle
Giuseppe Zanotti Design
Goffredo Fantini
Good, the Bad and the Ugly
Gruen Optika
Harry Zarin
Hazel's House of Shoes
Hervé Leger
Hiponica
Hyde Park Stationers
Isa
Jamin Puech
Jill Platner
J. Leon Lascoff & Son
Kangol
Kazuyo Nakano
Kein
Kids Foot Locker
Kieselstein-Cord
Kiton
Koh's Kids
Lace
La Layette et Plus
Lâle
Lederer de Paris
Legacy

Avant-Garde

Liliblue
Marithé + François Girbaud
Market NYC
Mary Adams The Dress
MoMA Design
Opening Ceremony
Other Music
Pleats Please
Prada
Roberto Cavalli
Samuel Jackson
Seven New York
Steven Alan
Sublime American Design
Takashimaya
Tekserve
30 Vandam
Yohji Yamamoto
Zero/Maria Cornejo

Celebrity Clientele

Aaron Basha
ABC Carpet & Home
Alain Mikli
Alexander McQueen
Annelore
Balenciaga
Barneys New York
BDDW
Bergdorf Goodman
Bergdorf Men's
Billy Martin's Western
Breguet
Burberry
Calvin Klein
Calypso
Carlos Miele
Carolina Herrera
Catherine Malandrino
Chanel
Chloé
Christian Louboutin
Chrome Hearts
Creed & Bond No. 9
DDC Lab
Dernier Cri
Dior Homme
Dior New York
Dolce & Gabbana
Donna Karan
Dylan's Candy Bar
Emilio Pucci
Fat Beats
Fendi
Filth Mart

Fragments
Fred Leighton
Fresh
Giorgio Armani
Good, the Bad and the Ugly
Gucci
Hermès
Hervé Leger
Hogan
HOLLYWOULD
Issey Miyake
Jeffrey New York
Jill Platner
Jimmy Choo
Jonathan Adler
Joseph
Judith Leiber
Kangol
Kiton
LaDuca Shoes
Lana Marks
La Petite Coquette
La Petite Princesse
Louis Vuitton
Lucky Wang
Lulu Guinness
Manolo Blahnik
Marc Jacobs
Marni
Martin
Mayle
Michael Kors
Michele Varian
Mish
Miu Miu
Moss
Oliver Peoples
Prada
Rafe
Ralph Lauren
Reem Acra
Robert Marc
Roberto Cavalli
Room
Rooms & Gardens
Santa Maria Novella
Shin Choi
Some Odd Rubies
Stella McCartney
Swiss Army
Todd Hase
Tod's
Unis
Urban Archaeology

Frequent-Buyer Program

Prato Fine Men's Wear
Saks Fifth Avenue
Sam Goody
Sharper Image
Tourneau
Toys R Us
West Side Kids

Hip/Hot Places

a.cheng
Adidas Originals
Agent Provocateur
Alain Mikli
Albertine
Alexander McQueen
American Girl Place
Amy Chan
Anna
Anna Sui
Apple Store SoHo
Arden B.
Armani Casa
Artsee
Azaleas
Baby Bird
Bagutta Life
Balenciaga
Bark
Barneys Co-op
Barneys New York
BCBG Max Azria
Betwixt
Big Drop
Bird
Blades Board and Skate
Bond 07 by Selima
Bottega Veneta
Breukelen
Burberry
Butter
Calypso
Calypso Enfant & Bebe
Camper
Cantaloup
Carlos Miele
Catherine Malandrino
Cécile et Jeanne
Cherry
Chloé
Christian Louboutin
Chrome Hearts
Chuckies
Club Monaco
Compact-Impact by TKNY
Costume National
Creed & Bond No. 9
C. Ronson

Custo Barcelona
D & G
Darling
delfino
DeMask
Dernier Cri
Destination
Diane T
Diane von Furstenberg
Diesel Denim Gallery
Diesel Superstore
Dior Homme
Dior New York
Doggystyle
Dolce & Gabbana
Dune
Dylan's Candy Bar
Earl Jean
Eidolon
Erica Tanov
Eugenia Kim
Eye Candy
Fab 208 NYC
Fat Beats
Fetch
Flight 001
Flying A
Foley & Corinna
Forréal
Fossil
Four Paws Club
Fragments
Fresh
G.C. William
Ghost
Giuseppe Zanotti Design
Goffredo Fantini
Good, the Bad and the Ugly
Gucci
H&M
Helmut Lang
Henry Lehr
HOLLYWOULD
Homer
Hot Toddie
Infinity
Intermix
Jack Spade
Jeffrey New York
Jill Stuart
Jimmy Choo
J. Lindeberg Stockholm
John Varvatos
Jonathan Adler
Jutta Neumann
Kangol
Kate Spade

Insider Secrets

Special Feature Index

Geraldine
Giselle
Goldin-Feldman
Good, the Bad and the Ugly
IF
Isa
Jammyland
Jay Kos
Jazz Record Center
Jill Platner
John Derian
Kavanagh's
Kazuyo Nakano
KD Dance & Sport
Kiton
Koh's Kids
Kremer Pigments
Lace
La Petite Princesse
Layla
Legacy
Lo-Fi
Lowell/Edwards
Lucky Wang
Magry Knits
Mariko
Market NYC
Mary Adams The Dress
Miele
Mika Inatome
Mini Mini Market
Morgan Library Shop
M Z Wallace
Neue Galerie
New York Replacement
Nom de Guerre
OM Boutique
Oriental Lamp Shade Co.
Otte
Pearldaddy
P.E. Guerin
Peter Hermann
Pieces
Premium Goods
Purl
Purple Passion/DV8
Push
Ray Beauty Supply
Rebel Rebel
Redberi
Religious Sex
Rico
Ro
Ruzzetti & Gow

Samuel Jackson
Scarlet Ginger
Scarpe Diem
Sean
Seigo
Shin Choi
SoHo Baby
Some Odd Rubies
Sorelle Firenze
Stackhouse
Stella
Stephen Russell
Suzette Sundae
Tatiana
Ted Baker
30 Vandam
Umkarna
Unis
Untitled
Urban Angler
Urban Archaeology
Yellow Door

Legendary

(Date company founded)
1730 Floris of London
1748 Villeroy & Boch
1752 Caswell-Massey
1760 Creed & Bond No. 9
1775 Breguet
1781 Asprey
1818 Brooks Brothers
1825 Clarks England
1826 Lord & Taylor
1831 Takashimaya
1835 Holland & Holland
1837 Tiffany & Co.
1838 C.O. Bigelow Chemists
1839 Crouch & Fitzgerald
1847 Cartier
1851 A La Vieille Russie
1851 Bally
1857 P.E. Guerin
1860 Chopard
1860 Frette
1863 Bernardaud
1870 Penhaligon's
1872 Bloomingdale's
1872 Shiseido
1873 Church Shoes
1873 Levi's Store
1878 Daum
1878 Dempsey & Carroll
1878 Salvation Army
1882 Danskin
1885 Turnbull & Asser

Only in New York

Saks Fifth Avenue
Scully & Scully
Sherle Wagner
Simon Pearce
Steuben
Takashimaya
Target
Terence Conran Shop
37=1
Tiffany & Co.
Uproar Home
Via Spiga
Victoria's Secret
Villeroy & Boch
Williams-Sonoma
William-Wayne
Yellow Door
Zabar's

Status Goods

Aaron Basha
Aedes De Venustas
Akris
Alan Moss
A La Vieille Russie
Alexander McQueen
Allen Edmonds
Amsale
Ann Sacks
Antiquarium Ancient Art Gallery
Armani Casa
Arredo
Artistic Tile
Asprey
A. Testoni
Au Chat Botte
Baccarat
Bagutta Life
Balenciaga
B&B Italia
Bang & Olufsen
Barbour by Peter Elliot
Barneys New York
Barton-Sharpe Ltd.
Belgian Shoes
Bellini
Bergdorf Goodman
Bernardaud
Boffi SoHo
Bonpoint
Borealis
Bottega Veneta
Botticelli
Breguet
Brioni
Buccellati
Bulgari

Burberry
Calvin Klein
Carlos Miele
Carolina Herrera
Caron Boutique
Cartier
Cassina USA
Catherine Memmi
Catimini
Celine
Cellini
Cesare Paciotti
Chanel
Chloé
Chopard
Christian Louboutin
Christofle
Clea Colet
Country Floors
Creed & Bond No. 9
Daum
Davide Cenci
David Webb
David Yurman
Dean & Deluca
De La Espada
Dennis Basso
Design Within Reach
Destination
Dior Homme
Dior New York
Dolce & Gabbana
Donna Karan
Donzella
Dunhill
Elizabeth Locke
Emanuel Ungaro
Emilio Pucci
Ermenegildo Zegna
Escada
Etro
Fratelli Rossetti
Fred Leighton
Frette
George Smith
Georg Jensen
Ghurka
Gianfranco Ferré
Givenchy
Graff
Gucci
Harry Winston
Helene Arpels
Henri Bendel
Hermès
Hervé Leger
Hickey Freeman

Yohji Yamamoto
Yumi Katsura
Yves Saint Laurent Rive Gauche

Tween/Teen Appeal

Abracadabra
Adidas Originals
Air Market
Alphabets
American Eagle Outfitters
Apple Store SoHo
Arden B.
Atrium
Barneys Co-op
Beacon's Closet
Bebe
Berkley Girl
Betwixt
Blades Board and Skate
Body Shop
Capezio
Charlotte Russe
Claire's Accessories
Compact-Impact by TKNY
David Z.
Domsey Express
Dylan's Candy Bar
EMS
Flying A
Forever 21
Fossil
Fye
G.C. William

Girl Props
HMV
Hooti Couture
Lord of the Fleas
M.A.C. Cosmetics
Marsha D.D.
Maxilla & Mandible
Metro Bicycles
Niketown
North Face
Paragon Sporting Goods
Paul Frank Store
Pearl River Mart
Perfumania
Puma
Quiksilver
Rags-A-GoGo
Rampage
Sanrio
Screaming Mimi's
Sephora
Sony Style
Stackhouse
Strawberry
Supreme
Tah-Poozie
Tokio 7
Tower Records/Video
Trash and Vaudeville
Urban Outfitters
Virgin Megastore
Yellow Rat Bastard

Eat. Drink.
Party. Shop.
(Welcome to New York!)